DRAFTING LEGISLATION

This book constitutes the first thorough academic analysis of legislative drafting. By placing the study of legislation and its principles within the paradigm of Flyvberg's phronetic social sciences, it offers a novel approach which breaks the tradition of unimaginative past descriptive reiterations of drafting conventions. Instead of prescribing rules for legislation, it sets out to identify efficacy as the main aim of the actors in the policy, legislative and drafting processes, and effectiveness as the main goal in the drafting of legislation. Through the prism of effectiveness as synonymous with legislative quality, the book explores the stages of the drafting process; guides the reader through structure and sections in their logical sequence, and introduces rules for drafting preliminary, substantive and final provisions. Special provisions, comparative legislative drafting and training for drafters complete this thorough analysis of the drafting of legislation as a tool for regulation. Instead of teaching the reader which drafting rules prevail, the book explores the reasons why drafting rules have come about, thus encouraging readers to understand what goal is served by each rule and how each rule applies. The book is aimed at academics and practitioners who draft or use statutory law in the common or civil law traditions.

Drafting Legislation

Art and Technology of Rules for Regulation

Helen Xanthaki

• HART •
PUBLISHING
OXFORD AND PORTLAND, OREGON
2014

Hart Publishing
An imprint of Bloomsbury Publishing Plc

Hart Publishing Ltd
Kemp House
Chawley Park
Cumnor Hill
Oxford OX2 9PH
UK

Bloomsbury Publishing Plc
50 Bedford Square
London
WC1B 3DP
UK

www.hartpub.co.uk
www.bloomsbury.com

Published in North America (US and Canada) by
Hart Publishing
c/o International Specialized Book Services
920 NE 58th Avenue, Suite 300
Portland, OR 97213-3786
USA

www.isbs.com

British Library Cataloguing-in-Publication Data
A catalogue record for this book is available from the British Library.

ISBN: 978-1-84946-428-4

Typeset by Compuscript Ltd, Shannon
Printed and bound in Great Britain by
Lightning Source UK Ltd

To Anna-Faye, my beautiful and
talented little darling

Table of Contents

Table of Cases xiii
Table of Legislation xxi

1. Legislation as a Means of Regulation: Effectiveness in Legislative Drafting 1
   - Introduction 1
   - The Nature of Rules for Regulation: Art or Technology? 10
   - The Universality of Rules for Regulation 16
   - Compilations of Rules for Regulation: Homogeneity versus Rigidity? 19
   - Conclusions 20
2. Drafting Instructions 21
   - What are Drafting Instructions? 22
   - Purposes of Drafting Instructions 24
   - The Four Principles of Drafting Instructions 27
   - What is the Content of Drafting Instructions? 29
   - Quality of Legislative Instructions 32
   - Style of Drafting Instructions 34
   - Conclusions: a Checklist for Quality Drafting Instructions 35
   - To Sum Up: Checklist for Legislative Instructions 36
3. The Legislative Plan: Designing a Legislative Solution 38
   - Designing a Legislative Solution: What is it? 39
   - The Advantages of Compiling a Legislative Plan 41
   - The Elements of Analysis in the Legislative Plan 44
     - Analysis of the Existing Law 44
     - Analysis of the Necessity of Legislation as a Solution to the Identified Social Need 46
     - Analysis of Potential Danger Areas 48
     - Analysis of the Policy Options and the Preferred Legislative Solution 51
     - Analysis of the Projected Interpretation of the Legislation 57
   - Initial Considerations of Structure: Thring's Five 'Golden Rules' 59
   - Conclusions 60
4. Structure of a Bill 61
   - The Theory: Lord Thring's Five Rules of Drafting Revisited 62
   - More Doctrine: Bergeron's Rules 65
   - The Practice: Thornton's Approach 66
   - Structure in Brief: the Traditional Style 67

Structure in Brief: Innovation 68
Arrangements in Parts 71
Headings 73
Sections 74
Marginal Notes 74
Marginal References 76
Table of Arrangements or Arrangement of Sections 76
Real Innovation: the Layered Approach 76
An Example of the Layered Approach in Action: The Succession to Crown Act 2013 (UK) 79

5. Clarity, Precision, Unambiguity and the Legislative Sentence 85
The Basics 85
Ambiguity and Vagueness 88
Semantic Ambiguity 92
Common Problems with Small Words: May, Shall, And/Or 92
Unless—Except 94
Scale Indicators 95
Terms Conveying Ranges of Numbers, Days, Dates and Ages 95
That and Which 96
Serial Commas and Ambiguity 98
Syntactic Ambiguity or Ambiguity at the Sentence Level 98
The Placement Problem 99
Modifiers of Nouns 100
Punctuation: Thornton's Four Rules of Punctuation 102
Gender-Neutral Drafting (gnd) 103

6. Plain Language 108
What is Plain Language? 108
Plain Language Aspect 1: Knowing your Audience 113
Plain Language Aspect 2: Easy Communication 116
Common Problems of Legislative Texts 117
Best Practices for an Easy Communication: Plain Language Innovations 123
The Debate: Concerns with Plain Language 125
Concern 1: Plain Language Lowers the Standards of Good Writing 125
Concern 2: Intelligibility 126
Concern 3: Plain Language Can only be Achieved if Certainty is Sacrificed 127
Concern 4: Plain Language Leads to a Loss of Established Meanings of Words Settled over Centuries of Judicial Interpretation 129
The Way Forward 130

7. Preliminary Provisions 132
The Structure of an Act 133
Preliminary Provisions: A Plain Language Approach 133
The Introductory Text (Formerly Known as Long Title) 139
Enacting Clause 141
Start Date (Formerly Known as Commencement) 143
Application Provisions 147
Innovations for the Future 147

8. Principal Provisions: the National, EU and International Dimension 149
Principal Provisions 149
Substantive Provisions 151
Administrative Agency Provisions 152
The EU Dimension: National Implementing Measures 152
The Choice of Form 154
The Choice of Language, Syntax and Structure 164
Summing up 168
The International Dimension: Implementing International Agreements 169
Innovation 174

9. Final Provisions 176
Saving Provisions 176
Transitional Provisions 179
Repeals and Consequential Amendments 182
Purpose Clause/Objectives 185
Commencement/Duration Provisions or Start/End Date 188
Short Title 190
Schedules 191
Schedule of Definitions 194
Other Schedules 196

10. Comparative Legislative Drafting 199
The Clichés 201
Statutory Interpretation 202
Rules of Interpretation and Construction in the Common Law: Ilbert's Rules 202
Rules of Interpretation and Construction in the Civil Law World 204
The End of the Cold War in (Statutory) Interpretation 204
Stare Decisis 205
Drafting Rules and Conventions 207
Conclusions 211

11. Time in Legislation 213
Prospective Provisions 214
Legalising Provisions 215
Retrospective Legislation 219
Retroactive Provisions 220
The Drafter and Legalising Provisions 220

12. Amending Provisions 223
Initial Considerations 224
Express and Implied Amendment 225
Direct and Indirect Amendment 226
Drafting Techniques for Direct Textual Amendments 231
Indirect Amendments 235
Amalgamating Indirect Referential Amendment with Direct Textual Amendment 238
Consequential Amendments 239
Implied Repeals 240

13. Penal Provisions 242
Drafting Instructions: Initial Considerations 243
The Legislative Plan 244
The Parts of a Penal Provisions 246
Rules of Construction 247
General Rules and Innovation 247
Expressing the Conduct 248
Sanctions 249
Special Circumstances 250
Defences 252
Special Considerations 253

14. Delegated Legislation 257
What is Delegated Legislation? 257
The Role of the Drafter in Delegated Legislation 260
Use of Delegated Legislation 262
Validity of Delegated Legislation 267
Construction 269

15. Drafting for Consolidation v Drafting for Codification 276
Codification 278
Consolidation 281
Codification versus Consolidation 284
Diverse Models and the EU 287

16. Taxation Legislation 290
Understanding Drafting Instructions: Initial Considerations for the Drafter 290

Analysing the Proposal 291
Designing the Law 292
Initial Design 298
Drafting 299
Verification 302
Use of Code 303

17. Extra-territorial Legislation 304
The Theory of Extra-territoriality: Realism, Liberalism and Beyond 306
Extra-territoriality in Practice 310
Blocking Legislation 314
Alternatives to Blocking Legislation 316
The Rules on Extra-territorial Legislation 317

18. Statutory Interpretation and Legislative Drafting 318
Current Techniques of Statutory Interpretation in the UK 320
The Drafters' Duty 327
Presumptions 328
Maxims 330
Drafting and Statutory Interpretation 330

19. Quality of Legislation Post-Lisbon and the Role of Parliaments 333
The EU's Regulatory Framework for Legislative Quality 333
The Post-Lisbon Smart Regulation Initiative 338
The UK Approach to Regulatory Quality 347
Modern Parliaments and Legislative Quality 351

20. Legislative Education and Training 354
Education and Training 354
Training versus Mentoring on the Job 358
Clinical Education and Training in Legislative Drafting 361
National versus Universal Training for Drafters 362
Conclusions 364

Index 366

Table of Cases

INTERNATIONAL

Permanent Court of International Justice

SS Lotus (France v Turkey) PCIJ Rep 1927, Series A, No 10 305

EUROPEAN UNION

Agrarproduktion Stabelow GmbH v Landrat des Landkreises Bad Doberan (C-504/04) [2006] ECR I-679 57

Amsterdam Bulb BV v Produktschap voor Siergewassen (50/76) [1977] ECR 137, [1977] CMLR 218 .... 160, 164

Asocarne v Council of the European Union (C-10/95) [1995] ECR I-4149 164

Atlantic Container Line AB v Commission of the European Communities (T-18/97) [2002] ECR II-1125, [2002] 4 CMLR 30 159

Booker Aquaculture Ltd (t/a Marine Harvest McConnell) v Scottish Ministers (C-20/00 & C-64/00) [2003] ECR I-7411, [2003] 3 CMLR 6, [2003] NPC 89 154

Commission of the European Communities v Belgium (102/79) [1980] ECR 1473, [1981] 1 CMLR 282, [1982] 2 CMLR 622 161

Commission of the European Communities v Belgium (239/85) [1986] ECR 3645, [1988] 1 CMLR 248 161

Commission of the European Communities v Denmark (143/83) [1985] ECR 427, [1986] 1 CMLR 44 161

Commission of the European Communities v France (C-327/98) [2000] ECR I-1851 157

Commission of the European Communities v France (C-38/99) [2000] ECR I-10941, [2001] Env LR 43 157

Commission of the European Communities v France (C-152/00) [2002] ECR I-6973 161

Commission of the European Communities v Germany (29/84) [1985] ECR 1661, [1986] 3 CMLR 579 162

Commission of the European Communities v Germany (C-96/95) [1997] ECR I-1653 161

Commission of the European Communities v Greece (C-365/93) [1995] ECR I-499 161

Commission of the European Communities v Greece (C-236/95) [1996] ECR I-4459, [1997] 1 CMLR 1029 161

Commission of the European Communities v Greece (C-214/98) [2000] ECR I-9601 157

Commission of the European Communities v Italy (39/72) [1973] ECR 101, [1973] CMLR 439 160
Commission of the European Communities v Italy (145/82) [1983] ECR 711, [1984] 1 CMLR 148 161
Commission of the European Communities v Italy (272/84) [1985] ECR 1057, [1987] 2 CMLR 426 168
Commission of the European Communities v Italy (420/85) [1987] ECR 2983, [1989] 1 CMLR 490 157
Commission of the European Communities v Italy (C-162/99) [2001] ECR I-541 161
Commission of the European Communities v Italy (C-49/00) [2001] ECR I-8575 .... 157, 166
Commission of the European Communities v Netherlands (C-339/87) [1990] ECR I-851, [1993] 2 CMLR 360 161
Commission of the European Communities v Netherlands (C-310/89) [1991] ECR I-138 161
Commission of the European Communities v Netherlands (C-144/99) [2001] ECR I-3541 .... 161, 162
Commission of the European Communities v Sweden (C-478/99) [2002] ECR I-4147 153
Commission of the European Communities v United Kingdom (C-441/00) [2002] ECR I-4699 157
Criminal Proceedings against Max Rombi and Arkopharma SA (C-107/97) [2000] ECR I-3367 154
Crispoltoni (C-133/93, C-300/93 & C-362/93) [1994] ECR I-4863 155
Ebony Maritime SA v Prefetto della Provincia di Brindisi (C-177/95) [1997] ECR I-1111, [1997] 2 CMLR 24 160
France v Commission of the European Communities (C-325/91) [1993] ECR 3283 162
Francovich v Italy (C-479/93) [1995] ECR I-3843, [1997] 2 BCLC 203, [1996] CEC 441, [1996] IRLR 355 337
Greece v Commission of the European Communities (C-86/03) [2001] ECR I-10979 57
Grimaldi v Fonds des Maladies Professionnelles (322/88) [1989] ECR 4407, [1991] 2 CMLR 265, [1990] IRLR 400 162
Hauptzollamt Bremen-Freihafen v Waren-Import-Gesellschaft Krohn and Co (74/69) [1970] ECR 451 167
Hauptzollamt Hamburg-Oberelbe v Firma Paul G Bollmann (40/69) [1970] ECR 69, [1970] CMLR 141 167
Internationale Handelsgesellschaft mbH v Einfuhr- und Vorratsstelle fur Getreide und Futtermittel (11/70) [1970] ECR 1125, [1972] CMLR 255 155
Marleasing SA v La Comercial Internacional de Alimentacion SA (C-106/89) [1990] ECR I-4135 326
Max.Mobil Telekommunikation Service GmbH v Commission of the European Communities (T-54/99) [2002] ECR II-313, [2002] 4 CMLR 32 .... 155, 156

Ministere Public v Guy Blanguernon (C-38/89) [1990] ECR I-83, [1991] BCLC 635, [1990] 2 CMLR 340 161
Portugal v Council of the European Union (C-149/96) [1999] ECR I-8395 166
R (Vodafone Ltd) v Secretary of State for Business, Enterprise and Regulatory Reform (C-58/08) [2010] ECR I-4999 57
Rothley v European Parliament (T-17/00) [2002] ECR II-579, [2002] 2 CMLR 30 164
Tempelman and van Schaijk (C-96/03 & C-97/03) [2005] ECR I-1895 57
Torfaen BC v B&Q plc (145/88) [1990] 3 CMLR 535 154
United Kingdom v Council of the European Union (C-84/94) [1996] All ER (EC) 877, [1996] ECR I-5755, [1996] 3 CMLR 671, [1997] ICR 443, [1997] IRLR 30 165
United Kingdom v Council of the European Union (C-150/94) [1998] ECR I-7235, [1999] 1 CMLR 367 156
Vereniging van Samenwerkende Prijsregelende Organisaties in de Bouwnijverheid v Commission of the European Communities (T-29/92 R) [1995] ECR II-289 155
Zuckerfabrik Watenstedt GmbH v Council of the European Communities (6/68) [1968] ECR 409, [1969] CMLR 26 164

DOMESTIC

Australia

A v Hayden (1984) 156 CLR 532 273
Amalgamated Society of Engineers v Adelaide Steamship Co Ltd (1920) 28 CLR 129 320
Certain Lloyd Underwriters Subscribing to Contract No IHOOAAQS v Cross [2012] HCA 56 322
Coco v R (1994) 179 CLR 427 273
Zheng v Cai [2009] CLR 239 322

Canada

Ruttan v Burk (1904) 7 OLR 56 (CA) 216

Ireland

DPP v Flannagan [1979] IR 265 321
People (Attorney General) v McGlynn [1967] IR 232 321

New Zealand

R v Royal (1993) 10 CRNZ 4 (HC) 85

United Kingdom

Adler v George [1964] QB 7, [1964] 2 WLR 542, [1964] 1 All ER 628, (1964) 128 JP 251, (1964) 108 SJ 119 321

Agricultural, Horticultural and Forestry Industry Training Board v Aylesbury Mushrooms Ltd [1972] 1 WLR 190, [1972] 1 All ER 280 209
Attorney-General v Lamplough, 47 LJQB 555, (1878) 3 Ex D 214 (CA) 193
Attorney-General v Wilts United Dairies Ltd [1921] 39 TLR 781 (CA) 263
Baines, Re, 41 ER 400, (1840) 12 A & E 227 193
Black-Clawson International Ltd v Papierwerke Waldhof-Aschaffenburg AG [1975] AC 591, [1975] 2 WLR 513, [1975] 1 All ER 810, [1975] 2 Lloyd's Rep 11, (1975) 119 SJ 221 (HL) 90, 141, 205, 325
Carter v Bradbeer [1975] 1 WLR 1204, [1975] 3 All ER 158, (1975) 61 Cr App R 275, [1975] Crim LR 714, (1975) 119 SJ 560 (HL) 203, 323
Case of Proclamations (1611) 12 Co Rep 74 273
Chandler v DPP [1964] AC 763, [1962] 3 WLR 694, [1962] 3 All ER 142, (1962) 46 Cr App R 347, (1962) 106 SJ 588 (HL) 75
Customs and Excise Commissioners v ApS Samex [1983] 1 All ER 1042, [1983] Com LR 72, [1983] 3 CMLR 194, (1983) 133 NLJ 281 325
Cooper v Motor Insurers' Bureau [1985] QB 575, [1985] 2 WLR 248, [1985] 1 All ER 449, [1985] RTR 272, (1985) 82 LSG 202, (1985) 129 SJ 32 (CA (Civ Div)) 319
Corkery v Carpenter [1951] 1 KB 102, [1950] 2 All ER 745, 66 TLR (Pt 2) 333, (1950) 114 JP 481, 48 LGR 648, (1950) 94 SJ 488 321
Dean v Green (1882) 8 PD 79 193
Dimond v Lovell [2000] QB 216, [1999] 3 WLR 561, [1999] 3 All ER 1, [1999] RTR 297, [1999] CCLR 46, (1999) 96(21) LSG 40, (1999) 149 NLJ 681, (1999) 143 SJLB 181 (CA (CivDiv)) 329
Entick v Carrington, 95 ER 807, (1765) 2 Wils KB 275, (1765) 19 St Tr 1029 273
Fisher v Raven [1964] AC 210, [1963] 2 WLR 1137, [1963] 2 All ER 389, (1963) 47 Cr App R 174, (1963) 127 JP 382, (1963) 107 SJ 373 (HL) 73
Fletcher v Birkenhead Corp [1907] 1 KB 205 (CA) 73
Gittus v IRC [1921] 2 AC 81, 90 LJKB 716 (HL); [1920] 1 KB 563, 89 LJKB 313 (CA) 193
H (A Minor) (Foreign Custody Order: Enforcement), Re [1994] Fam 105, [1994] 2 WLR 269, [1994] 1 All ER 812, [1994] 1 FLR 512, [1994] Fam Law 366 (CA (Civ Div)) 94
Heydon's Case (1584) 3 Co Rep 7a, 76 ER 1034 .... 203, 321
Heydon's Case, 74 ER 67, (1586) 1 Leo 72, (1584) 3 Co Rep 7a 31
HP Bulmer Ltd v J Bollinger SA (No 2) [1974] Ch 401, [1974] 3 WLR 202, [1974] 2 All ER 1226, [1974] 2 CMLR 91, [1974] FSR 334, [1975] RPC 321, (1974) 118 SJ 404 .... 203, 321
ICS (Investors Compensation Scheme) Ltd v West Bromwich Building Society (No 1) [1998] 1 WLR 896, [1998] 1 All ER 98, [1998] 1 BCLC 531, [1997] CLC 1243, [1997] PNLR 541, (1997) 147 NLJ 989 (HL) 203, 322

James Buchanan & Co Ltd v Babco Forwarding & Shipping (UK) Ltd [1977] QB 208, [1977] 2 WLR 107, [1977] 1 All ER 518, [1977] 1 Lloyd's Rep 234, [1977] RTR 457, [1977] 2 CMLR 455, (1977) 121 SJ 10 (CA (Civ Div)) 204, 325
JCS v West Bromwich Building Society [1998] 1 WLR 896........ 322
JH Rayner (Mincing Lane) Ltd v Dept of Trade and Industry [1990] 2 AC 418, [1989] 3 WLR 969, [1989] 3 All ER 523, (1989) 5 BCC 872, [1990] BCLC 102, (1990) 87(4) LSG 68, (1989) 139 NLJ 1559, (1989) 133 SJ 1485 (HL)........ 171
Jones v DPP [1962] AC 635, [1962] 2 WLR 575, [1962] 1 All ER 569, (1962) 46 Cr App R 129, (1962) 126 JP 216, 96 ILT 207, (1962) 106 SJ 192 (HL)........ 321
Kammins Ballrooms Co Ltd v Zenith Investments (Torquay) Ltd (No 1) [1971] AC 850, [1970] 3 WLR 287, [1970] 2 All ER 871, (1971) 22 P & CR 74, (1970) 114 SJ 590 (HL) 323
Kay v Goodwin, 130 ER 1403, (1830) 6 Bing 576........ 182
Lauri v Renad [1892] 3 Ch 402 (CA)........ 324
Litster v Forth Dry Dock & Engineering Co Ltd [1990] 1 AC 546, [1989] 2 WLR 634, [1989] 1 All ER 1134, 1989 SC (HL) 96, 1989 SLT 540, [1989] 2 CMLR 194, [1989] ICR 341, [1989] IRLR 161, (1989) 86(23) LSG 18, (1989) 139 NLJ 400, (1989) 133 SJ 455 (HL)........ 326
Magor and St Mellons Rural DC v Newport Corp [1952] AC 189, [1951] 2 All ER 839, [1951] 2 TLR 935, (1951) 115 JP 613 (HL)........ 205, 323, 324
Merkur Island Shipping Co v Laughton (The Hoegh Anapa) [1983] 2 AC 570, [1983] 2 WLR 778, [1983] 2 All ER 189, [1983] 2 Lloyd's Rep 1, [1983] ICR 490, [1983] IRLR 218, (1983) 133 NLJ 577, (1983) 127 SJ 306 (HL)........ 86, 184
Pepper (Inspector of Taxes) v Hart [1993] AC 593, [1992] 3 WLR 1032, [1993] 1 All ER 42, [1992] STC 898, [1993] ICR 291, [1993] IRLR 33, [1993] RVR 127, (1993) 143 NLJ 17, [1992] NPC 154 (HL)........ 75, 203, 322, 325
Phillips v Eyre (1870-71) LR 6 QB 1........ 216
Pickstone v Freemans plc [1989] AC 66, [1988] 3 WLR 265, [1988] 2 All ER 803, [1988] 3 CMLR 221, [1988] ICR 697, [1988] IRLR 357, (1988) 138 NLJ Rep 193 (HL)........ 325
Port Louis Corp v Attorney-General of Mauritius [1965] AC 1111, [1965] 3 WLR 67, (1965) 109 SJ 413 (PC) 269
Qualter, Hall and Co Ltd v Board of Trade [1962] Ch 273, [1961] 3 WLR 825, [1961] 3 All ER 389, (1961) 105 SJ 884 (CA) 73
R v Casement [1917] 1 KB 98, (1917) 12 Cr App R 99 (CA)........ 100
R v Chambers (William) [2008] EWCA Crim 2467 87
R v City of London Court Judge [1892] 1 QB 273 (CA) 320
R v Henn and Darvy [1978] 1 WLR 1031, [1978] 3 All ER 1190, (1979) 69 Cr App R 137, [1978] 2 CMLR 688, [1979] Crim LR 113, (1978) 122 SJ 555 (CA)........ 203

R v Lord Chancellor, ex p Witham [1998] QB 575, [1998] 2 WLR 849, [1997] 2 All ER 779, [1997] COD 291, (1997) 147 NLJ 378, (1997) 141 SJLB 82 263
R v Millward [1985] QB 519, [1985] 2 WLR 532, [1985] 1 All ER 859, (1985) 80 Cr App R 280, (1985) 149 JP 545, [1985] Crim LR 321, (1985) 82 LSG 923, (1985) 129 SJ 187 (CA) 329
R v Montila [2004] UKHL 50, [2004] 1 WLR 3141, [2005] 1 All ER 113, [2005] 1 Cr App R 26, [2005] Crim LR 479, (2005) 102(3) LSG 30, (2004) 148 SJLB 1403 75
R v Oakes [1959] 2 QB 350, [1959] 2 WLR 694, [1959] 2 All ER 92, (1959) 43 Cr App R 114, (1959) 123 JP 290, (1959) 103 SJ 373 (CA) 320
R v Pigg [1983] 1 All ER 6, [1983] 1 All ER 56, (1983) 76 Cr App R 79, [1983] Crim LR 177, (1983) 127 SJ 35 (HL) 323
R v Secretary of State for Social Security, ex p Joint Council for the Welfare of Immigrants [1997] 1 WLR 275, [1996] 4 All ER 385, (1997) 29 HLR 129, (1997) 9 Admin LR 1, (1996) 146 NLJ 985 (CA) 263
R v Secretary of State for Social Services, ex p Association of Metropolitan Authorities [1986] 1 WLR 1, [1986] 1 All ER 164, (1985) 17 HLR 487, 83 LGR 796, (1986) 130 SJ 35 209
R v Secretary of State for the Environment, Transport and the Regions, ex p Spath Holme Ltd [2001] 2 AC 349, [2001] 2 WLR 15, [2001] 1 All ER 195, (2001) 33 HLR 31, [2001] 1 EGLR 129, [2000] EG 152 (CS), (2001) 98(8) LSG 44, (2000) 150 NLJ 1855, (2001) 145 SJLB 39, [2000] NPC 139 (HL) 205, 321, 325
R v Secretary of State for the Home Department, ex p Leech (No 2) [1994] QB 198, [1993] 3 WLR 1125, [1993] 4 All ER 539, (1993) 137 SJLB 173 (CA (Civ Div)) 263
R (McCann) v Crown Court at Manchester [2002] UKHL 39, [2003] 1 AC 787, [2002] 3 WLR 1313, [2002] 4 All ER 593, [2003] 1 Cr App R 27, (2002) 166 JP 657, [2002] UKHRR 1286, 13 BHRC 482, [2003] HLR 17, [2003] BLGR 57, [2003] Crim LR 269, (2002) 166 JPN 850, (2002) 146 SJLB 239 .... 203, 321
R (Quintavalle) v Secretary of State for Health [2003] UKHL 13, [2003] 2 AC 687, [2003] 2 WLR 692, [2003] 2 All ER 113, [2003] 1 FCR 577, (2003) 71 BMLR 209, (2003) 153 NLJ 439 .... 203, 322
R (Westminster City Council) v National Asylum Support Service [2002] UKHL 38, [2002] 1 WLR 2956, [2002] 4 All ER 654, [2002] HLR 58, [2003] BLGR 23, (2002) 5 CCL Rep 511, (2002) 146 SJLB 241 .... 73, 324
River Wear Commissioners v Adamson (1877) 2 App Cas 743 (HL) 324
Rollo v Minister of Town and Country Planning [1947] 2 All ER 488, 63 TLR 499, (1947) 111 JP 534, [1948] LJR 23, (1947) 91 SJ 505 269

Stock v Frank Jones (Tipton) Ltd [1978] 1 WLR 231, [1978] 1 All ER 948, [1978] ICR 347, (1978) 13 ITR 289, (1978) 122 SJ 109 (HL) 203, 321
Stone v Yeovil Corp (1876) 2 CPD 99 (CA) 329
Sussex Peerage, 8 ER 1034, (1844) 11 Cl & F 85 (HL) 203, 207, 320
Sutherland Publishing Co v Caxton Publishing Co [1938] Ch 174, [1937] 4 All ER 405 (CA) 321
Victoria (City) v Bishop of Vancouver Island [1921] AC 384 .... 203, 321
Warburton v Loveland, 6 ER 806, (1832) 2 Dow & Cl 480 (HL) 320, 321
Wilson v First County Trust Ltd (No 2) [2003] UKHL 40, [2004] 1 AC 816, [2003] 3 WLR 568, [2003] 4 All ER 97, [2003] 2 All ER (Comm) 491, [2003] HRLR 33, [2003] UKHRR 1085, (2003) 100(35) LSG 39, (2003) 147 SJLB 872 .... 203, 205, 322, 325
Woking UDC (Basingstoke Canal) Act 1911, Re [1914] 1 Ch 300 (CA) 75
X (A Minor) (Adoption Details: Disclosure), Re [1994] Fam 174, [1994] 3 WLR 327, [1994] 3 All ER 372, [1994] 2 FLR 450, [1995] 1 FCR 135, 92 LGR 656, [1994] Fam Law 555, (1995) 159 JPN 80 (CA (Civ Div)) 323

United States

Cabell v Markham, 148 F 2d 737 (1945) 203, 322
Caminetti v United States, 242 US 470 (1917) 323
Frigaliment Importing Co v International Sales Corp, 190 F Supp 116, SDNY 1960 92
Kring v Missouri, 107 US 221 (1883) 219
Senate Concurrent Resolution No 10, Re, 137 Colo 491, 328 P2d 103 (1958) 102
State v Turchick, 436 NW 2d 108 (Minn App 1989) 102
Thompson v Utah, 170 US 343 (1898) 219
Timerlane Lambert Co v Bank of America, 549 F 2d 597 (9th Cir, 1976) 317
United States v Aluminium Co of America ('Alcoa'), 148 F 2d 416 (2d Cir, 1945) 307, 308
United States v Sisal Sales Corp, 274 US 268 (1927) 308
Whipple v Houser, 291 Or 475, 632 P 2d 782 (1981) 219

Table of Legislation

INTERNATIONAL

Treaty of Westphalia 1648 304
Vienna Convention on the Law of Treaties 1969
art 2(2)(d) 170
art 24(2) 170
art 25 170
art 26 .... 170, 171
art 31 170
art 32 .... 170, 173

EUROPEAN

EC Treaty
art 3b 155
European Convention on Human Rights 1950 .... 326, 327
art 4 243
art 5 243
art 9 243
art 10 243
art 11 243
Protocol 1 243
Protocol 4 243

Regulations
Regulation 2271/96 protecting against effects of the extra-territorial application of legislation adopted by a third country [1996] OJ L309/1
art 5 315

Decisions
Decision 93/662 adopting the Council's Rules of Procedure [1993] OJ L304/1 335
Decision 94/90 on public access to Commission documents [1994] OJ L46/58 167

DOMESTIC

Australia

Defence Act 1964
s 27 75
Flag Act 1953 248
Interpretation Act 1901–1966
s 13(1) 73
Interpretation Act 1987
s 15AC 130

Interpretation of Legislation Act 1984
s 36 ... 73
Mint Employees Act 1964
Pt 2 ... 72
Public Service Act 1999 ... 72
Queensland Legislative Standards Act 1992 ... 86

Canada

Interpretation Act, RSC 1985, c I-21
s 4 ... 69
s 44 ... 268

Malawi

Microfinance Act 2010 ... 143

New Zealand

Interpretation Act 1924
s 5 ... 75
(f) ... 73

United Kingdom

Antarctic Act 2013 (c 15) ... 143
Anti-terrorism, Crime and Security Act 2001 (c 24)
s 51 ... 314
Bill of Rights 1689 ... 273
Capital Allowances Act 2001 (c 2) ... 296
Child Maintenance and Other Payments Act 2008 (c 6)
sch 1 ... 105
Children and Young Persons Act 1933 (c 12)
s 99 ... 252
Clergy Discipline (Amendment) Measure 2013
s 6 ... 179
s 9 ... 229
Climate Change Act 2008 (c 27)
sch 2, para 10 ... 106
Consolidation of Enactment (Procedure) Act 1949 (c 33) ... 209
Corporation Tax Act 2009 (c 4) ... 296
Corporation Tax Act 2010 (c 4) ... 296
Counter-Terrorism Act 2008 (c 28) ... 106
Courts Act 1971 (c 23) ... 117
Crime and Courts Act 2013 (c 22) ... 146
s 61 ... 145
sch 8 ... 179
Crofting (Amendment) (Scotland) Act 2013 (asp 10) ... 227

Defamation Act 2013 (c 26)
s 4 253
Domestic Violence, Crime and Victims (Amendment) Act 2012 (c 4) 191
Energy Act 2004 (c 20)
s 102 313
Energy Act 2013 (c 32)
s 21 264
Enterprise and Regulatory Reform Act 2013 (c 24)
s 24 181
(3) 181
European Union (Croatian Accession and Irish Protocol) Act 2013 (c 5)
s 6 178
Export Control Act 2002 (c 28) 231
Finance Act 2013 (c 29) 140, 143
s 24 192
Forestry Act (Northern Ireland) 2010 (c 10)
s 33 251
Freedom of Information (Amendment) (Scotland) Act 2013 (asp 2) 191, 238
Growth and Infrastructure Act 2013 (c 27)
s 17(b) 264
s 35 188
Health and Social Care Act 2008 (c 14)
s 34(1) 106
High Hedges (Scotland) Act 2013 (asp 6) 191
Human Rights Act 1998 (c 42) 173, 206, 243, 322, 323, 325–27
s 3 .... 322, 327
Income Tax Act 2007 (c 3) 296
Income Tax (Earnings and Pensions) Act 2003 (c 1) 296
Income Tax (Trading and Other Income) Act 2005 (c 5) 296
Interpretation Act 1978 (c 30) 208
s 6 104
s 13 268
s 21(1) 257
Judicial Pensions Act 1981 (c 20) 270
Justice and Security Act 2013 (c 18) 191
Landfill Tax (Scotland) Act 2014 (asp 2)
s 29 252
s 41 266
Legal Aid, Sentencing and Punishment of Offenders Act 2012 (c 10)
s 33 253
Local Audit and Accountability Act 2014 (c 2)
s 2 266
s 23 .... 249, 250
Marine Act (Northern Ireland) 2013 (c 10)
s 34 253
Marriage (Same Sex Couples) Act 2013 (c 30) 143
s 21 143

Mesothelioma Act 2014 (c 1)
s 8 248
Mobile Homes Act 2013 (c 14)
s 4 253
s 15 178
Mobile Homes (Wales) Act 2013 (anaw 6)
s 5 .... 247, 248
(1) 248
(2) 248
sch 5 182
Offences against the Person Act 1861 (c 100)
s 9 311
Pensions Act 2008 (c 30)
sch 1 105
Presumption of Death Act 2013 (c 13)
s 21 178
Protection of Freedoms Act 2012 (c 9)
s 54 250
Protection of Military Remains Act 1986 (c 35)
s 3 312
Reading Borough Council Act 2013 (c iv)
s 9 252
Road Traffic Act 1972 (c 20) 117
Sexual Offences Act 2003 (c 42)
s 72 255
Statutory Instruments Act 1946 (c 36) 208
Succession to the Crown Act 2013 (c 20) 79–84
Supply and Appropriation (Main Estimates) Act 2013 (c 28) 141
Sustainable Communities Act 2007 (Amendment) Act 2010 (c 21) 141
Taxation (International and Other Provisions) Act 2010 (c 8) 296
Terrorism Act 2000 (c 11)
s 77 255
Transparency of Lobbying, Non-Party Campaigning and Trade Union Administration Act 2014 (c 4)
s 12 253
s 13 250
s 23 263
(1), (2), (3) 263
s 45 265
Treason Act 1351 (c 2) 100
Trusts (Capital and Income) Act 2013 (c 1) 191
Diplomatic Privileges Act 1964 incorporating the Vienna Convention on Diplomatic Relations 173
Water and Sewerage Services (Amendment) Act (Northern Ireland) 2013 (c 6) 191
Water Resources (Scotland) Act 2013 (asp 5)
s 56 179

Statutory Instruments

A31 Trunk Road (Cadnam–Verwood Interchange) (Temporary Restriction and Prohibition of Traffic) Order 2014 (SI 2014/311) ... 271
A38 Trunk Road (Eggington to Branston, Staffordshire) (Temporary Prohibition of Traffic) Order 2014 (SI 2014/277) ... 271
A556 Trunk Road (Turnpike Wood, Over Tabley-A56 Bowdon Roundabout) (Detrunking) Order 1996 (Revocation) Order 2008 (SI 2008/234) ... 272
Additionally-developed Oil Fields Order 2013 (SI 2013/2910)
art 1 ... 274
Appointment of Consultants (Amendment) Regulations (Northern Ireland) 2013 (SI 2013/114)
reg 5 ... 238
Armed Forces and Reserve Forces Compensation Scheme (Consequential Provisions: Subordinate Legislation) Order 2013 (SI 2013/591) ... 240
Building (Amendment) (Wales) Regulations 2014 (SI 2014/110) ... 275
Child Benefit, Child Support and Social Security (Miscellaneous Amendments) Regulations 1996 (SI 1996/1803) ... 232
Children's Homes and Looked After Children (Miscellaneous Amendment) (England) Regulations 2013 (SI 2013/3239) ... 227
Democratic People's Republic of Korea (European Union Financial Sanctions) Regulations 2013 (SI 2013/1877)
reg 21 ... 274
Export Control (Amendment) (No 2) Order 2010 (SI 2010/2007) ... 231
Extraterritorial US Legislation (Sanctions against Cuba, Iran and Libya) (Protection of Trading Interests) Order 1996 (SI 1996/3171) ... 312
Family Procedure (Amendment No 3) Rules 2013 (SI 2013/3204) ... 226, 227
Further Education Loans (Amendment) Regulations 2014 (SI 2014/290) ... 272
Health and Social Care Act 2008 (Primary Dental Services, Private Ambulance Services and Primary Medical Services) (Regulated Activities) (Transitory and Transitional Provisions) (Amendment) Order 2011 (SI 2011/2948)
art 4 ... 236
Judicial Pensions (Widows', Widowers' and Children's Benefits) (Amendment) Regulations 2014 (SI 2014/288) ... 270
Local Authorities (Executive Arrangements) (Functions and Responsibilities) (Wales) (Amendment No 2) Regulations 2013 (SI 2013/2902 (W 281)) ... 191
Maritime Security (Jersey) Order 2014 (SI 2014/265) ... 275
Merchant Shipping (Prevention of Air Pollution from Ships) Order 2006 (SI 2006/1248)
art 3 ... 312
Olive Oil (Marketing Standards) Regulations 2014 (SI 2014/195) ... 274
Police Act 1997 (Criminal Records) (Isle of Man) (Amendment) Order 2012 (SI 2012/2598) ... 231
Prosecution of Offences (Youth Courts Time Limits) Regulations 1999 (SI 1999/2743)
regs 4, 7 ... 254

Public Bodies (Abolition of the Commission for Rural Communities)
Order 2012 (SI 2012/2654) 232
Representation of the People (England and Wales)
(Description of Electoral Registers and Amendment)
Regulations 2013 (SI 2013/3198) 226, 236
Solvent Emissions (Scotland) Regulations 2010 (SSI 2010/236)
reg 2 237
Tobacco Products (Descriptions of Products) (Amendment) Order 2013
(SI 2013/2721)
art 1 273
Town and Country Planning (Development Management Procedure)
(England) (Amendment No 2) Order 2013 (SI 2013/1238) 232
Town and Country Planning (General Permitted Development)
(Amendment) (England) (No 3) Order 2013 (SI 2013/2147) 231

United States

Foreign Relations Law (Third Restatement) 1987 308
Indiana Constitution
art 4, s 20 86

1

Legislation as a Means of Regulation: Effectiveness in Legislative Drafting

INTRODUCTION

THE CONCEPT OF 'rules for regulation' may encompass all types of directions and prohibitions imposed by governments[1] in the exercise of their right and duty to run the state business through a pyramid of supports or a pyramid of sanctions, following the supportive regulation paradigm.[2] The term can be defined very broadly. It can allow for the inclusion of written and soft rules, although by definition both types have to be binding to be classified as rules; the inclusion of all types of sources of rules, be it the legislature or the executive according to procedural requirements; and the inclusion of any type of regulation, positive or negative (deregulation is a form of governing after all), active or passive (non-regulation is a form of governing after all), self-executable or enforceable.[3] The OECD includes in the term the full range of legal instruments by which governing institutions, at all levels of government, impose obligations or constraints on private sector behaviour, such as constitutions, parliamentary laws, subordinate legislation, decrees, orders, norms, licences, plans, codes and even some forms of administrative guidance.[4] But for the purposes of this analysis the term 'rules for regulation' is narrowed down and defined as written, binding, legal provisions of statutory law.

[1] It is precisely the involvement of government that stands out as the common theme for legal rules: see JC Dernbach, RV Singleton II, CS Wharton, JM Ruhtenberg and CJ Wasson, *Legal Writing and Legal Method* (Austin, Wolters Kluwer, 2007) 3.
[2] See esp J Braithwaite, 'The Essence of Responsive Regulation' (2011) 44 *University of British Columbia Law Review* 475, 482.
[3] But it excludes standards: see P Schlag, 'Rules and Standards' (1985–86) 33 *UCLA Law Review* 379.
[4] See OECD, 'Recommendation of the Council on Improving the Quality of Government Regulation' (Paris, 9 March 1995) C(95)21/Final; also see OECD, 'Building Capacity for Regulatory Quality: Stocktaking Paper', GOV/PGC (Paris, 2004) 11, 2.

But what exactly is the link between regulation and legislation or statutory law?[5] Although the relationship between regulation and legislation is quite simple and straightforward, it is rarely placed in a functional context.[6] And, as a result, it tends to remain in the theoretical drawers of academics rather than established in the brains of the actors of the policy process. Mousmouti and Voermans distinguish clearly between legislation and regulation:

> [L]egislative quality reflects an institutional view of legislation as an issue closely related to the constitutional principles of legality, effectiveness and legal certainty, while regulatory quality reflects a more instrumental view of legislation where quality mirrors the success of legislation in promoting economic development.[7]

Put simply, irrespective of the polity of each state, governments are there (elected, appointed or otherwise established) to run the business of governing the state. They take their place in order to ensure that the agenda that led to their placement in power is actually seen through.[8] Government agendas are seen through via policies aiming to produce the desired regulatory results:[9] the prevalent measure of policy success is the extent of production of the desired results.[10] Policies are conceived by policy-makers, normally in the first instance at the pre-election/appointment/establishment agenda-setting phase and later at the governing phase.[11] Normally policy agendas at the two stages coincide but of course this is not always the case,[12] either because a policy is abandoned in between stages, because a policy is not prioritised in the governing stage, or because a policy presents itself after the election/appointment/establishment in power stage. But, whatever the timing of their appearance, the fate of prioritised policies is to be put to

[5] See H Xanthaki, 'Quality of Legislation: an Achievable Universal Concept or a Utopian Pursuit?' in M Travares Almeida (ed), *Quality of Legislation* (Baden-Baden, Nomos, 2011) 75, 76–78.

[6] See ST Trautmann, 'Empirical Knowledge in Legislation and Regulation: a Decision-making Perspective' (2013) 1 *The Theory and Practice of Legislation* 533, 538–39.

[7] See M Mousmouti, 'Operationalising Quality of Legislation through the Effectiveness Test' (2012) 6 *Legisprudence* 191, 194; also W Voermans, 'Concern about the Quality of EU Legislation: What Kind of Problem, by What Kind of Standards?' (2009) 2 *Erasmus Law Review* 59, 223 and 225; and R Baldwin and M Cave, *Understanding Regulation: Theory, Strategy and Practice* (Oxford, Oxford University Press, 1999) 85.

[8] See OECD, 'Recommendation of the Council on Improving the Quality of Government Regulation' (n 4).

[9] The executive branch of government is no longer expected to confine itself to the mere making of proposals: it has to see them through: see J Craig Peacock, *Notes on Legislative Drafting* (Washington, REC Foundation, 1961) 3.

[10] See N Staem, 'Governance, Democracy and Evaluation' (2006) 12(7) *Evaluation* 7, 7.

[11] For a contra view, namely that most policies come about in response to sudden needs rather than from the manifesto commitments of the governing party, see M Zander, *The Law Making Process* (Cambridge, Cambridge University Press, 2005) 2, 7.

[12] On the dynamic nature of regulation, see C Radaelli and F de Francesco, *Regulatory Quality in Europe: Concepts, Measures and Policy Processes* (Manchester, Manchester University Press, 2007) 36.

effect.[13] Let me clarify: governments normally aim to actually to put their policies to effect; but a government's conscious choice to simply be seen to have put a policy to effect on paper rather than actually to have done so is an acceptable choice.[14] And so regulation, in the sense used in this analysis, is the process of putting government policies into effect to the degree and extent intended by government.[15] The regulatory tools available to government vary[16] from flexible forms of traditional regulation (such as performance-based and incentive approaches), to co-regulation and self-regulation schemes,[17] incentive- and market-based instruments (such as tax breaks and tradable permits) and information approaches.[18]

More often than not rule-making takes the form of legislation, although alternative means of rule- or law-making are becoming popular in the form of soft law. But legislation remains a choice offered to governments as a regulatory tool. And this is really what gives law legitimacy: its adoption by a formally authorised legislature.[19] Here the policy process narrows down to a legislative process, namely a process of, for civil lawyers, law-making or, for common lawyers, legislating. Here rules become artefacts with practical authority over enough persons within their scope of application that they can order these persons' affairs.[20] Here the policy becomes translated into legal concept and then expressed as a legislative text.[21]

This latter part is an even narrower circle within the legislative process, the drafting process. It is within the drafting process that drafters undergo each one of Thornton's five stages of drafting.[22] Here, policy officers and legal officers see their concept transform into written law, if and where appropriate.[23]

[13] OECD notes the importance of public sector management in ensuring policy effectiveness and economic efficiency under conditions of democratic accountability: C(2014)32 Recommendation of the Council on Effective Public Investment Across Levels of Government.

[14] And the choice is the government's not the drafter's: see P Delnoy, *Le rôle des légistes dans la détermination du contenu des norms* Report for the International Cooperation Group (Department of Justice, Canada, 2013) 3 www.justice.gc.ca/fra/apd-abt/gci-icg/publications.html.

[15] See National Audit Office, Department for Business, Innovations and Skills, 'Delivering Regulatory Reform' (10 Feb 2011) para 1.

[16] See Better Regulation Task Force (BRTF), 'Routes to Better Regulation: A Guide to Alternatives to Classic Regulation' (December 2005).

[17] See J Miller, 'The FTC and Voluntary Standards: Maximizing the Net Benefits of Self-Regulation' (1985) 4 *Cato Journal* 897.

[18] See OECD Report, Alternatives to Traditional Regulation (Paris, 2002) para 0.3; and also OECD, 'Regulatory Policies in OECD Countries: From Interventionism to Regulatory Governance' (Paris, 2002).

[19] See Y Blankt, 'The Reenchantment of Law' (2010–11) 96 *Cornell Law Review* 633, 639.

[20] See L Alexander and E Sherwin, *The Rule of Rules: Morality, Rules, and the Dilemmas of Law* (Durham, NC, Duke University Press, 2001) 188.

[21] A statute is the formal expression of legislative policy: see EA Driedger, *The Composition of Legislation—Legislative Forms and Precedents* (Ottawa, Ministry of Justice, 1976) xv.

[22] See H Xanthaki, *Thornton's Legislative Drafting*, 5th edn (West Sussex, Bloomsbury Professional, 2013).

[23] See National Audit Office, Department for Business, Innovations and Skills, 'Delivering Regulatory Reform' (n 15) para 2.5.

And so legislation is a mere tool for governing, or else a mere tool of regulation. This is the relationship between regulation and legislation. Legislation is one of the many choices[24] offered to governments in their pursuit of putting their policies to effect. But legislation cannot be 'reduced' to policy.[25]

If one takes this holistic picture of legislation as a tool for regulation into account, identifying the goal of the drafter as achieving 'quality in legislation' is a rather short-sighted and narrowly focused approach.[26] In application of Stefanou's scheme on the three processes,[27] drafters can only aim to perform well in their little, albeit crucial, part in the application of governmental policy better expressed as regulation.[28] Thus, the starting point of this chapter is that drafters pursue quality in regulation. This statement reflects the role of the drafter in the whole of the governing process, and strengthens the view that legislation is only one, in fact the last and least,[29] of the choices offered to governments in their attempt to regulate. This is what the EU calls the principle of necessity[30] in EU regulation.[31]

One of the most eloquent quotes on current thinking about legislation is attributed to Richard Heaton, First Parliamentary Counsel and Permanent Secretary of the Cabinet Office:

> I believe that we need to establish a sense of shared accountability, within and beyond government, for the quality of what (perhaps misleadingly) we call our statute book, and to promote a shared professional pride in it. In doing so, I hope we can create confidence among users that legislation is for them.[32]

[24] See A Flückiger, 'Régulation, dérégulation, autorégulation: l'émergence des actes étatiques non obligatoires' (2004) 123 *Revue de droit suisse* 159.

[25] P Westerman, 'Breaking the Circle: Goal-legislation and the Need for Empirical Research' (2013) 1 *The Theory and Practice of Legislation* 385, 411.

[26] For a detailed historical analysis of the term 'quality of legislation', see E Albanesi, *Teoria e Tecnica Legislative in Sistema Costituzionale* (Naples, Editoriale Scientifica, 2013) 45–54.

[27] See C Stefanou, 'Legislative Drafting as a Form of Communication' in L Mader and M Travares-Almeida (eds), *Quality of Legislation Principles and Instruments* (Baden-Baden, Nomos, 2011) 308; and also see C Stefanou, 'Drafters, Drafting and the Policy Process' in C Stefanou and H Xanthaki (eds), *Drafting Legislation: A Modern Approach* (Aldershot, Ashgate, 2008) 321.

[28] In fact, there is an emergence of a public interest in good quality of rules: see M De Benedetto, M Martelli and N Rangone, *La Qualità delle Regole* (Bologna, SE il Mulino, 2011) 23.

[29] See S Weatherhill, 'The Challenge of Better Regulation' in S Weatherhill (ed), *Better Regulation* (Oxford and Portland, Hart Publishing, 2007) 1, 19.

[30] See the French Circular of 2 Jan 1993 on the rules for the elaboration, signature and publication of texts in the Official Journal and the coming into force of the particular procedures of the Prime Minster, art 2.1.1.1; also see German *Gemeinsame Geschäftsordnung der Bundesministerien* (15 Oct 1976) as modified, art 40; German Manual of Judicial Formalities (1991) paras 26–28; Portuguese Deliberation of the Council of Ministers of 8 Feb 1989 on the approval of the general principles for the elaboration of projects of normative acts, art 1a.

[31] See R Haythorthwaite, 'Better Regulation in Europe' in Weatherhill (ed), *Better Regulation* (n 29) 20, 23.

[32] See R Heaton, 'Foreword' in Cabinet Office, Office of Parliamentary Counsel, *When Laws Become Too Complex* (16 April 2013).

But, if drafters pursue contributing towards the quality of governmental regulation, what does this contribution really entail? The diagram[33] below visualises these goals and their hierarchy.[34]

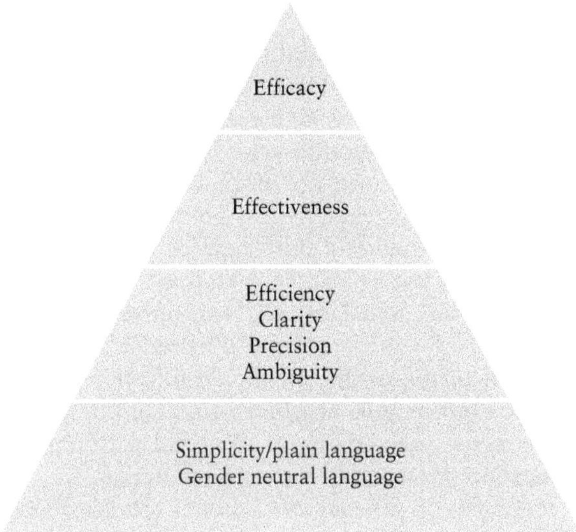

Figure 1.1: Legislative Drafting Virtues

The ultimate goal for regulation is efficacy. Efficacy is the extent to which regulators achieve their goal.[35] It is often confused with effectiveness, especially by experts outside the field of legislative studies, who have nonetheless much to offer in the analysis of the concept. W Bradnee Chambers, for example, offers a unique systematisation of the conceptual spectrum of what he calls effectiveness[36] and I call efficacy: the measure by which the performance data of the legislation match its objectives.[37] Bradnee Chambers distinguishes between rule-based positivist models of efficacy that look at the level of compliance achieved; socio-legal models[38] that assess efficacy by reference to the compliance of rules with societal norms

[33] See H Xanthaki, 'On Transferability of Legislative Solutions: the Functionality Test' in Stefanou and Xanthaki (eds), *Drafting Legislation: A Modern Approach* (n 27) 1.

[34] For a thorough analysis of the goals for drafters and the theoretical basis for their universality, see Xanthaki, ibid.

[35] ibid, 126; also see Mousmouti, 'Operationalising Quality of Legislation through the Effectiveness Test' (n 7) 200.

[36] Also see A Flückiger, 'L'évaluation législative ou comment mesurer lefficacité des lois' (2007) *Revue européenne des sciences sociales* 83.

[37] See W Bradnee Chambers, 'Towards an Improved Understanding of Legal Effectiveness of International Environmental Treaties' (2003–04) 16 *Georgetown International Environmental Law Review* 501, 531.

[38] Based on the theory that legislation is a tool for changing behaviour: see H Kelsen, 'Law as a Specific Social Technique' (1941) 9 *University of Chicago Law Review* 75, 79–80.

and values falling within the 'established milieu'[39] or by reference to their legitimacy leading to compliance;[40] the economic legal model that includes cost-efficiency as the measure of efficacy;[41] and international relations models that call for clearer distinctions between efficacy, implementation and compliance.

Taking into account the role of the drafter as a mere unit in the many actors of regulation (namely in the policy, legislative and drafting processes),[42] efficacy from the narrow point of view of legislative drafting can be defined as the capacity of a piece of legislation to achieve the regulatory aims that it is set to address.[43] Efficacy, as a measure of quality of legislation for the purposes of achieving the desired regulation, is not a goal that can be achieved by the drafter alone.[44] A wonderful draft may be capable of producing the desired regulatory effects, but bad implementation[45] and bad judicial application may interfere with its actual results.[46] Of course one has to accept that the extent of the margin for incorrect implementation and judicial application is directly linked to the quality of the draft,[47] but it is quite possible that the error in the draft may be attributed to a fault in the content of the pursued policy or in the calculations of the regulatory impact assessment made for the allocation of resources for implementation.

Within the umbrella of efficacy the drafter pursues effectiveness in legislation.[48] The term is used widely but often without a definition. For example the EU calls for accountability, effectiveness and proportionality as

[39] See I Jenkins, *Social Order and the Limits of Law: A Theoretical Essay* (New Jersey, Princeton University Press, 1980) 180.

[40] See TM Franck, 'Legitimacy in the International System' (1988) 82 *American Journal of International Law*, 705.

[41] See OK Young and MA Levy, 'The Effectiveness of International Environmental Regimes' in OR Young et al (eds), *The Effectiveness of International Environmental Regimes* (Massachusetts, MIT Press, 1999) 1, 4–5; also see OECD, 'Regulatory Policies in OECD Countries; from Interventionism to Regulatory Governance' (n 18); and also 'Background Note to the OECD Reference Checklist for Regulatory Decision Making' of OECD, 'Recommendation of the Council on Improving the Quality of Government Regulation' (n 4)

[42] See AE Black, *From Inspiration to Legislation: How and Idea Becomes a Bill* (New Jersey, Pearson Education Ltd, 2007) 123.

[43] See N Gunningham and D Sinclair, 'Designing Smart Regulation' 18 www.oecd.org/dataoecd/18/39/33947759.pdf; and also R Baldwin, 'Is Better Regulation Smarter Regulation?' (2005) *Public Law* 485, 511.

[44] See JP Chamberlain, 'Legislative Drafting and Law Enforcement' (1931) 21 *American Labor Legislative Review* 235, 243.

[45] See D Hull, 'Drafters' Devils' (2000) *Loophole* www.opc.gov.au/calc/docs/calc-june/audience.htm.

[46] See U Karpen, 'The Norm Enforcement Process' in U Karpen and P Delnoy (eds), *Contributions to the Methodology of the Creation of Written Law* (Baden-Baden, Nomos, 1996) 51, 51; also L Mader, 'Legislative Procedure and the Quality of Legislation' in Karpen and Delnoy (eds), *Contributions to the Methodology of the Creation of Written Law* 62, 68.

[47] See G Teubner, 'Regulatory Law: Chronicle of a Death Foretold' (1992) 1 *Social Legal Studies* 451.

[48] See C Timmermans, 'How Can One Improve the Quality of Community Legislation?' (1997) 34 *Common Market Law Review* 1229, 1236–37.

a means of achieving better law-making, but the term is not defined at all.[49] Similarly, the UK's Office of Parliamentary Counsel repeats its aspiration to effectiveness as a contribution to or in balance with accuracy, but does not define the term.[50] Mader defines effectiveness as the extent to which the observable attitudes and behaviours of the target population correspond to the attitudes and behaviours prescribed by the legislator.[51] Snyder defines effectiveness as 'the fact that law matters: it has effects on political, economic and social life outside the law—that it, apart from simply the elaboration of legal doctrine'.[52] Teubner defines effectiveness as term encompassing implementation, enforcement, impact and compliance.[53] Muller and Ulmann define effectiveness as the degree to which the legislative measure has achieved a concrete goal without suffering from side-effects.[54] In Jenkins' socio-legal model effectiveness in the legislation can be defined as the extent to which the legislation influences in the desired manner the social phenomenon which it aims to address.[55] Voermans defines the principle of effectiveness as a consequence of the rule of law, which imposes a duty on the legislator to consider and respect the implementation and enforcement of legislation to be enacted.[56] Mousmouti describes effectiveness as a measure of the causal relations between the law and its effects: and so an effective law is one that is respected or implemented, provided that the observable degree of respect can be attributed to the norm.[57]

For the purposes of drafting in its narrow sense, therefore, effectiveness is the ultimate measure of quality in legislation.[58] It simply reflects the extent to which the legislation manages to introduce adequate mechanisms capable of producing the desired regulatory results.[59] If one subjects effectiveness

[49] See European Commission, 'European Governance: Better Lawmaking' (Communication) COM(2002) 275 final; also see High Level Group on the Operation of Internal Market, 'The Internal Market After 1992: Meeting the Challenge—Report to the EEC Commission by the High Level Group on the Operation of Internal Market' SEC (92) 2044.

[50] See Office of Parliamentary Counsel, 'Working with OPC' (6 December 2011); and Office of Parliamentary Counsel, 'Drafting Guidance' (16 December 2011).

[51] See L Mader, 'Evaluating the Effect: a Contribution to the Quality of Legislation' (2001) 22 *Statute Law Review* 119, 126.

[52] See F Snyder, 'The Effectiveness of European Community Law: Institutions, Processes, Tools and Techniques' (1993) 56 *Modern Law Review* 19, 19; also F Snyder, *New Directions in European Community Law* (London, Weidenfeld and Nicolson, 1990) 3.

[53] See G Teubner, 'Regulatory Law: Chronicle of a Death Foretold' in L Lenoble (ed), *Einfuhrung in der Rectssoziologie* (Darmstadt, Wissenschaftliche Buchgesellschaft, 1987) 54.

[54] See G Muller and F Uhlmann, *Elemente einer Rechtssetzungslehre* (Zurich, Asculthess, 2013) 51–52.

[55] See I Jenkins, *Social Order and the Limits of the Law: a Theoretical Essay* (Princeton, Princeton University Press, 1981) 180; also see R Cranston, 'Reform through Legislation: the Dimension of Legislative Technique' (1978–79) 73 *Northwestern University Law Review* 873, 875.

[56] See Voermans, 'Concern about the Quality of EU Legislation' (n 7) 230.

[57] See Mousmouti (n 7) 200.

[58] See Xanthaki, 'On Transferability of Legal Solutions' in Stefanou and Xanthaki (n 27) 6.

[59] See Office of the Leader of the House of Commons, *Post-legislative Scrutiny—The Government's Approach* (March 2008) para 2.4.

of legislation to the wider semantic field of efficacy of regulation as its element, effectiveness manages to hold true even with reference to diverse legislative phenomena, such as symbol legislation, or even the role of law as a ritual. If the purpose of legislation is to serve as a symbol, then effectiveness becomes the measure of achieved inspiration of the users of the symbol legislation. If the legislation is to be used as a ritual, effectiveness takes the robe of persuasion of the users who bow down to its appropriate rituality.

In its concrete, rather than abstract conceptual sense, effectiveness requires a legislative text that can (1) foresee the main projected outcomes and use them in the drafting and formulation process; (2) state clearly its objectives and purpose; (3) provide for necessary and appropriate means and enforcement measures; and (4) assess and evaluate real-life effectiveness in a consistent and timely manner.[60]

But what about the means used for the achievement of effectiveness? Effectiveness can be achieved by use of two sets of tools: first, by efficiency, namely use of minimum costs for the achievement of optimum benefits of the legislative action;[61] and secondly, by clarity, precision and unambiguity. Efficiency refers to the choice of the most financially appropriate solution: as a result it is a preoccupation for the economists of the multi-disciplinary drafting team. In the context of legislation as a tool of regulation efficiency is a quality *sine qua non* of the regulation, and consequently the legislation that has been selected as the tool for the achievement of the regulatory goals. Clarity, or clearness,[62] is the quality of being clear and easily perceived or understood.[63] Precision is defined as exactness of expression or detail.[64] Unambiguity is certain or exact meaning:[65] semantic unambiguity requires a single meaning for each word used,[66] whereas syntactic unambiguity requires clear sentence structure and correct placement of phrases or clauses.[67] Clarity, precision and unambiguity offer predictability to the law. Predictability allows the users of the legislation, including enforcers,[68] to comprehend the required content of the regulation. Predictability of effect

[60] This is Mousmouti's effectiveness test: Mousmouti (n 7) 202.

[61] See R Posner, 'Cost Benefit Analysis: Definition, Justification, and Comments on Conference Papers' (2000) 29 *The Journal of Legal Studies* 1153.

[62] See Lord H Thring, *Practical Legislation: The Composition and Language of Acts of Parliament and Business Documents* (London, John Murray, 1902) 61.

[63] *See Compact Oxford English Dictionary of Current English* (Oxford, Oxford University Press, 2005).

[64] ibid.

[65] ibid.

[66] J MacKaye, AW Levi and W Pepperell Montague, *The Logic of Language* (Hannover, Dartmouth College Publications, 1939) ch 5.

[67] For the distinction between semantic and syntactic ambiguity, see R Dickerson, *The Fundamentals of Legal Drafting* (Boston, Little-Brown, 1986) 101 and 104; for an application of rules of logic to resolve syntactic ambiguities, see LE Allen, 'Symbolic Logic: a Razor-edged Tool for Drafting and Interpreting Legal Documents' (1956–57) 66 *Yale Law Journal* 833, 855.

[68] See A Seidman, R Seidman and N Abeyesekere, *Legislative Drafting for Democratic Social Change* (The Hague, Kluwer Law International, 2001) 255.

is a necessary component of effectiveness and indeed of the rule of law.[69] Thus, compliance becomes a matter of conscious choice for the user, rather than a matter of the user's subjective interpretation of the exact content of the legislation and, ultimately, the regulation.

At the third level of the hierarchy of goals for the drafter comes plain language and gender-neutral language. Plain language as a concept encapsulates a qualifier of language which is subjective to each reader or user.[70] Eagleson defines plain language as clear, straightforward expression, using only as many words as are necessary. It is language that avoids obscurity, inflated vocabulary and convoluted sentence structure. It is not baby talk, nor is it a simplified version of the English language.[71] According to Redish, plain English means writing that is straightforward, that reads as if it were spoken. It means writing that is unadorned with archaic, multi-syllabic words and majestic turns of phrase that even educated readers cannot understand. Plain English is clear, direct and simple; but good plain English has both clarity and grace.[72] Plain language takes into account design and layout, as well as language, and means analysing and deciding what information readers need to make informed decisions, before words, sentences or paragraphs are considered.[73] A plain language document uses words economically[74] and at a level that the audience of the particular text can understand. Sentence structure is tight. The tone is welcoming and direct. The design is visually appealing.[75] Common problems identified by the plain language movement are long sentences; passive voice;[76] weak verbs; superfluous words; legal and financial jargon; abstract words; and unreadable design and layout.[77]

Gender-neutral language is a tool for accuracy, as it promotes gender specificity in drafting[78] and before the courts.[79] Gender-specific[80] language

[69] See Sir S Laws, 'Giving effect to policy in legislation: how to avoid missing the point' (CALC Conference Hong Kong, 2009).

[70] See R Sullivan, 'Some Implications of Plain Language Drafting' (2001) 22 *Statute Law Review* 145, 149.

[71] See RD Eagleson, *Writing in Plain English* (Commonwealth of Australia, 1990) 4.

[72] See JC Redish, 'The Plain English Movement' in S Greenbaum, *The English Language Today* (New York, Pergamon Press, 1985) 125, 126.

[73] See BA Garner, *Legal Writing in Plain English* (Chicago, The University of Chicago Press, 2001) 10–13.

[74] See R Wydick, *Plain English for Lawyers* (Durham, NC, Carolina Academic Press, 1998) 9.

[75] ibid, 121–34.

[76] See Maine Manual on Legislative Drafting, ch 1, s 7http://www.maine.gov/legis/ros/Publications.htm.

[77] See Legislation Advisory Committee, 'Guidelines on Process and Content of Legislation 2001 (including the 2003 Supplement)' (Wellington, Ministry of Justice, May 2001, updated September 2003).

[78] See Commentary, 'Avoidance of Sexist Language in Legislation' (1985) 11 *Commonwealth Law Bulletin* 590, 590.

[79] See WB Hill Jr, 'A Need for the Use of Nonsexist Language in the Courts' (1992) 49 *Washington and Lee Law Review* 275.

[80] See S Petersson, 'Gender-neutral Drafting: Recent Commonwealth Developments' (1999) 20 *Statute Law Review* 35, 57.

serves in parallel with plain language as an additional tool for the promotion of precision, clarity and unambiguity.

This brief expose of the main principles of drafting and their placement in a pyramid of hierarchy presents interesting conclusions. The pursuit of drafters is their contribution towards efficacy of regulation. This is undertaken within the limited role of the drafter in regulation, and is defined as effectiveness. Thus, for drafting in its narrow sense quality in legislation is synonymous with effectiveness. Effectiveness in legislation is achieved via efficiency on the one hand, and clarity, precision and unambiguity on the other hand. Plain language and gender-specific language are both worthwhile tools for the achievement of clarity, precision and unambiguity.

THE NATURE OF RULES FOR REGULATION: ART OR TECHNOLOGY?

But what is the nature of rules for regulation? And how are they to be applied? Answering this question depends on the nature of drafting legislation, which is often evasively described as 'serious business'.[81] Dick describes it as 'legal thinking made visible'.[82] Dickerson views legislative drafting as 'the crystallization and expression in definitive form of a legal right, privilege, function, duty, status or disposition'.[83] Salembier distinguishes drafting from other forms of writing, in that its goal is not to entertain, to impress or to explain, but to set out the parameters for legal relationships in the clearest possible manner.[84]

If drafting is considered to be a pure form of art[85] or a quasi-craft,[86] then rules and conventions bow down to creativity and innovation. Drafting is a liberal skill that is bound by no rules and is developed through experience and subjective mentoring.[87] There is therefore no possibility of instruction on how drafting must be done for each possible set of circumstances that may occur in the future, and therefore there are no lessons to be learnt from rules of any kind; moreover, techniques, language and general approach change and must be allowed freedom to do so.[88] This is drafting as traditionally conceived in the common law world of the past, and in the civil law world even currently. Drafting is a liberal skill, which is possessed by

[81] See D Revell, 'Authoring Bilingual Laws: The Importance of Process' (2004) 29 *Brooklyn Journal of International Law* 1085.

[82] See RC Dick, *Legal Drafting* (Toronto, Carswell Publishers, 1972) 1.

[83] See R Dickerson, *Fundamentals of Legal Drafting*, 2nd edn (Boston, Little Brown, 1986) 3.

[84] See P Salembier, *Legal and Legislative Drafting* (Markham, Ontario, LexisNexis, 2009) 23.

[85] See Sir G Bowman, 'The Art of Legislative Drafting' (2005) *European Journal of Law Reform* 3, 3; also see K Gilberg, 'De l'Art de Mieux Légiférer' *Le Monde* (Paris, 17 Feb 2010) 1.

[86] See BG Scharffs, 'Law as Craft' (2001) 45 *Vanderbilt Law Review* 2245, 2339.

[87] Some would call it 'intuitive' rather than subjective: see O Korhonen, 'New International Law: Science, Defense or Deliverance' (1996) 7 *European Journal of International Law* 1, 13.

[88] See Scharffs, 'Law as Craft' (n 86) 15.

enlightened legal scholars who take part in drafting committees on behalf of a variety of governmental ministries and agencies drafting legislation.[89]

But this traditional approach to legislative drafting ignores its nature as a discipline of law,[90] and the decline of law as art and the rise of technique and regulation.[91] And, even within the ideal of multi-disciplinary drafting teams, drafting remains a mainly legal job. For those who reject the classification of law as art, law is a science: drafting, as a part of the science of law, can only be a science or maybe a technique.[92] And if drafting is indeed a science,[93] then there are rules that apply to it,[94] awareness of them is gained via professional development in courses and seminars,[95] and this awareness is so specialised that drafting is reserved to specialist professionals[96] usually gathered in a special department of the government, such as a Parliamentary Counsels Office.

In our choice of our subjectively preferred approach to law and drafting, Aristotle comes to the rescue. For Aristotle there are three possible options:[97] science as *episteme*;[98] art as *techne*; or *phronesis*[99] as the *praxis* of subjective decision-making on factual circumstances or the practical wisdom of the subjective classification of factual circumstances to principles and wisdom as *episthmh*.[100]

Phronesis has been translated as practical reasoning, practical wisdom, moral discernment, moral insight and produce.[101] In Aristotle's words, *phronesis* is an intellectual virtue that is 'reasoned, and capable of action with regard to things that are good or bad for man'.[102] It is 'the art of

[89] See C Nutting, 'Legislative Drafting: A Review' (1955) 41 *American Bar Association Journal* 76, 76.

[90] See F Ost and M van de Kerchove, *Jalons pour une theorie critique du droit* (Brussels, Publications des Facultes universitaires Saint-Louis, 1987) 52.

[91] See Shi-J Lavir, *The Modern Art of Dying: a History of Euthanasia in the US* (2005) 1–14.

[92] See J-C Piris, 'The Legal Orders of the European Union and of the Member States: Peculiarities and Influences in Drafting' (2006) *European Journal of Law Reform* 1, 1.

[93] See 'Editorial Review' (1903) 22 *Can Law Times* 428, 437.

[94] See C Langdell, *A Selection of Cases on the Law of Contracts* (1871) viii.

[95] See M Hoyt, 'Education, Training and Retention of Legislative Draftsmen in Canada' (1979) 5 *Commonwealth Law Bulletin* 260, 261; also see M Mulkey, 'Judges and Other Lawmakers: Critical Contributions to Environmental Law Enforcement' (2004) 4 *Sustainable Development Law & Policy* 2, 9.

[96] See R Dickerson, 'Professionalizing Legislative Drafting: A Realistic Goal' (1974) 60 *American Bar Association Journal* 562, 563.

[97] See M Griffiths and G MacLeod, 'Personal Narratives and Policy: Never the Twain?' (2008) 42 *Journal of Political Economy* 121, 126.

[98] *Episteme* is defined as scientific knowledge: see DW Hamlyn, 'Aristotelian Epagoge' (1976) 21 *Phronesis* 167, 167.

[99] See Aristotle, *Nichomachean Ethics*, bk VI, chs 5–11 (D Ross trans, 1980).

[100] See S-U von Kirchmann, *Die Werlosigkeit der Jursprudenz als Wissenschaft* (Berlin, Verlage von Julius Springer, 1848).

[101] See J Noel, 'On the Varieties of Phronesis' (1999) 31 *Educational Philosophy and Theory* 273, 273.

[102] See Aristotle, *Nicomachean Ethics* (n 99) 1140a24–b12, 1144b33–1145a11.

judgement'.[103] *Phronesis* can neither relate to things that are not capable of being changed, nor to goals that cannot be realised.[104] *Phronesis* is not knowledge about the unchangeable order of the world; it relates only to human affairs and, among them, again only to those which can be objects of meaningful deliberation.[105]

Phronesis concerns values[106] and goes beyond the analytical, scientific knowledge of *episteme* and the technical knowledge or know-how of *techne*. Voegelin writes that *phronesis* differs from the dianoetic virtues of *episteme*-science that draws conclusions from principles; from nous-intellect, which recognises first principles; and from *sophia*-wisdom, which, as a combination of science and intellect, refers to things divine.[107] *Phronesis* differs from artistic and technical skill-*techne*, because *techne* produces artefacts and thus is not action that has its end in itself.[108] *Phronesis* involves both rational choice and the process of reflective deliberation by which a rational choice is formed, and is a primary virtue of good citizenship.[109] *Phronesis* is supreme to *episteme* and *techne* as it is able to manage human affairs, including *episteme* and *techne* which cannot manage themselves.[110] *Phronesis* is most important also because it is that activity by which instrumental rationality is balanced by value-rationality.[111]

Episteme is defined by Aristotle as a demonstrative state (ie a state of mind capable of demonstrating what it knows). A person has scientific knowledge when their belief is conditioned in a certain way, and the first principles are known to them because if they are not better known to him than the conclusion drawn from them, he will have knowledge only incidentally.[112] *Episteme* concerns universals and the production of knowledge that is invariable in time and space and achieved with the aid of analytical rationality, and corresponds to the modern scientific ideal as

[103] See G Vickers, *The Art of Judgement: A Study of Policy Making* (London, Sage, 1995).
[104] See Aristotle, *Nicomachean Ethics* (n 99) 1140a32 ff.
[105] See E Voegelin, 'Phronesis as Deliberation' http://voegelinview.com/from-The-Collected-Works/natural-law-and-aristotle-what-is-right-by-nature-pt-3/Phronesis-as-Deliberation-Phronesis-as-Knowledge-of-What-is-Good.html; and also see Aristotle, *Nicomachean Ethics* (n 99) 1141b8 ff.
[106] A person with *phronesis* cannot fail to act correctly and a person to act correctly must have *phronesis*: see D Brosnan, 'Virtue Ethics in a Perfectionist Theory of Law and Justice' (1989) 11 *Cardozo Law* Review, 335, 344.
[107] See Voegelin, 'Phronesis as Deliberation' (n 105); and also see Aristotle, *Nicomachean Ethics* (n 99) 6.6–7.
[108] See Voegelin, 'Phronesis as Deliberation' (n 105) and also Aristotle, *Nicomachean Ethics* (n 99) 6.4.
[109] See S Heyman, 'Aristotle on Political Justice' (1992) *Iowa Law Review* 851, 862–63.
[110] See B Flyvbjerg and T Landman, *Real Social Science: Applied Phronesis* (Cambridge, Cambridge University Press, 2012) 2.
[111] See B Flyvbjerg, 'Phronetic Planning Research: Theoretical and Methodological Reflections' (2004) 5 *Planning Theory & Practice* 283, 285; also M Weber, *Economy and Society* (Berkeley, University of California Press, 1978) 85.
[112] See Aristotle, *Nicomachean Ethics* (n 99) 1139b18–36.

expressed in natural science.[113] And so law as *episteme* 'would be basic science aiming at universality and searching for generic truths or laws'.[114] *Techne* is defined by Aristotle as a truly reasoned productive state, whose practice is the study of how to bring into being something that is capable of being or not being.[115] And so *techne* is a craft or art that is concrete, context-dependent and variable. Its objective is the application of technical knowledge and skills according to a pragmatic instrumental rationality that Foucault calls 'a practical rationality governed by a conscious goal'.[116] Dunne sees *techne* as

> the kind of knowledge possessed by an expert maker: it gives him a clear conception of the why and wherefore, the how and with-what of the making process and enables him, through the capacity to offer a rational account of it, to preside over his activity with secure mastery.[117]

And law practised as *techne* would be a type of consulting aimed at arriving at better laws by means of instrumental rationality, where 'better' is defined in terms of the values and goals of those who employ the consultants, sometimes in negotiation with the latter.[118] *Phronesis* focuses on practical knowledge within the realm of ethics: 'phronesis is a true state, reasoned, and capable of action with regards to things that are good or bad for man … this quality belongs to those who understand the management of households or states'.[119] Persons with *phronesis* (*phronimo*i) are moved by a sense of the proper order among the ends pursued, which cannot be conceived as theoretical axioms but only grasped by phronesis.[120] And so phronetic law is concerned with reflection about values and interests with reference to *praxis* based on practical value-rationality.[121]

Aristotle distinguished the practical wisdom (*phronesis*) needed to work with practical knowledge (*praxis*) from the theoretical wisdom (*sophia*) and theoretical understanding (*episteme*) needed to carry out enquiry into timeless truths (*theoria*). *Praxis* is the kind of practical knowledge needed for the social and moral judgements made by the *phronimos* (the possessor of *phronesis*).

[113] See B Flyvbjerg, *Making Social Science Matter: Why Social Inquiry Fails and How it Can Succeed Again* (Cambridge, Cambridge University Press, 2001) chs 3–4.

[114] Drawn from Flyvbjerg's definition of planning as *episteme*: see Flyvbjerg, 'Phronetic Planning Research' (n 111) 283.

[115] *Nicomachean Ethics* (n 99) 1140a1–23.

[116] M Foucault, 'Space, Knowledge, and Power. Interview with Paul Rabinow' in P Rabinow (ed), *The Foucault Reader* (New York, Pantheon, 1984) 239, 255.

[117] J Dunne, *Back to the Rough Ground: Practical Judgement and the Lure of Technique* (South Bend, IN, University of Notre Dame Press, 1993) 9.

[118] Drawn from Flyvbjerg's definition of planning as *techne*: Flyvbjerg (n 111) 287.

[119] See Aristotle, *Nicomachean Ethics* (n 99) 1140a24–b12.

[120] See C Taylor, *Sources of the Self: The Making of the Modern Identity* (Cambridge, MA, Harvard University Press, 1989) 125 and 148.

[121] Drawn from Flyvbjerg's definition of planning as *phronesis*: Flyvbjerg (n 111) 287.

Aristotle also distinguished practical wisdom (*phronesis*) from the expertise (*techne*) needed to apply technical knowledge (*poiesis*) when making things.[122]

Is law *phronesis*? It can be.[123] And it predominantly is considered to be such.[124] Law as *phronesis* encourages continued uniform application, and thus supports certainty and the rule of law in the civil law tradition. Law as *phronesis* supports prudence or appropriateness, and hence stare decisis in the common law tradition. *Phronesis* can serve as a concrete guide to anyone wishing to ameliorate justice by urging the subject to answer the following questions: where are we heading to? Who wins and who loses, and by virtue of what mechanisms? What are desirable consequences? What can be done on this topic?[125] *Phronesis* supports probabilistic reasoning, as opposed to deductive reasoning, which can be defined as the selection of solutions made on the basis of informed yet subjective application of principles on set circumstances.[126] *Phronesis* is 'practical wisdom that responds to nuance and a sense of the concrete, outstripping abstract or general theories of what is right. In this way, practical wisdom relies on a kind of immediate insight, rather than more formal inferential processes'.[127] *Phronesis* provides the means to achieve the purpose.[128] And *phronesis* accommodates both legal *episteme* and *techno*-law.[129]

So, what is the nature of legislative drafting, as a sub-discipline of law? The debate between drafting as art and drafting as science seems to be false. It ignores relativity as the essence of legal science. Law, and consequently drafting as its discipline, is not part of the arts, nor is it part of the sciences[130]

[122] See Griffiths and MacLeod, 'Personal Narratives and Policy' (n 97) 126.

[123] But it can also be craft: see esp Scharffs, 'Law as Craft' (n 86) 2245; or art: see esp SG Pollock, 'The Art of Judging' (1996) 71 *New York University Law Review* 591; or science: see esp P Schlag, 'Law and Phrenology' (1997) 110 *Harvard Law Review* 877, 897.

[124] See SJ Burton, 'Law as Practical Reason' (1989) 62 *California Law Review* 747; also, WN Eskridge Jr and PP Frickley, 'Statutory Interpretation as Practical Reasoning' (1990) 42 *Stanford Law Review* 321, 353; DA Farber, 'The Inevitability of Practical Reason: Statutes, Formalism, and the Rule of Law' (1992) 45 *Vanderbilt Law Review* 533; B Leiter, 'Heidegger and the Theory of Adjudication' (1996) 106 *Yale Law Journal* 253; R Mohr and D Manderson, 'From Oxymoron to Intersection: an Epidemiology of Legal Research' (2002) 6 *Law Text Culture* 159, 174.

[125] See M Deschamps, 'L'acces a la justice, l'affaire de chacun' (2009) 50 *Cahiers de Droit* 248, 253.

[126] See E Engle, 'Aristotle, Law and Justice: the Tragic Hero' (2008) 35 *Northern Kentucky Law Review* 1, 4.

[127] See C Rideout, 'Storytelling, Narrative Rationality, and Legal Persuasion' (2008) 14 *Legal Writing: Journal of the Legal Writing Institute* 53, 75.

[128] See J Moss, 'Virtue Makes the Goal Right: Virtue and Phronesis in Aristotle's Ethics' (2011) 56 *Phronesis: A Journal for Ancient Philosophy* 204.

[129] See P Cserne, 'Introduction: Legislation, Legal Episteme, and Empirical Knowledge' (2013) 1 *The Theory and Practice of Legislation* 387, 391.

[130] For an analysis of the contra argument on law as a science, see M Speziale, 'Langdell's Concept of Law as Science: The Beginning of Anti-Formalism in American Legal Theory' (1980) 5 *Vermont Law Review* 1.

in the positivist sense.[131] Law, and consequently drafting is neither *episteme* nor *techne*. It is *phronesis*, an arty science, with principles and rules that may well apply, but only in principle. This is because *phronesis* supports particularity.[132] In other words, law, and consequently drafting, is a liberal discipline where theoretical principles guide the drafter to conscious decisions made in a series of subjective empirical and concrete choices. And, as it is phronetic, law is context dependent, in the sense that it can only inform on what might work in certain circumstances, but the decision about what to do in any specific circumstance will always depend on normative judgements that have to be made by those who are there.[133] It is also subject to revision as new perspectives are encountered: it is always revisable.[134]

In applying the description of phronetic social science and its distinction from *techne* and *episteme* onto legislative drafting, phronetic legislative drafting is centrally about decisions on how things can and should be done, and actually how to perform the task. It is not theoretical knowledge (*episteme*) because it is not about only what is true, but also about what would be good under the circumstances. It differs from technical knowledge (*techne*) in that it is concerned with evaluating and prescribing goals, and setting the means to achieve them.[135]

In other words, the art of drafting lies with the subjective use and application of its science, with the conscious subjective Aristotelian application and implementation of its universal theoretical principles to the concrete circumstances of the problem.[136] Being aware of these principles, the drafter has to decide in a conscious and informed manner how to apply them to the concrete future choices[137] that form part of their trade. And this can only be done if the drafter is aware of the theoretical principles that need to be applied, and of their hierarchy in the pyramid of principles.

Take for example, the notorious question of limits in the extreme use of plain language: do we need to substitute the term 'mens rea' in modern English in rules of criminal procedure or criminal evidence? If one refers to the hierarchy of principles in drafting, then plain language is clearly a tool

[131] See RR Formoy, 'Special Drafting' (1938) 21 *Bell Yard: Journal of the Law Society's School of Law* 3, 3, but see contra C Langdell, 'Harvard Celebration Speeches' (1887) 3 *Law Quarterly Review* 118, 123–24.

[132] See S Schwarze, 'Performing Phronesis: The Case of Isocrates Helen' (1999) 32 *Philosophy & Rhetoric* 78, 78.

[133] See Griffiths and MacLeod (n 97) 129.

[134] See H Arendt, *The Human Condition* (London and Chicago, University of Chicago Press, 1958) 129.

[135] See S Schram, 'Phronetic Social Science: an Idea whose Time has Come' in B Flyvberg, T Landman and S Schram (eds), *Real Social Science: Applied Phronesis* (Cambridge, Cambridge University Press, 2012) 15, 19.

[136] See W Eskridge Jr, 'Gadamer/Statutory Interpretation' (1990) 90 *Columbia Law Review* 609, 635.

[137] See M Curtis, 'A Better Theory of Legal Interpretation' (1950) 3 *Vanderbilt Law Review* 407, 423–24.

for clarity: thus, since the term 'mens rea' is clear to lawyers and judges as the main users of rules of criminal evidence or criminal procedure, plain language bows down to clarity, and there is no need for a substitution of the term with its plain language equivalent. Moreover, the introduction of a new term may distort clarity and hence effectiveness of the new legislation. Another example of another notorious question: what happens in the event of a clash between clarity and precision? Simply, in application of the pyramid, the criterion of choice is effectiveness: since clarity and precision are in the same grade of the pyramid, the drafter will need to select whichever one of these two principles serves effectiveness best.

THE UNIVERSALITY OF RULES FOR REGULATION

Having defined the main principles of drafting legislation, and therefore the main parameters to the drafter's task, it is important to identify in which legal context these apply. The term 'principle', as opposed to 'rule' and 'concept', is used to relay the semantic field of a constitutive element of a legal discipline or system that is indispensable to its functioning.[138] Although universality in its absolute sense can be claimed if models of jurisdictions from all families of law and all geographical areas are analysed, an analysis of this length can only attempt to demonstrate relative universality. The term reflects applicability of conclusions within the narrow barriers of Europe, but across the traditional common versus civil law divide.

In the hierarchy of goals set for the drafter, and consequently, principles by which drafters abide, effectiveness (as part of efficacy) comes at the very top. The crucial measure of quality for legislation is therefore, whether 'it does what it says on the tin', namely whether it achieves its purpose clause in the case of common law, or whether it achieves the will of the legislator in the case of civil law. Apart from the terminology used in the two systems of law, is there a real difference between the two concepts? The role of purpose clauses is to express in dry and tangible terms the objectives set for this piece of legislation, or in other words what the legislator intended with this law. Thus, there is hardly any difference between the two terms, at least for the purposes of this analysis: for the determination of the ultimate goal of the drafter, it is irrelevant whether the intent of the legislation or the legislator is found in the purpose clauses of the common law or in the *travaux preparatoires* of the civil law. The difference in the location of the intended objectives of the legislation does not alter the similarity of the criterion of effectiveness across the civil versus common law divide. Ultimately in both legal systems drafters

[138] See I Zajtey, 'Immutability of Rules and Principles of Legal Development: The Permanence of Roman Law Concepts' in V Gessner, A Hoeland and C Varga (eds), *European Legal Cultures* (Aldershot-Brookfield USA-Singapore-Sydney, Dartmouth, 1996) 67, 67.

must compose the law in a manner that best achieves the intended results. Effectiveness is the ultimate goal, the ultimate pursuit, the ultimate measure of quality and the ultimate principle in both systems of law.

This is an exciting start to the relative universality analysis that reflects recent conceptual trends,[139] but not necessarily unexpected: after all, if one reaches deep into the depths of philosophy of law, and strips the law of its national eccentricities, one is bound to discover universal truths. If one is to prove universality, albeit relative, of this analysis, one must look into the lower levels in the hierarchy of principles of drafting. This is where national or systemic eccentricities may sneak in and reflect the difference in style and legal concepts. But how does one determine whether clarity, precision and unambiguity apply in the selected jurisdictions? In view of the variety in the form of drafting conventions and principles in the different European jurisdictions, one would have to explore each legal system in detail in order to discover not only the letter of the law but also the spirit of the law as reflected in judicial practice, statutory interpretation and academic debate. Thankfully, it is not necessary to enter into the detail of past relevant studies.[140] In order to assess whether clarity, precision, unambiguity, plain language and gender-neutral drafting apply both in European common and civil law jurisdictions, one needs only look at the express principles of drafting included in easily traceable written sources of law.[141]

Clarity is expressly introduced in Austria, Belgium, France, Germany, the Netherlands,[142] Portugal, Spain and the UK.[143] Unambiguity is required

[139] See LM Friedman, 'The Concept of Legal Culture: A Reply' in D Nelken (ed), *Comparing Legal Cultures* (Aldershot, Ashgate, 1997) 33; also see LM Friedman, 'On the Emerging Sociology of Transnational Law' (1996) 32 *Stanford Journal of International Law* 65; LM Friedman, *The Horizontal Society* (Massachusetts, Yale University Press, 1999); C Schmid, 'The Emergence of a Transnational Legal Science in Europe' (2000) 19 *Oxford Journal of Legal Studies* 673; R Sacco, 'Legal Formants: A Dynamic Approach to Comparative Law (I)' (1991) 39 *American Journal of Comparative Law* 1, 4, 26–30 and 32; R Zimmermann, 'Savigny's Legacy: Legal History, Comparative Law, and the Emergence of a European Legal Science' (1996) 112 *Law Quarterly Review* 576.

[140] For the initial, and detailed, analysis of the subject see H Xanthaki, 'The Problem of Quality in EU Legislation: What on Earth is Really Wrong?' (2001) 38 *Common Market Law Review* 651, 661.

[141] For an unfortunately outdated presentation of legislative drafting rules in Europe, see R Pagano, *Le Direttive di Tecnica Legislative in Europa* vols 1 and 2 (Rome, Camera dei Deputati, 1997).

[142] See P Eijlander and W Voermans, 'Outlooks for Legislation: Introduction' (1999) 3 *Regel Maat* 120, 122; also see Dutch Minister of Justice *Legislation in Perspective* (The Hague, Ministry of Justice, 1991).

[143] See Austrian *Legistische Rechtlinien* (1990) art 7; *Belgian Circulaire de Premier Ministre* (23 April 1982) art 1; German *Gemeinsame Geschäftsordnung der Bundesministerien* (15 Oct 1976) as modified, art 35; German Manual of Judicial Formalities (1991) paras 33–39; Italian *Regole e suggerimenti per la redazione dei testi nomativi* (1991) art 2; Dutch *Aanwijzingen Voor de Regelgeving* (1992) art 218; Portuguese Deliberation of the Council of Ministers of 8 Feb 1989 on the approval of the general principles for the elaboration of projects of normative acts, art 7c; Spanish Guidelines on the form and structure of projects of laws (1991),

from Belgian, German, Italian, Portuguese, Spanish and UK drafters.[144] Precision and simplicity is a drafting principle in Austria, Belgium, Germany, Portugal, Spain,[145] and the UK.[146] Despite the common perception of a gap between civil and common law drafting, surprisingly for some, even at this level of hierarchy of goals for the drafter there is evidence of universality.

Thus, the tools used by drafters in order to achieve effectiveness as a measure of quality in legislation evidently break the barriers of civil versus common law. This is a surprising, albeit not novel,[147] finding indeed. Despite their many differences in style and conceptualisation, European drafters from both systems of law use the same tools to achieve the same aim. This may well be the result of European legal integration over the last 50 years,[148] leading inevitably to the common-alisation of civil law and to the civil-isation of common law. Whatever the origins of the phenomenon may be, the fact remains that the principles of drafting and their hierarchy in the pyramid of principles stands the tests of relative universality.

The argument is strengthened even further by the relative universality of the lowest grid of tools in the pyramid. Plain language as a tool for clarity, precision and unambiguity; and as an expression of the rule requiring consideration of the language accessible to the lay persons who will be the main users of the particular legislative text, is expressly introduced in the Netherlands, Portugal and the UK.[149]

approved by the Decision of the Council of Ministers of 18 Oct 1991 [1991] OJ 276, disposition 27774, 37235–37, 37235; Office of the Parliamentary Counsel, 'Drafting Guidance' (16 Dec 2011) 1–12.

[144] See Belgian *Circulaire de Premier Ministre* (23 April 1982) art 1; German *Gemeinsame Geschäftsordnung der Bundesministerien* (15 Oct 1976) as modified, art 35; German Manual of Judicial Formalities (1991) para 37; Italian *Regole e suggerimenti per la redazione dei testi nomativi* (1991) art 2; Portuguese Deliberation of the Council of Ministers of 8 Feb 1989 on the approval of the general principles for the elaboration of projects of normative acts, art 7c; Spanish Guidelines on the form and structure of projects of laws (1991), approved by the Decision of the Council of Ministers of 18 Oct 1991 [1991] OJ 276, disposition 27774, 37235–37; for an analysis of ambiguity under British law, see M Black, *The Labyrinth of Language* (London, Pelican Press, 1972) 107.

[145] See Austrian *Legistische Rechtlinien* (1990) art 1; Belgian *Circulaire de Premier Ministre* (23 April 1982) art 1; German *Gemeinsame Geschäftsordnung der Bundesministerien* (15 Oct 1976) as modified, art 35; German Manual of Judicial Formalities (1991) para 33; Portuguese Deliberation of the Council of Ministers of 8 Feb 1989 on the approval of the general principles for the elaboration of projects of normative acts, art 7c; Spanish Guidelines on the form and structure of projects of laws (1991), approved by the Decision of the Council of Ministers of 18 Oct 1991 [1991] OJ 276, disposition 27774, 37235–37.

[146] See *The Preparation of Legislation: Report of a Committee Appointed by the Lord President of the Council Chairman Sir David Renton* (Cmnd 6053, 1975) ch XI, art 14.

[147] See T Millet, 'A Comparison of French and British Legislative Drafting (with Particular Reference to their Nationality Laws)' (1986) 7 *Statute Law Review* 130, 153.

[148] See V Gessner, 'The Transformation of European Legal Cultures' in V Gessner, A Hoeland and C Varga (eds), *European Legal Cultures* (Aldershot-Brookfield USA-Singapore-Sydney, Dartmouth, 1996) 513, 516.

[149] The Dutch *Aanwijzingen Voor de Regelgeving* (1992) arts 54 and 218; Portuguese Deliberation of the Council of Ministers of 8 Feb 1989 on the approval of the general

Relative universality applies to all the grades in the pyramid of principles of drafting: from aim, to mechanism, to tools, drafters in Europe both in civil and common law jurisdictions apply the same principles. Whether they apply them in the exact same manner, one cannot be sure without an even deeper analysis. And, of course, some national eccentricities should doubtless be expected.

COMPILATIONS OF RULES FOR REGULATION: HOMOGENEITY VERSUS RIGIDITY?[150]

Having established the precise role of the drafter in the achievement of quality in legislation, and having identified the main mechanisms and tools available to drafters for that purpose, it is time to discuss whether manuals or compilations for rules for regulation can be of use.

In their colonial past former empires tended to offer drafting manuals to their colonies but never introduced one for themselves. This was a reflection of the conviction that newer countries with shorter traditions of drafting and law would require a starting point in their legal maturity and, therefore, would benefit from a manual.[151] However, the empire itself with its long and established legal tradition would not require a series of commands on how to draft because this came with the superior experience and wisdom they felt they possessed vis-a-vis their colonies. A very good example of this approach has been the British Commonwealth. Manuals have been offered, encouraged and introduced in most former colonies, which now form the Commonwealth; however, the UK still rejects the introduction of a manual for drafting applicable to its own territory. Although a parallel is unfair and indirect, nevertheless, the EU has taken a similar attitude, or at least appears to have utilised a similar vein of thought, with the newer Member States. Older Member States tended to be split in their introduction of manuals or compilations: only nine out of the fifteen older Member States currently introduce manuals or compilations of drafting conventions. However, newer Member States have been encouraged, and indirectly requested, to pass legislation on drafting laws as a means of responding to the Commission's wise insistence that implementation of the acquis for the purposes of accession means correct implementation of EU law with national implementing measures of good quality.

principles for the elaboration of projects of normative acts, art 7a; for the UK, see M Faulk and IM Mehler, *The Elements of Legal Writing* (London, Macmillan Press, 1994).

[150] See H Xanthaki, 'Drafting Manuals and Quality in Legislation: Positive Contribution towards Certainty in the Law or Impediment to the Necessity for Dynamism of Rules?' (2010) 4 *Legisprudence* 111, 122–26.

[151] See M Goodale, 'From the Trenches and Towers: Current Illusions and Delusions about Conflict Management—In Africa and Elsewhere' (2002) 27 *Law & Social Inquiry* 595, 598.

This line of thinking, which requires manuals for inexperienced legislatures and legislators alone, does not survive scrutiny. First of all, the passing of legislation on drafting or the introduction of a manual does not guarantee application of the rules,[152] and consequently cannot be seen as a guarantee of quality of legislation produced. Secondly, the need for manuals of drafting reflects the need for improvement of current legislative quality: in view of the increasing awareness of the problems of legislation in the EU and the so-called developed world, the argument of self-sufficiency in the experienced legal systems of Europe and the ex-colonial powers simply does not stand true. And thirdly, there is nothing dogmatic about drafting: 'the only matter on which it is wise to be dogmatic is that it is unwise to be dogmatic on nay drafting matter'.[153]

But does that mean that compilations of rules for regulation via legislation have no use? An affirmative answer to this question would negate any value in this book. Since legislative drafting is a phronetic discipline, compilations like the present serve the reader in identifying the principles that apply, albeit relatively, in dilemmas and questions faced in the task of legislating. They also allow the reader to prioritise between rules applicable in parallel. And ultimately they set criteria for the application of those rules, in implementing practical wisdom and professional experience. It is envisaged that this, in combination with the introduction of effectiveness as legislative quality, can assist the drafter in their task not in prescribing rigid rules but in enforcing phronetic choices.

CONCLUSIONS

The concept of rules for regulation is narrowed down to reflect the written rules of statutory law that put into effect policy choices made by the executive in the course of governing.

Regulation aims at efficacy, which is synonymous with regulatory quality.

Legislation as a regulatory tool aims at effectiveness, which is synonymous with legislative quality.

The objective of this compilation of rules is to contribute to awareness of the modern rules for legislation to regulate; to prioritisation of competing or parallel rules applicable in set circumstances; and to introduce effectiveness as the criterion of choice in selecting the most prudent or appropriate rule.

152 See MJ Rizzo, 'Which Kind of Legal Order? Logical Coherence and Praxeological Coherence' (1999) 9 *Journal des Economistes et des Etudes Humaines* 1, 2.

153 See D Greenberg, *Craies on Legislation—A Practitioner's Guide to the Nature, Process, Effect and Interpretation of Legislation* (London, Sweet and Maxwell, 2004) 303.

2

Drafting Instructions

GRANT THORNTON, ONE of the leading experts and innovators in the discipline of legislative drafting, systematises the legislative drafting process[1] into five stages:

1. Understanding the proposal.
2. Analysing the proposal.
3. Designing the law.
4. Composing and developing the draft.
5. Verifying the draft.[2]

In stage one the drafter begins with the reading and understanding of the request for the drafting of legislation sent to them by the instructing officers. In stage two the drafter proceeds with an analysis of the drafting request, which takes the form of a legislative plan. In stage three the drafter begins to identify the structure of the legislation. In stage four, and only then, the drafter puts pen to paper and drafts the requested legislation. Stage five concerns the internal and external verification of the first version of the draft legislation delivered within and outside the drafting team.[3]

The aim of this chapter is to analyse the start of the drafting process, namely the understanding of drafting instructions. Although these are drafted by policy and legal officers, and fall outside the scope of drafting *stricto sensu*, they do form part of the process of drafting legislation and are crucial for the successful completion of the drafting effort.[4] Drafting instructions are considered cryptic for policy and legal officers. They, as the whole of the legislative process, constitute a black box with little interest to the policy and legal officers, touching more on policy rather than legal science.[5] Being unaware of drafting conventions, which fall outside the scope

[1] For the distinction between the legislative and the drafting process, see C Stefanou, 'Drafters, Drafting and the Policy Process' in C Stefanou and H Xanthaki (eds), *Drafting Legislation: A Modem Approach* (Aldershot, Ashgate Publishing, 2008) 323.

[2] See H Xanthaki, *Thornton's Legislative Drafting*, 5th edn (West Sussex, Bloomsbury Professional, 2013) 145.

[3] See J Stark, *The Art of the Statute* (Littleton, F Rothman, 1996) 52–53.

[4] See R Fox and M Korris, *Making Better Law: Reform of the Legislative Process from Policy to Act* (London, Hansard Society, 2010) 86.

[5] See C-A Morand (ed), *Légistique formelle et matérielle* (Aix-en-Provence, 1999) 25.

of their training and tasks, policy and legal officers cannot possibly know what aim drafting instructions serve, how they will be used, and ultimately what should be included in them or not. Viewing them through the prism of the drafter as a means of contributing to effectiveness as legislative quality, drafting instructions respond to the common but rarely answered questions of legal and policy officers.[6] And this starts the drafting process exactly as it should continue:[7] with an unbroken dialogue between the actors of the drafting process (policy, legal and drafting experts), the disciplines involved in the process (policy, substantive law, legislative drafting) and the languages used by these experts in their disciplines (policy, law and drafting). After all, legislation is 'the product of many minds'.[8]

One note of clarification: although the terms policy, legal and drafting officers is used, this does not necessarily reflect three different persons. Although this is not so in the UK, in the Commonwealth it is possible for the same person to serve more than one role,[9] especially since these are not always distinguishable accurately.[10] It is precisely in this case that there is an increased need for the person serving all three functions to understand what the role of each function is, and when and why they serve under each 'hat'. Schizophrenic as it may be, the dialogue (or tri-alogue[11]) of the process takes place irrespective of how many physical persons are actually present in the debate! And it is the drafter's concern to ensure that the drafting process is followed religiously.[12]

WHAT ARE DRAFTING INSTRUCTIONS?

Drafting instructions are requests from the policy and legal officers to the drafting officers to proceed with the drafting of legislation within the

[6] See A Seidman, RB Seidman and N Abeyesekere, *Legislative Drafting for Democratic Social Change—A Manual for Drafters* (The Hague, Kluwer, 2001) 280.

[7] As things stand the drafting process is flawed: see Fox and Korris, *Making Better Law* (n 4) 13.

[8] See G Tanner, 'Confronting the Process of Statute-Making' in R Bigwood (ed), *The Statute: Making and Meaning* (Wellington, LexisNexis, 2004) 54.

[9] See TW Cain QC, 'The Legislative Draftsman in a Small Jurisdiction' (1993) 19 *Commonwealth Law Bulletin* 1237, 1238.

[10] But, there are calls for involving the drafter even at the drafting instructions stage as a means of ensuring quality of the instructions: see MV Petelo Fa'asau, 'Challenges Faced by Legislative Drafters in Samoa and Other USP Member Countries' (2012) 14 *European Journal of Law Reform* 191, 205.

[11] See P Regan, 'Enacting Legislation—a Civil Servant's Perspective' (2012) 34 *Statute Law Review* 32, 33.

[12] See V Vanterpool, 'A Critical Look at Achieving Quality in Legislation' (2007) 9 *European Journal of Law Reform* 167, 170.

parameters set.[13] The term is jargon for 'request'.[14] Within the realm of effectiveness, the drafter requires a precise understanding of the field under intervention, its function and logic, and an explicit diagnosis of the problem with evidence not only of the aim pursued but also its objectives:[15] the ultimate goal is the elaboration of an effective strategy of legislation withstanding pre- and post-legislative scrutiny.[16] Normally drafting instructions are collections of data provided to the legislative drafter by the policy and legal officers as a means of assisting the drafter to draft effective legislation within the parameters detailed by the government's policy-makers.[17] And so, by definition, drafting instructions normally include the request, the background materials leading to the policy and legal choices already made by the instructing officers, and any background information necessary for the comprehension of all aspects of the political decision to proceed with legislation and the choice of the proposed legal means for the achievement of government policy.

But often, in civil law jurisdictions[18] and even in the Commonwealth, drafting instructions are brief,[19] often oral,[20] and take the form of a Ministerial 'order' to the drafter of the legislation[21] on a broadly described topic.[22] There is little doubt that this stage of the drafting process is undermined by

[13] Lord Goldsmith described the role of a drafter as translating policy into legal text: see Lord Goldsmith QC, 'Parliament for Lawyers: An Overview of the Legislative Process' (2002) 4 *European Journal of Law Reform* 511, 513.

[14] See B Simamba, *How to Make Effective Legislative Proposals* (Indiana, AuthorHouse, 2012) 8.

[15] See Office of Parliamentary Counsel UK, 'Working with Parliamentary Counsel' (6 Dec 2011) para 132 www.gov.uk/government/uploads/system/uploads/attachment_data/file/62668/WWPC_6_Dec_2011.pdf.

[16] See A Flückiger and J-D Delley 'L'élaboration rationnelle du droit privé: de la codification à la légistique' in C Chappuis et al (eds), *Le législateur et le droit privé, Mélanges en l'honneur de Gilles Petitpierre* (Geneva and Zurich, Bale, 2006) 125–26.

[17] The government 'needs legislation to give legal effect to its policies, to clothe them with the force of law': see DR Miers and AC Page, *Legislation*, 2nd edn (London, Sweet and Maxwell, 1990) 11.

[18] See U Karpen, 'Instructions for Law Drafting' (2008) 10 *European Journal of Law Reform* 163.

[19] On the inadequacy of drafting instructions, see N Nand, 'Legislative Drafting, Distance Education and Its Contribution to Good Governance in the Pacific' (2008) www.wikieducator.org/images/3/37/PID 309.pdf; also see A Songa Gashabizi, 'The Challenges of Rwandan Drafters in the Drafting Process for Good Quality Legislation' (2012) 14 *European Journal of Law Reform* 280, 281.

[20] See J-D Delley, MT Christin Jochum and S Ledermann, 'La conception des lois: la démarche légistique entre théorie et pratique' (Geneva, CETEL, 2009) 23–24 http://archive-ouverte.unige.ch/unige:2026.

[21] See R Ikiriza, 'Instructions to Draft Legislation—A Study on Legislative Drafting Process in Rwanda' (2012) 14 *European Journal of Law Reform* 225, 226.

[22] See Petelo Fa'asau, 'Challenges Faced by Legislative Drafters in Samoa and Other USP Member Countries' (n 10) 204.

the legislative expediency normally attached to drafting.[23] And so in order to identify the elements of quality in drafting instructions that can promote effectiveness of the legislation as the end product, it is necessary to identify the purposes of drafting instructions. This can guide us to the appropriate content and consequently format.

PURPOSES OF DRAFTING INSTRUCTIONS

There is little doubt that the main purpose of drafting instructions is to determine and delimit what the draft bill is to contain. This is the opportunity of policy and legal officers to inform the drafter on the policy that the government intends to put to effect.[24] This is where the link between regulation and legislation is made. The more aware of the regulatory aims the drafter is, the closer the link between the regulatory aims and the legislative tools will be.[25] Going back to the doctrine of legislation as a means of regulation, the more aware of the real regulatory/policy aims the drafter is, the better equipped they are to pursue the legislative choices that best promote the policy and legal choices made by the instructing officers. And so the information offered to the drafter by the instructing officers at this stage can ensure that the legislative text as the end product and the probable outcomes of that end product match the desired policy aims.[26] In other words, the information offered here is crucial for the effectiveness of the legislative text and its contribution to the efficacy of the proposed regulation.[27] If the drafting choice is haphazard, and this of course would happen in cases where drafting instructions are a simple order to legislate, then the effectiveness[28] of the legislation can only be haphazard.[29] Unless the instructions are clear on the idea and objectives of the proposal,[30] 'it is sheer waste of time to embark upon drafting a piece of legislation'.[31] Eloquently pictured by J-D Delley and A Flückinger below, the sequence of

[23] See R Nawaqakuta, 'Challenges and Problems of Legislative Drafting in the Fiji Islands' (2003) *The Legal Lali* 13, 13–14.

[24] See RJ Martineau and MB Salerno, *Legal, Legislative and Rule Drafting in Plain English* (St Paul, MN, Thomson West, 2005) 93.

[25] See VF Nourse and JS Schacter, 'The Politics of Legislative Drafting: A Congressional Case Study' (2002) 77 *New York University Law Review* 575, 595.

[26] See D Elliot, 'Preparing Drafting Instructions for Legislation' www.davidelliott.ca/papers/preparingdrafting.doc

[27] NA Hashim, 'Consultation: A Contribution to Efficiency of Drafting Process in Malaysia' (2012) 14 *European Journal of Law Reform* 142, 148.

[28] And this will not be the drafter's fault: see A Ashworth, 'A Crystal Mark for Lawmakers' (1996) *Maryland Criminal Law Review* 149, 149.

[29] See M Mayer, *The Lawyers* (London, Harper and Rowe, 1967) 50.

[30] Clear drafting instructions ultimately serve the citizens: see P Salembier, *Legal and Legislative Drafting* (Toronto, ON, Lexis Nexis, 2009) 1.

[31] See VCRAC Crabbe, *Legislative Drafting* (London, Cavendish Publishing, 1993) 14.

phases in the drafting process is as follows: the instructing officers define the problem, determine the objectives of the requested law, identify alternative scenarios, and on the basis of 'prospective evaluation' (pre-legislative scrutiny) they choose the right solutions: drafting instructions are there to describe all of the above, thus allowing the drafter to put the chosen solutions to effect in preparation for 'retrospective evaluation' (post-legislative scrutiny) of the passed legislation.[32]

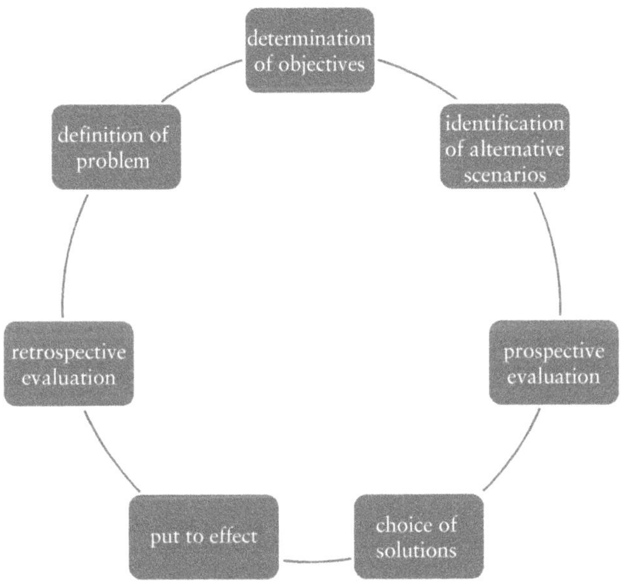

Figure 2.1: Sequence of phases in the drafting process

In addition to the main clear purpose of drafting instructions, these also serve a number of related purposes.[33] First, in the form of a memorandum to Cabinet or the Legislative Committee for the purposes of prioritisation or approval of the legislative proposal, they act as a key mechanism for the Cabinet's control over the legislative process by giving Ministers a more detailed view of how the policy that they are approving will be reflected in legislation: eg when Ministers from a European jurisdiction were presented with the plan for legislation to castrate paedophile repeat offenders in direct response to a particularly horrible case of paedophilia

[32] See J-D Delley and A Flückinger, 'La légistique: une élaboration méthodique de la legislation' in *Confection de la loi* (Paris, Presses Universitaire de France, 2005) 83, 84 http://archive-ouverte.unige.ch/unige:8307.

[33] See Privy Council Office, Government of Canada, 'Guide to Making Federal Acts and Regulations Preparing Bill-drafting Instructions for a Memorandum to Cabinet' (12 Feb 2003).

in the country resulting in the awful death of a number of young victims, the Cabinet or Committee requested that the measure be 'toned down' to ensure compliance with the human rights of the convicted. The result was legislation introducing the choice of chemical and reversible castration for those offenders who chose to live outside prison.

Secondly, still in the form of a memorandum to Cabinet or the Legislative Committee, drafting instructions provide an opportunity for other government departments to appreciate how, if at all, the proposals will affect them. This is particularly useful in jurisdictions where drafting is undertaken as a fragmented task by the various government departments, rather than centrally within an Office of Parliamentary Counsel. For example, in a southern European jurisdiction the Ministry of Transport requested the drafting of legislation allowing the early landing of charter flights in a particularly tourism-dependent island. The current requirement that flights should not land in the early hours of the morning was viewed as an irrelevant little victory for local residents who, we thought, managed to guarantee a good night's sleep. It was only when the Department for the Environment came to read the draft law, already before Parliament, that it was able to shed real light on the existing prohibition of early flights: the protected species of turtles known as careta-careta laid their eggs on that specific island in the early hours of the morning during the summer. And so the prohibition on early landings was not there to guarantee uninterrupted sleep for local residents, but to protect the reproduction of a species in danger of extinction.

Thirdly, drafting instructions provide an opportunity for the sponsoring department to think through its proposals.[34] Often legislation is introduced as a knee-jerk reaction to events that move public opinion so profoundly, that the government feels it imperative to respond quickly and actively. Although a responsive government is to be praised for its relevance to the people who elect it to power, legislation by definition needs to be cooler if it is to stand the test of time and generality that forms part of its constitutional mandate. And so putting pen to paper, either as a memorandum to Cabinet or as a detailed request to drafters, offers a unique opportunity for instructing officers to appreciate the details of the request and assess, in detail and in writing, the parameters of the request from a constitutional, ethical and international law perspective. This can lead to the fine-tuning of the request, or to the identification of sensitivities, political or legal, which would be useful for the drafter's awareness of points of danger or points to be avoided or thought through further.

Fourthly, drafting instruction in their final form can be juxtaposed to Cabinet authorisation of the policy in order to assess whether the proposed

[34] See Stark, *The Art of the Statute* (n 3) 13.

legislation actually does what Cabinet authorised, or whether additional authority must be sought for particular provisions of the Bill.

THE FOUR PRINCIPLES OF DRAFTING INSTRUCTIONS

In order to serve their five purposes adequately, drafting instructions must comply with four principles. First, they must contain sufficient background information to enable the drafter to see in perspective and in context the facts and problems that the legislative proposal is to serve. This is in response to their main purpose: drafters must be allowed to share the real policy objective pursued by government in order to ensure the desired match between their legislative choices and the desired regulatory aims. The table below introduced by the Attorney-General's Department in Brunei, and reiterated here verbatim, explains very eloquently what information is needed and what purpose it serves.[35]

Table 2.1: *Why* is legislation required?

Background information	This enables the Attorney-General to understand the problem and see the legislative scheme in perspective and context
Nature of the problem	Explain why the current law needs amending. Describe the nature of the problem (whether economic, political or social) that the legislative scheme is addressing or that is to be dealt with.
History or circumstances	The history or circumstances giving rise to the legislative scheme including where appropriate, any deficiencies in the operation of the existing law, any court decisions (especially recent ones) affecting its interpretation, illustrations of problems with the existing state of affairs.
Aim of the legislation or its principal objectives	This helps to enable the draftsperson to draft a law to give effect to or achieve the outcome that the Department intends.

[35] See Attorney-General's Department, *Guidelines on Drafting Procedure and Instructions for Ministries and Departments* (Brunei, Dar-es-Salam) para 4.2.1.

Secondly, the principal objects of the legislation should be clearly and fully stated[36] so that the drafter is in no doubt as to the spirit and intent of the proposed legislation.[37] In order to fully achieve their main aim, drafting instructions must share the true intent of the policy rather than the beautified often populist objectives presented to the electorate. One can draw a parallel from the medical profession: there is little point in visiting the doctor for a prescription against dizziness if diabetes is the underlying illness. Similarly, there is little point is seeking effective legislative solutions for allegedly excessive parking in wheelchair bays when the real policy is collection of additional funds for the government. At the end of the day, the drafter lacks legitimacy to judge government policy: popular or not, fair or not, 'correct' or not, this is what those elected to power have decided to introduce. And, at the end of the day, it is those elected who will carry the electoral praise or defeat at the end of their term. The drafter's duty is simply to put whatever policy is requested, in a manner that is constitutional, legal and as reasonable as possible.

Thirdly, the means whereby the principal objects are to be achieved should be set out: How will the legislation work in practice? What is the machinery envisaged? What powers and duties are considered necessary? These policy choices are normally considered by the instructing officers before the request for legislation is made. It assists the drafter no end to be aware of what policy and legal options have been considered, how they have been evaluated by the instructing officers and why the preferred choice has been introduced. This can also assist the drafter to understand fully what regulatory aim is sought.

And fourthly, instructions should refer to all known legal implications and difficulties. I will resist another doctor analogy. But in the same way that policy issues need to be shared with the drafter, legal issues need to be shared with them too. Drafters are not normally experts in the field of law of the requested text, and they require assistance by the substantive law experts to identify any legal implications arising from the request. It serves the effectiveness of the end product to face and deal with any difficulties of law at the stage of drafting rather than be surprised by them in the parliamentary reading or, even worse, the implementation stage. As a worst case scenario, the drafter's ammunition includes legislation in stages that can offer the government the opportunity to achieve the desired regulatory result later but surely.

[36] J Kobba, 'Criticisms of the Legislative Drafting Process and Suggested Reforms in Sierra Leone' (2008) 10 *European Journal of Law Reform* 219, 228.

[37] VCRAC Crabbe, 'The Role of Parliamentary Counsel in Legislative Drafting', (UNITAR Sub-Regional Workshop on Legislative Drafting for African Lawyers, Kampala, Uganda, 20–31 March 2000) 8; also see SL Trusty, 'The Value of Clear Instructions' (1946–47) 15 *University of Kansas Law Review* 9.

WHAT IS THE CONTENT OF DRAFTING INSTRUCTIONS?

The purposes of drafting instructions and the principles for drafting instructions are served by their inclusion of a large number of possible elements. One caveat: it is not necessary for all drafting instructions to include lengthy analyses of each and every one of the elements below. But the drafter is served well if they are aware of all possible elements, thus ensuring that what is left out in each case is actually not needed as opposed to erroneously forgotten.[38] In principle, drafting instructions must include the desired outcome, with or without specific ideas about how that outcome is to be achieved through legislation; or a detailed list of required legislative changes, with or without a well-articulated desired outcome; or any combination of those options.[39] Effective drafting instructions must be complete,[40] accurate and comprehensive in responding to the questions of what needs to be done, how it needs to be done and by what time it needs to be done.[41] More concretely:[42]

— Drafting instructions can begin with general factual background information on the current legislative solutions to the social problem that the new legislation aims to address, and the instructing officers' reasoning for their characterisation of the existing legal framework as inefficient. Media reports, political observations, court judgments, academic opinion and foreign sources can shed some light in this. Offering the drafter an insight into the existing legal framework as applied, or the lack of it, offers them an understanding of the mischief that they are called to rectify. After all, drafting instructions are all about the desired outcome, the mischief and the desired result.[43] Understanding what does not work, or works in an undesired manner, allows them to (1) ensure that legislation is indeed necessary; and (2) identify the most appropriate drafting tool: new legislation or amendment?

— The regulatory aims of the proposed legislation spell out the main criteria for effectiveness of the legislation: in an era where pre- and

[38] See BH Simnamba, *The Legislative Process: A Handbook for Public Officials* (Indiana, Author House, 2009) 13.

[39] See Office of Parliamentary Counsel, Australian Government, 'Working with the Office of Parliamentary Counsel—A Guide for Clients' (March 2008) para 53.

[40] But not too broad: see Lord Renton QC, 'Current Drafting Practices and Problems in the United Kingdom' (1990) 11 *Statute Law Review* 11, 13.

[41] See Office of the Queensland Parliamentary Counsel, 'A Guide for Effective Legislative Drafting Instructions', para 36.

[42] For a full checklist, see Office of Parliamentary Counsel UK, 'Checklist for Drafting Instructions' (26 Jan 2011); also Legislation Advisory Committee, 'Guidelines on Process and Content of Legislation' (Wellington, Ministry of Justice, 2001) annex 1; and Delley, Christin Jochum and Ledermann, La conception des lois' (n 20).

[43] See Office of Parliamentary Counsel UK, 'Checklist for Drafting Instructions' (26 Jan 2011) 1.

post-legislative scrutiny is becoming crucially important as a tool for the updating of the ever-increasing statute book, spelling out the regulatory aims sought offers drafters an understanding of what it is that they must achieve, and allows them to express them in the legislation as tangible criteria of its quality in the pre-and post-legislative monitoring cycles. Any comments on the possible scenarios for the achievement of the regulatory aims offer the drafter the opportunity to understand the rationale behind the legislative proposal, to question and hopefully confirm the selection of the policy choices made by the instructing officers, and to take any existing impact or cost/risk analysis into account when drafting purpose clauses, objectives provisions and monitoring provisions. Within the element above it is always useful to alert the drafter to legislative solutions drawn from other jurisdictions, their impact and possibly comments on their transferability to the jurisdiction served. Although borrowing from abroad has become increasingly popular amongst instructing officers and drafters, the practice does carry dangers of ineffectiveness, if the two jurisdictions do not share adequate commonality of needs and usefulness in the legislative solutions.

— Danger points must be raised in drafting instructions thus ensuring that the drafter does not miss them, and that consequently the end result does not introduce them haphazardly:
  — politically or ethically sensitive issues must be raised, thus inviting the drafter to deal with them adequately in the end result;
  — extra-territoriality as a departure from the norm must be raised clearly; and
  — similarly, commencement issues can be discussed at this early stage with specific reference to the date of entry into force, especially when the sponsoring department envisages commencement on a specified day, or on a day dependent on a specific event (eg the coming into force of another Act), on a day to be fixed by delegated legislation, with gradual or measured entry into force, retroactive or retrospective effect, or transitional arrangements.
— Following on from the point above, drafting instructions must raise any administrative or judicial review considerations, any decisions of an administrative character reviewable and by whom and any consultations with the Attorney-General.
— Legal opinions of the sponsoring department or any other legal officers must be attached, thus preventing duplication of effort, and informing the drafter on expert evaluations and interpretation.[44]

[44] See Office of Parliamentary Counsel UK, 'Working with Parliamentary Counsel' (n 15) para 139.

- Similarly, consultations with other departments are useful, especially when a legislative proposal impacts on another department's competence, or when a legislative proposal involves policy considerations for which another department is solely or jointly responsible.
- Affected provisions and consequential amendments must be raised, as early as at the first stage of drafting;[45] of course, the list cannot be final or exhaustive at this stage but identifying a basic list of consequential amendments and affected provisions enhances the drafter's awareness of the mischief, and informs them in their choice of the most appropriate drafting tool: lengthy amendments may call for repeal and re-enactment whereas a short list of amendments may direct the drafter to a simple amendment.
- Drafting instructions must also include procedural information on policy authority and legislative priority, thus pacifying the drafting office that the request must be included in their timetable with immediate effect.
- And finally, practical details, such as the name of instructor, contact details, planned leave etc offer a personal touch, which facilitates the required dialogue between instructing officers and drafters.

It is worth noting that the UK Office of Parliamentary Counsel requests the following points of content from drafting instructions,[46] which correspond to the mischief rule in *Heydon's Case*:[47]

- A brief introduction setting out:
  - the factual and political context in which legislation is being proposed;
  - the general purpose of the changes that are being proposed; and
  - the principal reasons for legislating.
- A description of the relevant existing law and of its application in practice.
- A description of the respects in which, and extent to which, the existing law prevents the implementation of the department's policy ('the mischief').

  A full description of the legal changes to which the Bill is to give effect in order to provide a remedy for the mischief ('the remedy').
- A description of the incidental and supplemental provisions needed to support the remedy.

[45] See Office of Parliamentary Counsel, Australian Government, 'Working with the Office of Parliamentary Counsel—A Guide for Clients' (n 39) paras 87–88.

[46] See Office of Parliamentary Counsel UK, 'Working with Parliamentary Counsel' (n 15) para 165.

[47] (1584) 3 Co Rep 7a20.

— A discussion of any parliamentary or other handling issues relevant to the drafting.
— Housekeeping matters.

QUALITY OF LEGISLATIVE INSTRUCTIONS

But let's go back to the original question for this chapter: what constitutes quality of drafting instructions? Two excerpts from two very different texts shed some light on the question of quality of legislative instructions. One originates from 1966 and was drafted by a military government in Nigeria, whereas the second stems from one of the most innovative and socially conscious recent textbooks in legislative drafting. Yet, despite their differences, both texts confirm that the quality of legislation as an end product is directly linked to the quality of drafting instructions, which cannot be offered in the form of a draft law.

> Drafting instructions should set out the requirements in plain language. They should give as fully as possible the purpose and background of the Decree and should state what existing legislation affects the subject. They must not take the form of a layman's Draft Decree. Where a proposal is based on an existing piece of legislation, whether of Nigeria or the United Kingdom or any other country, this fact should be stated, and the instructions should refer the draftsman to the legislation.[48]

And

> Unless the legislative drafting instructions and the theory and methodology that underpin them guide drafters in making an adequate empirical study of their countries' relevant social realities, their bills' impact in changing problematic behaviours will depend on plain luck.[49]

The practice of offering drafters raw or lay drafts instead of drafting instructions is very widespread in the Commonwealth (but not in the UK[50]), although no jurisdiction encourages lay drafts.[51] Instructing officers

[48] See Cabinet Office, 'Procedure for the Preparation of Federal Legislation under the Federal Military Government' (Lagos, May 1966) para 5(5).

[49] See A Seidman and R Seidman, *Legislative Drafting for Democratic Social Change: A Manual for Drafters* (The Hague, Kluwer Law International, 2001) 39.

[50] A number of jurisdictions reject lay drafts: for the UK see Office of Parliamentary Counsel, https://www.gov.uk/government/publications/guide-to-making-legislation; for Australia, see 'Legislation Handbook' http://www.dpmc.gov.au/guidelines/docs/legislation_handbook.pdf; for Canada, see 'Guide to Making Federal Acts and Regulations' http://www.pco-bcp.gc.ca/index.asp?lang=eng&page=information&sub=publications&doc=legislation/cabdir-dircab-eng.htm; for New Zealand, see Cabinet Manual 2008, www.cabinetmanual.cabinetoffice.govt.nz/7.19; for Australia also see 'Giving Written Instructions' www.opc.gov.au/about/docs/draftingminstructionsv05.pdf.

[51] See Sir W Dale, 'Canadian Draftsmanship, and the French Connection' (1984) 10 *Commonwealth Law Bulletin* 1865, 1866.

seem to prefer lay drafts to drafting instructions, mainly because they erroneously think that this will speed up the process of drafting, and perhaps guide the drafter to the result that instructing officers hope to achieve. This cannot be further from the truth.[52] A bad lay draft can only start a gradually increasingly frustrating friction between instructing officers and drafters, promoting a power game between offices, and leading to dangerous products.[53] As a result, even the defence of alleged expediency cannot stand at the side of lay drafts:[54] drafters have to undo what is badly done by untrained officers.[55]

Perhaps more importantly, the practice of lay drafts disregards and undermines the nature of legislative drafting as a phronetic discipline whose principles, contextualism and idiosyncrasy can only be appreciated and unlocked by trained drafters. In the same manner that one would not ask the best gynaecologist in the world to perform brain surgery, one cannot expect the best lawyer, or policy officer in the world to draft a good law. Drafters are trained and experienced in their discipline, which cannot and should not be reduced to a mere editing of the language of a text drafted by others. The stages of legislative drafting are paramount to the quality of the end result: so are drafting instructions. Drafters must be allowed to serve their task with a clear mind, uninfluenced by others even the most basic of questions, such as the necessity of legislation for the achievement of the policy goals, the appropriateness of the selected form of legislation, the structure of the legislative text and its composition.[56] Any attempt to usurp part of this task and part of the drafters' liberty to perform it unhindered can only harm the common goal of the drafting team (instructing policy officers, instructing legal officers and drafters) thus endangering the effectiveness of the produced legislative text.

[52] See D Elliot, 'Getting Better Instructions for Legislative Drafting' (the Pre-Conference Clinic on Writing Laws of the Just Language Conference, Victoria, British Columbia, 21 Oct 1992) www.davidelliott.ca/papers/getting.htm#8; also JF Wilson, 'The Preparation of Drafting Instructions' www.lawdrafting.co.uk.

[53] See J Hertin, J Turnpenny, A Jordan, M Nilsson, D Russel and B Nykvist, 'Rationalising the Policy Mess? Ex Ante Policy Assessment and the Utilisations of Knowledge in the Policy Process' (2009) 41 *Environment and Planning* 1185; for an interesting example of the tension between evidence-based policy-making and political considerations in the drafting of legislation, see RW Hahn and PM Dudley, 'The Disconnect between Law and Policy Analysis: A Case Study of Drivers and Cell Phones' (2003) 55 *Administrative Law Review* 127, 181.

[54] See R Muhamad, 'Instructions to Draft Legislation: A Study on the Legislative Drafting Process in Malaysia' (2011) *European Journal of Law Reform* 236, 256.

[55] See EA Driedger, *The Composition of Legislation*, 2nd edn (Ottawa, Department of Justice, 1957) xix–xx.

[56] See DL Revell, 'Enhancing the Legislative Process: The Value of the Legislative Drafter' (2011) 32 *Statute Law Review* 149, 154.

Without narrative drafting instructions the architecture of the resulting legislative text is pre-decided and pre-set by untrained officers, whose product can only be of questionable quality.[57] And so, the time has come for drafters around the world to follow the UK lead and simply ignore lay drafts.[58] One possibility would be to simply tear them up and return them to the instructing officers, a practice religiously followed by a recent former First Parliamentary Counsel in London. But this of course requires both stealth on behalf of the head drafter and also a fertile mentality in the civil service with appreciation of the specialist know-how and tasks performed by drafters. Another, perhaps more realistic, approach is for drafters to view lay drafts as drafting instructions only. In other words, drafters can read the lay draft and treat it in exactly the same manner that lawyers treat the flowery descriptions of the subjective take on events offered by clients: they note the description, fish out what is relevant and completely discard what is irrelevant or harmful for the case.

Is this enough? Well, a degree of damage is inevitable when a lay draft is part of the drafting process. The drafter can only attempt to discard parts of the lay draft: it is impliedly unavoidable that they are influenced by what they read; and, in a job where time is always scarce,[59] it is only human for them to use the lay draft as a starting point. But, ideally, drafters should use the lay draft as drafting instructions. And fill in the gaps to the missing elements by means of a legislative plan. This is the topic of the next chapter of the book.

Is what I am calling for possible? Of course it is. Drafters have been using international agreements and treaties critically as drafting instructions in the process of drafting national implementing measures. The technique is there: its application to lay drafts is merely a matter of practice.

STYLE OF DRAFTING INSTRUCTIONS

Drafting instructions must always be in the narrative form.[60] Lay drafts are dangerous and more often than not useless and misleading.[61]

Technical language should be avoided. Drafting instructions are addressed to the drafter whose expertise lies only in expressing the policy

[57] See Office of the Queensland Parliamentary Counsel, 'A Guide for Effective Legislative Drafting Instructions' (n 41) para 37.

[58] See I McLeod, *Principles of Legislative and Regulatory Drafting* (Oxford, Hart Publishing, 2009) 39.

[59] For drafters and officers alike, see W Iles CMG, 'Legislative Drafting Practices in New Zealand' (1991) 12 *Statute Law Review*, 16.

[60] See Office of Parliamentary Counsel UK, 'Working with Parliamentary Counsel' (n 15) paras 157–58.

[61] See G Eorsi, 'Unifying the Law (A Play In One Act, With A Song)' (1977) 25 *American Journal of Comparative Law* 658.

into effective legislation. Drafters are not aware of all fields of law. Drafters are not aware of terminology stemming from other disciplines. And so it is important for instructing officers to convey their message to the drafter clearly and accurately. If technical language cannot be avoided, perhaps due to the topic or content of the required action, explanations must be provided. These can in turn be used by the drafter in the definitions introduced in the legislative text.

Drafting instructions must be systematic; they must present the instructions in logical sequence, promoted by the sequence of elements introduced in this chapter.

And consistent language must be used.

Suggested amendments and repeals of existing legislation must be introduced clearly, perhaps in tabular form, which can then be replicated in the legislative text.

Most importantly, drafting instructions must not be in the form of draft legislation!

CONCLUSIONS: A CHECKLIST FOR QUALITY DRAFTING INSTRUCTIONS

Drafting instructions constitute the first part of the first stage of the drafting process. It is equally important for the effectiveness of legislation as the composition phase. Quality drafting instructions can serve as the foundation to the building that is legislation. They offer a unique opportunity for instructing officers to facilitate the task of the drafter, to set the process of drafting in a solid start, and to participate effectively in the drafting process. After all, legislation is the product of a joint effort within the 'Bill team'.

In order to lead to effective legislation, drafting instructions must begin by indicating the main objectives that the Bill is intended to achieve: this puts the drafter in the picture from the very beginning. They must contain all relevant background material relating to the proposals to be included in the Bill, including all known legal implications and difficulties. They must explain in detail how it is proposed to achieve the various objectives, but *not* in the form of draft provisions.[62] Drafting instructions must indicate the sources of ideas, where these are based on existing provisions, mentioning any known precedents on the statute book for the sort of provisions thought to be wanted. If any matters have not yet been decided, they must

[62] The drafter needs to know exactly what results they are required to achieve, and cannot discover this from someone else's attempt at drafting. On the other hand, an indication of how the necessary provisions *might* be framed is often helpful, since departmental lawyers have a working knowledge if the shape and layout of the existing law.

indicate what they are and when additional instructions in relation to them are likely to be given. They must indicate any existing legislation that will or may require amendment in order to give effect to the proposals. They must state any known consequential amendments or repeals. They must identify any transitional or saving provisions. If the Bill is to come into force on a future date, they must say when, or indicate how a date is to be appointed. Finally, if the Bill impinges on the activities of another department, they must indicate the extent to which that department has been consulted.

They *do* not and *should* not attempt to draft! It is misleading and less effective in achieving the purpose of instructions, which is to communicate information to the drafter.

TO SUM UP: CHECKLIST FOR LEGISLATIVE INSTRUCTIONS

1. *What is the precise problem?*
   a. What harm or other undesirable outcome do we want to prevent?
   b. Who or what is being harmed?
2. *What is the nature and scale of the risk from the harm?*
   a. How frequent or probable is the occurrence of the problem?
   b. How many people or situations are affected, and how seriously, when the problem occurs?
3. *What are the options for dealing with the problem?*
   a. What are the alternative courses of action, from doing nothing through to, eg a complete prohibition of specific activities?
   b. Are there any alternatives that do not involve a governmental body?
   c. Can the matter be dealt with without making any regulation?
4. *What is the likely impact of each option?*
   a. What is the probable benefit from each option; ie how far is it likely to reduce the estimated risk?
   b. To what extent should this be discounted because the reduction in risk is likely to be lessened by persons altering their behaviour in response to the option?
   c. To what extent should this be discounted because of indirect side-effects or other harms likely to flow from an option?
5. *What administrative mechanisms are needed?*
   a. Is the mechanism for implementing each option the most practical and effective?
   b. In so far as the mechanisms involve public services, is that option an efficient use of public resources, given other claims?

6. *What is the monetary value of the expected benefits?*
   a. In monetary terms, what is the value of the benefits that are expected to accrue from each option?
   b. To what extent is that value likely to be increased by other benefits in respect of which the monetary value cannot be fully calculated (ie because they are not marketed)?

7. *What are the estimated costs of each option?*
   a. Overall, what are the costs (recurring and non-recurring) to the government budget of implementing each option?
   b. What is the cost of providing the administrative mechanisms (in personnel and non-personnel expenditure) necessary for each option?
   c. What are the likely direct costs (recurring and non-recurring) to the private sector in complying with each option?
   d. What are the likely indirect costs to the private sector in complying with each option, eg in terms of reduced competitiveness?

8. *How cost-effective is each option?*
   a. How do the costs of each option compare with the expected benefits? Are they proportionate?
   b. How efficient are the administrative mechanisms necessary for each option, in terms of costs measured against the likely reduction in risk?
   c. Which option is the most cost-effective?

9. *What issues of distributive fairness and public perception are relevant?*
   a. Are the costs and benefits fairly distributed between different groups in the society?
   b. What are the public perceptions about the extent of the risk and the need to eliminate it?

3

The Legislative Plan: Designing a Legislative Solution

DRAFTING INSTRUCTIONS SIGNIFY the start of the legislative drafting process, in that they are received by drafters whose first task in the process is to understand them. Thornton includes them as stage one of the drafting process, thus marking their extreme importance for the effectiveness of the legislation as the end product, and stressing the need for the drafter to read them in detail and understand the policy goals pursued, the proposed mechanisms for the pursuit of the policy goals, the basic legal concepts relevant to the policy goals and the law reform requested as a means of pursuing the policy goals.[1]

However, it is Thornton's stage two that marks the beginning of the real work for drafters. Stage two is the analysis of the proposal. It takes place well before the drafter designs the law, composes and develops the drafts, and of course before the draft verification. Although it belongs still to the preparatory work before the law is actually drafted, it is equally crucial for the effectiveness of the legislation as drafting instructions.[2] In fact, in view of the frequent practice of using either simple commands or lay drafts instead of proper drafting instructions,[3] this stage is even more crucial for the end result because it allows the drafter to mend the inefficiencies of stage one by filling in the gaps of the instructions offered by instructing officers.[4] Here the aim of the drafter is to analyse the legislative proposal

[1] For a detailed analysis on the relationship between law and politics, see M Zambone, *The Policy of Law—A Legal Theoretical Framework* (Oxford and Portland, Hart Publishing, 2007).

[2] Law Drafting Division, Department of Justice, *Legislative Drafting in Hong Kong—Crystallization in Definitive Form* (2001) www.doj.gov.hk/eng/public/pdf/ldhkv2e.pdf; also see E Page, 'Their Word is Law: Parliamentary Counsel and Creative Policy Analysis' (2009) *Public Law* 790, 797.

[3] For an analysis of the inevitability of lay drafts in certain jurisdictions, see P Perry Biribonowoha, 'Efficiency of the Legislative Process in Uganda' (2005) 7 *European Journal of Law Reform* 135, 146–47.

[4] For a detailed insight in the disruption caused by lay drafts, see P Perry Biribonowoha, 'The Role of Legislative Drafting in the Law Reform Process' (2006) 32 *Commonwealth Law Bulletin* 601.

and design a legislative solution noting the relevant points in a research report.[5] The compilation of the legislative plan marks the end of stage two.

DESIGNING A LEGISLATIVE SOLUTION: WHAT IS IT?

Having received the drafting instructions, and having understood their policy and legal elements, the drafter now turns to the task of elaborating on the instructions, planting the first foundations for the legislation building. The task here is dual: one, to think about the choices made by the instructing officers as a means of internal quality control;[6] and two, to introduce own thoughts on the policy and law reform elements of the proposal with specific reference to if and how these may be translated to drafting.[7] There is inquisition and creativity involved in this process: the drafter is more than a scribe.[8] And so the draft goes through the same list of questions required for complete drafting instructions, and attempts to offer themselves and the drafting team a short list of acceptable answers to all questions that should have been answered adequately and acceptably in stage one. But at the same time the drafter takes the opportunity to begin considering the composition of the resulting legislation, asking further questions of law and policy, addressing questions of practicality and feasibility and creating the foundations of a ground, acceptable to all, upon which legislation will stand. This is the start of the tri-alogue within the drafting team: agreement at this stage saves immense time, resources, energy and goodwill later on.[9] Parkinson describes quite accurately the elements of the intellectual task involved in drafting: knowledge of conditions proposed to be regulated and determination of the exact evils requiring regulation; determination of the nature of the regulation required and the precise principles or rules which will effect such regulation; and phraseology of the new principles or rules and of necessary administrative provisions in apt and precise language which will fit them into existing principles of constitutional and statute law and make them reasonably clear to the executive and judicial officers who are to enforce them:[10] in other words, policy/law/legislative expression.

[5] See BR Atre, *Legislative Drafting* (Dehli, Universal Law Publishing Co, 2006) 88–89.

[6] Driedger advocates non-political drafting: see EA Drieger, 'The Preparation of Legislation' (1953) 31 *Canadian Bar Review* 33, 36.

[7] But the current prevalent view is that the drafter's work on policy instructions is political: see DA Marcello, 'The Ethics and Politics of Legislative Drafting' (1995–96) 70 *Tulane Law Review* 2437, 2441.

[8] See RJ Martineau and MB Salerno, *Legal, Legislative and Rule Drafting in Plain English* (St Paul, MN, Thomson West, 2005) 95.

[9] See Office of Parliamentary Counsel, *Working with the Office of Parliamentary Counsel: A Guide for Clients*, 2nd edn (Canberra, OPC, 2002) 24: para 87.

[10] See T Parkinson, 'Legislative Drafting' (1913) 3 *Proceedings of the Academy of Political Science in the City of New York* 142, 191 www.jstor.org/stable/1193363.

Stefanou pictures expertly the communication taking place between the members of the drafting team and the drafter during stage two of the drafting process, and beyond, in the graph below:[11]

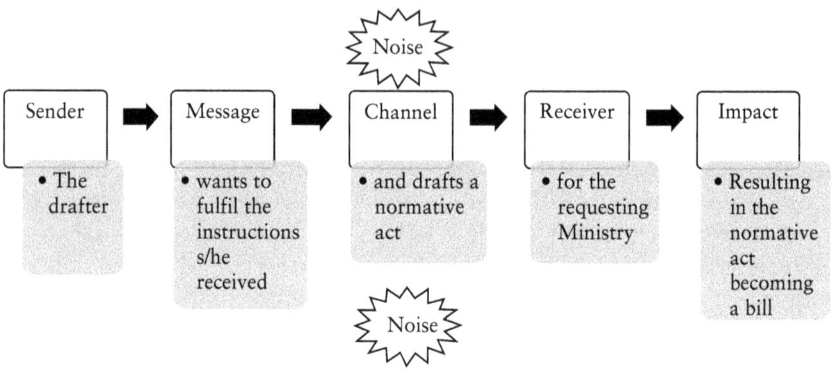

Figure 3.1: Communication within the drafting team

The compilation of mutually acceptable thoughts and agreed points is recorded in a legislative plan, also known as a legislative scheme[12] or a research report[13] or a commentary.[14] Whatever the term used, the plan involves a brief or longer report on the basic elements of the drafter's response to the drafting instructions.

The legislative plan can be complete and shared amongst the members of the drafting team. Or it can simply be a written sketch of the drafter's thoughts, private to them, and used solely for the purposes of assisting them in the composition of the legislation. As is the case with most aspects of phronetic legislative drafting, there is no rule here. The aim of the legislative plan is achieved simply by its compilation in whatever form: this is how the human brain begins to cope with complex intellectual tasks. The plan allows the drafter's thoughts to come through in a logical sequence, their interrelations explored at least prima facie, thus allowing its reader (drafter

[11] See C Stefanou, 'Is Legislative Drafting a Form of Communication?' (2011) 37 *Commonwealth Law Bulletin* 407, 414.

[12] See R Muhamad, 'Instructions to Draft Legislation: a Study on the Legislative Process in Malaysia' (2011) 13 *European Journal of Law Reform* 236, 241; also see L Levert, 'Bilingual and Bijural Legislative Drafting to be or not to be' (2004) 25 *Statute Law Review* 151; and EA Driedger, *The Composition of Legislation—Legislative Forms and Precedents* (Ottawa, Ministry of Justice, 1976) 1.

[13] See A Seidman and RB Seidman, 'ILTAM: Drafting Evidence Based Legislation for Democratic Social Change' (2009) 89 *Boston University Law Review* 435, 479.

[14] Office of Parliamentary Counsel UK, 'Working with Parliamentary Counsel' (6 Dec 2011) para 260 www.gov.uk/government/uploads/system/uploads/attachment_data/file/62668/WWPC_6_Dec_2011.pdf.ff.

or the whole drafting team) to follow the pattern of thoughts by the drafter. But there is a lot to be said for the compilation of a complete plan, shared amongst the members of the drafting team: this allows policy and legal officers to comment, rectify or confirm the drafter's initial thoughts, ensuring that the project is directed to a place acceptable to all. Having said that, the last thing that is needed is for the legislative plan to turn into yet one more bureaucratic layer in the drafting process, an 'audit trail',[15] a mere obligation to draft a memorandum to simply tick the box of stage two. And so ideally the legislative plan remains with the drafter who informally can invite comments by the team.

THE ADVANTAGES OF COMPILING A LEGISLATIVE PLAN

There are few who could argue that a legislative plan is a bad idea. After all, it cannot cause much harm. But, at a time where drafters are offered less and less time to complete their task, is a legislative plan a worthwhile activity in which valuable time is to be spent? Beginning with a legislative plan presents five advantages.

First, the legislative plan ensures that the end result of legislation is what is expected from their policy-makers. Although, at least in theory, the policy aims pursued by the instructing officers are clearly introduced and clarified in the drafting instructions, their translation from policy to substantive law and then to drafting may well lead to a loss of meaning.[16] Instead of waiting to discover such an unpleasant surprise at the verification stage of the first draft, the compilation of a legislative plan allows instructing officers to confirm that the drafting choices are agreeable to them, before any wastage of time and resources. For example, the policy aim of a requested law may be the eradication of poverty; this can be translated into substantive law as the introduction of a housing benefit for the chronically unemployed; in turn, the legislation may refer in the long title to the introduction of the housing benefit, and in the objectives clause may set as a measurable criterion of effectiveness the reduction of the number of homeless on the streets of the capital. As the legislative plan will demonstrate the translation of policy into law and then into legislative solution, the instructing officers can confirm that the objective is indeed the reduction of the number of homeless on the street rather than, for example, the increase in the number of previously

[15] ibid, para 263.

[16] Sir Stephen Laws confirms that 'this translation has risks of introducing obtuseness: (i) the necessary incompleteness of legislation; (ii) the risks from extrapolating a legislative solution from a failed non-legislative solution; (iii) the precedent trap, and (iv) the difficulty of hitting a moving target from a moving platform': see S Laws, 'Giving Effect to Policy in Legislation: How to Avoid Missing the Point' (2011) 32 *Statute Law Review* 1, 6.

homeless who now train and re-enter the job market. Thus, the legislative plan acts as the Bill's early quality control mechanism.

Secondly, a complete legislative plan identifies all elements of the proposed legislation, thus preventing disruption of drafting.[17] Before drafting is even attempted, the legislative plan offers prominence to the central elements of the proposed legislation, thus ensuring that central concepts are not missed, that the meanings attributed to them by all members of the drafting team are agreed upon and that the relationship between the requested Bill and Acts already in the statute book are exactly how the instructing officers envisaged and expected them to be. For example, in response to a request for legislation making trade in human organs an extra-territorial offence, the legislative plan will reveal that there is already legislation regulating transplants of human organs, that there is already a signed UN Convention on Trade in Human Organs that has been ratified and implemented by the jurisdiction and that the only point of law reform remaining for the drafter to deal with is the declaration of extra-territoriality of the existing offence. And so the policy goal may well begin as the eradication of the exploitation of the foreign poor by the citizens of the jurisdiction, the substantive law may call for a criminalisation of the extra-territorially committed offence and the drafter may well propose putting the policy and law reform into effect by an amendment to the existing Act adding the clause 'Utopia or abroad' in the definition of the existing offence. And, going back to the first point, this is the perfect stage of the process for the drafter to confirm that the legislative solution put forward is not only technically correct but also effective in its serving of the policy goal. The instructing officers may, and indeed must, argue that the mere amendment of the existing Act does not serve them very well, as users of the legislation may well miss the crucial change of law effected by the drafter, and that it may be more effective for the prevention of the extra-territorial offence but also for the investigation of the new offence to actually set it out in a separate section with a heading alerting them to extra-territoriality. Whichever view prevails at the end of the drafting process, it makes much more sense for this discussion to take place in stage two, rather than in stage five of the process, which will inevitably signify embarking on a new drafting effort, following stages two, three, four and five all over again.[18]

Thirdly, a complete legislative plan encourages the drafter to identify all elements of the requested legislation, and allows them to analyse each one separately and in turn. Logical structures and complete solutions are encouraged. By identifying the main elements of the legislation early on,

[17] Sir G Engle, '"Bills are Made to Pass as Razors are Made to Sell": Practical Constraints in the Preparation of Legislation' (1983) 4 *Statute Law Review* 7, 14 ff.

[18] See R van Gestel and J Vranken, *Kwaliteit van beleidsanalytische wetgevingsadviezen van de Raad van State* (The Hague, Boom Juridische Uitgevers, 2008) ch 2.

the drafter can alert their instructing officers to aspects of the legislation that may have been neglected or that may have been erroneously added in the drafting instructions. For example, a request for legislation regulating transport of goods via the sea needs to be evaluated in order to ensure that it is strictly sea transport that instructing officers aim at, rather than perhaps transport by sea and by the land's internal waterways. And at the same time, the identification of all possible elements of the requested legislation requires their prioritisation in the structure of the Bill. For example, robbery may also include armed robbery; and it makes sense at this early design stage for instructing officers to confirm whether they envisage that the legislation will address both robbery and armed robbery, whether they envisage a single Act dealing with both and whether they agree, as they should, that the section on armed robbery will follow the one on robbery. In fact, the drafting team may, at this point, decide to only deal with one element of the legislation or may decide to divide the legislation into distinct parts set in a rational sequence. And so, the legislative plan assists with the division of long instruments into distinct parts; with the introduction of a logical relationship between the parts and the whole; and with the identification of a rational sequence of normative provisions focusing only on the questions within the scope of the problem.[19] One caveat here: as the legislative plan is simply a first attempt of the drafter to deal with the request, there is absolutely nothing binding in its contents. There is nothing that can guarantee that the plan will not change with the further elaboration of the concepts: for example, upon the drafter's suggestion that both robbery and armed robbery may be included in the requested legislation, further analysis of statistics by the instructing officers may well lead to their decision to offer armed robbery a separate legislative solution with a specific policy objective driven by evidence-based analysis on the types of weapons used or the repeat offence policy of the instructing department.

Fourthly, by identifying the elements of the legislative solution, the design ensures that the drafter examines all relevant evidence and facts and that these facts are classified logically.[20] In jurisdictions where drafting instructions take a narrative form with multiple attachments of policy studies and policy and legal opinions it is possible that the drafter misses a document or piece of evidence. The legislative plan, which can briefly explain how each document has been used, or which may simply list the received document, can ensure that the drafter uses all documents sent by the instructing officers. In jurisdictions where drafting instructions are brief and without a

[19] See JC Dernbach, RV Singleton II, CS Wharton, JM Ruhtenberg and CJ Wasson, *Legal Writing and Legal Method* (Austin, Wolters Kluwer, 2007) 62.

[20] See A Seidman, RB Seidman and N Abeyesekere, *Legislative Drafting for Democratic Social Change—A Manual for Drafters* (The Hague, Kluwer, 2001) 88.

dossier of documents, drafters can identify the documents or data needed, and request them from the instructing officers.

Fifthly, compiling a legislative plan facilitates management of the drafting office, and delegation within the team. On the one hand, the legislative plan allows the drafter to set a realistic time table for the completion of the dossier, thus promoting better management of the drafting office. On the other hand, the legislative plan allows the team to agree on tasks and time-plans, thus promoting a good organisation of the task ahead.[21]

THE ELEMENTS OF ANALYSIS IN THE LEGISLATIVE PLAN

The elements of the legislative plan correspond to the content of drafting instructions, although the focus here is more at the drafting language and concepts rather than the policy and substantive law concepts.[22] They include:

- analysis of the existing law;
- analysis of the necessity of legislation;
- analysis of potential danger areas;[23]
- analysis of the policy options and the preferred legislative solution; and
- analysis of the practical implications of the legislative proposal, including projected statutory interpretation issues and an analysis of matters for which secondary legislation is likely to be needed to implement the draft law.

Let's focus on each element separately.

Analysis of the Existing Law

Amongst the very first considerations of the drafter is to ensure that they understand clearly and fully the current legal position on the topic of the requested legislation. At this point the drafter relies on the instructing legal officers, whose substantive law expertise can provide guarantees of accuracy and comprehensibility of the legal data offered to the drafter. In order to acquire the full picture the drafter needs to receive not just the list of relevant laws but a detailed description of what statutory law as applied by common law exists on the precise point of the requested legislation, and also on relevant neighbouring issues. What exactly does the drafter need to

[21] Office of Parliamentary Counsel UK, 'Working with Parliamentary Counsel' (n 14) para 252 ff.

[22] See HW Jones, 'Notes for a Legislative Research Checklist' (1950) 36 *American Bar Association Journal* 685.

[23] See H Xanthaki, *Thornton's Legislative Drafting* (West Sussex, Bloomsbury, 2013) 153.

know? Quite simply, the whole framework of the legal position: all relevant current laws as interpreted, implemented and supplemented by court decisions and academic opinion.[24] Comparative research can also be included at this point, especially in aid to the instructing officers' request for law reform.[25] But, of course, in order to ensure that the jurisdictions, institutions, laws or provisions identified by the policy officers as possible models for the drafter can be useful for the receiving jurisdiction, the drafter must be satisfied that the needs addressed by legislation are common between the foreign selected jurisdictions and the home jurisdiction, and that the legislative solutions of the model jurisdictions can be equally useful in the home jurisdiction.[26] A classical example would be the ineffectiveness of transplanting the laws on housing benefits from the UK to Greece: although the need to provide housing for the financially and socially vulnerable is shared by the two jurisdictions, housing benefits would not be equally effective in Greece where the close family structure and the availability of cheaper housing ensures that in the most part housing is not the main issue faced by the financially and socially vulnerable.

For the purpose of the legislative plan in the analysis of the request for legislation all requested laws must be considered as amending laws. It is very rare nowadays that legislation is introduced in a well sealed vacuum: knowingly or not, consciously or not, obviously or not, any proposal for new legislation touches upon existing legislation. And so the need to ensure a smooth surgical placement of the new legislation into the existing legal system in a manner that is as painless as possible makes the necessity for consideration of the relevant laws, for consequential amendments, and for repeals the rule rather than the exception. This generally accepted rule, principally supported by Thornton, ensures that drafters focus on the legal implications of the proposed legislation exercising acute alertness with regards to the analysis of existing law.

This analysis must reply to the following questions:

- What must be amended?
- What must be repealed? And how: express or implied repeals?

[24] For an eloquent analysis of the failings in the process of understanding the law before law reform, see N Des Rosiers, President Law Commission of Canada, 'A Just Law for All—Equality and Law Reform' (Canadian Congress on Criminal Justice, Halifax, Nova Scotia, 21 June 2001) www.restoringdignity.org/speech_desrosiersjune21.html.

[25] For the distinction between pure domestication of foreign laws and reception of foreign laws, see RM Lastra, 'Financial Law Reform in Emerging Economies' (2008) *Journal of International Banking Law and Regulation* 413, 419–20.

[26] See H Xanthaki, 'Foreword' (2011) 37 *Commonwealth Law Bulletin* 391, 393 ff; H Xanthaki, 'Legal Transplants in Legislation: Defusing the Trap' (2008) 57 *International and Comparative Law Quarterly* 659; L Mistelis, 'Regulatory Aspects: Globalization, Harmonization, Legal Transplants, and Law Reform—Some Fundamental Observations' (2000) 34 *International Lawyer* 1055; and of course O Kahn-Freund, 'On Use and Misuse of Comparative Law' (1974) 37 *Modern Law Review* 1, 18 and 12.

— What must be preserved?
— What must be added?

And this is exactly one of the points in the drafting process where drafting instructions in the form of a lay draft fail to provide the necessary background information to allow the drafter into a head start understanding of the legal position.

Why is such a good understanding of the law in theory and practice, in abstract and in context so vital for the drafting process? For two main reasons. First, it is only a comprehensive account of the legislation as applied that can offer the drafter the opportunity to identify the mischief, namely the specific point where the current law fails the user. Identifying the mischief allows the drafter to focus on this specifically, thus promoting a surgically accurate intervention to the legal system, in respect, as far as possible, of legal certainty as an expression of the rule of law. Secondly, a comprehensive presentation of the current legal position allows the drafter to proceed effectively to the next point of consideration at this stage, namely to the assessment of the necessity for legislation.

Analysis of the Necessity of Legislation as a Solution to the Identified Social Need

Legislation must be viewed as a solution of last resort. By definition, regulation is a breach of human liberty. Legitimately or not, every time a government regulates a new activity, they chip away at their citizens' freedom to act as they please. Even within Wintgens' concept of relative freedom without limitations for citizens,[27] there is little doubt that legislations adds a restriction to citizens' activities. And so legislation, as a strict regulatory tool with consequences including the imposition of fines or even imprisonment, constitutes a legitimate deprivation of citizens' freedom. As a result, legislation should not be undertaken lightly. 'Far from being paid for productivity, therefore, drafters should be paid for non-productivity'.[28] Much less so at a time where there are calls for the recognition of legislative negligence, which includes enacting defective legislation and failing to revoke or to amend out of date legislation.[29] The crucial importance of necessity

[27] See LJ Wintgens, 'Legitimacy and Legitimisation from the Legisprudential Perspective' in LJ Wintgens, *Legislation in Context: Essays in Legisprudence* (Aldershot, Ashgate, 2007) 3, 20.

[28] See D Greenberg, *Laying Down the Law* (London, Sweet and Maxwell, 2011) 155.

[29] See L Blake, J Pointing and T Sinnamon, 'Over-Regulation and Suing the State for Negligent Legislation' (2007) 28 *Statute Law Review* 218.

in all new legislation has been recognised by the regulators of the EU, who require that any new piece of legislation passes the necessity test.[30]

It is therefore necessary for the drafter to assess whether the identified social need can be addressed[31] by use of alternative means of regulation,[32] such as contracts and voluntary agreements, self-regulation, economic incentives and wider dissemination of information.[33] Drafters who strive to be faithful to their trade must begin with an instinctive negation to any request for further legislation, even though the process of legislating has already begun and the preliminary decision to proceed with legislation has already been taken.[34] Every drafter's response must be 'how can I avoid drafting this Bill?'[35] It truly serves statutory law better to decline drafting legislation rather than draft yet another law destined to be added to the now complex and remarkably long statute book: apart from the theoretical objection to legislation as a legitimate deprivation of citizens' right, new legislation adds to the unbearable volume of the statute book whose consequences include increasing complexity leading to incomprehensibility and ultimately ineffectiveness, and to an increasing loss of the value and importance of legislation when used as a ready and easy regulatory tool.[36]

[30] See esp *The Internal Market After 1992: Meeting the Challenge*. Report presented to the Commission by the High Level Group on the Functioning of the Internal Market (The Sutherland Report) EC COM (1992); also see Commission, *The Brussels Programme* COM (93) 545; *The Report of the Group of Independent Experts on Legislative and Administrative Simplification* (The Molitor Report) COM SEC (95) 1379; *Simpler Legislation for the Internal Market* http://www.europa.eu.int/comm/internal_market/simplification/index_en.htm; *Better Regulation—Simplification Initiative* http://europa.eu.int/comm/enterprise/regulation/better_regulation/simplifi cation.htm; and Commission, 'Smart Regulation in the European Union' (Communication) COM (2010) 543 final.

[31] The drafter must aim to diminish the 'uneven correspondence of lawmaking purpose and social outcome': see HW Jones, *The Efficacy of the Law* (Evanston, Northwestern University Press, 1969) 48.

[32] Legislation is often an insignificant instrument of control when compared to extralegal means of social control: see SF Moore, 'Law and Social Change: the Semi-autonomous Social Field as an Appropriate Subject of Study (1973) 7 *Law and Society Review* 719; also RD Schwarz, 'Social Factors in the Development of Legal Control: a Case Study of the Two Israeli Settlements (1954) 63 *Yale Law Journal* 471; and P Selznick, 'Legal Institutions and Social Controls' (1963) 17 *Vanderbilt Law Review* 79.

[33] See OECD, 'Law Drafting and Regulatory Management in Central and Eastern Europe' OCDE/GD(97)176, SIGMA PAPERS: No 18 (Paris, 1997) 14.

[34] See A Nicolaï, 'Schoonheid en effectiviteit: enkele observaties bij de kwaliteit van wetgeving' (2002) *RegelMaat* 39.

[35] See Marcello, 'The Ethics and Politics of Legislative Drafting' (n 7) 2444.

[36] See Department for Business, Innovation and Skills, *Delivering Regulatory Reform*, Report by the Comptroller and Auditor General (HC 2010–11, 758) 31, para 3.5 ff.

A lot of ink has been used by academics and regulators on the complexity of the statute book and the need to de-regulate and de-legislate.[37] The UK Government's 'Two for One' initiative, demanding the withdrawal of two current pieces of legislation in exchange for any new legislative proposal, is certainly moving in the right direction. But drafters cannot leave the decision on the necessity to legislate to instructing officers. Much as the aim to decrease the volume of legislation is common for all civil servants, it is the drafter who has the expertise to decide not when the policy objective necessitates further legislation, but when the legislative solution requires legislative intervention or not. Of course, this is a joint decision of the drafting team, with considerations that often go beyond drafting techniques. For example, in my work in Ukraine in the late-1990s and the early-2000s I was astonished to hear that the letter 'i' was introduced to the Ukrainian language by means of a law. From the point of view of pure drafting this seemed like a classic case of over-legislation. Of course, a circular amongst government officials and education authorities would have been equally effective. But the policy consideration behind the decision to legislate was revealed when the drafter at the Ministry of Justice informed me that it is precisely the letter 'i' that distinguished Ukrainian from Russian, thus upgrading the introduction of a letter to the alphabet as a paramount contribution to the enhancement of the self-determination efforts of the then newly established Ukrainian state that had only recently broken away from the then USSR. And, as a parenthesis, this is a good example to show that drafting does not work in a vacuum: policy and legal considerations come in the way of drafting purity, always in the pursuit of effectiveness of the resulting legislative text. This is also a good example to show how misguided purely international ad hoc consultancies tend to be in the drafting world: effectiveness carries a national meaning with eccentricities and requirements so inherently interwoven with the political, legal, social, financial, religious status and ethos of the home nation that any drafting attempt without a local component is doomed to haphazard success.

Analysis of Potential Danger Areas

Having satisfied themselves that legislation is indeed necessary for the extinction of the mischief, the drafter now turn their eye to potential danger areas. There is no limit to the nature or extent of danger areas that can crop up in a legislative effort. Constitutionality, legality, adherence with regional

[37] See E Donelan, 'European Approaches to Improving Access to and Managing the Stock of Legislation' (2009) 30 *Statute Law Review* 147, 153 and 161; also see A Flückinger, 'Régulation, dérégulation, autorégulation : l'émergence des actes étatiques non obligatoires' (2004) 123 *Revue de droit suisse* 159.

and international law and effectiveness issues are now at the forefront of a drafter's mind. Common danger areas include the following:

1. Constitutionality-related issues[38] include:
   a. issues of competence of the instructing department or of the bodies or agencies requested or required in the new legislation;
   b. proposals affecting personal rights (such as proposals affecting social benefits, pensions, access of citizens to activity regulated by statute, access to justice, electoral rights, freedoms or non-discrimination);
   c. proposals affecting private property rights (namely proposals granting powers of access to private property, search, seizure, detention or forfeiture of private property);
   d. proposals to introduce powers to the government without necessary parliamentary authority (such as proposals to introduce taxation legislation without specific parliamentary authority);
   e. proposals affecting the interests of other government departments or public bodies;
   f. proposals ignoring or clashing with case law, especially of the Supreme Court; or even
   g. proposals requesting vague enacting clauses for delegated legislation (for example a sweeping clause empowering the department to implement consequential and transitional provisions for a Bill).
2. Legality-related issues include:
   a. proposals for retrospective legislation;[39] or
   b. proposals for extra-territorial legislation.[40]
3. Issues related to compliance with regional or international law include:
   a. the expropriation of the property of foreign individuals without compensation;
   b. proposals of doubtful territorial or constitutional competence;
   c. proposals clashing with an international treaty to which the jurisdiction has acceded;
   d. proposals clashing directly or indirectly with legally binding regional legislation, such as EU law;[41] or

[38] For an analysis on the relevance of constitutional constraints to the drafter's basic legislative design, see J Zurcher, 'Basic Rules of Legislative Drafting' (1976–77) 7 *Manchester Law Journal* 131, 132.

[39] Criminal retrospective legislation must be viewed with extreme caution; civil retrospective legislation can be accepted if the law is certain and stable, it is general in character, and it is not subject to alteration in regard to specific individuals: see AL Goodhard, 'I think doctrine of precedent: the invitors and licensors' (1950) 66 *Law Quarterly Review* 374.

[40] In principle, extra-territorial legislation is a shock to the legal system; however, it may be imposed in the case of transnational social needs, such as for the regulation of transnational legislation.

[41] For examples with particular difficulties of 'marrying' EU and UK law, see J Steele, 'Remedies and Remediation: Foundational Issues in Environmental Liability' (1995) 58 *Modern Law Review* 615; also, B Pontin, 'Tort Law and Victorian Government Growth:

4. Issues related to best practices for effectiveness include proposals that are unnecessarily bureaucratic (such as proposals introducing complicated licensing or permit systems).
5. Issues of ethical or political sensitivity include proposals for the de-criminalisation of abortion in religious states, the de-criminalisation of homosexuality and the legalisation of gay marriages in most of Africa, the introduction of no fault divorce in strict Catholic states, or legislation related to minorities and minority rights.

It must be stressed at this point that the identification of such danger areas in the legislative proposal does not signify automatically an abandonment of the plan for regulation or even legislation in the field. Although these are issues to be dealt with with extreme caution and with extreme care, preferably with the opinion of the Attorney-General, the ultimate legitimacy to proceed with the planned legislation lies with those elected to carry out the government mandate. And these are not the drafters, not by any means. Of course drafters are legal officers and as such they have a duty to raise any objections of constitutionality or legality in their broadest sense with the other members of the drafting team. There are a number of options open to a drafter who finds themselves in a similarly unfortunate dilemma:

— The drafter may persuade the policy-makers that the proposals must be dropped as unconstitutional or illegal: this is what happens in an ideal world, and normally if the drafter can enlighten the instructing officers to the extent that they actually share the drafter's views of unconstitutionality or illegality.
— The drafter may proceed with the proposals risking legal challenge: the drafter can raise the problem issues orally and in writing, and can insist that an opinion of the Attorney-General, or equivalent, is sought. But the drafter is a lawyer with a subjective understanding and consequent view on the matter. If this does not coincide with the understanding, interpretation and consequent view of the independent government adviser on such issues, then the objection is considered withdrawn and the legislative solution is pursued. At this point the drafter may be asked to be relieved from the dossier for personal reasons, but the decision to remove them lies with the head of office, who may very well choose to keep the drafter in place.
— The drafter may seek an amendment to the constitution to accommodate the proposals. This is particularly relevant to constitutional

The Historiographical Significance of Tort in the Shadow of Chemical Pollution and Factory Safety Regulation' (1998) 18 *Oxford Journal of Legal Studies* 661; R Malcolm and J Pointing, 'Statutory Nuisance: The Sanitary Paradigm and Judicial Conservatism' (2006) 18 *Journal of Environmental Law* 37.

polities, where increased majority requirements are introduced for the purpose of constitutional amendments. In such circumstances, this option is only feasible where the problems are minor or procedural ones, or where the government shares the drafter's views and is prepared to complete the burdensome procedures for constitutional amendments. In the case of countries with uncodified constitutions, such as the UK, this option demands an amendment of the Act, constitutional or not,[42] that clashes with the legislative proposals. This can be undertaken within the proposed legislation in the form of a repeal or amendment of the pre-existing Act. But here again, the nature of the Act as constitutional renders the choice feasible only where minor amendments or small fine-tuning of the pre-existing Act is required.

— The drafter may find an alternative means whereby the proposals can be implemented. This is where the drafter demonstrate their technical skills. It is not always possible to fine-tune the proposed legislative solutions, but it may well be possible to use conscious vagueness as a means of acceptable political compromise.

— Finally, the drafter may resign their post, and exit the dilemma altogether.

Analysis of the Policy Options and the Preferred Legislative Solution

Having been persuaded that the requested legislation is indeed necessary in view of a true legislative mischief, and having analysed any basic danger areas, the drafter now turns their attention to the policy options considered by the instructing officers, to the preferred policy solution, and its translation into a legislative solution. The aim of the drafter's analysis here is to confirm the appropriateness of the policy option put forward in the requested legislation,[43] and to ensure that the legislative solution forming at this stage meets the policy objectives by translating accurately and appropriately to legislative expression.

In jurisdictions where the roles of policy officers, legal officers and drafters are clearly distinguishable the drafter's main task at this stage is to guarantee accuracy in the translation of policy language into legal language and ultimately into legislative expression. In jurisdictions where the three roles may be vaguely defined and perhaps even concentrated in less than three persons the task of the drafter treads into policy and substantive law,

[42] For an eloquent analysis of the meaning of constitutional statutes, see D Greenberg, 'Editorial: Constitutional statutes' (2007) 28 *Statute Law Review* iii.

[43] Policy-makers decide in principle on the basis of efficiency and equity: see RO Zerbe Jr, 'An Integration of Equity and Efficiency' (1998) 73 *Washington Law Review* 349, 350.

as they seek to evaluate possible policy options before translating them into legislative expression.

And, as a parenthesis, this is one more point where drafting instructions in the form of a lay draft fail the drafter miserably. A lay draft cannot offer a reflection on policy choices, nor can it invite the drafter to confirm the instructing officers' choice. In a lay draft the translation of policy into substantive legal concepts and then into legislative expression has already taken place, in the absence of the one actor in the drafting process that is qualified to undertake the task. Combined with a lack of comprehensive drafting instructions, lay drafts fail to make the link between the mischief and an effective policy/legal/legislative solution. And, as a result, far from guaranteeing effectiveness, they can only lead to haphazard legislative success.

Coming back to the drafter's task, most drafters are not at all equipped to deal adequately with the task of checking or, even worse, undertaking the selection of the most effective policy option expressed as the most appropriate legislative solution. Drafters tend to be lawyers, who are untrained in social science methodology.[44] It would be utopic to profess that this gap can be filled here, but it is worth mentioning that drafters have four methods for selecting the most appropriate legislative solution: practical wisdom, the end-means method of analysis, incrementalism and reason informed by experience.[45]

The Method of Selecting the Most Appropriate Legislative Solution

Practical wisdom is a method well within the parameters of Aristotelian *phronesis*.[46] When applied to problem solving in legislative drafting,[47] practical wisdom requires the application of theoretical know-how informed by experience in order to select the most appropriate legislative solution. Practical reason is an excellent method of selection of the most appropriate solution but it requires 'wise' members of the team, namely officers with an understanding of the phronetic nature of legislative drafting. Moreover,

[44] See RF Cranston, 'Reform through Legislation: the Dimension of Legislative Technique' (1978–79) 73 *Northwestern University Law Review* 873, 874; also see W Bussmann, 'Evaluation of Legislation: Skating on Thin Ice' (2010) 16 *Evaluation* 279; DL Faigman, 'To Have and Have not: Assessing the Value of Social Science to the Law as Science and Policy' (1989) 38 *Emory Law Journal* 1006, 1052 ff and 1079 ff.

[45] A Seidman and RB Seidman, 'Law in Aid of Development: "Hasty Legal Transplants" and the Fatal Race' (2006) 1 *Journal of Comparative Law* 282, 307.

[46] See A Seidman, RB Seidman and T Uate, 'Assessing Legislation to Serve the Public Interest: Experiences from Mozambique' (1999) 20 *Statute Law Review* 1.

[47] See C Sunstein, 'Interest Groups in American Public Law' (1985) 38 *Stanford Law Review* 29, 35–38.

it inevitably encompasses subjectivity, and it may lead to the solution that best represents majority ethos.[48]

In end-means analysis the drafter attempts to use whatever means are necessary to meet the desired, predetermined,[49] end result. In practice, the drafter invents as many routes to the objectives of the proposed legislative text as possible, and selects the most socially cost-effective[50] solution. This is the core of the problem and the heart of the dangerous paths that end-means analysis can take the researcher/drafter: social cost-effectiveness signifies the provision of a response to the social need under remedy, limited to solutions conforming with the values of those in power.[51] And so end-means analysis can lead to legislative solutions of doubtful ethical or moral standing.[52] Yet, within a modern polity respecting the rule of law and human rights, end-means analysis can be a good choice for the drafting team. It allows, in fact it invites, members of the team to bring to the table every conceivable legislative solution, which is assessed for effectiveness and prioritised on the same basis.

Incrementalism is a method of selection of legislative solutions that advocates extreme caution and gradual legislative action, giving credit to precedent and history.[53] As drafters cannot ensure knowledge of all possible situations, solutions and implications,[54] incrementalism encourages experimental legislation or legislation in stages, with regular post-legislative scrutiny cycles that can guarantee the almost inevitable damage limitation. Incrementalism is a shy method of selecting a legislative proposal, which, however, can prove extremely useful[55] when the gap between the current mischief and the final stage of the legislative solution renders the solution difficult to accept and or doubtfully implementable by citizens. It is on the basis of incrementalism that drafters would bridge the extreme gap between legislation that prohibits divorce altogether and legislation allowing no fault

[48] See N Levit, 'Listening to Tribal Legends: An Essay on Law and the Scientific Method' (1989) 58 *Fordham Law Review* 263, 294.

[49] See B Comly French, 'Council of the District of Columbia, Legislative Drafting Manual Revised Edition' (1982) 25 *Howard Law Journal* 735.

[50] See EL Rubin, 'Legislative Methodology: Some Lessons from the Truth-in-Lending Act' (1991) 80 *Georgetown Law Journal* 233.

[51] See RB Seidman, 'The Memorandum of Law' (1991) 15 *Seton Hall Legislative Journal* 334; also see E Rubin 'Legislative Methodology: Some Lessons from the Truth-in-Lending Act' in A Seidman, RB Seidman and T Wilde (eds), *Making Development Work: Legislative Reform for Institutional Transformation and Good Governance* (The Hague, Kluwer Law International, 1999) 157.

[52] See AE Anton, 'Legislation and Its Limits' (1979) 5 *Dalhousie Law Journal* 233, 233.

[53] S Levmore, 'Interest Groups and the Problem with Incrementalism' (2010) 158 *University of Pennsylvania Law Review* 815, 815.

[54] See R Cox, 'Social Forces, States and World Order beyond International Relations Theory' in R Keohane (ed), *Neorealism and its Critics* (New York, Columbia University Press, 1986) 208.

[55] See Y Listokin, 'Learning Through Policy Variation' (2008) 118 *Yale Law Journal* 480, 519–22.

divorce. This could be attempted via the gradual legalisation of divorce under specific circumstances (such as adultery, serious domestic violence etc), then the legalisation of divorce to the expense of the guilty party, and then finally through the introduction of true no fault, no guilt divorce. Incrementalism does not prescribe whether the stage of the legislative solution needs to be included in the same piece of legislation as parts with variable start and sunset dates, or whether the long-term undertaking of a government[56] would lead to successive separate pieces of legislation putting the end result into effect. But, at the end of the day, these are both viable choices.

Reason informed by experience is a method of selecting the most appropriate legislative solution under the realm of drafting as *phronesis*. Here the drafter is called upon to conduct research both in the jurisdiction and abroad as a means of developing new ways of doing things by reflecting on the facts presented by experience.[57] The questions asked are: (1) what is the social problem and whose behaviour creates it; (2) what are the explanations for this behaviour; (3) what are the proposed solutions; and (4) how these will be implemented and monitored.[58] In other words, the drafter makes use of evidence-based policy analysis undertaken by the instructing department.[59] This policy analysis assesses the effectiveness and cost of each policy option, thus leading by way of practical reasoning to the most appropriate one for the social problem at hand.[60] Reason informed by experience recognises the degree of subjectivity involved in the selection of legislative solutions,[61] and therefore invites all disciplines and experts to contribute to the common aim, which is of course the identification of the solution that has the most probability o leading to efficacy of the underlying regulation.

It would be difficult to prescribe a one-size-fits-all method of selecting a legislative solution in legislative drafting. Each one of them presents advantages and carries risks. End-means analysis may lead to outcomes of doubtful social fairness, whereas incrementalism seems a rather timid and short-term way to regulate. But there is a place for each of them: ends-means seems to be ideal in the context of financially geared legislative

[56] It is difficult for the government to 'precommit' regarding future law, and markets for hedging the risk of future law are undeveloped: see S Levmore, 'Precommitment Politics' (1996) 82 *Virginia Law Review* 567, 618–22.

[57] See Seidman, Seidman and Abeyesekere, *Legislative Drafting for Democratic Social Change: A Manual for Drafters* (n 20) 90.

[58] RB Seidman, A Seidman and N Makgetla, 'Big Bangs and Decision-making: What Went Wrong?' (1995) 13 *Boston University. International Law Journal* 435, 458–60.

[59] RB Seidman, 'Justifying Legislation: a Pragmatic Introduction to the Memorandum and Law, Legislative Theory, and Practical Reason' (1992) 29 *Harvard Journal on Legislation* 1.

[60] And law has been successful in effecting social change: see Y Dror, 'Law and Social Change (1959) 33 *Tulane Law Review* 787, 796–801; and M Evan, 'Law as an Instrument of Social Change' (1962) 2 *Estudios Sociologicus* 167.

[61] See R Munday, 'In the Wake of "Good Governance": Impact Assessments and the Politicisation of Statutory Interpretation' (2008) 71 *Modern Law Review* 386.

solutions, as it promotes efficiency; incrementalism has a lot to offer in cases of huge leaps of regulation. Practical wisdom has been criticised for its possible lean on conservatism, but this is not necessarily a bad attribute. What renders pure practical wisdom difficult to support is its inherent subjectivity. This is measured in the case of reason informed by experience, which advocates objective evidence-based analysis. But at the end of the day both theories stem from phronetic approaches to methodology and reflect the phronetic nature of legislative drafting.[62] There is little doubt therefore that the phronetic approach is more appropriate for the majority of drafts, and that reason informed by experience is the preferred version of that methodology because it combines a degree of objectivity with the concepts of virtue and the common good.

The Selection of the Best Legislative Solution

But what exactly is the process of analysis undertaken by the drafting team in the selection of the most appropriate legislative solution?

Within the context of the reason informed by experience method, the drafting team begins by identifying the reasons behind the problematic behaviours, which cause the social need that the proposed legislative text aims to address.[63] Once the link between the social phenomenon and its roots has revealed itself, the drafting team proceeds with the design of legislative solutions addressing the problematic behaviours behind the social need, which is addressed by the proposed legislation. And finally, the work completes with the identification of the monitoring and implementation mechanisms[64] that will ensure that after enactment the proposed legislative solution will be controlled for effectiveness and adjusted if and when necessary.[65]

Content of the Design of a Legislative Solution

The legislative solution is expressed in the legislative plan. But its elements do not necessarily coincide with those of the plan. The legislative solution

[62] They are often classed together as 'problem solving': see A Seidman and RB Seidman, 'Drafting Legislation for Development: Lessons from a Chinese Project' (1996) 44 *American Journal of Comparative Law* 1, 22.

[63] All laws refer to behaviour and prescribe repetitive behaviours: ibid, 6.

[64] For the EU model on post-legislative scrutiny and monitoring and valuation mechanisms, see mainly European Commission DG Markt, *Guide to Evaluating Legislation* (Brussels, March 2008).

[65] See E House, *Professional Evaluation: Social Impact and Political Consequences* (Colorado, SAGE Publications, 1993); also see A Shinkfield, *Systematic Evaluation: A Self-Instructional Guide to Theory and Practice* (Boston, Kluwer-Nijhoff Publishing, 1985) 167–68; W Clune II, 'A Political Model of Implementation and Implications of the Model for Public Policy, Research and the Changing Roles of Law and Lawyers' (1983) 47 *Iowa Law Review* 78–98.

has a narrower semantic field, which is delimited to the analysis of the policy options as expressed in the legislation. Issues of necessity of the legislation, suitability of the form of legislation planned and issues of practicability do not come into play here. But issues of constitutionality and legality remain in the drafter's focus, albeit as one of the elements for the evaluation of each policy-legal-legislative option.

The legislative solution includes the following elements:

1. identification of the causes of the problematic behaviours that lead to the social need under review;
2. preliminary choices of methodology:
    a. delimitation of the scope of the legislative solution: identification of the specific behaviour to be addressed and differentiation from other intertwined behaviours;
    b. history of the social problem as a means of understanding the elements for its regulation;
    c. comparative experiences as a means of identifying solutions offered elsewhere;
3. potential solutions to the problem by use of foreign experiences,[66] academic opinion and departmental analyses included in the drafting instructions remaining in 'the reason informed by experience' method of analysis;
4. conformity-inducing measures[67] (punishments; civil damages or penalties; rewards; indirect measures) and method of administration (creation of an organ to put the rule into effect and the creation of a fertile environment for that agency to function[68]);
5. description of the proposed solution;
6. ex ante evaluation of the proposed solution, defined as 'future oriented research into the expected effects and side-effects of potential new legislation following a structured and formalized procedure, leading to a written report; such research includes a study of the possible effects and side-effects of alternatives,[69] including the alternative of not regulating at all', and including the following:
    a. analysis of the effectiveness of the proposed legislative solution, namely juxtaposition of the social need to be addressed against the possible tangible outcome of the selected option;

[66] On the dangers of pure transplants, see F Dahan and J Dine, 'Transplantation for Transition—Discussion on a Concept around Russian Reform of the Law on Reorganisation' (2003) 23 *Legal Studies* 284, 310.

[67] See A Rose, 'Sociological Factors in the Effectiveness of Proposed Legislative Remedies' (1959) 11 *Journal of Legal Education* 470.

[68] See JP Chamberlain, 'Legislative Drafting and Law Enforcement' (1931) 21 *American Labor Legislation Review* 235.

[69] See J Verschuuren (ed), *The Impact of Legislation: A Critical Analysis of Ex Ante Evaluation* (Leiden/Boston, Martinus Nijhoff/Brill, 2009) 5.

b. analysis of the proposed solution's projected costs and benefits:[70] although effectiveness is synonymous with legislative quality, cost-efficiency remains of often equal importance[71] for efficacy of the underlying regulation;[72]

7. identification of the monitoring and feedback systems of the proposed legislation in the form of criteria of post-legislative scrutiny and, increasingly in modern drafting, a sunset clause encouraging the government of the day to act in order to prolong the Act's life,[73] if the post-legislative scrutiny has demonstrated that this is still useful.[74]

Analysis of the Projected Interpretation of the Legislation

The final consideration of the drafter in the legislative plan is the analysis of the projected statutory interpretation of the new provisions. The analysis of the interpretative implications of a legislative choice and the reasons for putting forward the specific solution may well be included in the drafting instructions. After all, the legal officers have the substantive law expertise required to appreciate what implications a choice of legal concept or terminology may have when they fall into their place in the legal system. However, the drafter must repeat this analysis both in order to supplement incomplete drafting instructions and to verify complete instructions.[75]

[70] For the EU model on measuring administrative burden, see Commission, 'Communication from the Commission on an EU Common Methodology for Assessing Administrative Costs Imposed by Legislation' COM (2005) 518 final; also see U Karpen, 'Implementation of Legislative Evaluations in Europe: Current Models and Trends' (2004) 6 *European Journal of Law Reform* 57.

[71] But not always equal: see eg L Heinzerling and F Ackerman, *Pricing the Priceless: Cost-Benefit Analysis of Environmental Protection* (Georgetown, Georgetown Environmental Law and Policy Institute, 2002); on efficiency see LA Kornhouse, 'A Guide to the Perplexed Claims of Efficiency in the Law' (1979–80) 8 *Hofstra Law Review* 591.

[72] For an interpretation of legislative quality with specific reference to the proportionality of the preferred legislative solution, see Case C-58/08 *Vodafone Ltd et al* ECR [2010] I-49991. See also Joined Cases C-96/03 and C-97/03 *Tempelman and van Schaijk* ECR [2005] I-1895; Case C-86/03 *Greece v Commission* ECR [2005] I-10979; and Case C-504/04 *Agrarproduktion Staebelow* [2006] ECR I-679.

[73] See Department for Business, Innovation and Skills, 'Delivering Regulatory Reform' (n 36) 30, para 3.4; also see H Scheffer, 'Evaluation and Assessment of Legal Effects Procedures: Towards a More Rational and Responsible Law Making Process' (2001) 22 *Statute Law Review* 132, 133.

[74] See R van Gestel and M-C Menting, 'Ex Ante Evaluation and Alternatives to Legislation: Going Dutch?' (2011) 32 *Statute Law Review* 209.

[75] See WN Eskridge Jr, 'Dynamic Statutory Interpretation' (1987) 135 *University of Pennsylvania Law Review* 1479; JR Macey, 'Promoting Public-Regarding Legislation through Statutory Interpretation: an Interest Group Model' (1986) 86 *Columbia Law Review* 223; WD Popkin, 'The Collaborative Model of Statutory Interpretation' (1988) 61 *Southern California Law Review* 543.

In the process of this type of analysis the drafter takes into account the Interpretation Act, presumptions and maxims of statutory interpretation in the home jurisdiction and court precedents relevant to the term or concept under review.

Now in an era of purposive interpretation the draft looks even further than a term or concept. As the courts may look at a variety of material both to determine the purpose of legislation and as an aid to its interpretation, the drafter must be aware of non-governmental material, governmental material and parliamentary material that may in the future be used for the purposes of interpretation.

Of course, in an ideal world statutory interpretation should not have been a concern for the drafter; after all good drafting minimises the need for interpretation. But realistically statutory interpretation often comes into play even with reference to a perfect draft: for example, conscious vagueness may call for further specification of a term or concept by the courts; or new circumstances may call for application of a provision on new objects that came to existence after the law was passed; and courts may have to resolve disputes on the application of the legislation in the set of circumstances surrounding a case.

And in our current era of legal globalisation, there is an additional parameter of projected statutory interpretation: the courts may refer to international treaties or regional legislation (for example, EU legislation) in order to determine the purpose or interpretation of domestic legislation that, directly or indirectly, implements them.

In addition to statutory interpretation, the drafter assesses the practicability of the requested legislation with reference to any delegated legislation likely to be needed to implement the requested legislation. It is better for this concern to arise at an early stage in the drafting process, although of course it may well crop up during the pure composition or even verification stages. But at the legislative plan, when the drafter identifies all elements of the proposed legislative solution, it makes perfect sense for the drafting team to agree whether delegated legislation may be needed for specific purposes, and which elements can be left aside to be dealt with there, rather than in the requested legislation. There is little to guide the drafting team on what must remain in primary legislation and what can be left aside for delegated legislation. In principle, the following issues are normally preserved for primary legislation:

1. appropriations of money;
2. significant questions of policy, including significant new policy or fundamental changes to existing policy;
3. rules that have a significant impact on individual rights and liberties;
4. provisions imposing obligations on citizens or organisations to undertake certain activities (for example, to provide information or submit

documentation, noting that the detail of the information or documents required should be included in subordinate legislation) or desist from activities (for example, to prohibit an activity and impose penalties or sanctions for engaging in an activity);
5. provisions conferring enforceable rights on citizens or organisations;
6. provisions creating offences which impose significant criminal penalties (imprisonment or fines equal to more than 50 penalty units for individuals or more than 250 penalty units for corporations);
7. provisions imposing administrative penalties for regulatory offences (administrative penalties enable the executive to receive payment of a monetary sum without determination of the issues by a court);
8. provisions imposing taxes or levies;
9. provisions imposing significant fees and charges (equal to more than 50 penalty units consistent with (6) above);
10. provisions authorising the borrowing of funds;
11. procedural matters that go to the essence of the legislative scheme;
12. provisions creating statutory authorities (noting that some details of the operations of a statutory authority would be appropriately dealt with in subordinate legislation); and
13. amendments to Acts of Parliament (noting that the continued inclusion of a measure in an Act should be examined against these criteria when an amendment is required).[76]

INITIAL CONSIDERATIONS OF STRUCTURE: THRING'S FIVE 'GOLDEN RULES'

The structure of a Bill will be discussed in detail in chapter five. But although duplication of effort is to be avoided, one cannot neglect to raise the drafter's thoughts concerning the design and structure of the requested legislation. For the purposes of comprehensibility, therefore, one must refer to the five 'golden rules' on structure put forward by Lord Thring:

1. Provisions declaring the law should be separated from, and take precedence over provisions relating to the administration of the law.
2. The simpler proposition should precede the more complex and in an ascending scale of propositions the less should come before the greater.
3. Principal provisions should be separated from subordinate provisions.

[76] See S Argument, 'Legislative Scrutiny in Australia: Wisdom to Export' (2011) 32 *Statute Law Review* 116, 135–36.

4. Exceptional provisions, temporary provisions and provisions relating to the repeal of legislation should be separated from the other provisions and placed by themselves under separate headings.
5. Procedure and matters of detail should be set apart by themselves and should not, except under very special circumstances, find any place in the body of primary legislation.

CONCLUSIONS

The second stage in the process of legislative drafting is 'understanding the proposal'. It refers to the drafter's elaboration on the drafting instructions, an intellectual process that begins the tri-alogue between policy, legal and drafting officers. This is the drafter's opportunity to ask questions, to fill in gaps, to bring to the table initial thoughts, to confirm and to receive feedback.[77] This is the drafter's opportunity to ensure that they understand fully the drafting instructions or, alas, to place the drafting process back into the straight and narrow after a bad start with laconic instructions or lay drafts.

At the centre of the drafter's consideration lies of course the legislative solution. This refers to the policy option put forward by the policy officers, as translated into substantive law by the legal officers. The drafter's task here is to confirm the accuracy of the translation and to translate the legal concept further into legislative expression. This is far from a technical task: translation here encapsulates creativity that can, and often does, fine-tune or change the underlying policy.[78]

In the process of this analysis, the drafter also considers the current legal status in the field of law under review as a means of identifying the mischief, the necessity of the legislation that can only be used as a solution of last resort, and the constitutional, legal and practicable constraints within which the drafting team must act.

All these elements are recorded in a self-addressed memorandum known as a legislative plan, or a legislative scheme or a research report. Whatever its designation, the legislative plan aims to assist the drafter in the organisation of thoughts, concepts and solutions in a manner that can be, if they so wish, shared within the drafting team.

The foundations of the architectural building of the requested legislation are set at this early stage before the drafter starts drafting. But of course nothing is written in stone, and all these thoughts, concepts and ideas are subject to continuous internal verification, and to the formal internal and external verification of stage five of the drafting process.

[77] Office of Parliamentary Counsel, *Working with the Office of Parliamentary Counsel: A Guide for Clients*, 2nd edn (n 9) 42, para D3.

[78] D Hull, 'Drafters' Devils' (2000) *Loophole* http://www.opc.gov.au/calc/docs/Loophole/Loophole_Jun00.pdf.

4

Structure of a Bill

HAVING UNDERSTOOD THE drafting instructions and analysed the proposal via the compilation of a legislative plan the drafter proceeds with stage three of Thornton's drafting process, namely with designing the law. This entails the early[1] identification of the appropriate legislative structure for the Bill as a whole in as much detail as possible, even down to the internal organisation of each particular clause or Schedule. As Sir George Engle states, 'it is not too much to say that good design, in this sense, is the essence of a well-drafted Bill'.[2]

At this point it would be necessary to state that the stages of the drafting process are neatly distinguished and classified for the purposes of their academic examination and study. However, they are not equally neatly distinguishable in practice: understanding and analysis are ongoing processes that continue throughout the drafting process even past the verification stage; and issues of design are conceived in stage three but they continue to spread into composition[3] and of course verification. Within the realm of fluidity of intellectual engagement with the legislative text, structure is considered mainly in stage three (design): but it cannot be amputated from stage four (composition) of which it forms an integral part.

Structure is not merely a technical concern. Prioritising the provisions within the legislative text ensures that the prime message of the communication that is drafting can be placed at the very beginning of the text, where the reader's attention is at its prime. This is not a novel concern. Drafting has a lot to learn from advertising in the techniques used to ensure that, whatever the abilities of the audience, they come out with one clear message. Similarly, in drafting the drafter needs to ensure that, whatever the abilities of the users, the prime message of the legislative text as an expression of the regulatory choice comes out loud and clear. If the message is a prohibition, then this is exactly what the user needs to take away from the legislative text; if the message is a declaration, then

[1] See AG Mackay, 'Some General Rules of the Art of Legal Composition' (1888) 32 *Journal of Jurisprudence (TT Clark)* 169, 178–79.

[2] See Sir G Engle, '"Bills are Made to Pass as Razors are Made to Sell": Practical Constraints in the Preparation of Legislation' (1983) 20 *Statute Law Review* 7, 14–15.

[3] See A Seidman, RB Seidman and N Abeyesekere, *Legislative Drafting for Democratic Social Change—A Manual for Drafters* (The Hague, Kluwer, 2001) 210.

this is what the user should 'hear'. This aim can be greatly facilitated by choices of structure.[4] Word choices, expression choices, gender-neutral language, everything that is immediately associated with the plain language movement are secondary to the prior concern of a plain structure.[5]

But what is it that drafters achieve with a plain structure? The goal of the drafter is to be effective, in other words to draft a legislative text that, with the synergy of the other actors in the legislative and policy process, can achieve the desired regulatory results.[6] Regulatory results, when pursued via legislation, require observance of the prescribed behaviour by the citizens. But in order to observe the new rules, citizens as users of the legislative text must be able to understand what it is that they must do or refrain from doing. This is the prime message of the legislative text. The question is how this prime message can be upgraded so that users can immediately identify it, and then of course understand it. Structure comes into play for the first part: the identification of the prime message. Placing it in a position of importance can allow it to shine through the inherent complexity of legislative structure and text. After all, users, including the courts, tend to rely on language and structure as primary carriers of meaning in legislative texts.[7] And so the aim of this chapter, as a contribution to the achievement of effectiveness towards the ultimate regulatory goal of efficacy,[8] is to offer the drafter techniques that facilitate the identification of the prime message of the legislative text. With a caveat: as Sir Geoffrey Bowman once said, sometimes there really is no right structure.[9]

THE THEORY: LORD THRING'S FIVE RULES OF DRAFTING REVISITED[10]

Placement of provisions within the text as a means of facilitating the user has been discussed by a number of prominent authors. Reference to relevant

[4] See Institute of Advanced Legal Studies, London University, 'The Template—A Guide for the Analysis of Complex Legislation' (1994) Research Working Paper Series.

[5] See B Bekink and Ch Botha, 'Aspects of Legislative Drafting: Some South African Realities (or Plain Language Is Not Always Plain Sailing)' http://repository.up.ac.za/xmlui/bitstream/handle/2263/3430/Bekink_Aspects(2007).pdf?sequence=1.

[6] And indeed without having to resort to the courts: see Law Reform Commission of Victoria, *Plain English and the Law* (Victorian Government Printer, Melbourne, 1987) 9.

[7] See E Garrett, 'Legal Scholarship in the Age of Legislation' (1999) 34 *Tulsa Law Journal* 679, 688.

[8] On the link between structure and efficacy as confirmed by Lord Cottonham, see G Wharton Pepper, 'Transitional Years in the University of Pennsylvania Law School' (1952–53) 101 *University of Pennsylvania Law Review* 169, 175.

[9] See Sir G Bowman, 'The Art of Legislative Drafting' (2005) 7 *European Journal of Law Reform* 3, 9.

[10] See Lord Thring, *Practical Legislation, The Composition and Language of Acts of Parliament and Business Documents* (London, 1902) 38; also see VCRAC Crabbe, *Legislative Drafting* (Oxford, Cavendish Publishing, 1998) 148–50.

literature cannot ignore the paramount word of Lord Thing. Lord Thring epitomises best practice in the prioritisation of provisions within a legislative text in logical order[11] in five rules. Under the first rule, provisions declaring the law should be separated from, and take precedence over, provisions relating to the administration of the law. In other words, the drafter must distinguish between the regulatory message and its administration. And then allow the regulatory message to take its prime place at the beginning of the legislative text, before and separate from the legislative provisions that involve the creation of the administrative structure within which the new law can be placed as a means of promoting its coming into effect. And so Lord Thring's advice is to:

— state the law, and then
— state the authority to administer the law, and then
— state the manner in which the law is to be administered.

There is little doubt that the rule is logical and serves the absorption of the message by the user. The question, and the difficulty in the application of the rule, is to identify what is the prime message as opposed to the administration of the law. Let us take the example of the law of inquest and the establishment of the office of Coroners. Which is the prime message? Is it the rules of inquest, in which case the establishment of the office is the administrative structure within which the law of inquest can be put to practice? Or is the establishment of the office the prime message, and its administration is the law of inquest as a list of functions under which the office can perform its new tasks? Needless to say that there is no unique answer here. In many jurisdictions the establishment of an agency such as the office is promoted to the prime message and often one finds the setting up of the office of Coroners first and then a statement of the law of inquest. In such cases the law, as it were, emanates from the authority rather than the other way round. But this is not always so. At the end of the day, the drafter needs to discuss with the policy and legal instructing officers what the policy aim is: if the policy aim is to regulate the so far unregulated forensic examination of crime as a means of achieving justice, then the law of inquest acquires prime importance. If the policy aim is to ensure that the law of inquest is observed in the process of a criminal investigation by a group of appointed trained individuals, then the establishment of the office is upgraded to the prime message and should take priority over the law of inquest. The difficulty is that in practice both messages compete in the drafting instructions. And it is up to the drafting team to decide what takes precedence. This rule is also expressed, albeit slightly differently, by

[11] See S Yueng, Ch Fung and A Watson-Brown, 'Traditional Drafting in Common Law Jurisdictions' (1995) 16 *Statute Law Review* 167, 173.

Coode who supports a 'genus to species order', also applied as 'rights to obligations to wrongs to remedies'.[12]

Lord Thring's second rule is that the simpler proposition should precede the more complex and, in an ascending scale of propositions, the less should come before the greater. And so, in principle, assault should be provided for before aggravated assault.

Lord Thring's third rule is that principal provisions should be separated from subordinate provisions. Subordinate provisions should be placed towards the end of the Act, while principal provisions should occupy their proper position in the narrative of the occurrence to which they refer. Principal provisions are those that declare the material objects of the Act. Subordinate provisions are those required to give effect to the principal provisions. They may deal with details, and thus complete the operation of the principal provisions. The third rule is often confused with the first rule. Although both rules classify provisions into two categories, and prioritise the prime category, they do not offer identical classifications. Rule one distinguishes between substantive and administrative provisions, whereas rule three distinguishes between principal and subordinate provisions. There is nothing to indicate that substantive provisions are always principal and that subordinate provisions are always of an administrative nature. Far from it: if the text is administrative in its content, then both the principal and the subordinate provisions will be administrative in nature. The message of rule one is that where there is substantive law, this should take precedence over its administration. If there is no substantive law, or if the content of the whole of the text is substantive or administrative, then priority must be given to the principal message. And this is the commonality between the two rules: the logic is that the drafter identifies the prime message and offers it priority. In this choice of the prime message, rules one and three can assist, albeit within the relativity of phronetic legislative drafting.

Equally useful is rule four. Exceptional provisions, temporary provisions and provisions relating to the repeal of Acts should be separated from the other enactments, and placed by themselves under separate headings. The rule is confirmed by Sir Courtney Ilbert.[13] The drafter's task is to distinguish between the body of the text, with its substantive and administrative, principal and subordinate provisions, and provisions that may well be of secondary importance to the main message but which, nonetheless, carry great significance to the full understanding of the legislative text. Provisions introducing exceptions to the text (such as savings), provisions that relate to time (entry into force, duration, transitional provisions), and provisions related to repeals (such as repeals, amendments, consequential repeals and

[12] See F Bowers, 'Victorian Reforms in Legislative Drafting' (1980) 48 *Tijdschrift voor Rechtsgeschiedenis* 329, 345.

[13] See Sir C Ilbert, *Legislative Methods and Forms* (Oxford, Clarendon Press, 1901).

amendments) are secondary to the main regulatory message and, in application of rule three, must be left aside for the later part of the legislative text. However, they can be of immense importance to the reader who can be alerted to their existence by their separate placement in provisions carrying the relevant heading. Combined with a table of arrangements as a road map, this technique can ensure that their non-prioritisation in the main text does not lead to the ignorance of these types of provisions by the users.

And rule five. Procedure and matters of detail should be set apart by themselves, and should not, except under very special circumstances, find any place in the body of the Act. At the end of the day, the drafter's task is to strip the text of anything that takes away the user's attention needlessly. And so offering the reader a bare text with a list of laconically expressed regulatory messages can facilitate the user's receipt of the main messages. But of course legislation usually involves more. Issues of relative detail must be foreseen. The dilemma between stripping the text of anything relatively unnecessary and being forced to leave aside crucial matters of detail is being addressed in rule five. And resolved by offering the drafter the opportunity of using Schedules, or even secondary legislation for that purpose. Which of the two is most effective is directed mainly by the envisaged longevity of the provision in question: if the drafter envisages that the provision will remain in place for the foreseeable future, then placing it in a Schedule would be ideal as a combination of downgrading it into a subordinate provision while offering it the legitimacy of parliamentary scrutiny; if the drafter envisages that the provision will have a short life, the providing for it via an enabling clause in secondary legislation will offer it flexibility in its amendment, but will carry the disadvantages of lower scrutiny inherent in secondary legislation.

MORE DOCTRINE: BERGERON'S RULES[14]

Bergeron places choices of structure under the umbrella of a logical sequence[15] of provisions within the legislative text. Bergeron focuses on the need for a rational order of provisions as a means of assisting the user to understand what constitutes a priority for the drafter. Within this prism, Bergeron stresses precedence of the provisions of the statute that are of a permanent nature over those expected to have a limited life. Presumably the rationale behind this is that amendments affect the text excessively when they refer to provisions at the beginning of the text; but one doubts whether this can serve as a criterion for the placement of provisions within the Act.

[14] See R Bergeron, *Rules of Legislative Drafting—Letters to Ukrainian Drafters* (Kiev, Department of Justice Canada and Ministry of Justice of Ukraine, 1999).

[15] On the concept of logical sequence of provisions, see NK Nanpoothiri, 'The Role of Parliamentary Counsel in Legislative Drafting' (2010) 36 *Commonwealth Law Bulletin* 57.

It certainly is a contributing factor to choices of placement of substantive and administrative provisions within the main body of the text. But the rule cannot be stretched to support the prioritisation of traditional preliminary provisions in the beginning of the text: the inconvenience of amending the first few provisions cannot be put at the same level of concern as the possibility of missing the target audience with the main regulatory message. In fact, placing the main regulatory message at the beginning seems to apply Bergeron's rule, as this would be the type of provision least expected to be amended later on in the Act's life.

Interestingly, Bergeron mentions the table of provisions showing the headings and the section titles. The table of provisions is not part of the statute but is included to make it easier to consult. This is a major tool for drafters in their pursuit to introduce user friendly structure. Tables of contents or tables of arrangement are becoming increasingly popular both as a means of offering a roadmap to the reader but also as a means of quality assurance of the structure in the verification stage of drafting.

Bergeron alerts drafters to the danger of over-dividing the text. As is the case with most things in drafting, keeping a balance between the need to divide a longer text to make it more accessible to the reader and the need to ensure that unity of communication is maintained is not an easy task. The statute is divided into parts only in those cases where the number of sections and the possibility of arranging them in categories constituting adequate conceptual units justify this. Only codes and other major statutes are divided into chapters.

THE PRACTICE: THORNTON'S APPROACH

Thornton takes stock of Lord Thring's rules but has the presence of mind to add an additional dimension to the prioritisation of legislative provisions, that of conventional practice. There is no doubt that consistency of practice within a jurisdiction undoubtedly facilitates the use of statutes by regular users.[16] 'But this should not deprive the drafter from the opportunity to try out different emerging techniques, whose benefits may outweigh the short-term imbalance of the transitional period between the old and new techniques come into force'.[17]

And this presents yet one more dilemma for the drafter. Ambushing the user with innovation may well be highly satisfying intellectually and academically. But surprise signifies doubt. And doubt is uncertainty. When this applies to law, the consequences can be dramatic both in the positive and

[16] On traditional approaches to structure, see BJ Ard, 'Interpreting by the Book: Legislative Drafting Manuals and Statutory Interpretation' (2010–11) 120 *Yale Law Review* 185, 191.

[17] See H Xanthaki, *Thornton's Legislative Drafting*, 5th edn (West Sussex, Bloomsbury Professional, 2013) 223.

negative senses of the word. This dilemma is highly relevant to the modern drafter. The increasingly louder academic voices, including mine, for a dry, bare text in the form of a succession of bullet-style commands clash rather violently with the traditional style of structure still dominant in much of the Commonwealth. And thus the increasing calls to drafters to at least weed out the text of useless (to the reader) preliminary provisions collide with the need to maintain a house style.

It would be a shame if house style were to prevail when clashing with effectiveness of the legislation. The first is there to feed the latter, rather than to chain it down to the ground of ineffectiveness. The examples of the UK, Australia, New Zealand, Canada and many more jurisdictions shine as models of modern legislative structure that depart from traditional house styles. But, of course, the manner in which this dramatic change is to be introduced cannot be sudden or unannounced to the users of legislation. And the balance between respect to tradition and exciting innovation in legislative structure is really a balance between dramatic change and smooth transition.

STRUCTURE IN BRIEF: THE TRADITIONAL STYLE[18]

In the current transitional period towards moving provisions from their traditional place in preliminary provisions at the beginning of Acts to final provisions at the end, one can only take the measured step of citing the traditional flowery style and then recommend an innovative bare one.

The traditional style of many jurisdictions in the Commonwealth is to include the following types of provisions under preliminary, main and final parts.[19] The list includes all possible provisions per part.

Preliminary provisions

— Long title
— Preamble
— Enacting clause
— Short title
— Commencement
— Duration/Expiry
— Application
— Purpose clause

[18] See New Zealand Law Commission, 'Legislative Manual: Structure and Style' (Report No 35, 1996); also Parliament of Canada, '16. The Legislative Process'—'Structure of Bills' www.parl.gc.ca/marleaumontpetit/DocumentViewer.aspx?Sec=Ch16&Seq=5&Language=E; also see A Watson-Brown, 'The Classification and Arrangement of the Elements of Legislation' (1997) 18 *Statute Law Review* 32, 45.

[19] See TK Viswanathan, *Legislative Drafting—Shaping the Law for the New Millennium* (New Delhi, The Indian Law Institute, 2007) 173.

— Definitions
— Interpretation

Principal provisions

— Substantive provisions
— Administrative provisions

Miscellaneous

— Offences and provisions ancillary to offences, such as time limit for prosecution, continuing offences, offences by corporations and vicarious responsibility
— Miscellaneous and supplementary provisions, such as evidentiary provisions, a power to make subordinate legislation, service of notices, powers of entry and search, seizure and arrest.

Final provisions

— Savings and transitional (these may also be placed in a Schedule if they are long)
— Repeals
— Consequential amendments (these may be placed in an annex especially if the repeals and consequential amendments are numerous and can conveniently be presented in a tabular form)
— Schedules

STRUCTURE IN BRIEF: INNOVATION

Within the context of legislative effectiveness and the use of structure as its facilitator, a drafter has to query the placement of each type of provision within the text. In application of Lord Thring's rules the drafter has to identify which types of provisions offer a prime message, can be classified as principal, and can therefore remain or be transferred to preliminary provisions. All other types of provisions must find their way to the bottom of the text under final provisions. The decision is not easy: although consistency of style is required as a means of forseeability and therefore predictability and certainty for the user, the introduction of a hard and fast rule in phronetic legislative drafting is an oxymoron in itself. But, in principle, one can identify these provisions that must remain in the preliminary part. Let's examine each one of the list above in brief.

Preliminary provisions must be short and absolutely necessary. After all, they are the one that competes with substantive provisions for the prime attention of the user. The long title, namely the description of the main mechanisms of law reform performed by the Act, must remain at the very beginning of the text. When technically correct, it serves as a unique introduction to the Act (indeed, the term 'introductory text' is found in the electronic publication of UK legislation) and it allows the user a quick assessment as to whether the Act is at all relevant to them or not. Similarly, the enacting clause is absolutely necessary as it confirms that the Act has complied with the procedural requirements for its constitutionality and legality; and, as a confession of weakness, the enacting clause also serves those of us used to reading legislation as a reminder of the long rich tradition of legislative practice. The short title is equally important as a statement of reference to the topic of the legislation and its distinction from other relevant Acts. Application provisions tend to remain high in the text simply because they are relevant to the user's decision on whether this is an Act worth reading, or whether this is not relevant to them at all.

But preambles tend to be seen as less significant, at least in Acts that do not carry a ceremonial robe. Experience from the newer and less fortunate jurisdictions around the world shows that a preamble can serve them well both during and post transition: in such circumstances preambles can serve as a vessel of confirmation of constitutionality by spelling out the required constitutional steps in the passing of the legislation and the legal basis upon which the legislation was passed. There is little doubt that this is a message of prime significance in circumstances where constitutionality and legality are or continue to be challenged rather more often than in circumstances of long-established political peace and continuity. Preambles can also serve as a confirmation of the necessity of the legislation in circumstances where legislation is used frequently and without much thought of its role as a solution of last resort. But of course this required confirmation of necessity may well be addressed adequately in stages one and two of the drafting process, and confirmed in the explanatory materials accompanying the legislation rather than in the text.[20]

Similarly, purpose clauses have lost their place in preliminary provisions. In fact they had reached a point of extinction due to the awful practice of piling into them political statements or vague expressions of catchy legislative intent. They are beginning to make a comeback as lists of measurable tangible criteria of effectiveness of the Act, and in that sense they may well remain in preliminary provisions, at least for a period of probation.

Apart from preambles and purpose clauses, where the arguments against their use tend to be prevalent, a number of types of provisions play between the preliminary and final parts of the text. Commencement provisions may be traditionally placed at the beginning of the text, but they seem to be moving towards the end in final provisions along with duration or expiry provisions. Definitions and interpretation provisions tend to feature in final provisions, or perhaps in Schedules hanging from a brief clause in

[20] For the dual purpose of the preamble, see Interpretation Act (Canada) RSC 1985, c I-21, s 4.

the preliminary section.[21] Admittedly there still is a distinction between substantial and subsidiary definitions: substantial definitions, namely definitions that define the scope and subject matter of a measure,[22] are often placed at the beginning of the text, whereas subsidiary definitions[23] tend to be placed at the bottom of the text. When it comes to commencement, definitions and interpretation provisions one would tend to suggest that these can and must be placed at the bottom of the text. There is an argument supporting their placement at the beginning where they introduce an exception to the general rule or practice: this would draw the reader's attention to a departure from the conventional. But, even then, a clear heading before the provision can alert the reader to the departure from the rule irrespective of where the provision is placed. If placement is with final provisions, the advantage of this practice is that they do not haunt the already overcrowded prime zone of preliminary provisions.

The body of the text includes principal provisions, both substantive and administrative in that order, and miscellaneous provisions.

Final provisions host what is not included in the preliminary part, plus savings, transitional, repeals and consequential amendments and any Schedules. In fact, Schedules are becoming increasingly popular as they offer the drafter the opportunity to include in the primary legislation text that is of secondary importance.

And so a recommended structure would be as follows:

- Preliminary provisions
  - long title
  - enacting clause
  - short title
  - purpose clause with tangible measurable criteria for effectiveness
  - hanging clause for definitions
  - application (where different from savings)
- Substantive and administrative provisions
  - principal provisions
  - subordinate provisions
- Final provisions
  - Savings
  - Transitional provisions
  - Repeals and consequential amendments
  - Purpose clause/Objectives

[21] On the division between jurisdictions on the placement of definitions, see Seidman, Seidman and Abeyesekere, *Legislative Drafting for Democratic Social Change* (n 3) 315.

[22] G Coode stated more than 100 years ago: 'Definitions should challenge attention by being placed before, not as is the more common practice, after, the matter to which they have reference'; see G Coode, 'On Legislative Expression' in EA Driedger, *The Composition of Legislation* (Ottawa, Edmont Clutier, 1957) 167, 225.

[23] See Ilbert, *Legislative Methods and Forms* (n 13).

  - Start/End provisions
  - Short title
  - Schedules
  - Definitions/Interpretation
  - Other Schedules

The analysis on the placement of provisions under preliminary or final continues in chapter seven where the innovative, some would say radical, approach on structure leads to the following:

- Preliminary provisions
  - introductory text
  - start/expiry date with hanging clause for a Schedule
  - hanging clause for definitions in a Schedule
  - application (where different from savings)
- Substantive and administrative provisions
  - principal provisions
  - subordinate provisions
- Final provisions
  - savings
  - duration/expiry provisions where not in preliminary or a Schedule
  - transitional
  - repeals
  - consequential amendments
  - purpose clause with tangible measurable criteria for effectiveness
  - short title
  - Schedules
  - enacting clause in the form of a signing statement.

ARRANGEMENT IN PARTS

But of course structure does not just refer to the division of the Act into preliminary, substantive/administrative and final provisions. Structure also refers to the division of the Act into smaller sets of provisions with unity of meaning, as a means of enabling the user to better, and easier, access the regulatory messages of the legislative text.

How does accessibility relate to the division of an Act into parts? The answer is through the promotion of clarity: clarity of presentation, clarity of structure and clarity of expression. Dividing an Act into parts promotes clarity of presentation, since parts and heading create a visual aid that allows the drafter to demonstrate the logic behind the Act, to maintain coherence of the legislative text and to stress the interrelation between the provisions of the text. Dividing an Act into parts promotes clarity of structure, since parts make it easier for the user to comprehend the structure and sequence of the contents of the legislative text: a part indicates the cohesive relationship of the provisions within it to one another and their separation from provisions in other parts. Dividing an Act into parts promotes clarity of expression; technically, it is useful to have a collective reference to certain sets of provisions.

This occurs frequently in legislation especially when aspects of the law apply differently with reference to time of entry into force, mode of entry into force, geographical application, scope of application or simply where a concept bears a different meaning in labeling definitions. Let's look at examples for each:

— different dates of entry into force: part 1 of this Act comes into force after 31 December 2013 and part 2 comes into force after 31 December 2014;
— different authority bring it into force: part 1 of this Act comes into operation by an order made by the Minister of Transport and part 2 comes into operation by an order made by the Minister of Labour;
— different geographical application: part 1 of this Act applies to Northern Ireland and part 2 applies to Scotland;
— different scope of application: part 1 applies only to licensing of domestic air services and part 4 applies only to the licensing of international air services;
— different concept in labelling definitions: 'Minister' in parts 2, 3 and 4 means the Minister of Labour and in part 5 means the Minister of Finance.

Of course there are cases where division in parts simply serves clarity: part 2 of the Mint Employees Act 1964 (Australia) is incorporated and shall be read as one with the Public Service Act. And so the drafter's criterion for arrangement in parts is not whether the Bill before them can be classified under any of the categories above, but simply whether in the design stage the drafter believes that arrangement in parts will make the Bill accessible to the reader.

And this is where the dilemma of the drafter actually lies: an overzealous effort to serve accessibility carries the danger of over-division, which prevents rather than promotes accessibility, and the danger of erroneous division, which confuses the reader through the placement of provisions in the wrong part. Erroneous division can be avoided if, at the first instance, the drafter can amass all preliminary provisions in part 1 entitled 'Preliminary' and all final divisions in a part entitled 'Final': what remains can then be divided on the basis of the prime regulatory message in application of the rules introduced by Lord Thring, Thornton and Bergeron. Over-division can be avoided if the drafter and their team assess what purpose it serves, and continues to serve, even after amendments,[24] throughout the drafting

[24] See MS Rafford, 'The Private Securities Litigation Reform Act of 1995: Retroactive Application of the RICO Amendment' (1997) 23 *Journal of Legislation* 283, 304; also see WM Graham-Harrison, 'An Examination of the Main Criticisms of the Statute Book and of the Possibility of an Improvement' (1935) 9 *Journal of the Society of Public Teachers of Law* 9, 30.

process, namely in the design, composition and verification stages. The task is greater in jurisdictions that also use subparts. Subparts also provide useful reference points and are helpful in larger and more complex Acts. They are identified by letter or number and may contain common definitions or purpose provisions. Subparts are numbered with a descriptive heading.

HEADINGS

Headings are intended to save users' time by helping them to find their way about the legislation.[25] And there is empirical evidence to show that they can serve their purpose well.[26] They should be accurate,[27] descriptive and they should be brief; but not so brief that they sacrifice clarity. Their language must be consistent with that of the enactment to which they relate. The recommended form is in Roman Capitals, with subheadings (also known as cross-headings) in italics, without a full stop at the end (what purpose would that serve?) and grammatically separate from the provision which follows immediately after. Their placement on the page seems to be indifferent to the user's understanding of the text.[28] In Australia headings are part of the Act.[29] In New Zealand headings are for reference purposes only.[30] In the UK the matter is still under debate, although the prevalent position is that headings only come into play when the text itself is not adequate.[31] In Canada tradition is not to amend headings even after amendments to the text, although this is now changing.[32] The discipline of drafting descriptive headings accurately can reveal the lack of the required unity between parts, subparts, sections and Schedules.[33] Reviewing headings at

[25] See BR Atre, *Legislative Drafting* (Dehli, Universal Law Publishing Co, 26) 56.

[26] See R Sullivan, 'Some Implications of Plain Language Drafting' (2001) 22 *Statute Law Review* 145, 149; also see M Kools et al, 'The Effects of Headings in Information Mapping on Search Speed and Evaluation of a Brief Health Education Text' (2008) 34 *Journal of Information Science* 833, 842–43; and S Wilhite, 'Headings as Memory Facilitators: The Importance of Prior Knowledge' (1989) 81 *Journal of Educational Psychology*, 115, 116 17.

[27] See R Carter 'Statutory Interpretation in New Zealand's Court of Appeal: When "May" Means "Must", Section Headings Affect Interpretation, and Latent Acts have Effect' (2001) 22 *Statute Law Review* 20, 29.

[28] See BH Simimba. 'Should Marginal Notes be Used in the Interpretation of Legislation?' (2005) 26 *Statute Law Review* 125, 125–26.

[29] See Interpretation Act 1901–1966, s 13(1); also see Interpretation of Legislation Act 1984, s 36.

[30] See Interpretation Act 1924 (New Zealand), s 5(f).

[31] See *Qualter, Hal and Co Ltd v Board of Trade* [1962] Ch 273 (CA), 11; also see *Fisher v Raven* [1964] AC 210; and *Fletcher v Birkenhead Corporation* [1907] 1 KB 205; but see contra *R (Westminster City Council) v National Asylum Support Service* [2002] 1 WLR 2956, [36].

[32] See Standing Committee on Environment and Sustainable Development, *Minutes of Proceedings* (14 May 2008) Meeting No 32.

[33] See New Zealand Law Commission, 'Legislation Manual Structure and Style' (n 18).

a late stage in the drafting process ensures that headings have remained consistent with changes in the draft.

Horn, in his detailed analysis of headings, states that they serve a vertical and a horizontal role: based on Stewart's doctrine Horn identifies the vertical role of headings as indicators of the contents of the section; and the horizontal role as their collective indication of the contents of the Act.[34]

SECTIONS

An Act is divided into numbered sections. A section must have a unity of purpose.[35] However, very long sections with numerous subsections, even with a unity of purpose, are difficult to read. Sections must therefore be kept to a manageable length. Each subsection must be relevant to the unifying theme of the section. As a general rule, if a section comprises more than one sentence, the drafter must present each sentence in a separate numbered subsection. However, two very closely related thoughts in separate sentences may be presented together in a single section or subsection, if that makes communication more effective. For example:

3. The applicant must apply within 2 weeks after receiving the notice. But, with the Minister's consent, the applicant may apply at any time after receiving the notice.

Note the use of *But* to link the two sentences, and to indicate the contrasting content.

Drafters must present the primary provision prominently in the first subsection of a section. Subsidiary matters follow. The design of a section should assume that the section will be construed as a unit. The relationship of subsections to one another is generally complementary and obvious. Qualifications and internal cross references such as 'subject to the provisions of subsection (1)' and 'in accordance with subsection (1)' must be kept to an absolute minimum.

MARGINAL NOTES[36]

Apart from division into parts, additional visual aids can facilitate the drafter's strive to offer clarity to the user. Traditionally, in the UK marginal

[34] See N Horn, 'Legislative Section Headings: Drafting Techniques, Plain Language, and Redundancy' (2011) 32 *Statute Law Review* 186, 192.

[35] While there is no specific rule regarding the content of Bills, there must still be a theme of relevancy among the various issues addressed in the Bill: see Speaker Lamoureux's ruling (Canada) *Journals* (6 May 1971) 531.

[36] See G Stewart, 'Legislative Drafting and the Marginal Note' (1995) 16 *Statute Law Review* 21.

notes could not be used for statutory interpretation,[37] but there are calls to extend their value after *Pepper v Hart*.[38] Marginal notes are used as a means of giving a concise indication of the contents of a section. The recommended form is brief, accurate and without necessarily being a full grammatical sentence. Marginal notes are not normally part of the Act,[39] and are not considered by Parliament[40] despite eloquent calls for a change of practice.[41] They refer to one section and can normally be found in the margin opposite the first line of the section:

Refusal to take oath	27. Section seventy-six of the Principal Act is repealed and the following section inserted in its stead:- '76. A man who is liable to enlist for service in the Citizen Forces shall not refuse or neglect to take an oath in accordance with the appropriate form set out in the Second Schedule to this Act when tendered to him by a Justice of the Peace or by an officer. Penalty: Imprisonment for six months.'[42]

Marginal notes represent headings but are placed next to, rather than above, the section to which they are attached. They are very helpful to the reader, provided that brevity and accuracy are observed. Given the choice between headings and marginal notes, the former seem to be more accessible to the users, as headings are a common form of labelling small sets of text in written texts outside legislation.[43]

[37] See *Chandler v DPP* [1964] AC 763; also see P St J Langan, *Maxwell on the Interpretation of Statutes* (Bombay, NM Tripathi Private Ltd, 1976) 10; but see contra New Zealand Interpretation Act 1999, s 5.

[38] See B Simamaba 'Should marginal notes be used in the interpretation of legislation?' (2005) 26 *Statute Law Review* 125.

[39] See House of Commons, *House of Commons Procedure and Practice* (Canada, 2009) www.parl.gc.ca/procedure-book-livre/document.aspx?sbdid=da2ac62f-bb39-4e5f-9f7d-90ba3496d0a6&sbpidx=5. For the UK, see Phillimore LJ in *In re Woking Urban District Council (Basingstoke Canal) Act 1911* [1914] 1 Ch 300, 322, where he said that 'I am aware of the general rule of law as to marginal notes, at any rate in public general Acts of Parliament; but that rule is founded, as will be seen on reference to the cases, upon the principle that those notes are inserted not by Parliament nor under the authority of Parliament, but by irresponsible persons'. But see contra judgments: *R v Montila and others (Appellants)* [2004] All ER (D) 386 (Nov).

[40] But see contra J Quick and RR Gharan, *Annotated Constitution of the Australian Commonwealth* (1901) 282.

[41] See S Bilika, 'Regina v Montila: Coming Full Circle on Marginal Notes' (2006) 16 *Caribbean Law Review* 260, 267.

[42] See Defence Act 1964 (Australia), s 27

MARGINAL REFERENCES

Marginal references are introduced in the text to provide the user with the reference to another price of legislation mentioned in the Act; or to indicate which part is found in the page. Marginal references carry an inherent risk of confusing the user, since they are not found in non-legislative texts. As a result, they are of doubtful value for lay users, and should be introduced in the simplest possible manner:

27 of 1968 Or 1968 c. 27	NOT	Cap.27 of 1968 or 1968 Chapter 27

TABLE OF ARRANGEMENTS OR ARRANGEMENT OF SECTIONS

This is a practice followed in some jurisdictions where marginal notes or headings are placed as a table of contents. The practice is highly recommended, as it provides a clear guide to the legislation in the form of a roadmap. Its success in serving effectiveness via clarity depends greatly on the accuracy of the headings or marginal notes that form the table's constituting elements.

REAL INNOVATION: THE LAYERED APPROACH[44]

But all these techniques seem to address the problem of approachability of legislation by means of structure influenced by the content and nature of the provision at hand. And so structure of legislative texts, as things stand, is decided on the basis of primary versus secondary regulatory messages, substantive provisions versus administrative provisions, or substance versus procedure. On what basis was this approach selected? Without empirical evidence to show its theoretical basis, one could fault it as haphazard. Admittedly, this is an approach based on logic, and philosophical and linguistic approaches to language and thought structure. But is it the only, or the best way, of approaching structure?

[43] But see contra, J Hartley and M Trueman, 'A Research Strategy for Text Designers: the Role of Headings' (1985) 14 *Instructional Science* 99, 149–51.

[44] The term, and to a certain extent, the concept is attributed to John Witing, Tax Director at the Tax Simplification Office. I am very grateful to John for his inspiration and the generosity with which he has shared it with me.

The 2013 Good Law Initiative of the UK's Office of Parliamentary Counsel in cooperation with the National Archives has offered an empirically led and methodologically sound insight into the profiles of legislative audiences. And so, finally, the profile of users of legislation has been revealed, to a great extent. Legislation is read by three main groups of users: lay persons seeking information on their rights and obligations; non-lawyers seeking guidance for the performance of their professional duties; and lawyers and judges interpreting and applying the law. This study can and must revolutionise the way in which legislation is drafted. Structure can now be approached by use of the people to whom it must speak. And so content of provisions must bow down to the profile of users.

This leads us to the concept of a layered approach to legislative drafting. So far, drafters have been lodged and squashed between the clashing stones of inherent legislative complexity and increasingly loud demands for simplicity of expression. An alternative, less rigid, approach to the drafting of legislative texts could be offered if one breaks free from the requirements of a unique and standard legislative language: this would allow drafters to imitate oral communication, and pitch the legislative text to the specific abilities and requirements of the precise audiences of each provision. The layered approach promotes the division of legislation into three parts, corresponding to each of the three profiles of legislative users identified eloquently by the Good Law Initiative. Part one of the legislation can speak to the lay persons: the content is limited to the main regulatory messages, thus conveying the essence of law reform attempted by the legislation, focusing gravely on the information that lay persons need in order to become aware of a new regulation, to comply with new obligations or to enjoy new rights. Part two of the legislation can speak to non-lawyers and other professionals who use the legislation in the course of their employment. Here one can see scope for further detail in the regulatory messages introduced, and for language that is balanced (technical, yet approachable to the professionals in questions). Part three of the legislation can then deal with issues of legislative interpretation, issues of procedure and issues of application, in a language that is complex but not quite legalese, as there is nothing to prevent all groups from reading all parts.

The layered approach is revolutionary, as it shifts the criterion for legislative structure from the content and nature of provisions to the profile of the users of each provision. And so when drafting, drafters have to decide to whom they are speaking in each case, and then place that provision to the relevant part. The layered approach is revolutionary because it offers a humanistic aura in drafting, making structure user-centred, and thus promoting a link between policy and effecting legislative text, but also enhancing and personalising the channel of communication between drafters and users. The approach reflects modern doctrines of linguistics, especially contextual language.

But it cannot be viewed as a complete departure from tradition, in that it continues to apply Lord Thring's five rules of structure. By requiring that part one includes the primary regulatory message, it promotes Lord Thring's rules that give precedence to the simpler proposition. And by structuring legislation into three parts, the layered approach complies with the other Thring rules that require division of provisions declaring the law (in part one or two) with provisions administrating the law (in part two or three accordingly); that principal provisions should be separated from subordinate provisions (in parts one and two); that exceptional provisions, temporary provisions and provisions relating to the repeal of Acts should be separated from the other enactments, and placed by themselves under separate headings (in part three); and that procedure and matters of detail should be set apart by themselves (either in part three of the layered approach, or in a Schedule).

Irrespective of whether it is truly innovative approach or an innovative interpretation of existing drafting doctrines, the layered approach seems to be one of the promising initiatives in the field of legislative drafting both from the perspective of structure but also from the perspective of language. One can of course see inherent weaknesses in the layered approach. First, one wonders whether the division of the legislative texts into parts with part one addressed to lay persons and including the bare central regulatory message leads to a patronising approach that results in a partial or, God forbid, fragmented and incomplete message to lay persons. But an optimist could counter-argue that placement of data in part one is an added bonus to lay users compared with the current state of affairs: at least the main message is easily identified, at a pronounced place, and in a language that is accessible to them. Compared to the current state of affairs, where all data are offered in the layered approach's part two or three language, this is certainly an improvement. And of course, there is nothing preventing the part one users from reading the rest of the text.

Secondly, although part one is distinctly different from parts two and three, and one can relatively easily identify the main essence of law reform, one wonders what really distinguishes between part two data and part three data. There is of course comfort in knowing that the text must still be read as a whole, and that there is nothing from preventing part two users from reading the whole Act. But one would need to balance faith in the abilities of part two users with the need to ensure that part three does not become a shell of definitions, repeals and consequential amendments: this would deprive the readers from at least part of the benefits of the layered approach.

Thirdly, the layered approach promotes inherent fragmentation of data. As a result, it rendered the use of explanatory notes reinstating the fluidity of information and the cross-fertilisation between parts an ever so crucial requirement.

Fourthly, a technical issue relates to the expression of direct amendments in part two. Direct amendments do not seem appropriate for part two, and a Keeling-type structure may be needed albeit in part two itself. One wonders then if the instructive direct amendment text should remain in part three. The logic is that part two people need to know what the law is right now without referring to other Acts but part three would benefit from direct instructing amendments and their surgical accuracy that renders them very appropriate for part three people. But is this not a consolidation exercise, and do the reasons for dropping Keeling Schedules in UK practice not apply here too?

AN EXAMPLE OF THE LAYERED APPROACH IN ACTION: THE SUCCESSION TO CROWN ACT 2013 (UK)

The text of the Act, as originally passed, is set out at the end of this chapter. The application of the layered approach would require the addition of a new part one addressed to lay persons and carrying the main regulatory messages, and the re-arrangement of the remaining sections in a part two addressed to civil servants and Palace staff, and a part three addressed to constitutional lawyers and judges. Without any attempt to tackle the layout of the new text, in order to remain focused on the structure and language, a suggested layered text may look like the one below:

Succession to Crown Act 2013

Table of Arrangements

Part 1
New sections redrafted

Part 2
Current sections 3(1), 3(2), 3 (3), 3 (5).

Part 3
Current sections 1, 2(2), 3 (4), 4, 5 (3), 5.

And now applied to produce a text:

Succession to Crown Act 2013

Part 1
1 The line to the throne of the United Kingdom is determined solely by the person's date of birth.
2 The gender of the person is irrelevant.
3 Marriage of the person to a Roman Catholic is irrelevant.
4 This Act is the law of the United Kingdom from [precise date].

Part 2

5 A person who, when they marry, will be one of the 6 persons in line to the throne must obtain Her Majesty's consent to the marriage.

(1) Her Majesty's consent is:

(a) signified under the Great Seal of the United Kingdom,

(b) declared in Council, and

(c) recorded in the books of the Privy Council.

(2) If Her Majesty does not consent to the marriage, the marriage is void and the person and their descendants from that marriage are disqualified from succeeding to the Crown.

(3) But the marriage is legitimate, and the person and their descendants from that marriage succeed to the Crown if—

(a) neither party to the marriage was one of the 6 persons next in the line of succession to the Crown at the time of the marriage,

(b) no consent was sought or notice given in respect of the marriage,

(c) it was reasonable for the person concerned not to have been aware at the time of the marriage that the Act applied to them, and

(d) no person acted, before the coming into force of this section, on the basis that the marriage was void.

Part 3

6 (1) This Act applies to persons in line to the Crown born after 28 October 2011.

(2) This Act does not give those persons or their desecendants precedence over any other person (whenever born).

7 This Act applies to marriages occurring before the time of its coming into force, where the person concerned is alive at that time (as well as in relation to marriages occurring after that time).

8 The Royal Marriages Act 1772 (which provides that, subject to certain exceptions, a descendant of King George II may marry only with the consent of the Sovereign) is repealed.

9 (1) The Schedule contains consequential amendments.

(2) References (however expressed) in any enactment to the provisions of the Bill of Rights or the Act of Settlement relating to the succession to, or possession of, the Crown are to be read as including references to the provisions of this Act.

(3) The following enactments (which relate to the succession to, and possession of, the Crown) are subject to the provision made by this Act—

Article II of the Union with Scotland Act 1706;

Article II of the Union with England Act 1707;

Article Second of the Union with Ireland Act 1800;

Article Second of the Act of Union (Ireland) 1800.

10 (1) Section 5 comes into force on [date when the Act was passed].

(2) All other sections come into force, together or separately, on the day and time set by an Order of the Lord President of the Council made by statutory instrument.

11 This Act is the Succession to the Crown Act 2013.

Ultimately, the layered approach is fertile ground for reservations on its feasibility, especially where long legislative texts are concerned. One wonders if sub-parts can be introduced in each of the current parts of complex texts, thus breaking down complex Acts and layering each of their existing parts. At the end of the day, the layered approach and indeed any legislative tool cannot be without problems, disadvantages and compromises. What remains to be seen is how committed we all are, as drafters but also as citizens, to the cause of better legislation. And whether the layered approach can be a plausible tool to contribute to that.

ELIZABETH II c. 20

Succession to the Crown Act 2013

2013 CHAPTER 20

An Act to make succession to the Crown not depend on gender; to make provision about Royal Marriages; and for connected purposes.

[25th April 2013]

BE IT ENACTED by the Queen's most Excellent Majesty, by and with the advice and consent of the Lords Spiritual and Temporal, and Commons, in this present Parliament assembled, and by the authority of the same, as follows:—

1 Succession to the Crown not to depend on gender

In determining the succession to the Crown, the gender of a person born after 28 October 2011 does not give that person, or that person's descendants, precedence over any other person (whenever born).

2 Removal of disqualification arising from marriage to a Roman Catholic

(1) A person is not disqualified from succeeding to the Crown or from possessing it as a result of marrying a person of the Roman Catholic faith.

(2) Subsection (1) applies in relation to marriages occurring before the time of the coming into force of this section where the person concerned is alive at that time (as well as in relation to marriages occurring after that time).

3 Consent of Sovereign required to certain Royal Marriages

(1) A person who (when the person marries) is one of the 6 persons next in the line of succession to the Crown must obtain the consent of Her Majesty before marrying.

(2) Where any such consent has been obtained, it must be—
   (a) signified under the Great Seal of the United Kingdom,
   (b) declared in Council, and
   (c) recorded in the books of the Privy Council.

(3) The effect of a person's failure to comply with subsection (1) is that the person and the person's descendants from the marriage are disqualified from succeeding to the Crown.

(4) The Royal Marriages Act 1772 (which provides that, subject to certain exceptions, a descendant of King George II may marry only with the consent of the Sovereign) is repealed.

(5) A void marriage under that Act is to be treated as never having been void if—
- (a) neither party to the marriage was one of the 6 persons next in the line of succession to the Crown at the time of the marriage,
- (b) no consent was sought under section 1 of that Act, or notice given under section 2 of that Act, in respect of the marriage,
- (c) in all the circumstances it was reasonable for the person concerned not to have been aware at the time of the marriage that the Act applied to it, and
- (d) no person acted, before the coming into force of this section, on the basis that the marriage was void.

(6) Subsection (5) applies for all purposes except those relating to the succession to the Crown.

4 Consequential amendments etc

(1) The Schedule contains consequential amendments.

(2) References (however expressed) in any enactment to the provisions of the Bill of Rights or the Act of Settlement relating to the succession to, or possession of, the Crown are to be read as including references to the provisions of this Act.

(3) The following enactments (which relate to the succession to, and possession of, the Crown) are subject to the provision made by this Act—

Article II of the Union with Scotland Act 1706;
Article II of the Union with England Act 1707;
Article Second of the Union with Ireland Act 1800;
Article Second of the Act of Union (Ireland) 1800.

5 Commencement and short title

(1) This section comes into force on the day on which this Act is passed.

(2) The other provisions of this Act come into force on such day and at such time as the Lord President of the Council may by order made by statutory instrument appoint.

(3) Different days and times may be appointed for different purposes.

(4) This Act may be cited as the Succession to the Crown Act 2013.

SCHEDULE

Section 4

CONSEQUENTIAL AMENDMENTS

Treason Act 1351

1 The Treason Act 1351 (declaration of offences to be adjudged treason) has effect as if—

(a) the first reference to eldest son and heir were a reference to eldest child and heir;

(b) the second reference to eldest son and heir were a reference to eldest son if the heir.

Bill of Rights

2 In section 1 of the Bill of Rights, omit—

(a) "or by any King or Queene marrying a papist";

(b) "or shall marry a papist";

(c) "or marrying".

Act of Settlement

3 In the Act of Settlement—

(a) in the preamble, omit "or marry a papist" and "or marrying";

(b) in section 2, omit "or shall marry a papist".

Regency Act 1937

4 In section 3(2) of the Regency Act 1937 (persons disqualified from becoming or being Regent), after "Crown" insert ", or is a person disqualified from succeeding to the Crown by virtue of section 3(3) of the Succession to the Crown Act 2013".

Supplementary

5 The amendments made by paragraphs 2 and 3 apply in relation to marriages occurring before the time of the coming into force of section 2 where the person concerned is alive at that time (as well as in relation to marriages occurring after that time).

Printed in the UK by The Stationery Office Limited under the authority and superintendence of Carol Tullo, Controller of Her Majesty's Stationery Office and Queen's Printer of Acts of Parliament

04/2013 29278 19585

Figure 4.1: Succession to the Crown Act 2013

5

Clarity, Precision, Unambiguity and the Legislative Sentence

THE BASICS

IN THE SAME way in which appropriate structure can inform clarity in the sense of quick comprehension,[1] language choices can also inform clarity, precision and unambiguity.[2] In turn, these promote and contribute to effectiveness, the ultimate goal for legislative drafters. And they do so in three main ways.

First, they render the law predictable,[3] thus promoting accessibility of the specific piece of legislation by lay users.[4] Certainty via predictability enhances clarity,[5] since everyone starts from common premises.[6] And those users who are inclined to comply with the law are offered the tools to understand what is required of them,[7] and thus comply with the legislation.[8] This promotes effectiveness of implementation.[9] Without clarity there are no

[1] See J Stark, 'Should the Main Goal of Statutory Drafting be Accuracy or Clarity? (1994) 15 *Statute Law Review* 207, 208.

[2] Clarity causes are volume, quality and perceptions of legislation: see Cabinet Office, Office of Parliamentary Counsel, *When Laws Become Too Complex* (16 April 2013) para 3 www.gov.uk/government/publications/when-laws-become-too-complex/when-laws-become-too-complex.

[3] See E Majambere, 'Clarity, Precision and Unambiguity: Aspects for Effective Legislative Drafting (2011) 37 *Commonwealth Law Bulletin* 417, 417.

[4] See B Bekink and C Botha, 'Aspects of Legislative Drafting: Some South African Realities (or Plain Language Is Not Always Plain Sailing)' (2011) 28 *Statute Law Review* 34, 65.

[5] On clarity via a balance of continuity and change, see Sir S Laws, 'Plus ça change? Continuity and Change in UK Legislative Drafting Practice' (2009) 11 *European Journal of Law Reform* 139.

[6] See Sir S Laws, 'Consistency v Innovation' (CALC conference, Hong Kong, 2009).

[7] See JP Martin, 'Development and Rights Revisited: Lessons from Africa' (2006) 3 *SUR: International Journal on Human Rights* 97.

[8] In *R v Royal* (1993) 10 CRNZ 4 (HC), Penlington J noted it is not a beach of the accused's right to legal assistance that they could not mount a sound defence without legal training where the accused has access to a lawyer; the question is whether this argument can be reversed where no access to a lawyer is possible.

[9] See MJ Rizzo, 'Which Kind of Legal Order? Logical Coherence and Praxeological Coherence' (1999) 9 *Journal des Economistes et des Etudes Humaines* 1, 2; also see R Craswell and JE Calfee, 'Deterrence and Uncertain Legal Standards' (1986) 2 *Journal of Law of Economics and Organization* 279, 281.

laws,[10] hence the void for vagueness doctrine.[11] Secondly, clarity, precision and unambiguity in the legal system offer democratic governments[12] the tool required to achieve transformation by means of legislation:[13] by offering clear regulatory messages within the law governments can achieve the fragmented regulatory goals of each legislative piece, which formulate the collage of regulatory goals expressing the transforming law reform.[14] This leads to policy effectiveness and possibly transformation. Unclear laws are the worst form of tyranny.[15] Thirdly, clarity, precision and unambiguity offer officers of the law the opportunity to understand correctly and fully the law, and consequently to apply it appropriately. This promotes directly the rule of law.[16] It is worth noting that for the New Zealand Law Commission availability, navigability and clarity constitute elements of accessibility,[17] which is directly linked to Fuller's interpretation of the rule of law.[18] It is interesting to note here that some jurisdictions introduce a statutory obligation to make the laws clear and understandable.[19] In the

[10] See T Hobbes, *Leviathan* (London, Andrew Crooke, 1651) ch XXXI Of the Kingdome of God by Nature, available via Project Gutenberg (Vancouver, 2002) www.gutenberg.org/wiki/Main_Page; also T Arnold-Moore, 'Public Access to Legislation and the Democratic Process' (paper for the Australian Electronic Governance Conference, Centre for Public Policy, University of Melbourne, 2004).

[11] See C Lockwood, 'Defining Indefiniteness: Suggested Revisions to the Void for Vagueness Doctrine' (2009–10) 8 *Cardozo Public Law Policy and Ethics Journal* 255.

[12] See S Krongold, 'Writing Laws: Making them Easier to Understand' (1992) 24 *Ottawa Law Review* 495, 501; for a direct link between democracy, the rule of law and clear laws, see *Merkur Island Shipping Co v Laughton* [1983] 2 AC 570 (HL).

[13] In the context of South Africa, see K Klare, 'Legal Culture and Transformative Constitutionalism' (1998) 14 *South African Journal of Human Rights* 147, 178–79.

[14] The clarity of law means overall consistency of their justificatory grounds and their intelligibility as justice-based reasons: see T Inoue 'The Rule of Law as Legislation' in LJ Wintgens, *Legislation in Context: Essays in Legisprudence* (Aldershot, Ashgate, 2007) 55, 71.

[15] See Lord Oliver of Aylmerton, 'A Judicial View of Modern Legislation' (1993) 14 *Statute Law Review* 1, 2; also see Parliamentary Counsel Office, *Public Access to Legislation, A Discussion Paper for Public Comment* (New Zealand, 1998) 6–8.

[16] See A Seidman, R Seidman and N Abeyesekere, *Legislative Drafting for Democratic Social Change* (The Hague, Kluwer Law International, 2001) 255; for specific reference to human rights related legislation, see M Arden, 'Modernising Legislation' (1998) *Public Law* 65, 75.

[17] New Zealand Law Commission, *Presentation of New Zealand Statute Law* (NZLC IP2, 2007) 8.

[18] See L Fuller, *The Morality of Law* (New Haven and London, Yale University Press, 1969) 39.

[19] The Indiana Constitution in its art 4, s 20 states: 'Every Act ... shall be plainly worded avoiding as far as practicable the use of technical terms'; similarly The Queensland Legislative Standards Act 1992 requires, in determining whether legislation complies with fundamental legislative principles, an assessment of whether the legislation is unambiguous and drafted in a sufficiently clear and precise way.

UK this is not the case, but accessibility is a condition of lawfulness.[20] And fourthly, vagueness costs.[21]

But clarity and precision are not always useful to the drafter. Although they do constitute tools leading to effectiveness, effectiveness is sometimes served by their misapplication. An anecdotal example of a demand from parliamentarians for complex language is reported by Bennion, who has used the term 'tried his best' to express clearly the technical term 'used his best endeavours': Bennion reports that in the House of Commons Gordon Oaks described the plain term as 'amateurish' and Dennis Howell called for 'better phraseology' than the proposed 'headmaster's phrase' in the House of Lords.[22]

Leaving aside for a moment the debate on plain alternatives as a means of serving clarity, vagueness can be useful when the drafter attempts to express in legislative terms a political disagreement that can endanger the actual existence of the legislation. If the choice is between no legislation[23] and inadequate legislation, effectiveness of regulation can side with inadequate legislation as a means of introducing at least a certain level of regulation.[24]

Another possible case requiring conscious vagueness could occur in a disagreement between policy officers and drafters.[25] Often an intransitive Bill leaving way to future ministerial regulation may unblock the process. This postpones decision-making post enactment thus allowing for further individualisation of the legislation at the moment of application.[26]

Moreover, often vagueness can serve in the pursuit of precision[27] by means of reference to context.[28] Reasonable precision may be achieved through the use of several general terms to narrow down the intended meaning to the area

[20] See D Greenberg, 'The Challenges of Understanding Legislation' Westlaw UK Annotated Statutes, where he quotes the Lord Chancellor's acknowledgement of the government's responsibility to ensure that satisfactory arrangements are made for the publication of the statute book, in order that the citizen may know by what laws he is bound; see HC Deb 13 June 1991, WA 613–14; also see Toulson LJ on the 'problem of substantial constitutional importance' relating to access to legislation, in *R v William Chambers* [2008] EWCA Crim 2467.

[21] See GK Hadfieldt, 'Weighing the Value of Vagueness: An Economic Perspective on Precision in the Law' (1994) 82 *California Law Review* 541, 546.

[22] See FAR Bennion, *Bennion on Statute Law* (London, Longman, 1990) 38.

[23] On an analysis of strict legislative construction as a means of stopping law reform, see J Willis, 'Statute Interpretation in a Nutshell' (1988) 16 *Canadian Bar Review* 20; also see R Pound, 'Common Law and Legislation' (1908) 21 *Harvard Law Review* 383.

[24] After all, the drafter's primary aim is to put effect to government policy: see E Sutherland, 'Clearer Drafting and the Timeshare Act 1992: A Response from Parliamentary Counsel to Mr. Cutts' (1993) 14 *Statute Law Review* 163, 163.

[25] See R Dickerson, *Fundamentals of Legal Drafting* (Boston, Little Brown and Company, 1986) 11.

[26] See G Christie, 'Vagueness and Legal Language' (1963–64) 48 *Minnesota Law Review* 885, 889.

[27] ibid, 895–96.

[28] See JA Corry, 'The Interpretation of Statutes' in E Driedger, *The Construction of Statutes* (Toronto, Butterworths, 1974) 203, 219–20.

of overlap of the terms used: use of a number of overlapping vague terms can allow the user to acquire precision and indeed clarity in the semantic field of the concept transmitted by sheer reference to the concrete area of overlapping semantic fields of the vague terms. Precision in spatial reference may be achieved through the overlapping of circles and the focusing of attention on the area which the several intersecting circles have in common.[29]

And finally, vagueness can serve in the very rarely justifiable cases where the drafter may wish to sneak into the legislation a degree of discretion for judges or enforcers. Judges are often called up to decide on a case by case basis issues that have not been possible to draft clearly in the legislative process.[30] The danger here is that judges may be ultimately called to legislate rather than apply: but there is always scope for specification via application, an action legitimately within the competence of the judiciary. And when it comes to vagueness allowing discretion to government officials and enforcers, the danger of inviting corruption is enhanced: but it often unavoidable to allow for example the Minister enhanced discretion to decide if naturalisation of a foreign citizen is acceptable. Whatever the reason behind vagueness in legislation, it is served much better when the law-makers and the courts are not antagonistic with each other.[31]

It is notable that in all these cases it is vagueness that seems justifiable, or even desirable,[32] but not ambiguity.[33] In order to explain why this is the case, it is necessary to define the two terms.

AMBIGUITY AND VAGUENESS[34]

Although there is widespread agreement that clarity, precision, and unambiguity should be pursued, their meaning, application and hierarchy (if any) in current drafting dilemmas is not equally clear. Clarity is defined as 'clearness or lucidity as to perception or understanding; freedom from indistinctness or ambiguity'.[35] The Law Reform Commission of Victoria argued that precision

[29] See I Richards, *The Philosophy of Rhetoric* (Oxford, Oxford University Press, 1965) 69–78.

[30] See A Miller, 'Statutory Language and the Purposive Use of Ambiguity' (1956) 42 *Virginia Law Review* 23.

[31] See Note, 'The Void-for-Vagueness Doctrine in the Supreme Court' (1960) 9 *University Pennsylvania Law Review* 67.

[32] See R Dickerson, 'Some Jurisprudential Implications of Electronic Data Processing' (1963) 28 *Law and Contemporary Problems* 53, 62.

[33] But see contra A Miller, 'Statutory Language and the Purposive Use of Ambiguity (1956) 42 *Virginia Law Review* 23; G Fraser, 'In Praise of Ambiguity' (2000) *Policy Options* 21, 25; and P Thomas, 'Legal Skills and the Use of Ambiguity' (1991) 42 *Northern Ireland Legal Quarterly* 14, 22–23.

[34] For a detailed analysis, see R Dickerson, 'The Diseases of Legislative Language' (1964) 1 *Harvard Journal on Legislation* 5.

[35] See C Soanes (ed), *Compact Oxford English Dictionary* (Oxford, Oxford University Press, 2003) 193.

and clarity are not competing goals: in its true sense, precision is incompatible with a lack of clarity.[36] For Gérard Caussignac 'clear' means easy to understand, intelligible, unequivocal or unambiguous.[37] And so Majambere is right in stating that that 'it is not possible to separate, clarity, precision and ambiguity when drafting'.[38] Kabba clarifies this point even further: in juxtaposing the definitions of clarity and unambiguity, one finds that the latter is part of clarity, as they share similar characteristics.[39] If one goes back to the pyramid depicting the hierarchy of drafting virtues, it becomes clear that clarity, precision and unambiguity all serve as techniques used for effectiveness, which have equal standing. And so in a dilemma, the drafter will implement whichever of these virtues best serves effectiveness based on the type of legislation that is being drafted, and the audience that it is drafted for.

Perfect words express a semantic field, namely a well defined, well described meaning. They can be pictured as perfect circles, with clear boundaries, and generally agreed semantic elements known as referents. Having clear boundaries and agreed referents offer perfect words the luxury of serving as tools of perfect communication: the message conveyed by the person who utters them is identical to the message received by their recipient. If one applies this to drafting as a form of communication, the use of perfect words by the drafter ensures that the reader and user of legislation attribute to legislative words the exact meaning intended by the drafter. And so the use of the word 'tree' conveys the message of a tall plant with leaves. And it distinguishes it from the concept of a bush or an animal. When established, this perfect communication detracts from the drafter's need to define, as the definition would be superfluous, and the judge has no need to interpret. But, unfortunately, perfect words do not really exist: it is not the word that defines the meaning, it is people who define a meaning.[40] And perfect communication in legislation is an even rarer phenomenon:[41] legislation is an expertise;[42] the high number and diversity of recipients leads to inherent possibilities of misunderstanding; and legislation as a form of written communication lacks the luxury of gesture and elaboration often afforded in oral face to face communication.

[36] See Law Reform Commission of Victoria, Report No 9, *Plain English and the Law* (1987) para 65.

[37] See G Caussignac 'Clear Legislation' (The International Cooperation Group, Department of Justice of Canada, 2005) 1 www.justice.gc.ca/eng/abt-apd/icg-gci/cl-lc/cl-lc.pdf.

[38] See Majambere, 'Clarity, Precision and Unambiguity (n 3) 419.

[39] See K Kabba, 'Gender-neutral Language: an Essential Language Tool to Serve Precision, Clarity and Unambiguity' (2011) *Commonwealth Law Bulletin* 427, 431.

[40] See J Waldront, 'Vagueness in Law and Language: Some Philosophical Issues' (1994) 82 *California Law Review* 509, 510.

[41] See L Del Duca, 'Introduction Symposium on the UCC, SEC, ALI, Federal Rules and Federal Government Simplification Experiences—Is It Time for a Model Set of Drafting Principles?' (2001) 105 *Dickinson Law Review* 205, 211; also see J McBaine, 'The Rule Against Disturbing Plain Meaning of Writings' (1942–43) 31 *California Law Review* 145, 147.

[42] See F Bennion, 'The Readership of Legal Texts' www.francisbennion.com.

So what can go wrong with words? Well, they can either suffer from disagreements on the referents attributed to them by their users in which case they are ambiguous, or from disrupted weak boundaries in which case they are vague. Both diseases are frequent, and destructive.

Ambiguity exists when a word can be interpreted in more than one way,[43] or the condition of admitting of two or more meanings, or being understood in more than one way, or of referring to two or more things at the same time.[44] And so ambiguous words can be pictured as two circles with an overlapping part. This is a symptom of their disease: the referents that can legitimately be attributed to them by the user may well vary from those offered to them by the recipient. Ambiguous words do not require uninformed or erroneous interpretation: by their very semantic nature they invite semantic diversity. An example of an ambiguous word is the word 'light': is a 'light truck' light in weight or light in color? Or the word 'shall': is it 'must' or is it 'will'? As you can see, the word can be legitimately used to convey either of the two messages. And so the recipient has a legitimate choice to select the one that they choose. It is the user's duty to refrain from using it altogether, knowing that the risk of conveying the wrong message is high. If the term is used, it makes sense to offer the antibody of a definition, thus ensuring that the choice of the user as to one of the word's legitimate messages is guided towards the right direction. But, of course, prevention is always better than cure, and so it makes sense for drafters to avoid the use of ambiguous terms at all costs. Having said that, a number of authors feel that all words are ambiguous and that the 'one word, one concept' notion is a fallacy.[45] Owing 'in part to the lack of precision of the English language, often more than one interpretation is possible'.[46]

Vagueness exists when there is doubt about where a word's boundaries are. Vague words can be pictured as a circle with interrupted boundaries that allow each user to insert varying referents to it. Here the problem does not lie with overlapping semantic fields offering uninvited choice of legitimate meanings. Here the disease is one of inadequate communication: the user is offered such a generic term, that their legitimate unilateral insertion of referents can lead to numerous semantic fields and numerous meanings. If ambiguity is a choice of two meanings, vagueness is a choice of any meaning. Vagueness is chaos. For example, the term 'blind': what degree of visual impairment is required? Or the term 'vehicle': does it mean mechanical vehicle or are animals used for transport also included in the

[43] See J Evans, *Statutory Interpretation: Problems of Communication* (Oxford, Oxford University Press, 1988) 73; also see FAR Bennion, *Bennion on Statutory Interpretation: A Code* (London, LexisNexis, 2008) 444–56.

[44] See *Webster's Third New International Dictionary* (Chicago, Encyclopedia Britannica, 1976) vol I, 66.

[45] See J Frank, 'Words and Music: Some Remarks on Statutory Interpretation' (1947) 47 *Columbia Law Review* 1259, 1263.

[46] See Lord Dilhorne in *Black-Clawson International Ltd v Papierwerke Waldhof-Aschaffenburg AG* [1975] AC 591, 622.

semantic field? But vagueness is benign chaos: unlike ambiguity it does not pretend to convey a specific message only to trap the recipient to one message only; instead, it invites the recipient to think exactly what is intended to convey, thus allowing conscious choices of referents.

Vagueness occurs as a result of the generic character of some words, like 'vehicle'. But additional causes include the readiness of some words to derive colour from their surrounding context: for example the word 'line' varies by reference to its use by a telephonist, a palmist, a schoolteacher or a fisherman. Other words are vague simply because of their inherent capacity to evoke emotional responses: for example in the common provision 'The penalty may be higher if the circumstances of the murder were especially loathsome' the term 'loathsome' is subjective, invokes emotional response, and can be perceived rather differently from person to person. In addition to the above, time and geography have a role to play in vagueness.

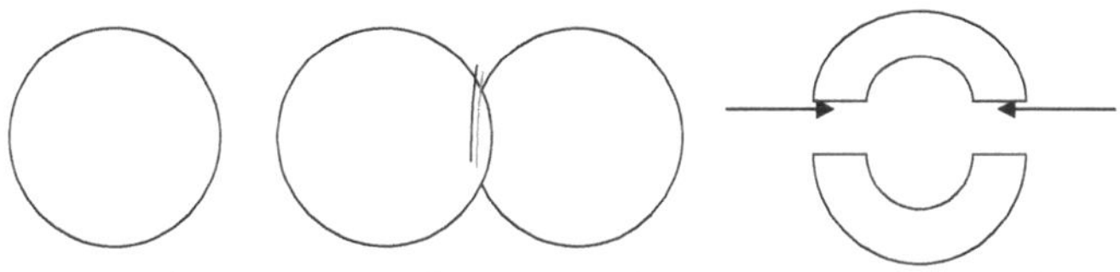

Figure 5.1: Depiction of Words and their Diseases

It is precisely its benign nature that renders vagueness a useful disease for drafters and legislators. Legislatures sometimes choose to be vague in order to allow for a political compromise or to let administrative agencies supply the specifics. But they rarely choose to be ambiguous. Benign or cancerous, ambiguity and vagueness remain drafting diseases that drafters must avoid. Needless to say that this is easier said than done. And on top of that, the striving to turn away from them can lead to equally tricky problems.

In an attempt to ensure well defined and single semantic fields per term, drafters can fall into the trap of over-exhaustiveness: in view of the inherent difficulties of selecting perfect words in legislation, drafters may resort to long exhaustive lists of referents per term used. This may promote precision of meaning. But at its extreme it can lead to an inadvertent exclusion of classes of concepts that the drafter intended to include in the semantic field conveyed. This is called over-precision, over-exhaustiveness, or—in the words of a former Chief Parliamentary Counsel to the Government in Ireland—over drafting:

> Precision in drafting is a worthy goal, but can be taken too far. It is frequently unnecessary to name every single thing you are forbidding or requiring. An overzealous attempt at precision may result in redundancy and verbosity. Drafting too precisely may create unintended loopholes.[47]

[47] See 'Legislative Drafting Manual' (unpublished, Dublin, 2001) para 4.4.

And so what is required, he continues, is the striking of a healthy balance between over-precision[48] and vagueness:

> Just as over drafting can affect a provision in unforeseen ways, under drafting is equally dangerous. Although it is often necessary or desirable to create a general or broad legislative standard or directive, beware of language that is so indefinite that it is meaningless or begs a challenge in court as invalid for vagueness. Generally, courts loathe declaring a law invalid on this ground, but careful drafting can eliminate the need for judicial scrutiny.

Of course, setting the golden medium is rather arbitrary. After all, drafting is phronetic and requires subjective choices. But one of the parameters that drafters must take into account is the context of the legislation. Some fields of law invite and require extreme clarity, precision and unambiguity, possibly owing to the need to convey a clear message whose non-implementation can lead to severe consequences for the user. Examples of this would be the criminal law, revenue law, business and commerce, or legislation where broad powers, such as powers of entry onto private premises, for example, could infringe basic human rights. On the other hand, generality and a degree of vagueness can be acceptable where it is desirable simply to chart directions and leave the courts to work out their detailed application on a case by case basis, as for instance in the law of contract.[49]

SEMANTIC AMBIGUITY[50]

Semantic ambiguity occurs when a single word has more than one meaning.[51] It is defined as the phenomenon where a word's inherent multiplicities of meaning derive from lexicographical usage and exist independently of context.[52]

Common Problems with Small Words: May, Shall, And/Or

Ambiguity often occurs with very common and very small words, words we never think about defining. 'May' and 'may not', and 'shall' with forms of 'be', can cause a number of problems.

48 See KE Tian, 'The Drafting of Statutes' (1974) 16 *Malaya Law Review* 196.

49 See J Burrows, *Statute Law in New Zealand* (Wellington, Butterworths, 1992) 63.

50 For an analysis of the concept of semantic ambiguity, see J MacKaye, *The Logic of Language* (London, Russell and Russell, 1965) ch 5.

51 Eg the parties to *Frigaliment Importing Co v International Sales Corp* (190 F. Supp. 116, S.D.N.Y. 1960) disagreed over the meaning of 'chicken'. Did the word 'chicken' in their contract include only broilers and fryers, or did it include stewing chickens as well?

52 See S Kloepfer, 'Ambiguity and Vagueness in the Criminal Law: an Analysis of Types' (1984–85) 27 *Criminal Law Quarterly* 94, 98.

'May' and 'shall' are often used interchangeably in language.[53] The problem of the false imperative, namely the use of 'may' for the imposition of an obligation, plagues legal language.[54] The ambiguity created by the erroneous use of 'may' is enhanced in legislation, and so it is the drafter's duty to ensure that 'may' is only used for the purposes of introducing a discretionary action.[55]

'Shall' is one of the most dangerous ambiguous words as it can convey both the future tense and the imposition of an obligation. Confusion over this can be detrimental in legislation. And in any case, 'shall' as an imposition of an obligation is only used by lawyers who have had to learn this technical meaning in their training.[56] This puts lawyers out of step with the language of the general community, as non-lawyers don't understand the special way lawyers use 'shall' in documents and laws.[57] This is exactly why the use of 'shall' is not recommended,[58] and must be eliminated altogether.[59] The Office of Parliamentary Counsel of England and Wales recommends a presumption in favour of an alternative to 'shall', both in new Acts but also in amendments of older Acts unless (a) they involve inserting text near existing provisions that use 'shall' in the same sense or (b) the use of an alternative would raise a real doubt that a different meaning was intended in an existing provision.[60] There is little doubt that 'shall' can be replaced by 'must', 'it is the duty of' or 'is to' when expressing an obligation.[61] But the use of the present tense as an alternative would make particular sense since legislation carries the context of a duty or obligation anyway.[62] But in amending Acts there is an argument for the retention of the dreaded 'shall': the possibility of ambiguity created by the use of two synonym terms

[53] For an example of a case confusing 'may' with 'must', see R Carter, 'Statutory Interpretation in New Zealand's Court of Appeal: when "May" Means "Must", Section Headings Affect Interpretation, and Latent Acts Have Effect' (2001) 22 *Statute Law Review* 20.

[54] See J Payne, 'The False Imperative' (2010) *The Legislative Lawyer* www.ncsl.org/legislators-staff/legislative-staff/legal-services/volume-xxvi-issue-2-the-false-imperative.aspx.

[55] See RJ Martineau, *Drafting Legislation and Rules in Plain English* (St Paul, MN, West, 1991) 81.

[56] See R Eagleson and M Asprey, 'Must we Continue with "Shall"?' (1989) 63 *Australian Law Journal* 75.

[57] See MM Asprey, 'Shall Must Go' (1992) 3 *Scribes Journal of Legal Writing* 79, 79.

[58] See A Watson-Brown, 'Do We Still Need "Shall"?' (1998) 28 *Hong Kong Law Journal* 29, 44.

[59] See P Butt, *Modern Legal Drafting: A Guide to Using Clearer Language* (Cambridge, Cambridge University Press, 2013) 269; also see J Kimble, *Lifting the Fog of Legalese* (St Paul, Carolina Academic Press, 2005) 159–60; B Garner, *Dictionary of Legal Usage* (Oxford, Oxford University Press, 2011) 954; M Asprey, *Plain Language for Lawyers* (Australia, Federation Press, 2010) 218.

[60] See Office of the Parliamentary Counsel, 'Shall' (March 2008) Drafting Techniques Group Paper 19 (final), paras 6 and 8.

[61] See R Redux, '"Shall" in Legislative Drafting' (1987) 104 *South African Law Journal* 186, 194.

[62] On the imperative of legislation, without reference to 'shall', see generally D Greenberg, 'Nothing will Come of Nothing' (2010) 30 *New Law Journal* 1084.

endangers the effectiveness of the amending Act enough to tip the balance towards clarity as opposed to plain language.

'And' and 'or' are words often causing confusion if it is unclear whether they reflect conjunction or disjunction.[63] As a result they are by their very nature ambiguous.[64] 'And' is normally[65] conjunctive. For example, 'This Act applies to doctors and nurses' indicates that both groups are within the field of application of the legislation. 'Or' is normally disjunctive. For example, 'Exchange of contracts may take place before or after payment' means that either options are acceptable. But 'or' has two possible meanings: it can either mean 'either ... or', or it can be 'or/and', thus causing ambiguity.[66] When it comes to 'and' or 'or' issues often arise simply because the drafter uses the terms wrongly, or because the placement of 'and' or 'or' as a means of expression of the legislative sentence is ambiguous,[67] or because courts fail to respect the general rule.[68] And so it is advisable for the drafter to be extra precise when using 'and' or 'or': often breaking the possibilities into three separate options; in addition, foreseeing the combination of the two obvious options, helps the reader. Although verbose and superfluous, it is much clearer to state that 'A doctor, a nurse, or a doctor with a nurse may conduct HIV tests in maternity wards with or without the subject's consent'. Moreover, 'and/or' is to be avoided.[69]

Unless—Except

These are terms of conditionality with one factor in common: negative conditionality. They provide for an eventuality arising, but they make no provision if it does not. For example 'unless X, A is entitled to B', or 'except X arises, A is entitled to B'. But the question remains: if X occurs, or X circumstances arise, what is A entitled to? And this is exactly the ambiguous point that the drafter must address clearly and effectively.

Some conditions may not be performed simultaneously, and in this case it is good form to list the conditions in chronological order. Since the legal

[63] See L Allen, 'Symbolic Logic: a Razor-Edged Tool for Drafting and Interpreting Legal Documents' (1956–57) 66 *Yale Law Journal* 833, 858.

[64] See MB Kirk, 'Legal Drafting: The Ambiguity of And/Or' (1970) 2 *Texas Tech Law Review* 235.

[65] See TJ Richards and RA Girlie, '"Or" and "And/or": a Discussion' (1989) 10 *History and Philosophy of Logic* 29.

[66] See L Goddard, 'The Exclusive "Or"' (1960) 20 *Analysis* 97.

[67] See S Wisotsky, 'How to Interpret Statutes—or not: Plain Meaning and other Phantoms' (2009) 10 *Journal of Appellate Practice and Process* 321, 327.

[68] In case *Re H (a minor)* [1994] 1 All ER 812 (CA) 'and' in 'Recognition and enforcement' was held to be disjunctive.

[69] See BA Garner, *Legal Writing in Plain English* (Chicago and London, University of Chicago Press, 2001) 112.

action cannot act upon the legal subject until the conditions have been performed or complied with the conditional clause must immediately precede the legal subject.[70]

Scale Indicators

Scale indicators introduce the start point, the end point, or the start and end point in a scale. Examples of scale indicators include the terms 'less than'; 'more than'; 'not exceeding'; 'exceeding'; 'above'; 'below'; 'over'; 'under'; 'before'; 'after'. The danger with scale indicators is that they do not automatically provide for the benchmark itself.

For example 'less than X, then A; and more than X, then B' provides for cases falling less and above X, but do not provide for cases that fall spot on X. And so the question is, what happens if it is X itself. The drafter needs to provide for these cases also. And so it would be clearer if the provision stated 'less than or at X' or 'X or more than X'. There is a trend in defusing the situation by providing for –X as a means of ensuring that X does not come into play at all. This is better expressed in ranges of dates.

Terms Conveying Ranges of Numbers, Days, Dates and Ages

Some other small words that cause trouble are the words we use to specify ranges of numbers, ages and dates: *to*, *through*, *between* and *from*. The problem with these words is that they do not adequately convey when exactly is the start and end of the range that they express.[71] But it is crucial for the drafter to convey exactly that information, and indeed in a very clear manner. Convention helps here, but not always.

For ranges of sections in bills, statutes or rules, it is acceptable and traditional to use a form such as 'sections 1 to 20' because the laws on statutory interpretation make clear what the range means. They specify that in ranges of sections, the form 'sections x to z' includes the first and last numbers and all sections between them. But, then again, it is worth thinking whether a lay user of legislation would be aware of the convention at all. And so it is advisable to keep the term for the purposes of learned users: a sudden change of expression can only give rise to questions and doubt. But at the same time the drafter must keep in mind that 'to' is ambiguous and perhaps

[70] See J Zurcher, 'Basic Rules of Legislative Drafting' (1976–77) 7 *Manitoba Law Journal* 131, 144.

[71] See B Simamba, *How Laws are Written and Applied* (Indiana, AuthorHouse, 2010) 32–33.

the term 'inclusive' can be added for the purposes of ensuring clarity even at a cost of superfluity.

However, 'to' is inappropriate for ranges of days. Instead, the term 'through' is gaining ground as it conveys pretty clearly the inclusion of the end point to the range conveyed. So, the phrase 'Monday through Friday' clearly includes all of Friday, whereas the phrase 'Monday to Friday' is ambiguous as to whether Friday is included. To be certain that Friday is included, the drafter could say 'Monday through Friday' or, even more clearly, 'Monday through Friday inclusive'. To exclude Friday, the drafter can write 'Monday through Thursday inclusive'.

For dates and for ranges of dates, Reed Dickerson offers innovative advice:

Table 5.1: Dickerson's Rules on Dates

Instead of ...	Say ...
From July 1, 2002, to ...	After June 30, 2002, and before ...
Between July 1, 2002, and ...	After June 30, 2002, and before ...
To (or until or by) June 30, 2002 ...	Before July 1, 2002 ...
... between the ages of 17 and 45 ...	... 17 years old or older and under 46 ...
... who is more than 17 years old ...	... who has passed his 17th birthday [or who is 17 years old or older] *unless you mean* ... who is 18 years old or older ...

The style of expressing dates can be adapted to a European style (so 1 July 2002) but the choice of legislative expression is quite novel, and rather clear.[72] At the end of the day the friction here is between clarity and brevity. And, in application of the pyramid of drafting values offered in chapter one, the prevalent suggestion can only favour clarity. Especially with reference to dates, whose significance in legislation is rather crucial. Perhaps Dickerson's expressions are too superfluous to follow, but the inclusion of the superfluous term 'inclusive' is certainly worth attempting.

That and Which

Another possible source of ambiguity is the word 'which' used without commas. The general rule is that 'that' is used to introduce restrictive clauses. 'That' restricts and defines the word that it modifies. A restrictive word, clause or phrase is necessary to the meaning of a sentence and is not set

[72] See VCRAC Crabbe, *Legislative Precedents—Volume II* (London, Cavendish Publishing Ltd, 1998) 14.

off by commas. An example of a restrictive clause is 'The court retains the weapon that was used in the alleged offense until the conclusion of the trial'. Here the drafter defines which weapon it is that the court must retain: it is none other than the particular weapon used in the alleged offence. The clause succeeds in defining that weapon, and in excluding any other weapon.

'Which', with commas, is used to introduce non-restrictive clauses. These do not restrict the word modified: they simply provide additional or descriptive information about the word modified. A non-restrictive word, clause or phrase is not essential to the meaning of a sentence and thus is set off by commas. An example of a non-restrictive clause is 'The Commission establishes the hearing date, which may be changed upon the request of either party'. Here the drafter does not attempt to define which is the hearing date established by the Commission, and does not prohibit the Commission from establishing other dates. Here the drafter introduces two separate clauses: the Commission establishes a hearing date; that hearing date may be changed upon the request of either party. Although, ideally, one would expect separation of the two clauses by punctuation or even by separate subsections, the drafter remains faithful in the separation of the two clauses by means of a secondary sentence. Although this is not a recommended form, nonetheless is it does not seem to confuse the reader much mainly because the comma separates the two concepts.

The problem becomes rather pronounced if the drafter uses 'which' without a comma. The problem is not the grammatical inconsistency, but the mixed and missed messages to the user, who remains unable to tell whether the clause defines the referent term or not. But the text cannot offer any guidance, making this a classic case of ambiguity. If possible, for example at the verification stage of the drafting, the drafter will have to decide whether to change 'which' to 'that', or to add commas. But quite often the best solution is to redraft the sentence entirely, and depart from the ambiguity via new legislative expression.

For example, in the sentence:[73]

> A report which is required to be available for inspection must be in a form convenient for photocopying

the user is left with two possible messages:

Either:

> A report, which is required to be available for inspection, must be in a form convenient for photocopying.

(In other words all reports must be made available for inspection, and all have to be in a certain form. For the purposes of achieving clarity the

[73] Example from the Minnesota Legislative Drafting Manual, para 10.11.

drafter could have expressed this as 'The office makes reports available for inspection; and maintains them in a form convenient for photocopying'.) Or:

> A report that is required to be available for inspection must be in a form convenient for photocopying.

(In other words, of all reports those that are required to be available for inspection must be kept in a form available for photocopying. And, by implication, all other reports need not be in that form. For the purposes of achieving clarity the drafter could have expressed this as 'The office makes the following reports available for inspection. These are kept in a form convenient for photocopying'.)

Serial Commas and Ambiguity

A final form of semantic ambiguity occurs from the placement of a comma before the conjunction in a series: 'All animals, tigers and lions'. The question is whether the comma introduces three separate concepts [animals, tigers, and lions] or whether it separates out two classes from an original generic concept (animals, namely tigers, and lions).

An example on legislation is:

The Commissioner assigns to the case two managers, a program specialist and a family visitor.

Here the question is whether the drafter intends to communicate that the Commissioner assigns four people to the case, namely two managers plus a program specialist plus a family visitor, or whether the Commission assigns two people on the case, namely one manager who is a programme specialist plus another manager who is a family visitor. Both interpretations are supported equally legitimately by the legislative expression chosen.

And so the answer here would be either the addition of 'plus' or 'and' after each of the persons assigned to the case, or a complete rewrite using a clear list of persons assigned.

SYNTACTIC AMBIGUITY[74] OR AMBIGUITY AT THE SENTENCE LEVEL[75]

This ambiguity arises from the way in which the meaning of a sentence is influenced by the intended relationships between individual words and

[74] See JL Montrose, 'Syntactic (Formerly Amphibolous) Ambiguity' (1962) *Modern Uses of Logic in Law* 65, 69, 70; also see PJ Fitzgerald, 'Law and Logic' (1963–64) 39 *Notre Dame Lawyer* 570.

[75] Martineau and Salerno also talk about contextual ambiguity, namely situations where it is unclear which of the two or more available alternatives are intended: see RJ Martineau and MB Salerno, *Legal, Legislative and Rule Drafting in Plain English* (St Paul, MN, Thomson West, 2005); but this seems to be included in ambiguity at sentence level.

phrases used in the sentence, as distinct from the way in which the meaning of the sentence is influenced by the meaning of the individual words and phrases.[76] A statement is syntactically ambiguous where its grammatical structure gives rise to uncertainties of reference. Syntactic ambiguity is the principal cause of the fallacy of amphiboly, and expressions in which it occurs are often not without aspects of humour, intended or not.[77]

Syntactic ambiguity is different from contextual ambiguity, which occurs within a text despite the unequivocation of meaning and syntax of the provisions in question. But syntactic ambiguity refers to the interrelation between provisions within the same text or amongst different texts. It is a matter related to statutory interpretation rather than the pursuit of clarity, precision and unambiguity, and so it will be covered in the chapter on statutory interpretation.

The Placement Problem[78]

Often ambiguity is the result of unclear sentence structure or poor placement of phrases or clauses. Here the ambiguity arises out of a loose combination of words such that it is not clear which word or phrase refers to which other word of phrase.[79] In legislative drafting this phenomenon, also known as syntactic discontinuity, is connected with the frequent use of the so-called qualifications in legislative provisions: there are simply too many adverbial constructions aiming to establish the scope of application of legislative rules, and often these are all fitted into a single sentence.[80] These constructions aim to promote clarity and precision; but attaching them all to the various words that they identify is a recipe for ambiguity. There is no doubt that to a certain extent syntactic discontinuity contributes to a greater complexity of the text and makes greater demands on the interpreter. The reason for this is that owing to syntactic discontinuity, the relations between individual clause elements throughout the legislative provision are less transparent and less explicit. The interpretation thus requires much analytical thinking and experience.[81]

For example, a sign about refunds at a local hardware store reads 'Store credit only after 90 days'. Does this mean that after 90 days, the customer can receive a refund only in the form of store credit? Or is the point that

[76] See R Engholm, 'Logic and Laws: Relief from Statutory Obfuscation' (1975–76) 9 *University of Michigan Journal of Law Reform* 322, 324.

[77] See Kloepfer, 'Ambiguity and Vagueness in the Criminal Law' (n 52) 102.

[78] Also known as 'ambiguity of reference' or 'amphibolous': see I Copi, *Introduction to Logic* (UK, Collier Mack, 1953) 70.

[79] See Allen, Symbolic Logic' (n 63) 860.

[80] See VK Bhatia, 'Cognitive Structuring in Legislative Provisions' in J Gibbons (ed), *Language and the Law* (New York, Longman Group UK Ltd, 1994) 136, 147–48.

[81] See J Mackinlay, 'Syntactic Discontinuity in the Language of UK and EU Legislation' (2004) 3 *English for Specific Purposes World* http://esp-world.info.

store credit is not available as a form of refund until 90 days have elapsed? The placement of 'only' makes the reader unsure.[82]

Phrases that specify time also need to be placed carefully. Consider this example:

> The public school district shall inform the non-public school of the type, level and location of health services that are to be made available to the non-public school students before 15 August.

Are services to be made available before 15 August, or is the district to inform the school before 15 August? Placing the words 'before 15 August' at the head of the sentence or after 'inform the non-public school' would make it clearer that the date is a deadline for supplying the information.

Another example comes from the infamous case of the trial of Roger Casement for treason[83] in the application of the Treason Act 1351. Roger Casement allied with the Germans during the First World War with an ultimate aim of serving an Irish revolution against the British, who were at war with Germany. The provision stated that 'if a man do levy war against our Lord the King in his realm, or be adherent to the King's enemies in his realm, giving to them aid and comfort in the realm, or elsewhere', he is liable for treason. The question was where '..., or elsewhere' referred to: was it attached to the location of the enemies of the King or was it attached to the location of the provision of aid and comfort? In other words was a person guilty of treason if they allied to the King's enemies who were at the time within the King's realm or elsewhere, or if they allied to the King's enemies within the realm, and they gave those enemies aid and comfort either in the King's realm or elsewhere? In the end, based on the comma in '..., or elsewhere' the Court found against Casement, who was 'hung on a comma'.

Modifiers of Nouns

Combinations of nouns and their modifiers are often a cause of trouble. A modifier is a word or group of words that makes the meaning of other words more exact by limiting, restricting or describing them. Modifiers allow the sender of communication to qualify the bare structure of a sentence [subject-verb-object], thus succeeding in offering complex meanings. The term modifier serves as a collective label for words and groups of words performing a comparable function. A modifier is a word or group of words that tells more about another word's meaning. Examples are the *escaped* prisoner; the executive officer *of the county*; an order *that has been signed by the governor*; an order *signed by the governor*; a document *stating the*

[82] See DR Woodworth, 'Musings on Precision in Legal Writing' (1966) 41 *Journal of the State Bar of California* 910, 911–12.

[83] See *R v Casement* (1917) 1 KB 98.

name of the accused. The basic rule is to keep the modifier as close as possible to what it is modifying, in order to allow the reader to attach it easily to the appropriate word. But a large number of modifiers within the same sentence leads to complexity, because the sentence itself becomes longer,[84] but also because it becomes increasingly difficult for the reader to retain the subject-verb-object structure without being distracted by the modifiers.

But in addition to these points, modifiers invite syntactic ambiguity owing to their dubious placement in the sentence and attachment to structural words. For example, the adjective 'married' is semantically clear but syntactically ambiguous in the clause 'A married woman or man may.'. The question is whether the drafter meant 'married man' or 'any man'. Participles as modifiers can also cause ambiguity. 'Immigration officers may deny entry to the country to persons who come from countries with swine flu.' But to whom is 'with swine flu' attached: the person or the country? Adverbs may cause similar problems, with 'only' being a common offender. 'A professor of law of this University only may offer references to alumni'. So does 'only' modify 'a professor of law of this University' or 'may offer references'. Phrases and clauses as modifiers are equally susceptible to the disease of ambiguity. 'No body corporate or company that is incorporated abroad' invites doubt as to whether 'incorporated in the Republic' modifies 'body corporate', 'company' or both?

And so questions often arise when there are more nouns than modifiers, or more modifiers than nouns, or when modifiers do not appear right next to the nouns they modify. Consider these three examples, all taken from Bryan Garner's *Advanced Legal Drafting*:

> solid wall or fence

Does *solid* modify just *wall*, or both *wall* and *fence*? In other words, does the phrase mean *solid wall or solid fence* or is the drafter distinguishing between a *solid wall* and a *fence*, which is usually not solid (in the sense of 'without holes')?

> charitable and educational institutions

Does this mean *charitable institutions and educational institutions*, or does it mean *institutions that are both charitable and educational*? One way to make the meaning clearer is to draft in the singular, so as to be able to write 'a charitable and educational institution' or 'a charitable or an educational institution.'

> to prevent piracy of original works by Americans

Does this mean original *works by Americans* or *piracy by Americans*? *By Americans* might not be modifying the nearest noun.

[84] See Sir W Dale, 'A London Particular' (1985) 6 *Statute Law Review* 11, 20.

A special problem with the placement of modifiers is the situation covered by the rule of last antecedent. In the phrase 'forms, reports, and other submissions that must be filed for review' do the words *that must be filed for review* apply to the words *forms* and *reports*, or do they only apply to other *submissions*?

The rule of last antecedent says that ambiguities like these are to be resolved by taking the problem phrase as applying only to the last item in the series.[85] Antecedents are nouns or phrases within a sentence that are later substituted by indefinite pronouns (it, they, etc) or demonstrative pronouns (that, this), or are modified within the sentence by adjectives, adverbs, or phrases. The rule suggests that a limiting clause in a phrase should ordinarily be read as modifying only the noun or phrase that it immediately follows.[86] But, a court is as likely to ignore the rule as to use it.[87]

PUNCTUATION: THORNTON'S FOUR RULES OF PUNCTUATION

Punctuation can cause ambiguity, even when the sentence presents no semantic ambiguities at word level. Thornton's advice on this is paramount. His four rules are to punctuate sparingly and with purpose; to punctuate for structure and not for sound; to be conventional; and to be consistent.[88]

Indeed, following the accepted rules of punctuation in legislative drafting assists the users to place the punctuation and the meaning in context. Little as they maybe, punctuation marks form part of the text, and for the purposes of statutory interpretation they are therefore equally[89] relevant as words.[90]

The placement of punctuation marks inside or outside quotes is another tool for clarity. Periods and commas inside quotes indicate that the punctuation is part of the matter being quoted. This is crucial in drafting amendments to bills. For example: 'This Act is the "Air Pollution Control

[85] See T Myers, 'Clearing up Ambiguity from a Series Modifier' (2011) 90 *Michigan Bar Journal* 52.

[86] See M Phelan D'Isa, 'Grammar Control: What Is a "Misdemeanor Crime of Domestic Violence" Under the Federal Gun Possession Statute?' (2008–09) 36 *Preview US Supreme Court Cases* 103, 105; also see T Clercq, 'Doctrine of the Last Antecedent: The Mystifying Morass of Ambiguous Modifiers' (1996) 2 *Legal Writing: Journal of the Legal Writing Institute* 81.

[87] See *State v Turchick*, 436 NW 2d 108 (Minn App 1989), in which the court interpreted the phrase 'headphones and earphones which are worn on both ears' without any reference to the rule.

[88] See H Xanthaki, *Thornton's Legislative Drafting* (West Sussex, Bloomsbury Professional, 2013) 37–39; also see R Wydick, 'Should Lawyers Punctuate?' (1990) *1 Scribes Journal of Legal Writing* 7, 23.

[89] But there is a view that punctuation marks are 'weak' signs of meaning, albeit part of the text: see The Hon Mr Justice VCRAC Crabbe, 'Punctuation in Legislation' (1988) *Statute Law Review* 87, 90 and 92.

[90] Although some courts have held that punctuation is not a part of a statute, the Colorado Supreme Court has interpreted a proposed constitutional amendment on the basis of punctuation (*In re Senate Concurrent Resolution No 10*, 137 Colo. 491, 328 P.2d 103 (1958)).

Act".' demonstrates that the period is not part of the Act's name. And that the example quoted here ends with the period, which is indeed part of the legislative sentence quoted as an example here.

Punctuation in bills based on an original Act form part of its language, and generally should not be changed, unless of course the intent of the drafter is to change the meaning or the concept communicated. The danger here is that, although a surgical amendment by use of a mere change of punctuation is highly commendable technically, users may miss the point of law reform undertaken: and so effectiveness of communication may be best served with a more obvious amendment, which admittedly would be technically clumsy.

The comma seems to present the most danger of ambiguity at sentence level. It is important to always use a comma in a series before a conjunction (or a semicolon if clauses of a series have punctuation within them). For example: 'No city, town, county, or city and county' may create the impression that 'city and county' is one of the subjects of the sentence, whereas 'city, and county' clarifies that either of them would be within the field of application of the provisions. This type of punctuation is not grammatically correct, but it does promote clarity in legislation, and does serve both the drafter and the user in their communication.[91] Although this form clashes with Thornton's rule on being conventional, it is however supported from the concept that the drafter punctuate for structure and not for sound.

The purpose of the comma as a punctuation mark is to separate or to enclose. A comma can separate long independent clauses joined by 'and', 'but', 'for', 'nor', 'or', 'yet'. It can separate an introductory modifying clause or phrase from what follows by a comma: 'At the end of the financial year, lecturers must submit'. Or it can separate items in a series: 'This section applies to banks, insurers, trustee firms, and corporate advisory firms.'. And the comma can also enclose non-restrictive modifying words or clauses: 'An investigator, appointed under section 403, may'; or parenthetical expressions interpolated as interruptions to the main stream of communication in the sentence: 'X or Y, as the case may be, encloses'.

GENDER-NEUTRAL DRAFTING (GND)

One of the two tools serving clarity, precision and unambiguity, and ultimately effectiveness of legislation is gender neutral drafting (gnd).[92] Gender-neutral language (gnl) refers to language which includes both sexes

[91] See SJ Hankin, 'Statutory Interpretation in the Age of Grammatical Permissiveness: an Object Lesson for Teaching why Grammar Matters' (2010) 18 *Perspectives* University of Maryland Legal Studies Research Paper No 2009-52.

[92] See D Greenberg, 'The Techniques of Gender-Neutral Drafting' in C Stefanou and H Xanthaki (eds), *Drafting Legislation: A Modern Approach* (Aldershot, Ashgate, 2008) 63.

and treats women and men equally. Traditionally, in our society, men have been the dominant force and our language has developed in ways which reflect male dominance, sometimes to the total exclusion of women. Gender-neutral language, also called non-sexist, non-gender-specific, or inclusive language, attempts to redress the balance.[93]

Admittedly, the mere reference to gnd seems to bring many a drafter around the Commonwealth to covert amusement.[94] It is often ridiculed as one more feminist invasion in legislative drafting, and it is often justified by reference to the provision common in many Interpretation Acts which foresee that '"he" includes "she"'.

Although it is quite tempting to ask whether the male of our species would accept a conversion to '"she" includes "he"', the main concern with gender-specific language is clarity and unambiguity.[95] With reference to clarity, it is any woman's right to consider that the statute does not apply to them if it is written in the male form: and although the Interpretation Act may say otherwise,[96] how many non-lawyers are aware of it or have read it in detail? And, after all, it is a consequence of the rule of law that women are clear in their understanding of which statutes apply to them and which do not. With reference to ambiguity,[97] 'he' can be both 'he' and 'she' in a great number of statutes, but equally 'he' is only 'he' where gender-specific language is actually appropriate.[98] For example, in jurisdictions where the military is exclusively male, one wonders whether the application of '"he" includes "she"' could lead to the admission of women in the army by broad interpretation of the male pronoun under the Interpretation Act, especially where there is no express provision to the contrary. And so within the modern drafter's striving to achieve clarity and minimise ambiguity, gender neutral language is a much pronounced demand. Mary Jane Mossman, a Canadian legal academic explains the reasons for non-discriminatory language in law as being important to promote accuracy in legal speech and writing; to conform to requirements of professional responsibility; and to satisfy equality guarantees in laws and the constitution.[99]

[93] See UNESCO, 'Guidelines on Gender-Neutral Language' (1999) http://unesdoc.unesco.org/images/0011/001149/114950mo.pdf.

[94] See WB Hill Jr, 'A Need for the Use of Non-sexist Language in the Courts' (1992) 49 *Washington & Lee Law Review* 275.

[95] See DT Kobil, 'Do the Paperwork or Die: Clemency, Ohio Style?' (1991) 52 *Ohio State Law Journal* 655; KW Graham Jr and CA Wright, 'Commenting on Gender Neutral Amendments to a Federal Rule of Evidence' (Federal Practice and Procedure, para 5231.1) (Suppl 1998).

[96] See eg UK Interpretation Act 1978, s 6.

[97] See WP Statsky, *Legislative Analysis and Drafting* (St Paul, MN, West Publishing Company, 1984) 183.

[98] See GG Corbet, *Gender* (Cambridge, Cambridge University Press, 1999) 21.

[99] See MJ Mossman, 'Use of Non-Discriminatory Language in Law' (1995) 20 *International Legal Practice* 8.

But, is it possible to draft in gnl? Gnl has been adopted by the New South Wales Office of Parliamentary Counsel in 1983, by New Zealand in 1985, by the Australian Office of Parliamentary Counsel in 1988, by the UN and the International Labour Organization roughly around 1989, by Canada in 1991, by South Africa in 1995 and by the US Congress, albeit not consistently, in 2001. In the UK gnl has been applied to all government Bills and Acts since 2007.[100] And so gnl is possible. It is also practicable,[101] provided that 'it comes at no more than reasonable cost to brevity or intelligibility'.[102] In fact, there is no technical reason why legislation should not be drafted in a way that avoids gender-specific pronouns.[103]

But what exactly does a switch to gnl entail? According to the guidance of the UK Office of Parliamentary Counsel it entails abandoning gender-specific pronouns to refer to a person who may be either male or female or neuter; and avoiding nouns that take a form that appears to assume that a man rather than a woman will hold a particular office, do a particular job or perform a particular role.[104]

From the point of view of terminology choices, the term 'man' is to be avoided. Originally, it meant 'human being' or 'person', but over the years it has come to mean only male humans. For many people, the generic use of 'man' causes ambiguity as to which of the two concepts it conveys: 'person' or 'male human'? Similarly, the term 'Chairman' generates distaste. 'Chairperson', 'convener', 'coordinator', 'moderator' or 'president' are possible alternatives, but the term 'chair' has emerged as the most accepted alternative in government, universities and business. If reference is made to the person chairing a meeting, 'the Chair' is a good choice. 'Madam Chair' or 'Mr Chair' defeat the object of gender neutrality and are best avoided. So, this type of gender-specific terminology can be avoided by a number of competing drafting techniques. The drafter can use neutral terms such as 'person' or 'individual', and can adopt neutral alternatives for masculine-based nouns[105] such as 'drafter', 'fire fighter', or 'chair'.[106]

[100] See Statement by Leader of House of Commons, HC Deb 8 March 2007 col 146 WS.

[101] See S Petersson, 'Gender Neutral Drafting: Recent Commonwealth Developments' (1999) 20 *Statute Law Review* 35, 57.

[102] See Office of the Parliamentary Counsel, 'Gender-Neutral Drafting Techniques' (Dec 2008) Drafting Techniques Group Paper 23 (final).

[103] See D Greenberg, *Craies on Legislation* (London, Sweet and Maxwell, 2008).

[104] See Sir S Laws, 'The Implementation of a Policy of Gender-neutral Drafting' (19 June 2007) RRDrafting note.fm.

[105] See UNESCO, 'Guidelines on Gender-Neutral Language' (n 92) 9.

[106] See eg the Pensions Act 2008, sch 1, and the Child Maintenance and Other Payments Act 2008, sch 1. But the use of 'chair' remains controversial: the New Zealand Law Commission *Legislation Manual Structure and Style* (1999), 48 (NZLC IP2, 2007), suggests 'chairperson' while avoiding 'chair'. In 2007 Conservative MP Ann Widdecombe declared: 'A chair is a piece of furniture. It is not a person. I am not a chair, because no one has ever sat on me': see T Branigan, 'Straw: Future Laws to be Gender Neutral' *Guardian* (9 March 2007) www.guardian.co.uk/gender/story/0,,2030075,00.html.

Pronouns carry difficult choices of language. 'He', 'his', 'him' or 'himself' are gender-specific terms and are to be used only when referring to a male person. Interpretation Acts or even concrete disclaimers in the text that masculine nouns and pronouns refer to both men and women are not adequate defence for using gender-specific language. And equally gender specific are female pronouns as choices reflecting both male and female. The prevalent in the US[107] 'he and she', 'he/she' or 's/he' to indicate that both sexes are included in the statement[108] may be unambiguous, but it is cumbersome, gender specific and clumsy.[109] Other techniques include repeating the noun; or omitting the pronoun;[110] or converting the noun to a verb form; or using passive voice; or using a relative clause; or using the plural noun followed by 'they';[111] or replacing the noun with a letter;[112] or using the singular noun followed by the plural 'they' rather than singular pronouns 'he' or 'she'.

The latter technique was favoured by authors prior to the nineteenth century[113] and is still common in contemporary English.[114] Although it has lost support in the recent 2014 version of the Office of Parliamentary Counsel's Guidance,[115] it is supported by authors as it is the most compatible with spoken English.[116] An example of it can be found in the Counter-Terrorism Act 2008: 'References in this Part to a person being dealt with for or in respect of an offence are to their being sentenced ... in respect of the offence'. And a further example comes from the Local Democracy, Economic Development and Construction Bill, Schedule 1, paragraph 2(3): 'The chair of the Boundary Committee for England holds office as chair ... in accordance with the terms of their appointment'. The technique is rather innovative, since it uses a grammatical error to draw the reader's attention to gender neutrality. But at the same time it demonstrates quite rightly

[107] See C Williams, 'The End of the "Masculine Rule"? Gender-Neutral Legislative Drafting in the United Kingdom and Ireland' (2008) 29 *Statute Law Review* 139, 139.

[108] But this has been criticised by Bentham who used this exact term for his definition of long-windedness: see J Bentham, 'Nomography or the Art of Inditing Laws' in J Bowring (ed), *The Works of Jeremy Bentham* (Edinburgh, William Tait, 1843) III: 231, 265.

[109] See R Wydick, *Plain English for Lawyers* (Durham, Carolina Academic Press 1994) 72.

[110] This is the prevalent technique in Australia: see 'Avoidance of "Sexist" Language in Legislation' (1985) 11 *Commonwealth Law Bulletin* 593.

[111] Eg 'The regulations may provide that participants may only carry on activities ... if they hold a permit' (Climate Change Act 2008, sch 2 para 10).

[112] Eg 'If a person (S) who is registered under this Chapter as a service provider in respect of a regulated activity carries on that activity while S's registration is suspended, S is guilty of an offence (Health and Social Care Act 2008, s 34(1)).

[113] See A Bodin, 'Androcentrism in Prescriptive Grammar: Singular "they", Sex Indefinite "he", and "he or she"' (1974) 4 *Language in Society* 129, 131–33; also see S Petersson, 'Gender Neutral Drafting: Historical Perspective' (1998) 19 *Statute Law Review* 93.

[114] See C Miller and K Swift, *The Handbook of Non Sexist Writing* (New York, Lippincott and Crowell, 1980) 38–40.

[115] See Office of the Parliamentary Counsel, *Drafting Guidance* (20 March 2014) 29–30.

[116] See D Schweikart, 'Gender Neutral Pronoun Redefined' (1990–91) 20 *Women's Rights Law Reporter* 1, 8.

that drafters must use grammar without being its slave. It is better to be inelegant than uncertain.[117]

And with this thought in mind, the drafter can select the gnd tool that best fits the overall goal of effectiveness.[118] But what does effectiveness mean in the context of gnd? Since the regulatory aim of the gnd policy is to redress the balance of gender inequality in society,[119] it seems that the choice of the most effective gnl tool is to be made on the basis of two criteria: one, clear inclusion of the female; and two, education of the public on the changed policy. This calls for a tool that quickly identifies the new position whilst at the same time reflecting gender neutrality or gender equality. On that basis the singular plural technique is ideal: it breaks the barriers of an inherent gender-specific language and uses a grammatically unconventional form to alert the user to the departure from gender specific to gender neutral. This book is written in singular plural.

[117] See JK Aitken and EL Piesse, *The Elements of Drafting* (Sydney, The Law Book Company Limited, 1995) 57.

[118] See H Xanthaki, 'On Transferability of Legislative Solutions: The Functionality Test' in C Stefanou and H Xanthaki (eds), *Drafting Legislation: A Modem Approach* (Aldershot, Ashgate, 2008) 1, 17; also see M Wilson, 'Sir William Dale Annual Memorial Lecture—Gender-Neutral Law Drafting: The Challenge of Translating Policy into Legislation' (2011) 13 *European Journal of Law Reform* 199, 207.

[119] See United Nations Development Programme, 'Drafting Gender-Aware Legislation: how to Promote and Protect Gender Equality in Central and Eastern Europe and in the Commonwealth of Independent States' (2003) 21.

6

Plain Language

WHAT IS PLAIN LANGUAGE?

IN THE DRAFTER'S pursuit for clarity, precision and unambiguity—as a means of achieving effectiveness of the legislative text—the drafter has two tools: gender-neutral language and plain language. Both contribute equally, mainly to clarity but also to precision and unambiguity.[1]

Plain language is defined by Butt as clear and effective for its audience'.[2] Plain English aims to promote uninhibited communication between the drafter, who is mostly a trained lawyer with drafting training and experience, and the user of the legislative text, who can be anything from a senior judge to an illiterate citizen.[3] The inequality in the understanding of common terms (whichever they may be) and certainly legal terms is obvious.[4] It is precisely this imbalance[5] that plain language aims to address. The difficulty in this form of communication is dual: first, the sheer length of the distance between the extremes of trained lawyers and drafters as a semiotic group[6] and of any illiterate citizens as users renders the identification of a common wavelength for communication a hopeless task; and, secondly, the identification of the exact level of understanding of the audience of each

[1] See Office of Parliamentary Counsel—Australian Government, *Plain English Manual* www.opc.gov.au; also see Law Reform Commission of Victoria, *Plain English and the Law* (1987) app 1: 'Guidelines for Drafting in Plain English: A Manual for Legislative Drafters'; UK Tax Law Rewrite, 'The Way Forward: Annex 1—Guidelines for the Rewrite' www.hmrc.gov.uk/rewrite/wayforward/tlra1.htm; and Office of Parliamentary Counsel, *Plain Language and Legislation* www.Scotland.gov.uk/Publications/2006/02/17093804/0.

[2] See P Butt, *Modern Legal Drafting: A Guide to Using Clearer Language* (Cambridge, Cambridge University Press, 2013) 103.

[3] See D Greenberg, *Craies on Legislation—A Practitioner's Guide to the Nature, Process, Effect and Interpretation of Legislation* (London, Sweet and Maxwell, 2004) 305.

[4] See Current Topics, 'The Problem of Drafting Styles' (1986) 60 *Australian Law Journal* 369.

[5] See R Flesch, *The Art of Readable Writing* (New York, Harper & Bros, 1949); also see S Chase, *The Power of Words* (New York, Harcourt Brace, 1954).

[6] 'A semiotic group is a group which makes sense (here, of law) in ways sufficiently distinct from other such groups as to make its meanings less than transparent to members of other groups without training or initiation': see B Jackson, 'Legislation in the Semiotics of Law' in H van Schooten (ed), *Semiotics and Legislation: Jurisprudential, Institutional and Sociological Perspectives* (Liverpool, Deborah Charles, 1999) 5, 6.

legislative text becomes all the more difficult as a result of the extreme diversity in the various users of legislation.

And so the use of plain language requires that the drafter addresses two separate but intertwined concerns. First, they must un-train, go back to the first few weeks in Law School before their initiation to legal terminology, mainly via precedents,[7] and remember how to speak and write as a non-lawyer. This is not an easy task. Especially since in the legal professions, where lawyers have fought hard for their rite of passage, non-legal terminology is considered inferior, uneducated and to a degree vulgar and imprecise.[8]

Secondly, the drafter must gu(ess-e)stimate the exact profile of the users of their legislative text, as a means of determining what the pitch of their communication must be. This involves identifying 'who will potentially read the legislation or whose activities it will control'.[9] Reverting to the allegedly homogenous community of 'ordinary users' is of course a fallacy.[10] In oral communication this is rather easier: one can see the recipient of the oral message, can adjust the pitch of the communication, and indeed one does so instinctively. Choices of words, choices of the depth of the communication and choices of references to relevant sources of information are undertaken on the basis of the pitch selected. And quite often one manages to offer diverse levels of pitch to groups of the audience, as required. Written language does not offer this luxury: there is a single text that carries the burden of communication for all audiences, learned or not. And this difficulty is much more pronounced in legislation, where a single written text must speak to a diverse audience. The internal conciseness, lack of digressions and examples so characteristic for legal texts 'seriously limit the possibility of any precise translation of the language in discourse into language of a legal text'.[11] Even with the undoubted help of the three main user profiles identified by the Good Law Initiative,[12] the legislative text must be able to speak to everyday citizens, to non-lawyers using the legislation in the course of their professional activities and to lawyers and judges. All at the same time, with a single text. The task is near impossible,

[7] See IML Turnbull, 'Clear Legislative Drafting: New Approaches in Australia' (1990) 11 *Statute Law Review* 161, 166.

[8] See LM Friedman, 'Law and Its Language' (1964–65) 33 *Georgetown Washington Law Review* 563, 567. Concerns of 'oversimplification' were also expressed in the survey conducted relatively recently in Australia: see Office of Parliamentary Counsel, 'Results of the 2010 Legislation Users Survey' (May 2010).

[9] See D Berry, 'Audience Analysis in the Legislative Drafting Process' (2000) *The Loophole* 61, 62, available at http://www.opc.gov.au/calc/docs/Loophole/Loophole_Jun00.pdf.

[10] See D Greenberg, *Laying Down the Law* (London, Sweet and Maxwell, 2011) 223.

[11] See W Cyrul, 'Lawmaking: between Discourse and Legal Text' in LJ Wintgens, *Legislation in Context: Essays in Legisprudence* (Aldershot, Ashgate, 2007) 52.

[12] See www.gov.uk/good-law.

and the demand on drafters rather unfair. But it can be done.[13] Hence the need for innovative approaches to legislation, such as the layered approach analysed in the chapter on structure. But before one looks at radical solutions, plain language seems to be the main tool that the drafter has in their effort to speak and be understood by the users of legislation.

The plain language movement may well have evolved as a single response to the remoteness and complexity of legal language. But it cannot be expressed as a standardised technical manual or a concrete list of rules that will always lead to legislation that is easily understood by all users.[14] This is because plain language itself is a concept that is extremely difficult to define: it means very many different things to different people and it is a relative concept.[15] Plain language encompasses all concepts that facilitate communication between the drafter and the user, whoever the latter may be. It is probably best to give representative descriptions as a starting point. Eagleson describes plain language as follows:

> Plain English is clear, straightforward expression, using only as many words as are necessary. It is language that avoids obscurity, inflated vocabulary and convoluted sentence structure. It is not baby talk, nor is it a simplified version of the English language.[16]

Redish offers an alternative definition:

> Plain English means writing that is straightforward, that reads as if it were spoken. It means writing that is unadorned with archaic, multi-syllabic words and majestic turns of phrase that even educated readers cannot understand. Plain English is clear, direct, and simple; but good plain English has both clarity and grace.[17]

For advocates of easy communication, both definitions suffer from vagueness. But this is less a matter of skill and more a matter of inherent unity in diversity. Plain language is the means of making a message understood and acted upon by the intended audience. Some plain language advocates go as far as requiring successful communication after the first reading. But this does not seem to be an inherent requirement of the plain language movement: understanding the message first time round is a good way of

[13] See contra K Larsen, *The Miss Grammar Guidebook* (Oregon, Oregon State Bar Association, 1994) 68–69; also see J Stark, 'Should the Main Goal of Statutory Drafting Be Accuracy or Clarity?' (1994) 15 *Statute Law Review* 207; and R Sullivan, 'Some Implications of Plain Language' (2001) 22 *Statute Law Review* 145, 180.

[14] See The Irish Law Reform Commission, 'Consultation Paper on Statutory Drafting and Interpretation: Plain Language and the Law' (LRC CP14–1999) 3.01; also see Law Reform Commission, 'Statutory Drafting and Interpretation: Plain Language and the Law' (LRC 61–2000).

[15] See RD Eagleson, 'Efficiency in Legal Drafting' (1989) *The Loophole* www.opc.gov.au/calc/loophole.htm.

[16] See RD Eagleson, *Writing in Plain English* (Commonwealth of Australia, 1990) 4.

[17] See JC Redish, 'The Plain English Movement' in S Greenbaum, *The English Language Today* (Oxford, Pergamon Press, 1985) 126.

encouraging the user to read further, and so it is a good tool for making the text inviting. But a text, much more so a legislative text, understood at the second or third reading is equally commendable. And so I would not go as far as demanding understanding after the first reading; or indeed understanding the legislation fully and completely. For me, an understanding of the main regulatory message, namely the gist of what the government wants to communicate as a means of achieving law reform, by every reader of the legislation, is good enough. For now.[18]

But what is certainly important in any analysis of plain language is to destroy the fallacy that comes by the very choice of its terminology: plain language is not only about language. Words, syntax, even punctuation are very important elements of it. But structure, layout, even the general look of the whole statute book—in paper or online—form part of the plain language movement. Hunt classifies plain language concerns under three categories: language, structure and style.[19] One could even add accessibility of the legislation: for example, there is little doubt that communication of the law to the citizen is greatly enhanced by the recent decision of the New Zealand Government to offer free access to the formal format of legislation electronically.[20] At the end of the day what falls under plain language is any tool, language, picture, image, anything that assists the user to understand the message expressed by government and conveyed by the drafter.[21]

And so plain language begins with the selection and prioritisation of the information that readers need to receive at the second stage of Thornton's drafting stages, namely during the analysis of the legislative proposal and the compilation of the legislative scheme: it requires reading all the data offered in the drafting instructions, weeding out what is unnecessary and selecting what needs to be kept in order to maintain the message intact but

18 See B Beking and C Botha, 'Aspects of Legislative Drafting: Some South African Realities (or Plain Language Is Not Always Plain Sailing)' (2007) 28 *Statute Law Review* 34, 65.

19 See B Hunt, 'Plain Language in Legislative Drafting: is it Really the Answer?' (2002) 23 *Statute Law Review* 24, 24.

20 Attorney general Chris Finlayson stated that: 'Access to official legislation online is important to anyone who needs to know what the law is, because of the assurance of accuracy that it provides' ... 'It also frees them from relying on potentially out-of-date printed legislation'. Not all legislation on the website is official: it applies only to legislation in PDF format, and only to PDFs that display the New Zealand Coat of Arms on the first page. But it includes the latest versions of all principal legislation enacted or made since 1931 (plus a few earlier Acts), and many other point-in-time versions. A printout of an official PDF is also official. These changes mean that the Parliamentary Counsel Office ceased publication of annual bound volumes of legislation after the 2013 volumes were printed, and traditional hard-copy reprints after the current programme was completed: official online legislation and print-on-demand renders them obsolete. See legislation.govt.nz/news.aspx#official.

21 See Office of the Parliamentary Counsel, 'Clarity in Drafting: Principles and Techniques' Drafting Techniques Group Paper 21 (final) (July 2008) www.cabinetoffice.gov.uk/parliamentarycounsel.aspx.

conveyed at the level needed for the users of the legislative text in question. It continues with choices related to structure during the third stage, namely the designing of the legislative solution: here it requires a simplification of the policy,[22] a simplification of the legal concepts that are involved in the realisation of the policy, and initial plain language choices of legislative expression (for example, a decision for direct textual amendments combined with a Keeling Schedule, or a repeal and re-enactment when possible). Plain language enters very much into the agenda in the fourth stage of compilation of the text. A plain language document uses words economically and at a level the audience can understand. Its sentence structure is tight. Its tone is welcoming and direct. And it remains on the cards in the fifth stage, that of verification. Here the drafting team verifies all of the above. And ensures that the design of the text is visually appealing and that the document is easy to read and looks like it is meant to be read. And so plain language extends from policy to law to drafting.

Perhaps the most precise definition of plain language comes from Watson-Brown:

> Plain English in writing legal documents is the style of writing in the English language that best conveys to the reader who is to do (or not to do) what and when to create the rights, privileges and powers and the corresponding obligations that a law gives rise to as the author requires. The concepts of 'who, what and when' may be supplemented by 'where' to indicate location or jurisdiction and 'how' to supply the mechanism necessary to give effect to the desired result.[23]

In the original definition Watson-Brown felt that since the rationalisation of the basis for the legislation should not form part of the text, it is not necessary in the text to explain 'why' the legislation is written. But he has recently revised this definition to suggest that it is indeed appropriate to explain 'why' in purpose clauses supplementing and strengthening the long title.[24] The fresher definition reflects the need to place the concept in context as a means of better communicating the message.

And as for the objectives of plain language, they are coherence, comprehensiveness, consistency, clarity and care.[25]

[22] See IC Meiklem, 'Legislative Expression and Transformational Generative Grammar' (1970) 5 *University of British Columbia Law Review* 57, 64; but plain language may not be useful where the policy is complex: see B Hunt, 'Plain Language in Legislative Drafting: An Achievable Objective or a Laudable Ideal?' (2003) 24 *Statute Law Review* 112, 121.

[23] See A Watson-Brown, 'Defining "Plain English" as an Aid to Legal Drafting' (2009) 30 *Statute Law Review* 85, 96.

[24] See A Watson-Brown, 'In Search of Plain English—The Holy Grail or Mythical Excalibur of Legislative Drafting' (2011) 33 *Statute Law Review* 7, 22–23.

[25] See R Macdonald, 'Plain English in the Law—a New Model for the 21st Century' (2004) 30 *Commonwealth Law Bulletin* 922, 926–27.

PLAIN LANGUAGE ASPECT 1: KNOWING YOUR AUDIENCE

So, plain language requires ease of communication to the audience. For example, the UK Tax Law Rewrite project went to great length in order to identify the users of tax legislation, as a means of drafting as a 'joint' venture.[26] But, which audience is that? Who are the people that are on the receiving end of the government's regulatory message? Who are the people whose social behaviour government targets as a means of achieving the desired policy? Who are those people whose cooperation and positive action government needs in order to achieve efficacy of regulation? Who are these people whose action, or—God forbid—non- or mal- action, makes government policy a success, or a failure? Who are the people to whom the legislation, as a tool for regulation, must speak and explain clearly what needs to be done, how and when? Whom is the drafter speaking to by means of a legislative text?

This is not an esoteric existential question for drafters. Far from it. Identifying the audience of legislation is excruciatingly necessary for the drafting team aiming to pitch the regulatory message at the right level of user general and legal sophistication.[27] I often order my English-speaking audience to 'καθιστε αμεσως κατω' with an increasingly loud and menacing voice as time passes and they inevitably fail to perform the task. This is exactly how users of legislation feel when the legislative text is intelligible for them. Those who never meant to listen and apply the law are lost anyway: accessibility of the message is irrelevant for their compliance. But those who wish to listen and comply remain aware that they are ordered to act in a certain way, but they have absolutely no way of knowing what it is that they are asked to do, by what means, and when. Unless I translate the command to the English equivalent, 'sit down immediately', my audience can simply not perform the task for me. And this is problematic for three reasons.

First, compliance with the legislative command is impossible, will not occur, and therefore the legislative text is ineffective and the underlying regulatory reform will not take place. This is confirmed by user testing experiments, such as the one undertaken by the Knight and Kimble team in the late-1990s[28] or the Canadian studies by Schmolka, or the UK's recent Better Law initiative. Secondly, the government and legislature that knowingly pass an intelligible piece of legislation entrap the citizens by asking them

[26] See D Salter, 'Towards a Parliamentary Procedure for the Tax Law Rewrite' (1998) 19 *Statute Law Review* 65, 68; also see Inland Revenue, 'The Tax Law Rewrite: The Way Forward'http://webarchive.nationalarchives.gov.uk/+/http://www.hmrc.gov.uk/rewrite/wayforward/menu.htm.

[27] See D Berry, 'Audience Analysis in the Legislative Drafting Process' (2000) *Loophole*, www.opc.gov.au/calc/docs/calc-june/audience.htm.

[28] See P Knight, *Clearly Better Drafting* (n7) 39.

to perform an impossible task (they do not understand it so how can they possibly do it?) and on top of that they impose penalties for non-compliance with that impossible task. Thirdly, the government that proposes a knowingly intelligible piece of legislation creates for voters the fraudulent impression that it has acknowledged the problem behind the legislative text, and that it has done something about it by legislating: the truth of course is that the government proposes an ineffective piece of legislation that cannot lead to regulatory efficacy.

And so knowing the legislative audience is a matter very relevant to democracy, the rule of law, citizens' rights and of course regulatory and legislative quality. But is there one audience of legislation? Can a drafter rely on the common notion of the 'lay person', the 'average man on the street',[29] the 'user'? The theoretical debate over this point has now been answered by the Good Law Initiative survey: at least three categories of people constitute the audience of legislation, and these are lay persons reading the legislation to make it work for them,[30] sophisticated non-lawyers using the law in the process of their professional activities and lawyers and judges. The categories identified may well be simplistic, but at the end of the day the diversity of each and every one of these groups can only allow for all-encompassing simplified profiles. And so the fallacy of speaking to 'an' or 'the' audience has now collapsed. But we are not much closer to identifying who the audience is, at least not without taking an extra factor on board.

Since the diversity of the audience prevents the drafter from attaching to it enough characteristics to identify the level of pitch of the legislative language, perhaps turning to a more objective and less diverse factor may do the trick. Having realised what the rough profiles of the audience are, the drafter can look at the topic of the legislative text itself as a means of steering towards the right user profile. Legislative texts are not all aimed at the same readers. Their primary audience varies.

For example, in drafting rules of evidence the drafter must be aware of the probability of judges and lawyers being the main audience of the text.[31] And so the language and terminology used can be sophisticated. And indeed, it must be sophisticated: if the drafter chose to paraphrase the term 'intent' or even 'mens rea' with a plain language equivalent such

[29] See D Murphy, 'Plain English-Principles and Practice' (Conference on Legislative Drafting, Canberra, Australia, 15 July 1992).

[30] See JJE Gracia, A *Theory of Textuality: The Logic and Epistemology* (Albany, State University of New York Press, 1995) 159–63 and 164–65; also see GLPi and V Schmolka, 'A Report on Results of Usability Testing Research on Plain Language Draft Sections of the Employment Insurance Act: A Report to Department of Justice Canada and Human Resources Development Canada' (unpublished, August 2000); and V Schmolka, 'Consumer Fireivorks Regulations: Usability Testing, TR1995-2e (Department of Justice Canada, unpublished, 1995).

[31] See BA Garner, 'Guidelines for Drafting and Editing Court Rules' (1997) 175 *Federal Rules Decisions* 169, 187.

as 'meaning to', then the primary audience of lawyers and judges would make the rather legitimate assumption that the drafter means something other than 'intent' and would not easily carry the interpretative case law of 'intent' onto 'meaning to'.

At the other extreme using the term 'mens rea' in a criminal law statute would ensure that most of the primary audience of lay persons whose behaviour would be regulated by the statute would completely miss the point about what is prohibited post enactment. A wonderful example demonstrating the diversity of audiences, and required consequent drafting styles, stems from taxation law: individual taxation legislation is primarily addressed to lay persons and must be drafted in plain language, whereas corporate taxation laws are primarily addressed to non-lawyer professionals or lawyers/judges and can be drafted using accepted terminology. Ultimately, the drafter cannot use the same drafting style when setting the price of the annual bacon subsidies and when introducing prosecution guidelines.

As a result, the drafter must identify the primary audience of the legislation with as much precision and accuracy as the topic allows. And for that purpose the help of policy officers can be invaluable, since they would have already been in contact with the primary stakeholders at the policy design stage. But could a primarily sophisticated audience serve as a 'carte blanche' for legalese? One would have to resist that temptation. Although it may well be mostly lawyers and judges using the new rules of evidence above, non-lawyers may need to, and in any case must, have access to the legislation too. After all, there is nothing to prevent a lay user from reading rules of evidence, especially in today's era when we are all used to researching on the internet and elsewhere about issues that relate to us. In the same manner that a person provisionally diagnosed with a minor or major illness will now look at the internet for further information, which could be addressed to clinicians or members of the public, the user of legislation is bound to research whatever is relevant to their case as a means of gaining the degree of information control that all of us have learnt to expect. As audiences become more specialised and more educated in technical areas, they expect texts that are targeted to their particular needs.[32] Moreover, since accessibility of legislation is directly linked to Bingham's rule of law,[33] passing inaccessible legislation under the feeble excuse that its primary audience possesses legal sophistication is not easily acceptable. And so legalese cannot be promoted even in cases of specialist legislation, such as rules of evidence. But in such circumstances there is an argument for either

[32] See KA Schriver, 'Plain Language through Protocol-Aided Revision' in ER Steinberg (ed), *Plain Language: Principles and Practice* (Detroit, Wayne State University Press, 1991) 148, 152.

[33] See Lord Simon of Glaisdale, 'The Renton Report-Ten Years On' (1985) 6 *Statute Law Review* 133.

the continued use of legal terminology or for the provision of a definition of the new plain language equivalent referring to the legal term used until now.

And what about the other extreme? How plain must legislation be? Even within the group profile of lay persons reading the legislative text in order to resolve a personal issue there is plenty of diversity. The private person will not be a trained lawyer, and will not be another trained professional using the legislation in the course of their work. But their sophistication, general and legal, can be very diverse, ranging from a fiercely intelligent and sophisticated user to a rather naïve illiterate and intellectually challenged individual. Whom does the drafter speak to? One would find it difficult to gauge the sophistication of the beast formerly known as 'the average man on the street'. Even if a drafter could identify such a person and attribute characteristics to them, are they to ignore the 'below averages' amongst us?[34] Going back to the aim of legislative drafting as the production of an effective text contributing to efficacy of regulation offers a rather lucid answer to this question. The drafter is speaking to each and every user who must comply with the new legislation: this includes the above averages, the averages and the below averages. Really the drafter speaks to each and every citizen or subject, provided that they remain legally capable. And so the level of plainness required is currently underestimated: the criterion currently used is the average person, whereas the real criterion must be the least sophisticated, below average citizen or subject. 'In the absence of instructions to the contrary, drafters are not only entitled to write for this audience but may even have a professional obligation to do so'.[35]

PLAIN LANGUAGE ASPECT 2: EASY COMMUNICATION

Having identified the audience for the specific piece of legislation, and having set the minimum level of sophistication expected from that audience, the drafter begins to create a plain language text. There are numerous tools that can allow them to achieve their aim, and most of them are common sense, or results of empirical research in user preferences within the jurisdictions served by the drafter. It is important to return to the phronetic nature of drafting here and to emphasise two things. One, what works in one jurisdiction may not work in another, even when the language is the same. For example, the term 'investigation' describing the first phase of criminal inquiries into an alleged offence may carry a variety of meanings according to domestic criminal procedure laws. And two, in the football game

[34] See J Kimble, 'Answering the Critics of Plain Language' (1994–95) 5 *The Scribes Journal of Legal Writing* 51, 59.

[35] See R Sullivan, 'The Promise of Plain Language Drafting' (2001) 47 *McGill Law Journal* 97, 114.

between effectiveness and plain language, effectiveness always wins or at least effectiveness should always be promoted. For example, in jurisdictions where the term 'shall' is used as a matter of practice, unilaterally departing from it in a single piece of legislation creates the legitimate impression that the drafter may not need to bind the users with the obligations introduced: otherwise, they would have used 'shall', right?

Common Problems of Legislative Texts

Long Sentences

Traditionally legal language is long-winded. Tiersma offers exceptional empirical evidence:

> One prominent feature of legal style is very long sentence. Bentham noted that lawyers favoured 'longwindedness' and suggested that 'the shorter the sentence the better'. His advice has been followed mainly in the breach. In the analysis of the British Courts Act of 1971, Marita Gustafsson found that the shortest sentence had 10 words and the longest had 179. Sentences in the Act had a mean length of 48 words. This contrasts to scientific prose, which according to one study had a mean length of 27.6 words, and dramatic texts, which in one corpus contained an average of only 7 words per sentence. Even lengthier sentences were found by Risto Hiltunen in his analysis of the first two parts of the British Road Traffic Act of 1972. Hiltunen calculated a mean sentence of length of 79.25; the shortest sentence had 7 words and the longest had 740. Similarly, in one set of jury instructions, the average sentence was 102 words long.[36]

Compare this with the US approach of no more than 30 words per sentence.[37]

Long sentences are not always problematic. In literature they create a rhythm that enhances the separate words' meanings.[38] But this is not the case with law. Long sentences in law inhibit comprehension of the text. There are several reasons for this: legal messages themselves are technical, already embedded in precedent and specialised meanings; the style of drafting is studied, evaluated and picked apart word by word, phrase by phrase; and the impact of any legal aspect of that story depends on accuracy, on believability, on the readers' clear understanding of the minute elements in the story.[39]

[36] See P Tiersma, *Legal Language* (Chicago, The University Chicago Press, 1999) 55–56.

[37] See Garner, 'Guidelines for Drafting and Editing Court Rules' (n 31) 187.

[38] See H Darmstadter, 'What's Wrong with Long Sentences?' (2002–03) 12 *Business Law Today* 36, 36.

[39] See T LeClercq, 'First Aid for Sentences, Part I: The Long Sentence' (1988) 51 *Texas Bar Journal* 814, 816.

The effect of long sentences in law is problematic. First, long sentences inevitably depart from the axiom of subject-verb-object,[40] or even the normalised if-then-else,[41] by inviting secondary sentences and other referents within the structure of the sentence. As a result they end up being long-winded thus preventing the reader from following the semantic flow of the communication sent by the drafter. Secondly, as a consequence of this, they invite syntactic ambiguity, a phenomenon directly linked to the existence of numerous referents within a sentence. And thirdly, with specific reference to the drafting of legislative texts they depart from the drafting convention of one meaning per legislative sentence.[42]

The question is, how long is a 'long' sentence. A clear-cut answer is of course impossible. For Tiersma length of the sentence is not even a good criterion for complexity: what is important really is how sentences are construed syntactically with regard to their information structure.[43] But it is generally accepted that the best sentences in English that are easier to comprehend are between 20 and 27 words long.[44] Anything longer is simply too long for the reader to retain fully and understand completely.

The true skill of the drafter is in the balance between the need to introduce single meaning short sentences following the subject-verb-object structure against the equally crucial link of offering the user guidance of the interrelation between meanings and sentences.[45] In that respect the grammatically incorrect but very effective '. And…' or '. But…' are incredibly useful. Alternatives to long sentences include repeating a key term such as the best antecedent of the pronoun; paraphrasing or summarising the antecedent of 'which'; changing dependent clauses to free modifiers; or dropping the 'which' plus its verb and turning the clause into an appositive.[46]

[40] See SE Rowe, '"Short and Sweet" Brings Clarity to Legal Writing' (2007) 68 *Oregon State Bar Bulletin* 11, 13.

[41] See P Ziegler, 'The Status of Normalized Drafting: the Need for Theory Building and Empirical Verification' (1989) 27 *Osgoode Hall Law Journal* 337, 341, fn 13.

[42] See F Bennion, *Statute Law* (London, Oyez Longman, 1983) 48; also see Renton Committee, *The Preparation of Legislation* (London, HMSO, 1975) 150; and GC Thornton, *Legislative Drafting* (London, Butterworths, 1987) 61.

[43] 'Sentences where the linear flow of information is repeatedly interrupted are likely to be more difficult to process than those where such interruptions are removed by opting for alternative syntactic arrangements. However, due to the independent status of sentence in statutory texts, alternative arrangements may not be available, and the result will often be a compromise between an ideal syntactic formulation and the desired information structure of a sentence'. See P Tiersma and L Solan, *The Oxford Handbook of Language and Law* (Oxford, Oxford University Press, 2012) 41–42.

[44] See N Lawler Dickhute, 'From Love Letters To Contracts, Punctuation Matters' (2002) *The Nebraska Lawyer* 32, 34.

[45] See GA Pennisi, 'All-inclusiveness in Legal Language. Cross-cultural Perspectives in Specialized Discourse' (2008) 14 *Studi e Ricerche di Scienze Politiche della Università degli Studi di Palermo*.

[46] See E Grodzins Romm, 'The Wicked Which of Long Sentences' (1985) 71 *American Bar Association Journal* 144, 144.

Passive Voice

Passive voice is often used as a means of introducing a message in a mellow, not direct, and therefore non accusatorial manner. For example, 'you have not paid your bill' is rather more aggressive than 'the bill has not been paid'. But legislation is not supposed to be mellow, kind, or polite: legislation is there to convey an authoritative command. And so passive voice has little place in the legislative ethos.

But it's not just a matter of ethos. Passive voice is a rather unforgiving device, as it urges the drafter to ignore the question 'who'.[47] Who is it that undertakes the action foreseen? And this promotes the erroneous idea that legislation is always addressed to 'a person' or 'anyone who'.[48] This cannot be further from the truth, and the practice—common as it is—results in over-regulating by failing to specify the circle of subjects that fall within the field of application of the text. And this can also impose obligations beyond the policy foreseen. For example 'a person who' may apply to a general criminal offence but would be absolutely inappropriate in the case of the imposition of an obligation to medically intervene to save a life: in that case 'doctors' or 'medical professionals' or 'doctors or nurses' would be the precise appropriate term. It is exactly this kind of concern that makes the use of passive voice as a gender-neutral drafting technique a rather unpopular choice: between gender-neutral language and clarity, clarity prevails.

Wordiness, ambiguity and monotony: the pitfalls of passive voice.[49] Moreover, passive voice leads to activism in statutory interpretation: the courts take it upon themselves to complete the legislative provision with details normally provided for by the use of active voice.[50] Yet, passive voice may have advantages at times. It can allow the drafter to place a long string of nouns at the end of a sentence, so that your reader does not wait too long for the verb of the sentence. For example,

> [t]he application is submitted by the prosecuting attorney of the county in which the offence was committed, or by the parole board, or by the chief executive officer of the facility or by the sheriff of the county from which the person escaped.

Of course, in such circumstances it is important for the drafter to remember the need to assign the duty of permission clearly either in the passive sen-

[47] See CM Kuzara, 'Plain English in Legislative Drafting' (1983) 62 *Michigan Bar Journal* 980, 981.

[48] See RJ Martineau, *Drafting Legislation and Rules in Plain English* (St Paul, MN, West, 1991) 68, 75.

[49] See KJ Sneddon and D Hricik, 'Pondering Passive Voice' (2008–09) 14 *Georgia Bar Journal* 72, 72.

[50] See AS Krishnakumar, 'Passive-Voice References in Statutory Interpretation' (2010–11) 76 *Brooklyn Law Review* 941, 950.

tence or in one of the sentences nearby. If the passive voice does not solve these specific problems, it should not be used.[51] Moreover, passive voice is helpful when the object, rather than the subject, is of substance for the meaning. Or when the drafter prefers to avoid assigning responsibility.[52] But this would constitute a case of intended vagueness as a form of political compromise rather than a purely drafting decision.

Weak Verbs and Nominalisations

The term 'weak verb' reflects verbs that do not denote an action, and are placed in a sentence alongside a noun that conveys an action indirectly.[53] For example 'hold a discussion' or worse 'a discussion is held' as opposed to 'discuss'.

The problem with weak verbs, apart from being superfluous, is that they fail to convey clearly the action, and the subject of that action.[54] 'Before making a decision, the Commissioner holds a discussion' is nowhere near as clear or direct as 'Before the Commissioner decides, they must discuss the issue with' The second option explains clearly who decides, who starts a discussion and invites the drafter to think about and foresee further details such as what it is that the Commissioner discusses and with whom. When combined with passive voice, a weak verb can be rather dangerous. 'A discussion must be held before the decision is made' fails to state who decides and who discusses, what and how.

A nominalisation is a type of abstract noun. In other words, it is the name of something that isn't a physical object but a process, technique or emotion. Nominalisations are formed from verbs: completion, introduction, failure, arrangement.[55] Nominalisations escort weak verbs, and thus they constitute part of the 'weak verb' phenomenon and they carry their share of the disease. And so nominalisations are often used instead of the verbs that they come from. And because they are merely the names of things, they sound as if nothing is actually happening in the sentence. Moreover, the use of nominalisations instead of base verbs invites surplus words 'to swarm like gnats'.[56]

[51] See Maine Manual on Legislative Drafting, ch 1, s 7http://www.maine.gov/legis/ros/manual/Draftman2009.pdf.

[52] See SE Rowe, 'Subjects, Verbs, Complete Sentences and Active Voice: Back to Basics' (2010–11) 71 *Oregon State Bar Bulleting* 13, 16.

[53] See GH Hathaway, 'Plain Language in Laws' (1999) 78 *Michigan Bar Journal* 582, 584.

[54] Drafters must use 'base' rather than 'weak' verbs for strong sentences: see F Georgann Wing, 'Where's the Verb?' (1989) 68 *Michigan Bar Journal* 150, 150.

[55] See JM Williams, 'An Excerpt from Style: Toward Clarity and Grace (Part Two)' (1992) 71 *Michigan Bar Journal* 196, 197.

[56] See RC Wydick, *Plain English for Lawyers* (Durham, NC, Carolina Academic Press, 2002) 25.

Superfluous Words

Since the reader's attention is at its prime with a short sentence of no more than 15 and 20 words, the choice of words used in it must be made with extreme caution. Weeding out words that are unnecessary for the meaning of the sentence is a task that allows the drafter to convey the message fully and without distractions.[57]

That it is the benign disease brought by superfluous words. The cancerous disease brought by superfluous words is over-precision, over-drafting, over-regulation and gold-plating. The more the drafter speaks, the more the legislation foresees: and this is problematic if it is not intended. But equally, over-precision carries an inherent risk of under-regulation and under-drafting: by attempting to foresee all possible cases falling within the term or sentence, the drafter may inadvertently exclude a case by forgetting or ignoring it either as a result of an error or as a result of the quite acceptable inability to foresee all possible circumstances at the time of drafting or in the future.

Legal or other Professional Jargon

Here the problem is the use of words that have a specialist meaning in a professional circle. Provisos are an example of legalese.[58] If the legislation is addressed exclusively or primarily to the members of that closed circle, then the use of jargon is not only expected but may well promote clarity as a plain language equivalent can be confusing to the users of that text. For example, attempting to replace the term 'mortgage' with 'a loan for the purchase of a home' would be counterproductive in a Bank of England text setting the rate of interest for banking and credit institutions: the users expect the Bank of England to use the term 'mortgage' and so the plain language equivalent refers them to interpret the plain language term as something other than a 'mortgage'.

But the problem with this simplified approach is that even specialist legislation is read by, even if not directly addressed to, lay users. And so maintaining the balance of plain but specialist language is a heavy burden for the drafter. Here the introduction of a plain language equivalent can be undertaken along with a definition correlating the two terms for the benefit of lay users who would find the plain term accessible, for the benefit of professionals who will enjoy the correlation, and for the benefit of lawyers and

[57] See RJ Martineau and MB Salerno, *Legal, Legislative and Rule Drafting in Plain English* (St Paul, MN, Thomson West, 2005) 53.

[58] See S Yuen-Ching Fung, 'The Rise and Fall of the Proviso' (1997) 18 *Statute Law Review* 104.

judges who would now be able to carry any interpretation of the previous term to the new plain language option.

Numerous Defined Terms

Just as over-drafting carries dangers of over-precision but also of exclusion of cases intended to be included in the provision, over-defining carries a risk of over- or under-regulation.[59]

But at the same time defining common terms or terms well understood by reference to previously passed legislation carries a risk of conflict within the statute book: the same term is defined in more than one statute and the definitions may not coincide. This leads to an unintended and non-conscious implied repeal of the pre-existing definition. This the courts and the users legitimately try to avert by attempting to interpret the two concepts in a manner that allows them to remain within the statute book: this is legislation by judges rather than the legislature, and legislation interpreted not for the purpose of putting the desired policy into effect accurately but for the purpose of compromising the two competing provisions. This may lead to ineffectiveness of the text, or, at least, to haphazard effectiveness by sheer luck.

Abstract Words

Abstract words invite vagueness, ambiguity or a combination of both. The result is a lack of clarity, precision and unambiguity. And this is a recipe for ineffectiveness of the text leading to its inability to convey the policy/regulatory message fully.

Unreadable Design and Layout

One cannot ignore the contribution of design and layout for the production of a plain language text, legislative or other.[60] Design allows the user to follow the thread of thought, the 'story' conveyed by the drafter. And this allows the user access to the underlying policy, the legislative choices made, and the rationale behind the text. This offers them the ability to read and interpret the text in context, thus making accessibility easier and more secure.

[59] See W Schiess, 'What Plain English Really Is' (2003–04) 9 *Scribes Journal of Legal Writing* 43, 73.

[60] See DC Elliott, 'A Model Plain-Language Act' (1992) 3 *Scribes Journal of Legal Writing* 51, 51.

A logical structure[61] is enhanced by the use of lists where appropriate. They are excellent for splitting information up. There are two main types of list: either a continuous sentence with several listed points picked out at the beginning, middle or end, known as 'sandwiches'; or a list of separate points.

Layout is equally crucial, as it offers the user the opportunity to focus on the main message, to understand key words and to feel invited to read the text.

Best Practices for an Easy Communication: Plain Language Innovations

Many a drafting convention stems from a clarity concern and a plain language ethos. But departures from established conventions as a means of promoting plain language are well worth noting here.

Present Tense over 'Will' and 'Shall'

The use of the present tense in legislation is a plain language requirement. Its choice is linked to the drafter's response on when does the legislative text speak? Although when the actual drafting takes place, the provision refers to the time in the future when the law will be passed, and the reader will read the text, and perhaps an agency will be established, this is not relevant for the drafter's choice of tense. The text must speak to the user in the present, whenever that present may occur in the future. In other words, there are two relevant moment in time, first the moment when the text is drafted and second the moment in the future when the text is read and used. But the second moment, which is the only one relevant for the choice of tense, takes place within the user's present (albeit in the drafter's future). This schizophrenic time warp is a cause of the commonly erroneous use of the future tense in legislation. And it is problematic because it creates obvious ambiguity: if the text is drafted in the future tense, does it bind the user who is reading it right now?

And so drafters must use the present tense, unless of course they have a reason to select another tense. It is possible to use the past tense, where required. This would suggest a time relationship between a prerequisite fact and the provision. For example, 'If, having been convicted of a felony, an alien is found physically incapable of being deported within the time prescribed by section 402, the alien may'. But, more often than not, the meaning can be expressed by use of terms such as 'before...' or 'after...'. For

[61] See Legislation Advisory Committee, 'Guidelines on Process and Content of Legislation 2001 (Including the 2003 Supplement)' (Wellington, Ministry of Justice, May 2001, updated Sept 2003).

example, 'Succession takes place after the heir's eighteenth birthday'. And so, although the future tense is rarely appropriate in drafting legislation, it is sometimes necessary: but the temporal point of reference is the time at which the law is applied, not when it is written and not when it takes effect. In any case, 'shall' does not convey the future tense.

This is an established drafting convention, at least in principle. The innovation brought in by the plain language movement concerns the increasing use of the present tense in legislation as a means of conveying an obligation, a 'shall' of the past.[62] For example, instead of stating that 'The Commissioner shall consult…' the drafter can simply state 'The Commission consults'. This is not an expression with great acceptance in the drafting world. Objections mainly refer to the need for the drafter to state the obligation in the provision. But is it really necessary? Legislation is compulsory, it introduces commands that must be complied with anyway.

The use of 'shall' other than as an expression of a concrete obligation—in which case it must be substituted by 'must'—is therefore superfluous.[63] And not just that: it creates the legitimate impression that where 'shall' is not used, the provision in not binding. One can only dread the time when the bindingness of a statute becomes a point of discussion, doubt or debate. Moreover, the inherent ambiguity of 'shall' would lead any open-minded drafter to the conclusion that the present tense as its plain language equivalent is a far better choice. With one caveat: as is the case with any unilateral departure from a drafting convention, the transfer from the dreaded 'shall' to the desirable, innovative and plain language present tense must be done consciously and in a manner offering the text predictability, for example with a clear, well published memorandum of the drafting office. The transfer may be burdensome in the beginning, and will inevitably invoke criticism from the traditionalist drafting and legal community, but it is certainly a project worth undertaking. Lay persons are not aware of the legal meaning of the term, whilst lawyers and judges are very much aware of the compulsory nature of legislation. Superfluous words distract the reader from the essence of the message, whist ambiguous words lead to lack of clarity. Why take that chance with a word that can be classified as both superfluous and ambiguous?

Positive Style

A drafting practice, still prevalent in most of Africa but thankfully increasingly rare in Europe, involves the use of the negative style of expression. For example, 'If a member does not send their payment by

[62] See L Dodova, 'A Translator Looks at English Law' (1989) 10 *Statute Law Review* 69, 77.

[63] See MM Asprey, 'Shall Must Go' (1992) 3 *Scribes Journal of Legal Writing* 79, 82.

the end of the month, the Board does not renew their membership of the scheme'. Or 'Persons other than the primary beneficiary may not receive these dividends'.

The problem here is that the negative style of expression complicates the sentence unnecessarily. It is much clearer to say 'Membership is renewed upon payment of membership fees before the end of each calendar month'. Or 'Only the primary beneficiary may receive these dividends'. And a double negative does not necessarily mean a positive. To quote from Sir Geoffrey Bowman: 'The appeal may proceed only if the tribunal has not certified that the appeal is not validly made' is not the same as 'The appeal may proceed only if the tribunal has certified that the appeal is validly made'.[64]

THE DEBATE: CONCERNS WITH PLAIN LANGUAGE

Concern 1: Plain Language Lowers the Standards of Good Writing

This concern stems from the view that plain language consists of monosyllabic words, very short sentences and a complete rejection of complex words or sentence construction. If this were true of plain language, then the criticism could be valid. It would certainly not be useful to draft statutes and legal documents in simplistic monosyllabic words. However, as other commentators have pointed out, this is to misunderstand plain language. As the Law Reform Commission of Victoria notes:

> Plain English involves the use of plain, straightforward language which avoids defects and conveys its meaning as clearly and as simply as possible[65], without unnecessary pretension or embellishment. It is to be contrasted with convoluted, repetitive and prolix language. The adoption of a plain English style demands simply that a document be written in a style which readily conveys its message to its audience.[66]

But, would it really be detrimental, if plain language did lower the standards of good writing? Is it that crucial for legislation to be drafted in an elegant and grammatically correct style? At the end of the day, language is simply a tool serving clarity and in turn effectiveness. More often than not, grammatical correctness enhances predictability of the text, thus promoting a common understanding of the concept as communicated and received. In that sense grammar is an ally for the drafter. However, given the choice

[64] See G Bowman, 'The Art of Legislative Drafting' (2005) 7 *European Journal of Law Reform* 3, 12.

[65] See Hon Mr Justice Nazareth, 'Legislative Drafting: Could our Statutes be Simpler?' (1987) 8 *Statute Law Review* 81, 92.

[66] See Law Reform Commission of Victoria, *Plain English and the Law* (1987) 39.

between grammatical correctness or elegance of style and clarity, then clarity is the obvious choice. Just as plain language and gender-neutral language are mere tools informing clarity, and thus when they clash clarity prevails, a clash between grammar and clarity can only be resolved with clarity as a clear winner. For example, the singular plural for gender neutrality.

Concern 2: Intelligibility

Plain language is often accused as an instigator of intelligibility for the lawyers and judges. Indeed, plain language seeks to depart from legalese and legal jargon, thus ambushing the torturously trained lawyer or judge with plain language equivalents. Legalese is wordy, unclear, pompous and dull;[67] it is overblown yet timid, homogeneous and swaddled in obscurity.[68] Most lawyers and judges would expect the term 'terminate' for a contract, and would cringe at 'end' as the plain language equivalent. There is little doubt that plain language requires that lawyers and judges, and indeed drafters, un-train from the incestuous language used in the closed legal circles[69] and return to the innocence of their years before law school. Unless they manage to do so, lawyers and judges may find the plain language text intelligible indeed. But whom should the legislative text speak to? To lawyers and judges? To lay persons? Or both, and then some?

Answering the question in not simple. Bennion believes that communicating the law to lawyers is vital. 'Unless they are clear about the nature and characteristics of legislative texts, there is not much chance that anyone else will be'.

> It may be positively dangerous to encourage non-lawyers to think they can understand legal texts unaided by expert advice ... [I]t takes a lawyer to know whether simple words in what should be a technical text really carry their apparent simple meaning.[70]

There is little doubt that lawyers and judges are vital users of legislation, and that the text must be clearly understood by them: after all, not only are they heavy users of the legislation, but they are called to interpret and apply it in the most complex of situations. But their needs must be balanced by the needs of the two other groups of users brought to light by the Good Law Initiative: lay persons and non-lawyer professionals. The legislation must speak to them, equally loud and clear as to lawyers and judges. And people choose to read and to keep reading 'only when they believe there

[67] See D Mellinkoff, *The Language of the Law* (Boston, Little, Brown & Co, 1963) 24.
[68] See L Friedman, 'How I Write' (1993) 4 *Scribes Journal of Legal Writing* 3, 5.
[69] See Lord Radcliffe, 'Some Reflections on Law and Lawyers' (1950) 10 *Cambridge Law Journal* 361, 368.
[70] See F Bennion, 'Don't Put the Law into Public Hands' *The Times* (London, 24 Jan 1995).

will be some benefit in doing so and only when they cannot get the same information in easier ways.'[71]

Balancing the pitch of the text for such diverse categories of persons with such extreme diversity of legal sophistication is very difficult indeed. If one had to compromise with a single text, then the balance would tilt towards lay users on the sole basis that non-lawyer professionals, and much more so lawyers and judges, possess the skills and training to understand a wider range of legislative expressions: it is easier for a lawyer or judge to understand a plain language text that for a lay person to understand legalese. The question of course is whether we actually have to compromise in a single style in a unique text, or whether the layered approach can offer the drafter the incredible possibility of communicating to each group the type of message useful to them, in the style of language that they are more comfortable with.

Of course, the layered approach, and indeed plain language in general, presupposes an agreement that the law must speak to non-lawyers too. In other words, the basis of plain language is that law must not be preserved for lawyers and that drafters must encourage non-lawyers to read the legislative text themselves in the hope that they can understand and apply it without necessarily resorting to a lawyer or judge. Reserving the legislation for the legal professions denies lay users access to the regulation expressed by the legislative text; as a result it is a violation of the rule of law. And so the solution to the problem is not to preserve the legislation for the skilled members of the legal profession, but to express the legislation in plain language thus making it accessible to as many users as possible.[72]

Concern 3: Plain Language Can only be Achieved if Certainty is Sacrificed

Plain language is often scorned for its clash with certainty. One of the major concerns attached to the adoption of a policy of plain language, is that drafting legal documents and particularly legislation in this style may lead to a loss of precision and certainty.[73] Gowers expresses this concern as follows:

> Legal drafting must therefore be unambiguous, precise, comprehensive and largely conventional. If it is readily intelligible, so much the better; but it is by

[71] See KA Schriver, *Dynamics in Document Design: Creating Text for Readers* (New York, John Wiley and Sons, 1997) 166.

[72] See Sir W Dale, *Legislative Drafting: A New Approach* (London, Butterworths, 1977) 331.

[73] See ML Turnbull, 'Problems of Legislative Drafting' (1986) 7 *Statute Law Review* 67; and Comment, 'Drafting Laws in Plain English, Can the Drafter Win' (1988) *New Zealand Law Journal* 25, 26.

> far more important that it should yield its meaning accurately than that it should yield it on the first reading[74]

It would be difficult to argue against Gowers' arguments convincingly. Effectiveness of legislation requires understanding and this is achievable irrespective of how many times one has to read the legislative text. But plain language is not really about first readings: this has been used as an expression conveying ease of communication. Plain language is not in conflict with precision as part of clarity, plain language promotes clarity and precision as its tool.

But it is true that the purposes of legislation are most likely to be achieved by a drafter who is ardently concerned to be intelligible. Intelligibility promotes easy communication and is therefore directly linked with the plain language movement. Far from resulting to intelligibility, plain language supports it as one of its main virtues.[75] But can this produce the opposite effect?

> The obligation to be intelligible, to convey the intended meaning so that it is comprehensible and easily understood by the affected parties, is best satisfied by writing with simplicity and precision… A law which is drafted in precise but not simple terms may, on account of its incomprehensibility, fail to achieve the result intended. The blind pursuit of precision will inevitably lead to complexity; and the complexity is a definite step along the way to obscurity.[76]

And so the irony is that in striving for precision at the expense of all other goals, and especially at the expense of clarity, precision is lost. This irony has led Lord Campbell of Alloway to go as far as state that: 'We should abandon that vain search for certainty in a statute, the cause of unintelligible and complex drafting which itself gives rise to uncertainty.'[77] This is a rather dramatic statement, but it is one that reflects the prioritisation of clarity above precision, which forms part of, and certainly above intelligibility. This leads to the conclusion that, when in clash with clarity, intelligibility and plain language must bow down. This is in accordance with the pyramid of drafting virtues: plain language and gender-neutral language lie below clarity, precision, and unambiguity. The latter are informed by the former and the former support the latter. Normally, plain language is on the same page with clarity, precision and unambiguity. In the extraordinary cases where they may clash, there is no doubt that clarity, precision and unambiguity prevail. And this is the only secure route to effectiveness. If one keeps effectiveness as the main and prevalent pursuit of legislative texts,

[74] See E Gowers, *The Complete Plain Words* (UK, HMSO, 1986) 7.
[75] See D Kelly, 'Legislative Drafting and Plain English' (1985–86) 10 *Adelaide Law Review* 409, 425.
[76] See Thornton, *Legislative Drafting* (n 42) 49.
[77] See Lord Campbell of Alloway, 'Law in Plain Language' (1983) *Law Society's Gazette* 621.

then the alleged clash is a non-issue: effectiveness requires clarity, precision and unambiguity at all costs, even when the drafter must sacrifice plain language and gender-neutral language to get to clarity, precision and unambiguity. And, although clashes should not occur, they tend to, especially with reference to traditional terms with an established meaning.

Concern 4: Plain Language Leads to a Loss of Established Meanings of Words Settled over Centuries of Judicial Interpretation

So, what prevails when the drafter is faced with a well-established archaic term within a plain language legislative document? The answer is quite clear, based on the argumentation of the previous drafting concern. When in conflict with clarity, precision and unambiguity, plain language bows down. Plain language advocates accept that there are certain phrases that have in fact attained this status. There is a small area of relative precision in the language of the law but they point out that the extent of this area of precision can be grossly overestimated.[78] Much of what are considered terms of art are only meaningless jargon.[79]

The question is when should established terms be retained and when is it time to replace them with a plain language alternative? This is a classic drafting dilemma, and—within the realm of phronetic legislative drafting—it a decision that is taken by the drafter on an 'ad hoc' (forgive me, 'on an individual basis'). Criteria for that decision are ease of communication, and the audience identified by the drafter: 'on an individual basis' is indeed an easier expression but the learned drafters and academics whom I expect (hope and pray) to read this book are perfectly able to comprehend the term 'ad hoc'. And so 'ad hoc' seems a more appropriate term as it carries with it a meaning long established in academic and professional writing. The same logic applies to the drafting of legislation. The added concern is that legislation will inevitably be read by a large audience, which inevitably includes lay persons. And so the demand for plain language is higher and therefore more pronounced. In rules of evidence the term 'ad hoc' could be forgiven but in criminal or individual tax statutes plain language equivalents must be preferred.

There is an added complication with reference to legislation amending an existing statute that includes archaic terms. What is the way forward here? Is effectiveness pursued by means of replacing all archaic terms, irrespective of where in the text they occur? Or is a surgical intervention limited to the

[78] See B Barr et al, 'Legalese and the Myth of Case Precedent' (1984) 64 *Michigan Bar Journal* 1136, 1137; also see S Johanson, 'In Defence of Plain Language' (1992) 3 *Scribes Journal of Legal Writing* 37, 39.

[79] See J Kimble, 'A Plain English Primer' (1987) 33 *The Practical Lawyer* 83, 86.

amendments required by the policy clients a better route to effectiveness? For a drafter a surgical intervention is preferred:[80] the lesser the bleed of the live organism that constitutes the legal system, the smoother the transition to the new legal status, and the more effective the legislative text. This would lead drafters to remain within the very strict drafting instructions related to the point of law reform introduced by means of amending the text, without expanding towards a modernisation of the terms used in the statute.[81] And this is a gallant approach. However, when the archaic terms used render the statute foreign to the reader and therefore challenge its effectiveness, terms need to be changed irrespective of how established they can be in law.[82] A classic example is the replacement of 'bastard children' with 'children born outside marriage': the archaic term challenged the modern user's level of tolerance and alienated the user and those to whom the law applied; established or not, such terms need to be replaced by a plain language term at any given opportunity. The Australian Interpretation Act 1987 facilitates this replacement of archaic terms with modern equivalents in section 15 AC, which expressly equates previous archaic terms with modern terms in amending legislation as long as they reflect the same concept. Following the Australian example would go a long way towards the practical application of plain language in existing legislation, via the opportunity of amendments.

THE WAY FORWARD

Plain language has revolutionised legislative drafting by turning drafters' attention to the wider legislative, as opposed to the restricted legal, audience. The question of whether legislation can and must be used by lay persons has become rather esoteric: legislation is and must remain accessible in application of the rule of law. Publication of legislation[83] is not adequate to guarantee its accessibility in application of the rule of law: statutes must be as approachable to the user as possible. And hiding behind the archaic notion that legislation can be accessible solely by means of extra-legislation explanatory materials[84] is equally unacceptable: the rule of law does not refer to accessibility of non-legislative texts but to accessibility of

[80] See Turnbull, 'Problems of Legislative Drafting' (n 73).

[81] See J Erasmus, 'Plain Language Drafting Meets Interpretative Principles and Rules: a Drafter's Perspective' (Conference of the Canadian Institute for the Administration of Justice, Ottawa, 9–10 Nov 1988).

[82] See P Butt, 'Modern Legal Drafting' (2002) 23 *Statute Law Review* 12, 15.

[83] Publication is currently the means of offering accessibility: see T Scassa, 'The Best Things in Law Are Free? Towards Quality Free Public Access to Primary Legal Materials in Canada' (2000) 23 *Dalhousie Law Journal 301*.

[84] See eg Bennion, 'Don't Put the Law into Public Hands' (n 70).

the legislative texts themselves. If this weren't the case, why is it that the legislative texts themselves are available freely online anyway? Helpful as they are, explanatory materials cannot and should not be used as a carte blanche for legislative convolution and complexity.

Plain language requires ease of communication and identification of the specific circle of users of the precise legislative text. Ease of communication is a much wider term than simply a choice of words. It requires accessibility of words, sentences, the whole text, its design, its layout and the statute book as a whole. As a result, plain language has a role to play in all aspects of legislative drafting, and even beyond that as it spreads onto policy formulation and the determination of the preferred policy and legislative solution.

However potent, plain language is a mere tool for clarity, precision and unambiguity. It is there to serve these three superior values of legislative drafting, and bows down when in conflict with either one of them. Effectiveness is served by plain language in principle, but when there is a friction, effectiveness is the ultimate goal.

So let us now explore how plain language is applied in drafting, starting with preliminary provisions.

7

Preliminary Provisions

IT IS NOW time to begin exploring in further detail the fourth of Thornton's stages of legislative drafting, namely the composition and development of the draft. Structure is the first consideration for the drafter who, having painstakingly completed the stages of analysis, understanding and design of the legislative text, is now finally[1] holding a pen in hand or perhaps pressing a button on their computer.

The structure of legislative texts is not just a matter of logical[2] or conceptual division of the legislative text. Concerns of plain language, in the broader sense, also come into play. Structure is a forum that can greatly enhance the approachability of legislation. Having discussed structure in general, and having analysed the suggestions for a layered approach, it is time to decide what type of provisions are to be included in the beginning of the text as preliminary provisions. Currently, structure is left to the parliamentary procedure[3] and the drafting tradition of each jurisdiction. There is a perfectly good reason why this is so: much of preliminary provisions entail archaic expressions reflecting the constitutional requirements for the classification of the text as legislation. And so a degree of sanctity or nostalgic adherence to tradition is not only understandable, but also highly desirable: it offers the text the seal of formality required to draw the users' attention to the gravitas of the text, and it reminds users of the long traditions of polity in the jurisdiction. Perhaps because of this, little debate is currently taking place on the placement of legislative provisions within the text: drafters simply use the traditional structure as the unquestionable format of each new legislative text.

Commendable as consistency may be, even for the approachability of the legislation by lay users, it is now time for drafters to consider carefully what needs to be placed in each part of an Act, and what can be either deleted or transferred towards the bottom of the text. The placement of provisions within the text must be reviewed on the basis of the most appropriate

[1] On the lengthy process before this actually happens, see R Dickerson, 'How to Write a Law' (1974) 1 *Notre Dame Journal of Legislation* 3, 4.

[2] See A Watson-Brown, 'The Classification and Arrangement of the Elements of Legislation' (1997) 18 *Statute Law Review* 32, 44–45.

[3] See FAR Bennion, 'Statute Law Obscurity and the Drafting Parameters' (1978) 5 *British Journal of Law and Society* 235, 238.

reflection of the prioritisation of messages sent to the user. And the need to use the valuable short attention span of the users for the purposes of passing on the main regulatory message needs to be recognised as a priority, or at least as a factor balancing consistency via respect to drafting traditions.

THE STRUCTURE OF AN ACT

Provisions are classified as preliminary, substantive, or final, with various sub-classifications available. Preliminary provisions can—but do not always—include the following types of provisions:

Preliminary provisions

1. Long title
2. Preamble (if a preamble is necessary)
3. Enacting clause
4. Short title (some jurisdictions only use a short title)
5. Commencement
6. Duration/Expiry
7. Application
8. Purpose clause
9. Definitions
10. Interpretation

The first point of note here is the length of this list. There simply are too many types of preliminary provisions to sustain the users' attention until, finally, the main message can be offered to them. As a result, legislative texts become user unfriendly and, perhaps most importantly, ineffective since they are less likely to be read all the way through to the main regulatory message buried somewhere in substantive provisions. And so the plain language's ease of communication task can only be fulfilled, if the main regulatory message is allowed to hit the user as close to the beginning of the text as possible. There is a lot to learn from advertising: the main message hits quickly; and then details follow. This can be achieved by the layered approach, but only partly: the layered approach refers to substantive provisions mainly, but the basic problem here is preliminary provisions. Let's examine each of the possible types of preliminary provisions to assess if they can remain where they are, or whether they can either be terminated or moved further down the text. Those remaining will be analysed in this chapter, and those moved will be explored in the chapter on final provisions.

PRELIMINARY PROVISIONS: A PLAIN LANGUAGE APPROACH

A plain language approach to preliminary provisions would direct the drafter to strip the text of unnecessary details at the very top, thus allowing them to have their full attention focused on the main regulatory message.

Currently legislation starts with a long title, which, when drafted properly, reflects the main mechanisms of law reform. Sir William Dale describes the role of the long title in the legislative text as a 'description of the contents of the Act'.[4] It does so in order to 'serve for the statute the purpose of words of introduction to strangers'.[5] The advantage of the long title, and perhaps its original task, was to offer the reader enough details to assess whether they need to read further. There is little doubt that the goal is quite worthwhile, and that this type of information is helpful to the reader, and thus deserves its place in a plain language Act. But there is equally little doubt that, in practice, long titles have ended up being vague and verbose. In their effort to avoid paraphrasing the main text, whilst covering all the main messages, drafters have entrapped, or trapped, themselves in the impossible task of telling the reader what is changing with the law without revealing the true message whose place is within the text. There are three possible answers to this inherent problem. The long title, as drafted currently, has become redundant. It furnishes the reader with archaically expressed non-data. 'Acts are invariably referred to not by their long title, but by their short title, and the remaining function of the long title appears to be to explain the general purpose of the Act'.[6] This makes the long title 'an unnecessary burden' for the user.[7] And so the long title in its current form can go.[8]

But is it the concept that must go, or the current application of it? Having a short description of the main point of law reform in a concrete list of affirmative and precise statements about what it is that the law does, without the horribly vague and superfluous '..., and connected purposes', remains a very attractive idea that serves the plain language approach very well. And so a concretely drafted long title can stay. So the first answer to the problem is to draft long titles appropriately, and leave them in the text. The second answer is to replace long titles with an introductory text that details the main points of legislation in the same manner as in the first answer. So this option involves renaming the long title, since the term confuses users in that it is not a title at all. And to draft the new 'introductory text' appropriately. The third answer takes into account the layered approach and the start of the text with the main regulatory messages for group one users, lay users.[9] If the layered approach is applied in drafting, the long

[4] See Sir W Dale, 'Legislative Drafting: A New Approach—Reviewing the Reviewers' (1981) *Statute Law Review* 69, 74.

[5] See PM Bakshi, *An Introduction to Legislative Drafting* (Mumbai, Tripathi Private Ltd, 1972) 15.

[6] See New Zealand Law Commission, *The Format of Legislation* (NZLC R27, 1993) 9.

[7] See DL Kennedy, 'Legislative Bill Drafting' (1946–47) 31 *Minnesota Law Review* 103, 109.

[8] See contra F Bennion, 'If It's Not Broke Don't Fix It: A Review of the New Zealand Law Commission's Proposals on the Format of Legislation' (1994) 15 *Statute Law Review* 163, 167.

[9] See further chapter 4.

title becomes redundant, irrespective of what it is named. And this is an advantage of the layered approach. For the purposes of this book, the second option is followed simply because the layered approach remains an academic concept, for now.

The preamble serves the drafter in offering them a place for statements of policy or intent,[10] of the necessity of the legislation, or of its legal basis, or of adherence to the constitutional procedural requirements detailed there. The role of preambles is to justify the enacting provisions.[11] Preambles have become largely redundant:[12] statements of policy or government intent are no longer forgiven in non-ceremonial legislation.[13] As Driedger stated: 'It is not the function of a draftsman either to originate or determine legislative policy'.[14]

Let's look at the types of provisions traditionally reserved for the preamble: they are now accommodated elsewhere. So, where necessary, policy issues can be explored in purpose clauses.[15] The justification of the necessity of legislation is addressed at the pre-drafting level, and need only be addressed within the law in the context of a federal construction where subsidiarity is a concern. The determination of the legal basis of legislation has no place in the text in jurisdictions with a long-established polity where frictions of competence are largely resolved. And similarly, a confirmation of adherence with the procedural requirements for a legitimate act is not needed within the context of long-established polity stability. In any case this is an issue covered by the enactment clause. As a result, preambles are rarely used in Europe and most of the Commonwealth.[16] And this is quite right: preambles have no place in modern legislative texts. Not only are they redundant, but they invite ambiguity: first, the legal value and bindingness of preambles remains a contentious issue,[17] and second, the risk of judicial activism via interpretation of provisions through the prism of the vague preamble sections is too enhanced. Bellis rings the bell of danger from preambles that are misused by law-makers, who insert elements other than

[10] See JO Frosini, 'Constitutional Preambles at the Crossroads between Policy and Law' (2013) 11 *International Journal of Constitutional Law* 813.

[11] See J-C Piris, 'Sir William Dale Annual Memorial Lecture—The Legal Orders of the European Union and of the Member States: Peculiarities and Influences in Drafting' (2004) 6 *European Journal of Law Reform* 1, 8.

[12] See Uniform Law Conference of Canada, 'Drafting Conventions' (1989) III; for an analysis of the Convention, see PE Johnson, 'Legislative Drafting Practices and Other Factors Affecting the Clarity of Canada's Laws' (1991) 12 *Statute Law Review* 1, 3.

[13] See *Report of the Renton Committee on the Preparation of Legislation* (Cmnd 1975, 6033) para 11.7.

[14] See EA Driedger, 'The Preparation of Legislation' (1953) 31 *Canadian Bar Review* 33, 36.

[15] See DJ Owens, 'A Handbook on Research and Drafting in Legislation' (1974) 1 *Notre Dame Journal of Legislation* 1, 21.

[16] See RC Bergeron, *Règles de Rédaction Législative* (Kiev, Ministry of Justice, 1999) 5.

[17] See O Duhamel, 'Igniting the Spirits' (2005) 1 *European Constitutional Law Review* 12.

a statement of reasons, so that preambles become 'almost a third kind of law-making'.[18]

But preambles continue to have a place in special legislation where legitimacy is indeed a concern both for the user and the drafter.[19] This includes constitutions and constitutional instruments;[20] in regional[21] or international legislation and national implementing measures; in legislation of an historic or ceremonial character; in private Acts of Parliament;[22] in statutory instruments;[23] and in decrees of military regimes. And preambles still have a place in the drafting of legislation for newly established jurisdictions, where polity stability remains in the balance: in such a context, it remains necessary to reassure the user that this text is actually legitimate (constitutional) and therefore binding.

In the exceptional circumstances where a preamble is necessary, it is important to draft it clearly. Brevity and consistency within the preamble provisions and also between the preamble and the text are paramount for legislative quality.[24] Operative provisions must not find themselves in the preamble.[25]

> It is not as a general rule advisable to enunciate the principle of an Act in a preamble, as the opponents of the Act are sure to select it as a battle-ground instead of dividing on the actual provisions of the Act.[26]

Currently preambles begin with 'Whereas'. The term is not clear to the non-lawyer, because in common language 'whereas' introduces an antithesis. And so simple statements, drafted as concretely as possible, are more user friendly. It would also be helpful to the user if the preamble clarified

[18] See R Bellis, 'Implementation of EU Legislation—An Independent Study for the Foreign and Commonwealth Office' (London, FCO, 2003).

[19] See Editorial, 'Contextual Legislative Elements as Fomites' (2004) 25 *Statute Law Review* xiii, xiii.

[20] See L Orgad, 'The Preamble in Constitutional Interpretation' (2010) 8 *International Journal of Constitutional Law* 714.

[21] For an analysis of preambles and recitals in EU law, see T Klimas and J Vaitiukaite, 'The Law of Recitals in European Community Legislation' (2008–09) 15 *ILSA Journal of International and Comparative Law* 61.

[22] Here preambles 'set out the facts on which it is founded and the circumstances that make it necessary. If the objects of the bill could be attained otherwise than by legislation, the preamble must state why legislation is preferred. The allegations in the preamble have to be proved to the satisfaction of the committee appointed to consider the bill': see DAS Ward, 'The Preparation of Acts of Parliament' (1965–68) 1 *Otago Law Review* 294, 295

[23] See Editorial, '... and all of its Enabling Powers' (2006) 27 *Statute Law Review* iii.

[24] This is a problem is EU legislation: see H Xanthaki, 'The Problem of Quality in EU Legislation: What on Earth is Really Wrong?' (2001) 38 *Common Market Law Review* 651, 653.

[25] See AA Farnsworth, 'The Interpretation of International Contacts and the Use of Preambles' (2002) *International Business Law Journal* 271, 273.

[26] See *Practical Legislation* (1902) 93, quoted by F Bennion in *Statutory Interpretation: A Code* (London, Butterworths, 2002) 624.

whether it is part of the text, or whether it can be taken into account for the interpretation of the provisions of the main text.

The enacting clause is a declaration of the legislative authority's agreement to the text. It is necessary both because it makes the legislation what it is, but also because it engulfs the text with the formality necessary to draw the reader's attention to the message and to invite respect and compliance. All that is needed in law is the enacting clause and the signature; everything else can go.[27]

The short title is the name of the Act. It is 'a guide to legislative intention'.[28] Traditionally its importance brought it to the very start of the legislative text. But the short title appears at the top of the text anyway, so introducing it as a provision in a section is a legal concern, not a user concern. And its importance is not lost by the placement of the legal provisions at the end, since the user can read the title at the beginning. On that basis, the short title is better placed in the final provisions.[29]

Commencement provisions and duration or expiry provisions express the life cycle of the legislative text. They are necessary data for the user, as they explain when their action is required and for what period of time. And so their place is with the preliminary provisions, with a caveat that technical duration or expiry clauses can find their way into the final provisions.

Application provisions express the field of coverage of the legislation. If they introduce data necessary for the reader to understand whether their circumstances are regulated by the legislative text, then there is an argument for including them in preliminary provisions.[30] But this would be rather exceptional as it is the drafter's task to identify plain language terms for the field of application: these promote clarity of understanding without overprecision; and so defining further is not always necessary.

Purpose clauses have fallen from grace simply because declarations of general policy intent are not suitable for legislative texts. And so it would make sense to state that purpose clauses can be left out of preliminary provisions. But recently purpose clauses have been offered a new lease of life,[31] at least conceptually: they can be optimal vehicles for listing the concrete and tangible criteria by which the effectiveness of the legislation will be evaluated at the pre- and post-legislative stage. Instead of including general, often emotional, statements, such as 'This Act aims to finally put an end to the carnage of innocent people on our streets as a result of accidents

[27] See 'Editorial' (n 23) iv.

[28] See VRAC Crabbe, *Legislative Precedents—Volume II* (London, Cavendish Publishing Ltd, 1998) 5.

[29] See TY Chan, 'Changes in Form of New Zealand Statute' (1975–78) 8 *Victoria University of Wellington Law Review* 318, 337.

[30] See J Zurcher, 'Basic Rules of Legislative Drafting' (1976–77) 7 *Manitoba Law Journal* 131, 135.

[31] See D Greenberg, *Laying Down the Law* (London, Sweet and Maxwell, 2011) 260.

caused by drivers who are under the influence of alcohol', the drafter can state that 'This Act aims to reduce the number of car accidents caused by alcohol by 25 per cent over a period of five years'. This latter provision can be enhanced by a sunset clause stating that the life of the Act will be extended only if there is a positive post-legislative evaluation of the results produced.[32] The advantage of this structure is that it forces periodic post-legislative evaluation of the legislation, and most notably on the basis of the criteria introduced by the original drafting team. And the combination of this statutory obligation for evaluation with a sunset clause renders successful evaluation of the effectiveness of the legislation necessary. Otherwise, the ineffective legislative texts die away, and the statute book is automatically cleared of unnecessary or unsuccessful laws. Needless to say, that this requires a general government policy and cannot be undertaken unilaterally by a sole drafter.

Definitions and interpretation provisions are traditionally placed in preliminary provisions, although there is a clear trend towards transferring them to final provisions. There are three drafting choices: their placement in preliminary provisions;[33] their placement in final provisions; or the introduction of a short preliminary provision directing the reader to a Schedule of Definitions. There has been extensive debate as to which definitions are best suited for preliminary and which for final provisions. Ilbert divides definitions into substantial and non-substantial definitions: the former define the scope and subject matter of the measure, come at the beginning of the legislative text.[34] But the classification of a definition as substantive or not is a rather arbitrary exercise. And the division of definitions can be rather confusing to the user[35] who, having classified the definition sought differently from the drafter, has failed to discover the one sought at the location expected, and has got the wrong impression that this definition is not offered at all. Yet even the 2014 version of the Office of Parliamentary Counsel's Guidance to Drafting seems to divide definitions into four categories with variable places in the structure of the Act: definitions of major concepts without which the reader cannot understand what follows, and definitions adopted for the sake of drafting convenience are to be placed at the beginning. But definitions of words or expressions which will be understood in general terms, but where a degree of certainty or clarification is needed, and definitions making, for convenience, a minor adjustment of what a word or phrase would otherwise mean can usually be left to the

[32] See U Karpen, 'On the State of Legislation Studies in Europe' (2005) 7 *European Journal of Law Reform* 59, 66.

[33] See B Simamba, 'The Placing and Other Handling of Definitions' (2006) 27 *Statute Law Review* 73, 82.

[34] See Sir C Ilbert, *Legislative Methods and Forms* (Oxford, Clarendon Press, 1901) 281.

[35] See IML Turnbull, 'Clear Legislative Drafting: New Approaches in Australia' (1990) 11 *Statute Law Review* 11.

end.[36] It seems to make sense simply to direct the reader to a Schedule of Definitions, at least as a temporary measure addressing the discrepancy between user expectation and the new trend of placement of definitions at the end of the text.

And so preliminary provisions are to include only:

1. the introductory text (formerly known as the long title);
2. enacting clause;
3. start date (formerly known as commencement); and
4. application, but only where necessary for the user.

Let us examine each of these types of provisions in detail.

THE INTRODUCTORY TEXT (FORMERLY KNOWN AS LONG TITLE)

The long title is a brief statement giving a short summary of the principal way or ways in which the statute will affect the law by indicating the central legal mechanisms it employs.[37] In other words the task of the long title is to list the main points of law reform.

The current application of this principle in most Commonwealth jurisdictions is rather broad, and long titles present vague descriptions of the main points of the legislative text. As a result, long titles do not inform the user of the main regulatory message; they simply state what the legislative text does: for example, it amends, it establishes a new agency, it regulates a field of activity, it prohibits or criminalises a behaviour, it implements an international treaty,[38] or it imposes a tax. The problem with this approach is that long titles do not allow the user to assess whether this is a piece of legislation relevant to them or not. A current long title could be 'to regulate broadcasting' but without explaining exactly what is the main content of the regulatory framework introduced by the legislation. The lack of a clear regulatory message for lay users,[39] and the inevitable technical language used in long titles renders them a rather esoteric tool of communication, mainly between drafting lawyers and user lawyers or judges. It is exactly because of the emptiness of their message and their user unfriendliness that long titles have lost ground in modern legislative drafting. And their misleading name does not help them much either: they need not be long, and in any case they are not titles.

[36] See Office of Parliamentary Counsel *Drafting Guidance* (20 March 2014) 39–40.

[37] See H Xanthaki, *Thornton's Legislative Drafting* (West Sussex, Bloomsbury Professional, 2013) 253.

[38] See WK Hastings, 'New Zealand Treaty Practice with Particular Reference to the Treaty of Waitangi' (1989) 38 *International and Comparative Law Quarterly* 636, 668.

[39] See eg J Hofman, 'Comments on the South African Law Reform Commission's Draft Interpretation of Legislation Bill' (2007) 124 *South African Law Journal* 479, 486.

However, they may now be offered a new lease of life. The name has to go, but the tool itself can remain, albeit dressed differently. The concept of having an introductory text at the very beginning of the legislation can serve the plain language drafting approach very well indeed: in a user friendly legislative text the most important messages are to be placed at the beginning of the text.[40] Provided that the content of the introductory text is informative for the user and plainly drafted. The introductory text can, and must, tell the reader the gist of the story behind the legislative text: what is being introduced, whom it applies to, and when from. This will indeed allow the user to figure out if this is relevant to them or not. And the language to be used must invite further reading: clear, precise and unambiguous. But this is a glimpse into the future.

For now, long titles require a revamp. The long title is part of the Act, and may be used in interpreting its provisions.[41] As a result, long titles must be carefully drafted, with clarity, precision and unambiguity. Their role in the legislative text is to list, briefly and precisely, the main points of law reform. And the legislative text must remain within the scope of the long title.[42] Their length is not necessarily related to the length of the statute itself.[43] The form used typically involves introductory words:

> An Act to [provide for] [authorise] [establish] [regulate] [prohibit] [impose a tax on] [amend].

For a plain language approach, long titles can be more specific. It is a good idea to avoid general terms, such as 'to regulate' or 'to introduce a regulatory framework'. And to leave out the common vague words expressing incidental purposes, such as 'and for related matters', or 'and for connected purposes', or the incredibly annoying 'and for purposes connected therewith'. An example of a beautifully crafted recent Act with a vague long title is the UK Finance Act 2013:

> An Act to grant certain duties, to alter other duties, and to amend the law relating to the National Debt and the Public Revenue, and to make further provision in connection with finance.

[40] See C Hand, 'Drafting with the User in Mind—a Look at Legislation in 1982–83' (1983) *Statute Law Review* 166, 167.

[41] See WM Graham-Harrison, 'An Examination of the Main Criticisms of the Statute Book and of the Possibility of Improvement' (1935) 4 *Journal of the Society of Public Teachers of Law* 9, 38.

[42] See S Yen Ching Fung and A Watson-Brown, 'Traditional Drafting in Common Law Jurisdictions' (1995) 16 *Statute Law Review* 167, 186.

[43] See P Mason, 'Legislative Bill Drafting—Correct Drafting Important' (1925–26) 14 *California Law Review* 298, 308–09.

In contrast to this, the Supply and Appropriation (Main Estimates) Act 2013 is rather more precise:

> An Act to authorise the use of resources for the year ending with 31 March 2014; to authorise both the issue of sums out of the Consolidated Fund and the application of income for that year; and to appropriate the supply authorised for that year by this Act and by the Supply and Appropriation (Anticipation and Adjustments) Act 2013.

Is it necessary to detail amendments in the long title? It is very useful to do so, as a means of drawing the user's attention to exactly which Act is being changed. But it is not a good idea to list each and every one of the Acts amended or repealed, simply because the job of the long title is balanced by the need for brevity. An excellent example of this practice is the long title of the UK Sustainable Communities Act 2007 (Amendment) Act 2010: 'An Act to amend the Sustainable Communities Act 2007'.

There is no reason to be frightened of amending the long title.[44] There is a silent drafting convention enrobing long titles with infallible immunity. There really is no reason why a substantive amendment of the original Act cannot be reflected in the long title: indeed, there is every reason for the amendment of the long title. However, and perhaps this is the basis for the drafting convention, an amendment to the long title may be a whisper of conscience: since the Act is being amended so heavily that even the long title needs amendment, does that signify that amending is technically under-drafting and that repeal and re-enactment might be a more appropriate tool? And so amending the long title is always a possibility. It is necessary where a new part is being added to the Act, where an existing part is repealed, where a new mechanism of law reform is being added, or where an existing mechanism is removed by repeal. But amending the main mechanism introduced by the long title is a sure sign that the amendment goes deep enough in the Act to require repeal and re-enactment, so that fresh authorisation by the legislature can be sought but also as a means of ensuring that the users understand fully the new legislation and appreciate the details of the departure from the previous text.

ENACTING CLAUSE

The enacting clause is a wonderful tool: its task is to state formally that the legislating authority has agreed to the measures introduced by the law.

[44] See Lord Simon of Glaisdale in *Black-Clawson International Ltd v Papierwerke Waldhof-Aschaffenburg AG* [1975] AC 591, 647.

'The enacting formula refers to the Parliament Acts to explain how what is enacted is an Act'.[45]

There is a varied formula in each jurisdiction which can be introduced in the constitution. This is inevitably drafted in the traditional drafting style of each jurisdiction, and may well take an archaic form. At this point the drafter is faced with a dilemma: on the one hand, the traditional format may be verbose and user unfriendly; but on the other hand changing the enabling clause and replacing it with a plain language equivalent deprives the text of predictability and creates ambiguity as to whether this text is indeed legislative or not. It is difficult to offer guidance. The drafter's decision is, once again, subjective, and so is the manner in which these clashing interests can be juggled to the benefit of the user. And the user of the Act often just needs a statement in the past tense saying that the Act has been enacted and giving the date of Royal Assent.[46]

But what does the enabling clause serve? The formula, Kurzon argues, is a speech act: specifically, it performs the speech act of enactment.[47] But to whom does it speak? There is no such oral declaration; indeed, there is no stage in the parliamentary process when the enactment formula is actually uttered.[48] So who is the user of the enacting clause and what do they get from it? Jackson identifies four distinct audiences with different semiotic needs, the public (including the lawyers): they rely on the self-evidence of a particular form of printing as authenticating the words of enactment. Secondly, the courts. They access the authenticated 'original' (the vellum copy). Thirdly, the legislative officers who supervise the documentation which leads to and authorises the vellum copy, including the Letters Patent. And fourth Parliamentarians, who are concerned primarily with the oral speech acts performed within Parliament, and indeed with the body language and gestures that go with them.[49] And so the needs addressed by the enacting clause are to offer authentication to users, who may not even read the text. This leads to the conclusion that the language of the enacting clause is irrelevant to the users, and so ceremonial formality is not a hindrance to communication. Whatever the decision on the language of the enacting formula may be, it cannot come as a unilateral departure from tradition by a sole drafter. Predictability most certainly demands a generalised change of drafting tradition, which must be declared openly to the public.

[45] See R Ekins, 'Acts of Parliament and the Parliament Acts' (2007) *Law Quarterly Review* 91, 99.

[46] See E Clive, 'Law-Making in Scotland: From APS to ASP' (1999) 3 *Edinburgh Law Review* 131, 138.

[47] See D Kurzon, *It is Hereby Performed ... Legal Speech Acts* (Amsterdam/Philadelphia, John Benjamin's Publishing Company, 1986) 10.

[48] See Y Maley, 'The Language of the Law' in J Gibbons (ed), *Language and the Law* (London and New York, Longman, 1994) 11, 20.

[49] See BS Jackson, 'Who Enacts Statutes?' (1997) 18 *Statute Law Review* 177, 203–04.

The UK enacting formula was used by the pre-1707 English Parliament. It can be traced back at least to the 1620s. The UK Antarctic Act 2013 is a standard sample of UK enabling clauses:

> Be it enacted by the Queen's most Excellent Majesty, by and with the advice and consent of the Lords Spiritual and Temporal, and Commons, in this present Parliament assembled, and by the authority of the same, as follows:—

Thus the Queen, or her vice-regal representative, in giving Royal Assent to a Bill, is acting with the advice and consent of both Houses.[50]

The UK Finance Act 2013 is a sample of an Act with ceremonial character, where formality is acceptable:

> Most Gracious Sovereign WE, Your Majesty's most dutiful and loyal subjects, the Commons of the United Kingdom in Parliament assembled, towards raising the necessary supplies to defray Your Majesty's public expenses, and making an addition to the public revenue, have freely and voluntarily resolved to give and to grant unto Your Majesty the several duties hereinafter mentioned; and do therefore most humbly beseech Your Majesty that it may be enacted, and be it enacted by the Queen's most Excellent Majesty, by and with the advice and consent of the Lords Spiritual and Temporal, and Commons, in this present Parliament assembled, and by the authority of the same, as follows:—

International examples offer simpler and clearer enacting clause formulae. Canada, New Zealand, Cyprus and Australia simply state that 'The Parliament of … enacts [as follows]:'. But the simplest enacting clause is found in Malawi's Microfinance Act 2010: 'I assent'.

START DATE (FORMERLY KNOWN AS COMMENCEMENT)

The Act's date of entry into force is of crucial importance to the reader. Yet, the current trend in the UK and elsewhere is to place commencement provisions at the end of the text.[51] For example, in the UK Marriage (Same Sex Couples) Act 2013 commencement is found in section 21 along with the short title. The reasoning behind this transfer of commencement provisions from the start to the end of the legislation is of course benevolent, and it is based on plain language teachings: the less the drafter places before the main regulatory message, the more attentive the user will be when the main regulatory message finally appears. But one wonders whether the start date, namely the date of entry into force, forms part of the main regulatory message anyway. In which case it makes perfect sense to include it in preliminary provisions.

In order to respond to this question it is necessary to explore the concept of the 'main regulatory message'. It can be described broadly as the

[50] See A Twomey, 'The Refusal or Deferral of Royal Assent' (2006) *Public Law* 580, 581.

[51] See SE Young, 'Shepardizing "English Law"' (1998) 90 *Law Library Journal* 209, 215.

essence of the policy priorities[52] expressed by the legislative text as a form of communication or, in a socio-legal robe, the change in user behaviour demanded by the legislation as a tool of law reform and ultimately regulation. What is it that can push the user to change their behaviour as prescribed by the legislative text? Seidman states that a user 'will likely obey a law' if a rule prescribes a change of behaviour; if they have the opportunity and capacity to obey the law; if the law is communicated to them; if their interests (including threat of sanction) encourage obedience; if they decide in a public, participatory process whether or not they will obey; and if their ideology (beliefs, values, tastes) is compatible with the desired behaviour.[53] These are the factors on the basis of which legislative messages are to be prioritised.

If one selects preliminary provisions on the basis of their relevance to the main regulatory message, then commencement, as the answer to the question when is the user required to start acting, is certainly an essential part of the main regulatory message.[54] And so, commencement has a well deserved place in preliminary provisions. With one caveat: if commencement is complex in the specific legislative text, then it makes sense to include the master commencement date in the preliminary provisions, along with a cross reference to further commencement dates in a Schedule, preferably in a tabular format. This practice balances the need for brevity and simplicity in the preliminary provisions with the need to keep all commencement provisions collated[55] in one place.

The general rules on the commencement of statutes and subsidiary legislation are commonly found in Interpretation Acts. Legislation may take effect upon being passed, after, or even before that, in the case of retrospective legislation.[56] Usually statutes come into force on the date of Royal Assent.[57] But commencement may be conditional on the date of assent of the Head of State; or can be postponed until later, for example when more time is needed to set up administrative arrangements, when subsidiary legislation,

[52] See DA Marcello, 'The Ethics and Politics of Legislative Drafting' (1995–96) *Tulane Law Review* 2437, 2442.

[53] See B Seidman, 'Drafting for the Rule of Law: Maintaining Legality in Developing Countries' (1987) 12 *Yale Journal of International Law* 84, 97; also see B Seidman, 'Why Do People Obey the Law? The Case of Corruption in the Developing Countries' (1978) 5 *British Journal of Law and Society* 45.

[54] But a commencement provision ordains nothing as to the state of the law before the commencement date. It neither approves, modifies nor reverses the law before the commencement date: it is simply silent. See PS Atiya, 'Common Law and Statute Law' (1985) 48 *Modern Law Review* 1.

[55] See 'Statute Law Society Working Party on Commencement of Acts of Parliament' (1980) 40 *Statute Law Review* 40, 53.

[56] See D Greenberg, *Craies on Legislation—A Practitioner's Guide to the Nature, Process, Effect and Interpretation of Legislation* (London, Sweet and Maxwell, 2004) 359.

[57] Publication is not always necessary to make law: see C Grant, 'Promulgation and the Law' (2006) 2 *International Journal of Law in Context* 321, 326.

on which the working of the Act depends, is made, or when explanatory material is prepared.[58] A rather extraordinary example of an Act with many possibilities of legislative expression for commencement is the UK Crime and Courts Act 2013, whose section 61 states:

Short title, commencement and extent

...

(2) Subject as follows, this Act comes into force on such day as the Secretary of State may by order appoint; and different days may be appointed for different purposes and, in the case of Part 4 of Schedule 16 and section 44 so far as relating to that Part of that Schedule, for different areas.

(3) Sections 17, 20 to 30 and 32 and Schedules 9 to 11, 13 and 14 come into force on such day as the Lord Chancellor may by order appoint; and different days may be appointed for different purposes.

(4) Subsection (3) does not apply to—

(a) Part 5 of Schedule 13, or section 20 so far as relating to that Part;

(b) section 26(2).

(5) Section 19 comes into force on the day after the day on which this Act is passed.

(6) Sections 26(2), 31 and 33 come into force at the end of the period of two months beginning with the day on which this Act is passed.

(7) Sections 34 to 39 come into force at the end of the period of one year beginning with the day on which a body is established by Royal Charter with the purpose of carrying on activities relating to the recognition of independent regulators of relevant publishers (as defined by section 41).

(8) An order which brings the monitoring provisions into force only in relation to a specified area may provide that they are to be in force in relation to that area for a specified period; and in this subsection and subsection (9) 'the monitoring provisions' means Part 4 of Schedule 16, and section 44 so far as relating to that Part of that Schedule.

(9) An order containing the provision permitted by subsection (8) may be amended by a subsequent order under subsection (2) so as to continue the monitoring provisions in force in relation to the area concerned for a further period.

(10) An order which includes provision for the commencement of section 49 or Schedule 19 may not be made unless the Secretary of State has consulted the Scottish Ministers.

(11) The following come into force on the day on which this Act is passed—

(a) Part 5 of Schedule 13, and section 20 so far as relating to that Part;

(b) section 43;

(c) section 48 (except subsection (6)(a));

(d) Part 2 of Schedule 18;

(e) sections 58 to 60 and this section;

(f) Schedules 24 and 25.

[58] For a classification of commencement provisions, see M Gobbi, 'When to Begin: a Study of New Zealand Commencement Clauses with Regard to those Used in the United Kingdom, Australia, and the United States' (2010) 31 *Statute Law Review* 153.

Whatever the need may be, the drafter's task is to introduce the commencement date in a simple and clear manner. It is imperative that the user understands very clearly when their rights and obligations begin, and when they need to amend their behaviour in order to comply with the new legislation. The formula of the UK Crimes and Courts Act 2013 manages the complete opposite. Before proceeding further, it is important to note here that the Act is a technical piece of legislation addressed mainly to lawyers and judges, hence the drafter's slip towards complexity. The example, unfair as it may be, is very valuable to illustrate exactly what wording is to be avoided in legislation addressed to lay users.

But even simple commencement provisions manage to confuse the users. Drafters have long hidden behind the practicalities of the legislative process. Admittedly it is almost impossible for the drafter to foresee when assent to the Act will take place or when the administrative arrangements for the law will be completed. But these arguments, much as they stand true, tilt the burden to the drafter's or the government's convenience rather than towards the need for clarity, precision and unambiguity. Effectiveness of the legislation can no longer be compromised simply because whatever Parliaments vote cannot be changed before commencement. At the end of the day, allowing the drafter to add the specific start date is not an addition against what Parliament voted: far from it; it is simply a clarification of Parliament's will. After all, a clerk in the Public Bill Office changes references to the year in cases where the Bill concludes its passage in the year subsequent to that in which it was introduced;[59] and so a change of commencement date is not unknown to parliamentary practice. As for commencement provisions that reflect the need to wait for a delegated instrument expressing ministerial confirmation that the administrative arrangements have been introduced or that delegated legislation has been completed, again this cannot be an obstacle to clarity, precision and unambiguity of commencement dates. Governments may choose to offer the whole package to Parliament thus facilitating precision in commencement dates. 'No Bill should be promoted if commencement is neither definite nor likely within a reasonable time'.[60] Or, perhaps more realistically, the drafter can replace the vague commencement provision with a precise one as soon as ministerial confirmation is offered. An ideal form for commencement would be: This Act comes into force after 31 December 2013.

Whatever form is used, there must be certainty whether an enactment is or is not in force. And in order to achieve this admirable aim the drafter has to reconsider whether the term 'commencement' is understood by lay users or not. The Good Law survey shows clearly that the term is not understood

[59] See F Bennion, 'Modern Royal Assent Procedure at Westminster' (1981) 2 *Statute Law Review* 133, 137.

[60] See A Samuels, 'Is it in Force? Must it be Brought into Force?' (1996) 17 *Statute Law Review* 62, 65.

by users. Perhaps it is not time to replace it with the plain language equivalent 'start date'.

APPLICATION PROVISIONS

Application provisions clarify the extent of the new regulation introduced by the legislative text: they can explore who, what, when and where the legislation regulates. Answering 'who' may refer to the persons to whom the law applies: the Crown, or specific circles of persons such as diplomats, residents, members of a profession etc. Answering 'what' may refer to specific areas of regulation, for example services as opposed to goods, or inland waterways as opposed to the sea. Normally the question 'what' requires the drafter to weed out of the legislation a part of the genre to which it applies. The question 'when' may refer to the points in time that are regulated by the legislative text, for example the past, the future, or a transitional period. And the question 'where' refers to the geographical extent of the legislative text's bindingness, for example, the UK or Northern Ireland.

The general rule is that legislative texts normally apply to all persons within the jurisdiction, to all parts of the regulatory field, to all prospective periods of time (now and in the future), and to the whole area of the jurisdiction of the state. Any departure from it must be clearly introduced and signposted to allow the reader to focus their attention and imprint it in their brains. The question is whether there is any scope in repeating the general rule in the legislative text. There is a persuasive argument supporting the view that even the general rule is worth repeating, simply because the user is not necessarily aware of it. It is doubtful whether the drafter needs to state that this Act applies to all persons in the UK, the whole of the UK, now and in the future. This would be superfluous. But clarifying any possible legitimate doubts for the user is a commendable practice. In the UK, post devolution, it does not harm to state where the Act applies to, simply because the complexity of the devolved constitutional structures may leave the user wondering whether the Act applies to them or not. Similarly, in legislation related to immigration it is worth stating that the Act applies to nationals and residents alike: the topic itself sheds doubt over this rather simple question. The subjective, phronetic decision of the drafter is required once again. But the answer must derive from the needs of the users rather than the drafter's legal training and expertise.

INNOVATIONS FOR THE FUTURE

The expression and layout of preliminary provisions are crucial for the user friendliness and accessibility of the legislative text. First impressions matter, and often the reader is discouraged from continuing owing to the current length and complexity of the preliminary part of the legislation. As a result, the user never makes it to the main regulatory message, thus endangering the effectiveness of the legislation and ultimately the efficacy of the regulation. On this basis, preliminary provisions are very fertile ground for modernisation. The problem is that for most drafters, lawyers and judges their sanctity renders them untouchable.

Nevertheless, a modern plain language approach would require that preliminary provisions are kept to a minimum, with an introductory text, an enacting clause, a start date and, where necessary, an application provision.

The introductory text may narrate the legislative story to the user offering them a summary of the main regulatory message of the legislative text, namely the main points of the information required in order that the user complies with the new legislation.

The enacting clause can take the form of 'I assent'. Or it can find its way to the end of the text where the signature of the Head of State can be. Although it is important that the user is in no doubt as to the bindingness of the text before them, the emblem of the state at the top of the legislative text, and its inclusion in the database of legislative texts may suffice. It is noteworthy that the electronic publication of UK legislation does not include the enacting clause, which can be found in the pdf file with the whole Act.

The start date must take the form of a clear statement of the precise date when the users' compliance begins. Complex commencement provisions can be collated all together within a cross reference to a Schedule.

Finally, application may clarify any doubt in the user's mind as to the personal, substantial, temporal or geographical extent of the legislative text's bindingness.

There is little reason why all of the above cannot be included in the introductory text as separate sections with headings in the form of questions, especially if the enacting clause is transferred to the signature part of the Act. This practice presupposes that the introductory text is part of the Act. A fictional example changing the mode of assessment of new students of the University of London from examination to one piece of coursework per module:

1. Introductory text
   (a) Students of the University of London submit one essay of 3500 words for each of the modules of their degree programme.
   (b) This is their only method of assessment per module.
2. When does this start?
   The new method of assessment applies to students enrolling for the first time in their degree programme from October 2013 onwards.
3. What about existing students?
   Existing students continue to be assessed by examination.

8

Principal Provisions: the National, EU and International Dimension

LET'S REMAIN WITH Thornton's fourth stage of legislative drafting, namely composing and developing the draft. Having considered preliminary provisions, which are commonly drafted at the very end, the drafter puts pen to paper, or hand on computer button, and begins to draft the principal provisions of the Bill, the substantive and administrative provisions. Just for the purposes of completion, the proposed structure of our Bill is:

— Preliminary provisions
— *Principal provisions*
  — *Substantive provisions*
  — *Administrative provisions*
— Final provisions

PRINCIPAL PROVISIONS

Principal provisions constitute the main body of the legislative text. They carry the regulatory message communicated by government and aiming to instigate law reform as a means of producing the desired regulatory results. Accordingly, principal provisions are of crucial importance to the effectiveness of the legislative text.

Principal provisions can be substantive or administrative. The division refers to their content and does not prioritise them automatically into primary and secondary respectively. In other words, substantive provisions refer to issues of substantive, as opposed to procedural, law. Administrative provisions refer to the procedural arrangements required to put the substantive provisions into effect. Substantive provisions tend to be of primary importance, normally. But administrative provisions can be equally at home as primary provisions, in legislative texts of a purely or mainly administrative content, or as subordinate provisions. The unfortunate thing is that the term 'principal' is used by Lord Thring to refer to primary provisions excluding administrative provisions, but by Thornton to refer to both substantive and administrative provisions. In other words, Lord Thring's principal provisions exclude administrative provisions whereas Thornton's primary provisions include administrative provisions. Hence the confusion. This book follows Thornton's concept of principal provisions, namely substantive and administrative provisions. There is a reason for this. At the end of the day, what this chapter examines is provisions within the body of the text. As these carry the regulatory message, at least at the moment, they are primary in nature. One caveat: the introduction of an introductory text in legislative texts may require a change of term as principal provisions would be expected to be within the introductory text placed in preliminary provisions. But then, even the term preliminary provisions would have to be amended too ...

The drafting of principal provisions is examined in the previous chapters of this book. Their effectiveness is served by clarity, precision and unambiguity. Plain language and gender-neutral language are wonderful tools for that purpose. Within plain language, design and layout play an important role. But language is not always on the side of law. Abstractly, law and language share three qualities: they are rule-governed symbolic systems; they are uniquely human; and they are essential to the fabric of society.[1] Here subjective choices between and amongst the values are required. The debate on which prevails[2] in abstract is really a methodologically flawed one: effectiveness decides in the concrete dilemma.

What do substantive provisions tells the user? From a regulatory perspective, they simply convey the regulatory messages. In other words, substantive provisions are used by the government to express to the user of the legislative text exactly how they are expected to act from the moment of enactment onwards. The legislative communication of the government entails an imperative: non-legislative means of regulation tend to entail an encouragement, a nudge for users to alter their ways and take on board the government's message. So, in an awareness campaign the vivid images of death caused by driving under the influence of alcohol urge drivers to think twice before they drink. But this educational direction is not prevalent in legislation, whose role is to force and enforce a change of behaviour. The imperative nature of legislation directs the manner in which it is drafted. One, the use of imperatives within the sentence is superfluous and repeating 'must' is not necessary. Two, the obligation imposed on the subjects of the legislative text requires clarity, precision and unambiguity in the composition of the text: who, what, how and when are crucial elements

[1] See B Danet, 'Language in the Judicial Process' (1980) 14 *Law and Society Review* 3, 3.

[2] See B Coleman, 'Are Clarity and Precision Compatible Aims in Legal Drafting?'(1998) 8 *Singapore Journal of Legal Studies* 376, 400.

of the message that must be pronounced and must be easily accessible by the users. This is where plain language, alongside knowing one's audience and easing communication, and gender-neutral language come into play. And three, legislation needs to be keep the balance between tradition, as a means of predictability, and innovation, as a means of directness and longevity.

All these balances and conflicts are addressed by the subjective choices of the drafter who is guided solely by their academic and professional training and their practical experience from continuing application of the know-how acquired by training.

SUBSTANTIVE PROVISIONS

Substantive provisions introduce rights, powers, privileges and immunities of persons to be benefited or regulated. These provisions are drafted as prescriptions, prohibitions, regulations or combinations of the above.

Statutory corporations must be introduced with care: their powers can only be those awarded to them by statute and those which are necessary for the completion of the purpose of incorporation (even if they are not directly awarded to them by statute).

Licensing and registration provisions must cover the appointment of a licensing authority, the object of its activity, the manner of application for the licence, the sanctions for breach of the obligation to obtain a licence or fraudulent behaviours in the procedure, appeals procedures, inspection issues, subsidiary legislation and any transitional regimes.

Powers and duties need attention also. Power is permissive and therefore the word 'may' is used. For example, 'The Minister may make regulations'. But the term 'may' carries an inherent necessity for accountability; it is the drafter's duty to identify the criteria by which the exercise of the power is to be undertaken. As a result, 'may' must be accompanied by the criteria upon which the power is to be exercised. Where there is no discretion, a duty is introduced by the present tense or the word 'must'. For example, 'The Minister appoints' or 'The Minister must appoint'. Here the drafter's task is to ensure that the duty will actually be undertaken. Enforcement of the duty, direct or indirect, must accompany its introduction in legislation: when must the Minister appoint? Within what period of time must the regulations be made? And, what happens if they are not: is the original primary Act capable of standing alone without regulations, or is it to expire? It is noteworthy that a power and a duty can be combined. For example, 'The Minister consults the Board of Directors, and may appoint a Deputy'. Or, 'The Minister may consult the Board of Directors, and appoints a Deputy'. In these cases, the drafter's task is to designate criteria for the exercise of the power.

ADMINISTRATIVE AGENCY PROVISIONS

The creation or extension of administrative agencies must be drafted within the framework of the constitution.

A checklist of administrative provisions includes:

- the department;
- department head;
- appointment and removal;
- compensation;
- powers and duties;
- classification of employees;
- rules;
- civil service status;
- reports; and
- relationship to local government.

THE EU DIMENSION: NATIONAL IMPLEMENTING MEASURES[3]

A separate category of principal provisions, which carry different concerns, is provisions implementing EU legislation. Since the EU is a 'goal regulator',[4] full compliance is a broader concept, 'which includes appropriate policies by national agencies, and even appropriate behaviour by street-level bureaucrats delivering services to citizens'.[5] Implementation is a middle concept that includes enforcement. And transposition is the technical task of regulating for the purposes of implementation that invites compliance. The task of transposition is rather complex from a quantitative point of view: the sheer number of binding instruments that require transposition suffices to demonstrate the volume of the task.[6] In addition to the quantitative difficulty of accession, from a quantitative perspective transposition is a multifaceted issue. When transposing, the drafter's

[3] For the complete analysis on this topic, see H Xanthaki, 'Transposition of EC Law for EU Approximation and Accession: The Task of National Authorities' (2006) 8 *European Journal of Law Reform* 89; and H Xanthaki, 'Technical Considerations in Harmonisation and Approximation: Legislative Drafting Techniques for Full Transposition' in M Andenas and C Baasch Andersen, *The Theory and Practice of Harmonisation* (Cheltenham, Edward Elgar, 2011) 536.

[4] See P Westerman, 'Breaking the Circle: Goal-legislation and the Need for Empirical Research' (2013) 1 *The Theory and Practice of Legislation* 385, 397–98.

[5] See R Thomson, R Torenvlied and J Arregui, 'The Paradox of Compliance: Infringements and Delays in Transposing European Union Directives' (2007) 37 *British Journal of Political Science* 685, 686; also see E Versluis, 'Even Rules, Uneven Practices: Opening the "Black Box" of EU Law in Action' (2007) 30 *West European Politics* 50.

[6] See J O'Reilly, 'Coping with Community Legislation—A Practitioner's Reaction' (1996) 17 *Statute Law Review* 15, 16.

autonomy is very restricted in terms of choosing the subject and the scope of the national legislation.[7] Even evaluation of transposition is a complex task, as it requires a detailed understanding of the relevant domestic legal systems and laws. Assessment of practical implementation is an even more difficult task, as it involves broader questions of policy, many and varied administrative acts, and other issues.[8] Whilst analysis of transposition is important, implementation is more important, as the success of a policy is ultimately judged by its impacts 'on the ground'.[9]

First, the dynamism of the acquis, especially when soft law is taken into account, signifies that the goalposts for transposition are inevitably being moved further away as time passes.[10] Every new EU legal instrument, every new judgment of the European Courts, every international agreement signed by the EU is added to the body of rights and obligations that form part of the acquis and that Member States must receive into their national legal order. Thus, national drafters and legislators require constant updating in the definition and delimitation of their concept of the acquis.[11] Secondly, EU instruments differ from the form of national, and international, legal measures. This renders the understanding of their legal value, their degree of bindingness and the depth of their enforcement requirements a rather complex task.[12] Thirdly, the terminology used in EU instruments tends to have an idiosyncratic meaning[13] with connotations that differ from those awarded to the same term in the national laws of Member States.[14] The identification of the elements of the concept utilised in the acquis and the nuances of variation with the national concept adds

[7] See G Maneva, 'Drafting for Accession: Bulgaria's Way to Success' (2005) 7 *European Journal of Law Reform* 111, 120.

[8] See R Macrory, 'The Enforcement of Community Environmental Laws: Some Critical Issues' (1992) 29 *Common Market Law Review* 347, 355.

[9] See A Jordan, 'The Implementation of EU Environmental Policy: A Policy Problem without a Political Solution?' in A Jordan (ed), *Environmental Policy in the European Union: Actors, Institutions and Processes* (London, Earthscan, 2002) 301; also see A Jordan, 'The Implementation of EU Environmental Policy: a Policy Problem without a Political Solution?' (1999) *Environment & Planning C: Government and Policy* 69.

[10] See R Wainwright, 'Techniques of Drafting European Community Legislation: Problems of Interpretation' (1996) 17 *Statute Law Review* 7, 9.

[11] The problem is becoming more pronounced as increasingly emphasis is placed on the use of alternative regulatory instruments, including self-regulation, co-regulation, open coordination, benchmarking, peer pressure, networks, standardisation and soft law: see LAJ Senden, 'Soft Law and Its Implications For Institutional Balance in the EC' (2005) 1 *Utrecht Law Review* 77.

[12] Even lists in annexes of EU directives must be transposed either expressly or in preparatory work in national implementing measures; see Case C-478/99 *Commission of the European Communities v Kingdom of Sweden* [2002] ECR I-4147.

[13] See S Chalton, 'The Transposition Into UK Law of EU Directive 95/46/EC (The Data Protection Directive)' (1997) 11 *International Review of Law Computers and Technology* 25, 27.

[14] See Th A Finlay, 'Community Legislation: How Big a Change for the National Judge?' (1996) 17 *Statute Law Review* 79, 80.

a layer of extra difficulty to the task of adequate and full transposition. Fourthly, as legislative texts are intertwined, the acquis may enter into aspects of national law that are outside the fields of regulation covered by the EU. In order to achieve the desired task of full reception and compliance without undue distortion to the national legal system, transposition must take into account the legal system as a whole, thus requiring amendments to all of its fields.[15]

The Choice of Form

In view of these complexities, how can transposition be achieved in practice? In responding to the task, from an exclusively legal point of view,[16] national authorities are faced with dilemmas concerning the choice of the type of national implementing legislative measure and dilemmas related to the means that can achieve quality of the national implementing legislation. The final decision concerning the means to be used for the achievement of transposition rests with the national authorities under the principle of autonomy. However, the principle of autonomy is balanced by the equally important principles of subsidiarity, proportionality, adequacy, synergy and adaptability. These are general principles of EU law, which form part of the acquis and touch upon all aspects of EU law and policy. Thus, the principles bind both EU institutions and Member States.[17] As a result, the principles dictate both the national implementing actions but also the monitoring and evaluation of national implementing measures by national and EU bodies.

The principle of subsidiarity dictates that the highest level of action is justifiable only when lower levels of regulation are inefficient for the

[15] See W-H Roth, 'Transposing "Pointillist" EC Guidelines Into Systematic National Codes—Problems And Consequences' (2002) 10 *European Review of Private Law* 761.

[16] At the domestic level, the *choice of national legislative instrument* is also a political one and individual ministerial styles affect this choice: see DG Dimitrakopoulos, 'The Transposition of EU Law: "Post-Decisional Politics" and Institutional Autonomy' (2001) 7 *European Law Journal* 442, 450.

[17] See JA Usher, 'The Reception of General Principles of Community Law in the United Kingdom' (2005) 16 *European Business Law Review* 489, 495. The requirements flowing from the protection of general principles recognised in the Community legal order are also binding on Member States when they implement Community rules: see Case C-107/97 *Criminal Proceedings against Max Rombi and Arkopharma SA, the party liable at civil law, and Union federale des consommateurs 'Que Choisir?' and Organisation generale des consommateurs (Orgeco), Union departementale* O6 [2000] ECR I-3367, [65]; see also Case 145/88 *Torfaen Borough Council v B & Q plc* [1989] ECR 3851; *Shrewsbury and Atcham BC v B & Q* [1990] 3 CMLR 535; C-20/00 and C-64/00 *Booker Aquaculture v The Scottish Ministers* [2003] ECR I-7411.

achievement of the goal.[18] When applied to transposition, subsidiarity has a dual meaning. Regulatory subsidiarity can be defined as an economy of approaches. Legislative subsidiarity can be defined as an economy of measures. In other words, when selecting the national implementing measure, national authorities may proceed with legislation only where other levels and forms of regulation are not efficient.[19] When selecting the form of the national implementing legal measure, national authorities go through the list of national legal forms in the hierarchy of normative measures from the bottom upwards: only when a personal administrative act is inefficient, will national authorities select a law and only when a law is inefficient, will they proceed with constitutional reform.[20]

The principle of proportionality guarantees that the level of regulation selected by national authorities reflects the effect or aim to be achieved.[21] In other words, regulatory proportionality in the transposition process supplements subsidiarity in ensuring correspondence between the national authorities' choice to legislate and the aim that the proposed legal instrument aims to achieve.[22] Legislative proportionality supplements legislative subsidiarity[23] and demands that the choice of form of the national implementing measure reflects its purpose.[24]

[18] See European Commission, 'Better Lawmaking 2004' Pursuant to Article 9 of the Protocol on the Application of the Principles of Subsidiarity and Proportionality (12th Report) COM (2005) 98 final and SEC (2005) 364, 2; also see G Davies, 'Subsidiarity: The Wrong Idea, in the Wrong Place, at the Wrong Time' (2006) 43 *Common Market Law Review* 63, 67; B Rodger and S Wylie, 'Taking the Community Interest Line: Decentralisation and Subsidiarity in Competition Law Enforcement' (1997) 18 *European Competition Law Review* 485; K Lenaerts, 'The Principle of Subsidiarity and the Environment in the European Union: Keeping the Balance of Federalism' (1994) 17 *Fordham International Law Journal* 846; N Farnsworth, 'Subsidiarity—A Conventional Industry Defence: Is the Directive on Environmental Liability with Regard to Prevention and Remedying of Environmental Damage Justified under the Subsidiarity Principle?' (2004) 13 *European Environmental Law Review* 176.

[19] Nevertheless, the UK tends to over-implement EU law: see J O'Keeffe, 'Making a Silk Purse Out of a Sow's Ear' (2006) 103 *Law Society Gazette* 14.

[20] It is noteworthy that no measure adopted before the entry into force of the second paragraph of art 3b of the EC Treaty may be reviewed by reference to that provision, since the latter would be endowed with retroactive effect. See Case T-29/92 *Vereniging van Samenwerkende Prijsregelende Organisaties in de Bouwnijverheid and others v Commission of the European Communities* [1995] ECR II-289, [12], [330]–[331].

[21] See Case 11/70 *Internationale Handelsgesellschaft* [1970] ECR 1125, 1148; see also The Law Society, 'EU Better Law-Making Charter' Better Law-Making Programme (2005) 5.

[22] When there is a choice between several appropriate measures recourse must be had to the least onerous, and the disadvantages caused must not be disproportionate to the aims pursued: see Case T-54/99 *max.mobil Telekommunikation Service GmbH v Commission of the European Communities* [2002] ECR II-313, [81]; see also Joined Cases C-133/93, C-300/93 and C-362/93 *Crispoltoni and Others* [1994] ECR I-4863, [41].

[23] See J Snell, 'True Proportionality' (2000) 11 *European Business Law Review* 50.

[24] See G de Búrca, 'The Principle of Proportionality and its Application in EC Law' (1993) 13 *Yearbook of European Law* 105; also see J Jans, 'Proportionality Revisited' (2000) 27 *Legal Issues of European Integration* 239.

The principle of adequacy balances subsidiarity and accentuates proportionality, albeit expressed in the negative form. Regulatory adequacy demands that the chosen means of regulation is capable of achieving the effect pursued. Legislative adequacy secures that the chosen form of legislation is capable of achieving the effect pursued. Although adequacy is a value to aspire to in the legislative process, true adequacy in legislative drafting can only be secured post hoc through a prospective evaluation of the proposed law,[25] namely through a cost benefit analysis and a retrospective evaluation in the form of monitoring of passed laws.

The principle of synergy promotes a holistic approach to the legal system. Regulatory synergy promotes coherence and interrelated functioning of diverse fields of law within the national legal system of the aspiring Member State. Legislative synergy promotes a holistic approach of the law on a concrete social phenomenon, thus ensuring that the new instrument falls smoothly into place upon its entry into force and that it combines its forces for the achievement of the aim of legislation on the social phenomenon in question.

The principle of adaptability completes the set of values pursued when transposing EU legislation. Legislative practice often requires flexibility in the choice of the appropriate instrument: parliamentary time is valuable and the selection of form may be based on the lighter procedural requirements of the form in question.[26] When combined with subsidiarity and proportionality, adaptability can reach dangerous extremes of under-regulation or under-authorised regulation produced without resort to parliamentary legitimatisation. However, when delimited by adequacy and synergy, adaptability can serve national governments to achieve results legitimately but without a waste of resources. Adaptability allows for experimental legislation or legislation in stages.

So, how can national authorities select the appropriate normative level? Three main considerations are taken into account for the application of the principles to the choice of form for the national implementing measures: the extent of legislative intervention required for full transposition; the type of the main EU instrument for transposition; and the object of the national implementing measure.

[25] Where the legislature is obliged to assess the future effects of rules to be adopted and those effects cannot be accurately foreseen, its assessment is open to criticism only if it appears manifestly incorrect in the light of the information available to it at the time of the adoption of the rules in question. See Case C-150/94 *United Kingdom v Council* [1998] ECR I-7235, [49]; *max.mobil Telekommunikation Service GmbH v Commission of the European Communities* (n 22) [84].

[26] Factors include the lourdeur of parliamentary procedures and the lack of parliamentary time: see J Usher, 'The Legal Framework for Implementation in the United Kingdom' in T Daintith (ed), *Implementing EC Law in the United Kingdom: Structures for Indirect Rule* (Chichester, John Wiley and Sons, 1995) 101.

The extent of legislative intervention required for the reception of EU instruments by the national law relates to the choice of a legislative, rather than an alternative,[27] means of regulation and to the choice of the legislative level.[28] If national law does not regulate the main object of the EU instrument under transposition, the need for regulation is undisputed.[29] In this case the five tests of legislative subsidiarity, proportionality, adequacy, synergy and adaptability have been passed at the EU level when the EU institutions produced the regulatory legal instrument in pursuance of a legislative process. Thus, the need for legislative regulation in the field must be taken for granted. Member States would have extreme difficulty[30] in making a legitimate and objectively plausible case for a refusal to proceed with legislative regulation on the basis of national intricacies.[31] As for the choice of national implementing legislative instrument, here selection is also limited exclusively to legally binding national forms of legislative texts. Delegated legislation could not commonly respond to the need for legal regulation in the cases of lack of former regulation at the national level, as—by definition—lack of prior regulation signifies lack of a primary instrument that would introduce the necessary authorising or enabling clause. As a result, primary legislation would be required for proportionate and adequate regulation. It would be uncommon for the task of transposition to end with the passing of a law, as transposition is a mere part of implementation. For reasons of synergy, the main law may commonly be supplemented by secondary legislative instruments that will deal with technical details arising from the application of the law. In this case delegated legislation would contribute to achieving legal proportionality and legal adaptability. Supplementing the main law with secondary legislation is absolutely necessary for reasons of adequacy with specific reference

[27] See HM Government, 'Transposition Guidance: How to Implement European Directives Effectively' (April 2013) 2.5–2.6.

[28] For a sociological analysis of compatibility of national norms and transposition, see A Dimitrova and M Rhinard, 'The Power of Norms in the Transposition of EU Directives' (2005) 9 *European Integration Online Papers* No 16 http://eiop.or.at/eiop/pdf/2005-016.pdf.

[29] However, transposition does not necessarily require EU provisions to be reproduced verbatim in a specific, express law or regulation; a general legal context may be sufficient, provided that it does effectively ensure the full application of the directive in a sufficiently clear and precise manner. See C-49/00 *Commission of the European Communities v Italian Republic* [2001] ECR I-8575. Nevertheless, faithful transposition is often required: see Case C-38/99 *Commission of the European Communities v French Republic* [2000] ECR I-10941.

[30] In Case C-327/98 *Commission of the European Communities v French Republic* [2000] ECR I-1851, [22]–[23], the ECJ held that national difficulties in transposition was not a plausible excuse for not passing implementing measures.

[31] National legislation is needed even when the activity regulated by the EU instrument does not take place in the Member State: see Case C-441/00 *Commission of the European Communities v United Kingdom of Great Britain and Northern Ireland* [2002] ECR I-4699; see also Case C-214/98 *Commission v Greece* [2000] ECR I-9601, [22]. However, national legislation may not be needed when the EU instrument is pointless for reasons of geography; see Case 420/85 *Commission v Italy* [1987] ECR 2983, [5].

to compliance with the Madrid Intergovernmental Conference administrative criterion. But the problems of piecemeal transposition must also be taken into account: lack of clarity and incomplete implementation.[32]

The same principles apply in the case of prior national regulation that is archaic or in radical and direct conflict with EU law. In these cases the options available for national implementing measures are limited to the passing of a core law supplemented by delegated legislation dealing with technical and administrative details.

In cases where there is prior national legislation in the field under transposition, national authorities tend to have a wider selection of options. At the regulatory level, the five tests are applicable to ensure that further regulation is indeed necessary. When prior national regulation is complete when compared with EU regulation, each of the tests must be repeated applying national circumstances. In view of prior national laws, is further regulation required? If so, would further regulation be proportionate to the aim that EU regulation sets out to achieve? Could it be that current national regulation is adequate for the achievement of EU aims? Would the proposed new regulatory measures be received smoothly? Is it necessary to regulate further or can a wider interpretation of current regulatory measures, perhaps with a simple addition of a reference to the EU instruments, lead to the desired effect? The answer to these questions will depend on the results of the comparative analysis between national and EU regulation.

If, and only if, the five tests are not passed at the regulatory level, will national authorities proceed with the same five tests at the legislative level. The extent of incompatibility of national law with the EU legislative text under transposition dictates the position of the selected national legal instrument in the hierarchy of sources of national law. Existence of prior national law in the field does not guarantee smooth transposition.[33] If the existing national law is incomplete, supplementing the existing law is necessary. This can be undertaken either via a repeal and re-enactment or by an amendment of the existing legislative text. Delegated legislation could be appropriate, where accommodated by an enabling clause in existing primary legislation, if complete transposition requires that: the aim of primary legislation is taken further; or that technical or detailed provisions implement the primary legislation; or that administrative arrangements are set; or that primary legislation is brought into force; or that the existing primary legislation is supplemented or amended.[34]

[32] See S Bell and L Etherington, 'Out of Sight, out of Mind: a Study of the Transposition and Implementation of the Groundwater Directive in the United Kingdom Environmental Law Review' (2007) 17 *Environmental Law Review* 6, 11.

[33] See M Kaeding, 'Determinants of Transposition Delay in the European Union' (2006) 26 *Journal of Public Policy* 229, 249.

[34] Nevertheless, national authorities cannot take adequacy to an extreme. This would be the case with transposition of directives through administrative circulars previously used in France

Moreover, the form of the EU instruments under transposition influences the choice of national authorities to a great extent. From a regulatory point of view, at least in theory, the five tests of subsidiarity, proportionality, adequacy, synergy and adaptability have already been met, and a decision to proceed with legislative regulation has been made at the EU level. Similarly, the level of legislative form selected by the EU has already taken into account the legal basis of the instrument but also the order of the selected form in the hierarchy of sources of EU law. And so, the EU instrument under transposition has already passed, at least in theory, the five tests. These choices of EU institutions in the EU legislative process direct the choices of national authorities in the national legislative process for the introduction of implementing measures.[35]

And so provisions of the constituting treaties are generally suitable for inclusion in national constitutions or constitutional principles. The logic behind this lies with the nature of treaty provisions as general: they are fundamental rules of law drafted in the vague style accommodated by national constitutions or constitutional documents. Most treaty provisions tend to introduce general principles of EU law that influence the interpretation and application of EU law in its entirety[36] and can be considered part of the general principles of national law. But most treaty provisions apply exclusively to EU citizens: and so there is an argument against express transposition of treaty provisions in the national constitutions that apply to both EU and third country nationals equally. So, when it comes to the provisions of the constituting treaties, the task of national authorities is dual: the negative task is to take out of the legislative equation articles related exclusively to the functioning of the EU; and the positive task is to identify articles that introduce rights and obligations that the treaties award to EU citizens but which subsequent EU law has extended to third country nationals. These are mainly provisions related to fundamental freedoms rather than to freedoms related to the internal market. It is only the former that require express inclusion in the constitution or constitutional principles. All other treaty provisions require silent transposition through their application to the interpretation and reception of all sources of EU law.

and the UK: see R Kovar, P Lagarde and D Tallon, 'L'éxécution des directives de la CEE en France' (1970) 6 *Cahiers de Droit Européen* 288.

[35] See J-L Sauron, *L'Application du Droit de L'Union Européene en France* (Paris, La documentation française, 2000) 40.

[36] The lack of any express provision to the same effect in the precise EC text does not mean that the general principle does not apply: see Case T-18/97 *Atlantic Container Line AB and Others v Commission of the European Communities* [2002] ECR II-1125, [39].

Regulations are directly applicable.[37] As they form part of the national laws of the Member States, they do not normally require transposition. In pursuance of the principle of synergy, regulations are drafted in a manner that allows their smooth reception by national laws as they stand. But this does not relieve national authorities from the task of evaluating regulations against existing national law.[38] Generally speaking there are four main types of national normative implementing measures for the transposition of regulations: concretising and/or complementing substantive measures; institutional and/or competence measures; procedural, controlling or penal measures; or adapting or derogating measures.[39] If regulations are in complete contrast with prior national legislation, the latter must be amended or repealed altogether. Implied amendment may be considered adequate for the purposes of transposition via statutory interpretation. But it hinders clarity in the national law of the Member State, and it cannot be condoned. Moreover, it may leave ground to judicial interpretation and application contrary to EU law,[40] which in turn may lead to judicial state liability claims. If regulations affect existing national law in part, the task of national authorities is to evaluate the extent and manner in which national law is changed by the reception of the regulation. In this case amendments via alteration, substitution or incorporation ensure synergy, while respecting adaptability. In the rare case where the regulation complies fully with prior national law, Member States may: remain inactive; or add a reference to the regulation in the purpose clause or explanatory materials of the national legal instrument; or introduce a national legislative text with a sole enacting provision cross referring to prior national laws and annex the regulation. The choice is subjective and depends on the extent of the need to draw the user's attention to the connection between the regulation and the national law.

Directives[41] require attention by national authorities, as they merely set aims to be achieved allowing national authorities to exercise their autonomy in the process of implementation.[42] Of course autonomy is not

[37] See Case 50-76 *Amsterdam Bulb BV v Produktschap voor Siergewassen* [1977] ECR 137; also Case 39-72 *Commission of the European Communities v Italian Republic* [1973] ECR 101.

[38] See C-177/95 *Ebony Maritime SA v Prefetto della Provincia di Brindisi* [1997] ECR I-1111.

[39] See R Kral, 'National Normative Implementation of EC Regulations. An Exceptional or rather Common Matter?' (2008) 33 *European Law Review* 243, 245.

[40] See AJ Gil Ibáñez, *The Administrative Supervision and Enforcement of EC Law: Powers, Procedures and Limits* (Oxford and Portland, Hart Publishing, 1999); on the political aspect of judicial interpretation, see F Snyder, 'The Effectiveness of European Community Law: Institutions, Processes, Tools and Techniques' (1993) 56 *Modern Law Review* 27.

[41] For a thorough analysis on every aspect of transposition of directives, see B Steunberg and W Voermans, *The Transposition of EC Directives* (Leiden, Universiteit Leiden, 2006).

[42] For an analysis of autonomy in the national legislative process, see JH Jans, 'National Legislative Autonomy? The Procedural Constraints Of European Law' (1998) 25 *Legal Issues of European Integration* 25.

boundless. The implementation of a directive requires 'the adoption of general measures of a legislative nature'.[43] National authorities must ensure full application,[44] not only in fact but also in law.[45] In application of this principle, for the transposition of directives national authorities cannot find refuge in a mere circular that can be amended by the administration at will,[46] or in a simple general provision in national legislation referring to EU law,[47] or in existing administrative practices,[48] or in the tolerance exercised by the administration under existing national rules and administrative rules that do not confer any right on individuals capable of being relied on before national courts.[49] Moreover, clarity and precision of terminology used cannot be relied upon on the definitions in preparatory materials.[50] And case law cannot fulfil the requirement of legal certainty of the provisions of a directive.[51] And of course national rules of statutory interpretation cannot be relied upon to complete the implementing measure indirectly.[52]

The rationale behind these restrictions to the autonomy of national authorities lies with the fact that the five tests were met at the time of the passing of the directive, and as a result the need for legislative regulation has been verified.[53] National authorities may leave the implementation of the objectives of the directive to social partners through collective agreements; but national authorities are still responsible for ensuring that the directive is fully implemented by adopting the appropriate legislative or administrative measures.[54]

[43] See S Prechal, *Directives in European Community Law. A Study of Directives and Their Enforcement in National Courts* (Oxford, Oxford University Press, 1995) 5.

[44] See Case C-365/93 *Commission v Greece* [1995] ECR I-499, [9]; see also Case C-144/99 *Commission v Netherlands* [2001] ECR I-3541, [17]: Member States may not justify breach of EU law on the basis of failure of other Member States to perform their obligations; see also C-38/89 *Ministere public v Guy Blanguernon. Reference for a preliminary ruling: Tribunal de police d'Aix- les-Bains* [1990] ECR I-83.

[45] See Case C-339/87 *Commission v Netherlands* [1990] ECR I-851.

[46] See Case 239/85 *Commission v Belgium* [1986] ECR 3645.

[47] See Case C-96/95 *Commission v Germany* [1997] ECR I-1653.

[48] See Case C-152/00 *Commission of the European Communities v French Republic* [2002] ECR I-6973. Member States may not plead provisions, practices or circumstances existing in their internal legal system in order to justify their failure to comply with obligations and time limits resulting from Community directives. See Case C-310/89 *Commission of the European Communities v Kingdom of the Netherlands* [1991] ECR I-138.

[49] See Case 102/79 *Commission v Belgium* [1980] ECR 1473; Case 145/82 *Commission v Italy* [1983] ECR 711.

[50] See Case 143/83 *Commission v Denmark* [1985] ECR 427.

[51] See Case C-236/95 *Commission v Greece* [1996] ECR I-4459.

[52] See Case C-162/99 *Commission v Italy* [2001] ECR I-0541.

[53] Even where the settled case law of a Member State interprets the provisions of national law in a manner deemed to satisfy the requirements of a directive, this cannot achieve the clarity and precision needed to meet the requirement of legal certainty. See *Commission v Netherlands* (n 44).

[54] See *Commission v Denmark* (n 50).

In the absence of prior national regulation, or when prior national legislation is in conflict with the provisions of the directive, the directive requires full transposition via legislative measures.[55] In cases of prior partial regulation, and in view of the detailed technical nature of most directives, they are commonly transposed via delegated legislation. But the power to use delegated legislation for the purposes of transposition must be included in the ratification of the Accession Act. In cases where the national legal system already secures the aims pursued by the directive, implementing measures are not necessary. This may be the case where the necessary legislation already exists in national law, or where principles of constitutional or administrative law render specific national legislation superfluous.[56] The condition for this is that the legal position arising from such principles is sufficiently precise and clear, and may be relied upon by individuals before the national courts.[57] A transposition tool commonly used by Member States is the transposition of several directives via a single national legal instrument, known as 'the national transposition package approach'. Although these are helpful for the reduction of the costs of coordination within the ministries,[58] their value as a technical drafting tool is questionable as they break the express link between a directive and 'its' national implementing measure. But they can also serve as an antidote to the extensive fragmentation of EU regulation.

Decisions are transposed via administrative acts or delegated legislation. The addressees of the decision are the subjects of the implementing measure, and this must be reflected in the national implementing measure.

Recommendations and opinions require no transposition, as they are not legally binding. However, they do serve as authentic interpretation of stronger, legally binding legislative texts[59] and they are subject to judicial review before the CJEU.[60]

Last but not least, judgments of the European courts, and especially persistent case law, is binding on Member States and must be included in national implementing measures.

[55] See Cabinet Office, Regulatory Impact Unit, 'Transposition Guide: How to Implement European Directives Effectively' (2005) 14.

[56] However, even where the settled case law of a Member State interprets the provisions of national law in a manner deemed to satisfy the requirements of a directive, this cannot achieve the clarity and precision needed to meet the requirement of legal certainty. See *Commission v Netherlands* (n 44) [21].

[57] See Case 29/84 *Commission v Germany* [1985] ECR 1661.

[58] See M Kaeding, 'Lost in Translation or Full Steam Ahead: The Transposition of EU Transport Directives across Member States' (2008) 9 *European Union Politics* 115, 123.

[59] See M Gardeòes Santiago, 'Las "comunicaciones interpretativas" de la Comisión: Concepto y valor normativo' (1992) 3 *Revista de Instituciones Europeas* 933.

[60] See Case C-322/88 *Grimaldi v Fonds des Maladies Professionnelles* [1989] ECR 4407; see also Case C-325/91 *France v Commission* [1993] ECR 3283.

Apart from the extent of legislative intervention required for full transposition and the type of the main EU instrument for reception, national authorities base their choice of national implementing measure on the nature and object of the field under treatment. In other words national authorities take into account the legal and legislative drafting criteria applicable for the selection of legal form in customary national legislative drafting. After all, transposition is ultimately a legislative drafting exercise. Legal criteria relate to the substantive field of law to which the implementing measure refers. Legislative drafting criteria refer to technical requirements for the classification of the national implementing measure as primary or executive legislation.

When it comes to legal criteria for the choice of form of the national implementing measure, national authorities identify the substantive field of law of the proposed measure. First, national legal custom[61] may require that regulation in specific areas of activity is reserved for special legal forms. This would be the case with the introduction of new crimes in the national legal order: this is traditionally reserved for criminal legislation. Secondly, areas of minor importance are rarely considered worthy of legislative intervention via primary legislation. In this case, regulation takes the form of delegated legislation, internal circulars or other lower forms of regulation. An example of such an area concerns the levels of compensation awarded to farmers whose crops have been destroyed by natural phenomena. Thirdly, areas of increased significance are commonly reserved for primary legislation. This refers to legislation affecting issues falling within the exclusive competence of the constitution and constitutional provisions, restrictions of citizens' rights, taxation, electoral issues or the establishment of a public body. But politics and economics also seem to play a role: governments tend to opt for primary legislation for the purposes of transposition at the beginning of their term; and wealthier countries seem to use primary legislation more.[62]

When it comes to legislative drafting criteria national authorities take into account technical drafting issues that affect the choice of form of the national implementing instrument. The main factor in favour of primary legislation refers to the need for parliamentary legitimatisation of the proposed measure in cases when there are special needs for democratic legitimacy: for example, a serious compromise of fundamental rights; or when important authority or powers are introduced and attributed; or when the measure is expected to have significant political, economic or social

[61] For an empirical study demonstrating the huge discrepancies in the national choices of implementing measures, see B Steunenberg, 'Turning Swift Policy-making into Deadlock and Delay National Policy Coordination and the Transposition of EU Directives' (2006) 7 *European Union Politics* 293, 295.

[62] See D Treutlein, 'What Actually Happens to EU Directives in the Member States?: A Cross-country Cross-sector View on National Transposition Instruments' CESifo working paper, No 2098 (2007) http://hdl.handle.net/10419/26143.

consequences; or when the proposed solutions are controversial politically. Another factor in favour of primary legislation refers to the characteristics of the proposed measure: a wide circle of addressees; general application;[63] or legal bindingness. The main factor in favour of delegated legislation is an enabling clause. The constitution or constitutional principles must not prohibit the delegation. The enabling clause must be introduced in primary legislation. The clause must delimit precisely the scope of the delegation. The clause must determine the aim and the means of the delegated instrument. Another factor in favour of delegated legislation is the characteristics of the proposed measure, namely the need for flexibility of regulation, the technical or detailed nature of the normative matter or the need for repetitive acts. What is surprising and therefore noteworthy is that the choice of primary legislation as a means of transposition does not delay the process at all.[64] But, whatever the choice on the form of the national measure, the drafter as an agent of the state cannot draft 'any measure which would conceal the Community nature and effects of any legal provisions from the person to whom it applies'.[65] And as a result, there must be visibility of the connection between the EU and the national legislative texts.

THE CHOICE OF LANGUAGE, SYNTAX AND STRUCTURE

The task of national authorities does not end with the choice of form of the national implementing measure. The EU has turned its attention to quality of EU and national implementing measures, and now requires that national legislative texts adhere to its rules for quality of legislation.[66] Unfortunately, there is no magic formula for achieving quality in legislation.[67] Each country has its own rules that are affected by the type of its legal system (is it a civil or a common law system?), the type of its polity (federal state?) and

[63] The wide circle of addressees and the wide application of the measure are judged on the basis of its true characteristics and not on the basis of its title. See Case T-17/00 *Willy Rothley and Others v European Parliament* [2002] ECR II-579, [61]; the mere fact, however, that the number and even the identity of the persons to whom a measure applies can be determined in no way implies that those persons must be regarded as individually concerned by that measure, where that measure applies to them as a result of an objective situation of law or fact specified by the measure at issue: see Case 6/68 *Zuckerfabrik Watenstedt v Council* [1968] ECR 409, [415]; see also Case C-10/95 P *Asocarne v Council* [1995] ECR I-4149, [30].

[64] See E Borghetto, F Franchino and D Giannetti, 'Complying with the Transposition Deadlines of EU Directives—Evidence from Italy' (2006) 1 *Rivista Italiana di Politiche Pubbliche* 7.

[65] See *Amsterdam Bulb BV v Produktschap voor Siergewassen* (n 37).

[66] See W Robinson, 'How the European Commission Drafts Legislation in 20 Languages' (2004) 53 *Clarity* 4, 6.

[67] Nevertheless, national drafting guidelines introduce similar standards of quality: see H Xanthaki, 'The Problem of Quality in EU Legislation: What on Earth is Really Wrong?' (2001) 38 *Common Market Law Review* 651.

the main aim of its legislators (to promote economic development, in which case legislation must serve corporations, or to protect its citizens, in which case legislation must be simple and approachable by all?).[68]

However, the EU has gone a long way in defining quality in legislation in a manner that is acceptable and receivable by all Member States.[69] Jean-Claude Piris has stated that there are two aspects to the issue of quality: quality in the substance of the law and quality in the form of the law. Quality in the substance of the law refers mainly to issues of legislative policy and covers tests of subsidiarity and proportionality, choice of the appropriate instrument, duration and intensity of the intended instrument, consistency with previous measures, cost/benefit analysis and analysis of the impact of the proposed instrument on other important areas of policy, such as SMEs, environment, fraud prevention etc. Quality in the form of the law concerns accessibility, namely transparency in the decision-making process, and dissemination of the law.[70] EU drafting rules can be classified into three categories: rules concerning the substance of the legislative text, rules related to the legislative process which leads to their passing and rules relevant to technical drafting issues.

As for the substance of the legislative text, EU legislation must be an essential and effective means of achieving the aim of the law in question: thus, alternative means of regulation, such as inter-trade agreements, must be encouraged, and so is abstinence from regulation in areas which do not fall within priority policy issues.[71] EU legislation must be proportional to the aim to be achieved,[72] and consistent with existing legislation. Moreover, it must take into account the particular needs of the users of the final texts: thus, it must determine the new rights and obligations introduced by it in

[68] See Rt Hon Lord Renton, 'The Preparation and Enforcement of Legislation in the Enlarged Community' (1996) 17 *Statute Law Review* 1, 3.

[69] See Commission, 'European Governance: Better Lawmaking' (Communication) COM (2002) 275 final; see also H Xanthaki, 'The SLIM Initiative' (2001) 22(2) *Statute Law Review* 108–18.

[70] See JC Piris, 'The Quality of Community Legislation: the Viewpoint of the Council Legal Service' in A Kellermann et al (eds), *Improving the Quality of Legislation in Europe* (Nijmegen, Martinus Nijhoff Publishers, 1998) 28.

[71] See 'General Guidelines for Legislative Policy': Communication of 9 January 1996 by the President of the Commission SEC (95) 2255; Commission, 'Towards A Reinforced Culture Of Consultation And Dialogue—General Principles And Minimum Standards For Consultation Of Interested Parties By The Commission' (Communication) COM (2002) 704 final; Commission, 'Updating And Simplifying The Community Acquis' (Communication) COM (2003) 71 final; Commission, 'Impact Assessment Guidelines of the European Commission' SEC (2005) 791; Interinstitutional Agreement of 16 December 2003 On Better Law-Making [2003] OJ C 321/1; Commission, 'On The Outcome Of The Screening Of Legislative Proposals Pending Before The Legislator' (Communication) COM (2005) 462 final; Commission, 'Implementing The Community Lisbon Programme: A Strategy For The Simplification Of The Regulatory Environment' (Communication) COM (2005) 535 final.

[72] Proportionality is defined as appropriateness to meet the needs; see Case C-84/94 *UK v Council* ECR [1996] I-5755, [47], [55], [57] and [58].

a manner which can be easily understood by lay persons. Furthermore, it must take into account the issue of transposition and the need for translation of the text into the many different EU official languages.

As for the legislative process, EU institutions must respect the principle of subsidiarity thus leaving it to Member States to regulate matters which are more effectively dealt with at the national level (another aspect of wise regulation).[73] The drafting process must be open,[74] transparent,[75] with full information of legislative dossiers available to all interested parties[76] and consultation must be as wide as possible. The legislative process must also be carefully planned and coordinated. Furthermore, planned legislation must be subject to cost analysis and already enacted laws must be monitored and evaluated.

As for the technical side of drafting, EU legislation must be clear,[77] unambiguous and simple; this is all the more important for texts which are going to be translated and transposed into 28 different legal orders. Clarity includes the use of plain language and the avoidance of too many cross references, and political statements without legislative character.[78] Unambiguity covers the use of the same term throughout the text, lack of unnecessary abbreviations and lack of pointless repetition of existing provisions. Simplicity incorporates lack of jargon, long sentences and imprecise references to other legal texts.[79] The title of legislative texts must be a full and clear indication of their subject matter. Preambles must only be used as means of justifying the enacting provisions in simple, non-repetitive

[73] See Commission, 'The Principle of Subsidiarity' (Communication) SEC (92) 1990. See also Interinstitutional Agreement of 25 October 1993 On The Procedures For Implementing The Principle Of Subsidiarity, 12 Bull EC (1993) 129, which has no binding effect and places no obligation on the institutions to follow any particular rules when drafting legislative measures: see Case C-149/96 *Portuguese Republic v Council of the European Union* [1999] ECR I-8395. See also Wainwright, 'Techniques of Drafting European Community Legislation: Problems of Interpretation' (n 10) 8.

[74] See Communication of the Council, the Parliament and the Economic and Social Committee, 'Openness in the Community' COM(93)258 final [1993] OJ C 166/4.

[75] See Interinstitutional Declaration On Democracy, Transparency And Subsidiarity, Bulletin EC, 10/93, 119–23; see also Resolution of the European Parliament of 6 May 1994 on the transparency of Community legislation and the need for it to be consolidated, A3-0266/94 [1994] OJ C 205/514.

[76] See Code of Conduct 93/730/EC Concerning Public Access to Council and Commission Documents [1993] OJ L340/41; also see Commission Decision 94/90/ECSC, EC and Euroatom of February 1994 on public access to Commission documents [1994] OJ L 46/58.

[77] When it comes to transposition, individuals should have the benefit of a clear and precise legal situation enabling them to ascertain the full extent of their rights and duties and, where appropriate, to rely on them before the national courts: see *Commission of the European Communities v Italian Republic* (n 29).

[78] See Opinion of the Economic and Social Committee of 5 July 1995 on plain language, [1995] OJ C 256/8.

[79] See Resolution of the European Parliament of 4 July 1996 on the report of independent experts on simplification of Community legislation and administrative provisions COM(95)288 final; see also A-4 0201/96 [1996] OJ C 211/23.

terms. Citations (namely the short title within the title) must provide the legal basis of the text, whereas recitals within the preamble must be used as a means of presenting the concise reasons for passing this piece of legislation. Moreover, there must be a very clear reference to the date of entry into force, which must be clearly distinguished from the date of the actual text. Furthermore, the practices of consolidation, recasting and informal consolidation must be actively pursued for already existing legislation. In their purity these drafting rules bind the EU and its institutions. However, it was as early as in 1998 the Commission in its *Better Lawmaking Report 1998: A Shared Responsibility*[80] that the role of Member States in the process of improving the quality of EU legislation was fully established. The Commission declared that Member States also have a role to play to complement the efforts of the institutions, as 'they are, after all, the main producers of legislation and hence the most direct cause of the burden [on firms]'. In fact, the correct transposition of EU directives was one of the eight main guidelines for action introduced by the report.[81]

On this basis there is little doubt that the rules for drafting legislation of good quality introduced by the EU are applicable to drafting national implementing measures. After all, the quality of the national implementing measure will be monitored and evaluated by the Commission and controlled by the CJEU, both of which are EU institutions whose perception of quality in legislation stems from the EU rules on legislative drafting. But national legislatures do have choices. For example, the scope of application of the national measure cannot depart from the EU one, unless expressly provided otherwise within the EU measure.[82] Clarification of ambiguous or vague terms within the EU instruments can make up for the flaws of EU text.[83] Moreover, identification of provisions already present in national law and avoidance of their inclusion in the implementing measure can reduce 'double banking', namely an unnecessary parallel regulation of the same topic in two legislative sources.[84] And exclusion of over-drafting in the national legislative text can avoid gold-plating, where this is not within the government's intent.[85] Gold-plating increases the burden resulting from

[80] See COM (1998) 715 final.

[81] ibid, point 1.8.3.

[82] See Case 40/69 *Hauptzollamt Hamburg-Oberelbe v Firma Paul G Bollmann* [1970] ECR 69, 79; also see Case 74/69 *Hauptzollamt Bremen-Freihafen v Waren-Import-Gesellschaft Krohn and Co* [1970] ECR 451, 459–60.

[83] On the flaws of EU texts, and directives specifically, under the prism of implementation, see M Kaeding, 'In Search of Better Quality of EU Regulations for Prompt Transposition: the Brussels Perspective' (2008) 14 *European Law Journal* 583.

[84] See Davidson Report drafted by Lord Davidson (1996) http://webarchive.nationalarchives.gov.uk/+/http:/www.hm-treasury.gov.uk/d/davidson_review281106.pdf.

[85] See P Kellett, 'Is the Better Regulation Agenda Producing Better Regulation?' (2009) 62 *Journal of Planning and Environment Law* 24, 25.

EU legislation, and endangers the competitiveness of national actors.[86] Drafters must ensure that: the national implementing measure does not extend the scope, concepts or substance of the EU legislative text; and that all derogations are taken into account. Piecemeal implementation is not good practice. But if the application of the system depends on a combination of a number of provisions adopted at Community, national and regional level, it is permissible for regional laws to incorporate some elements of the Community regulations involved, for the sake of coherence, and in order to make them comprehensible to those to whom they apply: at the end of the day the imperative is that 'the EU nature of the regulations, their direct applicability, and their direct effect are not disguised or otherwise compromised'.[87]

Summing up

Despite the vagueness of the task involved in the transposition of the acquis and the EU's avoidance to offer guidance, there are identifiable principles for complete transposition. Transposition in practice is a complex task both from a quantitative and a qualitative point of view. Problems tend to arise from the sheer volume of EU instruments forming part of the acquis, the dynamic nature of the acquis, the unique nature and form of EU instruments, the intricacies of EU terminology and the indirect effect of the acquis on aspects of national law seemingly unaffected by EU legislation.

Member States seem to be left to their own devices in the chaotic task of the choice of form, content and style of national implementing measures. This could not be further from the truth. In the choice of form national authorities can utilise the five tests of regulatory and legislative subsidiarity, proportionality, adequacy, synergy and adaptability. These dictate the choice made on the basis of the extent of legislative intervention required for full transposition; the type of the main EU instrument for reception; and the object of the national implementing measure.

In fact, the application of the five tests demolishes the simplistic correlation between particular forms of EU legislation with national forms: regulations often do require transposition via national law, and directives may not always require transposition. Each EU legal instrument must be considered ad hoc in the light of prior national legislation. This treatment requires accurate knowledge of the acquis, extensive experience in the workings of the national legal system and skills for the adaptation of the latter to the former.

[86] See HM Government, 'Transposition Guidance: How to Implement European Directives effectively' (n 27) 2.2.

[87] See Case 272/84 *Commission v Italy* [1985] ECR 1057, 1074.

However, complete implementation of the acquis from a substantive law point of view does not suffice for successful transposition. The quality of national implementing measures, pronounced since 1997, is equally important for the achievement of national implementing laws that are efficient, effective and enforceable, in other words that comply with both the Copenhagen and the Madrid criteria for accession. Drafting rules concern the substance of the legislative text, the legislative process leading to their adoption and technical drafting issues. As for the substance of the legislative text, legislation must be: an essential and effective means of achieving the aim of the EU instrument under transposition; proportionate to the aim to be achieved; and consistent with the national statute book. For the legislative process, national implementing measures must respect the principles of subsidiarity, openness, transparency and cost-efficiency. And on the technical side of drafting, national implementing measures must be clear, unambiguous and precise. They must also be capable of leading to effectiveness of national and, as a member of the implementing collective,[88] to effectiveness of EU regulation. This excludes the use of the 'copy out' technique[89] that is now used as standard even in the UK.[90] Drafters must recognise that elaboration, as opposed to copy out, is necessary for the effective transposition of an EU legislative instrument that introduces rights or obligations in an unclear or imprecise manner; that demands the creation of a criminal offence; or that involves sub-delegation via its application by administrative authorities. Finally, from the perspective of the UK post devolution, it is necessary to pitch the text to the right legislative authority.[91]

THE INTERNATIONAL DIMENSION: IMPLEMENTING INTERNATIONAL AGREEMENTS

Treaties are international agreements to legal bindingness between states: they can be included in one or more documents, and they are constituted

[88] See LJ O'Toole Jr, 'Multi-organizational Policy Implementation: Some Limitations and Possibilities for Rational Choice Contributions' in FW Scharpf (ed), *Games in Hierarchy and Networks: Analytical and Empirical Approaches to the Study of Governance Institutions* (Frankfurt am Main/Boulder, CO, Campus Verlag/Westview Press, 2003) 27.

[89] See L Ramsey, 'The Copy Out Technique: More of a "Cop Out" than a Solution?' (1996) 17 *Statute Law Review* 218; also see National Audit Office, *Lost in Translation? Responding to the Challenges of European Law* (HC 2005–06, 26); Cabinet Office Regulatory Impact Unit, 'Transposition Guide: How to Implement European Directives Effectively' (2005); L Etherington, 'Digging Beneath the Surface: Transposition, Implementation and Evaluation of European Environmental Law' (2006) 59 *Journal of Environmental Policy and Planning* 107.

[90] See HM Government, 'Guiding Principles for EU Legislation' BIS/13/774 (2013) point 5.

[91] For a detailed discussion, see A Ross, H Nash and CT Reid, 'The Implementation of EU Environmental law in Scotland' (2009) 13 *Edinburgh Law Review* 224.

de facto irrespective of their designation as treaties or not.[92] Their inherent difficulty for their drafter is the need to evoke bindingness from vague political statements, in all legal orders involved in the treaty. Treaties must be distinguished from memoranda of understanding (MoUs) which are not enforceable and do not require publication. Treaties require consent to be bound, expressed by signature, exchange of instruments, ratification or accession. Their entry into force can be on a specific date, or, under Article 24(2) of the Vienna Convention, as soon as all members have signed; provisional application is also possible under Article 25 of the Convention. Interpretation of treaties is foreseen in Articles 31 and 32 of the Convention,[93] and can be offered by means of an interpretative declaration, or political declarations or reservations[94] under Article 2(2)(d) of the Convention, which introduces basically a modification of the treaty without derogation.

Treaties become part of national law via two legislative processes, according to the prevalent theory of the jurisdiction.[95] Monism is based on Article 26 of the Vienna Convention and allows for their automatic inclusion in domestic law, thus rendering them enforceable before the national courts. For the purposes of drafting it is very important to note that treaties including offences require national implementation even in the monist scenario. Dualism, prevalent in common law jurisdictions and often considered the most effective method of implementation,[96] requires a second step in the legislative process for the purposes of implementation.[97] Conflicts between national and international law are resolved by reference to the national law.[98] Lord Oliver writes that treaty law is only part of English law when it

[92] See Sir F Berman, 'International Treaties and British Statutes' (2005) 26 *Statute Law Review* 1, 3.

[93] For an analysis of arts 31 and 32, see F Shaheed, 'Using International Law in Domestic Courts: Part 1: Domesticated Treaties' (2003) 8 *Judicial Review* 81.

[94] See Treaty Section, Legal Directorate, Foreign and Commonwealth Office, 'Treaties and MoUs: Guidance on Practice and Procedures' (April 2012) 7 www.gov.uk/government/publications/treaties-and-mous-guidance-on-practice-and-procedures.

[95] See K Hayes, 'General Principles: Judicial Implementation of International Human Rights Norms' in W Maina and W Wahiu (eds), *Human Rights Litigation and the Domestication of Human Rights Standards in Sub Saharan Africa* (Nairobi, AHRAJ Casebook Series vol 1, International Commission of Jurists, 2007) 17.

[96] See R Matemba, 'Incorporation of International and Regional Human Rights Instruments: Comparative Analyses of Methods of Incorporation and the Impact that Human Rights Instruments Have in a National Legal Order' (2011) 37 *Commonwealth Law Bulletin* 435, 436; also see G Gaja, 'Dualism Review' in J Nijman and A Nollkaemper (eds), *New Perspectives on the Divide Between National and International Law* (New York, Oxford University Press, 2007); P Capps, 'Sovereignty and the Identity of Legal Orders' in C Warbrick and S Tierney (eds), *Towards an 'International Legal Community'? The Sovereignty of States and the Sovereignty of International Law* (London, BIICL, 2006).

[97] See BR Opeskin, 'Constitutional Modelling: The Domestic Effect of International Law in Commonwealth Countries: Part I' (2000) *Public Law* 5, 5 and 6.

[98] See R Higgins, *Problems and Process: International Law and How We Use It* (Oxford, Oxford University Press, 1994) 205.

has been 'incorporated into the law by legislation'.[99] But even in the dualist scenario treaties remain binding and are applied in good faith irrespective of national implementation: 'pacta sunt servanta' under Article 26 of the Convention.[100]

Effect to international treaties is given via four methods:[101]

1. national implementing legislation may not refer to the international agreement, although it is advisable to clarify that its purpose is to give effect to the agreement;
2. national implementing legislation may refer to the international agreement and may give effect to it via separate substantive provision;
3. national legislation may include the international agreement in a Schedule for information purposes only; or
4. national legislation may set out the agreement in a Schedule and award it, or part of it, force of law.

This is fine, in theory. The question is what happens in practice? For that purpose, it is important for the drafter to use international treaties as a set of drafting instructions. This places the national drafter at stage one of Thornton's drafting stages. And it is a rather fortunate place to be, since the treaties will include policy intent, a reasonable structure and initial conceptual choices that the drafter can at least consider. But treaties infer the dangers of any lay draft. Choices have been made, and it is quite tempting for the drafter to simply copy what is there. This temptation is removed as soon as effectiveness comes into the equation.[102] The drafter needs to be aware of the fact the treaty was passed for the purposes of a different and much wider environment than the drafter's jurisdiction, and with an aim to iron out any difficulties stemming from national eccentricities. But this is exactly the context which the national drafter must serve and accentuate, all for the purposes of national effectiveness.

But, before proceeding further, what exactly is it that the drafter is pursuing? What criterion of effectiveness can be identified in the process of drafting for treaty or MoU domestication? Criteria include the technical nature of the treaty; its content; the better regulation ethos prevalent in the UK; and, last but by no means least, the policy decision concerning the extent of implementation, and the extent of the need to demonstrate to the

[99] See *JH Rayner (Mincing Lane) Ltd v Dept of Trade and Industry* [1990] 2 AC 418, 499F–500C.

[100] On monism and dualism, see O Tshosa, *National Law and International Human Rights Law: Cases of Botswana, Namibia and Zimbabwe* (Aldershot, Ashgate, 2001) 3.

[101] See FA Mann, 'The Interpretation of Uniform Statutes' (1946) 62 *Law Quarterly Review* 278.

[102] Otherwise domestication becomes an empty gesture: see C Heyns and F Viljoen, *The Impact of the United Nations Human Rights Treaties on the Domestic Level* (The Hague, Kluwer Law International, 2002) 1.

international community that implementation has taken place. This is a policy issue, and one on which the drafter has no role. Based on these criteria, the true purpose of the implementing legislation can be to comply fully with the international treaty, or to comply partially while respecting some national intricacies, or even to avoid effective compliance in practice. Each political goal is served by different techniques.

Avoiding compliance is not an ethical goal. After all, the implementation of international obligations is one aspect of the rule of law.[103] And in an ideal world countries sign international treaties in order to comply with them fully and on time. But this is not an ideal world and the drafter may be asked to draft a national implementing measure with haphazard effectiveness. The best way to achieve this is via the copy-paste technique. International texts are vague and incomplete by nature: and so they tend to be ineffective for the purposes of national implementation. Concepts and terms used may have a vague, ambiguous or no meaning for the national legal order: maintaining those without a national definition invites imprecision and ambiguity, which in turn makes effectiveness haphazard. Moreover, the placement of the national measure in the statute book and the determination of its relationship with existing texts are left to statutory interpretation by judges whose inclination is to offer gravitas to national laws.[104] If subtlety is not the preferred way forward, then the introduction of blocking measures is always a possibility: an international treaty is deprived of its teeth when it is escorted by the non-recognition or non-facilitation of mutual legal assistance, or the non-recognition of foreign judgments or the non-recognition of foreign orders.

But this is an extraordinary case of politically driven drafting, which raises issues of constitutionality and legality that the drafter must juggle, somehow. A more realistic aim for national implementing measures is to ensure partial compliance with the international treaty. Here the drafter's task is to identify the national eccentricities, to determine exactly what needs to be preserved, and to draft accordingly. For that purpose the drafter can use a variety of techniques. First, a new national implementing legislative text with both compliance and creative elements: this can balance the need for national implementation with a focus on the effectiveness of the points of the treaty that best serve national interests. Secondly, a national legislative text stating simply that the state incorporates into national law the international instruments by redrafting the provisions that require further implementation, and referring by number to the precise articles that can be left as they stand in the international text: this invites a focus on the international treaty as a

[103] See B Malkani, 'Human Rights Treaties in the English Legal System' (2011) *Public Law* 554, 567–68.

[104] See M Gobbi, 'Making Sense of Ambiguity: some Reflections to the Use of Treaties to Interpret Legislation in New Zealand' (2002) 23 *Statute Law Review* 47, 49.

means of interpretation and application of the national instruments, and is very useful as a proof that effective national implementation has taken place. Thirdly, an express statement that the purpose of the national implementing law is to achieve compliance with the relevant international instrument: this is a subtler way of referring to the international treaty as a whole inviting it to be used as a means of interpretation and application of the national text. Or fourthly, the drafter may choose to attach the international instrument in a Schedule: here focus is on the national instrument but reference to the international instrument is gracefully facilitated.

If the drafter's instruction is to ensure full compliance of the international treaty, then a replication of each one of Thornton's stages is meticulous and purposeful. The drafter must use the international instrument as a set of drafting instructions. They identify their response to these instructions by means of a legislative plan stating what is existing national law; what is already covered by national law; what is different in national law; what is not regulated in national law; which regulatory mechanisms are needed for each of the provisions that clash with international law; and which are the amendments and repeals needed for the smooth incorporation of the new national legislative text. When it comes to design, the drafter ensures that the regulatory mechanisms selected are appropriate. And this means that legislation is not always needed: in fact it is a solution of last resort. If legislation is needed, then the drafter moves to the composition stage.

The structure of the national implementing text serves national effectiveness. As a result, the structure of the international instrument is not always useful. The national intricacies of style and format are followed as a means of awarding predictability to the text. For example, preambles are not maintained; they are assessed subject to Article 32 of the Vienna Convention, which awards them interpretative value; as a result, they are either rejected as irrelevant to the national text, or transferred to preliminary or principal provisions. The national text follows national drafting style. And at the end it is verified internally within the drafting team, and externally within government.

And so in practice effective implementation can lead the drafter to four choices:

1. to do nothing, if there is no need for further legislation;[105] or
2. to pass an Act of Parliament incorporating the treaty wholly (eg the UK Diplomatic Privileges Act incorporating the Vienna Convention on Diplomatic Relations) or partially (eg the Human Rights Act 1998); or

[105] This is a sound approach from a drafting perspective but there is a substantive international law argument that the approach is incomplete, since 'As a consequence treaties are only part of English law if an enabling Act of Parliament has been passed': see I Brownlie, *Principles of Public International Law* (Oxford, Oxford University Press, 2003) 44–45.

3. to pass an Act of Parliament that contains the necessary powers to comply with the obligations arising from the treaty without necessarily incorporating the treaty itself; or
4. to pass delegated legislation to combine the incorporation of a number of treaties.

In the UK the practice is to implement treaties via amendment of existing law before the actual ratification of the treaty.[106] But, whatever the choice of national measure, its composition requires special attention and diverse treatment. For the purposes of full implementation, the drafter can state that the objective of the national text is the full implementation of the specific international instrument. For ease of reference they can attach the international instrument to the text of the national law to encourage reading them as a set. They can define all terms that need a correlation between national and international laws. They can structure the national law creatively and with the effectiveness of the regulation at the national level as the sole criterion. They can formulate the national law by use of best practices in drafting. Territorial application is often a concern, and the drafter must clarify it expressly. Similarly, it is worth clarifying in the text when the start date of the national law is, and what provisions are made for the period between the entry into force of the international instrument and the start date of the national measure. It is also worth clarifying the dispute resolution aspect of the international treaty structures, such as arbitration, before the courts, or via remedies analogous to breach of contract remedies in national law. Finally, amendment of the national legislation may require specific provision: it can remain within the power offered to the Foreign and Commonwealth Office in which case a specific provision with an enabling clause would be a good idea. Having finalised the composition, drafters can verify the quality of the national text by use of the producing foreign organisation.

Ultimately the vision for national implementation begins with negotiations at the international level. And so there is scope for a drafting team consisting of the negotiators, the national policy-makers, the national legal officers and the national drafters. This supports and serves the concept of international treaties as drafting instructions for national drafters.

INNOVATION

Drafting principal provisions, for whatever purpose, lies at the core of the drafter's task. But their success in that task is intertwined with the background work undertaken in the first three stages of Thornton's drafting

[106] See M Eaton, 'Enacting Treaties' (2002) 23 *Statute Law Review* 13, 13.

process. The drafter's aid is the pyramid of values leading to effectiveness, and its application in the inevitable clashes amongst these values that give rise to drafting dilemmas. The doctrine of phronetic legislative drafting recognises the subjectivity of the drafter's task, and acknowledges the subjectivity of their work. But this is balanced by the principles of legislative drafting, which, when serving effectiveness, come to the drafter's rescue.

Regional and international legislative texts are growing in number and volume. And they require special treatment. The need to use them as drafting instructions, rather than model laws, is currently submerged in the sea of practicalities that have led to the increasing use of delegated legislation for their implementation. It is questionable that practicalities must lead the debate. At the end of the day, regional and international legislative texts are no different from national drafting projects. In order to produce the desired regulatory results, they need to be drafted effectively, with clarity, precision, unambiguity and by use of plain language and gender-neutral language. And this requires their drafting from the Office of Parliamentary Counsel or the Foreign and Commonwealth Office. Departing from primary legislation for the purposes of domestication of regional or international instruments may be justified constitutionally, but it is completely unforgivable from a legislative quality perspective.

9

Final Provisions

HAVING DRAFTED PRELIMINARY and principal provisions the drafter turns their attention to final provisions. This is still within the context of Thornton's fourth stage of legislative drafting, namely composing and developing the draft. In application of the plain language requirements for short preliminary provisions, a large selection of provisions now rests with final provisions. This is the list:

- Preliminary provisions
- Principal provisions
- Miscellaneous
- Final provisions
  - Saving provisions
  - Transitional provisions
  - Repeals and consequential amendments
  - Purpose clause/Objectives
  - Start/End provisions
  - Short title (if this remains necessary)
  - Schedules
    - Definitions/Interpretation
    - Other Schedules

The list is long. But in the layered approach this would be a part addressed to the lawyers and judges that use the legislation. Even in the current legislative format the length of final provisions is a necessary evil, which, however, does not detract the user's attention from the main regulatory messages offered in the preliminary and principal provisions. Needless to say that not all types of final provisions are necessary in each legislative text: the drafter selects those appropriate for the task ahead.

SAVING PROVISIONS

Saving provisions preserve or 'save' a conceptual element that would otherwise be repealed or cease to have effect.[1] In other words, saving provisions

[1] See HR Millard, 'The Savings Clause: Some Problems in Construction and Drafting' (1954–55) 33 *Texas Law Review* 285, 285.

keep in being laws, rights or obligations that would otherwise disappear when an existing law is repealed.[2] Conceptually, saving provisions exclude a conceptual element from the field of application of a repeal necessary for law reform.[3]

It is precisely this link with the notion of application that classifies saving and application provisions under the same conceptual roof. Indeed, they both affect the subject or object of a principal provision that is affected by the legislative text. But saving provisions are exclusions from a concept,[4] whereas application provisions normally clarify the field of application of the legislative text: and so their main difference is the negative nuance of saving provisions as opposed to the positive nuance of application provisions. For example, a saving may exclude from the new law, and therefore save, applications submitted to an authority before the start date of the new legislative text even though the new procedure has not been followed. In contrast to this, an application provision clarifies that applications submitted to the authority before the start date of the new legislative text continue to be examined by the authority if the applicants submit the extra documents required by the new procedures. A second difference is perhaps more important and more practical: saving provisions refer to a secondary concept within the legislative text, whereas application provisions refer to either the main scope of the legislative text or a large part of it. For example, in a legislative text establishing a new agency and introducing powers the matter of pending applications is a secondary one: a saving provision can do the trick. But clarifying that the legislative text applies exclusively to England and Wales is a major issue, and requires an application provision.

One wonders whether drafters need to obsess with the distinction between application and saving: after all, it is the message that matters, not the title. Although this is quite correct and especially in final provisions one would expect lawyers and judges to be able to decipher the message communicated to them, it does make sense for drafters to identify which type is the provision before them. If it is a saving, then it is expressed as an exclusion, it refers to a minor part of the regulatory framework introduced by the new text, and it is titled as 'Saving provisions'. In this case, the drafter must then decide whether all saving provisions are to be placed together in final provisions, or whether they are better placed separately under the positive principal provision where the exclusion is attached. If the drafter drafts an application provision, then it must be expressed positively

[2] See AR Menard Jr, 'Legislative Bill Drafting' (1950–51) 23 *Rocky Mountain Law Review* 127, 138; also see VRAC Crabbe *Legislative Precedents—Volume II* (London, Cavendish Publishing Ltd, 1998) 31.

[3] See D Berry, 'The Importance of Getting Savings and Transitional Right: Two Contrasting Cases' http://www.opc.gov.au/calc/docs/Loophole/Loophole_Dec01.pdf.

[4] See R Muhamad, 'Savings Clause: Get It Right' (2011) 37 *Commonwealth Law Bulletin* 445.

and carry the title 'Application'.[5] Application provisions are really better placed in preliminary provisions: the user must be made aware as quickly as possible whether the text is worthy of further exploration, or whether it is totally irrelevant for their purposes. It is perhaps in response to this confusion between saving and application that geographical application is now expressed with 'extent'. For example: '(5) This Act extends to England and Wales only'.[6] Or, 'This Act extends to the whole of the United Kingdom'.[7]

Interpretation legislation normally deals expressly with saving provisions that are generally to be construed when legislation is repealed. Thus, the Maine Revised Statutes contain a general saving, namely a provision that preserves pre-existing rights that have vested before the change in the law. This is an example of a general saving[8] found in many jurisdictions around the world. There is a question as to whether these need to be repeated in legislative texts or not. There is no doubt that not repeating them does not disqualify them from applying to specific legislative Acts and constitutions or constitutional principles that apply in the whole statute book. But there is a question of approachability: Interpretation Acts and constitutional texts are not common reading for non-lawyers. The fact that something is mentioned in them does not necessarily mean that readers are aware of them, or that they can predict how they apply to the contents of each legislative text.[9] It is therefore advisable for the drafter to repeat them, where they are particularly relevant in legislation. And although cross references are considered to be bad practice as they are unclear to the user, a substantive provision with a cross reference and its specific application to the text does serve clarity in a most effective manner.

Since a repeal could otherwise destroy obligations, the saving clause must be tailored to the needs of a particular case.[10] Saving provisions are

[5] See Presumption of Death Act 2013, s 21:

21 Application to Crown

(1) This Act binds the Crown.

(2) But an application may not be made under this Act for a declaration in respect of Her Majesty.

[6] See Mobile Homes Act 2013, s 15.

[7] See European Union (Croatian Accession and Irish Protocol) Act 2013, s 6.

[8] For additional examples of general savings, see EM Million, 'Expiration or Repeal of a Federal or Oregon Statute or Regulation as a Bar to Prosecution for Violations Thereunder' (1944) 24 *Oregon Law Review* 25; also see DS Mitchell, 'In with the New, out with the Old: Expanding the Scope of Retroactive Amelioration' (2009) 121 *American Journal of Criminal Law* 1; and SC Day, 'Pitfalls on the Road to Salvation: The Kansas Saving Statute' (1990) 59 *Journal of the Kansas Bar Association* 19.

[9] See J Burrows, 'The Interpretation Act 1999' in R Bigwood (ed), *The Statute: Making and Meaning* (Wellington, Lexis Nexis, 2004) 224.

[10] See U Karpen, 'Instructions for Law Drafting' (2008) 10 *European Journal of Law Reform* 163, 180.

traditionally drafted by use of the term 'save'.[11] But this is a technical legal term whose departure from common language creates ambiguity for the reader. As a result, it is advisable to use more approachable terms: 'but', expressions of exclusion, or simply nothing in the text apart from a heading with 'saving'.[12] For example, 'The new procedure applies to all applications made to the Food Licensing Authority. But applications submitted before the start date of this law are not affected by the new requirements'. Or '(1) Except section 53 (and schedule 4), this Part comes into force on the day after Royal Assent'.[13] Or simply:

> *Saving of accrued pension rights etc*
> 10 (1) The amendments of the Superannuation Act 1972 made by Part 2 of this Schedule do not affect the operation of that Act in relation to employment of any of the following kinds by any person—
> (a) employment by SOCA;
> (b) employment as a member of the staff of the NPIA.
> (2) The amendments of the Police Pensions Act 1976 made by Part 2 of this Schedule do not affect the operation of that Act in relation to service of any of the following kinds by any person—
> (a) service as an employee of SOCA;
> (b) relevant service within paragraph (ca) or (cb) of section 97(1) of the Police Act 1996;
> (c) relevant service within section 38A(1)(ba) of the Police (Scotland) Act 1967;
> (d) service as a member of the staff of NPIA.[14]

TRANSITIONAL PROVISIONS

Transitional provisions deal with the passage from the previous regulatory regime to the new one. Their aim is to regulate issues whose timeline crosses the end of the previous legislative text and the start of the new legislative

[11] See Clergy Discipline (Amendment) Measure 2013, s 6:
(4) After subsection (3) there is added the following subsection—
'(3A) Where a notice of suspension is served under subsection (1)(c) or (d) above and it has not been revoked under subsection (2), the suspension shall continue until the expiry of the period of three months following service of the notice or until a penalty is imposed on the priest or deacon under section 30(1) above, whichever occurs earlier, save that a further notice of suspension under subsection (1)(c) or (d) may be served pending conclusion of any step taken under section 30(2) or (4), and this subsection shall apply in relation to the further suspension as it applied to the earlier suspension or suspensions'.

[12] See LE Filson and SL Strokof, *The Legislative Drafter's Desk Reference*, 2nd edn (Washington, CQ Press, 2009) 178, where the authors state that in drafting saving clauses every case is different, and there is no standard form.

[13] See Water Resources (Scotland) Act 2013, s 56.

[14] See Crime and Courts Act 2013, sch 8.

text. Transitional provisions are 'directions governing (the) application (of the new law) in time'.[15] They foresee how these issues are to be dealt with, by dissolving any confusion as to which regime applies and how. They smoothen the transition from the existing legislation to the new legislation, hence their name. They are necessary in tying up the loose ends that would otherwise be left dangling. What happens to cases already in the pipeline when a new system of appeal is instituted? How are licences granted under the old legislation to be affected by the new? What happens to the assets and liabilities of a body corporate whose constitution is being changed from a private company to a statutory corporation? A classic example of a transitional provision is one regulating the transfer of functions, property and staff from a now abolished agency to a newly established one:

> Sec. B-43. Transition provisions. The following provisions govern the transition of the Maine State Museum Bureau to the Maine State Museum.
>
> The Maine State Museum is the successor in every way to the powers, duties and functions of the former Maine State Museum Bureau.
>
> All existing rules, regulations and procedures in effect, in operation or adopted in or by the Maine State Museum Bureau or any of its administrative units or officers are hereby declared in effect and continue in effect until rescinded, revised or amended by the proper authority.
>
> All existing contracts, agreements and compacts currently in effect in the Maine State Museum Bureau continue in effect.
>
> Any positions authorized and allocated subject to the personnel laws to the former Maine State Museum Bureau are transferred to the Maine State Museum and may continue to be authorized.
>
> All records, property and equipment previously belonging to or allocated for the use of the former Maine State Museum Bureau become, on the effective date of this Act, part of the property of the Maine State Museum.
>
> All existing forms, licenses, letterheads and similar items bearing the name of or referring to the 'Maine State Museum Bureau' may be utilized by the Maine State Museum until existing supplies of those items are exhausted.[16]

Other examples of transitional provisions would be those dealing with the transfer of assets and liabilities, pending proceedings or interim arrangements. In view of the common content of these types of provisions with saving provisions, it is obvious why these transitional provisions are often confused with saving provisions. The Australian Office of Parliamentary

[15] See E Edinger, 'Retrospectivity in Law' (1995) 29 *University of British Columbia Law Review* 5, 5.

[16] See Legislative Council, Maine State Legislature, 'Main Drafting Manual' (2009) 20 www.maine.gov/legis/ros/manual/Draftman2009.doc.

Counsel states that there are many types of transitional provisions, since they can:

— modify the effect of the 'new' law; or
— modify the effect of the 'old' law (as it continues to apply by virtue of an application provision); or
— override the presumption against retrospectivity; or
— ensure that an amendment does not affect the interpretation of the 'old' law; or
— ensure that the repeal of an amending Act, or of amending provisions, does not affect the operation of amendments made by the amending Act or amending provisions.[17]

Transitional provisions deal with the passage from the previous regulatory regime to the new one. By definition therefore they have a limited life expectancy. And it is precisely this notion of limited time that they attempt to convey. As a result, transitional provisions come to an end, whereas saving provisions continue their life indefinitely, or at least until repealed. This is their main difference, and so this is the criterion for a classification of a provision under saving or transitional. But this is not always undertaken successfully. For example, section 24 of the Enterprise and Regulatory Reform Act 2013 has completely misnamed saving provisions as transitional. The provisions refer to the exclusion from the scope of the Act of disclosures, requests for information, proceedings and contracts of employment starting before the start date. This is not a transitional provision, it is a saving: these objects continue to be excluded indefinitely, and this is particularly evident in subsection (3).

> 24 Transitional provision
> (1) Section 10 does not apply in relation to a disclosure, or a request for information, made before that section comes into force.
> (2) Section 12 does not apply in relation to proceedings that are in the process of being heard by the Employment Appeal Tribunal when that section comes into force.
> (3) Section 13 does not apply where the effective date of termination of the contract of employment in question is earlier than the date on which that section comes into force.[18]

But inability or difficulty of classification of a provision as a saving or transitional is no excuse for dropping them under one section titled 'Saving and transitional provisions'. This may well salvage the drafter's professional dignity, but it creates ambiguity for the users including judges.

[17] See OPC Drafting Manual (Oct 2012) 12–13 https://www.opc.gov.au/about/docs/Drafting_manual.pdf.
[18] See Enterprise and Regulatory Reform Act 2013, s 24.

Equally puzzling is the invention of new classifications of provisions, such as in the heading 'SCHEDULE 5 TRANSITIONAL AND TRANSITORY PROVISIONS AND SAVINGS' in Schedule 5 of the Mobile Homes (Wales) Act 2013.

REPEALS AND CONSEQUENTIAL AMENDMENTS

Thornton believes, and very rightly so, that it is impossible to legislate in a vacuum.[19] Even when the topic of legislative reform appears to be brand new for the legal system, it still affects existing legislation in related or seemingly unrelated issues. In this sense, all legislation is to be treated as amending legislation. It is the drafter's duty to identify which existing legislative texts are affected by the new one, in total or as a part. And to repeal or amend accordingly. Otherwise the drafter introduces an 'unintended repeal by implication',[20] 'overlaps, and inconsistent terminology: in a word—confusion'.[21]

The effect of the repeal is the obliteration of the Act or section from the statute book. The classic statement is that of Lord Tindall:

> I take the effect of repealing a statute to be, to obliterate it as completely from the records of the parliament as if it had never passed; and, it must be considered as a law that never existed, except for the purpose of those actions which were commenced, prosecuted, and concluded whilst it was an existing law.[22]

This must be qualified: the rule applies especially to causes of action unknown at common law but created by statute, and 'in this respect embraces all transactions not past and closed'.[23]

Teasdale identifies the following circumstances giving rise to the necessity for repeal:

1. where the purpose underpinning the enactment has been overtaken by events, rendering it obsolete;
2. where there have been changes in social or economic circumstances since the original enactment came into being, rendering the legislation unnecessary;

[19] But see contra Bennion, who states that repealing an Act creates a vacuum to be filled by common law and therefore judge made law: see FAR Bennion, *Statutory Interpretation: A Code* (1997) pt IV, 222, 229.

[20] See R Izikira, 'Instructions to Draft Legislation: A Study on Legislative Drafting Process in Rwanda (2012) 4 *European Journal of Law Reform* 225, 231.

[21] See R Dickerson, 'How to Write a Law' (1955–56) 31 *Notre Dame Law* 14, 19.

[22] See Tindall CJ in *Kay v Goodwin* 6 Bing 576, 582 (1830).

[23] See MH Ruud, 'The Savings Clause: Some Problems in Construction and Drafting' (1954–55) 33 *Texas Law Review* 285, 290.

3. where provisions have become spent, in the sense that they were enacted for a specific purpose which has been activated and exhausted (for example, where transitional or saving provisions were enacted and they have ceased to be necessary);
4. where provisions have expired, or ceased to be in force, because they were time-limited (or they were expressed to be temporary) and no continuation Act was promoted;
5. where the enactment contained a 'sunset clause', which had the effect of discontinuing the Act's effectiveness, but did not repeal it;
6. where later legislation purported to supersede the earlier, but where the earlier was not repealed concurrently, or where references to specific Acts in the earlier legislation have been superseded by more modem legislation (including EU legislation);
7. where legislation was enacted, but has not been brought into force (by commencement order), usually for a substantial period, through change in circumstances; and
8. where legislation has fallen into desuetude[24] through lack of use, or it simply lacks practical utility.[25]

What is important to stress is that for the purposes of serving clarity the drafter must repeal and amend expressly in the form of an exclusive list of affected provisions gathered together in a single section placed in final provisions.[26] General provisions stating that anything in contrast to the new legislative text is amended are unclear and invite for judicial law-making.[27] This type of consequential amendment provisions is common in a number of jurisdictions: but they simply reflect the drafter's fear of missing something out rather than the drafter's strive to communicate fully the regulatory message to the user. Drafters are human and mistakes may happen: but, at the end of the day, offering an exclusive list of consequential amendments would not prevent a judge from construing an implied repeal or amendment, should the case absolutely necessitate. But at least it would limit necessity for this kind of judicial law-making to the absolutely necessary.

Repeals and consequential amendments are expressed by use of various terms. 'Repeal', 'revoke', 'rescind', 'delete' and 'cancel' are just a few samples. The drafter must keep in mind the legal requirement to 'repeal' primary legislation and 'rescind' delegated legislation. The question is, how

[24] But the doctrine is denied by W Chew, 'The Doctrine of Implied Repeal by Desuetude: a Legal Anachronism or Viable Principle?' (1984) 5 *Singapore Law Review* 139, 143.

[25] See J Teasdale, 'Consolidation or Something More?' (2009) 11 *European Journal of Law Reform* 157, 171–72.

[26] See DB Murray, 'When is a Repeal not a Repeal?' (1953) 16 *Modern Law Review* 50, 58.

[27] For the abandonment of this awful practice in the UK, see Sir N Hutton, 'Awful Statute Book of Great Britain' (1975) 2 *North Dekota Journal of Legislation* 1, 12.

this 'legal correctness' can be conveyed to the lay user clearly? Here radical innovation would call for 'delete' as a generic term. At the end of the day the term is generic enough to cover both sets of circumstances. A non-radical approach would call for the use of the same term throughout the text and the statute book, in application of the prevalent drafting convention of avoiding synonyms.

Repeals may take the form of a simple repeal, where the provision is no longer needed and no further legislative action is required in its stead; or of a repeal and re-enactment, where the provision is deleted and a new provision consolidates elements of the existing law with new elements but leaves the law essentially unchanged;[28] or of a repeal and replacement, where existing legislation is being remoulded to meet new circumstances in different ways.[29]

There seems to be a long-standing debate concerning the need to repeal Amending Acts or subsidiary legislation. The orthodox view from the point of view of constitutional theory is that Amending Acts do not have a life: they become alive on their start date when they are incorporated in the original Act. As a result, they do no need to be repealed since the original Act is repealed. This is a constitutionally correct view: Amending Acts are symbiotic organisms to the original Act, and their lives and expiry are intrinsically linked. And although there is an argument of clarity urging drafters to repeal original and Amending Acts alike, sometimes reflected by repeal provisions referring to 'Act... as subsequently amended', it is clear that amending Acts die along with the original Act. The question is what happens when the original Act is repealed before the start date of an Amending Act: is there a need for repealing expressly the Amending Act since it 'dies' before its incorporation to the original Act. The constitutional position is that the Act never existed, that the organism to which it would attach for oxygen dies at the moment of their joining, and that therefore the Amending Act never breathes at all. And so an express repeal is not needed. But from a clarity perspective, replying to this question requires balancing clarity with superfluity: and on the basis of the pyramid of virtues, clarity wins. As a result, although it is not necessary to do so, it is advisable for drafters to repeal expressly both the original Act, and the amending Acts not yet in force on the date of repeal.

The same applies with delegated legislation. There is little doubt that, unless otherwise expressly foreseen, delegated legislation ceases to exist when the original Act is repealed. And constitutionally this allows the

[28] 'Where possible, statutes or complete parts of statutes, should not be amended but re-enacted in an amended form so that those concerned can read the rules in a single document': see *Merkur Island Shipping Corporation v Laughton* [1983] 2 AC 570, 595.

[29] See DC Elliott, 'Getting Better Instructions for Legislative Drafting' 7 www.davidelliott.ca/legislativedrafting.htm.

drafter to avoid the tedious task of identifying all delegated legislation 'hanging' from the original Act, and of placing these in a list of repeals and consequential amendments. But there is a very serious issue of clarity and unambiguity here: in view of the abundance of delegated legislation in current legislative reality, it becomes near impossible for the reader to identify whether the original Act remains in the statute book, and to understand whether the delegated legislative text remains in force or not. There is no easy answer in practice. There is a clear academic call for an exclusive list of repeals and amendments of delegated legislation: if the drafter finds the task insurmountable, is there any doubt of its impossibility for the poor user? There is light in the tunnel, and this comes in the form of electronic publication of legislation: electronic databases of legislation can, with undeniable effort and resources, offer the possibility of linking primary to delegated legislation, thus allowing the drafter to simply take advantage of hyperlinks to delegated legislation in order to identify if and how these are affected by the repeal of the original Act. After all, one would expect the instructing officers of the client department to be aware of the relevant delegated provisions, to have identified them and read them, and to have taken them into account for the purposes of their drafting instructions. Otherwise, one is led to believe that the picture of existing legislation drawn in drafting instructions may not be a complete one. It is therefore hoped that, aided by technology and led by the clients, drafters will soon be able to have a list of delegated legislation hanging from the original Act, thus allowing them to include them in the repeal and consequential amendment provision. Clarity demands this.

PURPOSE CLAUSE/OBJECTIVES

The terms 'objects' and 'purposes' in this context are interchangeable.[30] Purpose clauses offer the user an insight of the reasoning of regulators, thus enhancing comprehension.[31] They express what purpose or objectives the legislative text pursues, and reflect the general ethos of legislative intent.[32] And so they can be 'perfect topic specifiers'.[33] They state what the statute intends to achieve.[34] And so they differ profoundly from a long title: the

[30] See D Berry, 'Purpose Sections: Why They are a Good Idea for Drafters and Users' (2011) 2 *The Loophole* 49, available at https://www.opc.gov.au/about/docs/Drafting_manual.pdf.

[31] See JD Bransford and MK Johnson, 'Contextual Prerequisites for Understanding: Some Investigations of Comprehension and Recall' (1972) 11 *Journal of Verbal Learning and Verbal Behaviour* 717; also see LMS Miller, JA Cohen and A Wingfield, 'Contextual Knowledge Reduces Demands on Working Memory During Reading' (2006) 34 *Memory Cognition* 1355.

[32] See B Drummond and P Marwood, 'Purposive Drafting in Finance Bill 2007' (2007) 4 *British Tax Review* 350, 354.

[33] IML Turnbull, 'Clear Legislative Drafting: New Approaches in Australia' (1990) 11 *Statute Law Review* 161, 169.

[34] See Lord Renton, 'Interpretation of Legislation' (1982) 3 *Statute Law Review* 7, 10.

long title tells the user what mechanisms of law reform are introduced in the legislative text, whereas an objectives or purpose clauses states what the desired regulatory results are. Long titles are factual and refer to the present; purpose clauses are pronouncements of future success.

And it is exactly this aspect of their role that has led them to treacherous paths.[35] Purpose clauses are operative provisions of the Act, and they must be expressed in clear, precise and unambiguous terms. They are to be drafted using the same precise and concise terms used elsewhere in legislation, and must focus on the results intended to be achieved rather than the means of achieving them. An example of good practice would state:

> The objectives of this Act are:-
> (a) to reduce the number of drivers with alcohol present in their blood when driving; and
> (b) to reduce the number of car accidents caused by these drivers.

Unfortunately purpose or objectives provisions have in the past been usurped by expressions of emotive political statement that should not have found their way into the legislative text.[36] In effect, they have been known to have been used instead of the now abolished preambles. An example of bad practice would state:

> The purpose of this Act is:
> (a) to curb the menace drunken drivers cause to themselves and to innocent drivers, passengers and pedestrians;
> (b) to reduce the carnage on the roads caused by such drivers;
> (c) to save lives.

The second example has no place in legislation. It takes away part of the attention span of the user, and offers them nothing in exchange. In fact its language invites for ineffectivess. It is exactly because of such language that purpose clauses have become very unpopular in the last decades. But one wonders whether they can acquire new kudos as perpetrators of innovation rather than reminders of their awful past.

Within the context of using legislation as a means of regulation one wonders[37] whether objectives provisions can set out in clear terms the tangible regulatory aims of the legislative text and the tangible measurable and concrete criteria by which these aims are to be achieved. If this were the case, objectives clauses would be directly linked to post-legislative

[35] See D Greenberg, *Craies on Legislation: A Practitioner's Guide to the Nature, Process, Effect and Interpretation of Legislation*, 9th edn (London, Sweet and Maxwell, 2008) 352; also see the detailed expose of J Barnes, 'Statutory Objects Provisions: How Cogent is the Research and Commentary?' (2012) 34 *Statute Law Review* 12.

[36] See Office of the Scottish Parliamentary Counsel, *Plain Language and Legislation* (2006) 40 www.scotland.gov.uk/Publications/2006/02/17093804/0.

[37] There are no empirical data on the user perspective of objects provisions: see Barnes, 'Statutory Objects Provisions: How Cogent is the Research and Commentary?' (n 35) 28.

scrutiny, as they would offer the policy officers of the instructing department the opportunity to articulate the concrete regulatory results desired and to then apply those in the planned post-legislative scrutiny exercise for the purposes of assessing the effectiveness of the legislative text.[38] All this would be with enhanced transparency as this would be in the public sphere.[39] But, most importantly, this exercise would contribute to a closure of the current gap between legislative intent and legislative effect.[40] In other words, in the drafting instructions clients would have to list what they hope to achieve by means of legislation, the drafter would have the opportunity to ascertain or reject legislation as a means of achieving the set regulatory results, the drafter would then incorporate the regulatory results in the legislation thus offering Parliament an insight into what is required, how it is hoped that this will be produced and on what basis the assessment of the success of the legislative text will take place at the post-legislative stage. Parliament could then use the criteria of assessment to evaluate the quality of the post-legislative exercise as a means of exercising meaningful parliamentary scrutiny, and then decide if the legislation can continue its life or whether it is has proven so inappropriate for the desired regulatory results that it should die and be deleted from the statute book. Here an end clause, known as a 'duration' or 'sunset' clause, could have the desired persuasive and empowerment effect. And so, a new mission for objectives provisions can offer them an unparallelled significance: their use as vessels of quality control of the whole regulatory cycle, from policy concept and formulation to legislative enactment and post-legislative scrutiny.

But of course to achieve in this new role objectives clauses must be drafted in concrete terms, and the criteria used must be deprived of political nuances and introduced as a matter of fact measures of scrutiny. There is little doubt that this requires a significant change in the ethos of drafting objectives clauses. But the elements of that are already here: presumably identifying measures of quality for post-legislative scrutiny apply the same ethos of concreteness and precision. And so what would be required really would be the incorporation of post-legislative scrutiny elements into the pre-legislative drafting process. Which in turn would recognise the role of the drafting process as a part of the legislative process, which is a part of the policy process.

[38] On the sunsetting policy, see Department for Business, Innovation and Skills, *Reducing Regulation Made Simple* www.bis.gov.uk/policies/better-regulation/better-regulation-executive/reducing-regulation-made-simple._

[39] See M Malik, 'From Conflict to Cohesion: Competing Interests in Equality Law and Policy' (2009) 187 *Equal Opportunity Review* 11, 12–13.

[40] See ER Beerworth, 'The Evaluation of Legislation' in R Tomasic (ed), *Legislation and Society in Australia* (New South Wales, Allen and Unwin, 1980) 66, 68.

COMMENCEMENT/DURATION PROVISIONS OR START/END DATE

The start and end of the life of an Act constitutes a primary regulatory message. Simple commencement and duration provisions are therefore placed in preliminary provisions. But the start and end date of legislation becomes all the more complex. And a long list of various start and end dates at the beginning of the text would defeat the object of the drafter striving to grasp the user's attention for that little window of opportunity offered in the first few minutes of their reading the legislative text. It is therefore advisable for the drafter to escort the 'master' start and end dates in preliminary provisions with a longer list of complex start and end dates either in final provisions,[41] or in a Schedule. The advantage of a Schedule is that the drafter can cross refer to it just below the 'master' start and end date. The choice between placement in final provisions or in a Schedule is made on the basis of the primacy of the message: if the start and end dates affect provisions introducing a primary regulatory message and readers must be made aware of that as it nullifies the start and end date to a great extent, then a Schedule would be preferable as the drafter will refer to it just below the start and end dates. In the context of the layered approach a Schedule is preferable if the exceptions to the master start and end date refer to provisions found in part one of the layered text. If not, then they can be placed in final provisions since the professional and legal users of groups two and three would certainly be aware of the need to read the whole text and to interrelate provisions throughout the text.

But why would a drafter provide for the end of the legislative text? After all, one of the traditional characteristics of legislation is that they apply generally for an indefinite period of time. End date provisions commonly

[41] See Growth and Infrastructure Act 2013, s 35:
35 Commencement
(1) Subject as follows, this Act comes into force on such day as the Secretary of State may by order appoint; and different days may be appointed for different purposes.
(2) Section 1(1) so far as it inserts the new section 62B, sections 4, 7, 9, 16, 19, 26, 32 and 33, this section and section 36, and Schedules 2 and 4, come into force on the day on which this Act is passed.
(3) Sections 11, 12, 17, 18, 29 and 30 come into force at the end of two months beginning with the day on which this Act is passed.
(4) Section 21(4) to (6) come into force on such day as the Scottish Ministers may by order appoint; and different days may be appointed for different purposes.
(5) The Scottish Ministers may by order make such transitional, transitory or saving provision as the Scottish Ministers consider appropriate in connection with the coming into force of section 21(4) to (6).
(6) The Secretary of State may by order make such transitional, transitory or saving provision as the Secretary of State considers appropriate in connection with the coming into force of any other provision of this Act.
(7) Power to make an order under subsection (5) or (6) includes power to make different provision for different purposes.

known as 'sunset clauses' declare that the Act at a set time 'ceases to have effect unless it is reauthorised'.[42] These are becoming extremely popular in legislation.[43] And this is an enlightened approach:[44] legislation is a tool for regulation, and its performance is judged against a concrete set of tangible measurable criteria for post-legislative scrutiny. It makes extreme sense for the regulator, namely the government, to assess the effectiveness of the legislative text periodically. And here the drafting profession can facilitate the concept of compulsory period post-legislative scrutiny by forcing government departments to conduct a post-legislative scrutiny exercise as a means of persuading Parliament that the legislative text is effective,[45] and can continue its life. Leaving this to government departments without the persuasive mechanism of a sunset clause may result in haphazard post-legislative scrutiny. Moreover, sunset clauses result in an automatic cleaning of the statute book every three or five years, depending on the duration of legislation. It makes perfect sense for end provisions to be inserted in legislation as standard, allowing for exceptions only where the possibility of a lack of legislative regulation, if the legislation dies unintentionally, may create regulatory chaos or unease. In the EU, sunset clauses are part of the Smart Regulation agenda and are becoming increasingly frequent. But, then again, sunset clauses on their own are not effective regulatory review weapons: they need to be supplemented by meaningful post-legislative scrutiny exercises undertaken on the basis of measurable criteria. For that, purpose clauses may come to the rescue.

Even in a more traditional approach to the innovative requirement for end dates by default, sunset clauses are necessary in five distinct types of legislation. First, legislation in stages can be useful in cases of controversial issues: for example, liberalising abortion in a deeply religious society may lead to a useless addition to the statute book without an incremental approach; liberalisation can start by allowing abortion exclusively where the mother's life is at risk, or where the embryo is a product of a criminal act; it can then expand to abortion up to nine weeks of gestation; and then it can proceed further. This incremental approach is served very well by means of a staggered start and end date of the intermediate regulatory regimes. Secondly, legislation that is experimental or whose benefits

[42] See EJ Gouvin, 'Are There Any Checks and Balances on the Government's Power to Check Our Balances? The Fate of Financial Privacy in the War on Terrorism' (2005) 14 *Temple Policy and Civil Rights Law Review* 517, 540.

[43] See HC Deb 1 July 2003 col 383 vol 26, Written Answer 217 from Greenberg (ed), *Craies on Legislation* (n 35) 384, para 10.2.4, note 7.

[44] For an analysis of the benefits of sunset clauses, see JE Finn 'Sunset Clauses and Democratic Deliberation: Assessing the Significance of Sunset Provisions in Antiterrorism Legislation' (2009–10) 48 *Columbia Journal of Transnational Law* 442, 447.

[45] See P Suber, 'The Paradox of Self-amendment: a Study of Law, Logic, Omnipotence, and Change' (1998) 14 www.earlham.edu/-peters/writing/psa/sec 14.htm.

are speculative or unpredictable would require an end date: throwing the legislative text into the statute book for a limited period of time can allow the text the opportunity to produce the desired regulatory results, thus earning its place within the statute book. Thirdly, legislation responding to a short-term need requires an end date: a classic example of this would be legislation offering aid to citizens suffering from extreme natural phenomena. And fourthly, authorisations to use emergency powers always come with an end date: they are a break from constitutional normality, and are tolerated only for a well defined short period of time.

There is a question as to whether Acts including sunset clauses need to be repealed after their expiry. Constitutionally, there is no doubt that the Act dies as soon as the end date occurs. But there is a question of best drafting practice. Although the repeal is not necessary from a legal perspective, nonetheless clarity is best served with an express repeal. The added value of this method is that the Act disappears from subsequent reprints of the statute book.[46]

SHORT TITLE

Short titles are the heading of the legislative text. Their task is to offer an agreed means by which to index and cite the legislative text. The short title of the legislative text is found both at the top above the text, and also in a provision now placed at the very end of the body of the text. Although one can see the need to provide for the title, it is time for drafters to consider whether this repetition is of service. It is time to get rid of the short title provision, and simply index or cite on the basis of the title found just above the table of contents or arrangements: whether this constitutes part of the text or not is certainly something that can be clarified perhaps by means of an announcement in Parliament just as the one offered for the introduction of gender-neutral language.

Irrespective of where the short title is in the text, it is drafted to express the name by which the law is to be known, without puns and sloganeering.[47] As a result, the title must be short, to the point, accurate, unique and distinctive, so that it cannot be confused with other titles.[48] In order to fulfil these qualities, the language of the title must be consistent with the content of the Act. The need to be brief does not justify abbreviations. In order to

[46] See AL Diamond, 'Repeal and Desuetude of Statutes' (1975) 28 *Current Legal Problems* 107, 124.

[47] See G Orr, 'From Slogans to Puns: Australian Legislative Titling Revisited' (2001) 22 *Statute Law Review* 160.

[48] For the US perspective, see BC Jones, 'Drafting Proper Short Bill Titles: Do States Have the Answer?' (2012) 23 *Stanford Law and Policy Review* 455.

achieve their goal successfully, the short title is drafted at the very end of the drafting process.[49]

Short titles include the year of introduction into Parliament in the case of a Bill; or of enactment in the case of an Act: eg Justice and Security Act 2013. It is common practice to add explanatory words in brackets to the short title. This is helpful when the drafter attempts to distinguish between various statutes on the same topic: in this case the specific aspect of the statute will be added in brackets, such as Trusts (Capital and Income) Act 2013; or when the Act applies to a specific geographical area only: in this case the statute's short title will have the geographical area in brackets, such as High Hedges (Scotland) Act 2013; or when the drafter amends an existing Act: in this case 'Amendment' will be in brackets, such as Domestic Violence, Crime and Victims (Amendment) Act 2012; or in combination of the above, such as Freedom of Information (Amendment) (Scotland) Act 2013, or Water and Sewerage Services (Amendment) Act (Northern Ireland) 2013, or even The Local Authorities (Executive Arrangements) (Functions and Responsibilities) (Wales) (Amendment No 2) Regulations 2013.

SCHEDULES

A Schedule, known as 'Annex' in some jurisdictions, is a convenient device for separating matters of secondary or technical detailed nature from the body of the legislative text. The logic behind the introduction of a Schedule is to leave aside any material that is of secondary regulatory value, thus enabling the user to focus on messages of primary regulatory importance.[50] The use of Schedules is a legitimate and helpful device for the clearer presentation and more effective communication of the content of legislation. The general practice is for matters of principle to remain in the sections of the statute, while lesser matters of machinery or detail may be arranged in Schedules. The principal purpose of this arrangement is to enable the presentation of the main sections of the enactment uncluttered by material of secondary or incidental importance. The use of Schedules can make a substantial contribution to effective communication by clearing away procedural and other distinct groups of provisions to Schedules in order to present the main provisions of the statute prominently and in a less cluttered package. So, Schedules free the main body of an Act from a possible charge of untidiness.[51]

[49] See DL Kennedy, 'Legislative Bill Drafting' (1946–47) 31 *Minnesota Law Review* 103, 109.

[50] See H Xanthaki, *Thornton's Legislative Drafting* (West Sussex, Bloomsbury Professional, 2013) 492–93.

[51] See VCRAC Crabbe, *Legislative Drafting* (Oxford, Cavendish Publishing, 1998) 145–47.

But it is important for the drafter to identify which provisions can remain in the text and which can be transferred to a Schedule. This is not too complex a task, if the drafter keeps in mind the logic behind the introduction of Schedules: matters of a subsidiary or consequential nature are suitable. Complex sets of provisions normally found in preliminary or final provisions can be transferred to a Schedule for start/end date; repeals and consequential amendments; transitional provisions; savings;[52] and also definitions. Other suitable material includes the composition of a body established by the legislative text; the procedure at meetings of such a body; lists of persons, items or places to which the legislation applies or does not apply; formulae for calculating taxes; tables setting out benefits or rates of taxes; images showing flags or traffic signs or plans; specification of forms (especially in subsidiary legislation); relevant articles or sections in a treaty or international agreement to be given the force of law; the form of international and other agreements.

The question here is why this type of material would be placed in a Schedule as opposed to delegated instruments. The drafter has a choice and a dilemma. There is little to separate the content of Schedules with that of delegated legislative texts: the common point is that they express matters of detail or a secondary nature. What is the distinguishing factor in this dilemma is longevity and practicality: if the drafter envisages that the material withstands the test of time, then primary legislation is preferable; but if the material seems to require early or periodic amendment, then delegated instruments offer the drafter a distinct advantage. But apart from this main point, the drafter must always keep in mind that, by their nature, some types of provisions are set aside for primary legislation because they require the pronounced parliamentary scrutiny offered to primary legislation: the introduction of new taxes or the introduction of new offences tend to be reserved for primary legislation, as they affect citizens' lives in such a detrimental manner that direct parliamentary legitimacy is needed before they can be enacted.

Although Schedules (note the conventional spelling, with a capital S) form part of the legislation, they cannot stand on their own and must be appended to a particular provision in the main body of the legislation. This is done by the use of what are called 'inducing words'. For an example of a beautifully drafted inducing provision, see the Finance Act 2013, section 24:

> 24 Gains from contracts for life insurance etc
> Schedule 8 amends Chapter 9 of Part 4 of ITTOIA 2005 (gains from contracts for life insurance etc).

[52] See G Thornton, *Legislative Drafting* (London, Butterworths, London, 1996) 140–41, 400–02, 425–26.

The provision is drafted simply, includes reference to the number of the Schedule hanging from it, and also, very crucially, includes a description of the content of the Schedule thus offering the user the opportunity to understand the content of the Schedule, and decide whether to read on or not. Moreover, it carries a descriptive heading.

In some jurisdictions the practice is followed of printing Schedules in a smaller print than that used for the remainder of the text. This is a practice to be avoided as it creates the erroneous impression that the contents of Schedules have lower importance to the remainder of the text. Schedules are as much part of the enactment as is the section introducing them, or indeed any other section.[53] As Brett J said in *A-G v Lamplough*: 'A schedule in an Act is a mere question of drafting, a mere question of words. The Schedule is as much a part of the statute, and is as much an enactment, as any other part'. Since an Act is to be read as a whole, a Schedule does not have 'second-class' status as compared to a section.

Consistency of design and content in Schedules is once again recommended as good practice.[54] Without it, a device intended only to facilitate easy communication may create ambiguity.[55] Matter should only be gathered together and presented in a Schedule, if it has some cohering and unifying feature.

But what if there is a conflict between a Schedule and the inducing section? In *IRC v Gittus* Lord Sterndale MR opined that:

> If the Act says that the Schedule is to be used for a certain purpose and the heading of the part of the Schedule in question shows that it is prima facie at any rate devoted to that purpose, then you must read the Act and the Schedule as though the Schedule were operating for that purpose, and if you can satisfy the language of the section without extending it beyond that purpose you ought to do it. But if in spite of that you find in the language of the Schedule words and terms that go clearly outside that purpose, then you must give effect to them and you must not consider them as limited by the heading of that part of the Schedule or by the purpose mentioned in the Act for which the Schedule is prima facie to be used. You cannot refuse to give effect to clear words simply because prima facie they seem to be limited by the heading of the Schedule and the definition of the purpose of the Schedule contained in the Act.[56]

[53] See *A-G v Lamplough* (1878) 3 ExD 214; on appeal, 47 LJQB 555, CA at 229; *IRC v Gittus* [1920] 1KB 563, 89 LJKB 313; affd sub nom *Gittus v IRC* [1921] 2 AC 81, 90 LJKB 716 (HL).

[54] See *Re Baines* (1840) 12 A & E 227; *Dean v Green* (1882) 8 PD 79.

[55] See C Hand, 'Drafting with the User in Mind—a Look at Legislation in 1982–83' (1983) 4 *Statute Law Review* 166.

[56] *IRC v Gittus* [1920] 1 KB 563, 576.

Schedule of Definitions

Schedules of definitions are becoming increasingly popular. One of the oldest examples is in the Reservoir Bill of 1974, 'where all the definitions are outlying ones, and tabulated indexing in a Schedule was adopted as the most convenient arrangement for the reader'.[57] There is no doubt that definitions must be collected in one place,[58] and arranged in alphabetical order. But, if a section contains a word with a particular definition which applies only to that section, the section can include the definition. The question, and heated debate, is whether definitions are best placed in preliminary or final provisions. It would be logical to assume that the user would benefit from definitions at the beginning, so that they would keep them in mind when reading on the text. But this view, traditionally prevalent in drafting, is giving way to the concern that definitions cannot be allowed to take up the primary attention of the users in the beginning of the text. At the end of the day, definitions are not of regulatory primacy: the main regulatory message is. This is a rather persuasive argument. But placing definitions in a Schedule offers the drafter the best of both worlds: a note in the beginning of the Act stating where definitions are found, and the actual definitions collected together in a Schedule. This is the optimal route.

A definition is used to give a standard meaning to words or phrases that occur frequently in an Act. Definitions are tools against uncertainty, ambiguity and repetition. As a result, they inform clarity and in turn effectiveness. But in order to do so, definitions cannot depart totally from the common concept of the word:[59] stating that 'for this purposes of this Act a man is a human female' creates obvious confusion and ambiguity. After all, representations get their meaning by actually co-varying with the things or states they represent in the real world.[60] A similar result derives from the use of the same term to reflect different semantic fields whether within the text or within the statute book: ambiguity is the disease in this case. Good definitions are sufficiently clear and precise to give reasonable notice of the elements of the term, whilst refraining from including elements that allow the term to operate outside its intended purposes.[61] Definitions cannot be

[57] See *The Preparation of Legislation*: Report of a Committee Appointed by the Lord President of the Council Chairman Sir David Renton (Cmnd 6053, 1975) (Renton Report) para 11.17.

[58] See B Simamba, 'The Placing and Other Handling of Definitions (2006) 27 *Statute Law Review* 73, 82.

[59] See MV Petelo Fa'asau, 'Challenges Faced by Legislative Drafters in Samoa and Other USP Member Countries' (2012) 14 *European Journal of Law Reform* 191, 199.

[60] See R Kukla, 'Cognitive Models and Representation' (1992) 43 *The British Journal of the Philosophy of Science* 219, 221.

[61] With reference to terrorism, see K Hardy and G Williams, 'What is "Terrorism"? Assessing Domestic Legal Definitions' (2011) 16 *UCLA Journal of International and Legal Foreign Affairs* 77, 81.

used to introduce substantive law: a common mistake in drafting is to state that 'For the purposes of this Act "Minister" is the Minister of Labour who is empowered to issue licences'. And of course definitions are to be used sparingly and only when needed: what is the point of stating that 'For the purposes of this Act "abroad" is a location outside the territory of Turkmenistan'?

Thornton's 10 Commandments on definitions are:

1. A word or expression is defined only if the definition will assist readers.
2. A definition does not include substantive matter.
3. A definition does not stipulate an outrageous or extravagant meaning.
4. A definition is, if possible, complete in itself.
5. A definition does not indulge in avoidable and unjustifiable referential legislation.
6. A term manufactured for the purposes of a definition must be as descriptive and helpful to readers as possible.
7. A definition of a term that is already defined in the interpretation legislation must not be repeated.
8. A definition need not state that it is to apply to grammatical variations and cognate expressions of the term defined.
9. A definition defines one word or expression only.
10. A word or expression that is not used in an enactment must not be defined.

Driedger suggests that definitions can be used to delimit, to narrow, to particularise general descriptions, to enlarge, to settle doubts and to abbreviate or shorten and simplify construction.[62] Definitions can be labelling, delimiting, extending, restricting or referential. The purpose of a labelling definition is to label a term used frequently in the legislative text thus avoiding useless repetition: eg 'The Minister' means the Minister of Labour. The purpose of a delimiting definition is to set the concrete boundaries of the semantic field of a normally vague or ambiguous concept: eg 'a month' means a calendar month. The purpose of an extending definition is to add an additional element to the common meaning of a term: eg 'floating restaurant' includes a floating bar. The purpose of a restricting definition is to remove an element of the common meaning: eg 'floating restaurant' excludes a floating bar. Finally, referential definitions cross refer to another Act: it is useful for the reader to receive not just a dry cross reference but also a repetition of the provision or a reiteration of its main topic, albeit without paraphrasing its content.

[62] See EA Driedger, *The Composition of Legislation—Legislative Forms and Precedents* (Ottawa, Ministry of Justice, 1976) 45–47.

Definitions can be descriptive or prescriptive: prescriptive descriptive definitions are expressed by means of the terms 'is' or 'means', and descriptive definitions are expressed by means of the terms 'includes' or 'excludes':[63]

> The descriptive definition recognizes uncertainty, incompleteness and the impossibility of fashioning a precise definition that will cover all-even unforeseen-instances. The prescriptive definition assumes that: (i) meaning can be assigned, (ii) meaning can be precise; (iii) there are essential characteristics of the instances that fall within the meaning of any term; and (iv) meaning can be articulated by a statement of required conditions or attributes. The prescriptive definition precludes doubt; any instance that lacks an element required by a prescriptive definition is excluded.[64]

And so using the term 'is' conveys the concept of an exclusive list of circumstances falling within the semantic field of the defined term:[65] as a result there is a risk of over-precision leading either to a generic vague definition or a narrower than intended concept. 'Means' conveys an exhaustive definition with comparable risks to 'is'. 'Includes' provides a partial definition with flexibility: the use of examples may guide the user to the correct application in unforeseen circumstances. Whatever the intent of the drafter is, they must choose between 'means' and 'includes'. Formulae such as 'means and includes' or 'includes only' are simply contradictory.

Other Schedules

Amongst the most frequently used Schedules is the so-called Keeling Schedule.[66] It is a device which 'sets out the wording of the enactment, indicating by bold type the changes proposed'.[67] In an Act with a Keeling Schedule a principal provision lists the direct textual amendments to a section, and directs the user to the Keeling Schedule, which restates the section putting the amendments into effect. As a result, the user has both a list of surgical amendments, and the new provision as it stands post-incorporation of these amendments. Thus, the Keeling Schedule is used where the changes made by the Bill in the previous enactments are exclusive textual amendments or repeals. The Keeling technique not only shows in the Schedule how the law will look once it is amended, but also makes clear, in the text of

[63] See T Haggard, 'Definitions' (2001) 80 *Michigan Bar Journal* 47, 47.
[64] See J Frazier Price, 'Wagging, not Barking: Statutory Definitions' (2012–13) 60 *Cleveland State Law Review* 999, 1013.
[65] See B Child, 'Stipulative Definitions: A Useful Drafting Tool' (1989) 68 *Michigan Bar Journal* 54, 54.
[66] It is named after Sir Edward Keeling, who, with Mr Justice Croom-Johnson, made the original proposal.
[67] See FAR Bennion, *Bennion on Statute Law* 56 www.francisbennion.com/book/statutelaw.htm.

the Bill itself, how the law is being amended.[68] And by doing so, it informs clarity[69] and legislative quality.[70]

Bennion has shown, however, that there are other difficulties in the use of the Keeling Schedule.[71] These mainly refer to the cluttering of the statute book with additional materials within the legislative text.[72] Moreover, Keeling Schedules are very time-consuming; and if the Bill is amended in Parliament, the change has to be reflected in the Keeling Schedule: as a result, Sir Geoffrey Bowman considers them 'a hostage to fortune' and prefers the informal departmental documents, or explanatory notes as alternatives.[73] Furthermore, issues arise from the variation in the timeline between the original provision and the amended Keeling Schedule.[74]

These are valid concerns of course. But the advantage of Keeling Schedules for the user is profound. And clarity prevails when in clash with brevity or indeed practicability. And so Keeling Schedules are a wonderful tool for drafters. Much more so since they inadvertently warn the drafter that it is time to repeal and re-enact when repeated or extensive amendments prevents their successful use.

The Jamaica Schedule was introduced by Bennion[75] when drafting tax legislation for the Jamaica Government in the early 1970s. But it has not really caught on anywhere else in the Commonwealth. The device aims to facilitate the user's awareness of the status of the Act's timeline. The Jamaica Schedule consists of two paragraphs: paragraph 1 of the Schedule states the master commencement date (the default start date); and subsequent paragraphs state provisions with individual start dates or provisions for which transitional provisions are required. As a result, each subsequent Amending Act amends not only the provisions in the body of the text but also the Jamaica Schedule as necessary to incorporate transitional provisions for the new amendments. The result of the reprint of the Act.

If it is updated by textual amendment, the whole history would be available in the Jamaica Schedule. Provided that the updated text is quickly available there would be no need for notes to commencement orders, for

[68] See the Renton Report (n 57) para 13.22.

[69] See C Carr, 'British Isles: Legislation' (1949) 31 *Journal of Comparative Legislation and International Law* 1949, 1; also see M Zander, *The Law-Making Process* (Cambridge, Cambridge University Press, 2004) 29.

[70] See R Cormacain, 'Keeling Schedules and Clarity in Amending Legislation' (2013) 15 *European Journal of Law Reform* 96, 105.

[71] See Bennion, *Bennion on Statute Law* (n 67) 56–57.

[72] See StJ Bates, 'Monitoring of Current Legislation by the Statute Law Society' (1981) 1 *Statute Law Review* 39.

[73] See Sir G Bowman, Select Committee on Constitution, Examination of Witness, Questions 340–59 (23 June 2004) www.publications.parliament.uk/pa/ld200304/ldselect/ldconst/173/4062301.htm.

[74] See A Samuels, 'Use of the Keeling Schedule' (1997) 18 *Statute Law Review* 250, 250.

[75] See Bennion, *Bennion on Statute Law* (n 67) 278–79.

the Jamaica Schedule is part of the Act and follows its numbering. The user can find the whole chronology of the Act in a single document. In other words, if the original Act is updated by textual amendment, its whole history is available in the Jamaica Schedule. And this eliminates the need for notes to commencement orders, as the Jamaica Schedule is part of the Act and follows its numbering.

10

Comparative Legislative Drafting[1]

ADMITTEDLY IT HAS only been in the last few years that academics and practitioners of legislative studies have finally come to the realisation that legislative drafting as a process and product is not a chauvinistic issue whose borders extend strictly within the jurisdictional barriers of national legislative competence. In a welcome complete departure from the overtly promoted ideology of legislative racism of the past, the legislative studies field has witnessed a widely shared turn towards universalism in the shape of the acceptance that quality of legislation is a universal pursuit which can be promoted (I would not dare say achieved) via the phronetic application of universally applicable rules. National eccentricities continue to be accommodated of course, but they constitute one of the many factors in legislative choices, a mere element of the sequence of informed decision-making that constitutes the task of phronetic legislative drafting or legisprudence. To be more precise, national characteristics of the jurisdiction, the legal system, but also the society that it serves, form part of the factors taken into account for the determination of which policy, legal and legislative solution could be most effective.

This comes at a time of political, legal and legislative globalisation[2] characterised by a multitude of regional and international legislative texts. But does this turn to universality mean that we can finally bury the hatchet between drafting in the common law versus law-making in the civil law style? Or is this a simplistic approach?[3] Although some comparative lawyers

[1] This chapter is an updated version of the following article: H Xanthaki, 'Editorial: Burying the Hatchet Between Common and Civil Law Drafting Styles in Europe' (2012) 6 *Legisprudence* 133.

[2] See B Markesinis, 'Learning from Europe and Learning in Europe' in B Markesinis (ed), *The Gradual Convergence: Foreign Ideas, Foreign Influences and European Law on the Eve of the 21st Century* (Oxford, Clarendon Press, 1993) 1, 30; also see B Markesinis, 'Judicial Style and Judicial Reasoning in England and Germany' (2000) 59 *Cambridge Law Journal* 294. But see contra P Legrand, 'European Legal Systems Are Not Converging' (1996) 45 *International and Comparative Law Quarterly* 52; and P Legrand, 'Against a European Civil Code' (1997) 60 *Modern Law Review* 44.

[3] See N Rescher, *Complexity: A Philosophical Overview* (New Brunswick, Transaction Publishers, 1998) 61; also see JH Merryman, 'On the Convergence (and Divergence) of the Civil Law and the Common Law' in JH Merryman, *The Loneliness of the Comparative Lawyer and Other Essays in Foreign and Comparative Law* (The Hague, Kluwer, 1999) 17, 27.

already talk about a converged[4] common and civil law legal system called the Western legal system,[5] the concept remains unknown in legislative studies.[6] But, at least in Europe, there is a noted convergence between common and civil law legislative drafting extending from conceptual approaches to actual drafting conventions.[7] Although this comes at a time opportune for universalism in legislative ideology,[8] this convergence seems to have occurred independent of this ideological change.[9] Aspects of legislative drafting in its constitutional foundations, the legislative process and the drafting tools employed by practitioners have converged, perhaps as a result of a combination of legal globalisation,[10] with regional legal integration,[11] and these changes seem to be leading us to the de facto demolition of one of the strongest fortresses of legislative history, the common versus civil law wall.[12] But is this actually true? In order to confirm that the hatchet can now be buried, let's identify the main 'civil-ised' clichés about common law, and the main 'common-alised' clichés about civil law, as a means of formulating the basis for an assessment of their continued prevalence or their de facto demolition.

[4] See C Schmid, 'The Emergence of a Transnational Legal Science in Europe' (2000) 19 *Oxford Journal of Legal Studies* 673.

[5] See W Tetley, 'Mixed Jurisdictions: Common Law vs. Civil Law (Codified and Uncodified)' (1999) 4 *Uniform Law Review* 591; also see R David, 'Existe-t-il un droit occidental?' in Mélanges HE Yntema, *Twentieth Century Comparative and Conflicts Law* (Leiden, AW Sijthoff, 1961) 56.

[6] See RC Dick, 'Comparisons in Legal Drafting' (1977–79) 4 *Estates and Trusts Quarterly* 195, 195.

[7] See contra Legrand, 'European Legal Systems Are Not Converging' (n 2) 52; also see G Teubner, 'Legal Irritants: Good Faith in British Law and How Unifying Law Ends Up in New Divergences' (1998) 61 *Modern Law Review* 11.

[8] See LM Friedman, 'The Concept of Legal Culture: A Reply' in D Nelken (ed), *Comparing Legal Cultures* (Aldershot, Dartmouth, 1997) 33; also see LM Friedman, 'On the Emerging Sociology of Transnational Law' (1996) 32 *Stanford Journal of International Law* 65; LM Friedman, *The Horizontal Society* (New Haven, CT, Yale University Press, 1999); Schmid 'The Emergence of a Transnational Legal Science in Europe' (n 4) 673; R Sacco, 'Legal Formants: A Dynamic Approach to Comparative Law (I)' (1991) 39 *American Journal of Comparative Law* 1, 4, 26–30, 32; R Zimmermann, 'Savigny's Legacy: Legal History, Comparative Law, and the Emergence of a European Legal Science' (1996) 112 *Law Quarterly Review* 576.

[9] E Örücü, 'Critical Comparative Law: Considering Paradoxes for Legal Systems in Transition' (2000) 4 *Electronic Journal of Comparative Law* http://www.ejcl.org/41/art41-1.txt.

[10] See W Voermans, 'Styles of Legislation and Their Effects' (2011) *Statute Law Review* 38, 53.

[11] See C Joerges, 'The Impact of European Integration on Private Law: Reductionist Perceptions, True Conflicts and a New Constitutional Perspective' (1997) 3 *European Law Journal* 378; also see C Joerges, 'Interactive Adjudication in the Europeanization Process? A Demanding Perspective and a Modest Example' (2000) *European Review of Private Law* 1; JE Levitsky, 'The Europeanisation of the British Legal Style' (1994) 42 *American Journal of Comparative Law* 347, 347.

[12] See Voermans, 'Styles of Legislation and Their Effects' (n 10) 51–52.

THE CLICHÉS

In the common law the aim of the drafter is precision[13] and accuracy.[14] The aim of the drafter is to provide a legislative text which encompasses all details on the topic[15] so that the text could, at least in theory, stand alone in the regulation of the phenomenon that it sets out to address. But statutes and codes are considered evil.[16] In the common law the drafter introduces a remedy in order to create a right, as remedies precede rights.[17] Drafting is viewed as a specialised trade, a technique, deserving attention and training.

A civil law drafting team aims to introduce the main legal concepts that are the necessary means for addressing a social phenomenon.[18] The team pursues brevity[19] as it rests confident that issues of detail or secondary issues will be regulated via secondary forms of law: a general provision[20] of the civil code will require ministerial decisions to complete the regulation on, for example, divorce. As a result, at least seemingly, the main aim of the civil drafting team is simplicity and concision.[21] The main aim of the civil drafting team is to strip the primary provision of all details[22] linking it to time as a means of creating a legislative phrase which will be equally applicable in the future when circumstances might change (for example, criminal procedural provisions on admissible evidence in the criminal trial must be equally applicable when technology allows new types of criminal

[13] See L-P Pigeon, *Rédaction et interprétation des lois* (Québec, Gouvernement du Québec, 1986) 19; also see L-P Pigeon, *Drafting and Interpreting Legislation* (Toronto/Calgary/Vancouver, Carlswell, 1988) 7.

[14] See J Stark, 'Should the Main Goal of Statutory Drafting Be Accuracy or Clarity?' (1994) 14 *Statute Law Review* 207; also see O Lando, 'On Legislative Style and Structure' (2006) 4 *European Review of Private Law* 475, 476; T Millet, 'A Comparison of French and British Drafting (with Particular Reference to their Respective Nationality Laws)' (1980) 1 *Statute Law Review* 130, 153.

[15] See Lando, 'On Legislative Style and Structure' (n 14) 476.

[16] See K Zweigert and H Kötz, *An Introduction to Comparative Law* (Oxford, Oxford University Press, 1998) 265.

[17] See WW Buckland and AD McNair, 'Roman Law and Common Law: A Comparison in Outline' (revised by FH Lawson) (Cambridge, Cambridge University Press, 1952) 399; also see Pigeon *Drafting and Interpreting Legislation* (n 13) 9.

[18] See J-EM Portalis, *Discours préliminaire au premier projet de Code civil (L'an VIII)* (Paris, Éditions confluences Voix de la cité, reprinted 1999) 18, 19.

[19] See Sir W Dale, *Legislative Drafting: A New Approach* (London, Butterworths, 1977) vii.

[20] See J Stark, 'The Proper Degree of Generality for Statutes' (2004) 25 *Statute Law Review* 77, 77; also see Sir O Khan-Freund, C Lévy and B Rudden (eds), *A Source-book on French Law* (Oxford, Clarendon Press, 1990) 233; B Dickson, *Introduction to French Law* (London, Pitman Publishing, 1994) 10–11.

[21] See JA Clarence-Smith, 'Legislative Drafting: English and Continental' (1980) 1 *Statute Law Review* 14, 21; also see W Tetley, *Marine Cargo Claims* (Montreal, Les Éditions Yvon Blais, 1988) 45.

[22] See C Pestalozza, 'Gesetzgebung im Rechtsstaat' (1981) 39 *Neue juristische Wochenschrift* 2081, 2084.

evidence such as videos, DVD etc).[23] In other words, the aim of the civil drafting team is to introduce primary provisions which will last the test of time. Legislative drafting is not a profession.[24]

Time to put these clichés to the test.

These conventions seem simplistic, even prima facie. Do they stand the test of closer scrutiny? Tetley's three themes of comparative analysis have been selected as case studies: rules of (statutory) interpretation, stare decisis and drafting conventions and techniques.[25]

STATUTORY INTERPRETATION

Rules of Interpretation and Construction in the Common Law: Ilbert's Rules[26]

Regard should be had to the general rules for the interpretation of statutes, as laid down in the ordinary textbooks. Among the most important of these are the following: an Act must be read as a whole; the language of one section may affect the construction of another; an Act may be interpreted by reference to other Acts dealing with the same or a similar subject matter. Hence the language of those Acts must be studied; the meaning attached to a particular expression in one Act, either by definition or by judicial decision, may be attached to it in another and variation of language may be construed as indicating change of intention; special provisions will control general provisions; where particular words are followed by general words (horse, cow, or other animal), the generality of the latter will be limited by reference to the former ('*ejusdem generis*' rule); subject to important exceptions, a guilty mind is an essential element in a breach of criminal or penal law; the words 'wilfully' or 'knowingly' must be inserted or, if not, perhaps implied; the legislature does not intend any alteration in the rules or principles of the common law beyond what it expressly declares; there is a presumption[27] that there is no intention to oust or limit the jurisdiction of the superior courts; there is a presumption that Acts of Parliament will not operate beyond the UK; there is a presumption that Parliament does not intend to contravene international law; the Crown is not bound by an

[23] See B Markesinis, H Unberath and A Johnston, *The German Law of Contract: A Comparative Treatise* (Oxford, Hart Publishing, 2006) 119.

[24] See Pestalozza, 'Gesetzgebung im Rechtsstaat' (n 22) 287.

[25] See W Tetley, 'Interpretation and Construction of the Hague, Hague/Visby and Hamburg Rules' (2004) 10 *Journal of International Maritime Law* 30.

[26] See Sir C Ilbert, *Legislative Methods and Forms* (Oxford, Clarendon Press, 1901) 250–51.

[27] On presumptions, see FAR Bennion, 'Threading the Legislative Maze—11' www.francisbennion.com.

enactment unless specially named; there is a presumption that statutes have no retrospective operation; and a power conferred on a public authority may be construed as a duty imposed on that authority ('may' = 'shall').[28]

Ilbert's rules detail clearly the basics of common law statutory interpretation but they only tell half the story. In the UK there never was a sole and unique method of statutory interpretation.[29] Instead of going down the comforting certainty of a civil law route of concrete, exhaustive and written (albeit inflexible and inherently general) compilations of statutory interpretation rules, the UK chose the familiar common law route of conventions. As these entered the system at various times historically, and were inevitably attached to specific cases, thus being limited by considerations of equity and fairness to the specific litigants, statutory interpretation rules tend to exist in parallel.

An analysis of the literal, mischief and Golden rules, and of course the purposive approach is undertaken in chapter 18.[30] But it is worth noting here that the literal rule evident in the *Sussex Peerage*[31] case demands adherence to the natural and ordinary sense of words.[32] The mischief rule, evident in *Heydon,*[33] requires identification of the problem that invited legislative intervention, and suppression of this mischief.[34] The Golden rule, evident in Lord Atkinson in *Victoria (City) v Bishop of Vancouver Island,*[35] requires the application of the litteral rule where possible and engagement with the mischief where necessary. The prevalent rule in the UK stems from *Pepper v Hart,*[36] and offers interpretative gravitas to the ordinary meaning of words, the context (subject matter, scope, purpose,[37] background of the Act, including Hansard).[38] This is purposive interpretation.[39]

[28] ibid, 5–6.

[29] See R Graham, 'A Unified Theory of Statutory Interpretation' (2002) 23 *Statute Law Review* 91, 134.

[30] See L Neville-Brown and F Jacobs, *The Court of Justice of the European Communities* (London, Sweet and Maxwell, 1998) 271.

[31] *Sussex Peerage* (1844) 11 Cl & F 85; 8 ER 1034.

[32] See Sir F Pollock, *Essays on Jurisprudence and Ethics* (London, McMillan, 1882) 85; also see Lord Reid, 'The Judge as Law Maker' (1972) 12 *Journal of the Society of Public Teachers of Law* 28; *Stock v Frank Jones (Tipton) Ltd* (1978) ICR 347, 354; *Bulmer Ltd v Bollinger* (1974) Ch 401, 425.

[33] *Heydon's Case* (1584) 3 CoRep7a; 76 ER 637.

[34] See *R (McCann) v Crown Court at Manchester* (2003) 1 AC 787, [16]–[18].

[35] *Victoria (City) v Bishop of Vancouver Island* [1921] AC 384.

[36] *Pepper v Hart* [1993] 1 All ER 42 at 50.

[37] See G MacCallum, 'Legislative Intent' in R Summers (ed), *Essays in Legal Philosophy* (Oxford, Blackwell, 1968) 237, 240.

[38] See Learned Hand J in *Cabell v Markham* (1945) 148 F 2d 737, 739; Lord Bingham in *R (Quintavalle) v Secretary of State for Health* (2003) 2 AC 687, §8; Lord Hoffmann in *ICS v West Bromwich Building Society* (1998) 1 WLR 896, 913; *Wilson v First County Trust (No. 2)*, [114]–[117].

[39] See Lord Diplock in *Carter v Bradbeer* (1975) 1 WLR 1204; *R v Henn and Darvy* (1978) 3 All ER 1190; also see J van Zyl Smit, 'The New Purposive Interpretation of Statutes: HRA Section 3 after Ghaidan v Godin-Mendoza' (2007) 70 *Modern Law Review* 294.

Rules of Interpretation and Construction in the Civil Law World

Mazeaud[40] states that when the text is clear, it should not interpreted but applied simply. When the text is obscure, the court must discover the intention of the legislator by examining the legislation as a whole and provisions immediately surrounding the obscure text. If such examination does not suffice, the court may refer to the preparatory studies to discover the thinking of the legislator (these studies are not binding on the court). When the text does not directly provide a solution, the court must rely on the text as a starting point from which to discover the law: the text remains the framework. The court may base its decision on general principles of law gleaned from the evolving jurisprudence. Such reliance must be made with circumspection and care. The court must not forsake the text in order to make equity its sole guide. The court may also turn to the rules of logic in shaping its reasoning. For example, exceptions are to be strictly construed; specific language supersedes the general.

Similarly, Mignault[41] advises to first refer to the text of the code itself. Only if there is ambiguity in the text of the code may one refer to the official codifiers' report (which is usually a statement by the drafters of the code as to the sources of each article). If there still remains any doubt, refer to the commentaries of recognised experts on the law. Only if all else fails, may one consider precedents. Finally, one may refer to the common law (*le droit anglais*), if the text in question has its origins in the common law.

The End of the Cold War in (Statutory) Interpretation

One contrasts the two 'diverse' positions of interpretation in sheer disbelief. Is the solution offered by the civil law not similar to that advocated in modern common law? As purposive interpretation is the new dogma of common law, the former gap between common and civil law in the sphere of interpretation has really narrowed.[42] The teleological method aims to identify the *telos* pursued by the legislator, whereas the purposive method aims to identify the intent of the parliament.[43] In other words, both methods seek to unveil the true aim of the law-makers and to interpret the text in order to give it effect. Now the specific tools that users may use for that purpose differ, in that purposive interpretation find refuge in exhaustively

[40] See H Mazeaud, *Leçons de Droit Civil* (Paris, Montchrestien, 1996) 172.

[41] See PB Mignault 'Le Code Civil de La Province de Québec et son Interprétation' (1935–36) 1 *University of Toronto Law Journal*, 104, 124.

[42] See *James Buchanan & Co Ltd v Babco Forwarding & Shipping (UK) Ltd* (1977) 2 WLR 107, 112.

[43] See Editorial, 'Legislative Intention' (2008) 29 *Statute Law Review* iii, iii.

listed sources which exclude the civil law's *travaux preparatoires*, parliamentary debates and historical and academic analysis. But at the end of the day the concept of statutory interpretation has finally converged.[44]

Does that lead to judicial law-making in the common law system, another one of the alleged divergences between the two legal systems? There are limits and restrictions inherent in the UK system of statutory interpretation whose legal value and consequent application in practice remains unaffected and continues to qualify all rules of statutory interpretation, including purposive interpretation.[45] First, interpretation is only invited when the meaning of words is unclear or disputed. So purposive interpretation is not needed and therefore not invited or tolerated for the purposes of everyday construction and application of the law. Interpretation is therefore limited to the extraordinary, albeit frequent, cases where there are either problems of drafting arising from the words of the statute alone, before any set of facts has been presented for its application; or problems of uncertain application arising in the process of applying the words of a statute to a set of facts.

Secondly, even under these exceptional circumstances judges can only use interpretation if there is a gap in the legislation or if the text requires clarification. One can argue that these are circumtances where the legislature omitted or failed to offer a complete legislative text. And so it is the judges' duty, not choice, to act in order to complete the legal and legislative picture.

Thirdly, judges continue to be bound by presumptions and maxims.[46] Even where judicial activism is necessary, judges do not work in a vacuum: they are constrained by constitutional, legal, and interpretative principles to which they have to adhere. And these suppress, or at least can suppress, a possible appetite for uncontrolled judicial activism.

And so another myth is demolished.

Stare Decisis

Stare decisis is defined as the common law principle under which inferior courts abide by or adhere to decisions of superior courts within the same jurisdiction on legal principles forming part of the ratio decidendi of the

[44] See Levitsky, 'The Europeanisation of the British Legal Style' (n 11) 369.

[45] See *Magor and St Mellons Rural District Council v Newport* (1952) AC 189, per Lord Simonds at 191.

[46] See *Black-Clawson International Ltd v Papierwerke Waldhof-Aschaffenburg AG* (1975) AC 591, per Lord Reid (HL 5 March 1975); *R v Secretary of State for the Environment, Transport & the Regions, ex p Spath Holme Ltd* (2001) 2 AC 349, per Lord Nicholls at 395; *Wilson v First County Trust (No 2)* (2004) 1 AC 816, per Lord Hope at [111].

case.[47] The purpose of stare decisis is to give uniformity, continuity and predictability to the law. In the common law world the principle is well established and traditionally it was considered one of the main characteristics of common law.[48] In the civil law world the judgment of a court is binding exclusively to the parties and only for the dispute heard by the court.

But in the common law of the UK the doctrine of precedent does not remain absolute or indeed purist in its stare decisis format. Nowadays decisions made in higher courts are binding upon courts below them, and to a certain extent on courts at the same level. So, Magistrates' Courts and County Courts are bound by decisions of the High Court, the Court of Appeal and the Supreme Court; but they are not bound by their own decisions, and they do not bind other courts. The Crown Court is bound by decisions of the Court of Appeal and the Supreme Court, but its judgments have mere persuasive value for the other courts, especially if the judgment is made by High Court judges sitting in the Crown Court. The High Court is bound by the Court of Appeal and the Supreme Court, and its judgments are binding upon inferior courts but not upon High Court judges. Moreover, High Court judgments are not always binding upon the Divisional Court (civil or criminal). The Divisional Courts of the High Court are bound by their own judgments, by judgments of the Court of Appeal, and of the Supreme Court. Their judgments are binding upon inferior courts (except the Employment Appeal Tribunal) and High Court judges sitting alone. The Court of Appeal (Civil Division) is bound by the Supreme Court, and by its own decisions, unless there was a serious omission flawing the decision, the decision conflicts with an earlier contradictory decision, or the previous Court of Appeal decision was overruled by the Supreme Court. Its judgments are binding on the Divisional Courts of the High Court, individual High Court judges and the inferior courts, including the Employment Appeal Tribunal. The Court of Appeal (Criminal Division) is bound by the Supreme Court and its own judgments, and is binding on lower courts. Finally, Supreme Court judgments are binding on all courts. The Supreme Court is persuaded by, but not bound by, inferior courts and, since 1966, is not bound by its own decisions. Moreover, in practice the Supreme Court may have to bow down to the European Court of Justice via the principles of supremacy and indirect effect, and the European Court of Human Rights by virtue of the Human Rights Act. This complex state of affairs demonstrates that the principle of precedent in its modern facet imposes a relative and at times subjectively defined obligation on common law judges to comply with precedent of specific courts. At the end of the day, the role

[47] The House of Lords in a 'Practice Statement (Judicial Precedent)' (1966) 1 WLR 1234, (1966) 3 All ER 77 (HL), proposed 'while treating former decisions of this House as normally binding, to depart from a previous decision when it appears right to do so'.

[48] See J Bell, 'Comparing Precedent' (1997) 82 *Cornell Law Review* 1243.

of precedent in common law is inherently limited since there are no limits upon the power of the parliament to make law, since judges must give effect to the parliament's intent, and since the only rule for the construction of Acts of parliament is that they should be construed according to the intent of the Parliament which passed the Act.[49]

As the common law doctrine of precedent seems to become ever more relative, precedents are becoming more relevant in the civil law context. Even in the civil law world judgments can reflect the prevailing interpretation and application of legal provisions. This happens in two cases. First, when the jurisprudence of the courts is persistent, this reflecting the commonly held view of national judges at various levels of courts. And secondly, when the Supreme Court expresses a view which is not contradicted by other Supreme Court judgments.[50] In other words, although in civil law theory the outcome of a case remains binding between the litigants of that case and for the purposes of that case alone, in practice persistent judicial interpretation mainly from the highest courts constitutes a very strong argument for the lawyers of future cases.

Although attributing this change of civil law tradition to a sole and specific causation would require extensive research, outside the scope of this chapter, it is probable that the invasion of the stare decisis principle in civil law is a direct result of the classification of CJEU judgments as sources of EU law.[51] Prevalence of EU law in the Member States signifies attribution of legal value to court judgments, namely those of the General Court and the CJEU, even in civil law jurisdictions. And continuous use of the General Court and CJEU judgments as sources of binding legal provisions even for civil lawyers allowed a silent invasion of stare decisis in jurisdictions, where previously jurisprudence was not even mentioned in courts.

DRAFTING RULES AND CONVENTIONS

The final theme of comparative analysis relates to the drafting rules and conventions prevalent in the common and civil law countries of Europe. One would expect to find a distinct common versus civil law ethos. After all, the choice is between two mutually exclusive objectives,

> namely the clarity of fuzzy law and the certainty of fussy law: broad principles may be readily understood but they are not readily applied, while detailed provisions

[49] See Tindall CJ in the *Sussex Peerage* case (1844) 11 Cl & F 85; 8 ER 1034.

[50] See DN MacCormick and RS Summers, *Interpreting Precedents: A Comparative Study* (Aldershot, Dartmouth, 1997).

[51] See V Fon and F Parisi, 'Judicial Precedents in Civil Law Systems: A Dynamic Analysis' (2006) 26 *International Review of Law and Economics* 519.

may provide immediate answers, but their complexity and volume make the law inaccessible to those who are bound by it.[52]

However, a closer analysis of the drafting conventions in Austria,[53] Belgium,[54] France,[55] Germany,[56] Italy,[57] the Netherlands,[58] Portugal,[59] Spain[60] and the UK[61] draws a very different story, one of commonality and similarity where drafting style is actually not defined by legal tradition. Clarity, simplicity, precision, accuracy and plain language are common standards of good quality of legislation both in the common and in the civil law drafting styles.[62] Moreover, consideration of the circle of persons which are the main users of the legislative text in question,[63] consideration of the interpretative problems which may arise from the text,[64] the need for consistency with existing legislation, avoidance of irrelevant provisions within the legislative texts and the use of uniform terminology within the text are all rules of drafting which are common within the legislative guidelines of European common and civil law jurisdictions.[65]

A closer comparative analysis of specific drafting conventions confirms our initial finding. The selection of legislation as a regulatory tool only as a solution of last resort, and provided that there is adequate justification for

[52] See L Campbell, 'Drafting Styles: Fuzzy or Fussy?' (1996) 3 *E Law—Murdoch University Electronic Journal of Law*, para 18 http://www.austlii.edu.au/au/journals/MurUEJL/1996/.

[53] See *Legistische Rechtlinien* (1990); also see A Shaefer, *Abkürzungen, Begriffe, Zitiervorschläge (Akronyme—internationale Einführung und umfangreiche Abkürzungssammlung)* (Vienna, Verlag Österreich, 2008).

[54] See Conseil d'Etat, *Technique législative* www.raadvst-consetat.be/?lang=fr&page=technique_legislative.

[55] See *Guide de légistique* (2013) www.legifrance.gouv.fr/Droit-francais/Guide-de-legistique.

[56] See Bundesministerium der Justiz (Hrsg), *Handbuch der Rechtsförmlichkeit* (Cologne, Bundesanzeiger, 2008) and online http://hdr.bmj.de/vorwort.html; also see H Kirchner, *Abkürzungsverzeichnis der Rechtssprache* (Berlin, De Gruyter Recht, 2008).

[57] *Formulazione tecnica dei testi legislativi* (2001) http://www.senato.it/application/xmanager/projects/senato/file/repository/istituzione/regole_testi_legislativi.pdf; also *Regole e suggerimenti per la redazione dei testi normativi* (2007) http://leggi.regione.abruzzo.it/docs/qualitaNorm/Regole_sugg_testi_normativi.pdf.

[58] See Circular of the Prime Minister, 'Guidelines for Legislation' (18 November 1992) http://wetten.overheid.nl/BWBR0005730/geldigheidsdatum_29-11-2013.

[59] See Deliberation of the Council of Ministers of 8 February 1989 on the approval of the general principles for the elaboration of projects for normative acts.

[60] See Spanish Guidelines on the form and structure for the schemes of projects of laws (1991); also *Normas sobre regimen de asesoramiento a las Comisiones del Congreso de los diputados y del Senato* (1989).

[61] See Consolidation of Enactment (Procedure) Act 1949, 41 *Statutes* 741; also Statutory Instruments Act 1946, 41 *Statutes* 717; Interpretation Act 1978, 41 *Statutes* 899.

[62] See R Pagano, *Introduzione alla legistica: l'arte di preparare le leggi* (Milan, Giuffrè Editore, 1999) 26–30.

[63] See M Ainis, *La legge oscura* (Bari, Laterza, 1997) 103.

[64] See V Fronsini, *Lezioni di teoria dell' interpretazione* (Rome, Bulsoni, 1993) 93; also see WA Leitch, 'The Interpretation Act: Ten Years Later' (1958) 16 *Northern Ireland Legal Quarterly* 215, 236–37.

[65] See Pagano, *Introduzione alla legistica* (n 59) 37–39.

the necessity and the timing of the legislative solution within the actual text is introduced in Belgium, France, Germany, Portugal and the UK. Equally common to European jurisdictions across the board is the principle of legality. Germany and Portugal expressly regulate that new legislation must comply with existing provisions, whereas in the UK legality is introduced in the form of a presumption.

Consultation as a form of pre-legislative scrutiny is introduced in Belgium, France, Germany, the Netherlands, Spain and the UK; although in the civil law tradition this usually involves the discussion of the draft law either by specialists in the field, or before the Constitutional Courts.[66] Regulatory Impact Assessments can be traced in the Finnish,[67] French, Dutch and UK[68] traditions, where the process of the cost and impact analysis is compulsory.[69]

As for rules related to the technical side of drafting, clarity of legislation is a principle common in Austria, Belgium, France, Germany, the Netherlands, Portugal, Spain and the UK. Unambiguity is required from Belgian, German, Italian, Portuguese, Spanish and UK drafters. Simplicity is a rule of drafting in Austria, Belgium, Germany, Portugal and Spain. It must be noted that in the UK simplicity is indeed pursued,[70] but not to the detriment of certainty in the law.[71] Plain language, namely consideration of language accessible for the main users of the particular legislative text, is expressly introduced in the Netherlands, Portugal and the UK.[72]

[66] See Belgian *Circulaire de Premier Ministre* (23 April 1982) art 28; French Circular of 2 Jan 1993 on the rules for the elaboration, signature and publication of texts in the Official Journal and to the coming into force of the particular procedures of the Prime Minster, art 1.7; German *Gemeinsame Geschäftsordnung der Bundesministerien* (15 Oct 1976) as modified, art 40; Dutch *Aanwijzingen Voor de Regelgeving* (1992) art 269; Spanish *Normas sobre regimen de asesoramiento a las Comisiones del Congreso de los diputados y del Senato* of 26 June 1989; for the common law approach to consultation, AD Jergensen, 'The Legal Requirement of Consultation' (1978) *Public Law* 290; also *Agricultural, Horticultural and Forestry Industry Training Board v Aylesbury Mushrooms Ltd* (1972) 1 All ER 280, (1972) 1 WLR 190; *R v Secretary of State for Social Services, ex p Association of Metropolitan Authorities* (1986) 1 All ER 164.

[67] For an analysis of the relevant Finnish tradition, see S Arkio, 'Assessment of Draft Legislation in Finland' in A Kellermann, G Ciavarini-Azzi, S Jacobs and R Deighton-Smith, *Improving the Quality of Legislation in Europe* (The Hague, Kluwer Law, 1998) 227.

[68] See Department of Trade and Industry, *Checking the Cost to Businesses: A Guide to Compliance Cost Assessment* (1999).

[69] See the French Circular of 21 Nov 1995 relating to the conduct of an impact study for projects of laws and decrees at the Council of the State; also the Dutch *Aanwijzingen Voor de Regelgeving* (1992) art 331.

[70] See BR Atre, *Legislative Drafting* (Delhi, Universal Law Publishing, 2006) 12.

[71] See *Report of the Renton Committee on the Preparation of Legislation* (Cmnd 1975, 6033) (Renton Report) ch XI, art 14; also see D Greenberg (ed), *Craies on Legislation* (London, Sweet and Maxwell, 2004) 307–08.

[72] See the Dutch *Aanwijzingen Voor de Regelgeving*, arts 54 and 218; also see Portuguese Deliberation of the Council of Ministers of 8 Feb 1989 on the approval of the general principles for the elaboration of projects of normative acts, art 7a; for the UK, see M Faulk and IM Mehler, *The Elements of Legal Writing* (London, Macmillan Press, 1994).

Only provisions of a legal nature may be included in legislative texts. Thus, political statements or declarations of intention have no place in legal texts in Austria, Belgium, France, Italy, the Netherlands and in the UK. Similarly, the avoidance of cross references or imprecise cross references is also introduced in Italy, Portugal and the UK. The requirement of the use of the same term when referring to the same concept is an expression of the principle of unambiguity and is expressly introduced in Austria, Belgium, Italy, the Netherlands, Portugal and the UK. On the basis of the same principle of unambiguity, unnecessary abbreviations are to be avoided in Germany, Italy and the UK as a by-product of clarity and precision. As an expression of the need for clarity and unambiguity, lack of pointless repetitions of existing provisions which is often followed by the use of different terms to reflect the same concept is to be avoided in the Austrian, Italian and Dutch guidelines, as well as in the UK by convention. Long sentences must be avoided in Austria, Germany and Italy; in the UK there is a convention against long sentences, as well as restrictions in the use of subordinate sentences (especially before the subject of the phrase or between the subject and the verb of the sentence) and against long sentences which are not split into paragraphs. Moreover, imprecise references to other legal texts are expressly prohibited in the Austrian, German, Italian, Dutch and Portuguese guidelines, and in the UK. The role of the title of legislative texts as a full, complete and clear indication of their subject matter, or perhaps better expressed as a complete and precise reflection of their true subject, is identical with the role of titles in Austria, Belgium, France, Germany, Italy, the Netherlands and Spain,[73] where a requirement for conciseness is added; similarly, in the UK it is now widely accepted that declarations as to the scope of the law must be in its provisions rather than in the title.[74] The practice of preambles is unknown in Austria, France, Germany and Greece and actively discouraged in modern UK drafting where, if used, they may not include declarations of purpose.[75] Furthermore, a clear date of entry into force, which must be clearly distinguished from the date of publication, is required in Austria, Belgium,

[73] Austrian *Legistische Rechtlinien* (1990) art 100; Belgian *Circulaire de Premier Ministre* (23 April 1982) art.20flect true subject; French Circular of 2 Jan 1993 on the rules for the elaboration, signature and publication of texts in the Official Journal and to the coming into force the particular procedures of the Prime Minster, art 1.3; German *Gemeinsame Geschäftsordnung der Bundesministerien* (15 Oct 1976) as modified, art 29; Italian *Formulazione tecnica dei testi legislativi* (1986) GU, no 123 of 29 March 1986, Ordinary Supplement, no 40, art 10; Italian *Regole e suggerimenti per la redazione dei testi nomativi* (1991) art 37; Dutch *Aanwijzingen Voor de Regelgeving* (1992) arts 98 and 105–07; Spanish Guidelines on the form and structure of projects of laws (1991), approved by the Decision of the Council of Ministers of 18 Oct 1991, OJ L 276 of 18 Nov 1991, disposition 27774, 37235-37, art 1.

[74] Renton Report (n 68) art 15; 44.

[75] Renton Report (n 68) art 11.6.

Germany, Italy and the Netherlands,[76] as well as in the UK by convention on commencement dates and duration clauses.[77]

The plethora of common principles, rules and regulations in the drafting of legislation across the common versus civil law divide constitutes the strongest indication of an approximation and convergence of their respective drafting styles. One could consider drafting techniques or conventions as a crucial case study for the purposes of proving the hypothesis of this chapter. As drafting rules tend to be considered to be intrinsically linked to the core sovereign-legislating ethos of each jurisdiction, proof of departure from chauvinist traditions demonstrates beyond doubt the end of legislative racism.

CONCLUSIONS

At least in Europe, there is a noted convergence between common and civil law legislative drafting extending from conceptual approaches to actual drafting conventions. The comparative analysis of (statutory) interpretation, the modern application of precedent, and drafting rules and conventions in the common and civil laws of Europe paint a clear picture of approximation and convergence, to the point where the sacred civil versus common law dividing wall is now critically shaken.

At the end of the day, what drafters pursue across the divide is legislative quality. There is now a universal definition for quality of legislation which is defined as effectiveness, or ability of the legislative product to produce the desired regulatory results, if synergy of all actors in the policy process actually occurs. This common concept of quality has led to a hierarchy of drafting values that extends beyond the common versus civil law divide and pursues clarity, precision and unambiguity as a means of promoting effectiveness, and gender-neutral and plain language as tools for the achievement of clarity, precision and unambiguity.

Does the final mutual agreement on a universal non-national, non-chauvinist concept of quality of legislation lead us to a standardisation of legislative drafting? This would not be possible. Within phronetic legislative drafting, where subjective choices based on theoretical awareness and practical empirical know-how constitute the backbone of legislative drafting as a task, standardisation is inconceivable. Even if legislative drafters were to

[76] Austrian *Legistische Rechtlinien* (1990) art 77; Belgian *Circulaire de Premier Ministre* (23 April 1982) art 121; German *Gemeinsame Geschäftsordnung der Bundesministerien* (15 Oct 1976) as modified, art 31; German Manual of Judicial Formalities (1991) para 307; Italian *Formulazione tecnica dei testi legislativi* (1986) GU, no 123 of 29 March 1986, Ordinary Supplement, no 40, art 18; Dutch *Aanwijzingen Voor de Regelgeving* (1992) art 178–80.

[77] VCRAC Crabbe, *Legislative Drafting* (Oxford, Cavendish Publishing, 1998) 138.

agree on rigid rules that disregard national eccentricities, this agreement would be self-destructive, as lack of adaptability and flexibility in drafting choices would render any rigid rule unable to serve the specific jurisdiction with the specific culture, the specific mores, the specific polity, the specific legal system, at the specific time; as a result, the rigid rule would be ineffective, and therefore adverse to, rather than supportive of, quality in legislation.

It is within this context of subjective prioritisation of legal conventions and empirical experiences that one must now evaluate the common versus civil law divide. This remains as one of the national eccentricities that drafters and legislators take into account when making drafting choices. The goal pursued is the same: effectiveness. The virtues pursued are the same: clarity, precision, unambiguity. The tools used are the same across the divide: gender-neutral language, plain language. What changes between common and civil law legislative drafting is simply the focus applied by the drafter. And so the hatchet between civil and common law drafting is buried. With a sigh of relief, academics and professionals can now look beyond this now demolished wall for best practices, for possible solutions, for legal transplants. But this would require the demolition of the last obstacle: legislative racism.

11

Time in Legislation

LEGISLATION IS DESTINED to operate throughout the passage of present and continue into the future. As a result it is asked to express time beyond real time.[1] The parallel levels of time in reality and legislative time create confusion not just for the reader but also for the drafter. This starts a vicious circle of ambiguity, which is accentuated by the difference between the drafter's time when writing the law, the reader's time when using the law, and the time expressed by the law itself. The present is fluid and has a different meaning when used at the time of drafting as opposed to the time of reading the law and then again as opposed to the present expressed within the law. The past and the future acquire similar parallel references in time. Yet, clarity of time is an essential element of clarity of legislation and, in consequence, effectiveness of legislation.

As if the varied notions of the past, the present and the future weren't enough of a complexity, the starting point of time references is also varied. As a rule legislation is prospective. It affects activities carried on in the future. But this simplest of legislative expressions encompasses four notions of time as its starting point: the time of drafting; the time of passing; the time of entry into force/commencement; and the time of usage of the law. In addition to this, it is often necessary to give legislative effect by reference to what has happened in the past.[2] In which case there are five notions of time as starting points: the pre-drafting past to which the law refers; the time of drafting; the time of passing; the time of commencement/entry into force; and the time of usage of the law.

It is not surprising that the expression of time in legislation is a rather tricky issue.

[1] For the interpretation of 'now' and time in legislation, see J Graboyes, 'Now, Voyager: Deixis and the Temporal Pragmatics of Statutes' (2009–10) 17 *George Mason Law Review* 1231, 1258.

[2] Necessity, not desirability, is the criterion for drafting retrospective legislation: see House of Lords Select Committee on the Constitution, *Banking Act 2009: Supplementary Report on Retrospective Legislation (Eleventh Report)* (HL 2008–09, 97) para 10.

PROSPECTIVE PROVISIONS

Prospective provisions are the rule.[3] They refer to legislative sentences applicable from the date of commencement (start date) of the legislation onwards. As a result, the rule is that the starting point for the classification of a moment in time as past, present, or future is the moment of commencement, namely the moment when the legislation comes into force. This is foreseen in the start provision, currently called the commencement provision. This can be found currently in the final provisions of an Act, but in the layered approach it could be found in preliminary provisions thus recognising its crucial importance for the regulatory message of legislative texts. Determining the start time as the criterion for the classification of other moments in time as past, present or future is a crucial aid to the drafter in their strive to select the appropriate tense.

Events that have already taken place, or will have taken place, before the start time are expressed in the past tense. Events that take place at the start time or close to that are expressed in the present tense. And events that will take place after the start time are, in principle, expressed in the future. This approach indicates that it is wrong to use the future tense for the determination of the composition of the board of an agency established by the Act: although the board does not exist yet at the time of drafting, it does exist at the crucial time of commencement. And so: the board 'includes' rather than 'will include' five members.

But is this right? The Act establishes the agency. The board of the agency comes into being after the establishment of the agency. Could it be that the future tense would be more appropriate in this case? The drafter has to balance the accuracy of time placement with the significant factor of relevance of the legislation to users whenever in the future the legislation is read. In other words, the legislative text must clearly show that it is applicable at the moment when any user reads it. It is for this reason that the use of present tense is the first port of call for the drafter. And, on balance, it prevails as a criterion of a choice of tense over the precision of the future tense in the example of the board of the agency above.

And so legislation is normally prospective.[4] And it is normally expressed in the present tense in order to convey clearly to the user the message that the legislative text applies at the moment when it is read.

[3] See NK Chakrabarti, *Principles of Legislation and Legislative Drafting* (Kolkata, R Chambray and Co Private Ltd, 2007) 194.

[4] On the prospectivity of legislation, see T Bingham, *The Rule of Law* (London, Penguin, 2011) 8; also see F Hayek, *The Road to Serfdom* (Chicago, University of Chicago Press, 1944) 22; J Raz, 'The Rule of Law and its Virtue' in *The Authority of Law: Essays on Law and Morality* (London, Clarendon Press, 1979) 214.

LEGALISING PROVISIONS

There is an additional reason why legislation is normally prospective. The law expects compliance with its demands at all times: but in order to comply with the law citizens need to be aware of its demands at the time when they decide to act in a certain manner.[5] Meddling with the law in the past changes its demands at a time when the citizens cannot change their behaviour. This is unfair to the citizen who wishes to comply and acts in compliance with the legislation as it stands at the time of their action: despite their best efforts the change of the law makes it impossible for them to comply. But it is also unsettling for the legal system: certainty in the law is seriously damaged when the law changes post facto.[6] This is of course linked to the rule of law and to constitutionality. And so provisions that are not prospective must be avoided.[7]

But there are exceptions to any rule, much more so in a phronetic legislative drafting. And there may indeed be compelling instances when the drafter needs to reach back in time and regulate past events or their effects.[8] Or, as David Slawson puts it, there are times when reliance on existing rules 'must be sacrificed to some extent to the need for change'.[9] As is the case with any departure from the norm, drafting legitimising provisions has to be undertaken expressly and with skill. The tool used by drafters to achieve regulation of past events or of their effects is a legalising provision.[10] A legalising provision is a statute passed either to cure defects in prior law or to save (validate) provisions or proceedings that, if the new legislation were to apply to them, would now be considered void.[11]

Natelson distinguishes four categories of legitimising laws: (1) curative laws, namely laws that match the provisions to existing expectation;[12] (2) laws that alter the future consequences of previous acts in unexpected ways, but do not change pre-existing obligations between people; (3) laws that unexpectedly alter the future consequences of previous acts so as to change pre-existing obligations prospectively; and (4) laws that unexpectedly alter

[5] See CB Hochman, 'The Supreme Court and Constitutionality of Retroactive Legislation' (1960) 73 *Harvard Law Review* 692, 693.

[6] See House of Lords Select Committee on the Constitution, *Nationality, Immigration and Asylum Bill Further Report (Seventh Report)* (HL 2001–02, 129) para 9.

[7] ibid, paras 6–8.

[8] House of Lords Select Committee on the Constitution, *Banking Bill (Third Report)* (HL 2008–09, 19) para 7.

[9] See WD Slawson, 'Constitutional and Legislative Considerations In Retroactive Lawmaking' (1960) 48 *California Law Review* 216, 226.

[10] See KN Chaturvedi, 'Legislative Retrospectivity and Rule of Law' (2013) 34 *Statute Law Review* 207, 218.

[11] See Office of Code Revision, Legislative Services Agency, *Form and Style Manual for Legislative Measures* (23 Sept 1999) 49.

[12] *Cf* J Héron, *Principes de droit transitoire* (Paris, Dalloz, 1996) 71–72.

the consequences of previous acts retrospectively.[13] But this classification suffers from a parallel application of more than one classification criteria: curative laws match the law with expectations, and they can do so with prospective, retrospective or retroactive statutes:[14] the qualifying criterion is one of intent rather than one of time of enactment and time of application. Similarly, laws that change pre-existing obligations prospectively are prospective statutes: reference to the event that gives rise to the law from the moment of enactment onwards is a classic example of a prospective law. Here time does not come into play, as the regulated are aware of the future consequences of their pre-existing obligations and have a choice whether to comply or not. For example, the imposition of a new obligation to register with the police any existing licensed guns is a prospective provision with new consequences that the licensee can opt to undertake by continuing to hold a licence or not.

It is generally accepted that legalising provisions are retrospective or retroactive. This is the classification confirmed by Salembier who divides statutes (not just legitimising ones) into those acting in the future on future events, namely prospective; those acting in the future on past events, namely retrospective; and those acting in the past on past events, namely retroactive.[15]

But it is worth noting that recently Cormacain identified three types of legalising provisions: retrospective, retroactive and Janus-faced provisions.[16] Janus-faced legislation stretches both into the future and into the past. Janus-faced legislation can be (1) retroactive, (2) retrospective, or (3) can interfere with existing rights. Janus-faced legislation can change the legal nature of a past event, and consequently it is 'truly a monstrosity'.[17] It is

> contrary to the general principle that legislation, by which the conduct of mankind is to be regulated ought, when introduced for the first time, to deal with future acts and ought not to change the character of past transactions carried out upon the faith of the then existing law.[18]

Cormacain's trichotomy confirms Munzer's trichotomy: a law is retroactive with respect to an act if and only if the law was created at a given time, the act was done before that time, and the law altered the legal status of

[13] See RG Natelson, 'Statutory Retroactivity: the Founders' View (2002–03) 39 *Idaho Law Review* 489, 494.

[14] Although in Canada when curative laws do not clearly express the intent to be retroactive the courts have on occasion refused to so apply them: see *Ruttan v Burk* (1904) 7 OLR 56, CA.

[15] See JP Salembier, 'Understanding Retroactivity: When the Past ain't what it used to be' (2003) 33 *Hong Kong Law Journal* 99, 102.

[16] See R Cormacain, 'The Lifespan of Legislation' Presentation at the Sir William Dale Legislative Drafting Clinic, IALS, London, (18 Oct 2013).

[17] See L Fuller, *The Morality of Law* (New Haven, Yale University Press, 1969) 53.

[18] See *Philips v Eyre* (1870) LR 6 QB 1, 23.

that act; a law is prospective if it applied to acts undertaken on or post its creation; and a law is partly retroactive and partly prospective if it is applicable to at least one act occurring before, and one occurring after, its creation.[19] There is little doubt that the trichotomy has sound basis. But one's view on it depends on the breadth of one's definition of retroactivity and retrospectivity: if it includes the possibility of prospective application, then Janus-faced or partially retroactive legislation is included in the concept of retroactive and retrospective. And this seems a rather persuasive view: retroactivity and retrospectivity depart from the norm by regulating pre-enactment events. But there is nothing requiring exclusivity to pre-enactment events: if anything, the rule is that a statute is prospective and so prospectivity can be expected, if not required, by the legitimising statute.

Perhaps on this basis the currently accepted classification of legalising provisions distinguishes between retroactivity and retrospectivity. The terms are often used interchangeably:[20] in the USA retroactivity seems to be the prevalent term covering both concepts;[21] in Australia retrospectivity seems to include retroactivity.[22] Recently Greenberg in *Craies* dismisses the distinction and states that a piece of legislation is retrospective if it has effect in relation to a matter arising before it was enacted or made.[23] But there is a difference between the semantic fields of the two terms.[24]

Retroactive provisions travel back to the past and change the law as it stood at the time of enactment: they require the intervention of a magic pen that travels back in time to delete and rewrite the provision. A retroactive statute changes the law from what it was. A retroactive statute is one that operates as of a time prior to its enactment. A retroactive statute operates backwards. And so a law validating the marriages solemnised in the past by an unauthorised person is retroactive, in that the marital status of the partners is considered to be 'married' from the moment the now validated marriage ceremony took place.

[19] See S Munzer, 'Retroactive Law' (1977) 6 *Journal of Legal Studies* 373, 381.

[20] See C Sands, 2 *Sutherland Statutory Construction* (Eagan, MN, Clark Boardman Callaghan, 1973) § 41.01.

[21] See eg S Munzer, 'A Theory of Retroactive Legislation' (1982–83) 61 *Texas Law Review* 425.

[22] See eg A Palmer and C Sampford, 'Retrospective Legislation in Australia: Looking Back at the 1980s (1993–94) 22 *Federal Law Review* 217, 218–19; also see D Gwynn Morgan, 'The Retrospective Dimension of the 2003–2004 Australian Personal Injuries Reforms' (2008) 29 *Statute Law Review* 53.

[23] See D Greenberg (ed), *Craies on Legislation: A Practitioner's Guide to the Nature, Process, Effect and Interpretation of Legislation*, 10th edn (London, Sweet and Maxwell, 2012) 491; also see in support O Gay, 'Retrospective Legislation' Standard Note SN/PC/06454, 14 June 2013.

[24] See EA Driedger, 'Statutes: Retroactive Retrospective Reflections' (1978) *Canadian Bar Review* 264, 268–69 and 276; also see R Sullivan, 'The Challenges of Transitional Law—the Canadian Experience' (2013) *The Loophole* 14 www.opc.gov.au/CALC/docs/Loophole/Loophole_March13.pdf.

Retrospective provisions do not alter the past: they simply alter the future effects of past events. A retrospective provision is prospective but it attaches new consequences to past actions. A retrospective provision changes the law not in regards to what is was when the event took place but in regards to what the effects of the past event will be in the future. And so, in the example above a retrospective statute would not validate the actual marriage but it may award a new marriage benefit to the partners in question.[25]

But of course a statute is not retrospective merely because it refers to matters in existence when the new legislation comes into force. Legislation introducing new requirements for the licensing of second-hand dealers who are already in business is not retrospective as it is merely regulating prospectively a present state of affairs. Similarly, a new law that imposes tax burdens on existing property owners for the coming year operates only prospectively.

Retroactive provisions return to the moment of enactment and change the law from that point onwards. Retrospective provisions look back at the point of enactment and attach new consequence from the point of enactment of the retrospective provision onwards. And prospective provisions look at events and consequences occurring after the enactment.

But of course prospectivity offers the regulated the opportunity to make an informed decision as to whether they will comply with the requirements of the law or not. This is not offered in the case of retroactive or retrospective provisions as the choice to act or omit has already taken place before the law is introduced.

This is precisely the source of unfairness that is inherent in legalising provisions both of a retroactive and retrospective nature.[26] The problem is enhanced in retroactive provisions as, at the time that the regulated made their behavioural choice, the law was different. And so the probability was that a perfectly sound choice of compliance with the law by a well-intending person suddenly turns to be a choice of non-compliance. But even in retrospective provisions there is an inherent unconstitutionality, especially in the case of criminal statutes. This is only excused if vested rights are not affected.[27] And so it is acceptable that non-remedial retroactive

[25] For a juxtaposition of retroactive and retrospective statutes, see GJ Demars, 'Retrospectivity and Retroactivity of Civil Legislation Reconsidered (1983) 10 *Ohio Northern University Law Review* 253, 255–57.

[26] If it is unfair to give legislation retrospective effect it must surely be equally unfair to make changes in judge-made law, whether it be a pure rule of the common law, or judicial interpretation of a statute, with retrospective effect: see R McManus QC, 'Predicting the Past: The Declaratory Theory of the Common Law—From Fairytale to Nightmare' (2007) 12 *Judicial Review* 228, 230.

[27] See B Smith, 'Retroactive Laws and Vested Rights' (1927) 5 *Texas Law Review* 231, 231; also see Dickson J in *Gustavson Drilling (1964) Ltd v Department of National Revenue* [1977] 1 SCR 271, 282; and D Greenberg, *Craies on Legislation—A Practitioner's Guide to the Nature, Process, Effect and Interpretation of Legislation* (London, Sweet and Maxwell, 2004) 392.

statutes may breach both the due process and the ex post facto principles of law, often expressly introduced by national constitutions. 'But in a remedial law due process may actually be promoted by extension of the remedy, and the ex post facto provision aims to curb penalties, not withhold benefits'.[28]

After all, the question of the retroactive or retrospective effect of a new law is not a question of adjudication. Its answer is not to be sought in judicial precedents.

> Retroactivity is in the first instance a question of legislative draftsmanship. When it becomes a problem, the problem is a failure of drafting, probably reflecting in turn a failure to give adequate attention to the policy choices involved.[29]

RETROSPECTIVE LEGISLATION

Retrospectivity tends to be expressed via savings or transitional provisions:[30] new effects to past events are exempted from the field of application of the previous regime, and are either 'saved' permanently or are treated differently temporarily in transitional provisions. At this point it is important to remember that savings provisions carry no concept of time or end, whereas transitional provisions incorporate a sense of duration or end.

Many constitutions contain basic rules making illegal the operation of a law which would make an act or omission a criminal offence if it was not so at the time of its commission;[31] or make a person liable to a criminal penalty greater than that which existed at the time of the offence.[32] For example, the House of Lords has stated that laws should not interfere retrospectively with criminal liability, with pending court cases, or with any benefits deriving from a judgment already obtained.[33] And the US Constitution bars retroactive delineations of crime, increases in grade of criminal activity, increased punishment and relaxed legal rules of evidence that favour the prosecution.[34] But, in

[28] See R Heimanson, 'Remedial Legislation' (1962–63) 46 *Marquette Law Review* 216, 224.

[29] See Linde J in *Whipple v Houser*, 291 Or. 475, 488, 632 P.2d 782 (1981).

[30] See E Edinger 'Retrospectivity in Law' (1995) 29 *University of British Columbia Law Review* 5, 5 and 11.

[31] For the Indian constitutional position, see Chaturvedi, 'Legislative Retrospectivity and Rule of Law' (n 10) 207.

[32] For an analysis of the prohibition of retroactivity as extending beyond the widely accepted exclusivity of criminal liability, see JN Eule, 'Temporal Limits on the Legislative Mandate: Entrenchment and Retroactivity' (1987) *American Bar Foundation Research Journal* 379, 427–28.

[33] See *Nationality, Immigration and Asylum Bill Further Report (Seventh Report)* (n 6) paras 7, 11 and 10 respectively.

[34] The latter alternative extends to procedural rules with similar detrimental impact: see eg *Thompson v Utah*, 170 U.S. 343 (1898) (size of trial juries); *Kring v Missouri*, 107 U.S. 221 (1883) (scope of trial following vacation of guilty plea); also see G Taylor, 'Retrospective Criminal Punishment under the German and Australian Constitutions' (2000) 23 *University of New South Wales Law Journal* 196.

addition to the time element of the statute, in order to be unconstitutional it has to adversely affect vested rights.[35]

And courts make the following presumptions unless clear words are used to rebut them: Parliament does not, without good reason, intend to alter the legal basis on which people have entered into lawful activities; and statutes do not intend to change the law from some prior date so as to cause the rights of people to be different from what they were conceived to be when they were acquired or exercised; and prior cases are to be treated as not subject to the new law.[36]

RETROACTIVE PROVISIONS

Retroactivity tends to involve negative nuances both from the point of view of the rule of law but also from the point of view of constitutionality.[37] But there are circumstances where even retroactive provisions can be not only useful but also desirable.

Retroactive provisions can serve the drafter to confer a benefit generally or on a specific section of society, without a corresponding liability: an example could be the backdated increase of pensions or benefits. Retroactive provisions can bring in provisions backdated to the date when public notice was given of the proposals: a classic example would be the enactment of a Finance Bill, whose provisions had been given temporary legal effect by a Provisional Collection of Taxes Order as from the date of the publication of the Bill. Retroactive provisions can validate technical or unintended irregularities: an example can be the removal of unintended restrictions resulting from previous interpretation of the law. Retroactive provisions can validate past events: examples include the validation of gay marriages taken place before the new legislation; or the validation of appointments of persons wrongly disqualified perhaps by a racist law.

THE DRAFTER AND LEGALISING PROVISIONS

The constitutionality of legalising provisions seems to be almost outside the scope of the legislative drafter's mandate. Although there is a duty on the

[35] See BJ George, Jr, 'When do the Ex Post Facto Clauses Cover the Retroactive Amendment of Procedural Statutes?' (1989–90) *Preview US Supreme Court Cases* 298, 299.

[36] See RS Summers, 'The Principles of the Rule of Law' (1998–99) 74 *Notre Dame Law Review* 1691, 1694–96; also see WA Leitch, 'Interpretation and the Interpretation Act 1978' (1980) 1 *Statute Law Review* 5, 11.

[37] See L Tremblay, *The Rule of Law: Justice and Interpretation* (Montreal, McGill-Queen's University Press, 1997); also see AC Hutchinson and P Monahan (eds), *The Rule of Law: Ideal or Ideology* (Toronto, Carswell, 1987).

drafter to draft within the boundaries of legality and constitutionality, the issue for the drafter is more focused on the technique to be used in order to offer constitutionality to whichever command is extended by the instructing officers of the client department.

But there is little doubt that retrospectivity and, to an even greater extent, retroactivity are danger areas for the drafter. They carry an inherently increased risk of unconstitutionality, illegality, unfairness, clash with the rule of law and, perhaps even more pronounced for the drafter, clash with certainty in the law.[38] The drafter's value is in avoiding retroactivity and retrospectivity[39] unless absolutely necessary,[40] and in ensuring that the expression of retrospectivity and retroactivity is of such increased and undoubted certainty[41] and precision[42] that the ambiguous content is remedied.

This requires a clear understanding of the concepts of retrospectivity and retroactivity, the ability to identify which of the two applies in each given case, and the capacity to select the most effective type of provision for the purpose: saving, application, or a provision within the body of the text headed accordingly.

There is very little in literature to carry the drafter's burden in that choice. Perhaps the only guiding principle is that of effectiveness: the drafter must identify the specific aspect of the message conveyed to the reader and use the provision that best expresses it.

If retroactivity or retrospectivity is a consequence of an exclusion of a circle of subjects or objects from the scope of application of the entire legislation, then an application provision may be best fit for purpose. But it is worth noting that substantive application provisions are confusing for the reader and that the message of exemption from the law is best carried where it is most obvious: in the short title. After all, the message to the user here is that the law is irrelevant to them: if this is the case, then this can be stated from the very top, the short title.

In the case of retrospective exemptions from a part of the Act or a section, a savings provision seems suitable. The scenario here is: before enactment the action in question was allowed; the new enactment repeals the previous enactment and introduces a new consequence to future identical actions; the retrospective provision extends the new consequences to the

[38] Certainty is an expression of the rule of law: see House of Lords Select Committee on the Constitution, *Regulatory Enforcement and Sanctions Bill (First Report)* (HL 2007–08, 16) para 6; also see House of Lords Select Committee on the Constitution, *The Cabinet Manual (Twelfth Report)* (HL 2010–12, 107).

[39] See *Nationality, Immigration and Asylum Bill Further Report (Seventh Report)* (n 6) paras 6–8.

[40] See *Banking Bill (Third Report)* (n 8) para 7.

[41] ibid, para 7.

[42] Retrospective and retroactive provisions must be drafted as narrowly as possible: ibid, para 7.

old actions and 'saves' them from the repeal. Here the drafter has a choice: either offer emphasis to the extension of consequences and the saving aspect of the message, in which case they use a saving provision, or offer emphasis to the retrospective aspect and use a section in the body of the text with a heading of 'retrospectivity'. Much relies on the context: an abolition of a benefit resulting from past actions, especially when a refund of already awarded benefits is required, is best expressed with a retrospective provision; maintenance of a benefit despite its prospective abolition is best expressed by a saving. The criterion is clarity, and the aim is effectiveness.

In the case of retroactive exemptions from a part of the Act or a section, a retroactive provision seems most appropriate. This would normally require a 'deeming' provision stating that the law is deemed to have started its application before its enactment. Here the departure from the constitutional and legal norm of certainty and legitimate expectations is such that the user would benefit from a clear and loud warning of the anomaly. A retroactive provision in the body of the text with a heading of 'retroactivity' seems to be the most honest and clear tool here.

Although not currently used, it is worth considering as an innovative concept using the heading 'retrospective saving'. This would indicate the duality of concepts in the text of the section. But of course this would be most beneficial to the professional users who are aware of the meaning of both terms. Plain language equivalents are difficult to identify but terms like 'exceptions from the new rules going back in time' could be tested.

12

Amending Provisions

AMENDING LEGISLATION IS often viewed as the perfect task for a novice drafter.[1] It involves minor changes to the text of the original Act, and this creates the erroneous impression that it is a minor drafting task. But this could not be further from the truth. The gravity of the drafter's task is not counted by the words produced: if anything, the number of words produced is geometrically opposite to the gravity of the task. The longer the drafter has considered the analysis, understanding and design of the law, the shorter the text will be. One word may be enough to amend a whole part of legislation: for example, replacing the term 'husband' with 'partner' requires a simple generic direct amendment but in order to reach that stage the drafter has already reviewed each and every piece of legislation where the original term was used to assess if a replacement is appropriate or not. And also, the change of a single term signifies a complete departure from a traditional to a liberal approach in the law on family, succession, welfare.

Lynch and Ziegler explain eloquently the three sources of uncertainty, and therefore technical intricacy, in the task of drafting amending legislation:

1. task diversity, which is caused by the sheer mass and diversity of legislative forms in the statute book;
2. task variability, which is the variation through time in the nature of the amendment task due to changes in the resources available for the undertaking of this process; and
3. task difficulty, which is a function of the complexity of the legislation amendments that are proposed.[2]

On the other side of the coin Thornton sees all legislation as amending legislation. And he is right: legislating rarely takes place in a vacuum.[3] Even in the case of new regulation expressed by innovative legislation, there is always the existing legal system to contend with. And this dynamic, live

[1] Or even, God forbid, the private sector: see St J Bates, 'Current Developments: Contracting out Legislation—the British Experience' (1996) 17 *Statute Law Review* 152, 153.

[2] See A Lynch and P Ziegler, 'The Amendment of Legislation' (1991) 12 *Statute Law Society* 48, 50.

[3] See R Tomasic, 'Towards a Theory of Legislation: Some Conceptual Obstacles' (1985) 6 *Statute Law Review* 84, 87.

organism is injured each and every time part of it, big or small, is being changed expressly or impliedly. And so the duty of the drafter, and the main criterion of effectiveness of the drafter's technical expertise in amendments, is to ensure that the injury takes place with surgical precision thus resulting in minimal bleeding. In other words, the quality of the amending laws depends gravely on the smoothness of their integration with the existing legal system. And the aim of the drafter in the process of drafting amending legislation is to maintain a coherent structure even after the amending legislation: amend in logical order, amend coherently.

INITIAL CONSIDERATIONS

But this is not the only consideration when amending legislation. Policy considerations are crucial to the amending project. It is crucially important for the drafter to apply Thornton's five stages of drafting in the case of amendments also. And this is so, because at the point of receiving the drafting instructions (hopefully in a narrative format), the decision on the legislative drafting tool to be used has not been made. It is important for the drafter to understand what policy is being pursued, what purpose the amending law is to serve, what the content of the proposed changes are, what is the existing law, and what mischief is to be addressed by the proposed legislation.[4]

Understanding the policy to be pursued is an integral part of the first stage of legislative drafting, and allows the drafter to be on the same page with the instructing officers in the drafting team. It conveys to the drafter the full picture of the aim to be achieved without any prejudiced filtering of information: this guarantees a conveyance of the whole picture without drafting pre-selections and pre-decisions made by the members of the drafting team who have not been trained in legislative drafting. Understanding the policy behind the request for amendment of the law includes a detailed understanding of the purpose to be achieved by the proposed amending legislation: in turn, this requires a description of the current law and the identification of the mischief to be addressed.[5]

It is only after the drafter considers all this detailed information that an informed decision can be made as to the necessity of legislation as a regulatory tool and the appropriateness of amendment as a drafting tool. Deciding on an amendment before this process has taken place, and much

[4] See JAL Bell, 'Extremist Drafting of Federal Statutes' (1990) 1 *Scribes Journal of Legal Writing* 31, 38.

[5] For an example of the goal pursued in the Florida constitutional amendment, see J Uhlfelder, 'The Machinery of Revision' (1978) 6 *Florida State University Law Review* 575, 577.

more so without the participation of the drafter, leads to haphazard quality of legislation and haphazard effects.[6]

Moreover, a request for amendment of existing legislation, even when the draft amendment is not included, is a form of lay draft. All arguments against lay drafts raised in the chapter on drafting instructions apply here too.

EXPRESS AND IMPLIED AMENDMENT

Statutes can be amended either expressly or impliedly. Express amendment is undertaken by replacing the existing provision with a new or updated one. This occurs by an Act or by subsidiary legislation based on an enabling clause in primary legislation. Express amendment promotes clarity, which of course contributes to effectiveness.

Amendment of statutes may also take place impliedly, namely as a consequence of inconsistences arising from an express amendment of an existing statute. Implied amendment is a result of statutory interpretation: it reflects the clash between two provisions, and requires the application of principles of interpretation in order to resolve the confusion. Implied amendment presupposes a drafting error: the drafter has failed to identify a consequential amendment and has failed to express this in the Act.

As a result, the user and the courts have the difficult task of trying to accommodate the parallel existence of two competing statutes. This can be achieved through the identification of a difference in the field of application of the existing and the amending provision, as a means of justifying the parallel existence of them both. The presumption is that the drafter intended to keep both statutes; otherwise they would and should have repealed the original provision. If the attempt to keep both statutes in parallel cannot work, then the users and the courts have no other option but to attempt to prioritise the competing statutes. This can be achieved through the application of statutory interpretation principles, such as the maxim that newer general provisions do not repeal older specific ones and so newer general provisions do not readily construe an implied amendment.

The tools are there, and the legal system will in the end find a way to settle the confusion caused by the implied amendment. But this is a clear transfer of the task and power to legislate from the legislature to the judiciary. And so implied amendments are a breach of the principle of separation of powers. This may be tolerated if the intent of the instructing officers and the legislature was to allow lengthy application to real cases to formulate the precise fields of application of the two statutes. This is an

[6] See VRAC Crabbe, *Legislative Precedents—Volume II* (London, Cavendish Publishing Ltd, 1998) 15.

expression of conscious vagueness that, although not best practice, can be of use to the legislature.

DIRECT AND INDIRECT AMENDMENT

Express amendments can be constructed either as direct or indirect amendments. In drafting the express amendment, the drafter may select to undertake a textual amendment of the existing legislation instructing the user what is changed and how.[7] The Family Procedure (Amendment No 3) Rules 2013 are a fantastic source of direct amendments. An example:

> Amendments to the Family Procedure Rules 2010
>
> 3. For rule 2.1, substitute—
> 'Application of these Rules
> 2.1. Unless the context otherwise requires, these rules apply to family proceedings in—
> (a) the High Court; and
> (b) the family court.'

Direct amendments may express repeals, alterations, substitutions, incorporations or a mixture of the above. An example of a direct amendment by repeal is found in the Freedom of Information (Amendment) (Scotland) Act 2013:

> 4. Historical periods
> (1) In section 59 (power to vary periods mentioned in sections 57 and 58) of the FOI Act—
> (a) in subsection (1), the words 'subsection (1) of section 57 or' are repealed.

An example of a direct amendment via alteration is traced in the Representation of the People (England and Wales) (Description of Electoral Registers and Amendment) Regulations 2013:

> Amendment in relation to communication of applications, notices etc.
> 5. (1) Regulation 5 is renumbered as paragraph (1) of that regulation.

An example of direct amendment by substitution is found in the Crofting (Amendment) (Scotland) Act 2013:

> (24c) ... (3) In subsection (3), for the words from 'land in respect' to the end substitute 'direction under section 24B(1) is revoked'.

[7] See Sir CT Carr, 'Legislation by Reference and the Technique of Amendment' (1940) 22 *Journal of Comparative Legislation and International Law* 12, 13.

An example of direct amendment via incorporation is found in the Children's Homes and Looked After Children (Miscellaneous Amendments) (England) Regulations 2013:

> Amendments to the Children's Homes Regulations 2001
>
> 4. In regulation 4, after paragraph (2) insert—
> '(2A) Where a children's home has a website, the registered person shall ensure that a copy of the statement of purpose is published on that website unless the registered person considers that such publication would prejudice the welfare of children cared for in the children's home.'

And an example of direct amendment using a combination of methods is in the Family Procedure (Amendment No 3 Rules) 2013:

> Amendments to the Family Procedure Rules 2010
>
> 23. In rule 9.5—
> (a) in paragraph (1)(a), for 'a designated county court' substitute 'the family court';
> (b) omit paragraph (2); and
> (c) in the words in parentheses at the end of the rule after '2004 Act' insert 'which is proceeding in the High Court'.

Direct amending as a drafting technique presents distinct advantages. As the aim of the drafter is effectiveness in the sense of smooth and precise incorporation of the existing legal system, direct amending offers increased clarity[8] and precision. The drafter instructs clearly on the action to be undertaken by the user, namely to insert or delete or substitute, and also on the elements of the phrase where the clear instructions apply. Narrative description of actions or locations where these apply can only cause confusion and doubt: clarity promotes certainty as to what needs to be done and where exactly. If the drafter has the skill to draft amendments properly, then punctuation can also be taken into account in the elements of textual change thus offering the user one additional layer of assistance in the comprehension of instruction and applicable text.

Direct amending assists precision in the drafting task. It reflects a meticulous elaboration of the role of each word or punctuation mark in the existing text, its juxtaposition to what the text should now be in order to reflect the drafting instructions, and ultimately it guides the reader as to exactly how this alignment with the new position is to be expressed by the law. Focusing on words and punctuation promotes this meticulous task and urges the drafter to consider precisely what, if anything, needs to be changed and how.

[8] See Sir W Dale, 'A London Particular' (1985) 6 *Statute Law Review* 11, 18.

It is precisely the surgical precision of direct amendments that offers drafters and instructing officers the luxury of touching only these parts of the text that absolutely need change. This promotes not just drafting excellence but also precision in the concepts under amendment: policy and legal officers become aware of the need to keep changes to the absolute minimum thus meddling with the legal system as little as necessary. This promotes fluidity and continuity in the law.

And it also ensures that when the legislature discusses the amendments all surrounding concepts and text remain outside the scope of parliamentary debate. This allows a surgical policy intervention by the legislature. And it can save parliamentary time.

Finally, direct amendments are in a format that supports later consolidation since they instruct the consolidating officer on the steps to be taken for the achievement of their task.[9]

In view of the advantages of direct textual amendments for the drafting team, the legislature and law reform officers, their prevalence in the Commonwealth is hardly surprising. But direct amendments carry a distinct disadvantage when viewed through the prism of untrained users: they are a complicated list of complex instructions referring to a text that the user does not have in front of them. And they amend the text of the law in a manner that can be imprecise for the lay user whose mind will always be in unrest not knowing for sure whether their application of the direct amendment to the text actually is what the drafter intended, and what the law now stands as.

The question is whether this distinct disadvantage weighs down on the advantages of direct amendments. As ever, effectiveness is the main criterion here, and the question is how clarity and precision are best served. The problem though is that what is clear for the trained professional may well be totally unclear for the lay user. And so a combination technique, namely one supplementing the direct textual amendment, can promote clarity for the lay user also. But what could these be? A variety of tools can be promoted: explanatory notes, comprehensive repeal and re-enactment, or even tools within the text of the amending statute itself. Let us explore them separately.

Explanatory notes are a wonderful way of bringing the user closer to an understanding, indeed an authentic interpretation and application, of the amending statute. Explanatory notes can explain the policy behind the amendments, the law reform pursued and the new terms used. In this way explanatory notes may form the bridge above the chasm of minimalism in law expression and possible maximalism of law reform. They can reflect

[9] See HH Marshall, 'The Commonwealth Legal Advisory Service: a Successful Experiment in Commonwealth Legal Cooperation' (1972) 21 *International and Comparative Law Quarterly* 435, 443; also see 'Current Developments' (1987) 8 *Statute Law Review* 191.

on the changes in real-life terms, thus offering the instructing officers the opportunity to draw examples of real people affected by the amendments in real life, also instructing and educating the executive officers expected to apply the amended law. But, in order for such explanatory notes to cover the gap between technical drafting precision and user intelligibility of the amending statutes, they have to: be fit for purpose; be accessible by lay users; and, perhaps more crucially in view of current UK practice, they have to actually be used by the lay users. As a relative professional in legislative drafting, I have little doubt that the majority of explanatory notes currently produced in the UK are fit for purpose: in fact, I confess to quite often resorting to them in order to understand the full picture of the change in the law. But lay users tend to be unaware of their existence and still unsure as to their interpretative value.

Another possible technique enhancing clarity for the users is that of repealing and re-enacting: the drafter deletes the original provision as amended, and redrafts from scratch a provision that expresses the original text and all subsequent amendments in a single text. An example can be found in section 9 of the Clergy Discipline (Amendment) Measure 2013:

> (5) For subsection (5) there is substituted the following subsection—
>
> '(5) The appointment of the Dean of the Arches and Auditor shall be for a period beginning with the date of the appointment and ending with the date on which he attains the age of seventy-five years, but—
>
> (a) he may resign his office by instrument in writing under his hand addressed to, and served on, the Archbishops of Canterbury and York,
>
> (b) he may be removed by the Archbishops of Canterbury and York jointly if the Upper Houses of the Convocations of the provinces of Canterbury and York each resolve that he is incapable of acting or unfit to act, and
>
> (c) he may continue to act as a judge for the purpose of any proceedings in either Court during the course of which he attains the age of seventy-five years as if the date of the conclusion of the proceedings were the date on which he attains that age.'

There is little doubt that this is immensely useful for the lay user, who has the expression of the law as it stands in the location where expected, namely within the text. Repealing and replacing heavily amended provisions offers increased clarity contrasted with amendments via a series of detailed insertions, omissions and substitutions. So the original text states:

> All cars, ships and planes must be registered by 1 August 2015.

The drafter's choice is to amend meticulously or to repeal and re-enact. Contrast the two possible drafts:

> In section 10:
>
> a. after 'cars' insert 'lorries'
>
> b. after 'ships' insert 'hovercraft'

c. after 'planes' insert '(including helicopters)'
d. for 'August' substitute 'September'
e. for '2014' substitute '2015'.

Or:

For section 10 substitute '10. All cars, lorries, ships, hovercraft and planes (including helicopters) must be registered by 1 September 2015.'

Clarity is enhanced by the choice to repeal and re-enact.[10] But repealing and re-enacting does not assist the reader in following the historical progression of the statute, and identifying the law as it stood at any of the moments of amendments in the past: not unless repeal and re-enacting takes place along with every amendment. This would occur in continuing revisions of the statute book, which however are scarce in the Commonwealth, as they require immense resources on an ongoing basis. And so repealing and re-enacting is a good technique but with inherent problems of practicability.

A form of repeal and re-enactment that takes place on a continuous basis is the technique of automatic consolidation of amended legislation.[11] The statute book reflects at any given time the full picture of the law as it stands post amendment. This becomes available either in a text that has official value, or in an official text as is the case with the Irish restatement. The value of the technique is evident and has been identified by a number of authors.[12] But, despite the application of the technique in a number of Commonwealth jurisdictions,[13] its heavy demand on resources renders it impracticable for the majority of jurisdictions.[14] Moreover, the disadvantages of repeal and re-enactments raised above apply here equally.

What combines the advantage of location within the text with a clean statement of the law as it stands post amendment is a combination of direct textual amendment with a restatement of the law. This can be achieved via direct textual amendments in the body of the amending Act combined with a Keeling Schedule at the bottom of the Act.[15] Yet, despite its great value for the user, Keeling Schedules have rarely been used in amending Acts. An analysis of UK

[10] For an analysis of consolidation, see Lord Simon of Glaisdale and JVD Webb, 'Consolidation and Statute Law Revision' (1975) *Public Law* 285.

[11] See T Arnold-Moore, 'Point in Time Publication for Legislation (XML and Legislation) Automating Consolidation of Amendments to Legislation in Common Law and Civil Jurisdictions' (2004) *Journées Internet pour le Droit* www.frlii.org/spip.php?article67.

[12] See A Wittfoth, P Chung, G Greenleaf and A Mowbray, 'AustLII's Point-in-Time legislation System: A Generic PiT System for Presenting Legislation' www.austlii.edu.au/austlii/help/pit/.

[13] See http://www.austlii.edu.au/au/legis/vic/consol_act/iola1984322/s16.html; http://www.legislation.gov.hk/index.htm; www.lawnet.com.sg.

[14] For an analysis of the position in a number of Commonwealth jurisdictions, see D Berry, 'Keeping the Statute Book Up to Date: a Personal View' (2010) 36 *Commonwealth Law Bulletin* 79.

[15] See A Samuels, 'Use of the Keeling Schedule' (1997) 18 *Statute Law Review* 250, 250.

legislation shows that Keeling Schedules are not included in amending Acts, but that explanatory notes direct the user to informal Keeling Schedules in the form of texts or tables of the law as applied post amendment. For example, the explanatory notes to the Police Act 1997 (Criminal Records) (Isle of Man) (Amendment) Order 2012 state that 'An informal Keeling Schedule setting out the provisions of the 2012 Act as they extend to the Island is published on the Ministry of Justice website to assist the reader at www.justice.gov.uk'. Although one can interpret this hesitance to include a Keeling Schedule within the Act as being in line with the current departure from the technique in UK legislation altogether,[16] one can nevertheless point out what a missed opportunity for clarity this is. The Keeling Schedule combines the sophisticated precision treasured by professionals with the clarity craved by lay users, especially in direct amendments. It can serve as the optimal tool for the drafter who already undertakes the task of applying the instructions to the text anyway. It is disheartening to see such a useful tool ignored.

Drafting Techniques for Direct Textual Amendments

The fact the direct textual amendments are focused on the facilitation of the learned used does not necessarily mean that they have to be cryptic. Far from it. There are a number of prevalent drafting techniques aiming to serve clarity and, thus, effectiveness.

The short title of the amending Act is no different from the short title of Acts in general. It needs to be short, precise, to the point and helpful for referencing purposes. Applied to amending Acts specifically, this requires that short titles of amending Acts state their nature as amending statutes, that they refer to the legislation being amended, and that they also offer additional distinguishing keywords for the reader including words in parenthesis and their date. For example, the Export Control (Amendment) (No 2) Order 2010 offers the reader a number of pieces of information: first, this is an amending act, hence the part 'Amendment'; secondly, the Act amends the Export Control Act to which the title refers; thirdly, the date of passing of the amending Act is 2010.

This specific example offers one additional piece of information, namely this is the second amendment to the same Act in the same year. But it does not include information on the specific topic to which amendments are made. The Town and Country Planning (General Permitted Development) (Amendment) (England) (No 3) Order 2013 includes all of the above plus an additional tip: the amendments refer to General Planning Development.

[16] There have been no Keeling Schedules in legislation in 2010, none in 2011, one in 2012, none in 2013 and none in 2014 so far.

The short title of the amending Act is one of the richest sources of information on their date, topic, number in a series of amendments and the original Act to which they refer. There is little doubt that well drafted short titles are excellent explanatory materials for the users. But concrete short titles may not be possible to draft in cases where one Act amends more than one statute, or refers to more than one topic. Before commenting on the technique to be used in such cases, it is worth stating that the short title of any Act is a mechanism of quality control. Being unable to find a precise title can serve as a loud warning for a possible construction that is too broad or without focus: coherence of the Act is under doubt, and clarity endangered; effectiveness is thus questioned. Mosaic laws are not best practice. But they are part of legislative reality. The drafter's job, when failing to avert such laws, is to identify a broad all-encompassing title with a series of clauses in parenthesis reflecting the precise topics addressed in the Act. More often than not the term 'Miscellaneous' is used: this is a true reflection of an Act that touches upon more than one topic; moreover, it refers the reader to the 'Miscellaneous' section of the statute book rather than placing the new Act under a general title that does not match the existing Acts under amendment.

Just as the short title of an amending Act can facilitate the user, a labelling definition of the amended Act may save the drafter from tedious repetition of the same short title within the text. For example, see Article 3 of The Town and Country Planning (Development Management Procedure) (England) (Amendment No 2) Order 2013:

> (3) In this article—
> 'the Planning Act' means the Town and Country Planning Act 1990.

Direct textual amendments can be constructed narratively, or in a table. An example of narrative direct amendment is found in the Child Benefit, Child Support and Social Security (Miscellaneous Amendments) Regulations 1996:

> Amendment of regulation 59 of the Adjudication Regulations
> 2. In regulation 59(1)(d) of the Adjudication Regulations (review of decisions involving payment or increase of child benefit), for the word '12' there shall be substituted the word '6'.

An example of tabular direct amendment is found in The Public Bodies (Abolition of the Commission for Rural Communities) Order 2012:

> SCHEDULE
>
> Repeals and revocations
> 4. The provisions mentioned in the Schedule are repealed or revoked to the extent specified.

SCHEDULE Article 4

Repeals and revocations
Table of repeals

Short title	*Extent of repeal*
Industrial Organisation and Development Act 1947	Section 5(3A)(c) (restriction on disclosure of information).
Superannuation Act 1972	In Schedule 1 (kinds of employment, etc, referred to in section 1), the entry relating to the Commission for Rural Communities.
House of Commons Disqualification Act 1975	In Part 2 of Schedule 1 (bodies of which all members are disqualified), the entry relating to the Commission for Rural Communities.

The tabular format, which has been gaining in popularity recently, is a visual aid tool that allows the reader to quickly pinpoint what is amended and to what extent. It presents all amendments, including repeals, in a compact and structured format that facilitates clarity and intelligibility. But tabular amendments may be counterproductive where the amendment is not solely a direct textual one.

Direct textual amendments benefit from placement of the reference to the section being amended at the beginning of the amending provision or as near as possible to it. The user needs to identify where to look before the instruction on the amendment is offered. And so, in contrast to the general rule on subject-verb-object, amendments are best expressed as 'In section 5(4) omit "goat"', as opposed to the bad practice of 'Omit "goat" in section 5(4)'.

Provisions being amended are best expressed in a simple and brief manner, thus allowing the user to concentrate on the substance of the amendment. And so it is best to say 'section 36(1)(b)', as opposed to the horribly complicated and agonisingly long 'paragraph (b) of subsection (1) of section 36'.

In application of the rule that one concept is expressed in a single legislative sentence, it is best to avoid offering multiple instructions for amendment in a single sentence. It is best to divide up into two subsections the currently conjoint 'In section 3 add "abc" and in section 4 omit the words after "def"'.

Punctuation is an intricate task in amendments: there is punctuation of the original provision, punctuation of the instruction to amend and punctuation of the actual amending provision. Punctuation is crucial for the clear communication between the drafter and the user. Grammar must not be a chain choking the drafter: it is a tool facilitating their work. And so a series of punctuation marks is not to be encouraged, where needed, rather than frowned upon: effectiveness is served by clarity rather than grammar.

The language of the amendment must be consistent with the language of the original text, at least in principle. As the amending text will be incorporated in the original text to form a new complete whole, the use of synonyms for the expression of the same concept creates ambiguity, a known impediment for clarity and therefore effectiveness. The question is, whether the modernisation of the term used in the original Act can ever be forgiven. Much depends on the focus of the drafter: if the task at hand is to succeed in as minimal a change of text as possible, then there is a logic in maintaining the same archaic term in the amending provisions too; if the task at hand is to achieve law reform, then it makes sense to bring the language of the original Act into life as it stands at the time of the amendment. This schism of prisms explains the frequent preference of legislative drafters in Offices of Parliamentary Counsel to ignore archaic terms and often to repeat them in the amendment, as opposed to the inclination of law reformers to modernise the text whilst amending. If effectiveness is used as the criterion of choice out of this dilemma, then an additional dimension is the extent of distaste of modern society to the archaic term in the original Act. Often the term 'elucidate' may remain in the amending text but terms such as 'bastard children' or 'the mentally or physically impaired' are simply too departed from currently accepted terminology and, hopefully, the mentality that new terms reflect. As a result, the implementation of the law is endangered by the distaste of society for the terms selected. This is surely a concern not just for law reformers but also for drafters.

The plain language agenda does not stop at the layout of amendments or the terminology used for concepts in the text. The terms used for instructing the amendment are also subject to tests of clarity, precision and unambiguity. And so consistency in a single simple term to reflect the instruction promotes effectiveness of the amending Act. The terms 'add', 'insert', 'replace', 'substitute' or delete seem easier to the lay user, as opposed to 'adjoin', 'append', 'affix', 'implant', 'interleave' or even 'repeal' or 'revoke'. With specific reference to the last two terms, it is worth noting that normally primary legislation is repealed, whereas delegated legislation is 'revoked'. This reflects the dependency of delegated legislation on a permission from the legislature to the executive: when the executive's licence to legislate is revoked, so are the delegated instruments produced on that basis. The constitutional value of the distinction is widely accepted. But one wonders whether the term 'delete' might be best for legislation: the term encompasses both concepts and the lay user is not left to wonder what the two terms actually mean and what is the distinction between them.

Following up on the plain language agenda, the common practice of complex and unnecessary words in amending provisions is best abolished. There is no point in saying that 'Section 26 of the Animals Act 1990 shall be hereby amended by the addition thereto immediately after the words "calendar year" of the following comma and words ", if the Director so certifies"'. This can be expressed in the simpler format of 'Section 26 of the Animals Act 1990 is amended by adding, after "calendar year", ", if the Director so certifies"'.

Finally, at the point of verification of the draft amendments the drafter need to assess whether the long title of the original Act may remain as is, or whether it needs to be amended to reflect the incorporation of the amending provisions. The mere suggestion that the long title may be amended seems to instil fear in traditional drafters: long titles seem to have been amongst those elements of the text that were deemed sacrosanct. But why is this the case? The tradition of leaving long titles, and indeed purpose clauses, outside amendment seems to stem from the correct view that even after amendment of the original Act long titles continue to reflect the main mechanisms of law reform introduced by the amending Act. Complete departure of the main mechanism of law reform signifies that the tool of amendment has been used incorrectly by the drafter: for an amendment of such contextual significance, constitutional order would request a repeal and re-enactment thus allowing the legislature to refresh its seal of legitimacy to the significantly altered new text. This is a persuasive argument. But it does not create an amnesty from amendment for long titles. If the drafter has supplemented the original Act with a new mechanism of law reform, as would be the case with the addition of a part in the Act, then the long title must be amended to reflect the change too. And so, when amendment of the long title becomes appropriate, the drafter can proceed with it provided that the amendment does not reflect such a radical departure from the original Act that repeal and re-enactment is actually the most appropriate way forward.

The same logic, and conclusion, applies to purpose or objectives clauses too. A complete departure from the existing objectives or purpose normally indicates the need for repeal and re-enactment. But if the drafter, having considered this alert, continues to feel that an amendment is appropriate, then an amendment to the purpose or objectives clause is equally suitable.

Indirect Amendments

Direct amendments offer enhanced clarity to the user.[17] And so it comes as no surprise to hear that they are the most common form of amendments in Commonwealth jurisdictions. But there are circumstances where even

[17] On the problems arising out of referential amendments, see J Teasdale, 'Statute Law Revision: Repeal, Consolidation or Something More?' (2009) 11 *European Journal of Law Reform* 157, 197.

direct amendments can be counterproductive. When general amendments are being made to a large number of statutes, the regulatory message is best conveyed by a holistic regulation on the issue in abstract, as opposed to a long and complex list of numerous amendments of the same term throughout the legal system. For example, when Member States of the Eurozone moved from their former national currencies to the Euro, an indirect amendment introducing a clear replacement of the term 'German mark' or 'French franc' with the term 'Euro' expressed far more effectively the notion of moving from one currency to another, as opposed to an incredibly lengthy list of millions of provisions of primary and delegated legislative instruments replacing the term in concrete.

Indirect amendments are clean and clear in such clean and clear circumstances. However, a sweep provision does not suffice, if clarity is pursued at all costs. Ideally, the initial indirect amendment has to be escorted at a later stage by direct amendments per part of the statute book, or per topic.

Indirect amendments are expressed by two means: either indirect referential amendment; or by comprehensive repeal and re-enactment.

Indirect referential amendment is the use of a narrative description of the amendments introduced without concrete instructions. An example is traced in the Representation of the People (England and Wales) (Description of Electoral Registers and Amendment) Regulations 2013:

> Revocations
> 2. The instruments listed in column 1 of Schedule 2 to these Regulations (which have the references in column 2) are revoked to the extent indicated in column 3 of that Schedule.

Indirect referential amendments are often preferable for clarity, especially if the task at hand is a lengthy list of instructions and interventions. Indirect referential amendments express the amendment introduced with generality appropriate to convey to the user the bigger picture and the bigger message.

They can also be very useful when extensive amending legislation is required and there is insufficient time to research the existing legislation. An example of this can be found in Article 4 of the Health and Social Care Act 2008 (Primary Dental Services, Private Ambulance Services and Primary Medical Services) (Regulated Activities) (Transitory and Transitional Provisions) (Amendment) Order 2011:

> (2) Article 3 applies to an application to which this article applies as if—
> (a) for all references to '1st April 2011' there were substituted '1st April 2013';
> (b) for all references to 'relevant regulated activity' there were substituted '2013 relevant regulated activity';
> (c) for all references to '31st December 2010' there were substituted '31st December 2012';
> (d) all references to article 2 and individual paragraphs of that article were interpreted as references to article 20 and its corresponding individual paragraphs;

(e) all references to 'this article' and individual paragraphs of article 3 were interpreted as references to article 3 and those paragraphs as applied by this article; and
(f) all references to article 5 and individual paragraphs of that article were interpreted as references to that article and those paragraphs as applied by the provisions of article 23.

Indirect referential amendments are also useful where all occurrences of a word in a legislative provision are to be amended. An example of this practice is found in regulation 2 of the Solvent Emissions (Scotland) Regulations 2010:

(e) in paragraph (2), in the definitions of 'adhesive', 'coating', 'ink' and 'manufacturing of coating preparations, varnishes, inks and adhesives', for 'preparation' and 'preparations' wherever they occur (including in the expression being defined) substitute 'mixture' and 'mixtures' respectively.

But indirect referential amendments lack the surgical precision of direct amendments: they can therefore carry vagueness or even ambiguity, which in turn creates confusion to the user and ultimately ineffectiveness via haphazard application. Moreover, they are not in a format appropriate for facilitating later consolidation. So clerks have to put them into effect even for the purposes of offering a clean picture of current law for government.[18] And, they are burdened with the common problem of any types of amendment: they are not meaningful to the user without a text superimposing the amending text onto the original Act. Of course this can always be counteracted by the provision of explanatory notes. But the problem with indirect referential amendments in particular is that, in contrast to direct amendments, they are not fertile for the magical, albeit currently ignored, Keeling Schedule that provides the final picture of the law to the user within the statute book.

It is precisely this weakness that comprehensive repeal and re-enactment aims to address. This is the second type of indirect amendment. It is a complex procedure involving two stages: repealing and re-enacting the legislation which is to be amended; and consolidating new provisions, amended versions of old provisions and re-enacted unamended provisions. The huge advantage of this type of amendment is no secret: the drafting team has a unique opportunity to review the effectiveness of the law and its elements, maintain those that are effective, get rid of those that have not served well and replace them with new elements. In other words, repeal and re-enactment, when undertaken properly in combination with an adequate post-legislative scrutiny of the original Act, can serve as a crucial tool for the promotion of legislative quality. The result of this immense, not to

[18] See D Johnstone, 'Current Development' (1980) 1 *Statute Law Review* 112.

mention time and resource consuming, process is legislation that has learnt from past mistakes, has adapted to requirements and has acquired every opportunity possible to serve the citizens well.

But, in order for the procedure to bear fruit, legislative quality must be observed both in the original Act and in the amendment procedure. In other words, the original drafters need to have identified the true policy pursuit of the instructing officers; the drafting team need to have identified and applied the most appropriate legislative solution; the texts need to have included a concrete list of tangible measurable criteria against which effectiveness of each aspect of the law is to be assessed; the government needs to have undertaken adequate post-legislative scrutiny of the original law and identified its weaknesses; and this needs to have served as the basis for the policy behind the amendment; finally, amendment needs to have indeed been the most appropriate tool for law reform in this case, and the construction of the amending Act needs to have observed the parameters of technical quality. Actually, in an ideal world this is exactly what takes place in the case of each and every amendment.

Does it, always? The disproportionality of the resources required with the seemingly minor task of amending legislation seems to indicate that repeal and re-enactment does not always follow this meticulous process. And it also guides us to the main disadvantage of the tool: when undertaken properly, it costs dearly. Another disadvantage stems from its main advantage: yes, it enables a fresh start to be made, but this opens the ground for parliamentary scrutiny and debate on provisions that it does not aim to change. And also, as legislation is in constant use, constant restructuring of the legislation may actually lead to confusion rather than legislative quality.

Amalgamating Indirect Referential Amendment with Direct Textual Amendment

It is worth noting that the classification of amendments as direct or indirect does not present the two species from mixing. An example of this common practice comes from regulation 5 of the Appointment of Consultants (Amendment) Regulations (Northern Ireland) 2013:

> Amendment of regulation 5 of the principal Regulations
>
> 5. In regulation 5 (Appointments to which the Regulations do not apply)—
> (a) for 'Board' wherever it occurs substitute 'Authority';
> (b) for paragraph (1)(a) substitute—
> '(a) appointed to a clinical academic post;'

Mixing different types of amendments in the same provision is a result of necessity not an educated choice: the drafter finds that the first aspect of the provision is better expressed via indirect referential amendment, whereas the second benefits from concrete direct amendment. But, despite the good reasoning behind the mixing of the two styles, the fact remains that the user remains confused by the interchange between concrete and abstract. And so breaking the provision down in a manner that takes this aspect of expression into account also promotes clarity for the user whose intellect is already challenged by lists of intelligible amendments.

CONSEQUENTIAL AMENDMENTS

If anything, the analysis of amendments has taught us that complexity is an inherent danger of the task. Much more so when one takes into account the interrelation between Acts within the same topic or even Acts seemingly untouched by the changes to other Acts. But the legal system is a complete whole. No Act exists in a vacuum. Every time an Act is amended, relevant Acts are touched: amendments are required to bring relevant Acts into line with the newly amended Act. Amendments that derive as a result of the amendment of another piece of legislation are called consequential amendments.

These are very common. But they cause a real headache to the drafter who needs to hunt them down and bring them to light. Consequential amendments come about as a result of the change imposed on the amended Act, but can refer to relevant or seemingly irrelevant Acts. This is the trap: consequential amendments crop up when least expected, often surprising not just the drafter but also the instructing officers whose substantive law expertise should have armed them with the ability to identify consequential amendments easily and quickly. It is precisely the difficult in identifying consequential amendments, and indeed doing so in an exhaustive list, that has caused the prevalence of bad practice in legislative drafting in the Commonwealth and beyond.

The first issue relates to the member of the drafting team whose task it is to identify consequential amendments. More often than not, especially in Africa and Asia, drafters are expected to devise the provision on consequential amendments almost single-handedly. There is little doubt that the drafting of the provision falls on the drafter's shoulders. But it is not fair to state that the content of the provision is the drafter's duty. The instructing officers of the client department are best equipped to identify consequential amendments, since they have both the substantive law knowledge of the law and its functioning within the field in question, but also because of the detailed research that they undertook at the stage of drafting instructions.[19] One of the main tasks of instructors is to

[19] See JC Peacock, 'Drafting a Proposed Statute' (1955) 1 *Practical Lawyer* 19, 29.

identify the mischief of the existing law, and propose ways to address it. It is within the auspices of this research that instructing officers, policy and law alike, need to dig out relevant laws and work out their interrelation with the Act under amendment. Without this process, drafting instructions are of doubtful quality. On the basis of this work, and their rich understanding of the substantive field of law on which they instruct the drafter, legal officers of the client department are in the best position to identify consequential amendments and suggest the best way to address the clash between them and the amended provision. And so the task of listing consequential amendments belongs to the instructing officers, with the drafter confirming of course.

Consequential amendments must be listed concretely and exhaustively. This is a task not necessarily proportionate to the actual text of the amending Act. For example, the Armed Forces and Reserve Forces Compensation Scheme (Consequential Provisions: Subordinate Legislation) Order 2013 has seven articles in its text and 54 articles of consequential amendments in its sole Schedule.

But the size of the task ahead can be no excuse for general indirect consequential amendments, such as 'All Acts and sections affected by these amendments are hereby amended'. This means absolutely nothing to the user. It simply is a transfer of legislative power from the legislature to the executive, and indeed one without even strictly drafted criteria for its exercise. Although one can almost visualise the relief of the drafter when this trick is accepted, the depth and extent of anomaly introduced in the legal system by this unforgivable vagueness leaves no ground for manoeuvre.

IMPLIED REPEALS

Similarly, implied repeals carry inherent vagueness. In traditional constitutional theory implied repeals are seen as a very narrow doctrine that reconciles older and newer enactments by minimally paring back older law where there is no plausible understanding of the laws that can avoid the inconsistency.[20] In more detail, they are defined as the deletion of a statute not expressly but via a 'subsequent inconsistent enactment which repeals the earlier to the extent of the inconsistency'; or via the statute's self-destruct mechanism of a duration provision; or via desuetude either as a result of non-usage or as a result of a change of circumstances.[21] Implied repeals are a form of implied amendment: their only difference is that

[20] See T Sedgwick, *A Treatise on the Rules which govern the Interpretation and Application of Statutory and Constitutional Law* (New York, John S Voorhies, 1857) 123–24.

[21] See W Chew, 'The Doctrine of Implied Repeal by Desuetude: a Legal Anachronism or Viable Principle?' (1984) 5 *Singapore Law Review* 139, 139.

implied amendments imply the intent to change the law, whereas implied repeals imply the intent to destroy the prior law.[22] And so, implied repeals are another invitation to the user to guess whether a relevant Act has been repealed in full or in part as a result of consequential amendment.[23]

There is no doubt that the legal system does provide a way around this anomaly, mainly via statutory interpretation. It prioritises competing Acts[24] on the basis of their hierarchy or their date of birth[25] or their generality. But this should come as no relief for the drafter. Implied repeals are to be used sparingly rather than creatively.[26] They are dangerous as they are breaches of the principle of the separation of powers: they call upon the judiciary to legislate. And they reflect a failure of the drafting team to achieve the main goal in amending legislation: the smooth transition from the previous to the post amendment regime.

[22] See ER Lanier, 'Statutory Construction: Effect of an Invalid Amendment of a Prior Statute' (1967) 16 *Journal of Public Law* 228, 229.

[23] See 'Recent Decisions: Statutory Construction—Effect of an Invalid Amendment on a Prior Statute' (1967) 6 *Journal of Public Law* 228, 229.

[24] See R Prebble, 'Constitutional Statutes and Implied Repeal: the Thobura Decision and the Consequences for New Zealand' (2005) 36 *Victoria University of Wellington Law Review* 291, 293.

[25] But see contra A Butler, 'Implied Repeal, Parliamentary Sovereignty and Human Rights in New Zealand' (2001) *Public Law* 586, 594.

[26] See JW Markham Jr, 'The Supreme Court's New Implied Repeal Doctrine: Expanding Judicial Power to Rewrite Legislation Under the Ballooning Conception of "Plain Repugnancy"' (2009–10) 45 *Gongaza Law Review* 437, 476.

13

Penal Provisions

PENAL PROVISIONS PRESENT pronounced challenges for the drafter. This is because the chasm between the inevitable complexities of penal legal norms against the very possible inexperience of the user reaches extreme boundaries. Penal provisions convey nuances of legal concepts that have acquired their precise meaning through centuries of statutory interpretation and judicial application: understanding the concepts and identifying their precise meaning within the context of the specific criminal statute is a triumph not just for any user but even for the most learned of criminal lawyers.[1]

But at the same time these complex concepts need to be conveyed in the simplest of manners, thus ensuring that the least educated, least intelligent, least able of citizens[2] has a good understanding of what they can and cannot do:[3] there are no margins for error in penal law, and the consequences of a possible mistake are detrimental to the freedom of the subject. And of course, consequences go beyond the subject:[4] prohibition of activities is not undertaken lightly, it is a solution of last resort,[5] used only when absolutely necessary and only if any other means of addressing the problem that society cannot tolerate[6] seem ineffective. This means that the reason for putting the prohibition in place must have been good, and therefore the danger for non-compliance grave.

This chasm between lay users and expert lawyers is so pronounced in penal law that Robinson sees no other way to reconcile their diverse demands than to draft one substantive criminal code for lay users and one

[1] See N Hutton, 'Mechanics of Law Reform' (1961) 24 *Modern Law Review* 18, 21.

[2] See D Husak, 'Ignorance of Law and Duties of Citizenship' (1994) 14 *Legal Studies* 105.

[3] But see contra F Bennion, 'If It's Not Broke Don't Fix It: A Review of the New Zealand Law Commission's Proposals on the Format of Legislation' (1994) 15 *Statute Law Review* 164, 165.

[4] See H Wechsler, 'The Challenge of a Model Penal Code' (1952) 65 *Harvard Law Review* 1097, 1098.

[5] See M Jefferson, 'Regulation, Businesses, and Criminal Liability' (2011) 75 *Journal of Criminal Law* 37, 37.

[6] See A Goodstein, 'Letting Armed Robbery Get Away: an Analysis of Wisconsin's Armed Robbery Statute' (1998) *Wisconsin Law Review* 591, 594.

procedural criminal code for the experts.[7] But of course this duality of audiences and sets of rules does not necessarily lead to a duality of texts:[8] the layered approach can apply here and accommodate the two statutes as part of one, thus offering access to the whole body of the text to both audiences. The layered approach would demand a plain language approach in the substantive part one but could allow for legal jargon, to an extent, in part two. But even the layered approach cannot serve as an excuse for unnecessary jargon, even in part two. And its huge advantage is that the lay audience can focus on the main regulatory message, thus optimising the opportunity to convey to the users the main regulatory message, namely what is prohibited, under which conditions, and what the punishment for non-compliance can be.

DRAFTING INSTRUCTIONS: INITIAL CONSIDERATIONS

At the stage of the legislative process where penal policy is being decided and legal officers articulate their drafting instructions, a number of initial considerations come into play.[9] Even in the case of a new criminal offence, the drafter does not work in a vacuum. There is a multitude of legislative layers that tackle issues directly linked with penal provisions starting from the very core of constitutionality and personal liberties, and expanding to the philosophy of the criminal justice system, its super goal,[10] and its cohesive approach to specific types of criminal offences. And these broad considerations arise from a multi-layered system of sources of criminal law and policy.

First, domestic standards are taken into account. These are expressed in the constitution, or the constitutional documents; in the Interpretation Act; in existing penal provisions be it within a code or in statutes; and, of course, in the rich case law of the criminal courts.

Secondly, regional standards are taken into account. These range from the European Convention on Human Rights (especially Articles 4, 5, 9, 10, 11 and Protocols 1 and 4) as applied by the Human Rights Act and by the case law of both the ECHR and the Court of Justice of the European

[7] See PH Robinson, 'Making Criminal Codes Functional: A Code of Conduct and a Code of Adjudication' (1996) 86 *Journal of Criminal Law and Criminology* 304; also see PH Robinson, 'Rules of Conduct and Principles of Adjudication' (1990) 57 *University of Chicago Law Review* 729; and M Dan-Cohen, 'Decision Rules and Conduct Rules: On Acoustic Separation in Criminal Law' (1984) 97 *Harvard Law Review* 625.

[8] PR Ferguson, 'Constructing a Criminal Code' (2009) 20 *Criminal Law Forum* 139.

[9] See G Stewart, 'Legislative Drafting: the Promulgation of Penal Provisions' (1997) 27 *Victoria University of Wellington Law Review* 487, 488.

[10] For a discussion on the theories of criminal justice, see N-D Barbu, 'Some Aspects Regarding the Prevention and Combating of Criminal Offences' (2013) 2 *Public Security Studies* 112.

Union.[11] And of course penal provisions derive from the rich loins of EU criminal law, and its increasingly complicated relationship, at least in the UK, with domestic law.

And thirdly, international (or is universal a better term?) standards are taken into account. And these relate to two different dimensions. On the one hand, instructing officers must take into account substantive criminal law instruments at the international level. UN conventions, bilateral and multilateral treaties, and other instruments of international law form an ever-increasing chunk of international regulation that applies to domestic legislative drafting. And, on the other hand, instructing officers can no longer neglect to apply the rule of law principles as these are expressed by certainty in the law, especially the criminal law. This enhanced notion of certainty in the law is promoted by clarity, precision and unambiguity of criminal laws, qualities that are both crucial and neglected in modern criminal laws.[12]

THE LEGISLATIVE PLAN

In order to cope with the task of drafting effective penal laws the drafter must begin with the legislative plan. Perhaps the most important question to be addressed in the plan is whether legislation is indeed necessary as a method of regulation and, if so, whether penal legislation is the most effective way forward. The drafter's instinct is to say no to both questions. And so they have to be persuaded by the instructing officers, preferably on the basis of evidence-based studies,[13] that other regulatory tools have been discussed and rejected. And that all lighter types of legislation, from soft law to civil legislation, have been studied and rejected as unable to meet the purpose set by the instructing officers: having said that, penal provisions must be introduced exclusively in primary legislation.[14]

Once the necessity of penal legislation is addressed, the drafter continues with an initial sketch of the main elements of the new penal provision. This details the objective and subjective elements of the proposed offence, focusing on the substantive penal law know-how transferred via the drafting instructions.

[11] See H Xanthaki, 'The UK Human Rights Act: a True Excuse for Judicial Law-making by the Law Lords?' (2012) 18 *Jura* 244, 246–47.

[12] See J Spencer, 'The Drafting of Criminal Justice Legislation—Need it be so Impenetrable?' (2008) 67 *Cambridge Law Journal* 585.

[13] See M Bohlander, 'Vicarious Criminal Liability of Parents for Offences Committed by Their Children' (2013) 177 *Criminal Law and Justice Weekly* 791, 792.

[14] See Law Commission, *Criminal Liability in Regulatory Contexts* (Law Com No 195, 2010) www.lawcom.gov.uk/docs/cp195-web.pdf.

It is again on the basis of the analysis offered by the instructing officers that sanctions are set, at least in principle. Instructing officers have an understanding of the penal system and a comparative awareness of what type and level of penalty similar or relevant offences currently carry. Proportionality can lead them to a good estimate of what the law should be.[15] A further issue to address at this point is the need to foresee additional sanctions, perhaps supplemental to the primary one, or sanctions imposed under special circumstances.

Once the basic plan of the provision is set, the drafter identifies the points already covered by the Interpretation Act or by general penal provisions. This could be the case with issues related to amnesty, early release or procedure. And so the next challenge is to decide whether there is any scope for deviation from the general penal procedures. Normally, deviation is to be justified by reference to effectiveness of the provision *in concreto*. But a change of policy may be creeping into the penal law thus requiring a departure from the current norm. The drafter's duty here is to alert the members of the drafting team that any deviation from the current norm is of surprise to the user, and needs to be expressed in a very clear manner. Which leads to a question: if there is no departure from the norm, must the drafter repeat the general provisions or is this superfluous? The question is not as straightforward as one might expect: there is little doubt that repeating the general provisions allows the Act to be self-sufficient. But Acts are meant to be read in conjunction with relevant Acts anyway. And so the bottom line is that paraphrasing the general provisions is an invitation to ambiguity, which is impossible to defend.

As for verbatim repetition or referential repetition, this may not cause harm but carries dangers: by referring to selective general provisions the user may acquire the legitimate impression that all other general provisions are inapplicable; and also repetition leads to a longer Act which may well detract the user's attention from the main regulatory message. The final answer to this dilemma can only be offered by reference to effectiveness. In principle, penal Acts envisaged as used by citizens without necessarily the need for legal advice are best presented with the general provisions thus ensuring that the user is aware of all relevant law: an example could be a Citizen's Arrest Act. But Acts designed to be used with a legal counsellor do not need to repeat or even refer to the general provisions: a typical example could be rules of criminal evidence.

[15] See ME O'Connell, 'Debating the Law on Sanctions' (2002) 13 *European Journal of International Law* 63; also see R Frase, 'Excessive Prison Sentences, Punishment Goals, and the Eighth Amendment: Proportionality Relative to What' (2004–05) 89 *Minnesota Law Review* 571, 624; and A von Hirsh, 'Proportionality in the Philosophy of Punishment' (1992) 16 *Crime and Justice* 55, 56 and 68–69.

And this leads to a final concern, that of amendments or repeals. If they are necessary, the drafter composes an exhaustive list thus preparing for the drafting of the final provisions of the Act. For penal laws specifically, there can be no excuse for implied amendments or implied repeals. Clarity is at the forefront of the drafter's pursuit. And this requires clarity in the relationship between the new Act and older Acts too.

THE PARTS OF A PENAL PROVISION

A penal provision introduces an offence. This is no easy task. The drafter's shopping list is both long and complex. Penal offences foresee two basic elements: first, the introduction of the offence; and second, the sanction.

The offence is introduced via the description of the conduct under prohibition, and the declaration of this conduct as an offence.

The description of the conduct includes objective and subjective elements. The objective elements describe the 'doing' part of the conduct. Is this about an action? Is this about an omission? Are there specific factual elements that must have taken place for the conduct to lead to the offence?

The subjective elements describe the 'thinking' part of the conduct. What level of intent is required? How is fault established? In principle, offences are divided into three classes: the first class includes offences where the mental element (known as mens rea) is a prerequisite for prosecution; the second class includes offences where proof of mens rea is not a prerequisite for prosecution, and the third class includes offences of strict liability where total absence of fault is not a defence. Mens rea is introduced by use of the terms 'knowingly', 'intentionally' or 'recklessly'.

And then what happens once both the objective and subjective elements are present, namely the declaration of the conduct as an offence? Without the express declaration of the conduct as an offence there is no offence: there can be no implied criminalisation, not even on the basis of the inclusion of the incomplete provision within a criminal statute.[16]

Once the offence is introduced, the provision deals with the sanction that may be imposed. The primary sanction is of course crucial as it constitutes an expression of the level of distaste that society places on the behaviour in question. It is set by the drafting team, and not solely the drafter, as it reflects the general criminal policy of the government, as detailed in the criminal law of the jurisdiction in question at the specific moment in time. The primary sanction can be a discharge, a fine, a community sentence or a prison sentence. On top of the primary sanction, the provision may introduce

[16] See F von Liszt, 'The Rationale for the Nullum Crimen Principle' (2007) 5 *Journal of International Criminal Justice* 1009, 1012.

supplementary sanctions, or sanctions imposed under aggravating or alleviating circumstances.

It is necessary to note that the long list of elements to be included in a penal provision should not be taken to require an equally long series of sections or subsections. A single section with a single legislative sentence may suffice. But setting out each of the elements of the provision in separate subsections seems to enhance clarity by drawing the user's attention to each of the crucial parts of the regulatory message: what behaviour is prohibited; that this behaviour constitutes an offence; and that this offence carries a penalty. For example, section 5 of the Mobile Homes (Wales) Act 2013 states that:

> 5 Prohibition on use of land as regulated site without site license
> (1) The owner of a regulated site must not cause or permit the site to be used as a regulated site unless the owner holds a license under this Part in relation to the land (a 'site license').
> (2) A person who contravenes subsection (1) commits an offence.
> (3) A person who is guilty of an offence under subsection (2) is liable on summary conviction to a fine.

RULES OF CONSTRUCTION

General Rules and Innovation

Penal provisions are no different from other types of substantive provisions: the rules are the same. Effectiveness leads the way, using clarity, precision and unambiguity. But in the case of penal provisions plain language is of enhanced value. And so simple terminology, contrasting layout and logical structure become all the more important as visual aids aiming to facilitate the user's inevitable struggle against legal semantics.

But one does wonder whether penal provisions could make use of additional visual aids. It is surprising that these have not been used in penal laws, certainly not to the extent used in planning laws for example. Yet the concept behind them would be the same. Having established that words offer limited clarity, could users make use of pictures? In other words, as language can narrate the conduct and its sanctions in a manner that carries inherent ambiguities, would pictures be able to offer the user the clear image of what behaviour is prohibited?[17] Depictions of crime and punishment have been drawn for centuries. Some of them have withstood the test of time, and have remained in peoples' brains as synonymous with

[17] See D Jerker, B Svantesson and S Greenstein, 'Preface' in D Jerker, B Svantesson and S Greenstein, *Internationalisation of Law in the Digital Information Society: Nordic Yearbook of Law and Informatics 2010–2012* (Denmark, Tutto, 2013).

the message that they convey. Expressive as Dante's *Inferno* may be, it is Botticelli's depiction of hell that has managed to convey sin and punishment in a loud and clear diachronical manner. And, although the suggestion that Schedules in penal laws could include pictures may sound extreme, how do penal laws differ from the online version of the Australian Flag Act 1953 with its colourful picture of a moving flag? And, in any case, does the possibility of finally conveying the penal regulatory message not make it worth studying, and even trying out, the Schedule with pictures idea? Innovative as the concept may be, policy officers have caught on with the advantages of image for the clarification of legislation.[18] It remains for drafters to follow.

Expressing the Conduct

Despite using the example of section 5 of the Mobile Homes (Wales) Act 2013 as a model for best practice from the point of view of listing the elements of the penal provision, the same section is the source of bad practice with reference to subsection (1) and the expression of the conduct. Here the drafter chooses to use the directory method, which introduces the offence via a command: 'must not'. Unfortunately this is a deficient method of expressing the conduct as it fails to declare the prohibition. In the example above this is done by use of subsection (2), which, however, is superfluous as it could have been expressed merging both subsections into one: 'it is an offence to ....', or 'whoever ... commits an offence'.

The better choice for the drafter would have been the declaratory method, the most popular method within the Commonwealth. Here the drafter states the behaviour to be criminalised, and declares the offence in a single combined legislative sentence. This is an express compliance with the principle of *nullum crimen, nulla poena sine lege*.[19] An example is found in section 8 of the Mesothelioma Act 2014:

> 8 Unauthorised disclosure of information: offence
> (1) A person involved in the administration of the scheme must not, without lawful authority, disclose information which—
> (a) was acquired in connection with the administration of the scheme, and
> (b) relates to a particular person who is identified in the information or whose identity could be deduced from it.
> (2) A disclosure is made with 'lawful authority' only if—
> (a) it is made for the purposes of the administration of the scheme,
> (b) it is made for the purpose of preventing or detecting crime,

[18] See eg EasyRead Service, 'Draft Bill on Care and Support' Ref ISL 151/12 (July 2012)https://www.gov.uk/government/uploads/system/uploads/attachment_data/file/216845/2900021-Care-and-Support-Bill-EasyRead-12.07.2012-WEB-ACC.pdf.

[19] See A Mokhtar, 'Nullum crimen, nulla poena sine lege: Aspects and Prospects' (2005) 26 *Statute Law Review* 41, 46–47.

(c) it is made in accordance with any enactment or an order of a court or tribunal,
(d) it is made for the purposes of proceedings before a court or tribunal, or
(e) it is made with consent given by or on behalf of the person to whom the information relates or the person's personal representatives.

(3) A person who breaches subsection (1) commits an offence (for penalties, see section 9).

Equally complete is the conditional method of expression of the offence. Here the drafter introduces the offence utilising a conditional clause. But the legislative sentence can become complicated. An example of the conditional method is found in section 23 of the Local Audit and Accountability Act 2014:

23 Offences relating to section 22

(1) A person is guilty of an offence if, without reasonable excuse, the person—
(a) obstructs the exercise of any power conferred by section 22, or
(b) fails to comply with any requirement of a local auditor under that section.

(2) A person guilty of an offence under subsection (1) is liable on summary conviction—
(a) to a fine not exceeding level 3 on the standard scale, and
(b) to an additional fine of not more than £20 for each day on which the offence continues after conviction for that offence.

Of the three methods of expression the declaratory method seems to offer the completeness and briefness favoured in the modern style of legislative drafting.[20] But, whatever the choice, the drafter must attempt to stick with a single method of expression within the same Act.[21]

Sanctions

The level of seriousness of the offence is a matter of policy.[22] The duty to select the level of seriousness of the offence lies mainly with the instructing officers. But ensuring that this policy is in compliance with existing legislation is the drafter's duty. Even within the constraints of policy the drafter has discretion in expressing sanctions.

Sanctions employ a steady and intermittent pressure pushing the citizen to a 'semi-automatic compliance'.[23] Setting the maximum penalty requires an analysis and consideration of penal policy; the social implications of the offence; any public and academic opinion on the level of clash between the

[20] Sir A Russell, *Legislative Drafting and Forms* (London, Butterworths, 1938) 46.

[21] See P Ferguson, 'The Drafting of Offence Provisions by the Scottish Parliament' (2011) 32 *Statute Law Review* 161, 174.

[22] See P Rossi et al, 'The Seriousness of Crimes: Normative Structure and Individual Differences' (1974) 39 *American Sociological Review* 224, 228–29.

[23] See J Davies, *Legislative Law and Process in a Nutshell* (St Paul, West Group, 1986) 145.

behaviour and *mores*;[24] the rehabilitation of offenders; and, in the case of setting the level of fines, the financial loss from the offence.[25]

Setting the minimum penalty requires consideration of the utility of minimum penalties as a matter of general penal policy. Although diminishing the level of discretion offered to judges leads to a delimitation of judge-made law, judges must be allowed discretion with regards to sanctions. The individuality of each case demands ad hoc considerations that cannot possibly be introduced in abstract by the drafter. Within this acceptable ground for manoeuvre, judges may well be served by the lack of a minimum penalty. Having one may lead the fair-minded judge to steer away from conviction in cases where the specific circumstances of the case render even the minimum penalty disproportionate to the offence committed. And so the lack of minimum sanctions is the norm both in UK Acts and in EU criminal laws. For example, section 54 of the Protection of Freedoms Act 2012 states that:

> (5) A person guilty of an offence under this section is liable—
> (a) on conviction on indictment, to a fine,
> (b) on summary conviction, to a fine not exceeding the statutory maximum.

Moreover, it is important to note that the drafter has a choice of civil penalties,[26] fines, imprisonment or all of those. For example, section 23 of the Local Audit and Accountability Act 2014 states that:

> (2) A person guilty of an offence under subsection (1) is liable on summary conviction—
> (a) to a fine not exceeding level 3 on the standard scale, and
> (b) to an additional fine of not more than £20 for each day on which the offence continues after conviction for that offence.

SPECIAL CIRCUMSTANCES

Penalties may be introduced in various levels with reference to corporate bodies. For example, section 13 of the Transparency of Lobbying, Non-Party Campaigning and Trade Union Administration Act 2014 states that:

> 13 Bodies corporate and Scottish partnerships
> (1) Where an offence under this Part is committed by a body corporate and is proved—

[24] See V Lee Hamilton and S Rytina, 'Social Consensus on Norms of Justice: Should the Punishment Fit the Crime?' (1980) 85 *American Journal of Sociology* 1117.

[25] See Sentencing Advisory Council, Preliminary Issues Paper, 'Maximum Penalties: Principles and Purposes' (Oct 2010) https://sentencingcouncil.vic.gov.au/sites/sentencingcouncil.vic.gov.au/files/maximum_penalties_preliminary_issues_paper.pdf.

[26] For the drafting of civil penalties, see RM White, '"It's not a Criminal Offence"—or is it? Thornton's Analysis of "Penal Provisions" and the Drafting of "Civil Penalties"' (2011) 32 *Statute Law Review* 17.

(a) to have been committed with the consent or connivance of a director, manager, secretary or other similar officer, or
(b) to be attributable to any neglect on the part of any such individual, the individual as well as the body corporate is guilty of the offence and is liable to be proceeded against and punished accordingly.

(2) Where the affairs of a body corporate are managed by its members, subsection (1) applies in relation to the acts and omissions of a member in connection with that management as if the member were a director of the body corporate

Various levels of sanctions can also be foreseen for a second offence, for offenders with accrued benefit from the offence, or for continuing offences. A wonderful example of a long list of such diverse sanctions is found in Schedule 2 of the Criminal Procedure (Consequential Provisions) (Scotland) Act 1995: what is even more interesting is that the Schedule takes a tabular, and therefore innovative, clear and unambiguous format:

...

NATIONAL ASSISTANCE ACT 1948 (C. 29) Offences under section 55(2) (obstruction).	Section 55(2) (as amended by Schedule 3 to the Criminal Justice Act 1967).	£10 for a first offence and £20 for a second or subsequent offence.

...

Continuing offences occur over a substantive period of time.[27] An example of a provision regulating a continuing offence is found in section 106 of the Wireless Telegraphy Act 2006. In this example the continuing offence is introduced as an accumulation of separate daily offences:

106 Continuing offences

... (2) The person is to be treated as committing a separate offence in respect of every day on which the use, or the failure or refusal, so continues.

(3) Subsection (2) does not affect the right to bring separate proceedings for contraventions of this Act taking place on separate occasions.

Section 33 of the Forestry Act (Northern Ireland) 2010 includes a rather more typical provision on sanctions for a continuing offence:

(3) Any person guilty of an offence under this section is liable on summary conviction—
(a) to a fine not exceeding level 4 on the standard scale or to imprisonment for a term not exceeding 6 months or to both; and
(b) in the case of a continuing offence, to a further fine not exceeding one-tenth of level 4 on the standard scale in respect of each day during which the offence is continued after conviction.

[27] See Notes, 'Continuing in Crime' (1969) 33 *Journal of Criminal Law* 130, 130.

An example of a provision discussing the parameters to be taken into account for the setting of the level of fines is section 9 of the Reading Borough Council Act 2013:

9 Levels of fixed penalties

... (3) In setting the level of fixed penalty under subsection (1) the council may

(a) in respect of relevant offences, take account of—

(i) any reasonable costs or expected costs incurred or to be incurred in connection with the administration of the provisions of Schedule 4 to the 1982 Act; and

(ii) the cost or expected cost of enforcing the provisions of that Schedule; or

(b) in respect of offences under section 6, take account of—

(i) any reasonable costs or expected costs incurred or to be incurred in connection with the administration of the provisions of that section; and

(ii) the cost or expected cost of enforcing the provisions of that section.

DEFENCES

The penal provision may well include a set of defences, namely a set of circumstances that preclude the offence from having taken place.[28] From a drafting perspective, defences are exceptions or savings from the general description of the elements of the offence. But, instead of a saving, the drafter more often than not chooses to introduce them in an express and clear manner, often expressed as 'It is a defence'.

Defences may refer to any exemption from the general rule, such as:

- Particular circumstances
  - eg section 29 of the Landfill Tax (Scotland) Act 2014 states that:
    (3) It is a defence, in relation to a claim under this section, that repayment of an amount would unjustly enrich the claimant.
- Age
  - eg section 99 of the Children and Young Persons Act 1933 states that:
    (4) Where a person is charged with an offence under this Act in respect of a person apparently under a specified age it shall be a defence to prove that the person was actually of or over that age.

[28] See J Gardner and M Gur-Arye, 'Offences and Defences: Selected Essays in the Philosophy of Criminal Law' (2012) 4 *Jerusalem Review of Legal Studies* 82; also see P Westen, 'Offences and Defences Again' (2008) 28 *Oxford Journal of Legal Studies* 563.

- Emergency action
  - eg section 34 of the Marine Act (Northern Ireland) 2013 states that:

    34 (1) A person is not guilty of an offence under section 32 or 33 if the act which is alleged to constitute the offence—

    ...

    (e) was necessary for the purpose of securing the safety of any vessel, aircraft or marine installation;

    (f) was done for the purpose of saving life.
- Action beyond control of the accused
  - eg section 4 of the Mobile Homes Act 2013 states that:

    (3) In proceedings against an occupier of land for an offence under subsection (1), it is a defence that the occupier had a reasonable excuse for failing to take the steps referred to in subsection (1) within the period referred to in that subsection.
- Mistake, accident, act of another and diligence
  - eg section 12 of the Transparency of Lobbying, Non-Party Campaigning and Trade Union Administration Act 2014 states that:

    (5) It is a defence for a person charged under any of subsections (1) to (4) to show that the person exercised all due diligence to avoid committing the offence.
- Protection of a higher value
  - eg section 4 of the Defamation Act 2013 states that:

    (1) It is a defence to an action for defamation for the defendant to show that—

    (a) the statement complained of was, or formed part of, a statement on a matter of public interest; and

    (b) the defendant reasonably believed that publishing the statement complained of was in the public interest.
- Exclusion of liability
  - eg section 33 of the Legal Aid, Sentencing and Punishment of Offenders Act 2012 states that:

    (5) It is a defence for a person charged with an offence under this section to prove that the person reasonably believed that the disclosure or use was lawful.

SPECIAL CONSIDERATIONS

The final dilemma for the drafter of penal provisions is to address the procedural aspects of the new offence. The first issue to be taken care of is the determination of the criminal court to which competence to deal with the new offence is to be awarded. The drafter does not legislate in a vacuum. It would make sense, from the point of view of the smooth functioning of the penal system as a whole to subject the new offence to the current rules of competence. But this does not mean to say that any departure from the norm is prohibited: special circumstances, such as perhaps the status of the accused or their connection to the courts of a specific locality, may lead the drafter to depart from the rules of competence or locality as a means of preserving and enhancing fair trial safeguards. And of course the nature of the new offence as indictable or summary is also a factor in the decision on competence.

The second procedural issue to be addressed is that of time limits, with the time limit for prosecution as the most common one. Again keeping to the general rule ensures compliance with the criminal law ethos of the jurisdiction. This enhances coherence in penal law, certainty in the law and respect for the rights of the accused. But special circumstances, for example the nature of the offence, may require a derogation in the form of possible extensions to the time limits at the discretion of the court or perhaps the Attorney-General. An example of a provision setting time limits is regulation 4 of the Prosecution of Offences (Youth Courts Time Limits) Regulations 1999:

> Overall time limit
> 4. In any case where a person's first appearance in a relevant court in connection with an offence is fixed to take place on or after 1st November 1999, the maximum period to be allowed to the prosecution for the completion of the stage beginning with the date fixed for that appearance and ending with the start of his trial in a relevant court in connection with the offence shall be 99 days.

Regulation 7 deals with the extension of the time limit:

> Application for extension of overall or initial stage time limit by the prosecution
> 7. (1) An application by the prosecution under section 22(3) of the 1985 Act for an extension of the time limit prescribed in regulation 4 above shall be made before the expiry of the prescribed limit.

The third issue refers to territoriality of the offence. This will be addressed in a separate chapter. But it is worth noting at this point that restrictions to the jurisdictional boundaries of states are currently being debated and placed under doubt with specific reference to global penal offences. As effectiveness of the criminal regulation is sought as the main regulatory goal, it makes increasing sense to regulate offences that have a cross-border or international nature via extra-territorial provisions. Examples of such offences are money laundering, trade in human organs, trade in human beings or terrorism. If extra-territoriality is a necessary element of effective regulation, the drafter needs to be aware of and comply with strict constitutional obstacles, and with the principles of conflict of laws.[29] For an example of an extra-territorial offence without even a cross-border nature, look at section 72 of the Sexual Offences Act 2003:

> Offences outside the United Kingdom
> (1) If—
> (a) a United Kingdom national does an act in a country outside the United Kingdom, and
> (b) the act, if done in England and Wales, would constitute a sexual offence to which this section applies,
>
> the United Kingdom national is guilty in England and Wales of that sexual offence.

The fourth issue refers to the onus of proof. If it is an offence to open a public house without a licence, who has the onus of proof? Does the defendant have to prove that they have a licence? Does the prosecutor have to prove that the defendant does not have a licence? Does the prosecutor have to prove prima facie that the defendant does not have a licence, and it is then for the defendant to prove that they actually do have one? Or does the defendant have to prove prima facie that they do have a licence, and it is then for the prosecution to prove that the defendant does not have a valid and legally authorised licence? The rule in Commonwealth jurisdictions is that the onus of proof lies squarely on the prosecution.[30] Section 77 of the Terrorism Act 2000 deals with the onus of proof as follows:

> (2) If it is proved that the article—
> (a) was on any premises at the same time as the accused, or
> (b) was on premises of which the accused was the occupier or which he habitually used otherwise than as a member of the public,
>
> the court may assume that the accused possessed (and, if relevant, knowingly possessed) the article, unless he proves that he did not know of its presence on the premises or that he had no control over it.

And, finally, what type of evidence is acceptable in the case of the new offence? Is a basic level of proof sufficient or is certified evidence required? And is the evidence irrefutable, namely conclusive, or refutable, and therefore subject to counter argumentation?

In all these issues the question goes back to the extent of reliance on general rules of criminal evidence introduced by means of a criminal code or a general penal statute. It is rather tricky for the drafter to keep the right

[29] See BJ Jr George, 'Extraterritorial Application of Penal Legislation' (1966) 64 *Michigan Law Review* 609; also see M Hirst, 'Jurisdiction over Cross-frontier Offences' (1981) 97 *Law Quarterly Review* 80.

[30] See N Brownyn, 'Criminal Behaviour' (1989) 14 *Legal Service Bulletin* 271, 273.

balance between the increased need for clarity in penal statutes against the equally enhanced need for a concentrated, brief, intelligible regulatory message. If the user is not expected to have the capacity to read the statute book as a whole, then repetition of the general rules may be preferable. In this case, the Act can be divided into a substantive and a procedural part. And the introduction of the offence can be placed at the very beginning of the Act where the user's attention is at its prime. An additional tool can be reference to the general provisions applied here and repetition of the text of the general provisions in a Schedule at the end of the Act. There is of course a clash between clarity and redundancy of the repeated text: but the pyramid of drafting values suggests that effectiveness is best served by clarity, and so repeating the provisions in a Schedule may lack elegance and lustre but does promote intelligibility of the regulatory message. There can be no compromise for clarity, not in general, and certainly not in penal provisions.

14

Delegated Legislation

WHAT IS DELEGATED LEGISLATION?

THE TERM 'DELEGATED' legislation is used to signify texts of binding legal nature that are passed by the executive[1] on the basis of an enabling clause in primary legislation. It is precisely the notion of delegation that is the focus of this chapter, and this is why the term 'delegated' was preferred to 'executive'[2] or 'secondary' or 'subordinate'[3] or other terms often used elsewhere: the drafter needs to be very much aware of the transfer of legislative power from the legislature to the executive.[4] And they need to ensure that the terms of this transfer are set out in detail in the enabling clause. And that the delegated text remains within the limitations of that enabling clause.

It is also important to clarify that the chapter has a dual focus. It explores the topic from the prism of the enabling clause in the primary legislation: this is where the intricacy of the drafting task lies. The chapter also explores the drafting of the delegated text. But phronetic legislative drafting, or phronetic nomography, of the delegated text itself entails a drafting task that differs very little from the drafting of primary legislation. As a consequence all comments on legislative drafting in the book apply to the drafting of delegated legislation.

There is nothing more important in the study of delegated legislation than exploring the nature of this delegation. The principle of separation of

[1] 'Delegation' in a federal environment is explained in G Appleby and S McDonald, 'Looking at the Executive Power through the High Court's New Spectacles' (2013) 35 *Sydney Law Review* 253; and in a devolved environment in C Reid, 'The Limits of Devolved Legislative Power: Subordinate Legislation in Scotland' (2003) 24 *Statute Law Review* 187; also see CT Reid, 'Who Makes Scotland's Law? Delegated Legislation under the Devolution Arrangements' (2002) 6 *Edinburgh Law Review* 380.

[2] But 'a simple source-based distinction between primary and delegated legislation is clearly inadequate, or at least incomplete': see A McHarg, 'What is Delegated Legislation?' (2006) *Public Law* 539, 544.

[3] The Interpretation Act 1978, s 21(1) provides that '"[S]ubordinate legislation" means Orders in Council, orders, rules, regulation, schemes, warrants or byelaws and any other instrument made or to be made under any Act'.

[4] See H Xanthaki et al, 'Legislative Techniques in Rwanda: Present and Future' (2013) 15 *European Journal of Law Reform* 95, 167.

powers assigns the power to legislate to the legislature. This is an exclusive power and an exclusive privilege to the legislature. Since delegated legislation refers to binding legal instruments produced by the executive, delegated legislation can only be viewed as a legitimate yet extra-ordinary departure from constitutional order. It involves a paradox: an, in principle,[5] constitutionally sound constitutional anomaly, or an unfortunate but inevitable infringement of the separation of powers.[6] The problem is that this anomaly is used so frequently that it is often viewed as nothing out of the norm. And that often delegation is so broad that the primary Act is a bare 'skeleton' legislation.[7]

But, in truth, delegation is a danger zone[8] for the drafter as it is clear departure of one of the sacrosanct constitutional principles prevalent in modern democracies.[9] But at the same time delegation is a useful drafting tool that contributes greatly to legislative and ultimately regulatory quality.[10] So much so that countries with excessive delegation have been called 'executive paradise'.[11] In order to serve its benevolent purpose, delegated legislation must be drafted in a manner that offers respect to the balance of powers of the state with specific reference to the delimitation of the authority to legislate in the enabling clause; and to the control of the legislative instrument by the judiciary.[12]

A section of the Draft Deregulation Bill currently (namely in March 2014) before the House of Commons, and already passed through the second reading, reads as follows:

> 65 Consequential amendments, repeals and revocations
>
> (1) The Secretary of State may by order made by statutory instrument make such provision as the Secretary of State considers appropriate in consequence of this Act.

[5] Provided that the following principles are met: reliability, predictability, openness, transparency, accountability, efficiency and effectiveness: see OECD Sigma Papers: No 27 'European Principles for Public Administration' (Paris, 1998).

[6] See HWR Wade, *Administrative Law* (Oxford, Clarendon Press 1967) 291.

[7] See Editorial, 'Scrutinizing Enabling Powers' (1993) 14 *Statute Law Review* xi, xii; also VCRAC Crabbe, 'Shorter Parliamentary Enactments and Longer Regulation' (1986) 7 *Statute Law Review* 4, 6.

[8] See Rt Hon Sir G Palmer, 'Deficiencies in New Zealand Delegated Legislation' (1999) 30 *Victoria University Wellington Law Review* 1, 36.

[9] See AF Bennett, 'Uses and Abuses of Delegated Power' (1990) 11 *Statute Law Review* 23, 25.

[10] On this Janus-faced nature of delegated legislation, see K Kabba, 'Judicial Review An Essential Tool for Curbing the Excesses and Abuse of Executive Action in Sierra Leone' (2011) 13 *European Journal of Law Reform* 312, 321.

[11] See L Zines, *Constitutional Change in the Commonwealth* (Cambridge, Cambridge University Press, 1991) 47.

[12] See PA Joseph, 'Delegated Legislation in New Zealand' (1997) 18 *Statute Law Review* 85, 103.

(2) An order under subsection (1)—
  (a) may include transitional, transitory or saving provision;
  (b) may repeal, revoke or otherwise amend or modify any provision of primary or subordinate legislation (including legislation passed or made in the same Session as this Act).

(3) A statutory instrument containing (whether alone or with other provision) an order under this section which repeals, revokes or otherwise amends any provision of primary legislation is not to be made unless a draft of the instrument has been laid before, and approved by a resolution of, each House of Parliament.

(4) A statutory instrument containing an order under this section which does not repeal, revoke or otherwise amend any provision of primary legislation is subject to annulment in pursuance of a resolution of either House of Parliament.

(5) In this section—
  'primary legislation' means—
  (a) an Act;
  (b) an Act of the Scottish Parliament;
  (c) a Measure or Act of the National Assembly for Wales;
  (d) Northern Ireland legislation;
  'subordinate legislation' means—
  (a) subordinate legislation within the meaning of the Interpretation Act 1978;
  (b) an instrument made under an Act of the Scottish Parliament;
  (c) an instrument made under a Measure or Act of the National Assembly for Wales;
  (d) an instrument made under Northern Ireland legislation.[13]

The draft provision offers a wealth of opportunities for comments: the necessity of subsection (2) in view of the generality of subsection (1); the negative style of expression of the requirement for any statutory instrument under this order to be approved by both Houses in subsection (2); the utility of subsection (4) as a separate subsection as opposed to its use to qualify the general subsection (1) within subsection (1); or even the utility of subsection (5) that conveys common knowledge instead of an application provision. But what is thankfully extra-ordinary with this draft section is the generality of the enabling clause in subsection (1). Although, when read in conjunction with subsections (2) and (4), the enabling clause in subsection (1) seems constitutionally palatable, the drafting of subsection (1) qualifies it as one of the most profoundly unconstitutional provisions that UK legislation has to offer. The problem of subsection (1) is that it transfers legislative power to the Secretary of State without any indication of the delimitations of this power: this abstract enabling clause fails to offer the Secretary of State any parameters of subject or time within which the delegation is to be exercised.

[13] See Draft Deregulation HC Bill (2013–14) [162] www.publications.parliament.uk/pa/bills/cbill/2013-2014/0162/cbill_2013-20140162_en_6.htm#pb17-l1g65. I am indebted to Jonathan Teasdale, Sir William Dale Fellow, for alerting me to this provision.

Ultimately the Secretary of State seems to be offered a carte blanche to legislate as thought appropriate in order to secure the application of the draft Act. And the seal of legitimacy of the resulting legislative instruments is transferred to the Secretary of State wholesale and seemingly without any control from the legislature. The construction of this enabling clause is exactly what drafters are to avoid.

It is only when the rest of the section is taken into account that the true extent of the transfer of legislative power becomes clear: the Secretary of State has the discretion to make statutory instruments that can include transitional, saving, amending or repeal provisions, subject to approval from both Houses. In other words, the enacting clause of subsection (1) conveys a false impression of general delegation, whereas the delegation of section 65 is limited on a number of bases: the executive body with the power to legislate (namely the Secretary of State); the type of resulting delegated instrument (namely statutory instrument); the type of provision in the statutory instrument (only transitional, saving, amending or repealing); and procedure (subject to approval from both Houses of Parliament). It would have been far better for the drafter to merge these subjections into one, thus offering the Secretary of State an accurate depiction of the limited power conveyed to them by section 65.

The problem in this section is one of construction. But in the many instances in Commonwealth jurisdictions where enabling clauses remain within the generality of subsection (1) without any further qualification, the problem is deeper and touches upon constitutionality, democracy and the rule of law.

THE ROLE OF THE DRAFTER IN DELEGATED LEGISLATION

And so the role of the drafter in the drafting of enabling provisions is to convey clearly the policy aims of the ministerial power[14] and the narrow limits of the delegation,[15] as a means of presenting the reflective reaction of the legislature to the legitimate constitutional anomaly of empowering the executive to legislate.

The role of the drafter in the drafting of the delegated instrument is to promote effectiveness of regulation. And in that respect drafting virtues to be promoted are clarity, precision and unambiguity.

[14] See House of Lords Select Committee on the Constitution, *First Progress Report (First Report)* (HL 2005–06, 30) para 6; also see House of Lords Select Committee on the Constitution, *Defamation Bill (Ninth Report)* (HL 2012–13, 86) para 6; also see VCRAC Crabbe, *Legislative Precedents—Volume II* (London, Cavendish Publishing Ltd, 1998) 48–49.

[15] See House of Lords Select Committee on the Constitution, *European Parliament (Representation) Bill (Fifth Report)* (HL 2002–03, 65) para 4; also see House of Lords Select Committee on the Constitution, *Age-Related Payments Act (Thirteenth Report)* (HL 2003–04, 172) para 6; and *Defamation Bill (Ninth Report)* (n 14) para 6.

But, since it is the executive that legislates, what is the role of legislative counsel? In the UK, delegated legislation is drafted in the relevant departments. And the legislative drafters intervene to guarantee consistency of style within the statute book as a whole. Moreover, delegated legislation is scrutinised by parliamentary scrutiny committees.[16] But delegated legislation does not undergo the extensive scrutiny of primary legislation since *ab definitio* it does not deserve lengthy debates on policy, substance and style. Moreover, scrutiny of delegated legislation both from Parliament and the courts is 'constrained by the weight of executive influence'.[17]

In the rest of the Commonwealth, delegated legislation is drafted by legislative drafters and is treated no differently from primary legislation. This is best practice: viewing delegated legislation as 'subordinate', which is the prevalent term in UK legislation, creates the impression that it is somehow less important for the users. This cannot be further from the truth. Delegated legislation now forms the bulk of legislative instruments regulating citizen activity. In fact, with the new policy of transposing EU legislation via delegated legislation, the life of citizens tends to be more directly affected by delegated legislation than it is by general framework type laws passed by the Houses of Parliament. Moreover, it is delegated legislation that is applied by most authorities in their interaction with citizens, thus rendering the possibility and danger of corruption all the more pronounced.[18] It is for these reasons that delegated legislation requires the attention and skill of the legislative drafter. The task is mammoth, and the resource implications of allocating all legislation to the Office of Parliamentary Counsel are extreme.

But this is not a valid reason for bypassing the quality assurances offered by the drafting of delegated legislation from trained drafters. It is another argument that tilts the scale towards the UK position on this: delegated legislation is by definition so technical that it is the legal officers of departments who possess the awareness of the law and the substantive law skills to cope with the challenge. Trying to transfer this technical legal know-how to the drafter may well be possible but would require time: but is it not precisely time and flexibility that led to the choice of delegated legislation in the first place?

And so the optimal solution to this problem seems to be the training of legal officers in the departments in drafting delegated legislation rather than relocating the task to the Office of Parliamentary Counsel. And then

[16] On the scrutiny of delegated legislation in the UK, see P Tudor, 'Secondary Legislation: Second Class or Crucial?' (2000) 21 *Statute Law Review* 149.

[17] See St J Bates, 'The Future of Parliamentary Scrutiny of Delegated Legislation: Some Judicial Perspectives' (1998) 19 *Statute Law Review* 155, 156.

[18] See A Seidman, RB Seidman and N Abeyesekere, *Legislative Drafting for Democratic Social Change—A Manual for Drafters* (The Hague, Kluwer, 2001) 351.

perhaps offering the parliamentary Delegated Legislation Committee the extra power and technical know-how to scrutinise delegated legislation not just on grounds of constitutionality but also of legislative quality,[19] whilst still maintaining an embargo on policy scrutiny.[20]

USE OF DELEGATED LEGISLATION

In principle, there is little that delegated legislation cannot do: the enabling clause can transfer any aspect of legislative power to the executive. And so, in principle, delegated legislation is only constrained by the limitations of legislative power. An example of such limitation is the relative restrictions in the areas of Crown privileges.[21]

But, at least in jurisdictions where delegated legislation is not subject to the same procedures of parliamentary scrutiny, one cannot ignore the ethical and constitutional obligation of governments to subject issues of policy to parliamentary scrutiny. This need to ensure that members of the legislature have the opportunity to discuss issues of policy or issues of pronounced importance for the country or its citizens serves as a voice of conscience for governments that are tempted by the practicable advantages of expediency offered by delegated legislation.[22] And it is the source of a number of maxims in the common law that require placement of criminal offences[23] or new taxes or expropriation measures or emergency measures[24] or rights of appeal[25] in primary legislation. And so it is noteworthy that a second limitation of delegated competence lies with the constitutional necessity to offer the opportunity for parliamentary scrutiny, and consequently

[19] For an in-depth analysis of parliamentary scrutiny, see J Simson Caird, R Hazell and D Oliver, 'Standards of the House of Lords Select Committee on the Constitution' (The Constitution Unit, UCL, 2013).

[20] See DJ Whalan, 'Scrutiny of Delegated Legislation by the Australian Senate' (1991) 12 *Statute Law Review* 87, 97.

[21] See generally HV Evatt, *The Royal Prerogative* (Sydney, Law Book, 1987) 30–31; and on privileges, see W Hohfeld, 'Fundamental Legal Conceptions as Applied in Judicial Reasoning' (1913) 23 *Yale Law Journal* 16, 30.

[22] See NK Chakrabarti, *Principles of Legislation and Legislative Drafting* (Kolkata, R Chambray and Co Private Ltd, 2007) 174–75.

[23] But during the Blair administration out of the 3000 new crimes and offences 1845 were introduced by delegated legislation: see K Stevenson and C Harris, 'Breaking the Thrall of Ambiguity: Simplification (of the Criminal Law) as a Human Rights Imperative (2010) 74 *Journal of Criminal Law* 516, 520.

[24] See S Yeo Meng Heong, 'Legislative Control of Emergency Powers in New Zealand and Britain: an Appraisal' (1984) 5 *Singapore Law Review* 112, 118.

[25] See House of Lords Select Committee on the Constitution, *Third Progress Report (Ninth Report)* (HL 2012–13, 151) paras 9–10.

offer legitimacy,[26] to issues that by their very nature require the increased legitimacy offered by parliamentary debate[27] and express legitimisation.[28]

What is it that delegated legislation can do then?

Its first and most common function is to advance the purpose of primary legislation. Here the legislature allows the executive to legislate further as a means of carrying the primary legislation into effect. But the transfer of legislative power cannot be so general[29] as to breach the rule of law principle: the rule of law 'prohibits delegated legislation that merely passes on its enabling powers or a substantial element of them'.[30] An example of such a provision is section 23 of the Transparency of Lobbying, Non-Party Campaigning and Trade Union Administration Act 2014. It is interesting to note that the general power of subsection (1) is thankfully detailed and delimited by subsections (2) and (3):

> 23 Power to make further provision
>
> (1) Regulations may make such provision as the Minister considers appropriate for the purposes of carrying into effect any provision of this Part.
>
> (2) Regulations under subsection (1) may in particular make provision (or further provision) about—
>
> (a) the date from which an entry in the register is to take effect;
>
> (b) the form and content of information returns under section 5;
>
> (c) the exercise of the Registrar's powers under section 6(6);
>
> (d) the removal of entries in other circumstances;
>
> (e) the minimum period between the date on which an information notice is served and the date which must be specified under section 9(4)(b);
>
> (f) other matters which must be specified in an information notice;
>
> (g) the cancellation of notices under section 9(7).
>
> (3) Regulations under subsection (1) may make provision permitting or requiring the Commissioners for Her Majesty's Revenue and Customs to supply to the Registrar, on request, such information regarding any person who is, or is required to be, registered under the Value Added Tax Act 1994 as is specified in the regulations.

[26] On legitimacy generally, see H Puender 'Democratic Legitimation of Delegated Legislation—a Comparative View on the American, British and German Law (2009) 58 *International and Comparative Law Quarterly* 353.

[27] See House of Lords Select Committee on the Constitution, *Sessional Report (First Report)* (HL, 16).

[28] On the constitutional scrutiny of delegated legislation, see *Attorney-General v Wilts United Dairies Ltd* [1921] 39 TLR 781 (CA); also see *R v Secretary of State for the Home Department, ex p Leech* [1994] QB 198 (HL); *R v Secretary of State for Social Security, ex p Joint Council for the Welfare of Immigrants* [1997] 1 WLR 275 (CA); *R v Lord Chancellor, ex p Witham* [1998] QB 575.

[29] See House of Lords Select Committee on the Constitution, *Age Related Payments Bill (Tenth Report)* (HL 2003–04, 124) para 10.

[30] See JM Keyes, 'From *Delegatus* to the Duty to Make Law' (1987–88) 33 *McGill Law Journal* 49, 88.

The second function of delegated legislation is to introduce technical or detailed provisions necessary for the implementation of primary legislation. Here the executive is offered the power to introduce detailed provisions on secondary issues. The reason behind selecting delegated legislation as a drafting tool, as opposed to a Schedule, is the flexibility of delegated legislation,[31] which can easily be amended periodically.[32] It is precisely this flexibility of delegated legislation that renders it suitable for the introduction of levels of fine or fees. An example is found in section 17(b) of the Growth and Infrastructure Act 2013:

> 17 Applications to amend registers: modification of power to provide for feesIn section 24 of the Commons Act 2006 (regulations about making and determination of Part 1 applications)—
>
> (a) omit subsection (2)(d) (provision for England and Wales in the same terms as the provision for Wales made by the new subsection (2B)), and
>
> (b) after subsection (2) insert—
>
> '(2A) Regulations under subsection (1) made by the Secretary of State may make provision as to the fees payable in relation to an application (including provision for a fee payable under the regulations to be determined by the person to whom the application is made or (if different) the person by whom the application is to be determined).
>
> (2B) Regulations under subsection (1) made by the Welsh Ministers may make provision as to the fee payable on an application (which may be a fee determined by the person to whom the application is made).'

The third function of delegated legislation is the introduction of administrative arrangements necessary for the implementation of primary legislation. Here the executive is asked to fill the gaps in primary legislation as a means of facilitating the implementation of the provisions of primary legislation. An example is section 21 of the Energy Act 2013:

> 21 Regulations: further provision
>
> (1) Regulations may make provision—
>
> (a) to require a CFD counterparty to enter into arrangements or to offer to contract for purposes connected to a CFD;
>
> (b) specifying things that a CFD counterparty may or must do, or things that a CFD counterparty may not do;
>
> (c) conferring on the Secretary of State further powers to direct a CFD counterparty to do, or not to do, things specified in the regulations or the direction.

[31] See E Scotford and R Oliver, 'The State of UK Environmental Legislation: Opportunities for Reform' (2013) 15 *Environmental Law Review* 225, 227.

[32] See JS Williams, 'The Making of Statutory Instruments' (1970) 8 *Alberta Law Review* 324, 325.

The fourth function of delegated legislation is to bring primary legislation into force. This is possible, and indeed quite frequent in the UK.[33] A UK example of this tool is found in section 45 of the Transparency of Lobbying, Non-Party Campaigning and Trade Union Administration Act 2014:

> 45 Commencement
>
> (1) The following provisions of this Act come into force on such day as the Minister may appoint by order made by statutory instrument—
> (a) Part 1, except as mentioned in subsection (3)(a);
> (b) in Part 2—
> (i) section 26(11) and (12) (definition of 'election material');
> (ii) section 31 (extension of power to vary specified sums);
> (iii) section 32 (recognised third parties);
> (iv) section 36 (third party expenditure in respect of candidates);
> (v) section 37 (candidate's personal expenses not to count for local election expenses limit in England and Wales);
> (vi) section 38 (functions of Electoral Commission with respect to compliance);
> (c) Part 3, except as mentioned in subsection (3)(c).
>
> (2) An order under subsection (1)—
> (a) may appoint different days for different purposes, and
> (b) may make transitional, transitory or saving provision.
>
> (3) The following provisions of this Act come into force on the day on which the Act is passed—
> (a) any provision of Part 1 which confers power to make regulations, for the purposes of the exercise of that power;
> (b) the provisions of Part 2 not mentioned in subsection (1)(b);
> (c) section 41, for the purposes of the exercise of the power to make subordinate legislation conferred by section 24ZB(3) of the Trade Union and Labour Relations (Consolidation) Act 1992 (which is inserted by that section);
> (d) Part 4.
>
> (4) Section 46 contains transitional provision relating to the commencement of the provisions to which subsection (3)(b) applies.
>
> (5) 'The Minister' means—
> (a) for the purposes of subsection (1)(a) and (b), the Secretary of State or the Lord President of the Council;
> (b) for the purposes of subsection (1)(c), the Secretary of State.

The final function of delegated legislation is to supplement or amend part of primary legislation. But a large number of Commonwealth jurisdictions[34]

[33] For India, see BR Atre, *Legislative Drafting* (Dehli, Universal Law Publishing Co, 2006) 225.

[34] For a comparative analysis on the validity of Henry VIII clauses, see GA Moens and J Trone, 'The Validity of Henry VIII Clauses in Australian Federal Legislation' (2012) 24 *Giornale di Storia Costituzionale* 133.

do not allow delegated legislation to amend primary legislation,[35] and these clauses, known as Henry VIII clauses,[36] are considered to 'blur the hierarchy of norms'.[37] In the UK they are rather popular but subject to strict tests of necessity,[38] specificity of purpose[39] and procedural and legal safeguards.[40] The latter include a super-affirmative parliamentary procedure when the Henry VIII powers touch upon a constitutionally sensitive issue.[41] Examples from the UK are found in section 41 of the Landfill Tax (Scotland) Act 2014:

> 41 Subordinate legislation
> (1) Any power conferred by this Act on the Scottish Ministers to make an order or regulations includes the power to make—
> (a) different provision for different cases or description of case or for different purposes,
> (b) such incidental, supplementary, consequential, transitional, transitory or saving provision as the Scottish Ministers consider necessary or expedient.

An interesting example of a power to amend primary legislation via delegated legislation is section 2 of the Local Audit and Accountability Act 2014. It is interesting to note that the provision follows best practice in that it sets out very clearly how the regulations of the Secretary of State may amend the Act: exclusively by adding, modifying or removing an entry:

> (2) Relevant authorities
> ....
> (3) The Secretary of State may by regulations amend Schedule 2 by adding, modifying or removing an entry relating to a relevant authority.

[35] For the position in the USA, see C Kitchen, 'Negative Lawmaking Delegations: Constitutional Structure and Delegations to the Executive of Discretionary Authority to Amend, Waive, and Cancel Statutory Text' (2012–13) 40 *Hastings Constitutional Law Quarterly* 525, 552 and 554; and M Barone Jr, 'Delegation and the Destruction of American Liberties: The Affordable Care Act and the Contraception Mandate' (2012–13) 29 *Touro Law Review* 795. For the South African position, see D Rudman, 'Delegation by Parliament of its Legislative Power: A South African Perspective' (CALC Conference, Nairobi, Kenya, Sept 2007) www.opc.gov.au/calc/docs/calc loopholeAugust2008.pdf.

[36] See generally Lord Rippon, 'Henry VIII Clauses' (1989) 10 *Statute Law Review* 205; NW Barber and A Young, 'The Rise of Prospective Henry VIII Clauses and Their Implications for Sovereignty' (2003) *Public Law* 112.

[37] See R van Gestel, 'The "Deparliamentarisation" of Legislation: Framework Laws and the Primacy of the Legislature' (2013) 9 *Utrecht Law Review* 106, 114.

[38] See House of Lords Select Committee on the Constitution, *Banking Bill (Third Report)* (HL 2008–09, 19) para 3.

[39] See House of Lords Select Committee on the Constitution, *Government's Constitutional Reform Programme (Fifth Report)* (HL 2010–11, 43).

[40] See House of Lords Select Committee on the Constitution, *Legislative and Regulatory Reform Bill (Eleventh Report)* (HL 2005–06, 194) para 35.

[41] See House of Lords Select Committee on the Constitution, *Crime and Courts Bill (Second Report)* (HL 2012–13, 17) para 7.

(4) Regulations under subsection (3) may add an entry relating to a person or body to Schedule 2 only if that person or body exercises functions of a public nature in relation to an area which is—
  (a) wholly in England, or
  (b) partly in England and partly in Wales.

...

(6) The power in subsection (5) includes power—
  (a) to amend this Act or provision made under it in its application to that person or body, or
  (b) to make provision for this Act or provision made under it to apply to that person or body with modifications.

VALIDITY OF DELEGATED LEGISLATION

It is the enabling clause that offers delegated legislation the legitimacy that this departure from the separation of powers requires. The enabling clause ensures that all parameters of the transfer of legislative power to the executive are expressed clearly and restrictively thus guaranteeing that the transfer is considered and approved by the legislature.[42] And so any invalidity of delegated legislation is traced back to the enabling clause.

The executive must act 'legally, rationally, reasonably, timely, within the limits and according to the criteria and intent of the legislature'.[43] And so delegated legislation may be attacked for invalidity on two main bases:

— invalidity related to the procedural aspects of the enabling clause: this occurs when the statutory provisions attached to the exercise of power were not fulfilled; or
— invalidity related to the substantive aspects of the enabling clause: this occurs when the exercise of power is not in its substance within the scope of the delegation.

Inability related to the procedural aspects of the enabling clause refers to a lack of legislative competence to authorise the transfer of legislative power to the executive. This competence refers to the time of the exercise of the power, or the person exercising the power, or the manner in which the power is exercised, or a combination of these.

Delegated legislation must be issued within the time limits foreseen in the enabling clause. If the State Secretary is offered a period of two years within which to issue regulations, they lack legislative competence to issue

[42] And this describes exactly what type of scrutiny parliaments must afford to enabling clauses: see D Kibirige Kawooya, 'Act of Parliament: The Role of Parliament in the Legislative Process A Commonwealth Perspective' (2010) 12 *European Journal of Law Reform* 32, 55.

[43] See M Pecaric 'Delegated Legislation—a Mixture of General Principles of Law and an Individual Mind' (2011) 5 *Vienna Journal on International Constitutional Law* 400, 413.

these regulations three years post enactment, and any such regulations suffer a procedural invalidity. In other words, the authorisation to exercise the power to legislate via delegated legislation must exist legitimately at the time that the power is exercised. If the primary legislation authorising the delegation has been repealed, the delegated legislation arising from it will suffer a serious procedural defect. Similarly, primary legislation authorising the delegation must not be amended at the time of exercise of the power. This can occur when primary legislation has been amended either by an amendment of the enabling primary legislation, or impliedly via other primary legislation. But interpretation legislation may under conditions allow limited power to proceed with delegated legislation based on primary legislation that has been passed but has not yet come into force: this is the case with section 13 of the UK Interpretation Act 1978. Or it may keep into being delegated legislation hanging from a repealed and re-enacted Act:[44] this is the case with section 44 of the Canadian Interpretation Act. Moreover, primary legislation may allow a timeframe for delegated legislation whose beginning and end is clearly determined and delimited. Thus, public officials may utilise delegated legislation to regulate matters within their *in materiae* authority within, and only within, the performance of their official duties within the time limits of their term of office. The person exercising the power must be the person to which the enabling clause transfers legislative power. In view of the sensitive role of delegated legislation, the law usually delimits the persons that may utilise the power to legislate via delegated legislation. Most jurisdictions follow the UK model, thus allowing the exercise of the power to pass delegated legislation exclusively to holders of public office. However, the use of sub-delegation is common[45] as a means of addressing urgent government needs for regulation of detailed or technical matters.[46] As the determination of the persons who can be entrusted with the power to legislate even though they do not form part of the legislature is an issue of constitutional importance, the drafter must be clear and precise in naming those who can delegate and sub-delegate.[47]

[44] See R Duperron, 'Interpretation Acts—Impediments to Legal Certainty and Access to the Law' (2005) 26 *Statute Law Review* 64.

[45] Sub-delegation by an administrative body to yet a further administrative or other body gives rise to grave concern as it 'may lead to a further multiplication of bodies which exercise legislative functions, but which have been selected for this important task by an administrative body and not by Parliament': see A Rabie, 'When Delegated Powers Become Plenary Powers' (1989) 5 *South African Journal on Human Rights* 440, 443.

[46] But sub-delegation of legislative powers remains unconstitutional: see House of Lords Select Committee on the Constitution, *Legislative and Regulatory Reform Bill (Eleventh Report)* (n 40) para 61.

[47] On restrictions to sub-delegation see JF Northley, 'Sub-delegated Legislation and *delegatus non potest delegare* (1953) 6 *Res Judicatae* 294, 303; also see J Willis, *Delegatus non potest delegare* (1943) 21 *Canadian Bar Review* 257; and SA De Smith 'Sub-delegation and Circulars' (1949) 12 *Modern Law Review* 37.

A distinction must be drawn between sub-delegation and signification: in the first case the person authorised has the power to legislate,[48] whereas in the latter case the policy decision is taken elsewhere and the person authorised may sign on behalf of the higher authority.

Although delegated legislation must be flexible and therefore some concessions from normal legislative process are possible, nevertheless statutory procedural requirements must be met. These may refer to consultation;[49] approval, consent or confirmation; or printing and publication of the delegated legislation.[50] Even where defects occur, they may not affect the validity of delegated legislation if they do not contravene mandatory provisions essential to the validity of the legislation.

Defects in the content of delegated legislation may refer to the source of the power[51] or the construction of delegated legislation. The first issue, known as ultra vires,[52] is extensively analysed in constitutional law. The second issue related to drafting techniques and requires extensive analysis here.

CONSTRUCTION

The construction of delegated legislation involves two levels of consideration: drafting the enabling clause in the primary legislation; and drafting the delegated text.

The enabling clause is a substantive provision, and therefore the chapter on substantive provisions, and indeed those on legislative drafting techniques,

[48] See D Greenberg, *Craies on Legislation—A Practitioner's Guide to the Nature, Process, Effect and Interpretation of Legislation* (London, Sweet and Maxwell, 2004) 123.

[49] See *Rollo v Minister of Town and Country Planning* [1948] 1 All ER 13; also see *Port Louis Corporal v Attorney-General of Mauritius* [1965] AC 1111; A Jergensen, 'The Legal Requirements of Consultation' (1978) *Public Law* 290; J Garner, 'Consultation in Subordinate Legislation' (1964) *Public Law* 105; G Crave, 'Consultation in Subordinate Legislation—a Victorian Initiative' (1989) 15 *Monash University Law Review* 95.

[50] Publication is highly advantageous for delegated legislation: see R Mkuye, 'Controls and Safeguards of Delegated Legislation: a Case Study of Tanzania (2007) 9 *European Journal of Law Reform* 205, 241; also see DJ Lanham, who argues that publication of delegated legislation is required not just by law but also by the maxim of non-ignorance of law in relation to delegated legislation. DJ Lanham 'Delegated Legislation and Publication' (1974) 37 *Modern Law Review* 510, 510; and See H Xanthaki, *Thornton's Legislative Drafting* (West Sussex, Bloomsbury Professional, 2013) 412–13.

[51] The doctrine of ultra vires basically posits that all administrative power is exercised within the limits of legitimacy: see D Tan, 'An Analysis of Substantive Review of Singaporean Administrative Law' (2013) 25 *Singapore Academy of Law Journal* 296, 298. But ultimately the deciding issue for ultra vires lies in the purposes of the governing statute: see E Ip, 'Economic Structure of Hong Kong Administrative Law: Efficiency and Legality of Government Decision-making since China's Resumption of Sovereignty' (2013) 12 *Washington University Global Studies Law Review* 227, 243.

[52] On the principle of ultra vires with specific reference to local authorities' decisions, see C Aguma, 'The Principle of *Ultra Vires* and the Local Authorities' Decisions in England' (2013) 15 *European Journal of Law Reform* 267.

applies. With one major difference: this is a departure from constitutional normality, and therefore the enabling clause must be drafted with constitutionality and precision at the forefront of the drafter's concerns. There is little doubt that effectiveness of the enabling clause directs the drafter to clarity, precision and unambiguity of:

— the precise power transferred;
— the time within which the power is to be exercised;
— the person to whom the transfer is made;
— the manner in which the transfer is to be exercised; and
— any discretion to make use of the power or not.

As the enabling clause 'speaks' mainly to the executive organ to which power is transferred, drafting is tuned to address group two in the layered approach, namely not necessarily lawyers but persons who use the primary legislation in the course of their professional capacity. As a result, some terminology is justified. But not to the extent where it renders the provision intelligible to group one lay persons who must be in a position to understand who regulated what, or indeed to group three persons who, as lawyers or judges, must be in a position to ascertain with precision what is transferred as a means of challenging and assessing the validity of the delegated legislation arising from the enabling clause.

And, since it is the limits to the delegation that are crucial for the implementation of the provision, it is precisely the conditions attached to the exercise of power in the enabling clause that must be expressly and precisely introduced. Here brevity bows down to precision.

As for the delegated instrument, the usual drafting conventions apply here too. The title must be informative and distinctive not just for administrative reasons but mainly for the users of the delegated instrument. The title of the primary legislation from which the delegated instrument hangs is kept as a means of quick reference and linkage. The precise angle which the delegated instrument regulates is introduced in parenthesis, thus encouraging a combination of easy indexing along with other relevant instruments but an equally easy distinction with increased precision of the sub-topic regulated in this specific text. And the year of the delegated instrument is set at the end of the title. For example, the Judicial Pensions (Widows', Widowers' and Children's Benefits) (Amendment) Regulations 2014 quickly informs the user that: (1) they hang from the Judicial Pensions Act (1981); (2) they relate specifically to widows', widowers' and children's benefits; (3) they amend former regulations (actually the 1987 ones) with the same title; and (4) they were issued in 2014. It is now easier to convey what a wealth of information the title can offer the user.

The preamble, which may possibly be forgiven here, serves as an opportunity to make the link between the enabling clause and the delegated instrument as a means of specifying the parameters of the enabling power in the primary legislation, and ensuring that procedural requirements have been met. In other words, the preamble addresses the possible point of invalidity, and describes how all these points are addressed adequately. For example, the 2014 (No 277) A38 Trunk Road (Egginton to Branston, Staffordshire) (Temporary Prohibition of Traffic) Order 2014 states:

> WHEREAS the Secretary of State for Transport, being the traffic authority for the A38 Trunk Road ('the A38') is satisfied that traffic on a length of that road, between Egginton and Branston, in the County of Staffordshire, should be prohibited because works are proposed to be executed thereon

Leaving aside the unfortunate verbosity of expression, the preamble explains that: (1) the Secretary of State for Transport is indeed the authority empowered to issue the Order; (2) the Secretary of State for Transport considers that traffic must be prohibited to facilitate works; and (3) issues the Order.

Useful as the preamble can be, one wonders whether it is found in some delegated instruments, mainly Orders and much less in regulations, as a matter of tradition rather than utility. A well drafted title can include all of the elements of the preamble, except perhaps the explanation of what criteria the executive organ used to exercise the discretion to issue the delegated instrument. There is an argument therefore that preambles have a purpose when the executive organ has a discretion to legislate in which case they must concentrate on the considerations undertaken for the purpose of issuing the delegated instrument.

The enacting provision is as much a set formula as the enacting provision in primary legislation. And so house style and tradition prevail. But there is a simpler way of stating that the executive organ legislates. Best practice is traced in the Further Education Loans (Amendment) Regulations 2014 which clearly and simply state who legislates, by what instrument, and on which primary enabling basis:

> The Secretary of State for Business, Innovation and Skills makes the following Regulations in exercise of the powers conferred by sections 22 and 42(6) of the Teaching and Higher Education Act 1998.

But one finds it difficult to justify the verbosity of complexity of the 2014 (No 311) A31 Trunk Road (Cadnam—Verwood Interchange) (Temporary Restriction and Prohibition of Traffic) Order 2014:

> NOW, THEREFORE, the Secretary of State, in exercise of the powers conferred by section 14(1)(a) of the Road Traffic Regulation Act 1984(a), hereby makes the following Order:-

Similarly, the common addition of 'and all other enabling powers' is as vague and useless as the common term 'and any connected purposes' in long titles: they serve no purpose at all, and in fact they create the impression that other enabling powers need to be identified in order to justify the legitimacy of the delegated instrument. And so there is vagueness but also ambiguity in the enacting provision of the 2008 (No 234) A556 Trunk Road (Turnpike Wood, Over Tabley-A56 Bowdon Roundabout) (Detrunking) Order 1996 (Revocation) Order 2008, which states:

> The Secretary of State for Transport makes this Order in exercise of powers conferred by sections 10 and 12 of the Highways Act 1980 and all other enabling powers

Few modern delegated instruments present purpose clauses. This can be attributed to the lesser value now afforded to purpose clauses in general but also to the correct view that delegated legislation absorbs the purpose clause of the primary legislation from which it hangs. There is validity in the view that the purpose clause of delegated legislation coincides with that of the primary instrument: after all, both form a package of regulation contributing to the same policy. And this certainly applies to delegated legislation that serves the first four purposes identified in the chapter, namely taking the aim of primary legislation further; or introducing technical or detailed provisions necessary for the implementation of primary legislation; or introducing administrative arrangements necessary for primary legislation; or bringing the primary legislation into force. But the fifth function of delegated legislation, namely supplementing or amending part of primary legislation, introduces an environment fertile for a separate purpose clause. In other words, when the primary legislation is amended or supplemented whilst remaining within the original policy of the primary Act,[53] the original purpose clause may be amended or supplemented also. It would not be appropriate to amend or supplement the original purpose clause in the primary legislation, as the amendment is effected via delegated legislation rather than amendment of the original primary Act. But it would make perfect sense to offer an addition to the purpose clause in the delegated instrument: then both the purpose clause and the text of the delegated instrument form a complete regulatory package with the primary Act. At the same time, there is an additional argument in favour of purpose clauses in delegated legislation of all functions where the purpose clause introduces the precise tangible criteria on the basis of which post-legislative scrutiny of the regulatory package is to take place. In other words, the new function of purpose clauses as criteria of post-legislative scrutiny applies to delegated

[53] The main objectives of the regulatory package must be included in the primary Act and not in delegated legislation: see House of Lords Select Committee on the Constitution, *Gangmasters (Licencing) Bill (Seventh Report)* (HL 2003–04, 108) paras 4–8; also see House of Lords Select Committee on the Constitution, *Armed Forces Bill (Thirteenth Report)* (HL 2005–06, 200) para 5.

legislation also, thus offering additional support to the addition of the now neglected tool of purpose clauses in both primary and delegated legislation of the type and kind that is fertile for post-legislative measurement of effectiveness.

Commencement provisions are necessary in delegated legislation and now tend to take the form of a precise date. For example, Article 1 of the Tobacco Products (Descriptions of Products) (Amendment) Order 2013 states:

> Citation and Commencement
>
> 1. This Order may be cited as the Tobacco Products (Descriptions of Products) (Amendment) Order 2013 and comes into force on 1st January 2014.

Definitions are rare in delegated instruments. They are introduced only when necessary, and they must not depart from definitions in the primary legislation. This stems from the prevalent approach of linking primary and delegated legislation into a single regulatory package: new concepts are mostly presented in the primary legislation where they are defined. And the maxim of one term to express a concept applies not just within the primary instrument but within the regulatory package as a whole. But there is scope for definitions in delegated instruments that amend or supplement primary legislation. And these are to be introduced frugally and only where they assist the user, as is the case with definitions in primary legislation also.

Delegated instruments may also include retrospective provisions, if this power is specifically introduced in primary legislation. Similarly, express power is needed for delegated legislation that binds the Crown, for creating offences,[54] for dispensing with the law,[55] or infringing fundamental common law rights such as the right to property[56] or the right to respect for private life.[57] These are issues that require enhanced parliamentary legitimacy and, as a norm, must be reserved for primary legislation. George Winterton refers to these as limits on the depth of the executive power.[58] The limits on the depth of non-statutory executive power have been driven by principles

[54] See House of Lords Select Committee on the Constitution, *Co-Operative and Community Benefit Societies and Credit Unions Bill (Nineteenth Report)* (HL 2008–09, 158) para 14; also see *Case of Proclamations* (1611) 12 Co Rep 74.

[55] See Bill of Rights 1689: 'the pretended Power of Suspending of Laws or the Execution of Laws by Regal Authority without Consent of Parliament is illegal'; also see *A v Hayden* (1984) 156 CLR 532, 580–81 (Brennan J).

[56] *Entick v Carrington* (1765) 19 St Tr 1029; also *Coco v R* (1994) 179 CLR 427, 435–37 (Mason C, Brennan, Gaudron and McHugh); but see contra House of Lords Select Committee on the Constitution, *Co-Operative and Community Benefit Societies and Credit Unions Bill (Nineteenth Report)* (n 54) para 14, which does not accept the use of delegated legislation for the creation of criminal offences.

[57] See House of Lords Select Committee on the Constitution, *Policing and Crime Bill (Sixteenth Report)* (HL 2008–09, 128) paras 11–15.

[58] See G Winterton, *Parliament, the Executive and the Governor-General* (Melbourne, Melbourne University Press, 1983) 29–30, 40–44.

of separation of powers, responsible government, accountability and the rule of law.[59] But there is nothing to stop Parliament from extending this capacity to the executive via an enabling clause in primary legislation. For example, Article 1 of the Additionally-developed Oil Fields Order 2013 made on 15 November states:

> Citation, commencement and interpretation
> 1. (1) This Order may be cited as the Additionally-developed Oil Fields Order 2013 and is treated as having come into force on 1st April 2013.

And regulation 21 of the Democratic People's Republic of Korea (European Union Financial Sanctions) Regulations 2013 states:

> The Crown
> 21. (1) These Regulations bind the Crown.
> (2) No contravention by the Crown of a provision of these Regulations makes the Crown criminally liable.
> (3) The High Court or, in Scotland, the Court of Session may, on the application of a person appearing to the court to have an interest, declare unlawful any act or omission of the Crown that constitutes a contravention of a provision of these Regulations.
> (4) Nothing in this regulation affects Her Majesty in her private capacity.
> (5) Paragraph (4) is to be read as if section 38(3) of the Crown Proceedings Act 1947(1) (meaning of Her Majesty in her private capacity) were contained in these Regulations.

And the Olive Oil (Marketing Standards) Regulations 2014 state:

> Offences and penalties
> 11. (1) A person is guilty of an offence if that person—
> (a) fails to comply with a compliance notice;
> (b) intentionally obstructs an authorised officer exercising a power under these Regulations;
> (c) fails, without reasonable excuse, to give any assistance or information that the authorised officer may reasonably require for the enforcement of the EU Regulations or the performance of that officer's functions under these Regulations;
> (d) knowingly gives false or misleading information to an authorised officer; or
> (e) without reasonable excuse, fails to produce a label, document or record, including—
> (i) the entry and withdrawal registers required to be kept under Article 7a of Commission Regulation (EEC) No 2568/91, and
> (ii) the documentation described in Article 7 of Commission Implementing Regulation (EU) No 29/2012,
>
> when reasonably required to do so by an authorised officer.

[59] See C Saunders, 'The Sources and Scope of Commonwealth Power to Spend' (2009) 20 *Public Law Review* 256, 259.

The signature, title and date must be included at the bottom of the text in a simple manner. For example, the Building (Amendment) (Wales) Regulations 2014 state:

Carl Sargeant

Minister for Housing and Regeneration, one of the Welsh Ministers

21 January 2014

And finally, where consent, approval or confirmation by an authority is required by the enabling provision, this must be introduced expressly but simply. The same formula as the one introduced above for the signature applies in these cases too. For example in the Immigration and Nationality (Fees) (Amendment) Order 2014:

Mark Harper
Minister of State
Home Office

3rd February 2014
We consent

David Evennett
Karen Bradley

Two of the Lords Commissioners of Her Majesty's Treasury

30th January 2014

In the UK, explanatory notes are used at the foot of delegated legislation to direct the user to the primary legislation and to assist them with the understanding of technical and detailed provisions that are included in the delegated text. This example is from the Maritime Security (Jersey) Order 2014:

EXPLANATORY NOTE

(This note is not part of the Order)

Various provisions of the Aviation and Maritime Security Act 1990 ('the 1990 Act') were extended to Jersey by the Maritime Security (Jersey) Order 1996 (S.I. 1996/2881) subject to modifications. This Order revokes and replaces that Order. In doing so, it provides for certain of the provisions of the 1990 Act to extend to Jersey with fresh modifications, specified in the Part II of the Schedule to the Order, that reflect—

(a) amendments to the 1990 Act made by the Merchant Shipping and Maritime Security Act 1997 in the United Kingdom; and
(b) legislative provisions made in Jersey by the Shipping (Jersey) Law 2002.

Explanatory notes serve as a unique tool that allows the drafter to offer the user a fuller glimpse of the whole regulatory package. As a result they contribute greatly to the drafter's main pursuit when it comes to delegated legislation: a constitutionally sound legislative transfer that regulates technical and detailed issues with convenient flexibility and expediency.

15

Drafting for Consolidation v Drafting for Codification

THE MULTITUDE OF legislative texts added to the statute book annually, in combination with the inevitability of prevalence of parliamentary realism over technical drafting idealism in the manner in which these new additions find their place in the statute book, create a collage of complexity in legislation. This is frustrating for the user who, irrespective of their legal training, is faced with a multi-layered legislative framework fragmented over numerous primary and delegated instruments especially where a timeline of legislation is needed. And, to add insult to injury, this folly is justified by reference to the presumption that Acts in the common law tradition are self-sufficient. Whatever its basis there is little doubt that the current state of the statute book leaves users in awe when attempting to ascertain what the legal position is in relation to their needs. And, let's not forget, lay users are 60 per cent of the users of www.legislation.gov.uk.

But tidying up the statute book is not an easy task, even in jurisdictions where there is a specialised Law Commission. The keepers of the statute book have a number of simple and more complex tools at hand: consolidation, codification, revision, repeal, rewrite, restatement and reprint. Their identification and detailed clarification is beautifully introduced by Jonathan Teasdale.[1]

Teasdale's table introduces mechanisms for weeding out provisions or whole texts that clog the statute book. There is intrinsic value in the complete listings of these mechanisms. But for the purposes of identifying the drafting techniques required for them, one needs to juxtapose them against each other and classify them under the prism of their drafter's tasks. Repeals are a type of amendment in essence, indeed mostly direct textual amendment; they may have as a secondary consequence the tidying up of the legislative text to which they refer but their primary aim is to dilute any ambiguity concerning a point of law that, without them, could have been regulated by parallel provisions. Because they relate to a single provision or a single

[1] See J Teasdale, 'Statute Law Revision: Repeal, Consolidation or Something More?' (2009) 11 *European Journal of Law Reform* 157, 195.

Table 15.1: Teasdale's Table 1

Statutory mechanism	Purpose
Consolidation ('pure', with minor amendment, and with more radical amendment)	To amalgamate existing statutory text, dealing with a single topic, in a single and coherent statute
Repeal	To remove from the 'live' statute book enactments which are obsolete, and to promote reform of statute law
Rewrite	To produce a form of enhanced consolidation, whereby existing enactments are amalgamated and updated with parliamentary authority
Restatement	To effect a consolidated text of existing enactments as an administrative exercise, without affecting existing law (either by amendment or repeal)
Reprint	To produce an informal updated statutory text (often by topic)
Revision (UK and overseas)	To facilitate the production of revised editions of the statutes (chronologically or by topic) by repealing the obsolete and running in parallel with programmes for statutory consolidation and restructuring

legislative text, they are in my mind classified under amendments rather than under holistic mechanisms of law reform. I can see them used as tools in the process of consolidation, rewrite or revision rather than as mechanisms for tidying up the statute book in their own right. Restatement and reprint involve mainly administrative arrangements of the text that enhance clarity but do not involve a drafting task other than an identification of a structure used as the sole means for enhancing clarity: consequently, they are mechanisms for consolidation in its broad sense. Codification, rewrite and revision are the true agents for drafting for the purposes of enhancing the legislative quality of the statute book; they all involve a creative drafting task leading to the introduction of a new text, and as such they can be broadly classified as consolidations of various extent.

And so from the drafting perspective one can classify Teasdale's mechanisms of law reform in two broad categories of drafting exercises: codification versus consolidation. Having stressed the variety of membership inhabiting these broad concepts, it is time to turn attention to their usage, advantages and disadvantages. The lens of analysis remains the effectiveness of the resulting legislative text as a means of enhancing legislative quality contributing to efficacy of regulation.

CODIFICATION

Codification is a broad term used inconsistently[2] to signify either the process of arranging, rationalising and enacting the collection of laws of a jurisdiction on a field of law; or the end result of the process, namely the systematic arrangement, exhaustive collection, updating and enactment of the collection of primary legislation in a field of law in a specific jurisdiction. Chakrabarti distinguishes codes into creative, consolidating, and consolidating and creative.[3] Codification presupposes the prior existence of a substantive number of Acts regulating the same or relevant issues, although some codifications have been based solely on existing judge-made decisions where codification is used to rationalise a line of common law where there has been little or no previous statutory intervention. These are collected, arranged in a logical sequence and supplemented by new provisions that either fill in any gaps or resolve vagueness, ambiguity or competing provisions. Codification signifies a break from the past: this has led Steiner to state that it suits better societies in transition or countries with existing codes.[4] The argument is strengthened by Samuels' initial, and now re-worked view that the English legal system is 'too mature' to lend itself to codification.[5] One can see why Steiner places codification within the context of transition: the ability to reform the legal system with a big bang is uniquely served by codification.[6] But that does not exclude its use in other contexts: codification carries advantages in dealing with the problem of excessive volume and complexity of legislation in any society and legal system. But Samuels does have a point here: codification may well be desirable but where does one start and what does one tackle first?

In other words, codification involves drafting on a large scale. Existing legislation is viewed as a form of learned drafting instructions, a plateau of technically informed texts. The task of the drafting team is to identify a structure for the code, to identify and arrange the contents of each part in a logical sequence promoting clarity and to ensure that any diseases arising from the compilation are resolved. Vagueness and ambiguity are addressed

[2] See J Vanderlinden, 'Qu'est-ce qu'un code?' (2005) 46 *Cahiers de Droit* 29; also see Clive who uses codification as a term reflecting both reforming and restating 'more or less comprehensive, well organised, legislated statement or restatement of the rules of law in a particular area, whatever the source of the rules and whether or not they are changed in the codification process': E Clive, 'Current Codification Projects in Scotland' (2000) 4 *Edinburgh Law Review* 341, 341–42; and E Clive, 'Thoughts from a Scottish Perspective on the Bicentenary of the French Civil Code' (2004) 8 *Edinburgh Law Review* 415, 415.

[3] See NK Chakrabarti, *Principles of Legislation and Legislative Drafting* (Kolkata, R Chambray and Co Private Ltd, 2007) 204–05.

[4] See E Steiner, 'Codification in England: The Need to Move from an Ideological to a Functional Approach—A Bridge too Far?' (2004) 25 *Statute Law Review* 209, 220.

[5] See A Samuels, 'Improving the Quality of Legislation' (1974) 3 *Anglo-American Law Review* 523, 533.

[6] See A Harmathy, 'Codification in a Period of Transition' (1997–98) 31 *University of California Davis Law Review* 783, 784.

but more at the macro-level of the code rather than the micro-level of words, clauses and sections within the membership of the code.

In consequence, best practice requires that the drafter organises sections or articles and chapters in a logical sequence. Any related material should be grouped together under relevant headings. Articles must be numbered in consecutive order. Substantive provisions must be placed in the text of the code, not in the introductory report, or in appendices. Headings for parts or chapters must only carry a substantive content. When amending a code, the drafter must only amend what should have been legislated in the original code but was not. And they should refrain from renumbering parts, chapters and articles. This is to ensure that the resulting code is comprehensive in scope, systematic in principle and accessible in its expression.[7]

Codification mainly aims to create a unique document in the field of law that it refers to, which encompasses legislative regulation as interpreted by the courts.[8] In other words, the goal is to offer a text that reflects the whole picture of regulation in this field. And this is exactly where the added value of codification lies: it facilitates the re-emergence of the principles and values of the law,[9] and the re-subscription of these principles and values to the common values and characteristics of the society in the name of which the legislature legislates.[10] In order to achieve this goal the drafter undertakes a quadruple task. First, they weed out any obsolete provisions, any repealed provisions, any possibly unconstitutional provisions and any provisions now incompatible with current international law and obligations. Secondly, they identify and resolve any contradictions in legislation. Thirdly, they identify and supplement any lacunae in the law. And fourthly, they put to effect any textual and consequential amendments.[11] And all these tasks point to the main duty of the drafting team, which is to promote effectiveness via clarity at the level of the code rather than each specific Act.

This also points to the objectives of codification. In general terms, codification may have three functions: formal simplification of the law; systematisation of the law; and reform of the law.[12] Clarity is at the forefront: the law becomes more accessible, comprehensible, consistent and certain.[13]

[7] See G Letourneau and SA Cohen, 'Codification and Law Reform: Some Lessons from the Canadian Experience' (1989) 10 *Statute Law Review* 181, 184.

[8] See L James, 'Restructuring the Labour Code in Lieu of Quality in Legislation Principles: Will the Use of a Code Prove Beneficial?' (2009) 11 *European Journal of Law Reform* 259, 268.

[9] See F Fairfax Stone, 'A Primer on Codification' (1954–55) 29 *Tulane Law Review* 303, 307.

[10] See M-J Longtin, 'La codification comme element ou source de justice' (2001) 42 *Les Cahiers de Droit* 667, 674.

[11] See P Ferguson, 'Constructing a Criminal Code' (2009) 20 *Criminal Law Forum* 139, 142.

[12] See D Tallon, 'Codification and Consolidation of the Law at the Present Time' (1979) 14 *Israeli Law Review* 1, 4.

[13] See CGB Nicholson, 'Codification of Scots Law: A Way Ahead, or a Blind Alley?' (1987) *Statute Law Review* 173, 177.

But it is set within a generic pursuit for modernisation or updating.[14] Codification serves updating when the existing fragmented legislation or any existing code no longer reflects the balance of the policy goals served by means of legislation. For example, a code on criminal law that does not include e-crimes and internet crimes no longer serves adequately its regulatory aim of compiling an exhaustive list of offences in the jurisdiction; users would be misled into thinking that these are the criminal laws in the jurisdiction, whereas huge chunks of important laws are not included there at all. Codification also serves updating when the existing laws or codes include superseded text, redundant provisions or conflicting provisions. Codification serves modernisation when the terms used in its membership are so archaic or obscure, that the regulatory aim pursued by the pre-existing legislation or code can no longer be served adequately. Users can no longer access the regulatory message sufficiently as their understanding of the provisions is severely inhibited by the language or arrangement used. It is obvious that most codes would come about for the purposes of updating rather than modernisation: when viewed under the prism of legal certainty, the large shake-up in the law resulting from the introduction of a new code or the amendment of a legislative text as basic as an existing code is rarely balanced by modernisation unless the current texts are severely inaccessible either in its parts or as a whole. On top of that, and strengthening the argument, owing to the size of codes the legislative process of codification or recodification of an existing code can often take a decade or longer.

The length of the process reflects the amount of resources required. The effort involved is such that codification rarely takes place at once in a single Bill. More often than not codification is undertaken gradually via positive law codification. This involves a process of revision and restatement of each part of the code separately, enacting each one as it is finished. At the end of the process all the parts or titles of the code are legal evidence of the current law. But even a staggered approach to codification presents a number of methodological, substantive and practical obstacles, as elaborated by Skinner:[15] its alleged incompatibility with the Anglo-American tradition[16] often termed 'codophobia';[17] the possible disruption of the hierarchy of sources of law; the possible distortion of substantive law and

[14] See PJ Omar, 'Lessons from the French Experience: the Possibility of Codification of Commercial Law in the United Kingdom' (2007) *International Company and Commercial Law Review* 235, 240.

[15] See C Skinner, 'Codification and the Common Law' (2009) 11 *European Journal of Law Reform* 225, 229–32.

[16] But see contra G Weiss, 'The Enchantment of Codification in the Common-Law World' (2000) 25 *Yale Journal of International Law* 435, 529.

[17] See L Farmer, 'Reconstructing the English Codification Debate: The Criminal Law Commissioners, 1833-45' (2000) 18 *Law and History Review* 397, 398.

the impairment of legal development;[18] and extensive demand on resources. But codification does not halt reforms of substance: 'it amounts to reform of a different kind, and should not be put forward as a hybrid'.[19] And 'the common law ... increasingly ... attempts to codify broad areas of law'.[20] Of all these arguments the latter one seems the most persuasive. Leaving aside the huge spending on resources in such a complicated humongous drafting task, the problem remains that by the time codification finishes, the dynamic and ever-changing law[21] may have already moved forward. Perhaps this is the source of the present view that codes 'state principles in short phrases' in a style that is 'succinct and inspiring, rather than to cover every eventuality'.[22]

J-L Warsmann, President of the French Commission for Constitutional Law, states that codification has proved its value as a technique for the rationalisation, organisation and presentation of whole areas of law. It is a tool for the improvement of access and legibility of regulation because it allows us to regroup dispersed texts while clarifying them, through the modernisation of their terminology, and through their reclassification in conformity with the hierarchy of norms. It assesses the coherence of texts between them and so facilitates the harmonisation of the state of the law. Despite the division of doctrine on the merits of codification for a constant law, the Conseil constitutionnel has declared that by its nature codification is likely to achieve 'the constitutional value of accessibility and intelligibility of law'.[23] After all, accessibility is intrinsically linked to the rule of law.[24]

CONSOLIDATION

Consolidation is a broad term used to signify either the process of arranging in a single text the current laws of a jurisdiction in a field of law or the end result of the process, namely the systematic arrangement and exhaustive collection of primary legislation in a field of law in a specific jurisdiction.

[18] See P LeGrand, 'Strange Power of Words: Codification Situated (1994) 9 *Tulane European and Civil Law Forum* 194, 213.

[19] See F Bennion, 'Codification of the Criminal Law—Part 2: The Technique of Codification' (1986) 1 *Criminal Law Review* 295, 298.

[20] See C Pejovic, 'Civil Law and Common Law: Two Different Paths Leading to the Same Goal' (2001) 32 *Vanderbilt University Law Review* 42, s 5.

[21] See *Report of the Renton Committee on the Preparation of Legislation* (Cmnd 1975, 6033) 85.

[22] See I Stewart, 'Mors Codicis: End of the Age of Codification?' (2012) 27 *Tulane European and Civil Law Forum* 17, 37.

[23] See J-L Warsmann, 'Simplifions nos lois pour guérir un mal français', Rapport sur la qualité et la simplification du droit, *La Documentation française* (Feb 2009) www.ladocumentationfrancaise.fr/rapports-publics/094000276/.

[24] See P Rickard-Clark, 'Access to Justice: Accessibility' (2011) 11 *Legal Information and Management* 159, 159.

Russell describes consolidation as the gathering into one Act of provisions contained in several Acts; but a 'scissors and paste arrangement of the existing Acts will not usually be sufficient' to serve conciseness and clearness.[25] Dickerson describes US codification Bills and their equivalent UK consolidation Bills as 'unified restatements of existing statutory law'.[26] Gretton defines it as 'the restating of statutory law, by repealing the grimy old enactments and replacing them with shiny new ones'.[27] It does not alter the substance of the law. It involves 'the preparation for re-enactment of a number of older statutes, dealing with the same or allied subject matter, in a single new Act rationally arranged and, as far as possible, expressed in modern language'.[28] The consolidated text can be binding or not. Consolidation presupposes the prior existence of Acts regulating the same or relevant issues; these are collected and arranged in a logical sequence, but without any alteration of content. It also requires that the law under treatment is settled before an attempt to consolidate it is even made.[29]

And here lies the difference between codification and consolidation in their pure sense: codification involves drafting on a large scale, whereas consolidation involves limited drafting in the form of creating a new clear structure of existing and untouched parts. The drafting task involved in consolidation lies in the pursuit of clarity by means of structure alone. Here existing legislation is viewed as the final draft of the parts of the consolidated documents, and so it resembles the task of structure verification in stage five of Thornton's drafting process. And this points to the main task of the drafting team, which is to promote effectiveness via clarity of structure alone.

This also points to the objectives of consolidation. It addresses the volume of statutes, their frequent change, their multiple amendments, drafting errors within the texts and of course the cumulative effect of these phenomena in the statute book.[30] Clarity is at the forefront of consolidation, exactly like codification. And, exactly like in codification, in consolidation clarity is set within a generic pursuit for updating. Consolidation serves updating when older legislation has been indirectly contextually supplemented by a newer Act regulating relevant issues in a newer context. For example, placing next to each other an older Act on fraud with a newer

[25] See Sir A Russell, *Legislative Drafting and Forms* (London, Butterworths, 1938) 64.

[26] See R Dickerson, 'Legislative Drafting in London and Washington' (1959) *Cambridge Law Journal* 49, 55.

[27] See G Gretton, 'Of Law Commissioning' (2013) 17 *Edinburgh Law Review* 120, 131.

[28] See N Marsh, 'Law Reform in the United Kingdom: a New Institutional Approach' (1971) 12 *William and Mary Law Review* 263, 280.

[29] See Sir E Caldwell, 'A Vision of Tidiness: Codes, Consolidations and Statute Law Revision' in B Opeskin and D Weisbrot (eds), *The Promise of Law Reform* (Canberra, Federation Press, 2005) 40, 44.

[30] See P Breuer, 'Consolidation and Confusion' (1988) 9 *Statute Law Review* 62, 62.

Act on e-crime allows the reader, by means of structure alone, to make the connection between fraud in its traditional form and fraud undertaken by means of the internet. Modernisation can be served by consolidation if the opportunity of consolidation is used to restate current Acts in gender-neutral language; or to restate, as an administrative exercise, current Acts without their obsolete or repealed provisions, or with their amended provisions with amendments put into effect.

This is exactly the value of consolidation in its pure form: without affecting the content of its constituting parts, the consolidated text offers the user clarity by restating the law as it now stands. In this respect, the consolidated text looks very much like an elaborate Keeling Schedule of grand scale. This undoubtedly involves careful drafting, aiming to render the law accessible to users whose legal skills do not allow them to put to effect amendments and repeals in a textual context. But it does not merit lengthy debate before the legislature, provided that it remains within the consolidation boundaries.[31] There is no doubt that consolidation promotes considerably understandability of the text, approachability of the law, reduction of the need for amendment[32] and consequently effectiveness of legislation. This makes it a very popular option: as Alec Samuels states, 'everyone is in principle in favour of consolidation'.[33] And according to Lord Hope of Craighead 'the idea that consolidation of that kind could ever be achieved seems to be becoming more and more fanciful'.[34]

Consolidation involves a lengthy process spent primarily in its research plan: the actual drafting seems disproportionate to that research,[35] which may explain why consolidation is often viewed as a mundane technical task of law reform. This law-mending task is in comparison with law-making 'less spectacular and less exciting ... but very important'.[36] And so consolidation is anything but mundane. First, in all types of drafting tasks preparation is the lengthiest but most crucial part. And secondly, immense skill is required to untangle the labyrinth of complex legislation, treat it and offer it to the user in a rational and accessible format.[37] The inherent difficulty of

31 See HC Deb 1968, vol 14, cols 347–65.

32 See A Lynch and P Ziegler 'The Amendment of Legislation' (1991) 12 *Statute Law Review* 48, 56–57.

33 See A Samuels, 'Consolidation: a Plea' (2005) 26 *Statute Law Review* 56, 56.

34 See Lord Hope of Craighead, 'Do We Still Need a Scottish Law Commission?' (2006) 10 *Edinburgh Law Review* 10, 27.

35 See LJH Beighton, 'Editorial—Tax Law Rewrite: Plans for 1998/99' (1998) *British Tax Review* 273, 274.

36 See DM Walker, 'The Second Annual Report of the Scottish Law Commission' (1968) *Scottish Law Times* (News) 2, 3; also see DM Walker 'The Scottish Law Commission under Review' (1987) 8 *Statute Law Review* 115, 118.

37 On the shortage of skilled drafters for consolidation, see 'Report of a Working party of the Statute Law Society on Consolidation of Enactments' (1984) 5 *Statute Law Review* 171, paras 15–16.

consolidation lies in the necessity to decide how to deal with problems caused by modifications, restrictions and constructions, especially with a large number of texts.[38] The intrinsic skill required is such that consolidation is mostly left to the wonderfully trained law reformers of a Law Commission.[39] For an analysis of the specific tasks see Teasdale's second table.[40]

Table 15.2: Teasdale's Table 2

Statutory mechanism	Criteria
Consolidation ('pure', with minor amendment, and with more radical amendment)	Enactments which have been subjected to complex amendment, which have been supplemented by related enactments, which contain obsolete material, and which need logical re-ordering
Repeal	Removal from the statute book of enactments (in whole or in part) which no longer have practical utility
Rewrite	As with consolidation (above), but involving the rewriting and reordering of complex statutory material which is outdated
Restatement	Pulling together of existing statutory material which has been amended piecemeal to produce a comprehensive text (but without removing obsolete material, unless formally repealed)
Reprint	Reprinting statutes as amended
Revision (UK and overseas)	Removal from the statute book of enactments (in whole or in part) which are obsolete, spent, unnecessary or superseded (but, non-UK, in tandem with programme of consolidation and restructuring)

CODIFICATION VERSUS CONSOLIDATION

Having presented codification and consolidation and their mechanisms and staggered tools, it is worth identifying their advantages and disadvantages from the point of view of effectiveness. These are schematically presented in the image below.

[38] See Irish Law Reform Commission, 'Legislation Directory: Towards a Best Practice Model' (LRC CP 49, 2008) 1.85.

[39] See E Donelan, 'European Approaches to Improving Access to and Managing the Stock of Legislation' (2009) 30 *Statute Law Review* 147, 181.

[40] See Teasdale, 'Statute Law Revision' (n 1) 196.

The scheme applies the pyramid of values in legislative drafting presented in chapter one to consolidation and codification in their pure forms. As a visual aid it facilitates the drawing of distinctions and identification of similarities between the two tools. Starting from specifics at the bottom of the scheme, one can see that consolidation serves plain language by means of introducing a single, holistic text in the field of law under consolidation. It may also contribute to gender-neutral drafting if the parameters of the specific consolidation so allow, but this is not necessary in all consolidations. Consolidation also contributes to clarity by introducing a single legislative instrument and by clarifying the law by means of a clearer structure. It promotes precision by deleting imprecisions but this is undertaken indirectly via the removal of imprecisions deriving from the removal of repealed provisions or texts. Consolidation contributes to unambiguity by deleting ambiguities but only indirectly, if these are caused by competing provisions or texts one of which has been repealed: in other words, if there are parallel provisions in the statute book which are not competing within a specific time but exist in the statute book together with reference to various points in the timeline, a consolidation exercise can juxtapose them and through the deletion of the now repealed provision or text can resolve the ambiguity with reference to current law. From the point of view of cost-efficiency consolidation assists both in the short term but also in the long term: a consolidated text is cost-efficient when compared with codification or with a fragmented tidying up of each of its constituent parts. For example, referring to the cost-efficiency of tax consolidation in Australia, D'Ascenzo stated that 'Consolidation involved transitional costs but the pot of gold at the end of this journey will be in the form of reduced complexity and increased flexibility in commercial operations'.[41] But of course one needs to take into account the prevalent need for regular periodic consolidations.[42] From the point of view of effectiveness, consolidation promotes approachable legislation, in other words legislation that is easier understood by the reader. But this refers to current law at the time of its completion.

Codification seems to be achieving more in-depth results. It is not only achieving approachability of legislation, it promotes true better regulation. The effectiveness of codification is the transformation that it achieves:[43] its innovative effect can accentuate its effectiveness.[44] But it is only cost-efficient in the long term, as the resources required in the short term are considerable: this may well classify codification as a solution of

[41] See M D'Ascenzo 'The Intent of the Consolidation Regime' (2005) 8 *Journal of Australian Taxation* 371, 380.

[42] See Law Drafting and Regulatory Management in Central and Eastern Europe, Sigma Papers: No 18.

[43] See A Battiau, 'Codification, atout ou danger?' (2013) 9 *Revista Stiinte Juridice* 18, 22.

[44] See JL Sourioux, 'Codification et autres formes de systématisation du droit à l'époque actuelle, Le Droit français' (1988) *Journal de la sociologie de legislation compare* 145, 147.

last resort.[45] But effectiveness is fed by means of clarity, precision and unambiguity. Codification serves clarity as it offers law in a single instrument and a clearer structure, just like consolidation; but in addition to consolidation it promotes clarity by means of clearer syntax, grammar and words. In other words codification offers the luxury of a re-examination of not only the structure of the codified instrument, but also the structure of each legislative part, the structure of each section, and the expression or parts, sections and clauses. Codification serves precision by filling in any gaps, by resolving vagueness, and by deleting imprecisions of all types and from all sources. Codification also promotes unambiguity by filling in any gaps in legislation, by resolving conflicts between and within texts, and by deleting ambiguities in the law and in the text. It achieves all this my means of plain language served by the placement of the whole law in a single text, and by use of homogenous structure, content, expression and terms. Moreover, it serves gender-neutral language as, at least in the UK, it applies this even in older legislative texts.

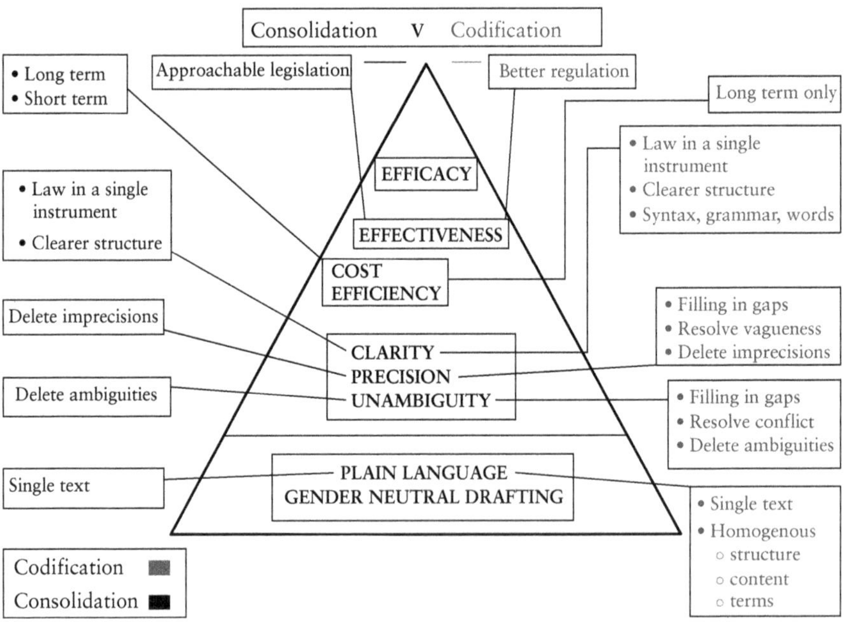

Figure 15.1: Consolidation v Codification

[45] See HR Hahlo 'Codifying the Common Law: Protracted Gestation' (1975) 38 *Modern Law Review* 23, 29.

To sum up, the choice between consolidation and codification can only be made through the careful and learned balancing of the need for effectiveness versus the need for cost-efficiency. Whichever principle feeds into efficacy of regulation the most will win the debate. For effectiveness codification presents clear and obvious advantage. But for cost-efficiency, consolidation wins the day, any day.

DIVERSE MODELS AND THE EU

The terms codification and consolidation tend to carry a jurisdiction-specific meaning, awarding them diverse levels of creative intervention to the tasks involved. It would be simplistic to distinguish between a civil versus common law meaning, as jurisdictions within the same family offer their own meaning to each term: the UK approach to consolidation is rather purist as opposed to the broad approach to consolidation in the USA. The EU has its own approach to the topic. It is worth discussing this briefly both because it constitutes a marriage between European civil and common law traditions, but mainly because understanding what each term means is a prerequisite of successful transposition for the purposes of national implementation of EU law.

Within the Commission's Better Regulation strategy the EU attempts to reduce the volume of EU legislation and to render it more readable and legally clear. For that purpose the EU uses codification, consolidation and recasting.[46]

Codification of existing legislation is bringing all amendments to a given law adopted at different times into one law.[47] It is defined in the 1994 Interinstitutional Agreement as 'the procedure whereby the acts to be codified are repealed and replaced by a single act containing no substantive change to those acts'.[48] Codification includes the deletion of all obsolete provisions, the harmonisation of the terminology used in the new Act and the determination of its recitals. The process enables the mass of the legislation to be reduced whilst maintaining the substance of the legislation.[49] The resulting texts are subject to formal decision-making and therefore they have legal status. They greatly facilitate access to legislation

[46] See W Voermans, C Moll, N Florijn and P Van Lochem 'Codification and Consolidation in the European Union: A Means to Untie Red Tape' (2008) 29 *Statute Law Review* 65, 74–75.

[47] See Communication from the Commission to the European Parliament, the Council, the European Economic and Social Committee and the Committee of Regions, 'Regulatory Fitness and Performance (REFIT): Results and Next Steps' COM(2013) 685 final, 1.

[48] See point 1 of the Interinstitutional Agreement on Better Law Making of 20 December 1994 [1996] OJ C 102, 2.

[49] See Communication from the Commission to the European Parliament and the Council, 'Codification of the Acquis communautaire' COM(2001) 645.

and reduce the volume of texts, especially for the purposes of transposition by the Member States.[50] Codification requires that the Acts in question are in a relative standstill, namely not subject to substantial amendments. Codification, also known as formal consolidation, can be horizontal when the new instrument incorporates several instruments in a field of law, or vertical when the new instrument incorporates a single instrument and its subsequent amendments.[51]

Consolidation of a legislative Act, like codification, brings together in a single text a basic legislative Act and all its amending Acts.[52] But these do not go through a formal decision-making process and as a result the text is neither binding nor authentic. Even so, they do offer users a reliable view of the current state of the law.

Instead of simply modifying the parts of the law that need to be changed, recasting presents the required amendments into a consolidated text together with all past amendments. Recasting modifies existing legislation whilst simultaneously codifying it in one consolidated text incorporating all previous amendments. In essence, the recasting technique permits the adoption of a new single legislative text that simultaneously makes the desired amendment, codifies that amendment with the unchanged provisions of the earlier Act and repeals that Act.[53] The new legal Act replaces and repeals the earlier Act. This is the prevalent method for simplification. But, the potential for use of this technique is constrained by several factors: first, it can be considered only for those Commission legislative initiatives that aim to amend existing legislation; and secondly, it is a technique that would be disproportionate in cases where legal texts are amended very often or where individual amendments are relatively limited, in which cases it would not be efficient to reproduce the whole text in a recast form.

From a UK perspective, EU codification and consolidation are types of UK consolidation: they do not affect the law but they differ on the procedure followed and the resulting authenticity of the text. On that basis one could state that EU codification is equivalent to UK consolidation in its pure form. And that EU consolidation is equivalent to a UK restatement. EU recasting is equivalent to a UK codification in its pure form. In fact, the Law Commission seems to have redefined its approach to codification[54] essentially adopting the EU's recasting model: giving the law a clearer

[50] ibid.

[51] See G Ciavarini Azzi, 'Better Lawmaking: the Experience and the View of the European Commission' (1998) 4 *Columbia Journal of European Law* 617, 625.

[52] See W Robinson, 'Drafting of EU Acts: A View from the European Commission' (2008) 10 *European Journal of Law Reform* 151, 159.

[53] See Interinstitutional Agreement of 28 November 2001 on a more structured use of the recasting technique for legal acts [2002] OJ C 77, 1, recital 5 and art 2.

[54] See Law Commission, *Simplification of Criminal Law: Public Nuisance and Outraging Public Decency* (Law Com No 193, 2010) 1.1.

structure; using more modern terminology; making the law in a given area more consistent with other closely allied areas of law; and making the law readily comprehensible to ordinary people by ensuring that it embodies sound and sensible concepts of fairness.[55] In essence the Commission is saying that an additional step of simplification (which may require some element of reform) should usually be the precursor to codification, certainly in the sphere of criminal law. Once piecemeal simplification has been undertaken attention can then turn to preparing a composite code.

The diversity of meanings attributed to the same term can only cause confusion for UK drafters and users. It may be reassuring to note that transposition would only come into play with reference to recasting, as this introduces new provisions. But all EU methods of law reform must be researched in depth and used by UK drafters as drafting instructions for the purposes of amending UK legislation. UK drafters must identify what has changed by virtue of EU recastings. Or what has been interpreted differently or amended or repealed by virtue of EU consolidations and, to a much lesser degree, EU codifications. Transposition can then be planned via the juxtaposition of EU texts to current UK law. That transposition does not necessarily require verbatim placement of the EU instruments in a unique text: transposition does require their smooth reception within the existing national legislative texts in whichever format best matches the national legal environment. And so for the UK, introducing a lengthy holistic EU unique instrument could create more uncertainty in the law and its hierarchical standing compared to national sources of law than the fragmentation of the EU instrument into more, but familiarly formatted UK Acts.

[55] See K Stevenson and C Harris, 'Breaking the Thrall of Ambiguity: Simplification (of the Criminal Law) as an Emerging Human Rights Imperative' (2010) 74 *Journal of Criminal Law* 516, 529.

16

Taxation Legislation[1]

TAXATION LEGISLATION PRESENTS some of the biggest challenges for the modern drafter. Just like criminal law, taxation law is complicated, complex and extends over a multitude of layers of regulation.[2] And just like criminal law, it has to be clearly understood by lay persons who have the obligation to implement it without having the opportunity to study it or specialise in it. On top of this, taxation legislation is notoriously fluid, as it is amended on a regular basis. This creates two additional layers of complexity: for the drafters time is a luxury that is not afforded to them, and so there is little scope for internal and external monitoring; for the users there is no time at all to get used to the new notions and understand them before they are once again amended.[3] It is perhaps in recognition of this unavoidable complexity that the UK has established the Office of Tax Simplification (OTS) whose work in researching and addressing some of the complexities of taxation law has advanced the debate considerably.

This chapter examines the drafting of taxation legislation using Thornton's five stages of drafting as a timeline for the discussion of particular problems. So, let's begin with policy, and the understanding of drafting instructions.

UNDERSTANDING DRAFTING INSTRUCTIONS: INITIAL CONSIDERATIONS FOR THE DRAFTER

Taxation is one of the most important areas of government as it relates to the main source of its revenue. Tax policy in an objective sense survives

[1] With my sincere gratitude to the Office of Tax Simplification at HM Treasury, and especially John Whiting, Tax Director; Jeremy Sherwood; and Caroline Turnbull-Hall for their immense generosity in offering me insight and documentation. John Whiting's 'layered approach' to legislation is the approach used in this book.

[2] See generally V Thuronyi, *Comparative Tax Law* (The Hague, Kluwer Law International, 2003); also see H Ault et al, *Comparative Income Taxation: A Structural Analysis* (The Hague, Kluwer Law International, 2004).

[3] See American Institute of Certified Public Accountants 'Guiding Principles for Tax Simplification; Tax Policy Concept Statement' (2002) 9 http://www.aicpa.org/interestareas/tax/resources/taxlegislationpolicy/advocacy/downloadabledocuments/tpcs%202%20-%20principles%20for%20tax%20simplification.pdf.

only in the language of the law. The drafting process involves a constant refinement of policy decisions. This is undertaken through the precise specification of tax policy during the drafting process. Therefore, the drafting process can be seen as the development of tax policy, which is inchoate at the beginning of the drafting process and fully realised only at the end of the process. Problems in existing legislation can arise from different sources: new tax policy choices; changes in the economy; improved techniques of tax avoidance, and earlier bad choices in policy, drafting and administration.[4]

The elements and principles of UK tax policy are:

— taxes should be efficient and support growth;
— taxes should be certain and predictable;
— taxes should be simple to understand and easy to comply with; and
— the tax system should be fair, reward work, support aspiration and ask the most from those who can most afford it.[5]

In other words the tax policy of the current government is to introduce a fair, rewarding and inspiring tax system promoting growth and cost-efficiency via the introduction of simple and understandable taxes introduced via predictable and certain legislation. If one were to analyse this from the point of view of drafting, the government requires drafters to regulate via legislation; as infrequently as possible (predictability and certainty); via accessible legislative texts (simple and understandable).

And so the super-goal of tax policy is to create a fair, rewarding and inspiring legal system. This is to be achieved by means of legislation as a tool for regulation. But taxation legislation must be certain, predictable, clear and understandable. Criteria of success of the regulation are economic growth, cost-efficiency of the measures and indicators showing citizen initiatives encouraged through taxation legislation. With these generic drafting instructions in the background of their specific ones, drafters start their analysis and the compilation of their legislative scheme.

ANALYSING THE PROPOSAL

Taxation policy is by definition complicated: it is spread over a variety of levels, it is sporadic and fragmented, it is ever-changing, and it is quite technical in nature. Detail is necessary but may detract from the main regulatory message that can be lost in the inevitably detailed provisions. This structure proves a challenge for most users: the tax professionals, the

[4] See RK Gordon and V Thuronyi, 'Tax Legislative Process' in V Thuronyi, *Tax Law Design and Drafting*, (International Monetary Fund, 1996) 1, 2.

[5] See HM Revenue and Customs, 'Creating a Simpler, Fairer Tax System' (15 Jan 2014) www.gov.uk/government/policies/creating-a-simpler-fairer-tax-system.

streetwise non-tax professionals and the lay persons. It is argued that tax complexity arises as a result of the organic development of the system that makes piecemeal reform difficult; as a result of governments' use of exogenous factors into the technical or objective system's design process; or as a result of the political costs of pursuing policy objectives openly thus leading to the covert use of the tax system.[6]

In order to address this complexity, even at the stage of analysis but perhaps more so at the design stage, the drafter focuses on two concerns: first, what must remain in primary legislation, what goes into delegated legislation, and what could be left to explanatory notes, policy documents or guidance; and second, how can the new legislative text fall into place within the existing complex legislative and regulatory framework. Let us begin with the first issue, that of arrangement.

DESIGNING THE LAW

Tax legislation is difficult to understand. The dilemma between placing provisions in primary or secondary legislation is always a balancing exercise between the constitutional need for increased parliamentary legitimacy for the introduction of new taxation obligations to citizens[7] and the need to strip the primary legislative text of unnecessary details that detract user attention from the gist of the regulatory message. It would be difficult to find support for exclusively delegated legislative solutions for taxation: apart from the constitutional aspect above, delegated legislation is by definition unapproachable to most users: this endangers citizen awareness of the new regulation, its implementation and ultimately the effectiveness of the regulation itself. But the length of detail required for most taxation laws render them prime candidates for unapproachable texts of technical detail at distasteful length. However, the need for lengthy analysis of new tax regimes, and the provision of numerous examples and scenarios of the application of taxation legislation is loud, and the practice would clearly serve approachability of legislation, as requested by policy-makers.

It is not usually considered appropriate to try to provide all the necessary details of tax legislation in the statute for reasons of accessibility; lack of the ability to foresee all the situations in which tax laws will be applied; and the need for flexibility often addressed by delegated legislation. And so, the answer to the problem lies in the extensive use of explanatory documents of various kinds that provide legislators, tax officials and taxpayers with an

[6] See M James, 'Tax Simplification: the Impossible Dream?' (2008) *British Tax Review* 392, 393.

[7] See D Morris, '"A Tax by any other Name": Some Thoughts on Money, Bills and other Taxing Measures: Part 1' (2001) 22 *Statute Law Review* 181, 205.

understanding of their purpose and intended operation. For example, the UK tax authorities issue extra-statutory concessions, explanatory booklets and statements of practice. Further guidance is offered by the Interpretation Act, at least for users who are aware of its existence and have access to it. And of course detailed explanatory notes are invaluable.

As for the smooth receipt of the new legislation by existing complex taxation laws, this does not differ much from other fields of legislation. Adherence to the local drafting style promotes compatibility between new and older laws. Holistic understanding of the tax law in its entirety allows for the identification of gaps, or overlaps, leading to the choice of the appropriate drafting tool: new legislation; amendment of the old legislation; or repeal and re-enactment. The use of solid terms and the avoidance of new terminology encourage certainty and understandability, but also compatibility. Good legislative quality fertilises effective taxation legislation. But what makes a tax law a good one? Thuronyi identifies the following criteria for a well drafted taxation law:

1. understandability, namely making the law easier to read and follow;
2. organisation, namely internal organisation of the law and its coordination with other tax laws;
3. effectiveness, namely the law's ability to enable the desired policy to be implemented; and
4. integration, namely consistency of the law with the legal system and drafting style of the country.[8]

These criteria are, of course, interrelated and overlapping. Organisation is important for understandability. Integration contributes to understandability. And all the criteria contribute to Thuronyi's notion of effectiveness. Moreover, Thuronyi's concepts play a different role in each of the first, second and third and fourth stages of drafting taxation legislation: as a prism of analysis of the drafting instruction they are relevant to stage two; as general concepts they direct the initial design of the draft in stage three; and of course as subjective drafting choices they are applied in stage four.

Understandability is an essential element of good taxation law. Complexity is the inherent weakness of legislation and it is much more pronounced in taxation legislation.[9] Identifying the sources of complexity of tax legislation is not simple. 'Neither tax simplification nor its mirror image, complexity, is

[8] See V Thuronyi, 'Drafting Tax Legislation' in *Tax Law Design and Drafting* vol 1 (International Monetary Fund, 1996) 1, 2 www.imf.org/external/pubs/nft/1998/tlaw/eng/ch3.pdf.

[9] But Donaldson argues that tax complexity is a necessary cost to providing an equitable taxing system: see SA Donaldson, 'The Easy Case Against Tax Simplification' (2003) 22 *Vancouver Tax Review* 645, 681; also see J Partlow, 'The Necessity of Complexity in the Tax System' (2013) 13 *Wyoming Law Review* 303, 306.

a concept that can be easily defined or measured'.[10] In December 2012 the Office of Tax Simplification made considerable advances in this field, and identified seven distinct indicators of complexity in taxation legislation, and of HMRC administrative or policy complexity.[11]

1. Legislative complexity;
   a. the number of sections and paragraphs;
   b. the number of pages of legislation in Tolley's 2011–12;
   c. the number of reliefs from OTS review;
   d. the number of Finance Acts (since 2000);
   e. the Gunning-Fog[12] readability index score;
2. HMRC guidance complexity;
3. Number of taxpayers impacted by the legislation;
4. Average ability of taxpayers involved in the area;
5. Avoidance risk;
6. Cost of compliance; and
7. HMRC operating costs.

The OTS index is used for the purposes of assessing existing legislation, draft legislation and as an evidence-based indication of which areas of tax legislation are considered to be particularly complex. The piece of legislation under review is given a 1–5 score for each of the individual indicators. The seven individual scores are all added up, and then divided by 150 to give a score out of 10, where 10 represents the most complicated tax area. Legislative complexity is scored differently by weighing up the individual factors to get a score out of 10, and then comparing this with the scores of other tax measures to grade it in a quintile so those in the 20 per cent highest score are given five, and the next 20 per cent are given four, and so on.

The index and its application are not for the faint-hearted. To start with, compiling it from what was a virgin field of methodological vacuum required innovation, progressiveness and boldness. But the result is undoubtedly excellent. The sources of complexity identified are indeed the most significant factors of complexity in legislation of any type, they are measurable and they lead to evidence-based grading on what has traditionally been an abstract concept. It is also worth noting that the awarding of a score in each type of complexity is not purely objective, thus allowing the mechanism a degree of subjectivity, which reflects the true nature of a phronetic legislative drafting. Of course, one could identify weaknesses in the index: and I presume the easiest one to identify would be the use of

[10] See EJ McCaffery, 'The Holy Grail of Tax Simplification' (1990) *Wisconsin Law Review* 1267, 1269.

[11] See OTS, 'The OTS Complexity Index' Fig 1 www.gov.uk/government/uploads/system/uploads/attachment_data/file/193493/ots_complexity_index_methodology_paper.pdf.

[12] This is a weighted average of the number of words per sentence, and the number of long words per sentence. An interpretation is that the text can be understood by someone who left full-time education at a later age than the index.

numbers of sections and paragraphs as elements of legislative complexity. It would be fair to state that a long simple text may be easier to understand compared with a short complex one: but it is equally fair to state that length of legislation is indeed a factor of complexity. And in any case in the index this is one out of five factors. And also it is one of the few measurable indicators of complexity anyway. It would be extremely interesting to see the index used further, and applied not just in taxation legislation but also beyond the field.[13] As it stands, it is an innovative tool that can lead to useful conclusions.

It is worth noting that the index has already developed into a version two.[14] The new version divides complexity into underlying, mainly policy and legislative, complexity and impact of complexity, mainly the cost of compliance to an individual taxpayer and the aggregated cost of compliance for all taxpayers. It is felt that this distinction can identify why a particular area has such a significant impact on taxpayers or HMRC; and reduces the double counting in the first iteration.[15] In version two these are sources of complexity:

1. Policy complexity:
   a. Number of exemptions plus the number of reliefs;
   b. The number of Finance Acts with changes (since 2000);
2. Legislative complexity:
   a. The Gunning-Fog readability index;
   b. Number of pages of legislation;
3. Operational complexity:
   a. Complexity of HMRC guidance;
   b. Complexity of information requirement to make a return, namely difficulty in gathering the information required for the taxpayer to meet their obligation.

The new version of the index does not include resource complexity indicators. It amends a few of the existing indicators: for example 1a has been expanded to include the number of reliefs. The 'number of sections and paragraphs' in the original index is discarded as it was decided entirely by the number of pages of legislation (which creates double counting). For the resource complexity indicators, cost of compliance and HMRC cost has

[13] But the Office of Parliamentary Counsel produced its own document with sources of complexity in 2013, and these do not coincide; see www.gov.uk/government/uploads/system/uploads/attachment_data/file/187015/GoodLaw_report_8April_AP.pdf.

[14] See OTS, 'The OTS Complexity Index—Version 2' www.gov.uk/government/uploads/system/uploads/attachment_data/file/250995/ots_complexity_index_version2.pdf.

[15] See D Ulph, 'Measuring Tax Complexity' (2013) www.gov.uk/government/uploads/system/uploads/attachment_data/file/193497/ots_david_ulph_measuring_tax_complexity.pdf; also see R Baron, 'Thoughts on the OTS December 2012 Document on a Complexity Index' (2013) www.gov.uk/government/uploads/system/uploads/attachment_data/file/193498/ots_richard_baron_complexity_index.pdf.

been aggregated into a single figure. It also offers quite extensive guidance as to what measurable criteria scorers should take into account. The use of numbers of sections and paragraphs is retained but with a comment that ideally one should count words. But the real innovation of the second version lies in the OTS' holistic approach to taxation legislation: the OTS' 2014 paper declares that complexity, albeit evil, cannot always be addressed by means of legislative drafting. Alternative or additional measures to combat complexity include a changing to the policy objective; the simplification of the business situation or transaction involved; or creating avoidance or non-compliance where additional complexity could have prevented it.[16]

The index is being developed further. But even at this stage it can be an immensely useful tool for identifying the causes of complexity of specific taxation legislative texts, and finding means to address them. Of course one could think of ways to improve this structure. For example, adding user testing exercises could offer the index an added safety net of accuracy in its results. But in legislation nothing is perfect. One must therefore embrace the admirable innovation of the index, and use it at length as a means of confirming it or improving it further.

Leaving the index aside, and coming back to understandability, it is quite interesting to address the issue of brevity or length in taxation legislation. It is questionable whether length is directly linked to complexity. Although one suspects that the longer a sentence the more complex it becomes, there have been few user-based studies related to the length of the legislative text as a whole. The length of sentences in the English legal system has been the subject of debate from linguistics and discourse analysis experts. Tiersma and Solan report that Hiltunen reports an average of about 45.04 words per sentence; whereas Kurzon reports a steady decline over the 20-year period 1970–90 from 92.50 (1970) and 45.06 (1980) to 37.06 (1990) words per sentence: these point to the conclusion that 'a trend towards shorter sentences is nevertheless apparent'.[17] The OTS' interim report on tax relief stated that volume of legislation does not necessarily lead to complexity, or the clarity and ease with which legislation can be interpreted and applied.[18] The rewritten Acts of the Tax Law Rewrite Project[19] amounted to 2413 pages of legislation, significantly increasing the length of legislation, but the use of plain language led to a more understandable text at least for those new to tax. And so length may well be an indicator of complexity but it

[16] See G Jones, P Rice, J Sherwood and J Whiting, 'Developing a Tax Complexity Index for the UK' www.gov.uk/government/uploads/system/uploads/attachment_data/file/285944/OTS_Developing_a_Tax_Complexity_Index_for_the_UK.pdf.

[17] See PM Tiersma and LM Solan, *The Oxford Handbook of Language and Law* (Oxford, Oxford University Press, 2012) 41.

[18] See OTS, 'Review of Tax Reliefs: Interim Report' (Dec 2010) www.hm-treasury.gov.uk/d/ots_review_tax_reliefs_interim_report.pdf.

[19] Capital Allowances Act 2001, Income Tax (Earnings and Pensions) Act 2003, Income Tax (Trading and Other Income) Act 2005, Income Tax Act 2007, Corporation Tax Act 2009, Corporation Tax Act 2010 and Taxation (International and Other Provisions) Act 2010.

does not necessarily signify complexity.[20] After all, going back to the pyramid of values in chapter one, clarity is a contributing factor to effectiveness along with precision and unambiguity: brevity does not feature there at all.

Staying with complexity, another contributing factor is transparency. A transparent statute is one that allows the user access to the rationale of the necessity of the legislative texts, and to the basic rules that it introduces. Linking policy to legislation is never easy: current mentality or processes see the two as divided by a huge canyon whose passing is not even afforded to the whole of the drafting team.[21] This may stem from the confidentiality of government policy documents. But modern legislative drafting requires that policies are revealed out in the open: this is viewed not as a generous pass to the prohibited canyon of confidential government policy but as a necessity for the effectiveness of the resulting legislative text, which must be drafted by drafters aware of the policy that they are expressing and implemented by users aware of why the new rules have come into play and what function they serve. In other words, modern thinking is that citizen behaviour is easier changed if the rationale behind the new demands is clearly explained and conveyed to them. The difficulty with taxation legislation is that the policy is harsh and unattractive: government introduces taxes to amass income rather than to offer services, but of course services cannot be offered without the amassed income. Harsh or not, government policy must be shared with the drafters and the users in a sincere and concretely measurable manner, as a means of testing the effectiveness of the legislative text. A concrete long title would go a long way in conveying the main mechanism of law reform, but an objectives or purpose clause with concrete measurable criteria for effectiveness would both convey the concrete policy goals and would serve as criteria of pre- and post-legislative scrutiny.

And this leads to effectiveness in its broader sense of contribution to the production of the desired regulatory results, rather than Thuronyi's narrow implementation notion. Ultimately, the effectiveness of taxation legislation lies with the number of taxpayers applying the new rules, the extent of compliance, the nature of statutory interpretation, the need for delegated legislation and amendments and the achievement of the concrete regulatory results introduced in the purpose clause of the law. Studies have shown that simplified tax legislation leads to a positive response for both novice and expert users, with the experts experiencing a more positive effect than the novices.[22] At this point it is worth remembering that purpose clauses have

[20] See OTS, 'Length of Tax Legislation as a Measure of Complexity' www.gov.uk/government/uploads/system/uploads/attachment_data/file/193496/ots_length_legislation_paper.pdf; also see JF Avery Jones, 'Tax Law: Rules or Principles?' (1996) 17 *Fiscal Studies* 63.

[21] On the abstract nature of tax policy, see P Kirchhof, 'Die Kunst der Steuergesetzgebung' (1987) 51 *Neue Juristische Wochenschrift* 3217, 3218.

[22] See R Woellner, C Coleman, M McKerchar, M Walpole and J Zetler 'Can Simplified Legal Drafting Reduce the Psychological Costs of Tax Compliance? An Australian Perspective' (2007) 6 *British Tax Review* 717, 717.

acquired a new role in pre- and post-legislative scrutiny, and that these require a complete re-think of their content and the manner in which they are drafted. Modern purpose clauses can facilitate an evidence-based decision on the utility of the legislative text, leading to an informed view on their review and ultimately sunsetting, if they are found to be ineffective.

Effectiveness requires that the drafter precipitate the application and statutory interpretation of the legislative text.[23] In other words, when drafting taxation legislation, the drafter is aware of the complex legislative and generally regulatory framework within which the legislative texts function. Taxation legislation is a field of law where clashing or parallel provisions are easily traced in the myriad of relevant texts, where complex notions meet voluminous legislative texts. Being aware of consequential amendments and repeals is anything but an easy task, and specialist policy officers and drafters need to depart from their own training, submerge to a lay user level, and guess what provisions may cause undesirable application or interpretation owing to the lack of tax expertise for users and, to a degree, judges. Ambiguity is never excused of course. But vagueness may come to the drafter's rescue, especially in pursuit of flexibility for the tax administration to respond to unanticipated cases.[24] For example, when drafting an income tax, one could list all the types of deductible business expenses: this would provide certainty, but not flexibility. It is better to provide a general rule, such as that all expenses incurred in the realisation of income subject to tax are deductible, with specified limitations. This general provision can be further specified by examples either in the legislation, following the Australian example, or in explanatory notes and policy guidance.

Ultimately, the pyramid of drafting virtues in chapter one applies here too: the tax drafter pursues effectiveness, by means of clarity, precision and unambiguity. Plain language and gender-neutral language are tools to get there.

INITIAL DESIGN

Keeping these principles in mind, the tax drafter proceeds with the initial design of the legislative text. Having decided what is to be placed in the primary legislation,[25] having identified streams of effectiveness, and having discussed main areas of concern for complexity, understandability, brevity and transparency, the drafter now looks into the initial draft of the design. There is nothing novel in designing a tax law: structure does not and should not differ from the structure of any legislative text.

[23] On the cautious approach to statutory interpretation of taxation legislation, see N Lee 'A Purposive Approach to Tax Statutes?' (1999) 20 *Statute Law Review* 124, 143.

[24] See J Sherwood, 'Tax Thresholds and Ceilings—the Numbers Game' (Dec 2012) www.gov.uk/government/uploads/system/uploads/attachment_data/file/193494/ots_tax_threshold_paper.pdf.

[25] See H Xanthaki, *Thornton's Legislative Drafting* (West Sussex, Bloomsbury Professional, 2013) 357.

And so grouping together relevant provisions on the same subdivision of the statute is helpful. This can be followed with any exceptions and special rules for particular cases. The extensive use of Schedules, especially Keeling Schedules, is commendable as it allows the drafter to keep the text short and free from details. The clear and precise introduction of powers and the proper use of delegated legislation are also crucial.

But taxation legislation is a prime example of a field of law where the use of the layered approach would be extremely beneficial. Having identified three main groups of users of legislation by means of user testing,[26] drafters can now begin to speak to each and every group separately. In other words, taxation legislation would be a prime candidate for a layered approach. This is supported by the fact that the introduction of the term is attributed to John Whiting, of the OTS. My approach to a layered text would be to accommodate three parts within the same legislative text with all parts being part of primary legislation. Part one would be addressed to lay users and in simple language would convey to them the main mechanism of law reform via a concrete long title, the objectives of the legislation via a concrete list of objectives with measurable criteria of achievement of the regulatory results, and the main regulatory message with clear instructions on what the rights and obligations of users are, and exactly what needs to be done to comply with them. Part two would be addressed to tax professionals with a language along the lines of current legislative language, with answers to questions on what is new, and how they are expected to comply and facilitate compliance of others. And part three would be addressed to tax specialists, tax lawyers and judges addressing issues of procedure, consequential amendments, transitional provisions (those not necessary for parts one and two) and other technical tax and legal details. This layered text would benefit from concrete explanatory notes highlighting the interconnection between parts and the relationship between this and pre-existing texts. Examples of profiles using and applying the new text would be extremely helpful. And policy documents and guidance would apply this even further.

DRAFTING

Irrespective of structure, drafting taxation legislation is indeed a difficult task that requires a purist drafter. Avoiding technical language needs to be balanced with the need to comply with widely accepted terminology. For example, concepts such as corporation, partnership, employee, contract and

[26] On the Good Law project, see www.gov.uk/good-law; also see 'Findings of User Testing of Legislative Texts: Results from Bunnyfoot of the Project Undertaken by The National Archives and OPC into Users of Legislation and how they Respond to Different Drafting and Presentational Approaches' https://bigdataforlaw.kahootz.com/gf2.ti/f/425314/11840293.1/PDF//TNA_OPC_legislation_study_user_testing_report_BF1481_v1.5.pdf.

mortgage are well defined by laws outside the tax laws, and it is appropriate to use these words rather than simpler words that might be more understandable to lay persons.

With frequent amendments comes the inevitable complexity of numbering heavily amended tax laws. Renumbering, an undisputed cause of ambiguity, is avoided by inserting new sections between the existing sections. However, this can lead to bizarre and confusing designations for sections. It is interesting to note the non-sequential numbering of the US Internal Revenue Code: this involves leaving a gap in section numbering between each division of the statute; if new sections are added, they can be named by using the unused section numbers. But of course this is of questionable effectiveness: what difference would it make to the user if the provision between 12 and 20 is designated as 13 or 12 bis?

Taxation legislation is plagued with numerous and often clashing definitions introduced by the same or various legislative texts, the Interpretation Act or even court judgments. Moreover, taxation definitions tend to refer not only to the whole Act, but they are part or section specific. The problem of definitions in taxation legislation is so pronounced that they were one of the focuses of the Tax Law Rewrite Project.[27] The elements of a good taxation definition as identified by the OTS are: clarity; focus on essential features; the use of an existing definition where possible; avoidance of circularity; avoidance of figurative or obscure language; and being affirmative rather than negative.[28] There is little to indicate that a tax drafter departs from good practices of drafting definitions in other fields of legislation: the only difference is that taxation legislation does not allow for mistakes. Difficult concepts require balancing between technical terms familiar to the practitioners[29] with simple language benefiting lay users. An index of tax definitions is considered a welcome innovation.[30] Perhaps a simplistic approach to the problem would be to invite the tax drafter to pitch the definition, and the language of the whole text, to the level of specialisation of the main bulk of users: personal income legislation calls for much simpler language when compared with corporation tax.

In principle, it is worth knowing that 'tax' describes both the process of levying money for government purposes and the money raised via this

[27] See Tax Law Rewrite 'The Way Forward' Annex 1: Guidelines for the Rewrite, www.hmrc.gov.uk/rewrite/wayforward/tlra1.htm.

[28] See M Scott and C Turnbull-Hall, 'Definitions in Tax Legislation and their Contribution to Complexity' (Sept 2013) www.gov.uk/government/uploads/system/uploads/attachment_data/file/246081/ots_review_of_definitions_in_tax_legislation.pdf, 28–29.

[29] See A Broke, 'Simplification of Tax or I Wouldn't Start from Here' (2000) 1 *British Taw Review* 18, 21.

[30] See OTS, 'Summary of Responses to the Report "Definitions in Tax Legislation and their Contribution to Complexity"' www.gov.uk/government/uploads/system/uploads/attachment_data/file/300384/OTS_definitions_project_summary_of_responses.pdf.

process.[31] 'Duty' signifies money raised by the customs and excise[32] from importation of goods into the country (import duty); from exportation of goods; from goods manufactured locally (excise duty); or from the estates of deceased persons (estate duty). 'Rate' refers to a tax raised for the purposes of local authorities, typically on the value of immovable property (rateable value) and payable annually in a lump sum or in instalments. 'Cess' is a tax raised for the purposes of local authorities. 'Toll' is a tax imposed on the use of roads. 'Levy' describes a tax authorised to be raised by subsidiary legislation for specific purposes.

The rate of tax can be expressed as a percentage of the value (eg income tax); or a fixed sum imposed by reference to a measurement, such as per weight, per volume, per time unit (eg petrol tax); or a sum related directly to the subject matter of the tax (eg poll tax); or as a set annual amount (eg vehicle excise duty).

The identification of the persons liable to pay tax depends on the nature of the tax. But it is the duty of the drafter to state clearly who is liable to pay the tax. The user of 'whoever' or 'those to whom this Act applies' is inadequate as a term expressing the circle of subjects of taxation provisions. Similarly, passive voice is inadequate.

A similar level of clarity is required for the determination of the moment in time where liability to pay tax arises. This can be an activity (eg the earning of a salary); or an event (eg death or a purchase). Either way this must be clearly introduced.

And the drafter must also foresee the moment in time when the tax is payable. This may coincide or differ from the moment in time when the tax liability arises. Tax may be payable when the liability to tax arises; or before (eg airport tax paid at the time of ticket issuance before the flight takes place); or after the moment in time where the tax liability arises (eg income tax is paid on an annual basis after the earning of a salary).

Any exemptions from payment must also be foreseen clearly, and indeed it is preferable to introduce them in the Act under the general rule. Unfortunately, in practice these are often left to delegated legislation: here convenience and flexibility overrides clarity.

The administrative arrangements for the collection of tax must be clearly introduced also. They can be expressed either as instructions of payment in part one of the layered text, or as administrative procedures in part two, if they are not relevant to lay users. When introducing the same arrangements as is the norm in the jurisdiction, the drafter balances brevity in

[31] See H Spitzer 'Taxes vs. Fees: A Curious Confusion' (2002–03) 38 *Gonzaga Law Review* 335, 357; also see OECD, 'Definition of Taxes' (Paris, 1996) www.oecd.org/daf/mai/pdf/eg2/eg2963e.pdf.

[32] See HM Revenue and Customs, *Excise Duty—Index* www.hmrc.gov.uk/briefs/excise-duty/index.htm.

avoiding repetition of existing provisions in existing legislation with clarity in repeating the same arrangements within the specific Act: there is scope for repetition if arrangements are addressed to lay users, as cross referencing creates complexity and inhibits effectiveness.

Offences and penalties may also be necessary for non-payment; partial payment; late payment; failure to account; false or misleading returns; tax avoidance; tax evasion; or obstruction of inspectors. Here the tax drafter resorts to the general principles for drafting criminal provisions.

VERIFICATION

The last stage in the drafting process is the verification of the legislative text. This is an opportune moment to discuss verification in brief. Drafts need to be verified as a means of achieving quality. Verification takes place internally, namely within the drafting team, and externally, namely by other interested departments and affected agencies. Scrutiny of the legislative text should be a continuous process throughout the drafting, particularly to improve its clarity and to check its practicability.

It is best practice to subject each version of a draft to scrutiny of legal form, clarity and comprehensibility. At the end of drafting, the final version of the law must be scrutinised on a wider range of matters, including a series of legal verifications.

And so each draft is checked for legal form, clarity and comprehensibility. This includes checks for compliance with house style on form, structure and layout; compliance with standard language usages, with comprehensibility and unambiguity; compliance with structural requirements for a logical ordering of the provisions facilitating clarity; and consistency with existing terminology. At the final stage additional legal verification checks also include checks for constitutional and legal compliance; compliance with international and regional treaties and their deriving obligations; and controls of effectiveness in the implementation mechanisms.

Legal verification checks include checks for compliance with the constitution, and in particular the norms that guarantee individual rights and freedoms; compliance with higher levels of law (eg that delegated legislation is consistent with primary legislation); and consistency with existing laws and procedures. A specific area of focus is the increasing use of retrospective taxation legislation. It is argued that tax laws made effective from the date of the budget announcement are probably in compliance with the constitutional principle of the rule of law; but tax laws made retrospective prior to any announcement 'grossly violate the minimum requirements of the rule of law'.[33]

[33] See GT Loomer, 'Taxing Out of Time: Parliamentary Supremacy and Retroactive Tax Legislation' (2006) *British Tax Review* 64, 90.

Implementation controls check that the text introduces adequate and effective operation provisions, with specific focus on mechanisms for the production of the desired regulatory results. Here mechanisms ensuring compliance are of prime importance. Moreover, implementation, enforcement and adjudication procedures must be fair, consistent, transparent, non-discriminatory and able to produce the desired regulatory results. Emphasis must also be placed on the verification of powers transferred via enabling clauses: the precise Minister must be determined concretely, the nature of the exercise of the awarded power as compulsory or optional must be clearly expressed, deadlines for the exercise of compulsory power must be clearly introduced and the elements of the power clearly described.

USE OF CODE

In view of the multitude of issues to be foreseen in tax legislation, one wonders whether codification or consolidation is fertile as a tool for clarity. The use of a taxation code facilitates the elimination of duplicative provisions. Lack of a code allows for possible ambiguities as definitions or administrative provisions repeated in separate laws may differ. Even consolidation of common provisions presents advantages for taxation legislation, as it facilitates rationalisation; it identifies general principles of taxation law carrying the main overarching regulatory messages of taxation policy and law;[34] and it ultimately promotes compliance via Thuronyi's understandability, organisation, effectiveness and integration.

The Tax Law Rewrite Project went a long way in consolidating taxation legislation in the UK. And equally so in Australia and New Zealand.[35] But, avid a supporter as one may be, the issue of complexity of taxation legislation remains. There is little doubt that complexity is inherent in tax law. The question is what antidote there is for this complex policy and law: the OTS has paved the way, but of course there is always more that can be done.[36]

[34] See R Gordon, 'Law of Tax Administration and Procedure' in V Thuronyi, *Tax Law Design and Drafting* vol 1 (International Monetary Fund, 1996) www.imf.org/external/pubs/nft/1998/tlaw/eng/ch4.pdf.

[35] See S James, A Sawyer and I Wallschutzky, 'The Complexities of Tax Simplification: Progress in Australia, New Zealand and the United Kingdom' (1998) 14 *Australian Tax Forum* 29.

[36] See A Sawyer, 'New Zealand's Tax Rewrite Program—in Pursuit of the (Elusive) Goal of Simplicity' (2007) 8 *British Tax Review* 405, 426.

17

Extra-territorial Legislation

TERRITORIALITY AND EXTRA-TERRITORIALITY are notions of international law. International law regulates the boundaries of a state. In principle, these coincide with its jurisdictional boundaries.[1] As a rule, a sovereign legislature[2] legislates in exclusivity[3] over the area over which it has authority.[4] This area covers the land mass and internal waters of the state; plus the territorial waters and the seabed beneath; and the airspace over both of the above.[5]

Of course this is no hard and fast rule. Exceptions to it have long been recognised in international and national laws. So both the common law, international custom and international agreements have extended the jurisdictional territory of states[6] to specific locations, such as the embassy of the state abroad, or to specific subjects or objects, such as the ships carrying the flag of the state, or to special status holders, such as diplomats or the military stationed abroad. This extension of jurisdictional territoriality can be permanent or it can address a short-term need. For example, the American hospital where the Dutch monarch was born was declared Dutch territory on a short-term basis thus ensuring that the monarch would acquire uniquely Dutch nationality as being born technically on Dutch soil. The topic has been the subject of lengthy analysis in international law literature,

[1] See S Elden, 'Contingent Sovereignty, Territorial Integrity and the Sanctity of Borders' (2006) 26 *School of Advanced International Study Review* 11, 11; also see J Agnew, 'Sovereignty Regimes: Territoriality and State Authority in Contemporary World Politics' (2005) 95 *Annual Association of American Geographers* 437, 437; G Lindell and Sir A Mason, 'The Resolution of Inconsistent State and Territory Legislation' (2010) 38 *Federal Law Review* 390.

[2] For the link between sovereignty and extra-territoriality, see *SS Lotus (France v Turkey)* PCIJ Rep 1927, Series A, No 10.

[3] See HG Maier, 'Resolving Extraterritorial Conflicts, or "There and Back Again"' (1984) 25 *Vanderbilt Journal of International Law* 7, 11.

[4] See M Akehurst, 'Jurisdiction in International Law' (1978) 46 *British Yearbook of International Law* 145, 179; also see WLM Reese, 'Legislative Jurisdiction' (1978) 78 *Columbia Law Review* 1587, 1587.

[5] The concept is based on the Treaty of Westphalia: see L Gross, 'The Peace of Westphalia 1648-1948' (1948) 42 *American Journal of International Law* 20, 28–29; also see K Raustiala, 'The Geography of Justice' (2005) 73 *Fordham Law Review* 2501, 2508.

[6] See AM Weisburd, 'Due Process Limits on Federal Extraterritorial Legislation?' (1997) 35 *Columbia Journal of Transnational Law* 379, 383.

and it touches upon drafting in circumstances where drafting instructions call for a departure from the rule of territoriality. As this is an increasingly frequent phenomenon,[7] this chapter aims to address extra-territoriality in legislation both extending jurisdictional boundaries abroad but also responding to extra-territorial laws imposed by foreign jurisdictions.

Despite the increasing challenges to territoriality, the presumption remains that laws made in one state do not extend to have effect abroad.[8] In other words, the presumption remains for territorial application of laws,[9] and against the extra-territorial operation of legislation.[10] It is worth noting here that the debate concerns legislation: the extra-territorial operation of the common law seems to be accepted widely since the common law with its reference to general principles is suited for international application.[11]

But before proceeding further with this, it is necessary to identify what is the meaning of the term extra-territoriality. The term signifies the exercise of jurisdiction by a state legislature beyond the geographical boundaries of state, as determined in international law. Extra-territoriality covers two types of laws. First, legislation that regulates the conduct of nationals abroad:[12] the most obvious example of extra-territorial legislation is taxation legislation that applies to own nationals irrespective of whether they reside within the geographical boundaries of the state of nationality or not. The second category of extra-territorial legislation refers to laws that apply to non-nationals outside the territory of the legislating country.[13] An example could be an extra-territorial provision on human trafficking extending the jurisdiction of the national authorities to prosecute and try human trafficking undertaken abroad by offenders of foreign nationality. In the first category of legislation one can identify the link, and relative legitimacy, of the regulation: by a choice of their nationality, own nationals are subjected to taxation legislation. In the second category of extra-territorial

[7] See Joint Committee on Foreign Affairs and Defence, Commonwealth of Australia, 'Australian—United States Relations: The Extraterritorial Application of United States Laws' (1983) http://webpac.auinfo.gov.au; also see PB Stephan, 'A Becoming Modesty—U.S. Litigation in the Mirror of International Law' (2002) 52 *DePaul Law Review* 627, 650–56.

[8] See AJ Colangelo, 'Constitutional Limits on Extraterritorial Jurisdiction: Terrorism and the Intersection of National and International law' (2007) 48 *Harvard International Law Journal* 121, 126.

[9] See TR Holbrook, 'Is the Supreme Court Poised to Assess the Extraterritorial Scope of US Patent Law?' (2014) 36 *European Intellectual Property Review* 212, 213.

[10] See W Estey, 'The Five Bases of Extraterritorial Jurisdiction and the Failure of the Presumption against Extraterritoriality' (1997–98) 21 *Hastings International and Comparative Law Review* 177, 178.

[11] See JA Meyer, 'Extraterritorial Common Law: Does the Common Law Apply Abroad?' (2013–14) 102 *The Georgetown Law Journal* 301, 307.

[12] See JA Meyer, 'Dual Illegality and Geoambiguous Law: A New Rule for Extraterritorial Application of US Law' (2011) 95 *Minnesota Law Review* 110, 123.

[13] See L Brilmayer and C Norchi, 'Federal Extraterritoriality and Fifth Amendment Due Process' (1992) 105 *Harvard Law Review* 1217, 1218.

legislation there is no visible link of choice: it seems that it is the universality of condemnation of human trafficking as a behaviour that is used as the link between foreign offenders acting abroad and the national legal system.

One can see why extra-territorial legislation is a controversial category of law.[14] Especially if one takes into account the inevitable trespassing of the legislating jurisdiction onto the existing and now clashing sphere of regulation and legislation from the geographically and jurisdictionally sovereign state on the land in which the activity was undertaken. Such is the unease of the international community with this inevitable clash that the extension of jurisdiction abroad is classed as an extra-territorial assertion of jurisdiction against, or within, the jurisdictional boundaries of another sovereign legislature. The legitimacy of this assertion, the requirement for an agreement of both jurisdictions involved, and the inevitable necessity of prioritisation of jurisdiction are burdened further by the relatively recent assertion of jurisdiction to regional or international legislatures. And so there is not only a clash between the home and legislating jurisdiction, there is the added complication of regional and international jurisdiction as a third legislating sphere.[15] On top of this, and perhaps more relevant to the legislative debate, regulation via extra-territorial legislation gives rise to concerns of bad regulation via fragmentation of the legislative tools used.[16]

THE THEORY OF EXTRA-TERRITORIALITY: REALISM, LIBERALISM AND BEYOND

International law theory presents conflicting approaches on the phenomenon of extra-territoriality. The traditional realist framework views states as opaque billiard balls[17] operating in a world of strictly national borders.[18] For the realist each state, and consequently, each jurisdiction, has well-defined

[14] Yet, Europe, for example, 'has come very close in a number of cases to exceeding its generally restrained methods'. See E Jardine, 'An Agreement between Australia and the European Union on Trade Practices: a Proposal' (1996) 4 *Trade Practices Law Journal* 67, 67.

[15] See P Schiff Berman, 'Global Legal Pluralism' (2007) 80 *South California Law Review* 1155, 1168; also see P Schiff Berman, 'The Globalization of Jurisdiction' (2002) 151 *University of Pennsylvania Law Review* 311, 329.

[16] See A Parrish, 'The Effects Test: Extraterritoriality's Fifth Business' (2008) 61 *Vanderbilt Law Review* 1455, 1490.

[17] See A Wolfers, *Discord and Collaboration: Essays on International Politics* (Baltimore, the Johns Hopkins Press, 1962) 19–24.

[18] See TJ Biersteker, 'State, Sovereignty and Territory' in W Carlsnaes et al, *Handbook of International Relations* (London, Sage, 2002) 157, 167; also see K Raustiala, 'The Evolution of Territoriality: International Relations and American Law' in M Kahler and BF Walter, *Territoriality and Conflict in an Era of Globalisation* (San Diego, University of California, 2006) 219, 220, 234–48; JG Ruggie, 'Territoriality and Beyond: Problematizing Modernity in International Relations' (1993) 47 *International Organisations* 139, 148; S Sassen, 'Territory and Territoriality in the Global Economy' (2000) 15 *International Society* 372, 373.

and impenetrable borders: inverting these borders as an unacceptable as extending them beyond their opaque definiteness. And so, a realist would find impossible to justify legislation regulating events that take place beyond state borders. To a realist legislation is necessarily and inherently subject to a presumption of territoriality. For the realist the classification of an action as lawful or unlawful can only be determined by the law of the jurisdiction where the action took place. And so, legislation is presumptively construed to be confined in its operation and effect to the territorial limits over which the legislature has general and legitimate power.

At the other end of the spectrum lies the liberal perspective. This banishes the concepts of territoriality and power. If realists focus on states as monolithic entities in their interaction with other states within an anarchic international system, liberals focus primarily on state society relations.[19] Universality and internationality is the name of a liberal's world. For some authors the notion that law should be tied to territory is an archaic remnant of a pre-globalised world.[20] State borders and jurisdictional boundaries play little role in the liberal agenda.[21] Instead of boundaries, interest is the focus of the liberal inquiry into jurisdictional space and extent. The state acts as the agent of individual and group interests.[22] The use of interest as a central notion for the delineation of jurisdictional power is a rather concerting concept. Whereas state boundaries are indeed opaque and, in principle, agreed as acceptable between states, interest can be self-introduced, self-declared and perhaps more worryingly self-exercised. Interest is such a vague term that it could be used by male fide states to exert legislative power over foreign nations without, or even against, their will. In other words, interest can be usurped to theorise or justify unilateral exertions of legislative territoriality within an as yet judicially unregulated international environment. But thankfully the notion of interest is not as arbitrary or vague as one could have feared.

The concept of interest in the liberal agenda is specified by means of the 'effects test'.[23] In the *Alcoa* case Judge Learned Hand interpreted effect

[19] See A-M Slaughter, 'International Law in a World of Liberal States' (1995) 6 *European Journal of International Law* 503, 508.

[20] See GB Born, 'A Reappraisal of the Extraterritorial Reach of US Law' (1992) 24 *Law and Policy in International Business* 1, 61–79; also see L Kramer, 'Vestiges of Beale: Extraterritorial Application of American Law' (1991) 501 *Supreme Court Review* 179, 184; A-M Slaughter, 'Liberal International Relations Theory and International Economic Law' (1995) 10 *American Journal of International Law and Policy* 717, 736; A-M Slaughter and DT Zaring, 'Extraterritoriality in a Globalized World' http://papers.ssrn.com/sol3/papers.cfm?abstractid=39380.

[21] See PS Berman, 'Dialectical Regulation, Territoriality, and Pluralism' (2006) 38 *Connecticut Law Review* 929, 932–38.

[22] See D Post, 'The "Unsettled Paradox": The Internet, the State, and the Consent of the Governed' (1998) 5 *Indiana Journal of Global Legal Studies* 521, 523.

[23] See WS Dodge, 'Extraterritoriality and Conflicts-of-Laws Theory: An Argument for Judicial Unilateralism' (1998) 39 *Harvard International Law Journal* 101, 141, 154.

as 'an effect to national commerce': a state's extra-territorial law-making power can be imposed on conduct that was intended to and did have an effect on national commerce.[24] The Third Restatement of American Foreign Relations Law confirms that a state may prescribe law in regard to extra-territorial conduct that has or is intended to have a substantial effect[25] within the state's territory or is directed against certain state interests, as long as its exercise of such jurisdiction is not unreasonable.[26] If one analyses these two famous statements of effect, one can identify three criteria for legitimacy of interest as used in the liberal agenda. First, the interest in question must affect the national commerce of the legislating jurisdiction: this is a factual criterion, and is therefore objectively provable by means of financial or statistical evidence of harm to national commerce. This criterion is now extended to non-commercial interests that are specific in nature: this excludes political or ideological motivation behind extra-territorial legislative action. Secondly, the effect on national commerce must be substantial and foreseeable:[27] this is a qualitative criterion, which is provable by means of qualitative or quantitative evidence demonstrating proportionality between the effect on national commerce and the legislative measure taken in response. Thirdly, the exercise of extra-territoriality must not be unreasonable: this is another qualitative criterion, which introduces a third sub-test, that of reasonableness.[28] Reasonableness is assessed on the basis of eight different factors including the closeness of the link between the regulated activity and the legislating state, the character of the regulated activity, and the likelihood of conflict with existing foreign regulation.[29] And so, even within the liberal framework extra-territoriality is defensible only if the legislative measure can pass the test of a substantial effect to commerce or other specific interest; the test of proportionality; and the test of reasonableness. Still, Slaughter suggests that the application of liberal

[24] See 148 F 2d 416 (2nd Cir, 1945); also see *United States v Sisal Sales Corp*, 274 U.S. 268 (1927); *United States v Aluminum Co of America* ('*Alcoa*'), 148 F.2d 416 (2d Cir 1945) (L Hand J).

[25] See L Kramer, 'Extraterritorial Application of American Law after the Insurance Antitrust Case: A Reply to Professors Lowenfeld and Trimble' (1995) 89 *American Journal of International Law* 750, 751.

[26] See Restatement (Third) of the Law: The Foreign Relations Law of the United States (1987), 402, 403 and 415.

[27] See R Weintraub, 'The Extraterritorial Application of Antitrust and Securities Laws: An Inquiry into the Utility of a Choice-of-Law Approach' (1992) 70 *Texas Law Review* 1799, 1825.

[28] Lowenfeld professes that US law should apply extra-territorially only if it is reasonable under the concept of international comity regardless of any effect in the US: see A Lowenfeld, 'Public Law in the International Arena: Conflicts of Laws, International Law, and Some Suggestions for Their Interaction' (1979) 163 *Recueil des Cours* 311, 373.

[29] See DB Massey 'How the American Law Institute Influences Customary Law: the Reasonableness Requirement of the Restatement of Foreign Relations Law' (1997) 22 *Yale Journal of International Law* 419, 427.

theory to questions of extra-territoriality is likely to result in something 'closer to a presumption of extra-territoriality than a presumption of territoriality'. In other words the effects test should reverse the presumption of territoriality.[30]

There is little doubt in in our era of globalisation and legal globalisation jurisdictional boundaries have lost much of their opaqueness.[31] There is little doubt that this has become necessary as a result of globalised phenomena that require globalised solutions. A prime example of that is cross-border crime such as human trafficking or money laundering. There is no point in hiding behind jurisdictional boundaries in the combat against these phenomena, when the only effective legislative option requires cross-border cooperation and cross-jurisdictional solutions. And so, territoriality seems to have lost its attractiveness in specific applications relating to cross-border regulatory demands. But at the same time the effects test is inherently undemocratic,[32] since it provides a source of sovereignty foreign to the consent of the regulated.[33] So does a rejection of territoriality lead necessarily to a presumption of extra-territoriality?

Or is non-territoriality or a-territoriality a plausible solution? The reach of legislation is confined and bounded ultimately by the network of those who have participated in its adoption and consented to its application. If that network is itself bound or defined by physical geography, the presumption of territorial reach and the power of the territorial agent are well-founded. But where the network of those who participated in the adoption of legislation crosses geographical borders, then so will the legislation itself. Let us examine this argument from a constitutional perspective: the legislature is awarded authority to legislate by the group of people who recognise themselves as citizens of the state to which the legislature belongs. This community of people has organised itself in a state and has agreed to concede legislative power to the legislature that is the agreed agency for regulating via legislation.[34] And they offer exclusive authority to their legislature of choice to regulate them and their activities.[35] In

[30] See WS Dodge, 'Understanding the Presumption Against Extraterritoriality' (1998) 16 *Berkeley Journal of International Law* 85, 99.

[31] See AL Parrish, 'Reclaiming International Law from Extraterritoriality' (2008–09) 93 *Minnesota Law Review* 815, 817.

[32] See M Gibney and RD Emerick, 'The Extraterritorial Application of United States Law and the Protection of Human Rights: Holding Multinational Corporations to Domestic and International Standards' (1996) 10 *Temple International and Comparative Law Journal* 123, 133.

[33] See D Post, '"Against Cyberanarchy"' (2002) 17 *Berkeley Technology Law Journal* 1365, 1385.

[34] See DR Johnson and D Post, 'Law and Borders—The Rise of Law in Cyberspace' (1996) 48 *Stanford Law Review* 1367, 1369–70.

[35] See MD Rosen, 'The Surprisingly Strong Case for Tailoring Constitutional Principles' (2005) 153 *University of Pennsylvania Law Review* 1513, 1616.

contrast to this, foreigners have not offered authority to be regulated via extra-territorial legislation made abroad.[36] Normally this community has organised itself within a state, and its geographical extent coincides with state boundaries.[37] But if the community exceeds the boundaries of the state, legitimacy to regulate via legislation is conceded to the regional or international organisation formed by the regional or international community. This justifies and legitimises regional and international law accordingly. Where a community is formed by reference to a specific interest, for example the regulation of electrical power deriving from a river crossing the boundaries of three states, this community concedes power to the three states to regulate via cross-border legislation. This is a basis of a bilateral or multilateral agreement.[38] Now, if the specific interest of a community in one state concedes authority to regulate via legislation this interest located outside state boundaries, then what is needed is the formation of a new community that carries legitimacy to concede legislative power. One part of the new community is the community whose interests abroad are regulated; and the second part is the community of the location of the new regulation. The first needs to concede legislative power to regulate their interests by their legislature of origin, even though they would normally expect regulation to stem from the foreign legislature. And the second needs to concede legislative power to the legislating legislature, whose regulatory power they have not authorised by means of agreement in principle. In other words, extra-territorial legislation requires legitimacy from the own citizens and from the foreign citizens. Extra-territorial legislation is a departure from the norm, and its legitimacy hangs with either a bilateral legislative measure or a unilateral measure with inherent bilateral agreement.

EXTRA-TERRITORIALITY IN PRACTICE

In England criminal conduct outside a state's area of authority was quite simply without legal significance. This leads to a presumption of territoriality,[39] but there is no doubt that statute law can reverse this effect. But, in the absence of international agreement, the claim to exercise

[36] See JK Powell, 'Prohibitions on Campaign Contributions from Foreign Sources: Questioning Their Justification in a Global Interdependent Economy' (1996) 17 *University of Pennsylvania Journal of International Economic Law* 957.

[37] 'The authority and legitimacy of a majority to compel a minority exists only within political boundaries': see JHH Weiler, 'Does Europe Need a Constitution? Demos, Telos, and the German Maastricht Decision' (1995) 1 *European Law Journal* 219, 222.

[38] The EU seems to use extra-territoriality upon agreement with recipient states: see J Scott, 'Extraterritoriality and Territorial Extension in EU Law' (2014) 62 *American Journal of Comparative Law* 87, 87.

[39] See GR Sullivan and CJ Warbrick, 'Territorial Jurisdiction: Criminal Justice Act 1993' (1994) 43 *International and Comparative Law Quarterly* 460, 460.

jurisdiction abroad is subject to legal and practical problems. First, state sovereignty will normally nullify the effect of extra-territorial legislation applying to foreign nationals abroad. And the application of any such law in practice will meet unsurpassable practical difficulties in the collection of evidence during investigation, in prosecution, and ultimately in bringing persons affected by it within the jurisdiction for the purposes of a criminal trial or even punishment. But recently there have been indications that some of the natural resistance to extra-territorial or transnational jurisdiction is being broken down by the need to deal with conduct that is harmful to British interests but which is not located or not wholly located within the state.[40]

But extra-territorial legislation applying to the state's own subjects abroad has been in existence for many years. An early example is section 9 of the Offences against the Person Act 1861:

> Where .... murder .... [is] committed on land out of the United Kingdom .... every offence committed by any subject of Her Majesty .... shall amount to the offence of murder .... [and] may be .... tried .... in any court .... in England .... in all respects as if such offence had been actually committed in that country.

In respect of civil matters, English law recognises that certain civil matters have to be dealt according to foreign law.[41] Examples are the law governing immovable property outside the jurisdiction or the validity of a marriage outside the jurisdiction. This is of course the realm of private international law or conflict of laws.[42]

And so, in practice, extra-territoriality is claimed to regulate the activities of own nationals on national transport outside the jurisdiction; to regulate the activities of nationals or their property outside the jurisdiction; or to regulate the activities of foreign nationals outside the jurisdiction. With reference to activities of own nationals in transport abroad, it is worth noting that jurisdiction is recognised by the common law in respect of things done on the high seas. But in practice jurisdiction is claimed by statute both with respect to the ships on the sea and on artificial installations such as oil rigs, and in the air outside the airspace of the jurisdiction. In addition, jurisdiction for nationals abroad is claimed in relation to certain serious crimes and to taxation. The rationale for such a claim is that persons subject to legislation in the state cannot evade it by moving themselves or their property outside it in order to commit offences there: in other words,

[40] See G Mullan, 'The Concept of Double Criminality in the Context of Extraterritorial Crimes' (1997) 1 *Criminal Law Review* 17, 19.

[41] See S Dutson, 'The Conflict of Laws and Statutes: The International Operation of Legislation Dealing With Matters of Civil Law in the United Kingdom and Australia' (1997) 60 *Modern Law Review* 668, 668.

[42] See S de Peuter, 'The Application of Foreign Public Law in Conflict of Laws: an Outline' (1990) 13 *International Business Law Journal* 79, 79.

individuals cannot be allowed to 'forum shop'. Typically, these offences are very serious, such as murder, or offences which have a direct effect on the home jurisdiction, such as official corruption, currency offences, customs offences, evasion of tax or assisting illegal immigration. All these seem quite legitimate exercises of extra-territorial jurisdiction justified by the link of nationality to the legislating state.

From a drafter's perspective, this type of extra-territoriality presents intricate challenges. The policy choice to proceed with extra-territorial legislation is a given, and, to a certain extent, so is the constitutionality of this choice.[43] But extra-territoriality is a departure from the norm. And so the user's attention must be drawn to extra-territoriality. The first dilemma for the drafter may concern the choice between primary and delegated legislation for the purposes of extra-territorial operation. Primary legislation is of course the most appropriate choice, as it ensures both increased parliamentary controls but also wider publicity for citizens and those foreign citizens affected by the extra-territorial operation of the legislation. But there are recent examples of delegation of extra-territoriality, and indeed some are expressed broadly.[44] The second dilemma is in the choice between a special Act on extra-territoriality against a general Act with extra-territoriality as an exception to a general rule. The main advantage of a special Act is the loud signposting of extra-territoriality as a major regulatory message. But in the UK the only piece of legislation in the statute book that includes extra-territoriality in its title is 'The Extraterritorial US Legislation (Sanctions against Cuba, Iran and Libya) (Protection of Trading Interests) Order 1996'. The advantage of a general Act is the holistic expression of the regulation in the field in question, which introduces a general rule and its exceptions. In the second case the drafter's focus is the best tool of clarity for the extra-territorial element of the general Act. Here a good method is a separately headed section dealing with all extra-territorial aspects of the Act. Most UK Acts are drafted like that.[45] There is a dilemma here of course: is it really more meaningful to separate out territoriality rather than to introduce it, for example, under defences in the form of 'It is not a defence that the act took place abroad'? This is one of the rare moments in drafting where marginal notes are desperately missed; but in their absence the gravitas of extra-territoriality seems to lean the balance towards a separate section with a separate heading.

[43] See ES Podgor, 'Globalisation and the Federal Prosecution of White Collar Crime' (1997) 34 *American Criminal Law Review* 325, 329.

[44] Eg The Merchant Shipping (Prevention of Air Pollution from Ships) Order 2006, art 3 states that 'Without prejudice to the generality of article 2, the regulations may in particular include provision—... (b) with respect to—...(ii) the extraterritorial operation of the regulations'.

[45] Eg The Protection of Military Remains Act 1986, s 3.

An example of good practice on this point is section 102 of the Energy Act 2004:

> 108A Extraterritorial operation of Act
> (1) Where by virtue of this Act an act or omission taking place outside Great Britain constitutes an offence, proceedings for the offence may be taken, and the offence may for all incidental purposes be treated as having been committed, in any place in Great Britain.
> (2) Provision made by or under this Act in relation to places outside Great Britain—
> (a) so far as it applies to individuals, applies to them whether or not they are British citizens; and
> (b) so far as it applies to bodies corporate, applies to them whether or not they are incorporated under the law of a part of the United Kingdom.

But things change with reference to extra-territorial legislation regulating foreign nationals outside the jurisdiction. It is here that the greatest possibility of a clash with other systems of law is likely to occur. Without a bilateral agreement, this legislation is likely to be able to be applied only to individuals who are only temporarily abroad and have domicile or habitual residence within the jurisdiction; or to foreign companies who trade within the jurisdiction but whose major assets are outside it. There is a body of international conventions and agreements under which jurisdiction is claimed over, inter alia, the activities of foreign nationals abroad. An example is legislation regulating off-shore installations, or international crimes such as air piracy. Another example is economic sanctions imposed on a country by the international community. Even this common practice gives rise to objections.[46] However, legitimacy of legislation falling under this category can neither be accepted nor rejected outright. It is precisely here that the existence of a legitimising community can make a difference: economic sanctions are a prime example of legitimisation by the international community to which even the country on which they are imposed has agreed to take part. International crimes are another such example. But legislation extending jurisdiction to foreign nationals abroad without a bilateral agreement of any sort is an example of legislation that lacks legitimacy, and cannot be considered acceptable.

The drafter's role in these cases is more that of a legal, constitutional and legislative adviser rather than that of a legislative technician. Here expression will not save the day. These are cases where constitutionality is far from secure, and so the drafter's main interventions would be in

[46] See R Meltzer and D Ross, 'Sanctions without Borders' (2013) 30 *International Financial Law Review* 30, 31.

understanding the drafting instruction, in analysing the proposal and in designing a legislative text that can be constitutionally palatable.[47]

An example of good practice on this point is section 51 of the Anti-terrorism, Crime and Security Act 2001:

> (1) Proceedings for an offence committed under section 47 or 50 outside the United Kingdom may be taken, and the offence may for incidental purposes be treated as having been committed, in any part of the United Kingdom.
> (2) Her Majesty may by Order in Council extend the application of section 47 or 50, so far as it applies to acts done outside the United Kingdom, to bodies incorporated under the law of any of the Channel Islands, the Isle of Man or any colony.

Whatever the status of such legislation under international law, the problem is that under the national law of the legislating country this type of legislation remains in the statute book, and can be applied or attempted to be applied. Apart from resorting to international courts or to sheer political pressure, jurisdictions under 'attack' by unilateral extensions of territoriality have very few tools to protect themselves and their citizens. Is there anything that drafters can do to defend their own statute book from such an unwelcome foreign penetration?

BLOCKING LEGISLATION

It is perhaps surprising to find that drafters seem to have far more effective tools of protection than policy officers, diplomats and lawyers. International fora may do the trick. But at the end of the day the statute book under 'attack' can and must defend itself effectively. Countries often enact retaliatory legislation to foreign extra-territorial legislation.[48] Blocking legislation[49] is used generically to describe the legislative mechanisms that countries have employed to counter the effects of unilateral assertions of extra-territorial jurisdiction:[50]

1. The first option is the passing of legislation that prohibits the giving of evidence and the production of documents in foreign proceedings. This ensures that any prosecution based on the extra-territorial foreign laws cannot be effective. The mechanism is an indirect but secure way of

[47] Legitimacy is a primary concern: see AL Parrish, 'Kiobel, Unilateralism, and the Retreat from Extraterritoriality' (2013) 28 *Maryland Journal of International Law* 208, 231.

[48] See V Lowe, 'The Problems of Extraterritorial Jurisdiction: Economic Sovereignty and the Search for a Solution' (1985) 34 *International and Comparative Law Quarterly* 724, 727.

[49] See PM Roth, 'Reasonable Extraterritoriality: Correcting the "Balance of Interests"' (1992) *International and Comparative Law Quarterly* 245, 251.

[50] See D Senz and H Charlesworth, 'Building Blocks: Australia's Response to Foreign Extraterritorial Legislation' (2001) 2 *Melbourne Journal of International Law* 69, 78.

making the foreign extra-territorial provision ineffective, and therefore depriving the policy behind it of any effect. And the added value of this option is that the passing of such legislation is wholly within the sovereign rights of the defending legislature.

2. The second option is the passing of legislation that aims to block or prevent the enforcement of foreign judgments. The aim of such legislation is to deprive the foreign legislation of effectiveness, and therefore to ensure that the policy behind the foreign legislation does not bear fruit. Again, this type of national legislation is wholly within the sovereign rights of the defending legislature, although there may be regional laws that may prevent such legislation from applying to the membership of the regional organisation in question.
3. The third option is the passing of national legislation prohibiting compliance with orders of foreign authorities. The logic and objectives of such legislation remains the same as the first two options. But legislation prohibiting compliance with the orders of foreign authorities may be presented as friendlier or more open internationally: national authorities will cooperate with foreign authorities at all stages of the investigation, prosecution and trial but recognition of the resulting judgment may legitimately be subject to reciprocity or to national evaluations of fairness of the foreign process.
4. The fourth option is compliance blocking, namely legislation prohibiting adherence to foreign extra-territorial legislation: for example, in the case of the EU Regulation on Covered Sanctions,[51] the EU allowed compliance under very strict conditions only.[52]
5. The fifth option is the passing of claw-back legislation, namely legislation allowing an entity that is the subject of a foreign judgment executed against its foreign assets to recover the judgment sum against assets of the foreign judgment creditor that are situated in the local jurisdiction.[53] This kind of legislation is retaliatory in nature, and reflects the clear and loud choice of the government under 'attack' to declare its distaste with the foreign government, and to act directly and openly against the foreign legislature.[54] The choice of claw-back legislation is political rather than legal in nature.

[51] See Council Regulation 2271/96 of 22 November 1996 protecting against effects of the extra-territorial application of legislation adopted by a third country, action based thereon and resulting therefrom [1996] OJ L 309/1, art 5.

[52] See HL Clark, 'Dealing with US Extraterritorial Sanctions and Foreign Countermeasures' (2004) 25 *University of Pennsylvania Journal of International Economic Law* 475, 476.

[53] See W Pengilley, 'United States Trade and Antitrust Laws: a Study of International Legal Imperialism from Sherman to Helms Burton' (1998) 6 *Competition and Consumer Law Journal* 187, 212–13.

[54] See G McFarlane, 'US Extra-territorial Legislation Puts Close Alliances under Strain' (1998) *Company Lawyer* 31, 32.

The role of the drafter in all types of responses to unilateral assertions of jurisdiction by foreign legislatures is defined by means of the precise drafting instructions. The first four types of legislation can be expressed with as much defiance as the policy officers choose to apply. At the low key end of the spectrum lies national legislation that accepts and encourages cooperation with the foreign authorities but makes this cooperation subject to a number of acceptable international tools of derogation: reciprocity, the double criminality rule,[55] controls of constitutionality and fairness in the foreign proceedings, compliance of the foreign proceedings with the national mechanisms of judicial process. All these may be acceptable under international law, but their expression and consequent application may be so wide that the general cooperation provision is ultimately cancelled in practice. At the other end of the spectrum lies national claw-back legislation or legislation of the three first options, which introduces a clear and unbroken rule of non-recognition of foreign proceedings, judgments and orders. But, however low key the national legislation is, the actual act of legislating in response to extra-territorial foreign legislation is a confrontational one.[56] The drafter must keep in mind that there are alternatives to blocking legislation, and must remind policy officers of the possibilities. This is not outside the normal duties of the drafter: it is within the drafter's duty to question the necessity of legislation, and warn against the many dangers of knee-jerk legislation.

ALTERNATIVES TO BLOCKING LEGISLATION

There are a number of alternatives to blocking legislation. In keeping with the principle that legislation is a solution of last resort, the drafter must examine whether these may be fruitful, before legislation is attempted.

First, it is always worth the government affirming the international law tenet that territory and nationality are the two traditional bases of national jurisdictional competence in international law.[57] Of course there are exceptions to this rule regulated by jurisdictional conflict rules in international law. These are applied on the basis of the doctrines of effect, reasonableness and comity. Effect allows any state to impose liabilities for activities

[55] See R Jennings, 'Extraterritorial Jurisdiction and the United States Antitrust Laws' (1957) 33 *British Yearbook of International Law* 146, 151; also see N Jareborg (ed), *Double Criminality: Studies in International Law* (Uppsala, Iustus Förlag, 1989); and in the context of extradition, see MC Bassiouni, *International Extradition and the World PublicOrder* (The Hague, Kluwer, 1974) 311.

[56] See J Yoon, 'International Law: Closing the Gap on Extraterritorial Jurisdiction one Way or the Other' (2001–02) 14 *Florida Journal of International Law* 503, 515.

[57] See I Brownlie, *Principles of Public International Law* (Oxford, Oxford University Press, 2008) 289.

undertaken outside its boundaries provided that these affect the territory of the state; however, extra-territorial legislation may not contradict the local law of the place where the offence was committed. The principle of reasonableness qualifies effects with a balancing requirement for interests.[58] Comity is a pragmatic principle of reciprocal expectation. However, comity is a discretionary behavioural principle, which is often abandoned in the application of black letter law:[59] this is a result of its imprecision and inherent vagueness.[60] Apart from these principles, additional alternatives to blocking legislation are diplomatic measures; international consultation, negotiations and agreements; and bilateral or multilateral trade or other agreements.

THE RULES ON EXTRA-TERRITORIAL LEGISLATION

A state can regulate the conduct or activity of its citizens or residents at all times, even when these are temporarily outside its geographical limits. Offences on board vessels or aircraft are normally regulated by the state of registry, although other bases of jurisdiction can be applicable. Activity by non-residents or non-citizens can be subject to the law of the forum provided that it affects the state in question and that the behaviour is a criminal offence in the jurisdiction where the primary offence has taken place. This latter rule applies also when the jurisdiction where the primary offence took place is neutral. George declares that these rules lead to concurrent jurisdiction rather than a choice of jurisdiction.[61]

Ultimately, extra-territoriality is a contentious chapter of international law with principles of fluid application. National legislation must recognise extra-territoriality as a departure from the norm. It is to be reserved to a small number of constitutionally justified circumstances, whose regulation by the national legislatures is not only internally constitutionally but also externally compliant with international law. The drafter's role in extra-territorial legislation is to question its necessity, to question its constitutionality and to question its prevalence when compared with other possible alternative measures capable of being effective towards the underlying policy goal. When it comes to drafting, clarity and unambiguity are the goals pursued, balanced by the task to attribute effectiveness to the extra-territorial policy aims.

[58] See *Timerlane Lambert Co v Bank of America*, 549 F 2 d 597 (9th Cir, 1976).

[59] See Note, 'Predictability and Comity: Towards Common Principles of Extraterritorial Jurisdiction' (1985) 98 *Harvard Law Review* 1310, 1317.

[60] See MD Ramsey, 'Escaping "International Comity"' (1997–98) 83 *Iowa Law Review* 893, 951–52.

[61] See BJ George Jr, 'Extraterritorial Application of Penal Legislation' (1965–66) 64 *Michigan Law Review* 609, 637.

18

Statutory Interpretation and Legislative Drafting

INTERPRETATION OF LEGISLATION is often defined as legislative construction. Sir George Engle professes that interpretation and construction mean the same thing. But Professor Crabbe distinguishes between interpretation and construction stating that construction is wider in scope than interpretation: 'it is directed at the legal effect or consequences of the provision called in question (and thus comes after interpretation)'.[1] Martineau and Salerno view construction as a dual task involving understanding of the statute and application of the interpretation to the facts of a case or situation.[2] It is fair to state that construction is the intellectual process of identifying the meaning of legislative rules by use; and so it can be undertaken either for the purposes of interpretation or for the purposes of application.

Application is the intellectual process of transferring the concepts and clauses of legislative provisions to the specific context of circumstances directed either by theoretical academic debate or by actual circumstances in everyday usage. And so application is synonymous with the use of legislation. Going back to the notion of the three Good Law personas, application is undertaken by lay users, by professional non-legally trained users and by lawyers and judges. Application does not require a debate or a dispute; it is a process of analysis and understanding. Statutory interpretation is set within an environment of debate or dispute. It is the process of settling disputes about the meaning of words. And it can be defined as the clarification of diseased legislative provisions, namely the clarification of ambiguous, vague or incomplete legislative provisions.

Consequently, statutory interpretation is of primary concern to lawyers and mainly judges. It is necessary for the clarification of ambiguity in legislation, for the delineation of vagueness in legislation and for the closure of any gaping holes in legislation. By use of these means, statutory interpretation

[1] See VCRAC Crabbe, *Understanding Statutes* (London, Routledge-Cavendish, 1994) 52.

[2] See RJ Martineau and MB Salerno, *Legal, Legislative and Rule Drafting in Plain English* (St Paul, MN, Thomson West, 2005) 104.

allows judges to 'legislate' through case law. And, where possible,[3] to declare laws as unconstitutional or obsolete.

Statutory interpretation is also necessary for parliaments. It is an intrinsic part of understanding the Bill in its provisions and as a whole,[4] and of course its relationship with existing and subsequent Acts. Identifying vagueness and deciding consciously whether it is required or not is another element of statutory interpretation in parliament.

Statutory interpretation seems irrelevant to the drafter. It occurs after the drafter's job is finished and the legislation has been produced. But statutory interpretation is the other side of the same coin to drafting. As statutory interpretation aims to cure textual diseases, it can be viewed as an evidence-based analysis of legislative quality. Of course this does not mean that any need for statutory interpretation is an indication of drafting failure. It may well be that the very aim of the drafter was to invoke statutory interpretation as a means of resolving conceptual issues that remained unresolved within the drafting team possibly for policy or political reasons. But the need for statutory interpretation is a hint that drafting may have failed or omitted to produce a precise, unambiguous or complete text. And since it is the drafter's pursuit to aim for exactly that, a precise, unambiguous and complete text, statutory interpretation must be in the mind of the drafter. As the drafter drafts, they precipitate, in so far as possible,[5] the manner in which the legislative text will be applied and interpreted. And so in that respect statutory interpretation is very much relevant to the drafter also. Being aware of the implications of interpretation when drafting allows the drafter the opportunity to fine-tune their expression to the tone that enhances the meaning that they wish to communicate.[6]

But, going back to the point above, an accurate prediction of future statutory interpretation, albeit possible, cannot guarantee legislative quality. It can avert problems arising from the words of the statute alone, before any set of facts has been presented for its application. But it cannot possibly avert problems of uncertain application of the legislation, such as problems arising in the process of applying the words of a statute to a set of facts.

[3] Not in the UK.

[4] See *Cooper v Motor Insurers' Bureau* [1985] QB 575.

[5] But this is not always possible: see R Carter, 'Statutory Interpretation Using Legislated Examples: Bennion on Multiple Consumer Credit Agreements' (2011) 32 *Statute Law Review* 86, 93.

[6] See RJ Martineau, *Drafting Legislation and Rules in Plain English* (St Paul, MN, West, 1991) 24.

CURRENT TECHNIQUES OF STATUTORY INTERPRETATION IN THE UK[7]

In the UK[8] there never was a sole and unique method of statutory interpretation.[9] Instead of going down the comforting certainty of a civil law route of concrete, exhaustive and written (albeit inflexible and inherently general) compilations of statutory interpretation rules,[10] the UK chose the familiar common law route of conventions. As these entered the system at various times historically, and were inevitably attached to specific cases, statutory interpretation rules tend to be exist in parallel.

Historically one can identify the literal, the mischief, the Golden and recently the purposive approaches to interpretation. Briefly the literal rule evident in the *Sussex Peerage* case[11] demands that, if the words in an Act are precise and unambiguous, judges must simply expound these words in their natural and ordinary sense. Where the language of an Act is clear and explicit, judges must give effect to it, whatever the consequences may be.[12] If the words of an Act are clear, judges must follow them even when they may lead to a manifest absurdity.[13] The court has nothing to do with the question whether the legislature has committed an absurdity.[14] 'It seems to this court that where the literal reading of a statute … produces an intelligible result, clearly there is no ground for reading in words or changing words according to what may be[15] the supposed intention of the parliament.'[16] As a response to the inequitable decisions[17] brought about by the strict application of the literal rule,[18] and the unattainable perfection demanded

[7] A first draft of this part appears in H Xanthaki, 'The UK Human Rights Act: a True Excuse for Judicial Law making by the Law Lords?' (2012) 18 *Jura* 244.

[8] For the Irish development of case law on statutory interpretation, see The Law Reform Commission 'Consultation Paper on Statutory Drafting and Interpretation: Plain Language and the Law' (LRC CP14–1999); and for the status of statutory interpretation in Singapore, see G Yihan, 'A Comparative Account of Statutory Interpretation in Singapore' (2008) 29 *Statute Law Review* 195, 196.

[9] See R Graham, 'A Unified Theory of Statutory Interpretation' (2002) 23 *Statute Law Review* 91, 134.

[10] On statutory interpretation in civil law jurisdictions, see G Carney, 'Comparative Approaches to Statutory Interpretation in Civil Law and Common Law Jurisdictions' (2014) 35 *Statute Law Review* 1.

[11] See (1844) 11 Cl & F 85; 8 ER 1034.

[12] See *Warburton v Loveland* (1832) 2 D & Cl (HL) 480, per Tindal CJ at 489.

[13] See *Amalgamated Society of Engineers v Adelaide Steamship Co Ltd* (1920) 28 CLR 129, per Higgins J at 161.

[14] See *R v City of London Court Judge* [1892] 1 QB 273, per Lord Esher MR at 290.

[15] See Editorial, 'Legislative Intention' (2008) 28 *Statute Law Review* iii, iii.

[16] See *R v Oakes* [1959] 2 QB 350, per Lord Parker CJ at 354.

[17] See *R v The Judge of the City of London Court* [1892] 1 QB 273 9 CA; also see Sir W Dale, *Legislative Drafting: A New Approach* (London, Butterworths, 1977) 296.

[18] See Sir F Pollock, 'Essays on Jurisprudence and Ethics' (London, MacMillan and Co, 1882) 85; also see Lord Reid, 'The Judge as Law Maker' (1972) 12 *Journal of the Society*

from the drafter,[19] the mischief rule[20] demands that the judge identifies the mischief or problem which led to legislative intervention, identifies the remedy now provided by the law, suppresses anything that would lead to continuance of the mischief[21] and finally advances the remedy according to the true intent of the legislator.[22] 'When the purpose of an enactment is clear, it is often legitimate, because it is necessary, to put a strained interpretation upon some words which have been inadvertently used'.[23] Of course, the assessment of the true intent[24] and the true remedy could be undertaken in departure from the literal meaning of the text. This could be of benefit to a judge trying to avert a judgment that would prove inequitable yet religiously compliant with the letter of the text. But it could possibly disrupt legal certainty and legitimacy if applied by an activist judge.

> It is a cardinal principle applicable to all kinds of statutes that you may not for any reason attach to a statutory provision a meaning which the words of that provision cannot reasonably bear. If they are capable of more than one meaning, then you can choose between those meanings, but beyond that you must not go.[25]

And so a combination of the mischief and literal rule produced the more equitable Golden rule.[26] Lord Atkinson[27] declared that:

> In the construction of statutes their words must be interpreted in their ordinary grammatical sense, unless they be something in the context, or in the object of the statute in which they occur, or in the circumstances with reference to which they are used, to show that they were used in a special sense different from their ordinary grammatical sense.

So, when the literal rule produces inconsistency or absurdity, the more creative and activist mischief rule can be used to correct the error.[28] But,

of Public Teachers of Law 28; and *Stock v Frank Jones (Tipton) Ltd* [1978] ICR 347, 354; *Bulmer Ltd v Bollinger* [1974] Ch 401, 425.

[19] See The Law Commission and the Scottish Law Commission, *Interpretation of Statutes* (Law Com No 21, 1969); (Scot Law Com No 11, 1969) 17.

[20] See *Heydon* (1854) 3 CoRep7a; 76 ER 637; also see *Corkery v Carpenter* [1951] KB 1, 102.

[21] See *R (McCann) v Crown Court at Manchester* [2003] 1 AC 787 (HL) [16]–[18].

[22] On legislative intent and mischief, see *R v Secretary of State for the Environment, Transport and the Regions, ex p Spath Holme Ltd* [2001] 2 AC 349 (HL).

[23] See *Sutherland Publishing Co v Caxton Publishing Co* [1938] Ch 174, per MacKinnon LJ at 201.

[24] See D Greenberg, 'The Nature of Legislative Intention and Its Implications for Legislative Drafting' (2006) 27 *Statute Law Review* 15, 28; also see RN Graham, 'A Unified Theory of Statutory Interpretation' (2002) 23 *Statute Law Review* 91, 134.

[25] See *Jones v DPP* [1962] AC 635, per Lord Reid at 668.

[26] See *Adler v George* [1964] QB 2, 7; also see *Warburton v Loveland* (1828) 1 Hud & B 623; for the prominent Irish cases see *People (Attorney General) v McGlynn* [1967] IR 232; *DPP v Flannagan* [1979] IR 265.

[27] In *Victoria (City) v Bishop of Vancouver Island* [1921] AC 384.

[28] Eg Case Comment 'Statutory Interpretation: Correction of Obvious Drafting Error' (2006) 170 *Justice of the Peace and Local Government Law* 623.

as stated in the Law Commission's 1969 report, the subjectivity of what is absurd and the lack of clear tests for the classification of a result as absurd rendered the Golden rule less popular in the UK compared to other common law jurisdictions (hence my quote of a Canadian case). In 1993, starting with *Pepper v Hart*,[29] senior UK judges[30] introduced the notion of a multi-dimensional interpretation of legislation taking into account the ordinary meaning of words under the literal rule plus the context, namely the subject matter, scope, purpose[31] and background of the Act, including parliamentary debate as evidenced in Hansard.[32]

Can the current prevalence of purposive interpretation be attributed to considerations of equity and fairness, or does it come as a direct or indirect consequence of the alleged increased liberties offered to UK judges via the Human Rights Act 1998 (HRA)? I find it difficult to support the view that it is the HRA that changed the approach of UK judges to a more activist approach of interpretation contributing to an alleged increased tolerance[33] of judge-made law in the general sphere of human rights.[34] Although an empirical analysis of each of the judgments produced in application of section 3 of the HRA would have made an eloquent argument either way,[35] this seems to me to be outside the scope of this chapter. And so one can only resort to qualitative analysis. Section 3 of the HRA introduces an interpretative duty only, it is not a judicial override, it introduces exemptions to the principle of precedent and it is still delimited by the ordinary meaning

[29] See [1993] 1 All ER 42, 50; [1993] AC 593 (HL).

[30] For Australian case law on purposive interpretation, see *Zheng v Cai* [2009] CLR 239, 446, 455; also see *Certain Lloyd Underwriters Subscribing to Contract No IH00AAQS v Cross* [2012] HCA 56, [25]–[26]. For the Hong Kong approach to purposive interpretation, see A Cooray and A Law, 'Legislative Guidelines on the Use of Extrinsic Materials in Statutory Interpretation: is Hong Kong Ready?' (2001) 9 *Asia Pacific Law Review* 23. For the Irish approach, see P Hunt, 'Statutory Interpretation: Pepper v Hart—the Irish Situation' (1996) 8 *Irish Tax Review* 17. For Canada, see JJ Magyar 'The Evolution of Hansard Use at the Supreme Court of Canada: a Comparative Study in Statutory Interpretation' (2012) 33 *Statute Law Review* 363.

[31] See G MacCallum, 'Legislative Intent' in R Summers, *Essays in Legal Philosophy* (Oxford, Blackwell, 1968) 237, 240.

[32] See Learned Hand J in *Cabell v Markham* (1945) 148 F 2d 737, 739; also see Lord Bingham in *R (Quintavalle) v Secretary of State for Health* [2003] 2 AC 687, [8]; Lord Hoffmann in *ICS v West Bromwich Building Society* [1998] 1 WLR 896, 913; and Lord Nicholls in *Wilson v First County Trust (No 2)* [2003] UKHL 40 [114]–[117]; also see R Greenfield, 'Statutory Interpretation since Pepper v Hart' (1995) 14 *Capital Tax Planning* 63; and I McLeod, 'The Use of Hansard in Statutory Interpretation' (1992) 156 *Local Government Review* 1021.

[33] Even if one accepts the argument that judges take into account their self-interests, including the cost of their interpretation choices to their reputation: see RNM Graham, 'What Judges Want: Judicial Self-interest and Statutory Interpretation' (2009) 30 *Statute Law Review* 38, 70.

[34] See P Brady, 'Convention Compatible Statutory Interpretation: a Comparison of British and Irish Approaches' (2012) 33 *Statute Law Review* 24, 25.

[35] For an individual case analysis, see J van Zyl Smit, 'The New Purposive Interpretation of Statutes: HRA Section 3 after Ghaidan v Godin-Mendoza' (2007) 70 *Modern Law Review* 294.

of words.[36] Moreover, it is interesting to note that purposive interpretation came about in 1993, about five years before the passing of the HRA. And so in terms of time, one could suggest that the moment was opportune. Admittedly purposive interpretation may be attributed, albeit in part, to the new judicial liberties resulting from the power to declare Acts incompatible by use of the HRA.[37] But purposive interpretation does not really depart from the UK tradition of statutory interpretation,[38] at least not by as much as some authors suggest.[39] As Lord Diplock had stated in the 1970s, purposive interpretation had already been the trend for three decades prior to the judgment.[40] After all, there can be no meaning detached from the author's intent.[41] And judges still have to, and largely do, comply with the limits set to them by the limited necessity of statutory interpretation, and by presumptions and maxims:[42] these delimit any alleged propensity to judicial activism, and set clear guidelines as to how statutory interpretation must take place irrespective of what rule is to be used.[43]

There are limits and restrictions inherent to the UK system of statutory interpretation whose legal value and consequent application in practice remains unaffected and continues to qualify all rules of statutory interpretation, including purposive interpretation.[44] First, interpretation is only invited when the meaning of words is unclear or disputed.[45] So purposive interpretation is not needed and therefore not invited or tolerated for the purposes of everyday construction and application of the law. Interpretation is by definition limited to the extraordinary, albeit frequent in practice, cases where there are either problems of drafting arising from

[36] For an eloquent and learned analysis on this point, see Arden LJ, 'The Interpretation of UK Domestic Legislation in the Light of the European Convention of Human Rights' (2004) 25 *Statute Law Review* 165, 177–78.

[37] See JA Holland and JS Webb, *Learning Legal Rules* (London, Blackstone Press, 2001) 227.

[38] See D Greenberg 'All Trains Stop at Crewe: The Rise and Rise of Contextual Drafting' (2006) 7 *European Journal of Law Reform* 31, 36.

[39] See G Bowman, 'Legislation and Explanation' (2002) *The Loophole* www.opc.gov.au/calc/docs/calc-june/audience.htm; also see G Slapper, 'Statutory Interpretation: a New Departure' (1993) 14 *Business Law Review* 56; and JH Baker, 'Statutory Interpretation and Parliamentary Intention' (1993) 52 *Cambridge Law Journal* 353.

[40] See Lord Diplock in *Carter v Bradbeer* [1975] 3 All ER 158; for old cases supporting purposive interpretation, also see *Kammins Ballrooms Co Ltd v Zenith Investments Ltd* [1970] 2 All ER 871; *R v Pigg* [1983] 1 All ER 56; and *Re X (A Minor) (Adoption Details: Disclosure)* [1994] 3 All ER 372.

[41] See C Walshow, 'Interpretation is Understanding and Application: The Case for Concurrent Legal Interpretation' (2012) 34 *Statute Law Review* 101, 123.

[42] And not just in the UK: see LA Marchili *Como Legislar con Sbiduria y Elocuencia—El Arte de Legislar Reconstruido a Partir de la Tradicion Retorica* (Buenos Aires, Editorial Dunken, 2009) 262–358.

[43] See F Bennion, 'A Human Rights Act Provision Now in Force' (1999) 163 *Justices of Peace* 164, www.francisbennion.com/pdfs/fb/1999/1999-011-threading-10.pdf.

[44] See *Magor and St Mellons Rural District Council v Newport* [1952] AC189, per Lord Simonds at 191.

[45] To quote an American case, see *Caminetti v United States*, 242 U.S. 470, 485 (1917).

the words of the statute alone before any set of facts has been presented for its application; or problems of uncertain application arising in the process of applying the words of a statute to a set of facts. Judges apply statutory law, they must not obstruct it.[46] Secondly, even under the exceptional circumstances determined above judges can only use interpretation for the purposes of clarifying ambiguous or vague legislation;[47] and supplementing the legal provisions in cases of a *casus omissus*.[48] But ambiguity, vagueness or incompleteness do not or should not happen inadvertently, at least not always. These are circumstances where the legislature has either consciously decided or unconsciously managed to bring itself to the unfortunate position of a textual failure. And so, in the circumstances, the judiciary has both the constitutional legitimacy and the legal duty to play an activist role as the applicator and interpreter of the law.[49] The means of achieving this is inevitably through case law. And even this case law is normally subject to a review both *in concreto* by the higher courts and *in abstracto* by general judicial practice: the judgment may be quashed or may be rejected by persistent contrary case law in future cases. Thirdly, judges continue to be bound by presumptions and maxims. These are discussed in some detail below. But for the purposes of this argument here it is important to note that, when using purposive interpretation, judges continue to work within the limits of constitutional and legal conventions. As a result, a later law continues to repeal an earlier law that is inconsistent with the later law. A new law continues to be prospective in character and not retrospective in operation.[50] Laws continue to be adopted for frequent and future cases. A liberal construction continues to be desirable in the interpretation of a statute. A passage continues to be best interpreted by reference to what proceeds and what follows it. The meaning of a doubtful word continues to be sought by reference to words attached to it.[51] There still is no need to interpret that, which has no need of interpretation. The express mention of one thing is still the exclusion of another. Statutes on the same subject matter are still to be read together. General words following particular or specific words are still construed as of the same kind or class as the particular or specific words. Perhaps more importantly, there still is a maxim that Parliament legislated for a reason. And that one must interpret the laws to give effect

[46] See Lord Devlin, 'Judges and Lawmakers' (1976) 39 *Modern Law Review* 1, 13.

[47] See M Troper, C Grzegorczyk and JL Gardies, 'Statutory Interpretation in France' in DN MacCormick and RS Summers, *Interpreting Statutes: A Comparative Study* (London, Dartmouth, 1991) 171, 190.

[48] See *Magor & St Mellons Rural District Council v Newport Corporation* [1951] 2 All ER 839.

[49] See M Vranken, 'Statutory Interpretation and Judicial Policy Making: Some Comparative Reflections' (1991) 12 *Statute Law Review* 31, 46.

[50] See *Lauri v Renad* [1892] 3 Ch 402, per Lindley LJ at 421.

[51] See *River Wear Commissioners v Adamson* (1877) 2 AC 743, per Lord Blackburn at 763; *R (Westminster CC) v National Asylum Service* [2002] 1 WLR 2956, per Lord Steyn at [5].

to the will of the Parliament.[52] These three points demonstrate effectively that UK judges[53] are not left to use purposive interpretation when and as they see fit or opportune. And that although alleged judicial activism can be attributed to the liberalism of statutory interpretation, at the end of the day this is well balanced by the checks and balances inherent to the UK Constitution.

But does that mean that the UK approach to statutory interpretation remains completely unmoved in the last few years? It would be fair to admit that the recent approach of UK judges to statutory interpretation has changed. Nowadays the interpretation of statutes spreads along 'a spectrum of judicial opinion ranging from strict literalism at one end to broadly based purposive interpretation at the other end'.[54] But this is not a direct and sole consequence of the introduction of the HRA. The new liberal approach to UK statutory interpretation simply reflects a conscious and unconscious influence of regional legal globalisation with specific reference to the European courts' teleological interpretation.[55] Even if one does not attribute the change fully to the Europeanisation of UK statutory interpretation, one must accept at least that the change has been accelerated by European ideas.[56] Lord Denning reassured his peers that the European schematic and teleological method of interpretation is 'not really so alarming as it sounds', since it merely means that European judges interpret legislation by going past and behind the design or purpose.[57] And Lord Bingham describes teleological interpretation as a process of 'supplying flesh to a spare and loosely constructed skeleton'.[58] And years before *Pepper v Hart*, Lord Oliver suggested that UK Acts passed to give effect to the UK's, then, EEC obligations fall into a special category and are to be interpreted purposively in order to ensure compliance with what was then EEC law.[59] If a purposive construction facilitates compliance with the then Community obligations,[60]

[52] See Editorial, 'Legislative Intent' (2008) 29 *Statute Law Review* ii; also see *Black-Clawson International Ltd v Papierwerke Waldhof-Aschaffenburg AG* [1975] AC 591, per Lord Reid; *R v Secretary of State for the Environment, Transport and the Regions, ex p Spath Holme Ltd* [2001] 2 AC 349, per Lord Nicholls at 395; *Wilson v First County Trust (No 2)* [2004] 1 AC 816, per Lord Hope at [111].

[53] And indeed US judges: see MD Goodman, 'Reconstructing the Plain Language Rule of Statutory Construction: How and Why' (2004) 65 *Montana Law Review* 229, 264–65.

[54] See Hon JJ Spigelman, 'The Intolerable Wrestle: Developments in Statutory Interpretation' (2010) 84 *Australian Law Journal* 822, 822.

[55] See JE Levitsky, 'The Europeanisation of the British Legal Style' (1994) 42 *American Journal of Comparative Law* 347, 371–72.

[56] See Greenberg, 'All Trains Stop at Crewe' (n 38) 32.

[57] See *James Buchanan & Co Ltd v Babco Forwarding & Shipping (UK) Ltd* [1977] 2WLR 107, 112.

[58] See *Commissioners of Customs and Excise v ApS Samex* [1983] 1 All ER 1042, 1056.

[59] See *Pickstone v Freemans Plc* [1989] 1 App Cas 66, 125–26 (1988).

[60] See EMH Hirsch Ballin, 'Reflections on Co-actorship in the Development of European Law-making' in EMH Hirsch Ballin and LAJ Senden, *Co-actorship in the Development of*

it will be applied even where it departs from the strict and literal application of the words used by the legislature.[61]

Can UK judges make law? Does the principle of precedent[62] really allow UK judges to form rigid legislative precedent thus allowing them to legislate, albeit within the limits quoted above? Although UK Supreme Court judgments are binding on all inferior courts, since 1966 they cannot bind the Court itself. And so although UK Supreme Court judges formulate a legal position that is carried down to all inferior courts, that legal position can change rather easily when the issue is reconsidered by virtue of another case. So, one could argue that compared to the omnipotence of the House of Lords before 1966, the possibility of introducing judge-made law offered to the Supreme Court is now rather diminished.

However, even before 1998, UK judges enjoyed a level of discretion that seems disproportionate to that allowed to their European civil law counterparts. Although the UK approach to the principle of the separation of powers prevents judges from declaring an Act obsolete or unconstitutional, the principle is not applied *stricto sensu*. In the past this allowed the Lord Chancellor's participation in all three functions of the state. And more recently UK judges have been offered unprecedented access to manipulation of national legislation as a means of squeezing it within the *telos* and text of EU legislation (under *Marleasing*[63]) and of the HRA.[64] But this new liberty should not be viewed narrowly. It is a similar liberty, and *onus*, offered to the national judges of the Member States of the EU and of the states signatory to the European Convention on Human Right (ECHR). It is not special to the HRA or indeed to UK judges. It can be attributed to the increasing demand placed on national judiciaries for smooth, and therefore inherently flexible, approximation between national and regional/international instruments resulting from legal globalisation.

So, has the approach of the Law Lords to statutory interpretation been radically changed by the HRA? Of course not. Suggesting that the implementation of the HRA has changed the ethos of UK statutory interpretation would disregard the continuing prevalence of the literal rule when the text is clear, the exceptional use of purposive interpretation when the text

European Law-making: The Quality of European Legislation and its Implementation and Application in the National Legal Order (The Hague, TMC Asser Press, 2005) 3, 15.

[61] See *Litster v Forth Dry Dock* [1990] 1 AC 546, 559.

[62] Common law judges ask themselves 'What did we do last time?': see TM Cooper, 'The Common and the Civil Law—a Scots View' (1950) 63 *Harvard Law Review* 468, 471.

[63] For an analysis of CJEU case law that led to *Marleasing*, see K Sawyer, 'The Principle of "interpretation conforme": How Far Can or Should National Courts Go when Interpreting National Legislation Consistently with European Community Law?' (2007) 28 *Statute Law Review* 165, 166–69.

[64] See The Home Office, *Rights Brought Home* (Cm 3782, 1997) para 2.7; also see P Sales and B Hooper, 'Proportionality and the Form of Law' (2003) 119 *Law Quarterly Review* 427.

is unclear or its application uncertain, the extraordinary use of statutory interpretation as a concept, and the continuing prevalence of maxims and presumptions that delimit the scope of any judicial activism made possible by section 3 of the HRA. UK judges simply enjoy, and suffer under, the obligation to marry national laws with EU legislation and the ECHR as expressed by the HRA. But this is a privilege worth offering to UK judges. The alternative would condemn the UK legal system to the chaotic uncertainty of an uncontrolled and dangerous series of implied repeals caused by inconsistencies between previous legislation and the HRA. And, after all, who would be called upon to pronounce these express repeals other than the same UK judges that are now accused of judicial law-making?

THE DRAFTERS' DUTY

But where does this leave drafters? Drafters cannot rely on the rules of construction unduly. These are a safety net that ensures that the legal system is not defenceless in the unfortunate event of a drafting error.[65] But they do not absolve drafters from the responsibility of producing effective legislation that is clear, precise and unambiguous.[66] Indeed, this is what rules of statutory interpretation[67] can facilitate: the production of an effective legislative text by means of allowing the drafter an insight in the manner in which their text can and probably will be received by the users. In other words, rules of statutory interpretation can guide the drafter in their inevitable struggle to foresee which of the many possible[68] interpretations of their message the user will choose when they decide to inhabit the world of the legislative text.[69] So drafters can prevent problems of interpretation from arising by doing their best to ensure that the draft does not raise any problems of drafting, and by detecting possible problems of uncertain application.[70] For this purpose drafters use rules of statutory interpretation to identify possible problems, make the instructing department aware of the possible issues involved, they find what result the instructing department wants to achieve, and finally draft it so that it

65 See J Stark, 'Understanding Statutes by Understanding Drafters' (2002) 85 *Judicature* 190, 191.

66 See D Greenberg, *Laying Down the Law* (London, Sweet and Maxwell, 2011) 265.

67 Statsky rejects the term 'rules' for canons of statutory interpretation on the basis that no court is required to apply a canon: see WP Statsky, *Legislative Analysis and Drafting* (St Paul, MN, West Publishing Co, 1984) 83.

68 See J Tontti, *Right and Prejudice: Prolegomena to a Hermeneutical Philosophy of Law* (Aldershot, Ashgate, 2004) 36–37 and 130–31.

69 See P Ricoeur, 'The Hermeneutical Function of Distanciation' in P Ricoeur, *From Text to Action: Essays in Hermeneutics, II* (London, The Athlone Press, 1991) 84–86.

70 See J Landis, 'A Note on "Statutory Interpretation"' (1930) 43 *Harvard Law Review* 886, 892.

is clearly achieved. In other words, rules of statutory interpretation are a drafting tool that facilitates the unearthing and subsequent avoidance of unintended vagueness, ambiguity and incompleteness, thus contributing to effective legislation.

PRESUMPTIONS

But what exactly is it that drafters must be aware of as rules of statutory interpretation? Presumptions are an excellent starting point. They are general principles of statutory interpretation expressing legislative communication rules that have become so widely accepted that the sender of the regulatory message can legitimately anticipate their application by the user in the event of application and statutory interpretation. Presumptions typically assist courts in circumstances where direct proof is difficult by attributing to the facts an arbitrary effect beyond their natural tendency to produce belief.[71] They can be viewed as 'inferences as to the existence of the presumed fact that the tribunal of fact is compelled to draw'.[72] In view of their cross-communication acceptance presumptions normally come to the aid of the user by reassuring them that the message received is what was intended to be delivered.[73] They also come of use to the drafter who can, to an extent, rely on presumptions to foresee with some certainty how the message expressed by them will be received by most users.

But there is a caveat. Presumptions are general rules, and exceptions to these rules are both possible and indeed useful. And so a presumption is the statutory interpretation equivalent to rebuttable evidence. There is nothing to stop the drafter from going against a presumption, as long as they are perfectly aware that this is exactly what they are doing. A conscious departure from a presumption is acceptable and commendable as it leads the drafter to the realisation that the provision has a different meaning. And consequently it directs the drafter to ensure that the reader is aware of the different meaning, and that the reader is aware of the scope of this difference.[74] There is no single agreed list of presumptions. And there are conflicting presumptions. But the fullest list can be borrowed from Crabbe.[75] There are presumptions of conformity to the common law, of conformity

[71] See RD Gordon, 'Fictitious Fraud: Economics and the Presumption of Reliance' (2013) 9 *International Journal of the Law in Context* 506, 510.

[72] See R Nazzini, 'The Wood Began to Move: an Essay on Consumer Welfare, Evidence and Burden of Proof in Article 82 Cases' (2006) 31 *European Law Review* 518, fn 32.

[73] On the nature of presumptions, see D Mendonca, 'Presumptions' (1998) 11 *Ratio Juris* 399.

[74] On the difficulty surrounding departure from presumptions by judges at the interpretation stage, see D Bailey, 'Die-hard Presumptions' (2004) 58 *Trusts and Estates Law & Tax Journal* 27.

[75] See VRAC Crabbe, *Understanding Statutes* (London, Cavendish Publishing, 1994) 119–77.

with the constitution, of conformity with international law.[76] And there is a presumption against the alteration of existing law. Any alteration of the existing law requires conformity with the constitution, case law, existing law, the jurisdiction of the courts and general principles of law. An Act is reasonable. There is a presumption against injustice. The presumption of consistency requires that the same idea be always expressed in the same manner. There is a presumption of certainty. There is a presumption against surplusage: useless words can be rejected by the courts.[77] Words have the same meaning throughout the Act,[78] which should be read as a whole.[79] There are also presumptions of finality of decisions, of conclusive evidence clauses, of mens rea,[80] of compliance with the principles of natural justice and of exclusivity of remedies.[81] And there is a presumption against ousting the jurisdiction of the courts. There is a presumption of equality of treatment of persons. Action or conduct is lawful unless declared unlawful by an Act. Consolidation Acts do not change the existing law. Retroactive operation of a statute is only awarded where the Act changes the law from a date prior to the date of its enactment. Retrospective operation of is awarded only where the Act attaches new consequences to an event that occurred prior to its enactment. Application to Crown or Republic is usually set in the Interpretation Act. Territorial operation is the rule.

The list of presumptions demonstrates that they are expressions of statutory interpretation conventions that are based on constitutional and legislative theory and practice. They are often quoted by judges but they remain unproven and unjustified by reference to concrete legislative texts. It is precisely this aspect of presumptions that makes them unreliable and fluid, at least from the viewpoint of the drafter of a precise and certain legislative text. But they also derive from constitutional and legislative custom over hundreds of years, thus rendering them a distilment of legislative and judicial wisdom that applies universally. And consequently they are not prone to radical or sudden change. Presumptions are the common law equivalent of general principles in civil law.[82] But they remain uncodified, in the sense of consolidated in a full and exhaustive list within a legislative text, and are therefore still established and reinforced through persistent statutory interpretation by the courts. And this seems to be a good option: an attempt to

[76] See I McLeod, *Principles of Legislative and Regulatory Drafting* (Oxford, Hart Publishing, 2009) 57.

[77] See *Stone v Yeovil Corpn* (1876) 1 CPD 691, 701.

[78] See *R v Millward* [1985] QB 519.

[79] See *Dimond v Lovell* [1999] 3 All ER 1, 10.

[80] Also see JE Stannard, 'A Tale of Two Presumptions' (1999) 21 *Liverpool Law Review* 275.

[81] On additional evidential presumptions, see A Craig, 'Evidential Presumptions' (2002) 152 *New Law Journal* 217.

[82] See TC Wegerich, 'Statutory Interpretation in Germany: the Continental Approach to Dealing with the Law' (1991/92) 15 *Holdsworth Law Review* 217.

codify rules of statutory interpretation in New Zealand was not successful, and according to Zander neither would a similar attempt be successful in the UK.[83]

MAXIMS

Maxims are no different from presumptions in that they are expressions of constitutional and legislative theory and practice mainly formulated via case law over hundreds of years.[84] But they differ from presumptions in that they are irrebuttable. In principle, they cannot be departed from. For example, a later law repeals an earlier law that is inconsistent with the later law. A new law must be prospective in character and not retrospective in operation. Laws are adopted to frequent, future cases. A liberal construction is desirable in the interpretation of a statute. A passage is best interpreted by reference to what proceeds and what follows it. The meaning of a doubtful word must be sought by reference to the meaning of words attached to it. There is no need to interpret that, which has no need of interpretation. The express mention of one thing is the exclusion of another. Statutes on the same subject matter are read together. General words following particular or specific words are construed as of the same kind or class as the particular or specific words. He who sticks with the letter of the law only gets to the bark of the tree.

Maxims are often interchangeable with presumptions. For example, the maxim of retrospectivity is qualified by the presumption of retrospective operation. As maxims also remain uncodified, their classification as maxims or presumptions is left to the judge who uses them for the purposes of interpreting legislation. Conviction to the universal application of the rule leads the judge to pronounce them as a maxim. Anything less sacrosanct is classified as a presumption, thus allowing the prospect of possible exceptions to the rule being introduced.

DRAFTING AND STATUTORY INTERPRETATION

Statutory interpretation, and indeed application, is distinct from drafting. It takes place well after the drafting of statutes is well and truly finished and the Act has been passed by Parliament. And so statutory interpretation forms part of the legislation agenda but not directly part of the legislative

[83] See M Zander, *The Law-Making Process* (London, Butterworths, 1999) 170.
[84] See RN Graham, 'In Defence of Maxims' (2001) 22 *Statute Law Review* 45, 68.

drafting debate. But, totally detaching the two would be as wrong as confusing them.[85]

Rules of statutory interpretation form part of the legislative environment within which drafting and the drafter operate. And, although these rules are not there to absolve the drafter from the responsibility of producing a clear, precise and unambiguous legislative text, they can facilitate the drafter in the formation of a pre-legislative perception on how users will perceive the legislative expression produced. In other words, awareness of the rule of statutory interpretation offers the drafter a window into the minds of users. This can direct the drafter to fine-tune the legislative expression to the prejudices of user comprehension.[86]

The dilemma is whether the draft need to repeat well-established interpretation conventions, or indeed provisions that can be found in an Interpretation Act. The dilemma is really between repetition and resulting wordiness on the one hand, and brevity of expression on the other hand. And the answer is not easily forthcoming. Interpretation Acts and rules of statutory interpretation are considered to be part of the legal environment within which the new Act will function. One cannot possibly repeat all relevant constitutional, legal and common law rules within an Act. But the danger of creating ambiguity and uncertainty via intended omission of cross references to the Interpretation Act or, even trickier if at all possible, to statutory interpretation rules is rather grave. One can only go back to the pyramid of drafting values. Brevity does not come into play at all, but clarity certainty does. It would seem therefore that, in principle, clarity would call for a repetition of provisions found in the Interpretation Act or in court precedents confirming presumptions or maxims.

But this is of course qualified by the estimated legal awareness of the specific audience of the legislative text. There is no point in repeating the concept of mens rea in the rules of procedure of criminal courts, a text mostly, if not exclusively, addressed to lawyers and judges. In fact paraphrasing the presumption invites the learned users of procedural rules to consider the possibility of a departure from the established definition and content of the concept. But can one expect the lay user to be aware of the existence of the Interpretation Act, let alone the content and interpretation of its provisions?

And if the drafter is to repeat the rules of interpretation for the lay user, where exactly will that be? Attempting to do so within the legislative text is a futile and ultimately counterproductive waste of resources: where does

[85] On the linkage between application and interpretation, see SD Smith 'That Old-Time Originalism' in G Huscroft and BW Miller, *The Challenge of Originalism: Theories of Constitutional Interpretation* (New York, Cambridge University Press, 2011) 240.

[86] See Sir A Russell, *Legislative Drafting and Forms* (London, Butterworths, 1938) 13.

one start and where does one stop cross referring and explaining?[87] Is it really possible to convey years of legal training on context and content to a lay user? And should the lay user actually have this training in order to understand what the government is asking them to do or omit?

The legislative text must speak to the user, lay or learned or anything between. Without the need for legal training and without the need for endless cross references to legislative texts that the user cannot access. It is here that publication of legislation can play a crucial role. The work of The National Archives on the use of patterns in legislative language is innovative and responds to this specific need: making users aware of the context of legislation by means of optional windows of information and clickable references to relevant texts.[88] In the meantime, the dilemma for the drafter remains. Keeping the balance between the need to convey complete information whilst keeping the text bare of data that is useless in practice for the untrained user is part of their duty. And part of the subjective job that is phronetic legislative drafting.

[87] See Office of the Parliamentary Counsel 'When Laws Become Too Complex: A Review into the Causes of Complex Legislation' 29 www.gov.uk/government/uploads/system/uploads/attachment_data/file/187015/GoodLaw_report_8April_AP.pdf.

[88] On access to legislation and its direct relevance to the rule of law, see R Cormacain, 'Accessing Legislation: 40 Years post-Renton' (2013) 19 *Web Journal of Current Legal Issues* http://webjcli.org//article/view/264/361.

19

Quality of Legislation Post-Lisbon and the Role of Parliaments[1]

IF ONE LOOKS at the quality of legislation as a regulatory tool diachronically, the notion of challenge becomes more of an understatement than a depiction of a grim reality. This book has dealt with the drafting of legislation and its provisions as a means of contributing to legislative quality, which feeds into regulatory efficacy and achieves successful regulation. It is now time to go back to the theme of regulation, focusing not on the introductory basics but on the advancement of the agenda via recent developments in the field. To this effect, both the EU and the UK have considerable innovations to offer; and, from a UK perspective, analysis of both fora is necessary for a holistic understanding of the content of regulatory quality in UK policy and law. And so, this chapter evaluates the advances made in the regulatory framework for quality of legislation post-Lisbon in the EU and the UK: the focus remains on regulation via legislation and lessons for drafters. As elements of this analysis have already been identified in chapter one, the book comes full circle here: as legislation is a tool for regulation, the book has addressed the eccentricities and details of good legislation, and now closes with the final developments in good regulation. Good legislation and good regulation feed into each other and place the quality argument within effectiveness and efficacy accordingly.

THE EU'S REGULATORY FRAMEWORK FOR LEGISLATIVE QUALITY[2]

The EU's long engagement with legislative quality is characterised by a strong UK political driving force behind the regulatory agenda.[3] Although

[1] For the original version of this chapter, see H Xanthaki, 'EU Legislative Quality post-Lisbon: the Challenges of Smart Regulation' (2014) 35 *Statute Law Review* 66.

[2] For a fuller analysis see H Xanthaki, 'The Problem of Quality in EU Legislation: What on Earth is Really Wrong?' (2001) 38 *Common Market Law Review* 651.

[3] Of course a number of initiatives deriving outside the UK have formed the agenda, such as the Dutch contribution with the Koopmans Report, the Scheveningen Conference and the Amsterdam IGC.

this could have led to a common law prevalence in drafting conventions, the emerging legislative style is a uniquely EU one. It balances admirably common and civil law structures, thus accommodating both families of law. But at the same time it respects the legal intricacies of EU law, such as the prevalence of consistent EU case law as a source of binding legal norms.

The framework within which this dynamic process takes place is via a long list of documents, mainly of non-binding nature, that set rules for the process and format of legislative drafting applicable to all EU institutions.

The first set of concrete quality-promoting rules is expressed in the 1992 Sutherland report.[4] Lord Sutherland sets five criteria that each new legislative measure must meet as a means of achieving legislative quality. These are: the need for regulatory action; the choice of the most effective course of action, be it legislative or alternative; proportionality of the measure to the desired regulatory results; consistency of the proposed measure with existing measures; and wide consultation at the preparatory stage.

But how could one put the Sutherland report into effect, with specific reference to drafting conventions and rules? Two months after Lord Sutherland's report, in December 1992, the European Council demanded clearer and simpler legislation.[5] In June 1993 the Council clarified these concepts, and introduced concrete measures for their attainment by use of a resolution on legislative quality: the resolution touched upon wording, structure and consistency with the content of existing legislation.[6] In an attempt to make legislation more accessible, the resolution called for clear, simple, concise and unambiguous wording. Practices encouraged by the resolution were: the use of the same term throughout the Act; the use of the accepted structure of chapters/sections/articles/paragraphs; compliance with the role of the preamble as a means of justification of the enacting provisions in simple terms; clear determination of the rights and obligations deriving from the Act; clear reference to the Act's date of entry into force; and consistency of the provisions of various Acts. Practices discouraged by the resolution were: the use

[4] See 'The Internal Market after 1992: Meeting the Challenge' Report to the EEC Commission by the High Level Group on the operation of the internal market SEC(92)2044; also Supplement to European Report no 1808 of 31 October 1992; Commission, 'Follow-up of the Sutherland Report' (Communication) COM(93)361 final and SEC(92)2227 fin; Opinion of the Economic and Social Committee of 5 May 1993, 'On the Commission Communication on the Operation of the Community's Internal Market after 1992: Follow-up to the Sutherland Report' [1993] OJ C 201/59; Commission, 'Follow-up to the Sutherland Report: Legislative Consolidation to Enhance the Transparency of Community Law in the Area of the Internal Market' (Communication) COM (93)361 fin; Commission, 'On the Handling of Urgent Situations in the Context of Implementation of Community Rules: Follow-up to the Sutherland Report' (Communication) COM (93)430 fin.

[5] See Edinburgh European Council, 'Conclusions of the Presidency' Bull EC 12/92, 7.

[6] See Council Resolution of 8 June 1993 on the quality of drafting of Community legislation [1993] OJ C 166/1, 1.

of unnecessary abbreviations; Community jargon; long sentences; imprecise references to other texts; too many cross references; political statements without legislative character; pointless repetitions of existing provisions; and inconsistencies with existing legislation. With specific reference to Acts amending earlier legislative texts, the resolution discouraged the inclusion of autonomous provisions, which could not be directly incorporated into the existing Act. The resolution is very similar to a legislative manual in the national context, but it is much shorter, and includes an imbalanced range of concrete conventions and general principles for drafters. Although the resolution cannot be attributed with originality or innovation in the prescribed drafting rules and conventions, its great value lies in its unprecedented, for the EU, focus on legislative quality, accessibility of legislation and the concept of set, clear criteria for the evaluation of EU legislative texts.[7] But a resolution carries little binding force, and therefore limited legal value; and in any case this resolution was of a general prescriptive character.

And so the onus was for the various actors of the legislative process to introduce concrete measures putting the Sutherland report and the resolution into effect in specific areas of law-making. Thus, in December 1994 the Council, the Commission and the Parliament set out to detail the guidelines of the resolution in a concrete, albeit still not binding, interinstitutional agreement on the official codification of legislative texts. The resolution and agreement are of course directly linked: the resolution declares that 'the general objective of making Community legislation more accessible should be pursued not only by making systematic use of EU consolidation but also by implementing the following guidelines'.[8] In June 1995, the Molitor Group applied the Sutherland report criteria to legislative and administrative simplification.[9] This was supplemented in 2003 by the notion of prioritisation for the purposes of simplification.[10]

And whilst this was going on the Commission took it upon itself to provide a more principled, but still not binding, stance on law-making. In 1995 and 1996 the *Better Lawmaking* reports[11] identified the regulatory

[7] These rules are also included in the Council Decision 93/662/EC of 6 December 1993 adopting the Council's Rules of Procedure [1993] OJ L 304/1.

[8] See Interinstitutional Agreement of 20 December 1994 on an accelerated working method for official codification of legislative texts [1995] OJ C 293/2, [1996] OJ C 102/2.

[9] See 'Report of the Group of Independent Experts on Legislative and Administrative Simplification: Summary and Proposals' COM (95) 288 final; also see Commission's comments on the report SEC (95) 2121 final; and the European Parliament Resolution of 4 July 1996, [1996] OJ C 211, 23.

[10] See Commission, 'Updating and Simplifying the Community Acquis' (Communication) SEC (2003) 165, COM/2003/0071 final.

[11] See *Better Lawmaking 1995*: Report of the Commission to the European Council [of Madrid] on the application of the principles of subsidiarity and proportionality, on simplification and codification CSE(95)580 Bull 11-1995, point 1.9.2; also see *Better Lawmaking 1996*: Report of the Commission to the European Council [of Dublin] on the application of the principles of subsidiarity and proportionality, on simplification and consolidation CSE (96)7.

aims of the EU's legislative policy: legislative quality, consistency, openness in the drafting process, a carefully planned and coordinated legislative process and thorough monitoring and evaluation of the legislation. In parallel to a focus on legislative quality at the EU level the Commission identified the crucial role of legislative quality in the national implementing measures as a key determinant of quality of EU regulation. This is evident in the Commission's 1996 SLIM (Simpler Legislation for the Internal Market) initiative, which, with the strong encouragement of internal market Ministers, targets simplification of both EU and national implementing legislation.[12] The theme was confirmed in June 1997 where the Commission's approach to simplification extended expressly to national measures also.[13] It was further confirmed in the Commission's 1997 *Better Lawmaking* report, which called upon the drafting authorities of the Member States 'to work towards the effective implementation of Community law and play an active part in the process of improving the quality of legislation'.[14] And again in the Informal Meeting of Internal Ministers of 13–14 February 1998, Ministers unanimously stressed their strong support for legislative simplification of national and Community rules.[15] The rationale of this policy was expressed clearly[16] in the 1998 *Better Lawmaking* report, *A Shared Responsibility*,[17] which pronounced Member States as 'the main producers of legislation and hence the most direct cause of the burden [on firms]'. In a series of documents the Commission extended its emphasis on the quality of legislative measures by the Member States to the need for monitoring and evaluation of transposition of EU instruments both pre and post accession.[18]

But what exactly are the elements of legislative quality, which the Commission so eloquently extended both to the EU and the Member States? The 1998 Commission Staff Working Paper entitled *Making Single Market Rules More Effective, Quality in Implementation and Enforcement*[19] clarifies the necessity for, purpose and content of quality in legislation: clear and

[12] See Commission, 'Simpler Legislation for the Internal Market (SLIM): a Pilot Project' (Communication) COM(96)204 final; also see Resolution of the European Parliament of 10 April 1997 on the Communication from the Commission to the Council and the European Parliament 'Simpler Legislation for the Internal Market (SLIM): a Pilot Project' COM(96)204 fin, A4-0108/97 [1997] OJ C 132/213.

[13] See COM(97)618 final, 2.

[14] See Bull EU 11-1997, point 1.1.1.

[15] See http://europa.eu.int/comm/dg15/en/update/general/camb.htm#1, 1.

[16] See Bull EU 5-1998, point 1.8.3.

[17] See COM(1998)715 final.

[18] See 'Annual Report 2007 on Monitoring the Application of Community Law' COM(2008)777; 'A Europe of Results—Applying Community Law' COM(2007)502; 'Annual Report 2006 on Monitoring the Application of Community Law' COM(2007)398 and Annex SEC(2007)976; 'Annual Report 2005 on Monitoring the Application of Community Law' COM(2006)416; 'Better Monitoring the Application of Community Law' COM(2002)725 (2002).

[19] See SEC(1998) 903 3–5.

simple legislation helps businesses and citizens to comply with the law without excessive burdens;[20] it facilitates its enforcement; and it addresses complaints of excessive red tape often leading to cases for damages, such as *Francovich*.[21] All this can be achieved by use of legislation that is easy to transpose and apply and takes into account the views of interested parties expressed in consultation under the 1998 Regulatory Policy Guidelines of the Commission and the 2002 General Principles and Minimum Standards for Consultation of Interested Parties by the Commission.[22] Accountability, effectiveness and proportionality were put forward as the main elements of better law-making in the 2002 Communication on European Governance: 'Better Lawmaking'.[23] Moreover, the Commission Communication to the European Council, 'Legislate Less to Act Better: the Facts',[24] emphasised the need to concentrate on policy priorities with strict application of the subsidiarity and proportionality principles (legislate less), the need for improved consultation procedures and the need for clearer, simpler and more accessible legislation (act better). These aims are achievable through the reduction of legislative proposals; the use of alternatives to legislation as a regulatory tool;[25] the quality of legislative drafting through the introduction of drafting guidelines for clear, coherent and unambiguous legislation; the simplification of legislation through SLIM; the appropriate use of formal consolidation (or codification, in today's terminology), recasting and informal consolidation;[26] easier access to information; proper

[20] For an analysis of administrative burdens, see Commission, 'Reducing Administrative Burdens in the European Union' 2008 progress report and 2009 outlook Commission working document COM(2009)16, Annexes EN; 'Reducing Administrative Burdens in the European Union' 2007 progress report and 2008 outlook Commission working document COM (2008)35; Commission, 'Action programme for reducing administrative burdens in the EU' (Communication) COM(2007)23 and Annexes SEC(2007)84 and SEC(2007)85; Commission, 'Measuring administrative costs and reducing administrative burdens in the EU Commission working document' COM(2006)691; EU Standard Cost Model, 'Operational Manual Assessing Administrative Costs set by EU Legislation'; Commission, 'EU common methodology for assessing administrative costs imposed by legislation' (Communication) COM (2005)518; Commission, 'Outline of the proposed EU common methodology and report on the pilot phase' (April–Sept 2005) Annex SEC(2005)1329; Commission, 'Minimising administrative costs imposed by legislation, detailed outline of a possible EU net administrative cost model' Annex to the Communication (COM(2005)97) on 'Better Regulation for Growth and Jobs in the EU' SEC(2005)175.

[21] See Case C-479/93 *Francovich* [1995] ECR I-3843.

[22] Also see Commission, 'Making Simple Market Rules More Effective' (Communication) COM(1998)296 final; and 'Towards a reinforced culture of consultation and dialogue—General principles and minimum standards for consultation of interested parties by the Commission' (Communication) COM(2002)704 (2002).

[23] See Commission, 'European Governance: Better Lawmaking' (Communication) COM/2002/0275 final.

[24] See eg the voluntary agreement between the Commission and European car manufacturers Bull EU 5-1998, point Institutional Affairs, 1.8.3.

[25] See Voluntary Agreement COM(1998)495.

[26] See 'Third progress report on the strategy for simplifying the regulatory environment Commission working document' COM(2009)17, Annex 6; 'First progress report on the

transposition; shared responsibility amongst institutions; and rationalising of national legislation.

The culmination of rules for legislative quality came with the 1998 interinstitutional agreement on common guidelines for the quality of drafting of Community legislation:[27] Community acts must be clear, simple, precise, concise and with homogeneous content. Drafting must be appropriate to the type of act concerned, and to the audience to whom it is addressed. Terminology must be internally and externally consistent. The standard structure of title—preamble—enacting terms—annexes if necessary) applies. The title offers a full indication of the subject matter. Citations set out the legal basis of the act. Recitals set out concise reasons for the chief provisions of the enacting terms without paraphrasing or reproducing them. Only clauses of a normative nature can be included in legislation. Internal and external references must be kept to a minimum. Repeals must be introduced expressly. Dates of transposition or enforcement must be introduced clearly as day/month/year. This was supplemented by the 2003 interinstitutional agreement on better lawmaking. But the 2003 agreement focuses only on: improving interinstitutional coordination and transparency; providing a framework for alternative regulatory instruments; increasing the use of impact assessments; and simplification of EU law.[28]

But the 1998 agreement remains non-binding and rather fragmented in its approach to legislative quality. It seems that on its own, and even in combination with the many relevant EU texts referred to here, the agreement and therefore the EU have failed to demonstrate what the elements of legislative quality must be.

THE POST-LISBON SMART REGULATION INITIATIVE

The fury of action for the achievement of legislative quality in the EU ends somewhere in 2003. Numerous policy documents continued to refer to *Better Regulation*, which continued to be at the forefront of the EU's governance debate, but a closer look at them shows beyond doubt a transfer from legislation as an autonomous product to legislation as a regulatory tool. This is of course exceptionally insightful as legislation is indeed a tool

strategy for the simplification of the regulatory environment Commission working document' COM(2006)690, Annex 2; Commission, 'Implementing the Community Lisbon programme: A strategy for the simplification of the regulatory environment' (Communication) COM(2005)535; Commission, Codification of the Acquis communautaire (Communication) COM(2001)645.

[27] See Interinstitutional agreement of 22 December 1998 on common guidelines for the quality of drafting of Community legislation [1999] OJ C 73, 1.

[28] See Parliament, Council and Commission Interinstitutional Agreement of 16 December 2003 On Better Law-making [2003] OJ C 321/01.

for regulation. But, unfortunately, in the EU this conceptual move led to a notable ignorance of legislation altogether at least from a drafting perspective. One could source the conceptual framework behind this movement as far back as 2001 and the Mandelkern Group report on *Better Regulation*.[29] It is notable that since 2001 the *Better Regulation* reports are pursuant to and therefore limited to proportionality and subsidiarity, whereas from 2007 even the title of *Better Regulation* reports has been usurped by subsidiarity and proportionality, thus excluding scope for legislative quality conventions and innovative assessments.[30] The 2008 'Second strategic review of Better Regulation in the EU' focuses solely on administrative burdens, legislative scrutiny, reducing the number of legislative instruments, and emphasising the shared responsibility of the EU and Member States.[31] Similarly, the 2009 'Third strategic review of Better Regulation in the EU' is another prime example of this move from legislation to regulatory agendas: although clear, precise and accessible legislation lies at the aether of regulatory reform, none of the recommendations address it: pre- and post-legislative scrutiny are the only focus.[32]

The most recent innovation in the field comes with the Smart Regulation Agenda.[33] The October 2010 Commission Communication on Smart Regulation constitutes the formal passing from the old Better Regulation Agenda to the new Smart Regulation Agenda.[34] The Commission identified three key messages in the Agenda. First, Smart Regulation is about the whole policy cycle, and thus touches upon the design of a piece of legislation, its implementation, enforcement, evaluation and revision. Secondly, Smart Regulation remains a shared responsibility between the EU institutions and the Member States. Thirdly, the views of users of regulation have a key role to play in Smart Regulation,[35] as consultation is an element of

[29] See Mandelkern Group on Better Regulation, *Final Report* (13 November 2001) http://ec.europa.eu/governance/better_regulation/documents/mandelkern_report.pdf.

[30] See 'Subsidiarity and Proportionality' Report 2011 (19th Report on Better Lawmaking 2011) COM(2012)373; 'Subsidiarity and Proportionality' Report 2010 (18th Report on Better Lawmaking 2010) COM(2011)344; 'Subsidiarity and Proportionality' Report 2009 (17th Report on Better Lawmaking 2009) COM(2010)547; 'Subsidiarity and Proportionality' Report 2008 (16th Report on Better Lawmaking 2008) COM(2009)504; 'Subsidiarity and Proportionality' Report 2007 (15th Report on Better Lawmaking 2007) COM(2008)586.

[31] See Commission, 'Second strategic review of Better Regulation in the European Union' (Communication) COM(2008) 33 final; COM(2008) 35 final; SEC(2008) 120; COM/2008/0032 final.

[32] See Commission, 'Third strategic review of Better Regulation in the European Union' (Communication) COM(2009) 16 final; COM(2009) 17 final; SEC(2009) 55.

[33] See H Xanthaki, 'The Regulatory Reform Agenda and Modern Innovations in Drafting Style' in L Mader (ed), *Regulatory Reform* (Baden-Baden, Nomos, 2013) 128.

[34] See Commission, 'Smart Regulation in the European Union' (Communication) COM(2010)543 http://eurlex.europa.eu/LexUriServ/LexUriServ.do?uri=CELEX:52010DC0543:EN:NOT.

[35] For an example of extensive consultation on administrative burdens, see Commission Staff Working Document, 'Monitoring and Consultation on Smart Regulation for SMEs

democracy.[36] In other words, the novelty of Smart Regulation refers to three main themes: (1) smart regulation throughout the policy cycle; (2) shared responsibility; and (3) stakeholder engagement.[37]

There is no doubt that Smart Regulation is revolutionary. The reaction of the experts to the Commission's agenda has been positive, although already need for further action has been identified. This includes the need to carry out impact assessments for every new regulatory proposal; to improve the informative value of roadmaps; to make the Commission's Impact Assessment Board more independent; to conduct systematic ex post-evaluations from the end users' perspective; to strengthen the role of the High Level Group; and to consult the public.[38] Smart Regulation presents obvious positive points. It follows Stefanou's identification of the drafting process as a part of the legislative process, which is a part of the policy process.[39] It confirms that EU regulation is a shared responsibility of the institutions and Member States. And it affirms the need for in-depth consultation. Focus is placed on the simplification of EU law via the reduction of administrative burdens past the expected 25 per cent cuts in red tape by 2012; evaluation of law effectiveness and efficiency ex ante via fitness checks on key areas (environment etc)[40] and via strategic general policy evaluations; selection of the 'the best possible' legislation through impact assessment;[41] improvement of implementation record via post legislative scrutiny, SOLVIT[42] and EU Pilot; and achieving clearer and accessible legislation via simple language, codification, recasting and e-access. These are worthy aims. And the Commission can show considerable success. For example,

Accompanying the document Communication from the Commission to the European Parliament, the Council, the European Economic and Social Committee and the Committee of the Regions Smart regulation—Responding to the needs of small and medium-sized enterprises' COM(2013) 122 final SWD(2013) 60 final.

[36] See http://ec.europa.eu/governance/better_regulation/smart_regulation/consultation_en.htm.

[37] See H McColm, 'Smart Regulation: The European Commission's Updated Strategy' (2011) 2 *European Journal of Risk Regulation* 9, 9.

[38] See 'Common Position Paper of the five European independent advisory boards for cutting red tape and better regulation', Adviescollege toetsing regeldruk (ACTAL), The Netherlands; Nationaler Normenkontrollrat (NKR), Germany; Regelrådet, Sweden; Regulatory Impact Assessment Board (RIAB), Czech Republic; Regulatory Policy Committee (RPC), United Kingdom www.regelradet.se/wp-content/uploads/2012/09/2012-Reaction-on-consultation-Smart-Regulation.pdf .

[39] See C Stefanou, 'Drafters, Drafting and the Policy Process' in C Stefanou and H Xanthaki, *Drafting Legislation: A Modern Approach* (Aldershot, Ashgate, 2008) 321.

[40] For examples of fitness checks, see http://ec.europa.eu/dgs/secretariat_general/evaluation/docs/fitness_check_en.pdf; also see http://ec.europa.eu/environment/water/blueprint/fitness_en.htm; and http://ec.europa.eu/transport/air/fitness_check_en.htm.

[41] On impact assessments, see http://ec.europa.eu/governance/impact/key_docs/key_docs_en.htm; http://ec.europa.eu/governance/impact/key_docs/docs/meg_guidelines.pdf; and http://ec.europa.eu/governance/impact/iab/members_en.htm.

[42] See http://ec.europa.eu/solvit/site/about/index_en.htm.

the EU's impact assessment system has been praised as first class.[43] The question is how these noble aims are going to be achieved.

Simplification of EU law is indeed a wonderful goal.[44] A depressing (or it is impressive?) 74 per cent of European citizens believe that the EU generates too much red tape.[45] And the Commission has responded to it via impact assessments and stakeholder consultation,[46] and via regular fitness checks undertaken within the Regulatory Fitness and Performance Programme (REFIT) of December 2012.[47] These initiatives have contributed to a reduction of red tape by well above the 25 per cent target set out in the Administrative Burden Reduction programme:[48] the precise figures correspond to a decrease of 25 per cent of burden in 13 priority areas equivalent to savings of EUR 30.8 billion with a further EUR 5 billion still pending adoption by the co-legislator.[49]

But simplification cannot be taken to mean simply a streamlining of legislation and a reduction of administrative burdens.[50] In fact, the Smart Regulation agenda neglects to address a number of crucial aspects of simplification without which reduction of administrative burdens cannot be achieved.[51] What about simplicity of the chosen policies? If a policy choice is complex in itself, then the reduction of red tape will not suffice to make

[43] See OECD, 'Sustainability in Impact Assessments—A Review of Impact Assessment Systems in selected OECD Countries and the European Commission' (Paris, 2011); European Parliament, 'Comparative Study on the Purpose, Scope and Procedures of Impact Assessments Carried out in the Member States of the EU' (2011); CEPS/University of Exeter, 'Regulatory Quality in the European Commission and the UK: Old Questions and New Findings' (2012).

[44] See 'Third progress report on the strategy for simplifying the regulatory environment' COM(2009) 17.

[45] See Eurobarometer Question QA16.4, 59: http://ec.europa.eu/public_opinion/archives/eb/eb79/eb79_anx_en.pdf.

[46] See 'Smart Regulation—Responding to small and medium-sized enterprises' COM(2013)122; also see Commission, 'Commission follow-up to the "TOP TEN" Consultation of SMEs on EU Regulation' (Communication) COM(2013) 446 final.

[47] See COM(2012)746 final.

[48] See SWD(2013)401 final.

[49] ibid, 4. This figure includes, for example, reduced inspection costs for the marketing of fruit and vegetables (EUR 970m), exempting micro-enterprises from the accounting directives and further modernisation of the overall regime (EUR 6471m), simplifying reporting changes to medicines, pharmacovigilance and applications for clinical trials (EUR 368m), reducing statistical requirements in intra EU trade, agriculture, industrial production etc (EUR 330m), VAT electronic invoicing, simplified refunds, one-stop-shop, special arrangements for SMEs and distance sales (EUR 26,000m). These examples refer to estimated burden based on the Commission proposal.

[50] See Commission, 'Action Programme for Reducing Administrative Burdens in the European Union' (Communication) COM(2007) 23 http://eur-lex.europa.eu/LexUriServ/LexUriServ.do?uri=CELEX:52010DC0543:EN:NOT; also see Commission, 'Regulatory Fitness and Performance (REFIT): Results and Next Steps' (Communication) COM(2013) 685 final, 1.

[51] For a demonstration on what is included in Smart Regulation, see European Commission, 'Communication from the President: The Working Methods of the Commission 2010-2014' C(2010) 1100, http://ec.europa.eu/commission_2010-2014/president/news/documents/pdf/c2010_1100_en.pdf.

it accessible to the citizens. What about simplicity in the selected regulatory means? Is the notoriously user unfriendly legislation not a most complex regulatory tool? And so reducing administrative burdens via legislation carries inherent complexity, which may well endanger the end result. What about the chosen drafting style as a means of simplifying the expression of a simple policy when a simpler regulatory tool is considered ineffective? A complex legislative style would diminish the actual effect of any simplification effort irrespective of what the percentage of administrative burdens in the simple policy chosen may be: if the users cannot understand the language of the law, how can they benefit from the opportunities created by a policy of reduced red tape? What about straightforward enforcement methods? And could one rely on a reduction of administrative burdens within the EU text, if the national implementing measures are complex and seize on any opportunity for discretion in the EU text in order to add further burdens? And finally could EU law be considered simple when the methods of pre- and post-legislative scrutiny utilised are inherently complex and therefore inaccessible for the users?

Similarly, evaluation of law effectiveness and efficiency ex ante is a fantastic initiative in theory.[52] It is defined as a judgement of interventions according to their results and impacts, and the needs they aim to satisfy.[53] But can it be achieved simply via fitness checks and general policy evaluations? In a legislative environment where the definition of effectiveness has not been provided conclusively, the goal that the regulatory team is supposed to be trying to achieve becomes a moving target, a vague and ambiguous goalpost, which carries a different meaning for the different actors in the regulatory process, much more so between EU and national levels.[54] But even where the concept of effectiveness appears clear, which are the specific criteria of effectiveness by way of successful regulation that must be used in reference to a specific piece of legislation? The application of the generic elements of the semantic field of the concept of effectiveness in the specific context of a piece of legislation as applied in the specific legal system that serves a specific society in a specific time is not an easy task, and should not really be ignored or left to chance. There is a dire need to ensure that the criteria for effectiveness of any piece of legislation are agreed between policy-makers, law experts and legislative drafters, and that they are clearly expressed in the legislation itself via perhaps their inclusion in a

[52] See The Evaluation Partnership, 'Evaluation of the Commission's Impact Assessment System Final Report 2007' 60 http://ec.europa.eu/governance.impact/key_docs/docs/tep_eias_finalreport.executive surnmary_en.pdf.

[53] See G Luchetta, 'Impact Assessment and the Policy Cycle in the EU' (2012) 3 *European Journal of Risk Regulation* 561, 572–573.

[54] For an example of descriptions for a strategy of evaluation without identifying evaluation of what and against what criteria, see Commission, 'EU Regulatory Fitness' (Communication) SWD(2012) 422 final; SWD(2012) 423 final, COM(2012) 746 final, 24.

purpose clause or an objectives article. These can then be carried through to post-legislative scrutiny. They can then be utilised to confirm effectiveness, thus allowing the text to continue its legislative life.

But how will ineffectiveness be addressed? What if the effectiveness criteria are not met by the piece of legislation at the pre-set time of post-legislative monitoring: will the legislation die an automatic death via perhaps a sunset clause, will it continue to plague the statute book as it stands until an enlightened decision-maker decides to address the problem, or will it lead to an automatic exercise of fine-tuning via perhaps an amending piece of legislation?

Moreover, Smart Regulation fails to identify the way in which, if at all, evaluation will take place at the Member State level. Here other considerations should also come into play. Will national scrutiny be compulsory or could the Member States be offered discretion on the basis of national sovereignty in the law-making process? Moreover, Smart Regulation fails to address the extent of any national scrutiny process, namely whether it must relate strictly to the national implementing measures or whether it can refer to the original EU text. This is rather crucial, especially in reference to national legislation, which departs from the policy and law of the EU by means of either a direct or indirect breach or even legitimately by means of an acceptable exercise of discretion as would be the case with the implementation of a directive. And what if the national scrutiny exercise identifies a flaw in the EU policy? Can that be reported back to the EU and will this result in any action at the EU level?

Moreover, the initiative fails to define efficiency. It is unclear whether this refers to a mathematical exercise involving financial cost or whether social and other impact must be calculated towards the reduction of burdens, or indeed how these can be calculated.

The improvement of the implementation record is a third worthy point of reference for Smart Regulation.[55] But once again one has to distinguish between the aim and the proposed methods for its achievement. Can implementation be improved solely via post-legislative scrutiny, availability of SOLVIT and the EU Pilot on clarification and assistance with the application of EU legislation?[56] What about clear guidance on the definition of complete transposition for new, older and aspiring Member States? What about clear guidance on the definition of quality in legislation for the purposes of EU drafting but also EU transposition? What about the establishment

[55] See Commission, '28th Annual Report on Monitoring the Application of EU Law' COM(2011) 588 final, 3.4.1 http://ec.europa.eu/eu_law/docs/docs_infringements/annual_report_28/com_2011_588_en.pdf .

[56] On EU Pilot, see Report from the Commission '29th Annual Report on monitoring the application of EU law (2011)' SWD(2012) 399 final, SWD(2012) 400 final, COM(2012) 714 final.

of national drafting offices with trained specialist drafters vetting (if not drafting) implementation measures on the basis of the UK model for drafting national primary legislation (Office of Parliamentary Counsel)? What about extending the scrutiny of implementation beyond substantive transposition to technical quality of transposition?

And finally, who would disagree with the election of the 'the best possible' legislation? But is this really achievable simply via impact assessments, clearer and accessible legislation, simple language, codification, recasting and e-access? What about opening the debate for a holistic approach to effectiveness in the sense of the use of legislation as a tool for regulation? What about setting a hierarchy of goals for the drafter? What about training drafters to achieve these goals? What about considering a central drafting office with trained drafters within EU institutions, including the Commission, the Council and the Parliament? What about training national drafters to contribute to the effort?[57]

And so even post Lisbon, EU legislative quality continues to face challenges which have remained unaddressed, for the most part. The analysis of the relevant EU initiatives, namely the Better Regulation agenda, identified a pause somewhere around 2003. Despite the fury of activity in the field of legislative quality before then, all initiatives from the EU after that date refer to legislative quality as an aim but have transferred the focus of attention to holistic regulatory quality thus leaving legislative quality aside.[58]

The move to regulatory quality as the main focus of the EU's better governance campaign is by no means a negative development in the field. Indeed, legislative quality is an intrinsic part of regulatory quality: without regulatory quality one cannot perceive the notion of legislative quality. As legislative drafting can only aspire to effectiveness, namely to the production of a legislative text that, with the cooperation and synergy of all other actors in the policy process, can achieve the regulatory aims, one cannot possibly expect it possible to produce quality legislation when the regulatory aims are erroneous or illegal, when the choice of legislation as a regulatory tool is inappropriate, or indeed when the implementation of the legislation has not been thought through. But at the same time one cannot possibly perceive regulatory quality without, in cases where legislation is the appropriate regulatory tool, legislative quality. To me, this is the great error of the EU's current strategy. By turning the focus of attention from legislation to regulation the EU seems to have forgotten about legislation

[57] For a full presentation of my critique to Smart Regulation, see H Xanthaki, 'Implementation of EU Legislation', Oral Evidence, Public Hearing at the Legal Affairs Committee of the European Parliament 'Better Regulation' Hearing (Brussels, 21 June 2011).

[58] See M Mousmouti, 'The Effectiveness Test' (2012) 6 *Legisprudence* 191, 196.

altogether, somehow trying to simply wish away the continuing problems of legislative quality.[59] The same conclusion is reached by the analysis of Smart Regulation, the 2010 EU initiative constituting the successor of Better Regulation.

What is even more disappointing is the 2020 Agenda for Europe, where not only Better Regulation but also Smart Regulation is ignored.[60]

The question is why the EU felt that it could move from Better Regulation to Smart Regulation, and then to a strategy for growth and competitiveness. From the perspective of legislative studies at least, neither of the two moves make sense. Why would the EU decide to leave Better Regulation and Smart Regulation aside, when neither of these agendas has born the desired fruits? Surely, one could not seriously support the argument that EU legislation and national implementing legislation, or indeed the EU regulatory environment has reached perfection.

Assuming that the latter is evident to all, the answer to this question must be sought in the determination of what actually were the desired regulatory aims for Better Regulation and Smart Regulation in the first place. Although most of us in the drafting and regulation world spent our time and energy dissecting each and every clause in these two agendas, rejoicing in the illusion of a possible focus to legislation and regulation, trying to understand what the new agendas and their clauses actually meant and how they could be achieved, we missed a crucial point: the purpose clause of both agendas, namely removing barriers to businesses and rendering them competitive against non-EU enterprises. Although we managed to ignore it totally, the expressly stated purpose of these agendas really was not to address the quality of legislation or the quality of regulation in the EU: it was simply to use legislative and then regulatory quality as a means of pursuing the policy aim of growth and competitiveness. It is precisely this aim which is repeated, and even more clearly expressed, in the 2020 Agenda for Europe.

So let us revisit our question: have the two agendas born fruit? If one contrasts them against their expressly stated purpose, in which case they can only be viewed as short- and medium-term measures or as initial steps leading to the 2020 Agenda, yes they have. With hindsight, and immeasurable disappointment, one can now see the revelation of the EU's strategy. The EU chose to regulate in stages in order to address competitiveness and growth for EU businesses, and it pursued the Better Regulation and then the Smart Regulation initiatives as simply the first and second stages of the final stage

[59] See C-H Montin, 'Smart Regulation in the European Union' http://montin.com/documents/smartregulation.pdf.

[60] See http://ec.europa.eu/europe2020/index_en.htm.

(the 2020 Agenda) for the originally conceived regulatory product, growth and competitiveness. The majestic concept of this long-term strategy has eluded me, and most of my drafting and regulation colleagues. Having seen its development, one can only praise the EU for its exemplary application of the legislation in stages tool. Moving from the generic specialised and politically innocent agenda of legislative quality, to the generic specialised and politically sensitive regulatory agenda, as a means of reaching the now politically acceptable but previously sensitive aim of growth and competitiveness is a brilliant policy strategy. The first two stages of the regulation putting this policy in effect have been successful, if one considers them as initial short-term stages of the wider competitiveness agenda: businesses now have some understanding of simpler, business-related EU laws (SLIM), and administrative barriers have been lifted via consultation, simplification and pre- and post-legislative monitoring. So Better Regulation and Smart Regulation can now be laid to rest, while work continues full steam ahead for pure growth and competitiveness.

But is this final revelation, or subjective realisation, that the EU was pursuing competitiveness and growth all along good news? I'm afraid not. What the EU has clumsily missed is a unique opportunity to finally balance its focus of attention on both businesses and citizens. While the first enjoy the fruits of Better Regulation, Smart Regulation and the 2020 Agenda for Europe, citizens are still facing the same issues of confusion stemming from the multitude of bad EU laws (not tackled by SLIM as they did not relate to SMEs), and bad regulation (not tackled by Smart Regulation since administrative burdens were not applicable). This imbalance may well have been intentional. After all, growth and competitiveness is a policy focused on businesses only. But how can this be justified within the focus on citizen and citizenship expressed clearly in the Treaty of Lisbon? How can it be accommodated within the emphasis on social equity for EU citizens so eloquently professed in the Treaty of Lisbon, which declares the passage from the internal market to a forum of citizenship, international justice, and peace?

My view is that the new challenge for Europe in the field of EU legislative studies is to apply Better Regulation, Smart Regulation and the 2020 Agenda for Europe to citizens, along with businesses, thus showing that the Treaty of Lisbon is not a list of good political intentions, but an accurate reflection of the new EU for its citizens and peoples. The challenge is to go back to Better Regulation and Smart Regulation and assess their success from the point of view of the citizens using the Treaty's citizenship concept as a focus. Transferring the focus from businesses to citizens would tint the picture of the effectiveness of these three regulatory initiatives with much darker colours. Because the amount of work that remains in order to make EU legislation and EU regulation palatable is daunting. But absolutely necessary.

THE UK APPROACH TO REGULATORY QUALITY

In the UK, regulatory reform started in essence with the 1997 Better Regulation Task Force principles aiming to cover any policy intervention, and its enforcement: proportionality; accountability; consistency; transparency; and targeting. A number of government initiatives flourished during that time making the link between better regulation and policy-making;[61] impact assessment;[62] written consultation;[63] implementation periods;[64] and enforcement.[65] The 2003 Better Regulation Task Force's 'Principles of Good Regulation'[66] linked better regulation with less legislation, and offered a number of regulatory alternatives: do nothing; advertising campaigns and education; using the market; financial incentives; self-regulation and voluntary codes of practice; and prescriptive regulation.

Regulatory reform took centre stage in the manifesto of the Coalition Government as evident in 'The Coalition: our programme for government' document.[67] The government undertook to cut red tape[68] by introducing a 'one-in, one-out' rule whereby no new regulation is brought in without other regulation being cut by a greater amount;[69] to end the culture of 'tick-box' regulation and instead target inspections on high-risk organisations through co-regulation and improving professional standards; to impose sunset clauses on regulations and regulators to ensure that the need for each regulation is regularly reviewed; and to give the public the opportunity to challenge the worst regulations. Such was the importance attributed to better regulation that the Prime Minister in his letter of 6 April 2011 to all Cabinet Ministers declared that:

> We need to tackle regulation with vigour to free businesses to compete and create jobs, and give people greater freedom and personal responsibility. … I want us to be the first Government in modern history to leave office having reduced the overall burden of regulation, rather than increasing it.

61 See 'Cabinet Office Guidance on Policy-making' www.policyhub.gov.uk.

62 See 'Better Policy Making: a Guide to Regulatory Impact Assessment' www.cabinetoffice.gov.uk/regulation/scrutiny/betterpolicy.htm.

63 See 'Code of Practice on Written Consultation' www.cabinet-office.gov.uk/servicefirst/2000/consult/code/ConsultationCode.htm.

64 See 'Guidance on Implementation Periods' www.sbs.gov.uk/content/pdf/implementation-guidelines.pdf.

65 See 'Enforcement Concordat' www.cabinetoffice.gov.uk/regulation/PublicSector/enforcement/Enforcement.htm.

66 See http://webarchive.nationalarchives.gov.uk/20100407162704/http:/archive.cabinetoffice.gov.uk/brc/upload/assets/www.brc.gov.uk/principlesleaflet.pdf.

67 See 'The Coalition: our Programme for Government' www.gov.uk/government/uploads/system/uploads/attachment_data/file/78977/coalition_programme_for_government.pdf.

68 For further information on the Red Tape Challenge, see www.redtapechallenge.cabinetoffice.gov.uk/home/index.

69 See www.bis.gov.uk/assets/biscore/better-regulation/docs/o/11-671-one-in-one-out-methodology.

In order to achieve this aim the UK Government introduced a one-in two-out approach. It also undertook to use regulation for the achievement of its policy objectives only where: non-regulatory approaches cannot lead to satisfactory outcomes; cost benefits analysis demonstrates a clear margin of superiority of regulation to alternative, self-regulatory or non-regulatory approaches; or the regulation and the enforcement framework can be implemented in a fashion which is demonstrably proportionate, accountable, consistent, transparent and targeted.[70]

The promise to allow public participation to the cause is formulated in the initiative known as The Red Tape Challenge, which encourages the private sector to help identify existing regulations that they believe should be removed from, or amended on, the statute book. The Coalition Government reports that since 2011 its deregulation efforts have outweighed the costs of new domestic regulation by over -£850 million: the bulk of the regulatory savings delivered through private pensions' indexation in the First Statement of New Regulation has now been offset by pensions' automatic-enrolment. Excluding private pension reform, regulatory savings to business since 2011 are expected to be at least -£160 million.[71]

The number of Acts passed in 2012 is only 20 with a total number of pages of 1886:[72] this is a new low after the peak of the late-1990s and early-2000s. But, whilst the number of Acts has decreased since the 1980s, the mean average number of pages per Act has increased significantly, from 37 and 47 pages during the 1980s and 1990s respectively, to 85 in the past decade; if one compares these numbers with the 1950s when the average was 16, a trend of fewer but longer Acts becomes evident.[73] One could contribute this increase to plain language drafting and to the increasing amounts of white space and bigger margins leading to 20 per cent fewer words on a page.[74] However, there is an undeniably crucial factor to be taken into account: over the last 30 to 40 years the number

[70] See Department for Business, Innovation and Skills, 'Better Regulation Framework Manual' (July 2013) 4 www.gov.uk/government/uploads/system/uploads/attachment_data/file/211981/bis-13-1038-better-regulation-framework-manual-guidance-for-officials.pdf.

[71] See HM Government, 'One-in, One-out: Third Statement of New Regulation' (July 2012) www.bis.gov.uk/assets/biscore/better-regulation/docs/o/12-p96b-one-in-one-out-fourth-statement-new-regulation.pdf.

[72] See HL Library Note LLN 2013/008, 'Volume of Legislation', 4.

[73] See HL Library Note, LLN 2011/028, 'Volume of Legislation'.

[74] See R Heaton, House of Commons Political and Constitutional Reform Committee, *Ensuring Standards in the Quality of Legislation, First Report* (HC 2013–14, 85 incorporating HC 2012–13, 74-i to vii) Question 64.

of statutory instruments has steadily increased.[75] And so the volume of legislation, including primary and delegated, seems to be fighting its ground in practice.[76]

Within the context of regulatory reform in the UK each government department now has a Better Regulation Unit whose task is to cut red tape and reduce regulatory overload.[77] Thus, the task of controlling the developing new regulation remains within the competent department.[78] Oversight of these units is undertaken via the 2009 Regulatory Policy Committee (RPC),[79] which provides independent scrutiny of proposed regulatory measures, and the 2010 Cabinet sub-committee entitled the Reducing Regulation Committee, which demands a robust case for each new regulation. The RPC undertakes its duty via the provision of external and independent challenge on the evidence and analysis of regulations presented in impact assessments supporting the development of new regulatory measures proposed by the government.[80] At the same time the Better Regulation Executive within the Department for Business, Innovation and Skills leads regulatory reform by identifying and supporting the positive outcome of regulation, whereas the National Audit Office researches and reports on aspects of regulatory reform, such as impact assessment,[81] administrative burdens reduction or the business aspect of

[75] See R Cracknell and R Clements, 'Acts and Statutory Instruments: the Volume of UK Legislation 1950 to 2012' HC Standard Note SN/SG/2911, 2.

[76] And not just in the UK: see R Pagano, *Introduzione alla legistica—L'arte di preparare le leggi* (Milan, Giuffre, 1999) 6.

[77] For evidence of this policy see Department for Environment Food and Rural Affairs, 'Better regulation evidence plan 2011/12' (Joint Evidence Plan with Defra and Environment Agency) (April 2011) www.defra.gov.uk/publications/files/pb13490-ep-better-reg.pdf.

[78] For an example of Better Regulation with specific application to the environment, see Department for Environment, Food and Rural Affairs, 'Red Tape Challenge—Environment Theme Proposals' (March 2012) www.defra.gov.uk/publications/files/pb13728-red-tape-environment.pdf.

[79] For the 2012 Report of the Committee, see http://regulatorypolicycommittee.independent gov.uk/wp-content/uploads/2011/09/Rating Regulation-July-2011-FINAL-A.pdf.

[80] See www.bis.gov.uk/assets/biscore/better-regulation/docs/o/12-p96b-one-in-one-out-fourth-statement-new-regulation.pdf; also see RPC, 'Rating Regulation: An Independent Report on the Analysis Supporting Regulatory Proposals, January–June 2011', 7 http://regulatorypolicycommittee.independent.gov.uk/wp-content/uploads/2011/09/Rating-Regulation-July-2011-FINAL-A.pdf.

[81] For the latest depiction of the government's approach on impact assessments, see Department for Business, Innovation & Skills 'Impact Assessments: Guidance for Government Departments' (27 Feb 2014) www.gov.uk/government/collections/impact-assessments-guidance-for-government-departments.

regulation. The many steps ensuring regulatory quality for measures of domestic and EU origin are demonstrated in the two graphs below:[82]

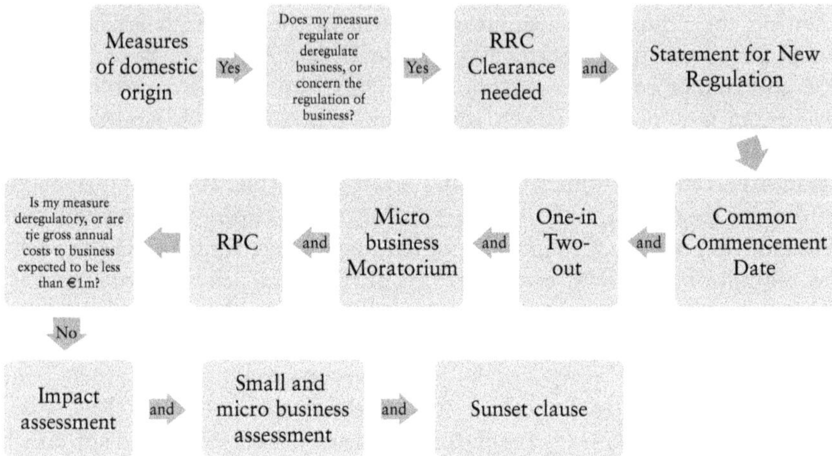

Figure 19.1: Schematic Process of New Regulations: Domestic Measures

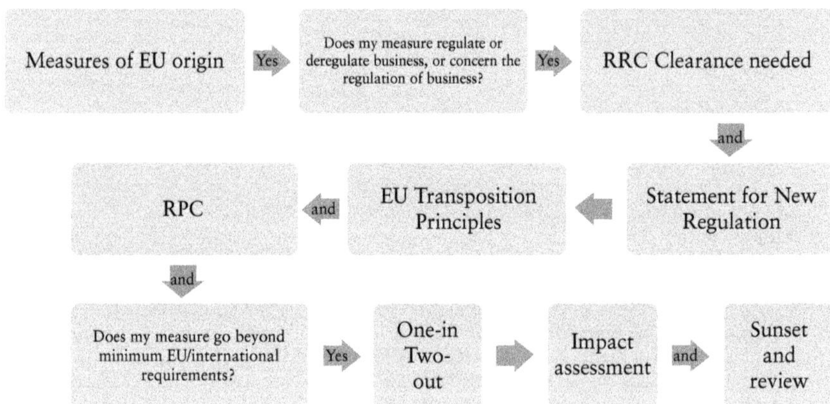

Figure 19.2: Schematic Process of New Regulations: Measures of EU Origin

There is little doubt that the UK has been very active in the field of regulatory reform. This is evidenced by a recent OECD review of the UK's Better Regulation policy implementation which pronounces the regulatory

[82] The source of both graphs is Department for Business, Innovation and Skills, 'Better Regulation Framework Manual' (July 2013) 6 and 7 www.gov.uk/government/uploads/system/uploads/attachment_data/file/211981/bis-13-1038-better-regulation-framework-manual-guidance-for-officials.pdf.

reforms in the UK as impressive.[83] Points of excellence identified by the OECD include the effective balance between policy breadth and the stock and the flow of regulation; the breadth and depth of ex ante impact assessment exercises before regulation; the effective risk-based enforcement of regulation; and the extensive application of the EU's Better Regulation initiatives in the UK.[84] Points in need of further reinforcement identified by OECD include the need to reinforce initiatives for citizens and public sector workers as a means of balancing the use of business as the main policy actors; the need to apply in practice even further the excellent existing transparency and consultation processes; and the need to develop a longer-term strategy of regulation.

MODERN PARLIAMENTS AND LEGISLATIVE QUALITY

Although the striving of governments for legislative quality has been the subject of much debate in the last two decades, the contribution of modern parliaments to this cause has not been documented. 'Parliament should at least be a partner in the process of setting the standards of what constitutes a well prepared piece of legislation, rather than permitting the executive to determine this from bill to bill'.[85] Parliaments are expected to scrutinise legislative drafts,[86] but there has been little analysis on what legislative quality is,[87] and what are the precise and concrete criteria for its scrutiny at pre- and post-legislative stages.[88] If the UK Houses of Parliament are excellent showcases for the identification of processes of pre-legislative scrutiny[89] that can effectively contribute to effectiveness of legislation as legislative quality.[90] Pre-legislative scrutiny gives Parliament and stakeholders in the wider society an opportunity to influence the Bill's content before it is passed,[91] thus offering the opportunity to address issues of legislative

[83] See www.oecd.org/dataoecd/61/60/44912018.pdf.

[84] For a listing of such policies and their implementation in the UK, see www.bis.gov.uk/policies/bre/improving-eu-regulation/guiding-principles-eu-legislation.

[85] See House of Commons Political and Constitutional Reform Committee, *Ensuring Standards in the Quality of Legislation, First Report* (n 74).

[86] See U Villani, 'L'impatto del trattato di Lisbona sul ruolo deo parliament nazionali' in C Decaro and N Lupo, *Il 'Dialogo' tra Parliamenti: Obiettivi e Risultati* (Rome, LUISS University Press , 2009) 407, 410–11.

[87] See A Brazier, S Kalitowski and G Rosenblatt with M Korris, *Law in the Making: Influence and Change in the Legislative Process* (London, Hansard Society, 2008) 193–94.

[88] See A Flückinger, 'Concluding Remarks: Can Better Regulation be Achieved by Guiding Parliaments and Governments? How the Definition of the Quality of Legislation Affects Law Improvement Methods' (2010) 4 *Legisprudence* 213, 213.

[89] See A Kennon, 'Pre-legislative Scrutiny of Draft Bills' (2004) *Public Law* 477, 492.

[90] For an excellent analysis on this issue, see A Samuels, 'Ensuring Standards in the Quality of Legislation' (2013) 34 *Statute Law Review* 296.

[91] See Law Commission, 'Post-Legislative Scrutiny' (Law Com 302, 2006) (Cm 6945, 2006).

quality ante facto.[92] Effectiveness must be at the forefront of pre-legislative scrutiny, and this involves evidence-based, empirical research.[93]

What criteria of legislative quality are used in the UK Parliament?[94] In May 2013 the UK's House of Commons assigned the Political and Constitutional Reform Committee with the task of reporting on 'Ensuring standards in the quality of legislation'. Richard Heaton, First Parliamentary Counsel, stated that pre-legislative scrutiny of draft Bills (in committee before the Bill is finalised) is 'one of the best ways of improving legislation and ensuring that it meets the quality standards that Parliament and the public are entitled to expect'. But not all Bills are suitable for pre-legislative scrutiny.[95] Still only a minority of Bills are published in draft and fewer are discussed in committee: in 2013 out of the 58 government post-legislative scrutiny memoranda[96] only three were the subject of dedicated reports by committees, although there has been some other post-legislative scrutiny activity.[97] As far back as 1992, the Rippon Commission concluded that there is not enough post-legislative review of the working of Acts.[98] More recently the government undertook the obligation to extend post-legislative scrutiny to all Acts.[99] It is also interesting to note that a Code of Legislative Standards is currently being drafted. The House of Commons Political and Constitutional Reform Committee concluded that:

> Parliament must have a stronger role as a partner with the Government in setting and monitoring standards of legislation. This will require a change of attitude by parliamentarians in asserting their role and 'caring more' about legislative standards, and in using existing processes and documents, such as Impact Assessments, more effectively. It may also require the creation of new mechanisms to assist them in the performance of their legislative duties. A change in attitude by Government is also required in its work with Parliament.[100]

[92] See HC Deb 24 Feb 2004 vol 418 col 17WH (Phil Woolas MP, Deputy Leader of the House of Commons).

[93] See P Westerman, 'Breaking the Circle: Goal-legislation and the Need for Empirical Research' (2013) 1 *The Theory and Practice of Legislation* 385, 413.

[94] For a full analysis, see H Xanthaki, 'Legislative Drafting: The Birth of a New Sub-discipline of Law' (2013) 1 *IALS Student Review* 57.

[95] See L Clapinska, 'Post-Legislative Scrutiny of Acts of Parliament' (2006) 32 *Commonwealth Law Bulletin* 191, 203.

[96] See Cabinet Office 'Guide to Making Legislation' (June 2012) pt 40.

[97] See Liaison Committee, *Select Committee Effectiveness, Resources and Powers: Responses to the Committee's Second Report* (HC 2012–13, 911) 12.

[98] See Hansard Society Commission (chaired by Lord Rippon), 'Making the Law' (Nov 1992) para 316; also see Commons Modernisation Committee, *The Legislative Process* (HC 1997–98, 190); Lords Constitution Committee, *Parliament and the Legislative Process* (HL 2003–04, 173); Commons Modernisation Committee, *The Legislative Process* (HC 2005–06, 1097).

[99] See Leader of the House of Commons, 'Post-legislative Scrutiny—The Government's Approach' (Cm 7320, 2008); also see Constitution Committee, *Parliament and the Legislative Process* (HL 2003–04, 173-I) paras 167–68, 171, 180, 189 and 285.

[100] See House of Commons Political and Constitutional Reform Committee, *Ensuring Standards in the Quality of Legislation, First Report* (n 74) para 28.

And so what must parliaments check for? There is a long list of basic quality principles that can serve as a checklist for modern parliamentarians, who strive to contribute to legislative quality:

1. Preliminary provisions
   a. Title: brief, accurate, to the point, unique, distinctive
   b. Preamble: exclusively legal provisions on legal basis and legislative process
   c. Enacting clause: according to house style
   d. Commencement: clear date
   e. Objectives provision: measurable criteria of post-legislative scrutiny
2. Substantive provisions
   a. Wording:
      i. Clarity
      ii. Precision
      iii. Unambiguity
   b. Content
      i. Within the scope of the constitution/law/legislation
      ii. Objectives achievable via means foreseen
      iii. Post-legislative scrutiny cycle/sunset clause
3. Final provisions
   a. Savings and transitional: these may also be placed in a Schedule if they are long
   b. Repeals
   c. Consequential amendments: these may be placed in an annex especially if the repeals and consequential amendments are numerous and can conveniently be presented in a tabular form
   d. Annexes

There is a direct link between quality of legislation and certainty in the law, and ultimately the rule of law and human rights. Demanding that citizens comply with bad laws knowingly can be viewed as a form of entrapment of citizens. Is it not within the mandate of parliaments to defend the rights of citizens to clear, precise and unambiguous legislation as a means of achieving effective regulation?

And so, although it is the task of the executive to draft legislation of good quality, modern parliaments have a crucial role to play in scrutinising the product offered to them by the executive. Policy considerations set aside, parliaments have to scrutinise legislation under the prism of legislative quality also. Legislative quality is synonymous with effectiveness of legislation. It is imperative for the modern parliamentarian to become aware of what is effectiveness, and how it can be achieved. The effort of training in legislative quality is great. But the rewards for the country are certainly worth it.

20

Legislative Education and Training[1]

EDUCATION AND TRAINING

Finally, I turn to the question of training. Having examined in depth what are the elements of good regulation and good legislation as a means of regulation, it is worth concluding with a brief reference to training and education in this field of legislative studies.

The eternal debate between those, mainly older, traditionalists[2] who profess that drafting can only be learnt on the job[3] and those innovationists who recommend a combination of formal and on the job training[4] remains lively. In order to take a stance on this continuing discussion one must inevitably turn to the nature of legislative drafting. This has been analysed in chapter one. But it is worth reminding oneself of the basic elements of each party to the debate.[5]

The prevailing view, mostly within the common law world, is that drafting is a pure form of art[6] or a quasi-craft.[7] It is this approach to the

[1] For the original version of this chapter, see H Xanthaki, 'Duncan Berry: A True Visionary of Training in Legislative Drafting' (2011) *The Loophole* 18 and also see H Xanthaki, 'EU Legislative Quality post-Lisbon: the Challenges of Smart Regulation' (2014) 35 *Statute Law Review* 66.

[2] See MM Hoyt, 'Education, Training and Retention of Legislative Draftsmen in Canada' (1979) 5 *Commonwealth Law Bulletin* 260, 273; also see J Ewens, 'Legislative Draftsmen: Their Recruitment and Training' (1983) 57 *Australian Law Journal* 567, 567–70.

[3] This is the prevalent view in the Commonwealth: see D Hull, 'Commonwealth Survey of Terms and Conditions of Service of Legislative Draftsmen' (1984) 10 *Commonwealth Law Bulletin* 1357, 1359.

[4] See D Berry, 'Legislative Drafting Training in the Hong Kong Department of Justice' (2005) *The Loophole*, www.opc.gov.au/calc/papers.htm#CALCpapers2005; also see C Parkhill, 'Best Practices for Developing Drafting Team Expertise—Australia: Publications and Presentations' (Canadian Institute for the Administration of Justice conference, Ottawa, 11–12 Sept 2008).

[5] For an analysis on the science v art debate, see H Xanthaki, 'On Transferability of Legislative Solutions: the Functionality Test' in C Stefanou and H Xanthaki (eds), *Drafting Legislation: A Modern Approach—in Memoriam of Sir William Dale* (Aldershot, Ashgate-Dartmouth, 2008) 1.

[6] See BG Scharffs, 'Law as Craft' (2001) 45 *Vanderbilt Law Review* 2339.

[7] See C Nutting, 'Legislative Drafting: A Review' (1955) 41 *American Bar Association Journal* 76.

discipline that supported the mentoring style of training for drafters. If drafting is an art or a craft, then creativity and innovation lie at the core of the task. Rules and conventions bear relative value, and the main task of the drafter is to learn the craft from those with more experience. If one believes that drafting is an art, then formal training is not relevant to drafters. In other words, if experience is the only thing that really matters, then simply time spent by a senior may offer the apprentice the only opportunity to learn on the job. But is drafting really a liberal skill possessed by enlightened legal scholars who take part in drafting committees on behalf of a variety of governmental ministries and agencies drafting legislation?[8]

Or is drafting a science[9] or technique?[10] This is the prevailing approach in most of the civil law world. If drafting is a science, then there are formal rules and conventions whose inherent teleogenesis manages to produce predictable results, provided that the application is correct. If this approach is followed, then there is plenty of scope for formal training. Drafters may learn the rules and conventions of their science, and the correct way in which these are applied in order to produce predictable results.

The real question is of course whether one is bound to a strict choice between art or science. If one sees drafting as a sub-discipline of law, then there must be a third option: law is not part of the arts, nor is it part of the sciences[11] in the positivist sense.[12] In science rules apply with universality and infallibility: gravity applies everywhere in the world (ok, on earth), and at all times. Law is different. 'All law is universal but about some things it is not possible to make a universal statement which will be correct ... the error is not in the law nor in the legislator but in the nature of the thing'.[13] But rejecting the view that drafting is a science does not necessarily confirm that drafting is an art. Art tends to lack any sense of rules. In the pursuit of aesthetic pleasure, art uses whatever tools are available. Art is anarchic. But drafting is not. Of course its rules are not rigid, but they are present. The use of synonyms is a principle by which drafters abide, mainly to serve clarity. There may be exceptions to all rules

[8] See F Ost and M van de Kerchove, *Jalons pour une Theorie Critique du Droit* (Brussels, Publications des Facultés universitaires Saint-Louis, 1987) 52.

[9] See contra 'Editorial Review' (1903) 22 *Canadian Law Times* 437.

[10] See contra J-C Piris, 'The Legal Orders of the European Union and of the Member States: Peculiarities and Influences in Drafting' (2006) 8 *European Journal of Law Reform* 1.

[11] For an analysis of the contra argument on law as a science, see M Speziale, 'Langdell's Concept of Law as Science: The Beginning of Anti-Formalism in American Legal Theory' (1980) 5 *Vanderbilt Law Review* 1.

[12] See RR Formoy, 'Special Drafting' (1938) 21 *Bell Yard: Journal of the Law Society's School of Law* 3; but see contra C Langdell, 'Harvard Celebration Speeches' (1887) 3 *Law Quarterly Review* 123.

[13] See Aristotle, E.N., 5.10.1137b13–24.

of drafting, but this does not mean that there are no rules. And these rules carry with them a degree of relevant predictability, since the latter is one of the six elements of theory.[14]

Since drafting is neither pure science nor pure art, what is it? For Aristotle[15] all human intellectuality can be classified as[16] science as *episteme*; art as *techne*; or *phronesis*[17] as the *praxis* of subjective decision-making on factual circumstances or the practical wisdom of the subjective classification of factual circumstances to principles and wisdom as *episteme*.[18] Law and drafting seem to be classical examples of *phronesis*, as they are liberal disciplines with loose but prevalent rules and conventions whose correct application comes through knowledge and experience. Drafting as *phronesis* is 'akin to practical wisdom that comes from an intimate familiarity with contingencies and uncertainties of various forms of social practice embedded in complex social settings'.[19] In other words, the art of drafting lies with the subjective use and application of its science, with the conscious subjective Aristotelian application and implementation of its universal theoretical principles to the concrete circumstances of the problem.[20] *Phronesis* supports the selection of solutions made on the basis of informed yet subjective application of principles on set circumstances.[21] *Phronesis* is 'practical wisdom that responds to nuance and a sense of the concrete, outstripping abstract or general theories of what is right. In this way, practical wisdom relies on a kind of immediate insight, rather than more formal inferential processes'.[22]

But who are the *phronimoi*[23] drafters, namely these who possess practical wisdom? The drafter's task involves mainly analysis,[24] namely principled

[14] See B Flyvbjerg, *Making Social Science Matter: Why Social Inquiry Fails and How it Can Succeed Again* (Cambridge, Cambridge University Press, 2001) 39.

[15] See Aristotle, *Nichomachean Ethics*, bk VI, chs 5–11 (D Ross trans, 1980).

[16] See M Griffiths and G Macleod, 'Personal Narratives and Policy: Never the Twain?' (2008) 42 *Journal of Philosophy of Education* 121, 126.

[17] See Aristotle, *Nichomachean Ethics*, bk VI, chs 5–11 (n 15).

[18] See S-U von Kirchmann, *Die Werlosigkeit der Jursprudenz als Wissenschaft* (Berlin, Verlage von Julius Springer, 1848).

[19] See B Caterino and SF Schram, 'Introduction' in SF Schram and B Caterino (eds), *Making political science matter: Debating knowledge, research, and method* (New York, New York University Press, 2006) 8.

[20] See W Eskridge Jr, 'Gadamer/Statutory Interpretation' (1990) 90 *Columbia Law Review* 635.

[21] See E Engle, 'Aristotle, Law and Justice: the Tragic Hero' (2008) 35 *Northern Kentucky Law Review* 4.

[22] See C Rideout, 'Storytelling, Narrative Rationality, and Legal Persuasion' (2008) 14 *Legal Writing: Journal of the Legal Writing Institute* 75.

[23] See RG Wright, 'Whose Phronesis? Which Phronimoi? A Response to Dean Kronman on Law School Education' (1995–96) 26 *Cumberland Sumford Law Review* 817, 817.

[24] See EC Page, 'Their Word is Law: Parliamentary Counsel and Creative Policy Analysis' (2009) *Public Law* 790, 797.

and conceptual analysis of policy[25] with a view to avoiding traps and suggesting solutions,[26] and the choice of the appropriate rule or convention that delivers the desired results within the unique circumstances of the specific problem at any given time. In other words, the drafter needs to be aware of the multitude of often clashing rules and conventions; the drafter needs to identify the most relevant set of circumstances applicable to the problem; and the drafter needs to have the theoretical knowledge and practical experience to promote the rule or convention that best delivers under the mostly unique circumstances of the problem and within the specific jurisdiction in question.[27] In other words, as drafting entails both elements of art and elements of science, the drafter's task entails both identification of all relevant circumstances and rules; and promotion of the most appropriate rule. And so the skills required are both an understanding of the relevant rules and wisdom through experience in the application of the most appropriate rule. These are the main skills that training in drafting must deliver. And they form the core of the reasoning behind the argument that training in drafting must be both academic and practical, both formal and via mentoring. But before we explore this further, let us clarify which are the rules of drafting, and what is the basis of the drafter's subjective choice when selecting the most appropriate one.

In other words, which is the ultimate criterion whose correct application leads the drafter to the appropriate choice between rules and drafting conventions? Which criterion is used to produce quality of legislation? The answer, of course, is effectiveness. Since legislation is a regulatory tool, a good law contributes its best to the achievement of the policy that it serves. As a law on its own cannot produce adequate regulatory results without synergy from the other actors of the policy process,[28] a good law is one that, with synergy, is capable of producing the regulatory results required by policy-makers.[29] Effectiveness is the criterion that drafters use when selecting the most appropriate drafting rule for the problem before them. This qualitative definition of quality in legislation respects and embraces the subjectivity and flexibility of both drafting rules and conventions and, ultimately, of phronetic legislative drafting.

[25] See E Moran, 'Foreword: Special Issue on Legislative Drafting' (2010) 36 *Commonwealth Law Bulletin* 1, 6.

[26] See G Bowman, 'Why is there a Parliamentary Counsel Office?' (2005) 26 *Statute Law Review* 69, 71.

[27] See VCRAC Crabbe, 'Drafting in Developing Countries: the Problems of Importing Expertise (1992) 4 *African Journal of International and Comparative Law* 630, 645.

[28] See JP Chamberlain, 'Legislative Drafting and Law Enforcement' (1931) 21 *American Labour Legislation Review* 235, 243.

[29] See L Mader, 'Evaluating the Effect: a Contribution to the Quality of Legislation' (2001) 22 *Statute Law Review* 119, 126.

TRAINING VERSUS MENTORING ON THE JOB

In the realm of the pursuit of quality in legislation within phronetic legislative drafting, the choice of the most appropriate style of training becomes rather obvious. Drafting is phronetic: it is basically a series of subjective choices made by the drafter. These subjective choices are, or must be, based on two separate yet overriding and intertwining skills: know-how and experience. And thus, in order to prepare for the task ahead, drafters must be encouraged to train in a manner that cultivates these two skills, their knowledge and their experience in drafting.

Experience in drafting is what can flourish through mentoring by an experienced, open and didactic senior, which is not always available or provided.[30] This is the one aspect or skill that drafters acquire as apprentices. This aspect of drafting acknowledges the arty elements of the drafter's task. And the nature of this type of training is professional, one could even call it vocational. It is true to state that drafters learn more from each other than from manuals.[31]

But this is not enough. Pure mentoring training would reduce drafting to 'a *techne* as application of technical knowledge and skills according to a pragmatic instrumental rationality'.[32] In other words, by isolating experience as a sole skill for drafters, one simply ignores the second element of a drafter's task: knowledge and understanding. And this can only be explored through formal 'classroom training'[33] offered in postgraduate academic programmes, which are prepared under the guidelines and the aegis of reputable postgraduate educational institutions. After all, their staff are trained in education techniques, their programmes are assessed on consecutive cycles of independent scrutiny, and teaching is what they do anyway. The academic aspect of drafting training is equally important, if not more so, than the vocational aspect of their training. This reflects the science elements of phronetic drafting.

It is academic training, or formal training, that allows drafters to understand the concept of quality in legislation; to become aware of what choices drafting entails; to identify the virtues or values that a drafter pursues; and the criteria and bases upon which these choices are made. And this is in an abstract context. The application of this academic or theoretical context in

[30] See K Pattchett, 'Preparation, Drafting and Management of Legislative Projects' (Workshop on The Development of Legislative Drafting For Arab Parliaments, Beirut, 3–6 Feb 2003) para 32.

[31] See R Cormacain, 'An Empirical Study of the Usefulness of Legislative Drafting Manuals (2012) 2 *The Theory and Practice of Legislation* 205, 221.

[32] See B Flyvbjerg, 'Phronetic Planning Research: Theoretical and Methodological Reflections' (2004) 5 *Planning Theory and Practice* 283, 286.

[33] The term is attributed to VCRAC Crabbe, 'Teaching Legislative Drafting: The Commonwealth Experience' (1998) 19 *Statute Law Review* 113, 115.

true examples, in practice, comes with experience and through vocational training. Without this academic theoretical background the drafter simply lacks the theoritisation of experience: the link between examples and the reasons behind the solutions offered, and any lessons learnt for the future are lost, as apprenticeship involves isolated and case-based education. But without vocational training and practical application the theory is equally lost, as there are no concrete cases to channel lessons learnt and reasoning explained.

The dual nature of drafting, and the dual skill required, makes it impossible to consider a drafter trained without formal academic instruction in combination with lengthy[34] practical hands-on experience.[35]

What aspects of training must educational institutions provide?[36] Drafting is a sub-discipline of law that requires as a prerequisite a global understanding of law. As a result drafting can only be taught in a postgraduate environment. Of course elements of drafting and statutory interpretation must be offered to undergraduate students of law but this will inevitably be more of a taster and a skills-oriented tuition. One cannot begin to discuss effectiveness and quality in legislation without having awareness of the sources of law, their hierarchy in the legal system, the constitution or constitutional principles, and administrative structures. It is at postgraduate level that students can explore the main concepts of drafting and the general principles on which drafting choices are made. And of course this must be set within an analysis of the legislative environment: drafting is only part of the legislative process that is part of the policy process. And appreciation of law as a mere tool for regulation cannot be undertaken without an exploration of the policy context within which law is expected to function and deliver results effectively. With reference to legislative drafting as a part of legislative studies, what is required from formal training is not the provision of concrete answers to concrete drafting questions: after all, it is doubtful that such answers exist, at least uniformly and generally applicable.[37]

What is required from training is the explanation of the role of the drafter in the drafting, legislative and policy processes, the introduction of the main theoretical principles of drafting,[38] and the setting of these principles in a hierarchy. In other words, what is required from drafting instruction is the

[34] Training is a protracted business stretching to six or seven years and more: see GP Nazareth, 'Legislative Draftsmen: A Continuing Dearth' in Annex to Paper LMM(83)6) in Commonwealth Secretariat, Meeting of Commonwealth Law Ministers (Colombo, Sri Lanka, 14–18 Feb 1983): Memoranda (Commonwealth Secretariat, London, 1983) 129, 131.

[35] See S Lortie, 'Providing Technical Assistance on Law Drafting' (2010) 31 *Statute Law Review* 1, 17.

[36] For an analysis of elements of training, see D Miers and A Paget, 'Teaching Legislation in Law Schools' (1980) 1 *Statute Law Review* 23, 24 ff.

[37] See G Bowman, 'The Art of Legislative Drafting' (2005) 7 *European Journal of Law Reform* 3, 15.

[38] See WD Lewis, H Hall, E Freund and S Williston, 'Report of the Special Committee on Legislative Drafting' (1920) 6 *American Bar Association Journal* 503, 504.

use of theory as a guide (not a script) for drafters in the making of subjective choices. This type of training, which respect and reflect the nature of drafting as an arty science or a liberal discipline, may assist the drafter in the development of a homogenous[39] drafting style in the jurisdiction.[40] This may prevent drafting surprises, namely circumstances, like the unilateral placement of definitions at the end, rather than the traditional beginning, of the legislation But, at the same time, this type of training respects and recognise the dynamic nature of legal rules,[41] the dynamic and evolving nature of drafting conventions, which, for the purposes of achieving effectiveness, require looseness, flexibility, innovation and change.[42]

Does the need for mentoring somehow negate the need for formal academic training? The answer is of course no.[43] One can draw analogies between drafters and brain surgeons. Just as brain surgeons need to have undergraduate medical training (academic and applied) followed by specialised postgraduate formal education with vocational training in the operating theatre, drafters need undergraduate law training (academic and applied) followed by specialised postgraduate training in legislative studies combined with hands-on experience in a drafting office supervised by an experienced senior. That level of specialisation and length of training time is necessary for the provision of all the skills required from drafters.

There is no arrogance in comparing drafters with neurosurgeons. Both are subspecialties of professional disciplines. And there is no notion of hierarchy between lawyers and drafters, just as there is no such notion between general medical practitioners and neurosurgeons. The analogy between drafters and neurosurgeons is based simply on the type of superspecialisation required in order to perform adequately; the only difference is that nobody questions the specialised skills of a neurosurgeon, whereas there are still those who feel that any lawyer (often even non-lawyers) can draft adequately. Just as few sane individuals would ask a foot specialist to undertake brain surgery, few sane individuals should be asking untrained professionals to draft. One should expect judges and lawyers to be bad in drafting (unless trained of course), exactly as one should expect drafters to be bad in court (unless trained and practising of course).

[39] See D Le May, 'Pour un manuel de legistique' (1980) 21 *Cahiers de Droit* 995; also see G Ciavarini Azzi, 'Better Lawmaking: The Experience and the View of the European Commission' (1998) 4 *Columbia Journal of European Law* 624.

[40] See 'Interview with Norm Larsen, Draftstoevsky (comments)' (2000–02) 28 *Manitoba Law Journal* 205; also see J Kobba, 'Criticisms of the Legislative Drafting Process and Suggested Reforms in Sierra Leone' (2008) 10 *European Journal of Law Reform* 231.

[41] See B Deffains and M Obidzinski, 'Real Options Theory for Law Makers' (2009) 75 *Recherches économiques de Louvain* 117.

[42] See W Holdsworth, *A History of English Law*, vol XII (London, Methuen and Co Ltd, 1938) 157.

[43] See B Simamba, 'Improving Legislative Drafting Capacity' (2002) 28 *Commonwealth Law Bulletin* 1125.

CLINICAL EDUCATION AND TRAINING IN LEGISLATIVE DRAFTING

At the crossroads between formal training and mentoring lies clinical education. This has been neglected in the training offered to legislative drafters.[44] The ideal structure is a legislative drafting clinic, such as the Sir William Dale Drafting Clinic, a forum where clients can receive pro bono legislative drafting services offered by trainee drafters.

The symbiotic nature of the legislative drafting clinic benefits clients and trainees alike.[45] It offers trainees the unique opportunity to come into contact with real clients and receive real files. It offers them the opportunity to participate in the drafting process in practice. And it allows them a unique chance to apply their theoretical knowledge in practice. And all this without the pressure of a professional environment of assessment, and with unique supervision from seniors who have themselves been holistically trained both in the theory and practice of legislation. In other words, a legislative drafting clinic presents the impressive advantage of mentoring but with the added value of mentoring from adequately trained seniors, who are removed from national eccentricities of tradition and style, and can apply international trends for legislative quality. This addresses the main disadvantage of pure mentoring, which tends to regurgitate the same traditional drafting style, thus repeating, rather than de-rooting, the national evils of past drafting errors and inadequacies of the jurisdiction.

For the clients a drafting clinic presents a unique prospect of receiving free legislative drafting services. The quality of the work is not necessarily of the highest standard but the clinic, by its very structure, guarantees informed legislative choices and the production of a legislative text that is modern and progressive in style. Moreover, clients have the privilege of participating in the training of young drafters, thus contributing to legislative quality in vulnerable jurisdictions.

For the jurisdictions receiving clinic drafts and for professional drafters in that jurisdiction the clinic can offer a showcase of modern legislative drafting techniques, a chance to view and review innovative legislative texts keeping what is useful for the jurisdiction and rejecting what is not effective there.

[44] There is a small number of excellent clinics in the field: see Columbia University School of Law Legislative Drafting Research Fund, www.law.columbia.edu/llm_intro/grad_studies/Research#93175; also see Boston University School of Law, 'Legislative Programs' www.bu.edu/law/central/jd/programs/clinics/legislative/index.shtml; CR Feldblum 'The Joy of Teaching Legislation' (2004) 7 *New York University Journal of Legislation and Public Policy* 31, 36–37.

[45] See K Kerrigan and P Plowden, 'Who Benefits?—Case Management and Clinical Education' (1996) 30 *Law Teacher* 315, 328.

Here lies the disadvantage of the clinic exercise: effectiveness of legislation is very much a relative concept. The legislative text has to 'work' within the specific legislative environment and for the specific jurisdiction at the specific time.[46] 'Nationalisation' of the draft is therefore absolutely necessary, if effectiveness is to be served. In other words, the draft produced by the clinic is inevitably a form of legal transplant: useful but in need of 'naturalisation' within the local environment.

And so ideally the clinic must work either with a local drafter as a trainee or with the client in constant communication with the clients to ensure a match. Actually, for the purposes of a match it makes sense for the senior or the trainee to have some experience in the client jurisdiction. For example, at the Sir William Dale Clinic the file is assigned to a drafter of the jurisdiction or to a jurisdiction that is familiar to the senior. This does lead to a rejection of many a number of requests, but it is impossible to serve the clinic's functions with ineffective draft laws.

It is time, at least within the drafting community for a start, to embrace drafting as a sub-discipline of law, and drafting skills as specialised professional skills.[47] And to finally welcome the specialised combined formal and mentoring training as a necessity for drafters. But where in the world can this type of training take place?

NATIONAL VERSUS UNIVERSAL TRAINING FOR DRAFTERS

Is drafting so nation-focused that training must definitely relate to the national eccentricities of the jurisdiction that the student will serve? Or are there universal values in legislative drafting which can be promoted and explored in institutions outside the home jurisdiction?

Effectiveness, as synonymous with quality in legislation, and therefore the ultimate pursuit for drafters worldwide, is universal. The universality of the notion of quality in legislation is linked to the universality of legal rules. And so, if the pursuit of quality in legislation is universal, can the training required to enhance knowledge of that pursuit be equally universal?

If one follows the view that legal systems, despite their national eccentricities, can learn from each other,[48] then the question here is not if quality

[46] See O Kahn-Freund, 'On Uses and Misuses of Comparative Law' (1974) 37 *The Modern Law Review* 1, 1; also see D Berkowitz et al, 'The Transplant Effect' (2003) 51 *The American Journal of Comparative Law* 163.

[47] See D Dewhurst, LA Levert QC and A Zariski, 'Producing Legislative Counsel: Ways and Means' (2012) 33 *Statute Law Review* 339, 353.

[48] See P de Cruz, *Comparative Law in a Changing World* (London and New York, Routledge-Cavendish, 2007) 513–14; also see E Örücü, 'Critical Comparative Law: Considering Paradoxes for Legal Systems in Transition' (2000) 4(1) *Electronic Journal of Comparative Law* http://www.ejcl.org/41/abs41-1.html.

is transferrable but how.[49] Watson[50] claims that legal rules are equally at home in many places, irrespective of their historical origins and connection to any particular people, any particular period of time or any particular place.[51] Others qualify Watson's anarchic borrowing from anyone and anywhere with the qualifier that like must be compared with like,[52] namely with countries at the same evolutionary stage.[53] Others allow transferability on the basis of differences, as only differences enhance our understanding of law in a given society.[54]

Jhering, Zweigert and Kötz[55] view the question of comparability through the relative prism of functionality.[56] For them transferability is not a matter of nationality, but of usefulness and need.[57] It is precisely this notion of functionality that supports transferability on the basis of effectiveness.[58] The objective of a good law is to effectuate adequate reform along the lines requested by the government of the day. If the reform requested applies to more than one jurisdiction, then the notion of effectiveness breaks the geographical boundaries of a single jurisdiction. And transferability is not only possible, but also desirable. In the current era of integrative legal globalisation[59] transnational problems require urgent transnational solutions. Nowadays integrative transnational approaches seem to be no longer a luxury but a realistic response. Trade in human organs, organised crime, terrorism and paedophilia cross national borders and therefore require a-national solutions. Borrowing laws

[49] For an in-depth analysis on borrowing and the drafting process, see H Xanthaki, 'Legal Transplants in Legislation: Defusing the Trap' (2008) 57 *International and Comparative Law Quarterly* 659.

[50] For an analysis of the term, see E Öcürü, 'Critical Comparative Law: Considering Paradoxes for Legal Systems in Transition' (1999) 59 *Nederlandse Vereniging voor Rechtsvergelijking* 59; also see E Öcürü, 'Law as Transposition' (2002) 51 *International and Comparative Law Quarterly* 206.

[51] See A Watson, 'Legal Transplants and Law Reform' (1976) 92 *Law Quarterly Review* 80; also see A Watson, *Legal Transplants: An Approach to Comparative Law* (Edinburgh, Scottish Academic Press, 1974); also see A Watson, 'Legal Transplants and European Private Law' Ius Commune Lectures on European Private Law, no 2.

[52] See H Gutteridge, *Comparative Law* (Cambridge, Cambridge University Press, 1949) 73; also see WW Buckland and AD McNair, *Roman Law and Common Law* (Cambridge, Cambridge University Press, 1936).

[53] See C Schmidthoff, 'The Science of Comparative Law' (1939) 19 *Cambridge Law Journal* 96.

[54] See F Teubner, 'Legal Irritants: Good Faith in British Law or How Unifying Law Wends up in New Divergences' (1998) 61 *Modern Law Review* 11; also see JWF Allison, *A Continental Distinction in the Common Law: A Historical and Comparative Perspective on English Public Law* (Oxford, Clarendon Press, 1996) 16.

[55] See K Zweigert and H Kötz, *Einführung in die Rechtsvergleichung* 3. neubearbeitete Auflage (Tübingen, JCB Mohr, 1996).

[56] See K Zweigert and K Sier, 'Jhering's Influence on the Development of Comparative Legal Method' (1971) 19 *American Journal of Comparative Law* 215.

[57] See K Jhering, *Geist des römischen Rechts, vol 1* (1955) 8–9.

[58] For an analysis of functionality in legislative drafting, see Xanthaki, 'Legal Transplants in Legislation' (n 49).

[59] See LA Mistelis, 'Regulatory Aspects: Globalization, Harmonization, Legal Transplants, and Law Reform—Some Fundamental Observations' (2000) 34 *International Lawyer* 1059.

already applied elsewhere simply offers the drafting team the opportunity to propose and apply policy and legislative responses with unprecedented insight into the possible results to be produced.

The pyramid of virtues pursued by the drafter promotes effectiveness as the common highest pursuit for drafters, while allowing them to select the most appropriate tools within the constitutional, political, legal and cultural constraints of the specific society at the specific time. Thus, the qualitative functional definition of quality reflects the integrative nature of our era of globalisation, while emphasising the need for naturalisation of legislative concepts. As a result, it promotes true universality rather than superficial standardisation. Diversity in drafting does not signify drafting nationalism. It is simply a reflection of the inherent subjective prioritisation of drafting virtues within the same hierarchical step of the ladder, based solely on national eccentricities, rather than an alleged rigid civil versus common law divide. But if common versus civil law barriers are demolished, what is it that explains diversity of drafting styles and choices?

If one views drafting as a series of subjective choices, what explains diversity of law as the product can only be diversity in the factors that influence these choices. The nature of the legal system is one, but only one of those influencing factors. But what shines through diversity is universality:

— in the concept of quality of legislation;
— in the virtues that contribute to quality; and
— in their hierarchical classification.

After all, in the sphere of Aristotelian *phronesis* virtues are moral universals that are indeterminate. Thus phronetic drafting involves the virtue of effectiveness as a moral universal. Effectiveness as a virtue is indeterminate. But, like all *phronesis*, drafting includes a mental-moral habit which, by mediating universals in the particular case, makes them determinate.[60] Thus, effectiveness as quality in legislation is universal and as such indeterminate. In order to attribute to it specific elements one needs to place it within the context of legal system, culture, legislative environment and policy.

CONCLUSIONS

Drafting is a phronetic sub-discipline of law, which deserves to be recognised as such. Drafting is not simply academic, just as drafting is not simply a technical science. Drafting encompasses both ends of the spectrum, as it is a liberal art, a phronetic discipline.

[60] See J Dunne, *Back to the Rough Ground* (Notre Dame, University of Notre Dame Press, 1993) 311.

Phronetic legislative drafting, in the Aristotelian sense, requires that drafters select the most appropriate subjective choice for the solution of the problem that they face at any given time. In other words, drafting is prudence: just as a judge applies the most appropriate legal norm for the circumstances of the case, a drafter applies the most appropriate theoretical drafting principle for the circumstances of the concrete drafting issue that they are called to address.

In order to complete this task adequately, a drafter needs to possess two distinct skills: (1) awareness and understanding of theoretical drafting principles, their purpose, their application and expected results from their use; and (2) experience in the application of drafting principles in concrete cases within the jurisdiction that they currently serve, and beyond.

To acquire the first skill, a drafter needs to have completed a formal academic training in the theory of legislative drafting, both in abstract and applied. This formal training is best offered by academic institutions with experience in academic training, with independent assessment of staff and training offered, and by staff with both academic excellence in the field of legislative studies and teacher training. The use of know-how from other jurisdictions by means of international and comparative experience is useful.

To acquire the second skill, a drafter needs to have completed mentoring training on the job within the jurisdiction of choice by an experienced senior with both long service in that jurisdiction and mentoring skills.

All that is needed is understanding: understanding of the nature of legislative drafting, understanding of what it involves, and how it is to be tackled. It is my inner hope that this book has managed to add to the debate, thus promoting the new sub-discipline of law that I call phronetic legislative drafting.

Index

abbreviations, unnecessary:
  EU countries' legislation, in, 210
accountability in legislation, 4, 6–7
acquis and EU legislation, 153–4
Acts of Parliament:
  structure of, 71–3, 133
  2012, passed in, 348
adaptability and EU legislation, 156
adequacy and EU legislation, 156
administrative agency, creation of, 152
ambiguity:
  definition, 90
  semantic *see* semantic ambiguity
  serial commas and, 98
  syntactic *see* syntactic ambiguity
  vagueness and, 88–92
amending legislation:
  definition, 232
  Thornton on, 223–4
amending provisions, 223–41
  approaches to, 223–4
  direct amendment, 226–35
    advantages, 227–8
    disadvantages, 228
    example of, 226–7
  express amendments, 225–6
  implied amendments, 225–6
  indirect amendments, 235–8
    expression of, 236
  initial decisions, 224–5
audience of legislation:
  diversity, 114–15
  identifying, 114, 115
  plain language and, 113–16
  sophistication, 116
Australia, gender neutral language, 105

Bergeron's Rules, 65–6, 72
'Better Law Initiative' (UK), 113
Better Lawmaking reports, 167, 335–6
Better Regulation reports, 338–9, 344–6
Better Regulation Task Force Principles (UK), 347
Better Regulation Unit (UK), 349
bill structure, 61–84
  arrangement of provisions and sections, 70–1, 74
  arrangement of sections, 74
  Bergeron's Rules, 65–6
  headings, 73–4
  introduction, 61–2
  layered approach, 76–84
  marginal notes and references, 74–5, 76
  over-division of sections, 72–3
  punctuation in, 103
  Thornton's five stages of drafting and, 66–7
  Thring's rules and, 68–71
  traditional arrangement of provisions, 67–8
blocking legislation, 314–16
  alternatives to, 316–17
  claw-back legislation, 315
  compliance blocking, 315
  methods of, 314–15

Cabinet and drafting legislation, 25–7
Canada:
  gender-neutral language, 105
  headings in bills, 73
  plain language, user testing, 113
citations in EU legislation, 167
civil drafting teams, 201–2
civil law and statutory interpretation, 204
clarity (clearness), 8
  consolidation and codification, in, 282–3
  definition, 88–9
  EU legislation, of, 166
  European countries, in, 17, 209
  repealing and re-enacting amendments, 229–30
codification, 278–81
  advantages, 285–6
  aims, 279
  benefits, 281
  clarity and, 282–3
  consolidation, distinguished from, 282
  definition, 278
  effectiveness and, 284–7
  EU, 287–8
    UK differences and, 288–9
  functions of, 279
  modernisation and, 280
  positive law codification, 280–1
  unambiguity and, 286
  updating and, 280
'codophobia', 280–1
Cold War in statutory interpretation, 204–5
comity, 317
commas, 103

common law:
  doctrine of precedent, 206–7
  statutory interpretation, 202–7
comparative legislative drafting, 199–212
  aims and clichés, 201–2
  introduction, 199–200
  statutory interpretation, 202–7
compliance and international treaties, 172
conduct:
  conditional method of expression, 249
  declaratory method of expression, 248
  directory method of expression, 248
  expression of, 248–9
  objective elements, 246
  offence, declaration as, 246
  subjective elements, 246
consequential amendments, 239–40
consolidation, 281–4
  advantages, 285
  clarity and, 282–3
  codification, distinguished from, 282
  definition, 281–2
  effectiveness and, 284–7
  EU, 288
    UK differences and, 288–9
  objectives, 282–3
  plain language and, 285
  process, 283–4
  Teasdale's mechanisms 284 (table), 284
  unambiguity and, 285
  value, 283
copy-paste technique (legal drafting), 172
corporate bodies, penalties for, 250–1
court judgments and doctrine of precedent, 206–7
Court of Justice of the European Union (CJEU) and legislative drafting, 167
cross-references in EU countries, 210

defences:
  examples of, 252–3
  penal provisions for, 252–3
definitions, schedule of, 194–6
  definition of, 194–6
  placement of in Act, 194
  Thornton's Commandments, 195
delegated instruments, 270–5
  commencement provisions, 273
  definitions in, 273
  enacting provision, 271–2
  preamble, 270–1
  purpose clause, 272
  retrospective provisions, 273
  title, 270
delegated legislation, 58, 257–75
  construction, 269–75
  definition, 257
  delegated instruments *see* delegated instruments
  delimitation of legislative power 258–60
  drafter's role, 260–2
  enabling clause, 267–8, 269–70
  EU legislation and, 158, 261
  exercising of, 268
  final provisions and repeals, 184–5
  Henry VIII clauses, 266
  implementation of, 157
  invalidity of, 267
  legal officers, drafting by, 261
  legislative drafting criteria, 164
  national law's incompatibility with EU legislation, 158
  primary legislation, amending, 272
  range of powers, 260
  separation of powers, 257–8
  time limits, 267–8
  uses of, 262–7
  validity of, 267–9
Dickerson's rules on dates, 96
direct textual amendment, 230–1
  consistency of language with original, 234
  drafting techniques, 231–5
  expressing 233
  indirect referential amendment, amalgamation with, 238–9
  narrative, example of, 232
  placement of, 233
  plain language and, 234–5
  punctuation and, 233–4
  tabular example, 232–3
doctrine of precedent:
  common law, in, 206–7
  court judgments and, 206–7
'double banking' (EU legislative drafting), 167
drafters:
  delegated legislation, role in, 260–2
  legislative plans,
    solutions for, 50–1
  legislative provisions and, 220–2
  policy options, analysis of, 51–2
  preferred legislative solutions, 51–2
drafting:
  generally, 10–11
  law and, 11–15
  lay (raw) drafts, 32–3, 34
  manuals for, 19–20
  phronetics and, 15
  rules for, 11–15
drafting conventions and rules, 207–11
drafting instructions, 22–32
  checklist, 25–7

content of, 29–32
departmental consultations over, 30–1
factual background, 29
introduction, 22–4
legislative amendments, 31
politically sensitive information, 30
principles, 27–8
purposes of, 24–7
quality of, 32–4
regulatory aims of legislation, 29–30
sponsoring department and, 26
style, 34–5
UK Office of Parliamentary Counsel guidance, 31–2
drafting process, 21–37
instructions for *see* drafting instructions
introduction, 21–2
phases of, 25
stages of, 21
Thornton's stages, 3
drafting rules, 207–11
dualism, 170

EC Commission and drafting legislation, 167
EC Regulations and legislative drafting regulations, 163
education and training:
legislative drafting and, 354–7
mentoring and, 358–60
effectiveness and ineffectiveness, 16–17, 362–4
codification and consolidation, 284–7
definition, 7
Europe, in, 18
evaluation of law of, 342–3
functions of, 8
legislation and, 6–9
legislative drafting and, 87
penal provisions, in, 247
taxation legislation, 297–8
transferability and, 363
'effects test', 307–9
definition 307–8
interest (extra-territoriality), 307–9
presumption of territoriality, 308–9
efficacy and legislation, 5–6
efficiency, 8
electronic publication, advantages, 185
enabling clauses, 267–8
delegated legislation, 269–70
end date, 188–90
financial provisions, 189
post-legislative scrutiny, 189
sunset clauses, 188–90
end-means analysis, 53, 54–5
entry into force, 72
date, EU countries' legislation in, 210–11
episteme, 11, 12–13
episthmh, 11
EU codification, 287–8
EU consolidation, 288
EU directives:
implementation, 160–2
transposition of, 162
EU instruments, transposition of, 159
EU law:
regulatory framework, 333–8
simplification of, 340–2
EU legislation:
acquis and, 153–4
adaptability and, 156
adequacy and, 156
delegated legislation and, 261
implementation, 152–64
international law and, 153–4
interpretation of legislation, 58
national law and, 153–4
incompatibility with, 158
principles of, 154
quality of *see* quality of EU legislation
regulation of, 344–5
EU legislative policy, 335–8
EU regulations, 160
EU treaties and national constitutions, 159
European Council and Sutherland Report (1992), 334–5
evidence-based analysis, 55
existing law:
amending law as, 45
analysis of, 45–6
legislative plan, in, 44–6
explanatory notes, 228–9
extra-territorial foreign legislation:
enforcement of judgments prevented, 315
non-compliance with foreign authorities, 315
prosecutions, ineffective, 314–15
extra-territorial legislation, 304–17
blocking legislation, 314–16
concluding remarks, 317
introduction, 304–6
extra-territoriality:
bilateral and unilateral legislative measures, 310
definition, 305
drafters' perspective and roles, 312–14
England, in, 310–11
jurisdiction outside national boundaries, 311–12
legislation under, 305–6
liberalism and, 307
realism and, 306–7
reasonableness and, 308

final provisions, 176–98
application provisions, 177–8

commencement, 188–90
consequential amendments *see* final provisions; repeals
duration provisions, 188–90
end date, 189
Jamaica Schedule, 197–8
Keeling Schedule, 196–7
listed, 176
objectives *see* final provisions; purpose clauses
purpose clause, 185–7
examples, 186
repeals, 182–5
Amending Act and, 184
causes, 182–3
delegated legislation, 184–5
terms for, 183
saving provisions *see* saving provisions
schedule of definitions *see* definitions
schedules *see* schedules
short title, 190–1
start date, 188–90
transitional *see* transitional provisions
fines, setting of, 252

gender-neutral drafting (GND), 103–7
gender-neutral language (GNL), 9–10, 103–5
International Labour Organisations and, 105
principal provisions and, 150
United Nations and, 105
'gold plating' (EU legislative drafting), 167–8
Good Law Initiative 2013 (UK), 77

Henry VIII clauses, 266
Human Rights Act:
and statutory interpretation, 326–7
purposive interpretation, effect on, 322–3

Ilbert's rules, 202–3
imperatives, substantive provisions and, 150–1
implementing legislation:
delegated legislation, 157
international treaties, compliance with, 172
implied repeals, 240–1
incorporation and substantive provisions, 151
incrementalism, 53–4
indirect referential amendment, 236–8
definition, 236
direct textual amendment, amalgamation with, 238–9
example of, 236–7
use of, 237
weaknesses, 237–8
innovation:
principal provisions, in, 174–5
tradition in legislation and, 151
interest (extra-territoriality), 307–9
commercial interests, 308
'effects test', 307–9
non-commercial interests, 308
International Labour Organisation and gender-neutral language, 105
international law:
definition, 304
drafting legislation in Ukraine, 48
EU legislation and, 153–4
exceptions to, 304
international treaties:
definition, 169–70
implementing legislation's compliance, 172
incorporation in national law, 170–1
interpretation of legislation, 58
Memoranda of Understanding, distinguished from, 170
national implementation methods, 171
ratification and entry into force, 170
interpretation of legislation, 318
EU legislation, 58

Jamaica Schedule, 197–8
Janus-faced legalising provisions, 216–17
jargon, 121–2
judges and penal provisions, 250

Keeling Schedule, 196–7, 230–1

law and *phronesis*, 14–15
law reform and Teasdale's mechanisms, 176–7
layered approach (bill structure), 76–84
elements of, 77
example of, 79–84
taxation legislation and, 299
Thring's rules and, 78
weaknesses of, 78–9
legal drafters and plain language, 109–10
legal drafting and revision tools, 276–7
legalising laws, categories of, 215–16
legalising provisions, 215–19
drafters and, 220–2
past events, regulation of, 215
unfairness of, 218–19
'Legislate Less to Act Better: the Facts' (EU report, 2002), 337–8
legislation:
accountability and, 4
aims of, 27–8
amending *see* amending legislation
background information, 27
blocking *see* blocking legislation
circumstances behind, 27–8

construction of, 318
delegated *see* delegated legislation
effectiveness and *see* effectiveness
'effects test', 308–9
efficacy and, 5–6
existing *see* existing legislation
implementing *see* implementing legislation
policy and, 4
post-Lisbon legislation, parliamentary role, 333–53
primary, issues for, 58–9
projected interpretation, 57–9
provisions, types of, 64–5
reasons for, 27–8
regulation and *see* legislation and regulation
schedules, in, 65
simple and complex propositions, 64
social needs and, 46–8
Stefanou's processes, 4
time in *see* time in legislation
legislation and regulation, 1–20
definition, 2–3
introduction, 1–10
Legislative Committee and drafting legislation, 25–6
legislative drafting:
analysis and, 356–7
art or science, 355
basic principles, 85–8
clinical education, 361–2
comparative *see* comparative legislative drafting
criteria for, 163–4
education and training, 354–7, 362–4
effectiveness of legislation, 87
EU, concluding remarks, 168–9
implementation of treaties, 171–2
knowledge and understanding, drafters', 358, 359
mentoring versus training, 358–60
national implementation measures *see* national implementation measures
'nationalisation' of drafts, 362
perfect words, 89
phronetic, 257
predictability and clarity, 85–6
principal provisions, 149–75
pronouns, 106
quality of, 364
rule of law, achieving, 86–7
statutory interpretation, 318–32
tenses used, 214
training methods, 358–9
transforming law reform, 86
vagueness, use of, 87–8
legislative plan, 38–60
advantages of, 41–4
analysis of, 44–59
communication plan for, 40
constitutionally-related issues in, 49
consultation for, 39–40
danger areas in, 48–51
designing, 39–41
documents required, 43–4
drafters' solutions, 50–1
drafting teams' plans, 44
effectiveness of proposals, 56
ethical issues, 50
international law, compliance with, 49
introduction, 38–9
legally-related issues, in, 49
penal provisions, for, 244–6
policy options, 51–7
political sensitivity, in, 50
preferred legislative solution, 51–7
proposed legislation, elements of, 42–3
regional law, compliance with, 49
translating policy into law, 41–2
legislative quality and parliament, 351–3
legislative solutions:
design of, 55–7
elements of, 56–7
most appropriate selections, 52–5
preferred, 51–2
selection of, 55
legislative texts in European countries' legislation, 210
liberalism:
extra-territoriality and, 307
liberal agenda and, 308
licensing authority, appointment for, 15
Making Single Market Rules More Effective, Quality in Implementation and Enforcement 1998 report, 336–7

marginal notes and references, 74–5, 76
maxims, 330
presumptions, compared with, 330
maximum penalty, 249–50
'may' considered, 151
Memoranda of Understanding:
international treaties, distinguished from, 170
mens rea 15–16
proof of, 246
mentoring and training, 358–60
modifiers defined, 100–1
monism, 170
'must' considered, 151

national authorities, legislative drafting criteria, 163–4
national implementation measures, 172–4
drafters' options, 173–4
drafting techniques, 172–3

national law and EU legislation, 153–4
  incompatibility with, 158
national legal customs, legislative drafting criteria and, 163
new penal offences:
  criminal court to be used, 253–4
  evidence required for, 255–6
  onus of proof, 255
  territoriality of offence, 254–5
  time limit for, 253–4
New Zealand:
  gender-neutral language, 105
  headings in bills, 73
Nigeria, drafting legislation, 32
nominalisations, 120
noun modifiers, 100–2
numbering (tax legislation), 300

offences:
  continuing, 251
  introduction of, 246
  penal *see* new penal offence
Office of Tax Simplification (OTS), 290, 294–6
over-exhaustiveness of language, 91
over-precision of language, 91–2
  vagueness and, 92

Parliament:
  legislative quality and, 351–3
  post-Lisbon legislation and, 333–53
penal offence, new *see* new penal offence
penal provisions, 242–56
  amendments and, 246
  defences, 252–3
  domestic and regional standards considered, 243–4
  drafting stages, 245
  effectiveness in, 247
  initial considerations, 343–4
  instructing officers' roles, 244, 245
  introduction, 242–3
  judges' discretion, 250
  legislative plan, 244–6
  offence details analysed, 241
  parts of, 246–7
  penal procedures, deviation from, 245
  repeals and, 246
  special circumstances, 250–2
  special considerations, 253–6
  visual aids and pictures in, 247–8
perfect words defined, 89
phronesis, 11–12, 13–15, 52–3, 54, 356
  law and, 14–15
  praxis and, 13
  techne and, 14
placement problem (syntactic ambiguity), 99–100
plain language, 9, 15–16, 108–31
  archaic terms, 129–30
  audience of legislation, 113–16
  consolidation, 285
  definition, 108–12
  design of text, 122–3
  direct textual amendment, 234–5
  easing communication, 116–25
  European countries' legislation, in, 18, 209
  intelligibility, 126–7, 128
  jargon, 121–2
  layered approach, 127, 134–5
  legal drafters and, 109–10
  nominalisations, 120
  over-defining, 122
  passive voice, 119–20
  precision, 127–9
  preliminary provisions, 133–9
  principal provisions, 150
  sentence length *see* sentence length and structure
  'shall',
    obligation and, 124
    present tense and, 123–4
  standards of good writing, 125–6
  superfluous words, 121
  Thornton's drafting stage 2, 111–12
  tradition and innovation in legislation, 151
  user testing experiments, 113–14
  weak verbs, 120
  'will' and present tense, 123–4
plain language movement, 110
policies:
  definition, 2–3
  legislation and, 4
political statements of intention in European countries' legislation, 210
'post-legislative scrutiny', 25, 352–3
post-Lisbon legislation, parliament's role, 333–53
praxis, *phonesis* and, 13
preambles, 135–7
  EU legislation, in, 166–7
  European countries' legislation, in, 210
precision (drafting principle), European countries, in, 18
pre-legislative scrutiny, 25, 351–2
  European Countries' legislation, in, 209
preliminary provisions, 132–48
  application provisions, 137, 147
  commencement *see* preliminary provisions, start date
  definitions in, 138–9
  enacting clause, 137, 141–3
    audiences aimed at, 142
  interpretation, 138

introduction, 132–3
introductory text, 139–41
long title, 134–5, 139–41
amendments, 141
minimum number of, 148
plain language approach, 133–9
preamble, *see* preambles
purpose clauses, 137
short title, 137
start date, 137, 143–7
ambiguity, 146
example, 145
importance, 144
positioning, 143
types, 133
presumptions:
constitutional and legislative basis of, 328–9
exceptions, 328
listed, 328–9
maxims, compared with, 330
primary legislation, 263–7
administrative arrangements, 264
amendment of, 265–7, 266–7
delegated legislation and, 272
entry into force, 265
implementation of, 157
legislative drafting criteria, 163
technical provisions, 264
principal provisions, 149–51
administrative, 149–50
definition, 149
EU, 152–64
gender-neutral language, 150
plain language and, 150
substantive, 149–51
principle of necessity, 4
prior national legislation, 158
pronouns, legislative drafting, in, 106
proportionality:
EU legislation and, 6–7, 155
'prospective evaluation', 25
prospective provisions, 214
provisions, amending *see* amending provisions
punctuation:
direct textual amendment, 233–4
Parliamentary Bills, in, 103
Thornton's four rules of punctuation, 102–3
purpose clauses, 16–17
as quality control, 187
purposive interpretation, 202–3, 322–5
Human Rights Act, influence of, 322–3

quality of EU legislation, 164–6
form of law, 165
substance of law, 165–6

realism, extra-territoriality and, 306–7
reasonableness, extra-territoriality and, 308
Red Tape Challenge, 348
referential repetition, 245
regulation:
definition, 3
and legislation *see* legislation and regulation
Regulatory Fitness and Performance Programme (2012) (REFIT), 341
regulatory framework:
documents supporting, 334–8
EU law and, 333–8
Regulatory Impact Assessments in European countries, 209
Regulatory Policy Committee (RPC) (UK) 349
regulatory quality control (UK), 347–51
one-in two-out approach, 348
regulatory tools, types of, 3
repeals and re-enactments, 229–30
example of, 229–30
implied, 240–1
'repetition of provisions', EU countries legislation, in, 210
retroactive exemptions, 222
retroactive legalising provisions, 216–18
retroactive provisions, 220
retroactivity, drafters and, 221
'retrospective evaluation', 25, 352–3
retrospective legalising provisions, 216–18
retrospective legislation, 219–20
retrospectivity:
drafters and, 221
saving provisions and, 221–2
RPC *see* Regulatory Policy Committee
rule of last antecedent, 102
rule-making, 3
'rules for regulation', 1, 10–16
manuals for, 19–20
universality, 16–19
rules of construction, 247–50
general rules, 247–8
rules of inquest, 63

sanction, 246–7, 249–50
introduction of, 246
maximum and minimum penalty considerations, 249–50
'semi-automatic compliance' 249
types of, 250
saving provisions, 176–9
and application compared, 177–8
interpretation legislation and, 178
retrospectivity, 221–2
terms used, 179
Schedules, 191–8
contents, 192

delegated instruments compared, 192
inducing section, conflict with, 193
secondary legislation, implementation of, 157–9
semantic ambiguity, 92–8
'and' considered, 94
dates and ages, expression of, 95–6
days, repetition of, 95–6
'except' considered, 94–5
'may' considered, 93, 151
'must' considered, 151
number ranges, 95–6
'or' considered, 94
scale indicators, 95
serial commas and ambiguity, 98
'shall' considered, 93–4
'that' considered, 96–7
'unless' considered, 94–5
'which' considered, 97–8
sentence length and structure:
advice for drafters, 117
European countries' legislation, in, 210
long sentences, 117–18
separation of powers, delegated legislation, 257–8
Shared Responsibility, A (1998 report), 336
short title, amending act of, 231–2
Simpler Legislation for the Internal Market (SLIM), 336
simplicity:
EU legislation, of, 166–7
European countries' legislation, in, 18, 209
Sir William Dale Drafting Clinic, 361, 362
SLIM initiative (1996) *see* Simpler Legislation for the Internal Market
Smart Regulation, 338–46
agenda, 339–40
definition, 339–40
legislative evaluation, 343
reaction to, 340–1
social needs, legislation and, 46–8
soft law, 3
SOLVIT, 340, 343
South Africa, gender-neutral language, 105
sponsoring departments, legal opinions of, 30
stare decisis, 205–7
definition, 205–6
purpose of, 206
states, state-society relations, 307
statutory interpretation:
application defined, 318
case law, 324
civil law, 204
Cold War in 204–5
common law, in, 206–7
construction defined, 318
conventions, and, 324–5
drafters' considerations and, 318–19
European influence, 325
Golden rule, 321–2
Human Rights Act, 326–7
legislative drafting and, 318–32
limits, 323–5
literal rule, 320
mischief rule, 320–1
precedent, 326
presumptions *see* presumptions
purposive interpretation *see* purposive interpretation
recent approaches, 325
rules, use of, 327–8
technique, 320–7
usefulness in drafting, 330–2
subsidiarity, EU legislation and, 154–5
substantive provisions:
definition, 151
educational nature of, 150
imperatives, used in, 150–1
'may', use of, 151
'must', use of, 151
regulatory nature of, 150
superfluous words, use of, 121
Sutherland Report 1992, 334–5
European Council and, 334–5
synergy, EU legislation and, 156
syntactic ambiguity, 98–102
introduction, 98–9
noun modifiers, 100–2
placement problem, 99–100

Tax Law Rewrite Project, 300, 303
taxation legislation, 290–303
complexity, 293–7
and brevity, 296–7
and transparency, 297
definitions in, 300
design of, 292–8, 298–9
drafting criteria, 293
drafting requirements, 299–302
effectiveness, 297–8
existing legislation, and, 293
issues covered, 301–2
layered approach, 299
numbering, 300
Office of Tax Simplification complexity index, 294–6
version 1, 294–5
version 2, 295–6
policy *see* taxation policy
quality assurance, 302–3
taxation code advantages, 303
Thuronyi's drafting criteria, 293
types of taxation, 300–1
understandability, 296–7
verification, 302–3

taxation policy, 290–1
  analysis, 291–2
  principles, 291
Teasdale's mechanisms of consolidation, (table) 284
Teasdale's mechanisms of law reform, 276–7, (table) 277
techne 11, 13, 356
technical language, 34–5
territoriality:
  a-territoriality, 309
  extra-territoriality *see* extra-territoriality
  jurisdictional, 304–5
  non-territoriality, 309
  presumption of 'effects test' and, 308–9
Tetley's themes of comparative analysis, 202
'The Coalition: our programme for government' document, 347
Third Restatement of American Foreign Relations Law, 307
Thornton's four rules of punctuation, 102–3
Thornton's five stages of drafting, 3, 21
  amending legislation, 223–4
  drafting process, 3
  stage 1, 38, 171
  stage 2, 2, 38, 111–12
  stage 3, 3, 61, 112
  stage 4, 132, 149–75, 176
  stage 5, 282, 290–303
  Thring's rules and, 66–7, 68–71
Thornton's ten commandments on definitions, 195
Thring's golden rules, 59–60
  application of, 62–5
  bill structure and, 68–71
  layered approach and, 78
  principal provisions, 150
Thuronyi drafting criteria (tax law), 293
time, legislation, in, 213–22
  introduction, 213
  legalising provisions *see* legalising provisions
  prospective provisions, 214
  starting points, 213
transferability, effectiveness and, 363
transitional provisions, 179–82
  examples, 180–1
  functions, 181
  lifetime, 181
transposition, 152–3
  analyses and evaluation of, 153
  EU opinions, 162
  EU recommendations, 162
2020 Agenda for Europe, 345–6
'Two for One' initiative (UK), 48

UK:
  clarity in, 17
  drafting conventions and rules, 208–9
  headings in bills, 73
  plain language in, 18
  precision (drafting principle) in, 18
  pre-legislative consultation, 209
  Regulatory Impact Assessments, 209
  regulatory quality control, 347–51
  simplicity (drafting principle) in, 18
  unambiguity in, 17–18
UK Office of Parliamentary Counsel:
  drafting instructions, 31–2
  gender-neutral language advice, 105
Ukraine, drafting legislation in, 48
unambiguity, 8
  codification and, 286
  consolidation and, 285
  EU legislation of, 166
  European countries' legislation, in, 17–18, 209
  semantic, 8
  syntactic, 8
understandability, and sentence length (taxation legislation), 296–7
United Nations, gender-neutral language, 105
universality, 16–19
  relative universality analysis, 17

vagueness:
  ambiguity and, 88–92
  defined, 90–1
  legislative drafting, in, 87–8
  over-precision and, 92
verbatim repetition, 245
verbs:
  tenses, choice of, 214
  weak, clarity and, 120
verification, 302–3
visual aids, penal provisions, in, 247–8

Lightning Source UK Ltd.
Milton Keynes UK
UKHW020621110619
344223UK00009B/368/P

9 781849 464284